American Movie Critics

An Anthology
From the Silents Until Now

AMERICAN
MOVIE CRITICS

An Anthology
From the Silents
Until Now
Expanded Edition

Edited by Phillip Lopate

A Special Publication of
The Library of America

Introduction, headnotes, and volume compilation © 2006, 2008 by Literary Classics of the United States, New York, NY. All rights reserved. No part of this book may be reproduced commercially by offset-lithographic or equivalent copying devices without the permission of the publisher.

Some of the material in this volume is reprinted with permission of holders of copyright and publication rights. For acknowledgments, see page 731.
Distributed to the trade by Penguin Group (USA), Inc.

This book is set in Caslon 540, with Americana headings.

A hardcover edition of this book was published by The Library of America in 2006. First paperback edition published 2008.

Library of Congress Control Number: 2007936330
ISBN 978-1-59853-022-3

10 9 8 7 6 5 4 3 2

Printed in the United States of America

*American Movie Critics:
An Anthology From the Silents Until Now*
was published with support from the
Sidney J. Weinberg, Jr. Foundation.

Contents

II. Masters and Moonlighters: The Late 1930s, World War II, and the Postwar Era

III. The Golden Age of Movie Criticism: The 1950s through the 70s

Introduction

This book celebrates film criticism as a branch of American letters. Movies may be only a hundred years old, but already they have generated in this country a body of extraordinary critical writing that honors the best belletristic traditions of our nonfiction prose. It is arguable, in fact, that in the last fifty years more energy, passion, and analytical juice have gone into film criticism than into literary criticism, or probably any other writing about the arts. This anthology attempts to uncover the narrative trajectory by which the field groped its way from the province of hobbyists and amateurs to become a legitimate profession.

◆

A good place to begin our story is 1915, the year D. W. Griffith released *The Birth of a Nation* and Vachel Lindsay published what is generally considered the first serious work of American film criticism, *The Art of the Moving Picture*. Lindsay was a poet who defended the then-controversial proposal that movies could be an art form. Having originated as entertainments for immigrants and laborers, movies were widely dismissed as crude spectacles. While this class bias receded as audiences came to include the middle classes and fleapits gave way to movie palaces, a lingering snobbery persisted: that the medium was a debased fad, somewhat akin to mass hypnosis. Early film reviewers (when not simply acting as plot-summary shills for the studios), embarrassed to be seen wasting their energies on this upstart novelty, adopted a facetious, condescending tone, lest the writer be seen as taking such sentimental hogwash too seriously.

Film was viewed as pushing its way into the pantheon established for centuries-old artistic traditions such as classical music, painting, and the ballet. Lindsay, an enthusiastic movie buff, tried to bridge films and the older arts by making analogies between cinematic techniques and sculpture or painting-in-motion. He had a Whitmanesque belief in movies as a democratic art, alongside a sort of Great Man theory of human progress (his designated film genius was D. W. Griffith). Lindsay envisioned Griffith's and Douglas Fairbanks' films as having somewhat the same effect that "Emerson's 'Address on the American Scholar' was said to have had on certain American people—a great turning point." Since Emerson's speech had rallied American writers to declare their independence from Old World models, Lindsay was clearly hoping for a similar result—claiming, in effect, that the speedy, non-elitist art of the motion picture was a quintessentially American expression.

Other intellectual, highbrow critics who came after Lindsay, writing for aesthetic quarterlies and left-wing journals such as *Close Up, Hound and Horn, Experimental Cinema*, and *New Masses*, took a dimmer view of American movies and looked to the German, Swedish, and Russian national cinemas for artistic breakthroughs. Harry Alan Potamkin, one of the era's most important film critics, began his 1929 appreciation of Carl Dreyer's *The Passion of Joan of Arc* by saying: "We are always waiting in the cinema for the eventual film which will be the vindication of the major cinema devices. We are always waiting for the film down to essentials and yet conveying a profound human experience . . . Where is the motion picture—we are always asking—profound in its exploitation of performance, and profound in its transmission of experience?" This prayerful incantation sums up the restlessness of a generation of film buffs longing to see movies liberated from the Hollywood assembly line in order to become a more personal, mature, and socially progressive art form.

From the silent era onward, a clash arose between seeing movies as a lively universal entertainment—the people's best friend—and as a dangerously numbing, escapist drug for the masses. Both viewpoints had valid points and articulate spokespersons. For instance, writer Gilbert Seldes boldly defended the popular culture of his day—movies, jazz, comic strips, radio, and so on—in his book *The Seven Lively Arts* and found in the knockabout silent comedy of Mack Sennett and the Keystone Kops his cinematic standard. Seldes' God of the movies was Charlie Chaplin.

One argumentative thread that ran through early film criticism was the attempt to justify the medium by defining its essence, singling out elements that seemed to make it unique. Gilbert Seldes argued that film must distance itself from what he regarded as the destructive influence of its older sibling, the theater. (The very fact that an early name for a motion picture was "photoplay" suggested how much work the young medium had to do to establish its own identity.) Left-wing critics such as Potamkin and Dwight Macdonald, drawing on the example of Eisenstein and fellow Soviet directors, placed a larger emphasis on montage, or rapid cutting; this was certainly something, they argued, that could be done only in film. Others looked to the close-up as the heart of the cinematic enterprise, or emphasized the mobile camera. The truism that film was primarily a *visual* medium, a way of telling a story through pictures, proved somewhat simplistic in retrospect with the introduction of sound and spoken dialogue. Many purists, such as theoretician Rudolf

Prided the pure visual

Arnheim, regarded sound film as a catastrophe, nipping silent cinema's promise in the bud. (Subsequently, each new technological advance—color, cinemascope, 3-D, digital—has been greeted with alarm as an undermining of film's essence. As it turns out, movies are more varied and multiform: some naturalistic, others theatrically stylized; some employing close-ups or montage, others neither. Today, film might be summarized, in John Simon's words, as "a totally visual and totally aural medium—in this ambidextrousness lies its glory.")

The early decades of film criticism drew many moonlighters—playwrights such as Robert E. Sherwood, poets such as Vachel Lindsay and William Troy, filmmakers such as Pare Lorentz—who tried their hand at it for a few years, then moved on to their preferred métier. Critics from other arts weighed in with occasional blasts of opinion. There were also specialized takes: Hugo Münsterberg approached film from a trained psychologist's perspective in his pioneering 1916 book *The Photoplay: A Psychological Study*. Cecilia Ager staked out the "woman's angle" by critiquing films as a branch of fashion; poet Melvin B. Tolson was one of many black newspaper film critics addressing the concerns of an African-American readership.

The first working film critic who put everything together, it seems to me, was Otis Ferguson of *The New Republic*. What Ferguson "got," while so many other critics of his day were busy lamenting the low level of American movies, was the genius of the Hollywood system, the almost invisible craft and creativity of the average studio movie. He singled out the eccentric artistry of a Jimmy Cagney, Fred Astaire, Mae West, Walt Disney, Alfred Hitchcock, Humphrey Bogart, as well as the quiet virtues of foreign films. Then unfortunately he died, torpedoed while in the navy in World War II.

Early Auteur Theory?

James Agee took over during and after the war years, first in *The Nation*, later for *Time*, as the most compulsively readable of the 1940s critics. Agee, a marvelously engaging, self-questioning writer, was less in sync with Hollywood fantasy than Ferguson, and tried to will a more realistic film into being by articulating his enthusiasms for Italian neo-realism, documentaries, and location shooting. His rich, metaphorical prose nudged film reviewing in a more classical-essay direction. W. H. Auden, the great English-American poet, famously declared that though he did not care much for movies and rarely saw them, he read Agee religiously: "In my opinion, his column is the most remarkable regular event in American journalism today."

Another writer who helped make film criticism more rigorous and respectable in the postwar period was Robert Warshow, who wrote serious, morally probing essays on movies for quarterlies such as *Partisan Review* and *Commentary*. Warshow displayed a sure instinct for film aesthetics, though he was often unfairly characterized as a "sociological" critic because he used movies as a springboard for analyzing traits in the national character (see his brilliantly suggestive "The Gangster as Tragic Hero").

The impetus for reading national character into films had been sparked by Siegfried Kracauer's 1947 study *From Caligari to Hitler*. "It is my contention," wrote Kracauer, "that through an analysis of the German films deep psychological dispositions in Germany from 1918 to 1933 can be exposed—dispositions which influenced the course of events during that time and which will have to be reckoned with in the post-Hitler era." The United States military even commissioned studies about the ways that mass psychology was reflected in movies, thereby employing film criticism as an intelligence-gathering tool. Martha Wolfenstein and Nathan Leites, Barbara Deming, Hortense Powdermaker, and others decoded the tensions in American culture by analyzing popular films' narrative tropes.

Inevitably, this concentration on movies' plots as sociological treasure troves provoked a formalist backlash. In emphasizing the movie's script or "literary" values, argued the formalists, something was lost: proper attention to composition, lighting, camera movement, art direction, the actor's costume and body language—in short, film's visual allure. The old chicken-and-egg argument regarding form and content had reemerged. While it was of course impossible to separate form strictly from content, the dispute had its periodic uses, since each film critic did tend to allot different proportions of interest to a film's dialogue or "message" and its cinematic technique.

One film critic who brought a trained painter's eye to his accounts of what transpired onscreen was Manny Farber, who took over for James Agee at *The Nation*. Farber was a true maverick, whose quirky, corkscrewing prose style took you into the push-pull of the screen's rectangle, the director's characteristic groupings of actors or background/foreground preferences. He was drawn to the Hopperesque atmospheres in American action movies and B pictures, which he called "underground movies" because the cultural Establishment generally ignored them; he was as eager to puncture the bloated reputations of "problem pictures" with social messages, perennially nominated for Best Picture Academy Awards, as he was to celebrate the incidental pleasures of a Howard Hawks aviation movie or a Raoul Walsh western. Farber was also astute at charting the unconscious mutations in an era's moviemaking practices.

Andrew Sarris, who started out in the mid-1950s, was another important American critic who looked at filmmakers' visual styles as a clue to their moral meanings. In doing so, he took a leaf from French critic André Bazin, who had favored the flowing *mise-en-scène* (deep-focused, often mobile long shots) approach over montage and close-ups, and from the young *Cahiers du Cinéma* critics (François Truffaut, Jean-Luc Godard, Claude Chabrol, Eric Rohmer, Jacques Rivette), about to become the French New Wave, who adored Hollywood movies. Sarris, too, championed the Hollywood directors who had managed to retain their individual spark in the face of impersonal studio production practices, and he welcomed the mature, adult viewpoint of European art cinema in his own version of *auteurism*. As Sarris understood it, the "auteur theory" was an attempt to account for the quality in a film by designating its main author, usually the director, based partly on analysis of past track records. "Hence, the auteur theory is a theory of film history rather than film prophecy," wrote Sarris. In attempting to bring order to American film history, he ranked directors in categories of achievement, positing a new canon that provoked considerable disagreement.

Film critics, an obstinately intuitive lot who mistrust systems to begin with, were especially dubious about a list that found any merit in commercial potboilers and seemed susceptible to glossing over weaknesses of performance or script in the interests of confirming some signature, personal style. (See Stanley Kauffmann's mixed review of Max Ophuls' *Lola Montes*.) One critic taking particular umbrage at the auteur theory was Pauline Kael, who wrote a maliciously funny, if unfair, polemic, "Circles and Squares: Joys and Sarris," against what she saw as its boys' club favoritism: "When a famous director makes a good movie, we look at the movie, we don't think about the director's personality; when he makes a stinker we notice his familiar touches because there's not much else to watch." Kael's detractors pointed out that she went on to acquire her own pet directors, such as Sam Peckinpah, Bernardo Bertolucci, and Brian DePalma. She also developed a huge, loyal following at *The New Yorker*, during which time she opened readers' eyes to the new, roller-coaster style of American film in the 1970s. Given permission to write "long," Kael pushed American film criticism further into a new zone of essayistic headiness.

The 1960s and 70s, whether because of the remarkable bounty of good films, or the rising interest in film culture, or both, spawned a golden age in American movie criticism. Alongside Farber, Sarris, and Kael, there were the cultured, resolutely non-film buff critics, such as Stanley Kauffmann, John Simon, William S. Pechter, Dwight Macdonald; there were the writers who focused more intently on questions of sexuality and gender, such as Parker Tyler, whose book *Screening the Sexes* paved the way for gay film studies, and Molly Haskell, whose pioneering *From Reverence to Rape* explored the treatment of women in movies; there were the proponents of experimental, avant-garde film such as Jonas Mekas and P. Adams Sitney. All united in disdaining the *New*

York Times' powerful but (to their mind) hopelessly square Bosley Crowther, the Colley Cibber of American film criticism. When Crowther was finally forced to retire after lambasting the hippest film of the season, *Bonnie and Clyde*, the *Times* replaced him first with Renata Adler and subsequently with Vincent Canby, who proved to be the best daily reviewer this country has ever had.

From the mid-1970s onward, along with daily or weekly responses to the latest releases, an impressive body of more measured, reflective film criticism about older movies began to accumulate: Walter Kerr's lively analysis of silent comedians, Arlene Croce's peerless study of the Fred Astaire–Ginger Rogers films, wise books by Stanley Cavell, James Harvey, and Elizabeth Kendall on the romantic or screwball comedies of the 1930s and 40s, among others. Some critics, such as the adventurous Jonathan Rosenbaum and David Thomson, who kept updating his magisterial *Biographical Dictionary of Film*, went back and forth, responding to new movies while refining their long-range historical perspective. Increasingly, film critics' judgments about the cinematic past became an important piece of their rhetorical armature and their standards for evaluating new work.

The proliferation of film studies programs in universities, from the 1970s onward, also began to exert an influence on American movie criticism. In a field earlier populated by self-taught amateurs and enthusiasts, a graduate degree suddenly seemed to bestow expertise. With this new crop of film-scholar graduates came sets of theoretical terms and concepts, smuggled into hurried review prose. The last twenty-five years have also been affected by postmodernism, as seen in the eclectic, mockingly decentered criticism of J. Hoberman and Geoffrey O'Brien, or the adoption of false personae (Paul Rudnick aka Libby Gelman-Waxner). In keeping with trends in cultural studies, issues of gender (Carrie Rickey) or race (Armond White, bell hooks) have also received critical emphasis. The sociological school of film criticism, which had seemed long ago put to rout by the formalists and auteurists, has revived, as young critics again look for clues to the ideological construction of films. In other words, film critics no longer are inclined to choose between form and content: everything is political, everything is aesthetics.

What can we say about the current status of film criticism? Many complain that the prestige or "clout" of film critics has declined from a high point in the 1960s and 70s. It is certainly true that, with the shrinking number of general-interest magazines and the greater emphasis on graphic design over copy, fewer venues exist now for thoughtful, sustained film criticism; there seems precious little middle ground between the consumer guide/sidebar squib and the academic article, with its abstruse jargon. Some have argued that film criticism matters less today because movies matter less—are simply not as good as they used to be. Susan Sontag, one of our best off-and-on film critics, even went so far as to mourn "the death of cinema." While brilliant, overpowering, innovative movies continue to be made every year, what does seem to have declined is the support apparatus for the medium: the art-movie houses, the 16mm film university circuit, the number of foreign films distributed, the film-buff magazines, the general public's level of interest in film history.

With the diminished prestige of the European art movie (household names such as Fellini, Antonioni, Bergman, Buñuel, Truffaut, and Fassbinder have yielded few popular successors), contemporary film critics are torn between responding to the latest Hollywood mega-hit and trolling the backwaters of Asia, Africa, the Middle East, and the avant-garde for a new pantheon. The elegant stylist Stuart Klawans, in *The Nation*, will alternate between reviewing *Gladiator* one week and the latest unreleased masterpiece by Taiwanese director Hou Hsiao-hsien the next. The discerning Gilberto Perez, writing in quarterlies, will do an in-depth consideration of the experimentalist Ernie Gehr one month and the Iranian master Abbas Kiarostomi the next. A new breed of film critics, made understandably impatient with old-fogy laments for the 1960s and 70s, has set about to advocate work that is firing up younger audiences: delirious, visually gorgeous, sensation-drunk movies by David Lynch, Wes Anderson, Wong Kar-wai, Quentin Tarantino, Baz Luhrmann, Tsai Ming-liang, Sofia Coppola, and others. These open-ended yet oddly claustrophobic, self-referential films often have an inner pulse that resembles rock music more than classic film narrative. In any event, the art of film is changing; and fortunately there are still film critics such as Kent Jones and Manohla Dargis who are alert enough to explain, as Manny Farber did so often in the past, how that ground is shifting.

"I should like to inquire why we as the nation that produces the movies should never have developed any sound school of movie criticism," wrote Otis Ferguson in "The Case of the Critics." Since he wrote that sentence in 1941, I think it can be safely asserted that we *have* developed a sound school of American movie criticism—thanks to Ferguson himself, James Agee, Robert Warshow, Manny Farber, Parker Tyler, Andrew Sarris, Pauline Kael, and those who have followed in their wake. The best of that criticism belongs as much to the canon of American nonfiction prose as it does to the history of film reception.

◆

Perhaps it is the time to ask: What is the job of a film critic?

First of all, the film critic is a *critic*. If we look at other fields of criticism we see a great deal of overlap. The literary critic F. O. Matthiessen wrote that the valuable book review "should furnish exposition and description; it should enable you to feel concretely what is being described; and it should give you in the process an evaluation," or "analytical insights, as you went along," while placing the work "in relation to what has been previously accomplished in the same field." According to Eric Bentley, the theater critic is "someone who knows almost everything relevant to theater," and is "an alert person not over-burdened with hostility or with a desire to please or be cute. He is as receptive as possible. . . . An attempt must be made at fairness, as in a court of law."

But film criticism has particular demands alongside those addressing other art forms. How, given such a complexly collaborative medium, to disentangle the different aspects that go into moviemaking (acting, direction, screenplay, sound, cinematography, art direction, editing); how also to suggest career patterns and shifts, by considering to what degree the film under review fits this actor's, director's, or studio's previous output; how to situate it in terms of its genre, and consider along those lines its originality or triteness; how to address its implicit social or political meanings, which may need to be teased out of its glossy surface; how to analyze the mass audience's response, which may differ from your own. All this often within a thousand words or less, sometimes juggling three films per column. Space limitations foster a style of witty compression. The critic learns to come at a film from a distinct angle or setup. Hence, the tendency for film criticism to move in an essayistic direction, as the writer gropes for some opening paragraph that can help generalize about the example(s) under discussion.

A premium is placed on the film critic's ability to translate visual representation into crisply vivid verbal descriptions. Further professional considerations include: how do you structure a piece of film criticism so that it builds toward a satisfying conclusion? How do you sustain tension—by coming out swinging, by staging a bout between your ambivalences, or by deferring an overall judgment as long as possible? How do you evolve a stylish prose that is textured, surprising, contemporary without pandering, neither too lightweight nor too solemn? How do you maintain enough resilience not to suffer burnout or get overly crabby, given the vast preponderance of bad movies?

The film critic cannot be solely preoccupied with identifying instances of film art because too many movies are clearly not artistic in any manner. It won't do to sound piously outraged at each instance of a movie's failing to rise to the level of art. Working critics have to develop philosophies about "trash" or "bad movies"—see Pauline Kael and J. Hoberman on the subject—and strategies for writing about entertaining junk, either by isolating those gifted cameos or enjoyable moments that rise above the general mediocrity or by employing a variety of ironic, satiric, humorous tones to illuminate the triumph of tripe. Still, how do you find something fresh to say about the unremarkable commercial pictures that accomplish what they modestly set out to do, but frankly elicit no new exciting thoughts? How do you maintain the integrity to speak your mind, resisting coercions from the movie industry, your editor, your peer group, and the public?

The critic should not be expected to predict which films the audience will love; the critic is only supposed to give an intelligent accounting of his or her response. In 1935, Otis Ferguson noted wryly that *Variety* kept a mid-year box score for "true critics," a category from which he, writing for *The New Republic*, was excluded: "Every quarter *Variety* lines up the leading daily reviewers and gives them their report cards, having kept a careful check on how the critic seemed to like a picture as against whether the picture seemed to make money. By this standard his review is either 'right or wrong.' . . . So there they all are, *Variety*, the nine New York critics, and the four Chicago critics, all in black and white, and their relative worth carried out to three decimal places. And all one of them has to do if he wants to find out whether he is a good critic is to look himself up in the list. Incidentally, all he has to do if he wants to *be* a good critic is keep his ear to the ground for rumors, his eye peeled for double-truck advance ads, and his nose out for the way films are going financially before they break in New York—as reported weekly in *Variety*. It is absolutely wonderful."

One reason why small-circulation publications such as *The Nation* and *The New Republic* played such a disproportionately large role in nurturing good film critics was that they were immune from industry arm-twisting, since studios did not bother to place ads there. Their wages may have been piddling, but these critics enjoyed independence, a literate readership, and a platform from which to develop a voice.

Critics for large publications enjoy massive readerships and better pay, but can face harsher pressures. When the *Los Angeles Times*' film critic Kenneth Turan panned *Titanic*, which then went on to become the biggest hit in Hollywood history, the movie's director, James Cameron, demanded that Turan be fired because he seemed obviously out of touch with popular taste. Turan replied calmly: "Film critics, general opinion notwithstanding, are not intended to be applause meters. Just as restaurant critics don't send couples seeking that special anniversary meal to McDonald's on the 'everybody goes there, it must be the best' theory, the overall mandate of critics must be to point out the existence and importance of other criteria for judgment besides popularity."

What are these "other criteria"? They tend to be devised on the run by each critic. Dwight Macdonald said that he had initially come up with five rules for measuring the quality of a film: "1) Are the characters consistent, and in fact are there characters at all? 2) Is it true to life? 3) Is the photography cliché, or is it adapted to the particular film and therefore original? 4) Do the parts go together; do they add up to something; is there a rhythm established so that there is form, shape, climax, building up tension and exploding it? 5) Is there a mind behind it; is there a feeling that a single intelligence has imposed his own view on the material?" Later, he tossed most of these criteria out, deciding that they were arbitrary and limited to only one kind of film. He substituted two others: "(A) Did it change the way you look at things? (B) Did you find more (or less) in the second, third, *n*th time? (Also, how did it stand up over the years, after one or more 'periods' of cinematic history?)" Macdonald clearly had grown wary of being suckered by his own transient enthusiasms, and was more interested later on in the long view—which films would survive as classics through multiple viewings.

Pauline Kael, by contrast, claimed that she never saw a movie more than once if she could help it. Her criteria were based more on parsing in tranquility her first-time visceral responses to the viewing experience. (She was aided by a phenomenal memory.) Andrew Sarris, in this way Kael's polar opposite, never stopped mulling over, re-viewing, and changing his mind about certain movies.

Manny Farber once told an interviewer that as a critic he found the role of evaluation "practically worthless. The last thing I want to know is whether you like it or not; the problems of writing are *after* that. I don't think it has any importance; it's one of those derelict appendages of criticism. Criticism has nothing to do with hierarchies." For Farber, it would seem, the job of the film critic was not necessarily to render a judgment, but to stage in print a processing of his complicated thoughts about a movie, in the attempt to understand better what he made of it.

All critics seem to agree that the critic is not there to give pointers to the filmmaker so that his work will improve in the next go-round. Most critics profess humility enough to understand that their words may have little effect on shaping the next generation of films. (In spite of this, it can be argued, the aes-

[handwritten marginalia: Various ways of defining]

thetic ambitions of American cinema in the past few decades have been profoundly shaped by the viewpoints of a handful of our film critics.)

The job of the American film critic is complicated by the fact that virtually
all Americans regard themselves as astute judges of movies. With good reason:
we grow up seeing hundreds of motion pictures in theaters and on television,
so that by our teenage years we know the current crop of actors, directors, and
genres, and even some of the classics. Pressed for time, we cannot help but
approach a reviewer as a consumer guide, singling out the best Friday-night
date choices and zeroing in on four stars and letter grades. In part, we are
looking for a mirror, someone like ourselves who is reasonably tasteful and not
too picky.

In his essay "A Critical Credo," John Simon asks: "What constitutes good
criticism? Perhaps it is easiest to begin by defining the commonest kind of bad
criticism, which is not criticism at all but reviewing. Reviewing is something
that newspaper editors have invented: it stems from the notion that the critic
is someone who must see with the eyes of the Average Man or Typical Reader
(whoever that is) and predict for his fellows what their reaction will be. To this
end, the newspapers carefully screen their reviewers to be representative common men, say, former obituary writers or mailroom clerks, anything but trained
specialists."

In the past, it would seem that *not* knowing much about movies served as
a qualification for a film reviewing post. The public, feeling already informed,
resisted the notion of film appreciation as a specialized field of study that might
necessitate historians, theorists, mavens. Yet however much satirists may poke
fun at the snobbish devotee of "the cinemaah," writing well about movies does
require historical knowledge and formal cultivation. How, then, does a film
critic assert authority in the face of the public's resistance to cinematic expertise? (The answer is: tactfully.)

Though university departments with their courses and degrees have
greatly altered the landscape of film studies in the last forty years, becoming a
film critic still seems largely a matter of knack, luck, and bluff. You can't just
hang out a shingle and wait for customers. Assuming you have gotten a foot in
the door, you must then earn respect as a *writer* and convert readers to the regular habit of perusing (if not agreeing with) you, largely on the basis on producing entertaining, convincing critical prose. It is a literary performance, in
the final analysis: What is involved is the operation of one art form (literature)
on another (the movies). Film critics, who must represent the visual in verbal
terms, start out for this reason somewhat on the defensive, knowing they
can be charged with a primarily writerish, or "literary," take on a movie.

"Exasperated by my unyielding stance toward *Titanic*, a friend recently informed me that I 'care too much about words.' To that charge I'm forced to plead guilty," wrote Kenneth Turan.

Third, the film critic is also a human being, who brings to the job all sorts of autobiographical quirks. Some critics willingly insert personal details in the midst of analyzing a movie, and we come to form an intimate picture of them. Andrew Sarris will remark offhandedly about his childhood and parents in Queens; Vincent Canby tells us he was in the army; we learn from Pauline Kael that her Western rancher-father was a Republican and an adulterer. We also glean the critic's other interests: that Otis Ferguson loves jazz, Manny Farber is knowledgeable about painting and prizefighting, Stanley Kauffmann has a deep feeling for the theater, Stanley Cavell is devoted to Emerson, James Agee seems interested in everything. Renata Adler, preparing herself to become the *New York Times* critic, commented: "The best criticism I read was still by writers who simply felt moved by film to say something about it—without reverent or consistent strategies, putting films idiosyncratically alongside things they cared about in other ways." Paradoxically, the really good film critic has to show an interest in something else besides movies; a well-stocked mind remains the mark of the true essayist.

Reading a favorite film critic regularly, you learn to make adjustments for blind spots and to sense, for whatever obscure biographical reasons, which forbidden desires or deadly sins the writer is most likely to condone or condemn. Being human, film critics also fall in love. Because movies are so sensually seductive, they encourage a falling-in-love response, which may or may not always yield the best critical writing. Sometimes the critic becomes smitten with a particular performer, and may even mischievously draw attention to the infatuation. Critics must be hypersensitive to their subjective responses as a starting-point. In addition, all film critics place mental bets on certain moviemakers to be the future hope, the cutting edge, just as all film critics write off certain attention-getting "comers" as irredeemably overrated. It then becomes the critic's task to admit at least the possibility that those already mentally dismissed as hacks might conceivably succeed with their next film. Conversely, loving a performer or filmmaker beyond measure may lead to overreactions in the opposite direction, as though the failure to live up to the critic's expectations were not just a disappointment but a betrayal.

The film critic we trust and read regularly becomes a kind of old friend whose conversation we cherish and to whom we turn eagerly for opinions and advice. Stanley Cavell said it best: "the writing about film which has meant something to me has the power of the missing companion. Agee and Robert

Warshow and André Bazin manage that mode of conversation all the time; and I have found it in, among others, Manny Farber, Pauline Kael, Parker Tyler, Andrew Sarris." In this sense, the best film criticism verges on the personal essay, where the particular topic matters less, in the long run, than the companionable voice.

Just as the personal essay tradition invites practitioners to engage with their illustrious ancestors, so film critics seem to be forever looking over their shoulders at their predecessors and contemporaries. Sometimes the dialogue becomes more contentious than reverential. In reviewing the literature, I am struck by how many times a film critic has felt the need to launch an assessment of a movie by ridiculing or denouncing the opinions of some colleague. This fraternal dissing popped up constantly in the 1960s and 70s, when so much seemed at stake regarding movies that taste differences were rarely accorded a civil disagreement. In retrospect, Sarris, Kael, Farber, Tyler, Macdonald, Kauffmann, Simon, Schickel, Pechter, Haskell, et al., were obviously all fine critics and passionate film-lovers, engaged in a collective effort to shore up the art; but that ardent, monotheistic era inspired the zealous striking down of any potential false gods. The rush to puncture the latest prestige movie was part of the same syndrome, which persists to this day. Some film critics still feel the need to position themselves as maverick outsiders against a putatively smug cultural establishment. This combative strategy is but one of the many tried-and-true ways to insert tension into a film review.

Much ink has been expended on the difference between film reviewing and film criticism. It's been said that the former is addressed to those who have not yet seen the movie, the latter, to those who have (or as though this were the case). The reviewer is caricatured as a vulgar, thumbs-up consumer guide; the critic, seen as more of an armchair intellectual. In truth, film reviewing at its best is every bit as demanding and rigorous as the most leisurely film criticism. In this collection I take the position that, at their highest levels, there is no hard line between the two. Personally, I admire as much the man-about-town, deadline prose of the *Times'* Vincent Canby as I do the measured philosophical reflections by Harvard's Stanley Cavell about classic Hollywood movies.

◆

My main criterion for selection has been personal: I either liked or didn't like the way a piece of criticism was written. In that respect, I have focused on film criticism as an art in itself—the magnet for strong, elegant, eloquent, enjoyable writing—rather than as a conduit for film theory. Not that film theory need necessarily be turgidly written; but the lay reader's pleasure is rarely where it places its emphasis. Similarly, in restricting the emphasis to film criticism, I have excluded chapters from film histories, such as those by Terry Ramsaye, Lewis Jacobs, Arthur Knight; excerpts from screen biographies, research studies, memoirs about working in movies, or on-the-set journalism; I have scanted fan magazines and trade journals.

I have concentrated, in my selections, on practicing film critics. However, the movies being such a dominant medium in modern American life, it has perforce attracted the occasional attention of our country's finest writers; and so I have included a smattering of criticism done by great kibitzers such as Edmund Wilson, Paul Goodman, James Baldwin, and John Ashbery.

Another criterion I adhered to, in order to focus the project, was that the critic be American, either born or naturalized. (The volume's title does not refer to the provenance of the movies under discussion, but to the author of the criticism.) By this logic, I have been forced to exclude such wonderful English critics as Graham Greene, Raymond Durgnat, and Anthony Lane, while including David Thomson, who was born in England but immigrated to California. Such ground rules may sound petty, but any attempt to anthologize all the glorious film criticism written worldwide would have required a set of gargantuan tomes. Even limiting the field to American critics, I faced stringent space limitations in keeping to a single manageable volume; consequently I have had to omit the work of many able contemporary film critics (myself included). I might add that in any anthology seeking to honor the historical development of a literary form, the present is always the hardest period to evaluate. However, much as I was tempted to lop off the parade at 1975, I concluded in the end that some present voices needed to be included in this collection to represent at least a sampling of the very fine film criticism that continues to be written today.

Although I've followed a more or less linear progression forward, from the silent era to today, I have organized the book by individual film critics rather than by the strict chronological composition of each critical piece. In other words, I've put all of Farber, Kael, or Sarris together in his or her own section, even though each of these writers spanned several decades—the reason being that I wanted to highlight each critic as an individual stylist. Also, it made no sense to divide the book thematically because the same critic might discuss several films from different genres in a single piece.

One further criterion, or prejudice, which I am almost embarrassed to admit, guided my selections: Did I agree or disagree with the critic's assessment of a film? I found that if I disagreed too strenuously, it was difficult for

me to include the critique. But subtler shades of disagreement seemed tolerable and indeed welcome. The selections that follow offer many opportunities
to compare conflicting viewpoints. Charlie Chaplin is a case study: I have
included half a dozen responses to his movies, ranging from worshipful to worried to sardonically critical. Readers may also be surprised to discover that films
they regard as unassailable classics, such as *Citizen Kane*, were greeted in their
day by more guarded or dismissive responses. Is it possible to say, then, that
some critics were more "right" than others, given the present consensus on
these films? I think not. The critical reservations registered then still have resonance, and a curious appeal. In some cases we can allow for the earlier critic's
"wrongheaded" judgment by considering the historic context underpinning
that response. In others we might permit an earlier critic's skepticism to correct our own tendency to accept as perfect and indivisible the miracle of an old,
nostalgically cherished film.

◆

There has been much speculation about what future influence the Internet will have on American movie criticism. As the number of newspapers and
periodicals that employ regular film critics has shrunk in recent years, the
growth of e-magazines and other websites has picked up some of the slack. But
since many of these websites have still not figured out a way to turn a profit,
the question remains: How is an Internet film critic to make a living from
writing reviews and extended criticism? The tentative answer (except for a
dozen lucky souls) is: You're not. Then again, film criticism has often been
more an avocation than a paying job: in the past, cinephiles who wrote for quarterlies and highbrow journals often had to supplement their scant fees with day
jobs, teaching posts, and other free-lance writing assignments.

Today, young people, many of whom remain fascinated by movies, have
taken to the Internet to air their views. Personal film criticism blogs prolifer-
ate, and while some seem driven merely by ego, others testify to the fact that
film culture is alive and well. There are websites devoted to obscure art-house
directors, or even a single film. Communally speaking, the Internet becomes
a meeting place for aficionados, connoisseurs, film geeks, and film buffs, who
can finally ruminate uncensored, with all the esoteric shadings of their mental
obsessions.

The lack of remuneration for most Internet film criticism curiously opens
up a vast sphere of freedom to the hobbyist blogger, who may chatter on about
a film to heart's content, without worrying about word counts. It is often

observed that the Internet encourages a sort of unedited stream-of-consciousness. Often, the result is sloppy, self-indulgent, inelegant writing. Still, by working out one's thoughts, hesitations, and skepticisms in this circular fashion, the amateur can hone the craft of film criticism in a non-pressured situation and acquire professional polish.

Much of the writing by professional film critics that one sees on the Internet is no different, stylistically speaking, from the kind encountered in print: it is taut, clever, economical, and opinionated. If most film criticism on the web is finally glibly unmemorable, the same could be said for the majority of print reviews. Indeed, the best web practitioners, such as Stephanie Zacharek, Charles Taylor, and Andrew O'Hehir, have traversed effortlessly back and forth between the Internet and print media.

One of the most intriguing web phenomena in recent years occurs when distinguished film critics, such as David Bordwell and Dave Kehr, voluntarily operate their own blogs in order to establish dialogue with readers and fellow practitioners. The blog also permits a practiced critic like Bordwell to use a more casual, conversational writing style than he might employ in, say, a monograph or textbook. The utopian conversation in cyberspace that ensues seems to invite a democratic parity among speakers, though the teacher-student model cannot help but persist as well, given the eminent authority of the blog operator. Manners may become somewhat ragged, as intruding bloggers "pile on" and Oedipal challenges erupt between Young Turks and graybeard patriarchs. At its best, however, one senses a new form of criticism emerging, produced by a sort of collective mind that keeps adjusting, reexamining, and inserting layers of judgment about a movie.

As digitalized delivery systems replace film projection, as motion pictures are downloaded on demand or seen on cell phones, as video games and other audiovisual entertainments challenge the supremacy of movies, film critics today (see the new pieces by Bordwell and Nathan Lee) increasingly analyze the fate of movies in the larger context of technological innovation and media saturation. Then again, movies have always been mutating, redefined in turn by the coming of sound, color, widescreen, or computerized editing, and the perspective of the film critic has evolved alongside these changes.

◆

All anthologies feed on the bones of prior anthologies. I would like to acknowledge the invaluable orientation I received from *Garbo and the Night Watchmen*, edited by Alistair Cooke (1937), *Film: An Anthology*, edited by

Daniel Talbot (1966), *American Film Criticism: From the Beginnings to Citizen Kane*, edited by Stanley Kauffmann with Bruce Henstell (1972), and *Awake in the Dark*, edited by David Denby (1977). Among the many friends and colleagues, too numerous to list, who offered their suggestions during the making of this book, I want to single out Meredith Brody, Tom Luddy, Richard Pena, Pierre Rissient, and Mark Street. A very special thanks to Myron Lounsbury for his tireless suggestions and photocopies. I also thank my intern, Jennie Yabroff, who was invaluable in tracking down reviews and sharing enthusiasms. And of course my editors, Geoffrey O'Brien and Max Rudin, for their enthusiastic support and erudite, honest feedback.

Phillip Lopate

1

◆

Pioneers

The Silent Era and the
Transition to Sound

Vachel Lindsay

The Bard of Springfield, Illinois, Vachel Lindsay (1879–1931) crisscrossed the United States three times in his twenties, selling his rhymes for bread, hobo-style, and spreading what he called "the gospel of Beauty." He later became a celebrity of the lecture circuit, reciting the aurally bravura, jazz-rhythmic poems such as "The Kalyope Yell," "General William Booth Enters Into Heaven" and "The Congo" that made him famous and earned him a permanent place in poetry anthologies. In addition to his twelve volumes of poetry, Lindsay wrote the first work of film aesthetics in America, *The Art of the Moving Picture*, a summary of what the movies had done so far as of 1914 and were capable of in the future. He divided films into categories such as the Action Film, the Intimate Film, and the Film of Splendor. Lindsay was an enthusiastic pitchman for the movies, and sought to legitimize them by comparing each category to the traditional visual arts (Sculpture-in-Motion, Painting-in-Motion, Architecture-in-Motion) and to literature (the drama, the lyric, the epic). He was guilty of rhapsodic exaggeration at times; yet, as can be seen in the chapter below, "The Photoplay of Action," he was also clear-sighted and funny about the genre's limitations, which he described in vigorous, peppery prose.

Decades after the poet's death, film scholar Myron Lounsbury discovered, along with scattered articles of film criticism, a second, unpublished manuscript by Lindsay, a sequel to *The Art of the Moving Picture* written in 1925 which he called *The Greatest Movies Now Running* (and which Lounsbury retitled *The Progress and Poetry of the Movies*), from which the second entry is excerpted. In it Lindsay lambastes the country's "beehive" conformity, while singling out Douglas Fairbanks and D. W. Griffith as harbingers of a new American Renaissance.

◆

The Photoplay of Action

Let us assume, friendly reader, that it is eight o'clock in the evening when you make yourself comfortable in your den, to peruse this chapter. I want to tell you about the Action Film, the simplest, the type most often seen. In the mind of the habitué of the cheaper theatre it is the only sort in existence. It dominates the slums, is announced there by red and green posters of the melodrama sort, and retains its original elements, more deftly handled, in places more expensive. The story goes at the highest possible speed to be still

3

credible. When it is a poor thing, which is the case too often, the St. Vitus dance destroys the pleasure-value. The rhythmic quality of the picture-motions is twitched to death. In the bad photoplay even the picture of an express train more than exaggerates itself. Yet when the photoplay chooses to behave it can reproduce a race far more joyously than the stage. On that fact is based the opportunity of this form. Many Action Pictures are indoors, but the abstract theory of the Action Film is based on the out-of-door chase. You remember the first one you saw where the policeman pursues the comical tramp over hill and dale and across the town lots. You remember that other where the cowboy follows the horse thief across the desert, spies him at last and chases him faster, faster, faster, and faster, and finally catches him. If the film was made in the days before the National Board of Censorship, it ends with the cowboy cheerfully hanging the villain; all details given to the last kick of the deceased.

One of the best Action Pictures is an old Griffith Biograph, recently reissued, the story entitled "Man's Genesis." In the time when cave-men-gorillas had no weapons, Weak-Hands (impersonated by Robert Harron) invents the stone club. He vanquishes his gorilla-like rival, Brute-Force (impersonated by Wilfred Lucas). Strange but credible manners and customs of the cave-men are detailed. They live in picturesque caves. Their half-monkey gestures are wonderful to see. But these things are beheld on the fly. It is the chronicle of a race between the brain of Weak-Hands and the body of the other, symbolized by the chasing of poor Weak-Hands in and out among the rocks until the climax. Brain desperately triumphs. Weak-Hands slays Brute-Force with the startling invention. He wins back his stolen bride, Lily-White (impersonated by Mae Marsh). It is a Griffith masterpiece, and every actor does sound work. The audience, mechanical Americans, fond of crawling on their stomachs to tinker their automobiles, are eager over the evolution of the first weapon from a stick to a hammer. They are as full of curiosity as they could well be over the history of Langley or the Wright brothers.

The dire perils of the motion pictures provoke the ingenuity of the audience, not their passionate sympathy. When, in the minds of the deluded producers, the beholders should be weeping or sighing with desire, they are prophesying the next step to one another in worldly George Ade slang. This is illustrated in another good Action Photoplay: the dramatization of The Spoilers. The original novel was written by Rex Beach. The gallant William Farnum as Glenister dominates the play. He has excellent support. Their teamwork makes them worthy of chronicle: Thomas Santschi as McNamara, Kathlyn Williams as Cherry Malotte, Bessie Eyton as Helen Chester, Frank Clark as Dextry, Wheeler Oakman as Bronco Kid, and Jack McDonald as Slapjack.

There are, in The Spoilers, inspiriting ocean scenes and mountain views. There are interesting sketches of mining-camp manners and customs. There is a well-acted love-interest in it, and the element of the comradeship of loyal pals. But the chase rushes past these things to the climax, as in a policeman picture it whirls past blossoming gardens and front lawns till the tramp is arrested. The difficulties are commented on by the people in the audience as rah-rah boys on the side lines comment on hurdles cleared or knocked over by the men running in college field-day. The sudden cutbacks into side branches of the story are but hurdles also, not plot complications in the stage sense. This is as it should be. The pursuit progresses without St. Vitus dance or hysteria to the end of the film. There the spoilers are discomfited, the gold mine is recaptured, the incidental girls are won, in a flash, by the rightful owners.

These shows work like the express elevators in the Metropolitan Tower. The ideal is the maximum of speed in descending or ascending, not to be jolted into insensibility. There are two girl parts as beautifully thought out as the parts of ladies in love can be expected to be in Action Films. But in the end the love is not much more romantic in the eye of the spectator than it would be to behold a man on a motorcycle with the girl of his choice riding on the same machine behind him. And the highest type of Action Picture romance is not attained by having Juliet triumph over the motorcycle handicap. It is not achieved by weaving in a Sherlock Holmes plot. Action Picture romance comes when each hurdle is a tableau, when there is indeed an art-gallery-beauty in each one of these swift glimpses: when it is a race, but with a proper and golden-linked grace from action to action, and the goal is the most beautiful glimpse in the whole reel.

In the Action Picture there is no adequate means for the development of any full grown personal passion. The distinguished character-study that makes genuine the personal emotions in the legitimate drama, has no chance. People are but types, swiftly moved chessmen. More elaborate discourse on this subject may be found in chapter twelve on the differences between the films and the stage. But here, briefly: the Action Pictures are falsely advertised as having heart-interest, or abounding in tragedy. But though the actors glower and wrestle and even if they are the most skilful lambasters in the profession, the audience gossips and chews gum.

Why does the audience keep coming to this type of photoplay if neither lust, love, hate, nor hunger is adequately conveyed? Simply because such spectacles gratify the incipient or rampant speed-mania in every American.

To make the elevator go faster than the one in the Metropolitan Tower is to destroy even this emotion. To elaborate unduly any of the agonies or seductions in the hope of arousing lust, love, hate, or hunger, is to produce on the screen a series of misplaced figures of the order Frankenstein.

How often we have been horrified by these galvanized and ogling corpses. These are the things that cause the outcry for more censors. It is not that our moral codes are insulted, but what is far worse, our nervous systems are temporarily racked to pieces. These wriggling half-dead men, these over-bloody burglars, are public nuisances, no worse and no better than dead cats being hurled about by street urchins.

The cry for more censors is but the cry for the man with the broom. Sometimes it is a matter as simple as when a child is scratching with a pin on a slate. While one would not have the child locked up by the chief of police, after five minutes of it almost every one wants to smack him till his little jaws ache. It is the very cold-bloodedness of the proceeding that ruins our kindness of heart. And the best Action Film is impersonal and unsympathetic even if it has no scratching pins. Because it is cold-blooded it must take extra pains to be tactful. Cold-blooded means that the hero as we see him on the screen is a variety of amiable or violent ghost. Nothing makes his lack of human charm plainer than when we as audience enter the theatre at the middle of what purports to be the most passionate of scenes when the goal of the chase is unknown to us and the alleged "situation" appeals on its magnetic merits. Here is neither the psychic telepathy of Forbes Robertson's Cæsar, nor the firebreath of E. H. Sothern's Don Quixote. The audience is not worked up into the deadly still mob-unity of the speaking theatre. We late comers wait for the whole reel to start over and the goal to be indicated in the preliminary, before we can get the least bit wrought up. The prize may be a lady's heart, the restoration of a lost reputation, or the ownership of the patent for a churn. In the more effective Action Plays it is often what would be secondary on the stage, the recovery of a certain glove, spade, bull-calf, or rock-quarry. And to begin, we are shown a clean-cut picture of said glove, spade, bull-calf, or rock-quarry. Then when these disappear from ownership or sight, the suspense continues till they are again visible on the screen in the hands of the rightful owner.

In brief, the actors hurry through what would be tremendous passions on the stage to recover something that can be really photographed. For instance, there came to our town long ago a film of a fight between Federals and Confederates, with the loss of many lives, all for the recapture of a steam-engine that took on more personality in the end than private or general on either side, alive or dead. It was based on the history of the very engine photographed, or else that engine was given in replica. The old locomotive was full of character and humor amidst the tragedy, leaking steam at every orifice. The original is in one of the Southern Civil War museums. This engine in its capacity as a principal actor is going to be referred to more than several times in this work.

The highest type of Action Picture gives us neither the quality of Macbeth or Henry Fifth, the Comedy of Errors, or the Taming of the Shrew. It gives us rather that fine and special quality that was in the ink-bottle of Robert Louis Stevenson, that brought about the limitations and the nobility of the stories of Kidnapped, Treasure Island, and the New Arabian Nights.

This discussion will be resumed on another plane in the eighth chapter: Sculpture-in-Motion.

Having read thus far, why not close the book and go round the corner to a photoplay theatre? Give the preference to the cheapest one.

1915

The Artistic Position of Douglas Fairbanks and *The Thief of Bagdad* Production

Douglas Fairbanks is an interesting and approved figure, interesting because of the merit and energy of his enterprises, approved in general by the motion picture world, approved in a special way by the author of this book because he is not "incorporated." He has had an individual career as an actor and producer, when even the best movies had a department-store atmosphere and the technical methods of a "Board of Control." Movies, like skyscraper-architecture, at best have a suggestion of the factory.

There is much to say for Douglas Fairbanks that I will not put down in this chapter. He had a long preliminary career as a kind of giant, superhuman flea, jumping hurdles with a Billy-Sunday agility in a costume of modern, Arrow-collar cool correctness. The time was when he seemed to be turning out these productions every two weeks. This is the first Douglas Fairbanks period, and there is much more to be said for it than these light words might indicate. He put into it the genius of columnists like Stoddard King, Franklin P. Adams, Don Marquis, Christopher Morley, Ted Robinson, and worked as fast.

His second period, which now continues with increasing glory, began with a costume production called *The Mark of Zorro*. This was a Spanish, Old California swashbuckling play, which I remember as being as adequate and interesting as any sword show I ever beheld on the stage. The main merit of the movie was that it was a direct challenge to all the Hollywood moralizers who said there was no such thing as a successful costume show. This aphorism cheerfully wiped out history as ruthlessly as the sword of Genghis Khan or Attila the Hun. The sword of Fairbanks in *The Mark of Zorro* was a definite challenge to the wisdom of Hollywood. As a motion picture, it was generally praised by the critics, though the moral victory was not especially emphasized.

Next came *The Three Musketeers*, a better production than any stage version I have seen, and I have seen Salvini the younger in his prime. If we think of the general principles of movie construction, and the unbroken law that the race—the hurdle race—is the fundamental plot, it is easy to see why *The Three Musketeers* is better for the screen than for the stage. It starts on the highway, with an inn scene, and goes galloping down the highway, with pursuits through the woods of France, the streets of Paris, across to England and back, one immortal hurdle race—the last thing that can be done on the stage, but the fundamental thing that can be done with a photoplay plot.

Douglas Fairbanks, in *The Three Musketeers*, again defied Hollywood's mandate that history is a failure and costumes are an abomination to the American people, even though these same are endorsed by *The Saturday Evening Post* and Henry Ford. Evidently this was Fairbanks' own decision. There is too clearly the thought of one man for two men to have thought it out. We have further evidence that Douglas Fairbanks is his own master in the third costume play, *Robin Hood*, the production of which, as a moral action in the face of the despisers of history, is to be even more praised, because to continue in a good action is more difficult than to begin.

Of the three productions, I myself could least approve of *Robin Hood*. It was on the borders of department-store splendor. Fairbanks was not sufficiently an orchestra leader. The thing seemed to fall apart of its own weight, though in general the critics approved of this pageant as of the other more energetic productions, and it certainly did not fail of popular appeal. There were many interesting episodes, fine passages, but *Robin Hood* remains in my memory more as evidence of the tenacity of purpose of Douglas Fairbanks, the good public citizen, than as an item in motion picture history. But things have reached the point in America where anyone, living a national life, who can survive the beehive tendency, is, indeed, a sturdy soul. So, now when the fourth production appears—*The Thief of Bagdad*, in my opinion the greatest movie so far in movie history—still the choice of Douglas Fairbanks, obviously representing his personal policy, I am very much thrilled by the victory of the young amateur statesman in the face of massive formulas and over-organized bee-hive corporations. There are only a few men alive in American politics who are themselves—not patented. Al Smith, the Governor of New York, emerges as a person, and not a copyrighted character, not an advertisement, not a formula, not a corporation. William Allen White emerges as an editor, who is as much his own man as editors were in the days of Andrew Jackson. When Douglas

Fairbanks has the initiative to put on his fourth production with a policy that represents his own pride and not the acquisitiveness of a Board of Control, he puts himself in a class with Andrew Jackson, or Al Smith or William Allen White, or any other statesman whose name means individuality.

There is much to say for Fairbanks as an artist, but I have been discussing his patriotism only. He represents "The Star Spangled Banner," "The Battle Hymn of the Republic," and "America the Beautiful."

I compare *The Thief of Bagdad* always with Griffith's *Intolerance*. Anita Loos once said to me that *Intolerance* was "a bathtub full of diamonds." I do not think she would object to being quoted, or Griffith would object to the compliment. It was a humorous way of proclaiming that there were enough suggestions in *Intolerance*, to producers of imagination, to last the motion picture world for fifty years. There are moments when I would compare it with an eruption of Vesuvius; it was such a long, hot blast of genius. If what we are looking for in this world is new, titanic, creative force, it is folly to compare *Intolerance* with *The Thief of Bagdad*. There was more originality in *Intolerance* in fifteen minutes than in the whole *Thief of Bagdad* pageant. And *The Thief of Bagdad*, obviously, in its greatest moments, with definite and unvarying taste, picked the best effects of *Intolerance* and used them.

On the other hand, *The Thief of Bagdad* production was pure "movie." It was not defaced by amateur history, by amateur poetry, by amateur literature, by special pleading, by long rivers of sentimentality, or by any other lack of self-control. Griffith was not only guilty in these directions, but, in a practical way, he almost ruined his show by crowding into an afternoon what it would take about four afternoons to see and a lifetime to study right. Reels were turned unmercifully fast to cover the whole ground. I attended *Intolerance*, I suppose, twenty times in many cities, with more suspense, more mesmerized attention, than I ever expended upon any other work of art whatsoever. It was the beginning of a lifetime education cut all too short. We must all see and keep studying that film. Yet one can honestly say that in many, many ways, *The Thief of Bagdad* is an advance. I am attending it as frequently with no exhaustion whatever. Both productions are having the same effect on our minds, dear friends, as Emerson's "Address on the American Scholar" was said to have had on certain New England people—a great turning point.

1925

Hugo Münsterberg

Hugo Münsterberg was born in Danzig, Prussia, in 1863 and died in Cambridge, Massachusetts, in 1916. A classically trained psychologist, his experiments impressed William James, who lured him to Harvard University where he taught and wrote many texts on applied psychology. In 1915 he became entranced with movies and set about trying to understand the psychological experience of watching a movie, which led to his pioneering book *The Photoplay: A Psychological Study*. In it Münsterberg suggested that film transforms the external world into the mechanics of the mind, including memory, imagination, attention, and emotion. He also detailed how the spectator participates imaginatively in a succession of "flat pictures" to create the illusion of continuous movement and depth—how film and individual consciousness interact. But Professor Münsterberg was also concerned, as we see below, with the potential of movies to exert positive or unwholesome moral influences on spellbound audiences. The danger he saw was less through the exposure of innocent minds to crime or vice than through "the trivializing influence of a steady contact with things which are not worth knowing." How then, he asked, do we harness film's enormous potential to educate the public and raise the cultural tone without preaching sermons?

◆

The Function of the Photoplay

Enthusiasts claim that in the United States ten million people daily are attending picture houses. Sceptics believe that "only" two or three millions form the daily attendance. But in any case "the movies" have become the most popular entertainment of the country, nay, of the world, and their influence is one of the strongest social energies of our time. Signs indicate that this popularity and this influence are increasing from day to day. What are the causes, and what are the effects of this movement which was undreamed of only a short time ago?

The economists are certainly right when they see the chief reason for this crowding of picture houses in the low price of admission. For five or ten cents long hours of thrilling entertainment in the best seats of the house: this is the magnet which must be more powerful than any theater or concert. Yet the rush to the moving pictures is steadily increasing, while the prices climb up. The dime became a quarter, and in the last two seasons ambitious plays were given before audiences who paid the full theater rates. The character of audiences, too, suggests that inexpensiveness alone cannot be decisive. Six years ago a keen sociological observer characterized the patrons of the picture palaces as "the lower middle class and the massive public, youths and shopgirls between adolescence and maturity, small dealers, pedlars, laborers, charwomen, besides the small quota of children." This would be hardly a correct description today. This "lower middle class" has long been joined by the upper middle class. To be sure, our observer of that long forgotten past added meekly: "Then there emerges a superior person or two like yourself attracted by mere curiosity and kept in his seat by interest until the very end of the performance; this type sneers aloud to proclaim its superiority and preserve its self-respect, but it never leaves the theater until it must." Today you and I are seen there quite often, and we find that our friends have been there, that they have given up the sneering pose and talk about the new photoplay as a matter of course.

Above all, even those who are drawn by the cheapness of the performance would hardly push their dimes under the little window so often if they did not really enjoy the plays and were not stirred by a pleasure which holds them for hours. After all, it must be the content of the performances which is decisive of the incomparable triumph. We have no right to conclude from this that only the merits and excellences are the true causes of their success. A caustic critic would probably suggest that just the opposite traits are responsible. He would say that the average American is a mixture of business, ragtime, and senti-mentality. He satisfies his business instinct by getting so much for his nickel, he enjoys his ragtime in the slapstick humor, and gratifies his sentimentality with the preposterous melodramas which fill the program. This is quite true, and yet it is not true at all. Success has crowned every effort to improve the photostage; the better the plays are the more the audience approves them. The most ambitious companies are the most flourishing ones. There must be inner values which make the photoplay so extremely attractive and even fascinating.

To a certain degree the mere technical cleverness of the pictures even today holds the interest spellbound as in those early days when nothing but this technical skill could claim the attention. We are still startled by every orig-inal effect, even if the mere showing of movement has today lost its impres-siveness. Moreover we are captivated by the undeniable beauty of many settings. The melodrama may be cheap; yet it does not disturb the cultured mind as grossly as a similar tragic vulgarity would on the real stage, because it may have the snowfields of Alaska or the palm trees of Florida as radiant back-ground. An intellectual interest, too, finds its satisfaction. We get an insight into spheres which were strange to us. Where outlying regions of human interest are shown on the theater stage, we must usually be satisfied with some standardized suggestion. Here in the moving pictures the play may really bring us to mills and factories, to farms and mines, to courtrooms and hospitals, to castles and palaces in any land on earth.

Yet a stronger power of the photoplay probably lies in its own dramatic qualities. The rhythm of the play is marked by unnatural rapidity. As the words are absent which, in the drama as in life, fill the gaps between the actions, the gestures and deeds themselves can follow one another much more quickly. Happenings which would fill an hour on the stage can hardly fill more than twenty minutes on the screen. This heightens the feeling of vitality in the spectator. He feels as if he were passing through life with a sharper accent which stirs his personal energies. The usual make-up of the photoplay must strengthen this effect inasmuch as the wordlessness of the picture drama favors a certain simplification of the social conflicts. The subtler shades of the motives naturally demand speech. The later plays of Ibsen could hardly be transformed into photoplays. Where words are missing the characters tend to become stereotyped and the motives to be deprived of their complexity. The plot of the photoplay is usually based on the fundamental emotions which are common to all and which are understood by everybody. Love and hate, gratitude and envy, hope and fear, pity and jealousy, repentance and sinfulness, and all the similar crude emotions have been sufficient for the construction of most scenarios. The more mature development of the photoplay will certainly overcome this primitive character, as, while such an effort to reduce human life to simple instincts is very convenient for the photoplay, it is not at all necessary. In any case where this tendency prevails it must help greatly to excite and to intensify the personal feeling of life and to stir the depths of the human mind.

But the richest source of the unique satisfaction in the photoplay is probably that esthetic feeling which is significant for the new art and which we have understood from its psychological conditions. *The massive outer world has lost its weight, it has been freed from space, time, and causality, and it has been clothed in the forms of our own consciousness. The mind has triumphed over matter and the pictures roll on with the ease of musical tones. It is a superb enjoyment which no other art can furnish us.* No wonder that temples for the new goddess are built in every little hamlet.

The intensity with which the plays take hold of the audience cannot remain without strong social effects. It has even been reported that sensory hallucinations and illusions have crept in; neurasthenic persons are especially inclined to experience touch or temperature or smell or sound impressions from what they see on the screen. The associations become as vivid as realities, because the mind is so completely given up to the moving pictures. The applause into which the audiences, especially of rural communities, break out at a happy turn of the melodramatic pictures is another symptom of the strange fascination. But it is evident that such a penetrating influence must be fraught with dangers. The more vividly the impressions force themselves on the mind, the more easily must they become starting points for imitation and other motor responses. The sight of crime and of vice may force itself on the consciousness with disastrous results. The normal resistance breaks down and the moral balance, which would have been kept under the habitual stimuli of the narrow routine life, may be lost under the pressure of the realistic suggestions. At the same time the subtle sensitiveness of the young mind may suffer from the rude contrasts between the farces and the passionate romances which follow with benumbing speed in the darkened house. The possibilities of psychical infection and destruction cannot be overlooked.

Those may have been exceptional cases only when grave crimes have been traced directly back to the impulses from unwholesome photoplays, but no psychologist can determine exactly how much the general spirit of righteousness, of honesty, of sexual cleanliness and modesty, may be weakened by the unbridled influence of plays of low moral standard. All countries seem to have been awakened to this social danger. The time when unsavory French comedies poisoned youth lies behind us. A strong reaction has set in and the leading companies among the photoplay producers fight everywhere in the first rank for suppression of the unclean. Some companies even welcome censorship provided that it is high-minded and liberal and does not confuse artistic freedom with moral licentiousness. Most, to be sure, seem doubtful whether the new movement toward Federal censorship is in harmony with American ideas on the freedom of public expression.

But while the sources of danger cannot be overlooked, the social reformer ought to focus his interest still more on the tremendous influences for good which may be exerted by the moving pictures. The fact that millions are daily under the spell of the performances on the screen is established. The high degree of their suggestibility during those hours in the dark house may be taken for granted. Hence any wholesome influence emanating from the photoplay must have an incomparable power for the remolding and upbuilding of the national soul. From this point of view the boundary lines between the photoplay and the merely instructive moving pictures with the news of the day or the magazine articles on the screen become effaced. The intellectual, the moral, the social, and the esthetic culture of the community may be served by all of them. Leading educators have joined in endorsing the foundation of a

Universal Culture Lyceum. The plan is to make and circulate moving pictures for the education of the youth of the land, picture studies in science, history, religion, literature, geography, biography, art, architecture, social science, economics and industry. From this Lyceum "schools, churches and colleges will be furnished with motion pictures giving the latest results and activities in every sphere capable of being pictured."

But, however much may be achieved by such conscious efforts toward education, the far larger contribution must be made by the regular picture houses which the public seeks without being conscious of the educational significance. The teaching of the moving pictures must not be forced on a more or less indifferent audience, but ought to be absorbed by those who seek entertainment and enjoyment from the films and are ready to make their little economic sacrifice.

The purely intellectual part of this uplift is the easiest. Not only the news pictures and the scientific demonstrations but also the photoplay can lead young and old to ever new regions of knowledge. The curiosity and the imagination of the spectators will follow gladly. Yet even in the intellectual sphere the dangers must not be overlooked. They are not positive. It is not as in the moral sphere where the healthy moral impulse is checked by the sight of crimes which stir up antisocial desires. The danger is not that the pictures open insight into facts which ought not be to known. It is not the dangerous knowledge which must be avoided, but it is the trivializing influence of a steady contact with things which are not worth knowing. The larger part of the film literature of today is certainly harmful in this sense. The intellectual background of most photoplays is insipid. By telling the plot without the subtle motivation which the spoken word of the drama may bring, not only do the characters lose color but all the scenes and situations are simplified to a degree which adjusts them to a thoughtless public and soon becomes intolerable to an intellectually trained spectator.

They force on the cultivated mind that feeling which musical persons experience in the musical comedies of the day. We hear the melodies constantly with the feeling of having heard them ever so often before. This lack of originality and inspiration is not necessary; it does not lie in the art form. Offenbach and Strauss and others have written musical comedies which are classical. Neither does it lie in the form of the photoplay that the story must be told in that insipid, flat, uninspired fashion. Nor is it necessary in order to reach the millions. To appeal to the intelligence does not mean to presuppose college education. Moreover the differentiation has already begun. Just as the plays of Shaw or Ibsen address a different audience from that reached by *The*

Old Homestead or *Ben Hur*, we have already photoplays adapted to different types, and there is not the slightest reason to connect with the art of the screen an intellectual flabbiness. It would be no gain for intellectual culture if all the reasoning were confined to the so-called instructive pictures and the photoplays were served without any intellectual salt. On the contrary, the appeal of those strictly educational lessons may be less deep than the producers hope, because the untrained minds, especially of youth and of the uneducated audiences, have considerable difficulty in following the rapid flight of events when they occur in unfamiliar surroundings. The child grasps very little in seeing the happenings in a factory. The psychological and economic lesson may be rather wasted because the power of observation is not sufficiently developed and the assimilation proceeds too slowly. But it is quite different when a human interest stands behind it and connects the events in the photoplay.

The difficulties in the way of the right moral influence are still greater than in the intellectual field. Certainly it is not enough to have the villain punished in the last few pictures of the reel. If scenes of vice or crime are shown with all their lure and glamour the moral devastation of such a suggestive show is not undone by the appended social reaction. The misguided boys or girls feel sure that they would be successful enough not to be trapped. The mind through a mechanism which has been understood better and better by the psychologists in recent years suppresses the ideas which are contrary to the secret wishes and makes those ideas flourish by which those "subconscious" impulses are fulfilled. It is probably a strong exaggeration when a prominent criminologist recently claimed that "eighty-five per cent of the juvenile crime which has been investigated has been found traceable either directly or indirectly to motion pictures which have shown on the screen how crimes could be committed." But certainly, as far as these demonstrations have worked havoc, their influence would not have been annihilated by a picturesque court scene in which the burglar is unsuccessful in misleading the jury. The true moral influence must come from the positive spirit of the play itself. Even the photodramatic lessons in temperance and piety will not rebuild a frivolous or corrupt or perverse community. The truly upbuilding play is not a dramatized sermon on morality and religion. There must be a moral wholesomeness in the whole setting, a moral atmosphere which is taken as a matter of course like fresh air and sunlight. An enthusiasm for the noble and uplifting, a belief in duty and discipline of the mind, a faith in ideals and eternal values must permeate the world of the screen. If it does, there is no crime and no heinous deed which the photoplay may not tell with frankness and sincerity. It is not necessary to deny evil and sin in order to strengthen the consciousness of eternal justice.

But the greatest mission which the photoplay may have in our community is that of esthetic cultivation. No art reaches a larger audience daily, no esthetic influence finds spectators in a more receptive frame of mind. On the other hand no training demands a more persistent and planful arousing of the mind than the esthetic training, and never is progress more difficult than when the teacher adjusts himself to the mere liking of the pupils. The country today would still be without any symphony concerts and operas if it had only received what the audiences believed at the moment that they liked best. The esthetically commonplace will always triumph over the significant unless systematic efforts are made to reënforce the work of true beauty. Communities at first always prefer Sousa to Beethoven. The moving picture audience could only by slow steps be brought from the tasteless and vulgar eccentricities of the first period to the best plays of today, and the best plays of today can be nothing but the beginning of the great upward movement which we hope for in the photoplay. Hardly any teaching can mean more for our community than the teaching of beauty where it reaches the masses. The moral impulse and the desire for knowledge are, after all, deeply implanted in the American crowd, but the longing for beauty is rudimentary; and yet it means harmony, unity, true satisfaction, and happiness in life. The people still has to learn the great difference between true enjoyment and fleeting pleasure, between real beauty and the mere tickling of the senses.

Of course, there are those, and they may be legion today, who would deride every plan to make the moving pictures the vehicle of esthetic education. How can we teach the spirit of true art by a medium which is in itself the opposite of art? How can we implant the idea of harmony by that which is in itself a parody on art? We hear the contempt for "canned drama" and the machine-made theater. Nobody stops to think whether other arts despise the help of technique. The printed book of lyric poems is also machine-made; the marble bust has also "preserved" for two thousand years the beauty of the living woman who was the model for the Greek sculptor. They tell us that the actor on the stage gives the human beings as they are in reality, but the moving pictures are unreal and therefore of incomparably inferior value. They do not consider that the roses of the summer which we enjoy in the stanzas of the poet do not exist in reality in the forms of iambic verse and of rhymes; they live in color and odor, but their color and odor fade away, while the roses in the stanzas live on forever. They fancy that the value of an art depends upon its nearness to the reality of physical nature.

It has been the chief task of our whole discussion to prove the shallowness of such arguments and objections. We recognized that art is a way to overcome nature and to create out of the chaotic material of the world something entirely new, entirely unreal, which embodies perfect unity and harmony. The different arts are different ways of abstracting from reality; and when we began to analyze the psychology of the moving pictures we soon became aware that the photoplay has a way to perform this task of art with entire originality, independent of the art of the theater, as much as poetry is independent of music or sculpture of painting. It is an art in itself. Only the future can teach us whether it will become a great art, whether a Leonardo, a Shakespeare, a Mozart, will ever be born for it. Nobody can foresee the directions which the new art may take. Mere esthetic insight into the principles can never foreshadow the development in the unfolding of civilization. Who would have been bold enough four centuries ago to foresee the musical means and effects of the modern orchestra? Just the history of music shows how the inventive genius has always had to blaze the path in which the routine work of the art followed. Tone combinations which appeared intolerable dissonances to one generation were again and again assimilated and welcomed and finally accepted as a matter of course by later times. Nobody call foresee the ways which the new art of the photoplay will open, but everybody ought to recognize even today that it is worth while to help this advance and to make the art of the film a medium for an original creative expression of our time and to mold by it the esthetic instincts of the millions. Yes, it is a new art—and this is why it has such fascination for the psychologist who in a world of ready-made arts, each with a history of many centuries, suddenly finds a new form still undeveloped and hardly understood. For the first time the psychologist can observe the starting of an entirely new esthetic development, a new form of true beauty in the turmoil of a technical age, created by its very technique and yet more than any other art destined to overcome outer nature by the free and joyful play of the mind.

1916

Carl Sandburg

From 1920 to 1928, another major poet from Illinois, Carl Sandburg (1878–1967), was the regular movie critic for the *Chicago Daily News*. Every Sunday he would watch movies, then write his reviews and a weekly film-reflections column, devoting the rest of the week to other work. During this prolific period he also finished the first volume of his Pulitzer Prize–winning biography of Abraham Lincoln, *The Prairie Years*, his fourth volume of poetry, and his study of folk music, *The American Songbag*. But, as is clear from *The Movies Are*, Sandburg's posthumously collected film reviews and essays, he brought dedication, professionalism, and a sophisticated eye to movie criticism. Fellow-Chicagoan Roger Ebert, contrasting Vachel Lindsay and Sandburg, notes in his introduction to that collection: "Sandburg takes the view not of a theorist but of a daily newspaperman whose job is to steer readers toward the good movies and away from the bad ones." Among the masterpieces he hailed when they first came out were *The Cabinet of Dr. Caligari*, *Nanook of the North*, and *What Price Glory?* In energetic, juicy reviews such as the one he did for *Manhandled*, Sandburg seems to be working up a movie review like one of his poems, stringing together images with rhythmic force to convey the special atmosphere of a picture he admires.

◆

The Cabinet of Dr. Caligari

The most important and the most original photoplay that has come to this city of Chicago the last year is being presented at the Ziegfeld Theater this week in *The Cabinet of Dr. Caligari*. That is exactly the way some people say it.

The craziest, wildest, shivery movie that has come wriggling across the silversheet of a cinema house. That is the way other people look at it.

It looks like a collaboration of Rube Goldberg, Ben Hecht, Charlie Chaplin and Edgar Allan Poe—a melting pot of the styles and techniques of all four.

Are you tired of the same old things done the same old way? Do you wish to see murder and retribution, insanity, somnambulism, grotesque puppetry, scenery solemn and stormy, wild as the wildest melodrama and yet as restrained as comic and well-manipulated marionettes? Then it is you for this Caligari and his cabinet.

However, if your sense of humor and your instinct of wonder and your reverence of human mystery is not working well this week, then you should stay away from the Ziegfeld Theater because you would go away saying Caligari and his cabinet are sick, morbid, loony.

Recall to yourself before going that Mark Twain is only one of numerous mortal philosophers who has declared some one streak of insanity runs in each of us.

Only two American motion picture artists have approached the bold handling, the smash and the getaway, the stride and rapidity of this foreign made film. Those two artists are Charlie Chaplin and D. W. Griffith.

It is a healthy thing for Hollywood, Culver City, Universal City, and all other places where movie film is being produced that this photoplay has come along at this time. It is sure to have healthy hunches and show new possibilities in style and method to our American producers.

This film, *The Cabinet of Dr. Caligari*, is so bold a work of independent artists going it footloose that one can well understand it might affect audiences just as a sea voyage affects a shipload of passengers. Some have to leave the top decks, unable to stand sight or smell of the sea. Others take the air and the spray, the salt and the chill, and call the trip an exhilaration.

There are two murders. They are the creepiest murders this observer has thus far noted in photoplays. Yet the killings are only suggested. They are not told and acted out fully. (No censor could complain in this respect.) As murders they remind one of the darker pages of Shakespeare, of *Hamlet, Macbeth* and again of the De Quincey essay on "Murder as a Fine Art."

Then a sleepwalker is about to kill a woman. He drops the dagger instead and carries her away across house roofs down a street. Oh, this sad sleepwalker and how and why he couldn't help it.

This is one of the few motion picture productions that might make one say, "Here is one Shakespeare would enjoy coming back to have a look at."

However, be cheerful when you go to see this. Or else terribly sad. Its terrors and grotesques will match any sadness you may have and so comfort you. But if you go feeling real cheerful and expecting to be more cheerful, you may feel yourself slipping.

The music is worked out well. The orchestral passages run their tallies of chord and rhythm and silence—they growl or they are elated—with the story running on the silversheet.

When it's a crackerjack of a production and the observer feels good about it he mentions the screen as a silversheet. Whereas if it's otherwise he says celluloid. Personally, in this instance, one says silversheet.

Yes, we heard what a couple of people said going out. One said, "It's the craziest movie I ever went to." The other one said, "I don't know whether I want this for a steady diet, but it's the best picture I've seen in a long while."

Cubist, futurist, post-impressionist, characterize it by any name denoting a certain style; it has its elements of power, knowledge, technique, passion, that make it sure to have an influence toward more easy flowing, joyous, original American movies.

1921

Nanook of the North

That photoplay *Nanook of the North*, is one of the few films that has come along the past year which is worth going to see once, twice, three times and more if you feel like it.

It is a classic that takes its place in the film world as a sort of parallel of *Robinson Crusoe* in the book world.

Every child that enjoys books and pictures about travel, and every grown person who would like to travel, should see the picture for the way it sweeps one out and away from the things just around the corner, carrying you to a cold, wild, white corner of the earth.

The film is the product of the Revillon Freres corporation. They are a big fur selling concern with headquarters in Paris, France. They have stations and outposts at several points in the far north where the fur-bearing animals live.

An Englishman who seems to have an Irish name, Robert Flaherty, a fellow of the Royal Geographical Society, went up into the Hudson Bay district under auspices of the Revillon Freres corporation.

The idea of Flaherty was to make a picture that would be a first-rate travel picture and at the same time tell a story, weave through as a drama. This he has done, thoughtfully, amazingly well.

If there ever was a fellow of the Royal Geographical Society who ought to have a medal and a string of medals, besides his own satisfaction and joy as an artist and a scientist, Flaherty is the man.

Nanook of the North is a novel and a poem and a biography and an epic. It takes the curse off motion pictures to the extent that those who anathematize the movies without making an exception of *Nanook of the North* thereby display merely their own pathetic ignorance of one picture product that stands comparison with the things of highest excellence produced by other arts.

Nanook is a magnetic and loveable character. His wife, Nyla, their children, their dogs, their pups, their snow houses, they too are magnetic and loveable.

Jack London wrote of the "white silence" of the north. Nansen, Steffanson, Amundsen and Shackleton have conveyed to us some of the airs of the region where the people make no wood nor iron, plant no crops, eat no vegetables nor fruit.

But the classic that excels them all in its delivery of the character and atmosphere of that region is *Nanook of the North*, a movie.

It is a work of genius to throw this informative material into the shape of a living, tingling drama. One may hear the children ripple with laughter at various places in this picture play.

Nanook comes in a seal hide canoe. He is landing. He seems to be alone. He goes to the canoe, dips down through the one big hole in the top of the canoe and brings out his wife, with a fine naked baby in a pouch on her back, goes back again for two husky boys one by one, and last of all the pup they are raising. Of course, the children laugh. It has magic and surprise.

The final scene shows the family sleeping in a snow house while outside the wolf dogs howl as the snow piles on their hair. We see the wind sweeping long levels of snow. We flash inside the snow house and the last of the film is the sleeping face of Nanook, peaceful, masterly, ready with his brood around him, ready for anything.

We have seen him trap a live fox and bring the live fox up out of the snow with his bare hands. We have seen him harpoon a walrus and drag forth a seal from under the ice. We have seen him driving the snarling dogs through a fierce blizzard with his Nyla and the little ones. It was a stroke of dramatic art to show him last of all sleeping with peace and understanding on his face.

1922

A Woman of Paris

The first picture of which Charlie Chaplin is the author and the director—but in which he does not act—is starting its run at the Orpheum Theater.

It is nine reels long, has the scope and extent of a novel, and is the most important photoplay since *The Cabinet of Dr. Calgari* and *The Golem*.

The outstanding point about this production is that the people in it come out of shadows and go back into shadows a good deal the same way that characters do for us in life.

Before any people are shown there is an old French stone house, which seems to say, "I am a house; all houses have human mysteries; I am still puzzling over the births, deaths, marriages, crimes and benedictions that have been known across my doorways."

The story is simple. A boy and a girl in a French provincial town are betrothed. Her father doesn't want the marriage. Fate sends the girl to Paris alone. Two men contend for her there. She goes back to a changed life.

As a story it is told on the screen in the same way that a man might tell about things that happened to the people who lived next door neighbor to him many years ago; the years have passed so the story has had time to happen; and in his heart and mind there is charity and understanding; they were all people; what happened just happened; it hurts to tell it, yet they were all loveable people and the story must be told because they all had ways that were loveable, notwithstanding hard or mean things they did.

This picture is so big hearted and simple, so fine and sure in its handling of people and laying the blame on nobody, that there will be some moviegoers a little mixed up about it; they are those who want either straight melodrama or straight comedy.

And *A Woman of Paris* is neither; it is as dark and mixed as life, or the Book of Ruth or the Book of Esther in the Old Testament.

Edna Purviance has the leading role. The leading men are Charles French and Adolphe Menjou. Other players are Carl Miller and Lydia Knott.

1924

Manhandled

In *Manhandled*, showing at McVicker's Theater this week, is an artistic and well-worked out opening scene. There are other scenes well worked out, but the opening in *Manhandled* is as good a one as this reviewer has seen in any picture this season.

Feet, hundreds of feet—in shoes—ladies' and misses' shoes—are coming down a stairway.

Sort of queer these feet are—they belong to people—and the people are working girls in a factory, stepping down to punch the clock and quit for the day.

Next the heroine—Gloria Swanson as a working girl—steps out on the street and gets her clothes all splashed by a passing motor car.

Into a New York subway car she steps and is there manhandled, her hat stepped on, her pocketbook and vanity case knocked on the floor of the car.

She gets off and goes home and takes off her shoes.

This is very well done.

The removal of shoes by a young woman who has been in a subway jam requires careful and refined pantomimic art.

And they do it here very humanly and sweetly.

One might almost go back and see *Manhandled* a second time, because of the knack and skill, the refined grace with which Gloria Swanson removes her shoes.

It is as good as the fellow in that O. Henry story who worked in a hat shop, cleaning hats, and each sweltering summer evening went straight home and placed his bare feet against a brick wall and read stories of the sea, the cool, kind ocean.

The husband of the heroine enters. He is an inventor working on a motor car accessory. During two weeks he has refused to go out of an evening with her, because he must work on his invention.

But she has new clothes and is anxious to go stepping.

From there on the developments start.

Tom Moore, Lilyan Tashman, Paul McAllister, Arthur Hausman, Ian Keith and Carrie Scott are members of the cast. It is of Allan Dwan direction. Arthur Stringer wrote the story, from which Frank W. Tuttle did the screen play.

1924

The Temptress

It is not the way of Greta Garbo to eat rose leaves in order to show filmgoers that she is an idle, destructive female. Vampires used always to do this. Some of them yet register wantonness by consuming a big bowl of deep red roses while they roll their eyes at some helpless he-man who is being sent simply off his nut by the sight of so much beauty.

Greta Garbo tempts in her own way, very cool of manner, very easy and very, very sure. Where Lya De Putti is all fire and flesh, Greta Garbo is half-myth, the spirit of unmoral, not immoral, love, wavering and trailing through the picture, *The Temptress*, like the essence of all siren hearts over time.

In *The Temptress* she may be seen to take a nominal husband to protect her vampiring raids among the fatuous bankers of Paris, also she may be seen to lead one banker to dramatic and howling suicide. And, moreover, for six whole reels she sets an engineering camp in the Argentine so mad with desire that a mammoth dam is destroyed by jealous rivals, friends saber each other to death and two men duel viciously with wicked blacksnake whips.

For all the deaths she occasions, reputations she wrecks and lifeworks she ruins this heroine of Blasco Ibáñez somehow is urged upon you as blameless, as sinned against rather than sinning, as the traditional female whose mere beauty causes sin to flourish.

Greta Garbo, slim, pale, like willows turning yellow in autumn, is the one actress, sure enough, to put into this role if it is to be made plausible. Gowned to kill, directed in such a manner that her face is full into the camera most of the time, she scores a downright triumph.

Antonio Moreno, Roy D'Arcy, Lionel Barrymore, Marc MacDermott, Robert Andersen—all good people for their roles—have a lot to do in this long special from Metro-Goldwyn-Mayer's workshops. Fred Niblo, who made *Ben-Hur*, worked on this and shows again his talents for arresting, vivid scenes and his inabilities to humanize plot.

Presentation is at the Roosevelt Theater, where Greta Garbo may be recommended as something indeed for all adults to look upon.

1926

What Price Glory?

One moment you're in the busy whirl of traffic in Randolph Street, the next you're away off in France living again the war as vividly, as dramatically, as real as you'll ever be able to live it eight or one hundred years after it's over.

That's the Aladdin transformation which awaits one who steps into the Garrick Theater to see the screen version of *What Price Glory?* William Fox, with Raoul Walsh directing and the help of a lot of men who have had a friendly speaking acquaintance with the late party over there, have taken this graphic tale of the great conflict and turned out a masterpiece that's hard to tell from the original.

It is the story of the comedy, the drama, the tragedy, the harshness, the cruelty and the futility of the war as it was lived by the men—and the women—who fought it. It isn't overplayed and it isn't theatrical. It is the war in stark reality—except, perhaps, in that melodramatic ending, which, let's hope, they put in more as a theoretical "kick" rather than to be swallowed as an actuality.

Strangely enough, comedy forms the greater part of this masterful yarn of the war, rich, uproarish, screaming comedy. But the drama and tragedy is there, drama that thrills and tragedy that grips. The battle scenes, of which there are many, tell the grim story of war as no tongue or pen will ever tell it. They are some of the greatest at which a camera has ever clicked, either in the real or make-believe. That "big push," the streaming over the top, the confusion, the terror, the spitting machine guns, the roaring, tearing, thundering barrages, are enough to make any ex-participant want to dive for the nearest shell hole.

The story, of course, revolves around those two hard-boiled, swearin' leathernecks, Capt. Flagg and Sergt. Quirt, and their eternal clash over the feminine spoils of war. Victor McLaglen is the batter-nosed, foul-mouthed, hardened captain and Edmund Lowe is the tough sergeant. They are everything Laurence Stallings and Maxwell Anderson must have had in mind when they wrote the story. Dolores Del Rio is the charming, chic, delectable Charmaine who reminds you so much of the girl you left behind—over there.

The cussin' in the stage play that shocked pious souls is there, too. Not in subtitles, but it's there—if, like the preacher's son, you know all the words and can read lip movements.

Maybe you missed the big show and wished you hadn't. Maybe you didn't miss it and wished you had. Either way you'll be sorry if you miss *What Price Glory?* It's war as real as you'll ever see it, and withal it's a sermon on peace, for in it you'll find, as nearly as you'll ever find, the answer to that question—what price glory, anyway?

Here is a strange matter.

Here is a motion picture with homely ruffians for heroes, with a faithless flirt for heroine, with an unorthodox ending and with blasphemy and profanity and suggestion coursing through it—here is a picture rich with all the taboos, achieving the unquestioned triumph of the season.

What Price Glory? violates every maxim in the screen director's guidebook and literally bowls over the very people for whom these guidebooks were prepared.

Housewives, grandmothers, orthodox matrons in hundreds sit thrilling and weeping and shaking with laughter most strangely and inexplicably in the Garrick Theater these days. They have never done anything but flee from such factors in real life. They have never loved drunken, carnal screen characters before. Probably they never will again. But they do these days in the Garrick.

The thing is sheer magic, sheer necromancy in its heroizing of two battered, foul-tongued professional soldiers. Capt. Flagg and Sergt. Quirk come to the screen as stronger, better rounded characters than to the stage. Laurence Stallings and Maxwell Anderson made them famous. Raoul Walsh and William Fox made them immortal. It is the camera that must receive the credit. It is the camera that erects, in its shots of Flagg's head, such a statue to the ancient professional soldier as Phidias could never have done.

Here is the secret for the incredible popular triumph of *What Price Glory?* on the screen. It rises above the appeals of patriotism, sentiment, humor, and romance—although it has all those things—to shake the whole emotional structure of spectators with an epic portrait of two fascinating and violent men. It rises to the heights of doing the professional soldier as he has waited 5,000 years to be done, without gloves, without patronage and with sure, certain truthfulness.

The professional soldier swears, he wastes his leisure on scarlet women, he drinks, he carouses, he is vulgar and brutal.

Well, he was so in the camps of Caesar, Alexander, Napoleon and Frederick the Great.

The hard-boiled fighting man violates every canon of the respectable civilian. Well, it was so in the legions of Gustavus Adolphus, of Cyrus the Great and William Tecumseh Sherman.

The man who fights as a trade, rather than for any flag or slippered burgher, has his kindly moments, his codes of honor, his manliness in odd moments in battle lulls.

This was true in the ranks of Hannibal and Marshal Ney.

What Price Glory? soars above all rules and canons of picture making because it holds to these truths. The broken-nosed head of Flagg as it comes through the smoke, cool, bitter, deadly, while young marines drop, drop, drop behind him and Germans shoot, run and fall before him, is the head of Caesar.

The face Flagg turns to the light of love Charmaine as he comes out of the trenches on leave is the face all professional warriors have turned to the crimson vivandiers since war was war.

Becoming the tale of two age-old characters, romance, adventure, humor all become merely obligators to a saga, a hero-song.

From the moment *What Price Glory?* begins until it ends it can do nothing, say nothing that is not in the epic mold. Victor McLaglen may be a good actor but he is something finer than that here. He is Capt. Flagg; he is Caesar. Edmund Lowe may be close to him in artistry but he is almost as completely Sergt. Quirk, Alexander the Great kissing Persian camp-followers after the day's red work is done. Dolores Del Rio suddenly seems to be a great actress. She is nothing of the kind. She is merely the perfect sweetheart of those laughing, faithless men who seldom marry because they are too busy defending whole populations of women whom they never see, nor care to see.

1926

Robert E. Sherwood

Robert E. Sherwood (1896–1955) is best known for his work as a playwright. Three of his biggest stage successes (*Idiot's Delight*, *Abe Lincoln in Illinois*, and *There Shall Be No Night*) received Pulitzer Prizes. But before his career as a dramatist, he was film critic for *Life* (then a humorous weekly) from 1920 to 1928. One of the first American movie critics to win a wide, loyal readership, he mastered his self-designated role as the audience's representative and consumer guide, perfecting a light, joshing reviewing style that took nothing too seriously. Later, he utilized what he had learned about film structure by writing the screenplays for *The Best Years of Our Lives* and *The Ghost Goes West*.

◆

The Ten Commandments

Emotional, intellectual or corporeal, there must be an end to all human qualities. The term "mortal," by which each dweller upon this earth is known, is in itself an admission of temporal limitations. A man may not live forever, nor may his sentiments, his point of view, or his prejudices. There is an end to the world, and to all things associated with it.

In view of which I have long realized that sooner or later I should be compelled to change my mind about those subjects upon which my opinion has been most firmly fixed: the day would come, I knew, when I should have to utter praise for a Cecil B. DeMille picture.

By an odd coincidence, this happens to be the day.

Mr. DeMille, in his time, has mutilated the works of many writers—from James Matthew Barrie to Alice Duer Miller—has sacrificed their ideas to make a Hollywood holiday. But when, in *The Ten Commandments*, he approached the words of God, he became suddenly overwhelmed with the idea that it would be better to set them forth unchanged. In this, Mr. DeMille displayed commendable originality; for no literary work has had rougher treatment from the public at large. If the mighty Cecil had seen fit to step on the Ten Commandments, he would at least have had plenty of precedent for the act.

However, there they are, all ten—count 'em—ten, presented on the screen just as they were revealed to Moses on the jagged crest of Mount Sinai. No star of the stage or the films has ever enjoyed a more spectacular entrance than that which is arranged for the Ten Commandments. Great masses of clouds form, are rent by streaks of lightning, and then are dissolved into the flaming words of God. Each of the Commandments swirls out of the heavens and hits the spectator squarely between the eyes—and each, it must be recorded, earns an equal storm of applause.

The Ten Commandments may not exercise as much influence as they should, but they are certainly good theater.

The picture itself is divided into two parts: the first, a biblical spectacle which shows, educationally, how the Commandments were made; the second, a modern story, designed to demonstrate how they are broken.

There is a vast difference, superficially and fundamentally, in the style with which these two portions have been treated. In the biblical prologue, Mr. DeMille puts on the dog heavily—reflecting the gorgeous extravagance of Pharaoh's court in pictures of incredible magnificence. Some of these are in color, and others in the usual photographic tints, an inconsistency which detracts materially from the realism of the spectacle. There are other remarkable scenes, of the Israelites wincing under Egypt's lash, of the Exodus, of the Red Sea being parted in the middle, and of the worship before the Calf of Gold.

This is all great stuff, and profoundly stirring—but it is not so very far ahead of *Intolerance*, which D. W. Griffith produced eight years ago. It is full of mechanical tricks which, while marvelous in themselves, remain just tricks: an audience invariably loses some of its illusion when it murmurs, "How did DeMille do *that?*"

In the modern story, however, Mr. DeMille displays a directorial genius which is comparable with that of Charlie Chaplin in *A Woman of Paris*. He recounts a narrative of singular absurdity, but does it so effectively that every character and every situation, however impossible, is made to seem eminently real.

The Ten Commandments, in its later stages, lacks all the bizarre ostentation which has been part and parcel of every DeMille movie since the *Don't Change Your Husband* days. He tells his story simply and with great vigor, relying on the subtle eloquence of reality rather than the megaphone blatancy of excessive splurge.

He is aided throughout the picture by the deft work of his cameramen, by the superb plot construction and subtitles of Jeanie Macpherson, and by the general excellence of the cast. Of the many stars who appear, Rod La Rocque stands out vividly. His performance of an unregenerate youth who flouts the Ten Commandments is one to be remembered as long as we old cronies sit around the fire and discuss the movies of yesteryear. Leatrice Joy is (of course) splendid, Richard Dix is seriously convincing, and Charles de Roche gives a glamorous portrait of Pharaoh the Magnificent.

From all the players, Mr. DeMille's production has derived an unusual degree of ability, sincerity, and inspiration. I'm not going to say that they "live their parts," because I don't want to steal any of *Dulcy's* stuff; but at least, they make a good bluff at it.

Here endeth to-day's lesson, and let no man say that I have never praised a DeMille production.

You may now bring forth a Jackie Coogan picture that I may pan, and my record for impartiality will be complete.

1923

Greed

Ferocity, brutality, muscle, vulgarity, crudity, naked realism, and sheer genius are to be found—great hunks of them—in von Stroheim's production, *Greed*. It is a terribly powerful picture—and an important one.

When von Stroheim essayed to convert Frank Norris's *McTeague* into a movie, he assumed what is technically known as a man-sized job. There was absolutely nothing in this novel of entertainment value, heart interest, or box-office appeal—none of the qualities that are calculated to attract the shrewd eye of the movie mogul.

Nevertheless, there were the elements of fierce drama in *McTeague*, and these have been taken by von Stroheim and turned loose on the screen. He has followed copy with such extraordinary fidelity that there is no scene in the picture, hardly a detail, that is not recognizable to those who have read the book.

The acting in *Greed* is uneven: Gibson Gowland is practically perfect as McTeague, as are Zasu Pitts and Jean Hersholt as Trina and Marcus Schouler; but von Stroheim has been guilty of gross exaggeration in his treatment of the subordinate characters. They are an artificial lot, derived from the comic strips rather than from reality.

Atmospherically, *Greed* is marvelous. The costumes, the settings, and the properties are just as Norris described them. McTeague wears a plaid cap which may be rated as the most appropriate article of attire ever displayed on the screen.

There are two defects in *Greed*—one of which is almost fatal.

In the first place, von Stroheim has chosen to be symbolic at intervals, and has inserted some very bad handcoloring to emphasize the goldenness of gold. This detracts greatly from the realism of the picture.

In the second place, von Stroheim has been, as usual, so extravagant with his footage that *Greed* in its final form is merely a series of remnants. It has been cut to pieces—so that entire sequences and important characters have been left out. Thus the story has a choppy quality; many of its developments are abrupt. We see Trina in one instant the tremulous young bride, and in the next the hard, haggard, scheming shrew of several years later. The intervening stages in her spiritual decay are not shown, although von Stroheim undoubtedly included them originally.

This is von Stroheim's own fault. He must learn to acquire some regard for the limitations of space. *Greed*, I understand, was produced in forty reels, which would take eight hours to unwind; and the eight-hour day for movie fans has not yet dawned—thank God!

Von Stroheim is a genius—*Greed* establishes that beyond all doubt—but he is badly in need of a stopwatch.

1923

Edmund Wilson

Arguably America's greatest literary critic, Edmund Wilson (1895–1972) wrote a number of masterworks on an impressive variety of subjects, such as *Axel's Castle* (literary modernism), *To the Finland Station* (revolutionary socialism), and *Patriotic Gore* (the Civil War). From 1925 on, he was *The New Republic*'s all-purpose reviewer, penning movie, theater, dance, and art criticism, backstage sketches of the Follies, and political commentary, all collected in *The American Earthquake*. Though skeptical of the typical Hollywood product, Wilson was fascinated with Charlie Chaplin (as we see in this lively, analytical piece on *The Gold Rush*) and even wrote a ballet for him, which the comic respectfully declined, saying he only performed his own material. *fan boy*

◆

The New Chaplin Comedy

The fundamental device of American moving-picture humor is what is technically known as the "gag." A gag is a comic trick, the equivalent in cinema action of the spoken gag of the stage. When Buster Keaton on a runaway motorcycle knocks the ladder out from under a house painter and goes off with the bucket of paint on his head, or when a clothesline, strung between two houses, on which Harold Lloyd is escaping, is cut at one end by an enemy and Harold, still clinging to it, swings into a room below where a séance of spiritualists are awaiting a materialization, this is a movie gag. Inventing such tricks is today one of the principal professions of the film industry. In Hollywood, the gag-writers of the comic stars are among the most influential and the most envied members of the community; for without them the stars would be nothing. There are moments when Buster Keaton gives evidence of a skill at pantomime which his producers do nothing to cultivate; but one may say of these comics in general that they hardly need to be actors any more than Baby Peggy, Rin-Tin-Tin, Strongheart or Silver King.

The one performer of Hollywood who has succeeded in doing anything distinguished with this primitive machinery of gags is, of course, Charlie Chaplin. In the first place, he is, I believe, the only comic star in the movies who does not employ a gag-writer: he makes everything up himself; so that, instead of the stereotyped humor of even the best of his competitors, most of whose

tricks could be interchanged among them without anyone's knowing the difference, he gives us jokes that, however crude, have an unmistakable quality
of personal fancy. Furthermore, he has made it a practice to use his gags as
points of departure for genuine comic situations. Thus in his latest picture, *The
Gold Rush*, there is a cabin—with Charlie and his partner in it—which is blown
to the edge of a cliff while the occupants are asleep. This in itself is a gag like
another: for any other screen comedian it would have been enough to startle
the audience by showing them the little shack rocking on the dangerous brink
and then, by acrobatics and trick photography, to follow this with similar shudders. But Chaplin, given his gag, the same kind of thing as Lloyd's clothesline,
proceeds to transport his audience in a way of which Lloyd would be incapable,
by developing it with steady logic and vivid imagination. Charlie and his companion wake up: the panes of the shack are frosted; they do not realize what
has happened; Charlie sets out to get breakfast, but whenever he moves to the
side of the room where his heavy companion is lying—the side hanging over
the abyss—the house begins to tip. He puts this down, however, to dizziness—
he has been drunk the night before—and goes resolutely about his business.
But when his companion—the gigantic Mack Swain—gets up and begins to
move around, the phenomenon is aggravated: "Do you have an illusion that
the floor is tipping?"—"Ah, you notice that, too, do you?" They jump on it to
see if it is standing solid; but as Charlie is jumping on the overhanging side
while Swain is holding it down on the other, they do not at once find out what
is wrong, and it is some time before the fatal combination—both men on the
projecting side—almost sends them over the cliff. They rush back to the safe
side of the room, and Charlie goes to the door—which has been frozen tight in
the night—to see what is going on: after a struggle, it suddenly flies open, and
he falls out into the void, only saving himself by a clutch at the sill. His companion rushes down to save him, but by the time he has pulled him in, their
double weight has set the cabin sliding: it is anchored now only by a rope which
has caught fast to something not far from the cliff. Charlie and his companion,
abject on their bellies, try to crawl up the terrible floor, now at an angle of sixty
degrees. At first, though the eyes of his companion are popping, Charlie
remains cool and sensible. "Just go easy! A little at a time." But no matter how
little they attempt, every movement makes the cabin slip. And so on, through
a long passage of pantomime.

Conversely, however, the gag is sometimes resorted to by Chaplin to break
up the non-farcical sequences—ironic or even pathetic—that are becoming
more frequent in his comedies. Thus the love story in *The Gold Rush* is, on the
whole, treated seriously, but from time to time enlivened by such low comedy

incidents as that in which Charlie accidentally saturates his bandaged foot with kerosene and then has it set on fire by a match dropped by one of the ladies. In these sequences, it sometimes happens—as in parts of *The Pilgrim*, his previous film—that such gags in the straight situations produce a jarring effect. They seem to be introduced in order to hold Chaplin's old public, who expects their full allowance of "belly laughs." He has never dared desert this public, who first saw him in the Mack Sennett comedies and who still go to him for the same sort of entertainment that they find in Fox and Christie comedies. Yet in proportion as his reputation has grown with the sophisticated audience and the critics, his popularity has hardly gained—it has not even, perhaps, held its own—with this original popular audience, who do not seem to feel any difference between Chaplin himself, on the one hand, and his imitators and rivals, on the other. They seem, in fact, to be coming to prefer the latter. Buster Keaton and Harold Lloyd have, in a sense, carried gagging far beyond Charlie Chaplin. Their films have more smartness and speed; they cultivate more frightening mechanical devices. With their motorcars, their motorcycles, their motorboats, their airplanes, their railroad trains, their vertiginous scaling of skyscrapers and their shattering cataclysmic collisions, they have progressed a long way beyond Chaplin, who has made no attempt to keep up with them, but continues with the cheap trappings and the relatively simple tricks of the old custard-pie comedy. For Chaplin is even more old-fashioned than the old-fashioned Mack Sennett movies; he is as old-fashioned as Karno's Early Birds, the unusual music-hall turn in which he originally appeared and which was at least a school for actors, not for athletes.

What turn Charlie Chaplin's career will take is, therefore, still a curious problem. He is himself, I believe, acutely aware of the anomaly of his position. In the films, he seems hardly likely to play an important role in the artistic development of the future. His gift is primarily the actor's, not the director's or artist's. All the photographic, the plastic development of the movies, which is at present making such remarkable advances, seems not to interest Chaplin. His pictures are still in this respect nearly as raw as *Tilly's Punctured Romance* or any other primitive comedy, and it is only when the subject is sordid—as in *Pay Day*, with its crowded city streetcars taking people home after work and its suffocating slatternly city flat—that the *mise en scène* in Chaplin's comedies contributes in any way to their effectiveness. The much-praised *A Woman of Paris* was handicapped particularly, it seemed to me—since it did not have Chaplin as the central figure—by this visual lack of taste. It was intended as an attractive, a serious picture, yet, for all the intelligence he brought to directing it, he allowed it to go out as if naked in its flat light and putty make-up. He is jealous of his independence in this as in other matters. He is very unlikely to allow himself to be written for, directed or even advised. If he is not carrying along his old public, he will unquestionably in time have to give it up; but whether he will then simply retire from the screen or try something altogether different, it is impossible to predict. In the meantime, it may be that his present series of pictures—*The Kid*, *The Pilgrim* and *The Gold Rush*—with their gags and their overtones of tragedy, their adventures half-absurd, half-realistic, their mythical hero, now a figure of poetry, now a type out of the comic strips, represents the height of Chaplin's achievement. He could scarcely, in any field, surpass the best moments of these pictures. The opening of *The Gold Rush* is such a moment. Charlie is a lone adventurer, straggling along after a party of prospectors among the frozen hills: he twirls his cane a little to keep his spirits up. On his way through a narrow mountain pass, a bear emerges and follows him. Any ordinary movie comedian, given the opportunity of using a bear, would, of course, have had it chasing him about for as long as he could work up gags for it. But Charlie does not know that the bear is there: he keeps on, twirling his cane. Presently the beast withdraws, and only then does Charlie think he hears something: he turns around, but there is nothing there. And he sets off again, still fearless, toward the dreadful ordeals that await him.

1925

H. L. Mencken

H. L. Mencken (1880–1956) was one of the greatest American men of letters, equally respected as a journalist, editor, essayist, and critic. Unafraid to provoke the public or part company with accepted opinion (characteristically titling his essay collection series *Prejudices*), Mencken weighed in with skepticism and sardonic humor on the so-called "liveliest art" in the piece below. Interestingly, it was the movies' rapid editing strategies that most put him off, an opinion that would later be fruitfully elaborated by the great French cinephile André Bazin.

◆

from
Appendix from Moronia

1927

Note on Technic

Having made of late, after a longish hiatus, two separate attempts to sit through movie shows, I can only report that the so-called art of the film still eludes me. I was not chased out either time by the low intellectual content of the pictures on display. For one thing, I am anything but intellectual in my tastes, and for another thing the films I saw were not noticeably deficient in that direction. The ideas in them were simply the common and familiar ideas of the inferior nine-tenths of mankind. They were hollow and obvious, but they were not more hollow and obvious than the ideas one encounters in the theater every day, or in the ordinary run of popular novels, or, for that matter, in the discourses of the average American statesman or divine. Rotary, hearing worse once a week, still manages to preserve its idealism and digest carbohydrates.

What afflicts the movies is not an unpalatable ideational content so much as an idiotic and irritating technic. The first moving-pictures, as I remember them thirty years ago, presented more or less continuous scenes. They were played like ordinary plays, and so one could follow them lazily and at ease. But the modern movie is no such organic whole; it is simply a maddening chaos of discrete fragments. The average scene, if the two shows I attempted were typical, cannot run for more than six or seven seconds. Many are far shorter, and very few are appreciably longer. The result is confusion horribly confounded.

How can one work up any rational interest in a fable that changes its locale and its characters ten times a minute? Worse, this dizzy jumping about is plainly unnecessary: all it shows is the professional incompetence of the gilded pants-pressers, decayed actors and other such half-wits to whom the making of movies seems to be entrusted. Unable to imagine a sequence of coherent scenes, and unprovided with a sufficiency of performers capable of playing them if they were imagined, these preposterous mountebanks are reduced to the childish device of avoiding action altogether. Instead of it they present what is at bottom nothing but a poorly articulated series of meaningless postures and grimaces. One sees a ham cutting a face, and then one sees his lady co-star squeezing a tear—and so on, endlessly. These mummers cannot be said, in any true sense, to act at all. They merely strike attitudes—and are then whisked off. If, at the first attempt upon a scene, the right attitude is not struck, then all they have to do is to keep on trying until they strike it. On those terms a chimpanzee could play Hamlet, or even Juliet.

To most of the so-called actors engaged in the movies, I daresay, no other course would be possible. They are such obvious incompetents that they could no more play a rational scene, especially one involving any subtlety, than a cow could jump over the moon. They are engaged, not for their histrionic skill, but simply for their capacity to fill the heads of romantic virgins and neglected wives with the sort of sentiments that the Christian religion tries so hard to put down. It is, no doubt, a useful office, assuming that the human race must, should and will go on, but it has no more to do with acting, as an art, than being a Federal judge has with preserving the Constitution. The worst of it is that the occasional good actor, venturing into the movies, is brought down to the common level by the devices thus invented to conceal the incompetence of his inferiors. It is quite as impossible to present a plausible impersonation in a series of unrelated (and often meaningless) postures as it would be to make a sensible speech in a series of college yells. So the good actor, appearing in the films, appears to be almost as bad as the natural movie ham. One sees him only as one sees a row of telegraph poles, riding in a train. However skillful he may be, he is always cut off before, by any intelligible use of the devices of his trade, he can make the fact evident.

In one of the pictures I saw lately a principal actor was George Bernard Shaw. The first scene showed him for fifteen or twenty seconds continuously, and it was at once plain that he had a great deal of histrionic skill—far more, indeed, than the average professional actor. He was seen engaged in a friendly argument with several other dramatists, among them Sir James M. Barrie and

Sir Arthur Wing Pinero. Having admired all these notorious men for many years, and never having had the honor of meeting or even witnessing them, I naturally settled down with a grateful grunt to the pleasure of feasting my eyes upon them. But after that first scene all I saw of Shaw was a series of fifteen or twenty maddening flashes, none of them more than five seconds long. He would spring into view, leap upon Barrie or Pinero—and then disappear. Then he would spring back, his whiskers bristling—and disappear again. It was as maddening as the ring of the telephone.

There is, of course, a legitimate use for this off-again-on-again device in the movies: it may be used, at times, very effectively and even intelligently. The beautiful heroine, say, is powdering her nose, preparing to go out to her fatal dinner with her libidinous boss. Suddenly there flashes through her mind a prophylactic memory of the Sunday-school in her home town far away. An actress on the stage, with such a scene to play, faces serious technical difficulties: it is very hard for her—that is, it has been hard since Ibsen abolished the soliloquy—to convey the exact revolutions of her conscience to her audience. But the technic of the movies makes it very easy—in fact, so easy that it requires no skill at all. The director simply prepares a series of scenes showing what is going through the heroine's mind. There is the church on the hill, with the horde of unhappy children being driven into its basement by the town constable. There is the old maid teacher expounding the day's Golden Text, II Kings, II, 23–24. There is a flash of the two she-bears "taring" the "forty and two" little children. There is the heroine, in ringlets, clapping her hands in dutiful Presbyterian glee. There is a flash of the Sunday-school superintendent, his bald head shining, warning the scholars against the sins of simony, barratry and adultery. There is the collection, with the bad boy putting in the suspenders' button. There is the flash showing him, years later, as a bank president.

All this is ingenious. More, it is humane, for it prevents the star trying to act, and so saves the spectators pain. But it is manifestly a poor substitute for acting on the occasions when acting is actually demanded by the plot—that is, on the occasions when there must be cumulative action, and not merely a series of postures. Such occasions give rise to what the old-time dramatic theorists called *scènes à faire*, which is to say, scenes of action, crucial scenes, necessary scenes. In the movies they are dismembered, and so spoiled. Try to imagine the balcony scene from "Romeo and Juliet" in a string of fifty flashes—first Romeo taking his station and spitting on his hands, then Juliet with her head as big as a hay-wagon, then the two locked in a greasy kiss, then the Nurse taking a drink of gin, then Romeo rolling his eyes, and so on. If you can imagine it, then you ought to be in Hollywood, dodging bullets and amassing wealth.

If I were in a constructive mood I'd probably propose reforms, but that mood, I regret to say, is not on me. In any case, I doubt that proposing reforms would do any good. For this idiotic movie technic, as I have shown, has its origin in the incompetence of the clowns who perform in the great majority of movies, and it would probably be impossible to displace them with competent actors, for the customers of the movie-parlors appear to love them, and even to admire them. It is hard to believe, but it is obviously so. A successful movie mime is probably the most admired human being ever seen in the world. He is admired more than Napoleon, Lincoln or Beethoven; more, even, than Coolidge. The effects of this adulation, upon the mime himself and especially upon his clients, ought to be given serious study by competent psychiatrists, if any can be found. For there is nothing more corrupting to the human psyche, I believe, than the mean admiration of mean things. It produces a double demoralization, intellectual and spiritual. Its victim becomes not only a jackass, but also a bounder. The movie-parlors, I suspect, are turning out such victims by the million: they will, in the long run, so debauch the American proletariat that it will begin to put Coolidge above Washington, and Peaches Browning above Coolidge.

Meanwhile, they are ruining the ancient and noble art of the dramatist— an art that has engaged the talents of some of the greatest men the world has ever seen. And they are, at the same time, ruining the lesser but by no means contemptible art of the actor. It is no advantage to a movie ham to be a competent actor; on the contrary, it is a handicap. If he tried to act, as acting has been understood since the days of Æschylus, his director would shut him off instanter: what is wanted is simply aphrodisiacal posturing. And if, by any chance, his director were drunk and let him run on, the vast majority of movie morons would probably rush out of the house, bawling that the film was dull and cheap, and that they had been swindled.

1927

H.D.

The poet H.D., born Hilda Doolittle (1886–1961), was first associated with the Imagist school championed by Ezra Pound. Like Pound an American expatriate, she wrote several pieces of impassioned film criticism for *Close Up*, an English-language film journal published in Switzerland, the most notable being her review-essay of Dreyer's *The Passion of Joan of Arc*. In this extraordinary critique—intensely subjective, almost confessional stream-of-consciousness, yet formally elevated in tone—she worked through an understanding of her moment-to-moment somatic responses to the film, her emotional surrenders and intellectual resistances. H.D.'s prolific oeuvre includes novels, prose accounts of her dealings with Ezra Pound and Sigmund Freud, translations of Euripides, and a body of poetry including the much-admired wartime trilogy *The Walls Do Not Fall*, *Tribute to the Angels*, and *The Flowering of the Rod*.

◆

The Passion of Joan of Arc

The *Passion and Death of a Saint* is a film that has caused me more unrest, more spiritual forebodings, more intellectual rackings, more emotional torment than any I have yet seen. We are presented with Jeanne d'Arc in a series of pictures, portraits burnt on copper, bronze if you will, anyhow obviously no aura of quattrocento gold and gold dust and fleurs-de-lys in straight hieratic pattern, none of your fresco that makes the cell of Savonarola make the legend of Savonarola bearable even to this day. Jeanne d'Arc is done in hard clear line, remorseless, poignant, bronze stations of the cross, carved upon mediæval cathedral doors, bronze of that particular sort of mediæval fanaticism that says no and again no to any such weakening incense as Fra Angelico gold and lilies of heavenly comfort. Why did and why didn't this particular Jeanne d'Arc so touch us? Jeanne d'Arc takes us so incredibly far that having taken us so far, we are left wondering why didn't this exquisite and superb piece of screen dramatisation take us further? Carl Dreyer, a Dane, one of the most superb of the magnificently growing list of directors, is responsible for this odd two-edged sort of feeling. His film, for that, is unique in the annals of film art. The passion of the Jeanne is superbly, almost mediumistically portrayed by Mlle Falconetti. Heart and head are given over to inevitable surrender. Heart broke, head bowed. But another set of curious nerve-reactions were brought into play here. Why is it that my hands inevitably clench at the memory of those pictures, at the casual poster that I pass daily in this lake-side small town? Is it necessary to be put on guard? *Must* I be made to feel on the defence this way and why? Also why must my very hands feel that they are numb and raw and bleeding, clenched fists tightened, bleeding as if beating at those very impregnable mediæval church doors?

For being let into the very heart, the very secret of the matter, we are left out of . . . something. I am shown Jeanne, she is indeed before me, the country child, the great lout of a hulking boy or girl, blubbering actually, great tears coursing down round sun-hardened, wind-hardened, oak-tree hardened face outline and outline of cheek hollow and the indomitable small chin. Jeanne is first represented to us, small as seen from above, the merest flash of sturdy boy figure, walking with chained ankles toward judges (too many) seated in slices above on ecclesiastical benches. Jeanne is seen as small, as intolerably sturdy and intolerably broken, the sort of inhuman showing up of Jeanne that from the first strikes some note of defiance in us. Now why should we be defiant? I think it is that we all have our Jeanne, each one of us in the secret great cavernous interior of the cathedral (if I may be fantastic) of the sub-conscious. Now another Jeanne strides in, an incomparable Jeanne, indu-bitably a more Jeanne-ish Jeanne than our Jeanne but it just isn't our Jeanne. Worse than that it is a better Jeanne, a much, much better, more authentic Jeanne than our Jeanne; scathing realism has gone one better than mere imag-inative idealism. We know we are out-witted. This is a real, real Jeanne (poor Jeanne) little mountain Newfoundland puppy, some staunch and true and incomparably loyal creature, something so much more wonderful than any greyhound outline or sleek wolf-hound is presented us, the very incarnation of loyalty and integrity . . . dwarfed, below us, as if about to be tramped or kicked into a corner by giant soldier iron-heeled great boots. Marching boots, marching boots, the heavy hulk of leather and thong-like fastenings and cruel nails . . . no hint of the wings on the heels of the legions that followed the lily-banner; the cry that sang toward Orleans is in no way ever so remotely indi-cated. We are allowed no comfort of mere beatific lilies, no hint of the mem-ory of lover-comrade men's voices, the comrades that Jeanne must have loved loyally, the perfect staunch child friend, the hero, the small Spartan, the very Telisila upon the walls of that Argos, that is just it. This is *no* Telisila upon the walls of Argos, no Athene who for the moment has laid aside her helmet for other lesser matters than that of mere courage and fidelity. This is an Athene stripped of intellect, a Telisila robbed of poetry, it is a Jeanne d'Arc that not only pretends to be real, but that is real, a Jeanne that is going to rob us of our own Jeanne.

Is that the secret of this clenching of fists, this sort of spiritual antagonism I have to the shaved head, the stares, defiant bronze-statue, from the poster that I pass on my way to market? Is it another Jeanne in me (in each of us) that starts warily at the picture, the actual *portrait* of the mediæval girl warrior? The Jeanne d'Arc of Carl Dreyer is so perfect that we feel somehow cheated. This must be right. This must be right . . . therefore by some odd equivocal twist of subconscious logic, *I* must be wrong. I am put in the wrong, therefore I clench my fists. Heaven is within you . . . therefore I stand staring guiltily at bronze figures cut upon a church door, at freizes upon the under-gables of a cathedral that I must stare up at, see in slices as that incomparable Danish artist made me see Jeanne in his perhaps over-done series of odd sliced portraits (making particularly striking his studies of the judges and the accusers of Jeanne, as if seen by Jeanne herself from below) overwhelming bulk of ecclesiastical political accusation. I know in my mind that this is a great tour de force, perhaps one of the greatest. But I am left wary, a little defiant. Again why and why and why and just, just why? Why am I defiant before one of the most exquisite and consistent works of screen art and perfected craft that it has been our immeasurable privilege to witness?

One, I am defiant for this reason (and I have worked it out carefully) and with agony I and you and the baker's boy beside me and Mrs. Captain Jones-Smith's second maid and our own old Nanna and somebody else's gardener and the honeymoon boy and girl and the old sporting colonel and the tennis teacher and the crocodile of young ladies from the second pension to the left as you turn to the right by the market road that branches off before the stall where the old lady sells gentians and single pinks and Alpenrosen each in their season (just now it is somewhat greenish valley-lilies) are in no need of such brutality. No one of us, not one of us is in need of this stressing and stressing, this poignant draining of hearts, this clarion call to pity. A sort of bugle note rises and with it our own defiance. I am asked to join an army of incorruptibles to which long and long since, I and the baker's boy and the tennis champion in the striped red sash have given our allegiance. This great Dane Carl Dreyer takes too damn much for granted. Do I *have* to be cut into slices by this inevitable pan-movement of the camera, these suave lines to left, up, to the right, back, all rhythmical with the remorseless rhythm of a scimitar? Isn't this incomparable Dane Dreyer a very blue-beard, a Turk of an ogre for remorseless cruelty? Do we have to have the last twenty four hours' agony of Jeanne stressed and stressed and stressed, in just this way, not only by the camera but by every conceivable method of dramatic and scenic technique? Bare walls, the four scenes of the trial, the torture room, the cell and the outdoors about the pyre, are all calculated to drive in the pitiable truth like the very nails on the spread hands of the Christ. Do we need the Christ-nails driven in and pulled out and driven in and drawn out, while Jeanne already numb and dead, gazes dead and numb at accuser and fumbles in her dazed hypnotized manner towards some solution of her claustrophobia? I am shut in here, I want to get out. I want to get out. And instead of seeing in our minds the very ambrosial fields toward which that stricken soul is treading, foot by foot like the very agony toward skull-hill, we are left pinned like some senseless animal, impaled as she is impaled by agony. This is not *not* good enough. There is some slur on the whole of human consciousness, it is necessary to stress and stress and stress the brute side of mystic agony this way. Somehow, something is wrong here. An incomparable art, an incomparable artist, an actress for whom any but praise were blasphemy . . . and what happens?

I do not mind crying (though I do mind crying) when I see a puppy kicked into a corner but I do mind standing aside and watching and watching *and* watching and being able to do nothing. That is something of the antagonism I think that crept in, that is something of the something that made me feel I ought to go again, to be fair, to be *sure* what it was that upset me, perhaps cowardice on my own part, some deep sub-conscious strata or layer of phobia that I myself, so un-Jeanne-like, was unwilling to face openly. I said to myself next morning I will get this right, I am numb and raw, I myself watched Jeanne d'Arc being burnt alive at Rouen last night . . . and I myself must go again . . . ah, that is just it. We do not go and see a thing that is real, that is real beyond realism, AGAIN. I said I will go again but I did not go again. I did not and I don't think I failed any inner "light", any focus of consciousness in so ceding to my own new lapse. I can NOT watch this thing impartially and it is the first film of the many that I have consistently followed that I have drawn away from. This is perhaps the last and greatest tribute to the sheer artistry and the devilish cunning of the method and the technique of Carl Dreyer. I pay him my greatest compliment. His is one film among all films, to be judged differently, to be approached differently, to be viewed as a masterpiece, one of the absolute masterpieces of screen craft. Technically, artistically, dramatically, this is a masterpiece. But, but, but, but, but . . . there is a Jeanne sobbing before us, there is a small Jeanne about to be kicked by huge hob-nailed boots, there is a Jeanne whose sturdy child-wrist is being twisted by an ogre's paw because forsooth she wears a bit of old hard hammered unwieldy bulk of gold upon one finger, there is a numb hypnotized creature who stares with dog-like fidelity, toward the sly sophist who directs her by half-smile, by half-nod, by imperceptible lift of half an eye brow toward her defaming answer, there is a Jeanne or a Joan whose wide great grey eyes fill with round tears at the mention of her mother ("say your pater noster, you don't know your pater noster? you do? well who taught it to you?") there is Jeanne or Joan or Johanna or Juana upon Jeanne or Joan or Johanna or Juana. They follow one another with precision, with click, with *monotony.* Isn't that a little just it? There is another side to all this, there is another series of valuations that can not perhaps be hinted at consistently in this particular presentation of this one kicked little puppy of a Jeanne or a Joan or a Johanna. Isn't it just that? Isn't the brute side of the flawless type, the Jeanne d'Arc of all peoples, of all nations, the world's Jeanne d'Arc (as the world's Christ) a little too defiantly stressed, a little too acutely projected? I know after the first half of the second reel all that. I know all, all that. Just that round child face lifted "who taught you your pater noster?" gives me all, all that. I do not mean to say that there could have been any outside sort of beatific screen craft of heavenly vision. I don't mean that. But Jeanne kicked almost, so to speak, to death, still had her indomitable vision. I mean Jeanne d'Arc talked openly with angels and in this square on square of Danish protestant interior, this trial room, this torture room, this cell, there was no hint of angels. The angels were there all the time and if Jeanne had reached the spiritual development that we must believe this chosen comrade of the warrior Michael must have reached, the half-hypnotized numb dreary physical state she was in, would have its inevitable psychic recompense. The Jeanne d'Arc of the incomparable Dreyer it seems to me, was kicked towards the angels. There were not there, nor anywhere, hint of the angelic wing tip, of the winged sandals and the two-edged sword of Michael or of the distillation of maternal pity of her "familiar" Margaret. Father, mother, the "be thou perfect" perfected in Jeanne d'Arc as in the boy of Nazareth, were in no way psychically manifest. Such psychic manifestation I need hardly say, need be in no way indicated by any outside innovation of cross lights or of superimposed shadows. It is something in something, something behind something. It is something one feels, that you feel, that the baker's boy, that the tennis champion, that the army colonel, that the crocodile of English and Dutch and mixed German-Swiss (come here to learn French) feels. We are numb and beaten. We won't go a second time. The voice behind me that says wistfully, taken unawares, "I wish it was one of those good American light things" even has its place in critical consciousness. For all our preparation, we are unprepared. This Jeanne d'Arc is sprung on us and why should it be? There is a reason for most things. I think the reason is that it doesn't link up straight with human consciousness. There is a gap somewhere. We criticise many films, sometimes for crudity, sometimes for sheer vicious playing up to man's most febrile sentiment, sometimes for cruelty or insincerity. We criticise Jeanne d'Arc for none of these things.

The Jeanne d'Arc of the incomparable artist Carl Dreyer is a class by itself. And that is the trouble with it. It shouldn't be.

1928

Alexander Bakshy

Russian-born Alexander Bakshy (1885–c. 1951), a drama critic and translator, was also the first regular film critic for *The Nation*. In a prescient early piece written in 1913, "The Kinematograph as Art," he heralded the artistic possibilities of the new medium, and in his subsequent criticism he was always on the lookout for those elements that were uniquely cinematic. In "The 'Talkies,'" he welcomed the new technology's impact on the movies. Bakshy may sound somewhat dry and high-minded today, refusing as he did to surrender even partway to the enchantments of the average movie. "Not only are there woefully few [films] that are worthy of serious consideration, but if you happen to be a film critic you are obliged to stop and analyze the incessant flow of bilge issuing from the film factories of Hollywood and elsewhere as if it were really to be measured by the standards of intellectual and artistic achievement," he lamented in his last movie review in 1933. Bakshy had importance beyond acting as consumer guide; as his younger disciple Harry Alan Potamkin put it: "He is not a weathercock but a prophet."

◆

The "Talkies"

It is a sad reflection on the limitations of intellectuals and artists all over the world to see history repeat itself in the contemptuous resentment with which they are greeting the arrival of the talking picture. Just as twenty years ago when the silent movies began to stir the world, so today the patrons of art and the theater refuse to see in the talking picture anything but another vulgar product of our machine civilization. But so, too, does history repeat itself in the eagerness of the commercially minded not to miss their share in the windfall of the talking picture, however little they may understand the problems which arise from the use of the new medium, or be able to see where to look for their solution. Thus between the incompetence of the commercial entertainer and the superior self-righteousness of the intellectual, the talking picture is apparently doomed to grope blindly for several years before it reaches anything that may be properly described as an original form of drama. That it will reach this goal eventually does not seem to me in the least doubtful.

In the meantime let us consider the prospects of the talking picture. So far its greatest successes have been scored in a field which does not quite come under the definition of "talking." Pictures like *The Singing Fool* or *My Man* are really "song pictures." The fact, however, that they succeed in conveying their appeal to the audience is vastly significant. Lacking as they are in color and depth, they still capture something of the personality of the artist. No doubt Al Jolson and Fannie Brice are more intimately felt and radiate more genuine warmth when one sees them on the stage. At the same time even on the screen they are unmistakably their peculiar and likable selves. The loudspeaker, though still very imperfect, serves them much more loyally than it does the "talking" actors, since singing reproduces better than speech.

With the inevitable technical improvement in the production of human voice and in the effects of color and stereoscopic depth, the song picture of today will naturally expand into a full-blown musical comedy. So long as this *genre* of entertainment rests its appeal on the singing of popular stars and the gyrations of pretty chorus girls, the screen musical comedy will be able to depart little from the orthodox methods of the stage. In this respect it is in the same boat as the screen drama which would also take the stage for its model. For it has been laid down by our aestheticians that in copying the stage the talking picture would lose all claim to be regarded as a medium of art. Though why should it? A perfect copy is obviously as good as the original, and it is absurd to claim that no reproduction can be perfect. Besides, in the case of the talking picture one does not so much copy an original stage production as imitate the stage form—which, if a sin, is certainly not a cardinal one.

At present the trouble with the talking picture is to be found less in its attempts to imitate the stage than in its numerous technical imperfections. It is safe to predict that within the next ten years these will be removed. And it is only then that the real aesthetic problem of the talking picture will become apparent. The ability to give a perfect imitation of the stage or to create a new and completely original dramatic form means nothing unless it is inspired by the genuine spirit of art. It is here that one becomes seriously alarmed. In the coming fight between Hollywood and Broadway it is ten to one that the former will be victorious. But if the defeat of the Broadway journeymen can hardly be regarded as a great loss to art, the victory of the Hollywood robots will undoubtedly endanger the future of drama on the stage as well as on the screen. The talking picture is merely a mechanized tool; but the Hollywood manufacturers of films represent mechanized brains, and what this means to art we have already learned from the experience of the silent movies.

In this rather dismal picture of the future there are two important factors which have yet to be taken account of, and which are likely to counteract if not completely overcome the influence of Hollywood. The first of these is the remarkable growth in volume and quality of amateur production together with the rapid spread of little cinema houses. Before many years are past these developments will seize the artistic leadership in the movies and will force Hollywood to accept their superior standards. The second factor is the inevitable evolution of the talking picture in accordance with the laws of its own nature. This undoubtedly will exercise a far-reaching influence on Hollywood methods. When the talking-picture mechanism is made perfect the really important development will be along lines which are already beginning to reveal themselves and which will definitely direct the talking picture away from the stage and toward a new, authentic motion-picture drama.

This evolution is inevitable. It is dictated by the inner logic of the medium. Analogies between the stage and the screen assume that they deal with the same material. But they don't. The material of the screen is not actual objects but images fixed on the film. And the very fact that they have their being on the film endows these images with properties which are never found in actual objects. For instance, on the stage the actor moves in real space and time. He cannot even cross the room without performing a definite number of movements. On the screen an action may be shown only in its terminal points with all its intervening moments left out. Similarly, in watching a performance on the stage the spectator is governed by the actual conditions of space and time. Not so in the case of the movie spectator. Thanks to the moving camera he is able to view the scene from all kinds of angles, leaping from a long-distance view to a close-range inspection of every detail. It is obvious that with this extraordinary power of handling space and time—by elimination and emphasis, according to its dramatic needs—the motion picture can never be content with modeling itself after the stage. The fact that it has now acquired the power of speech will certainly not make it any more willing to sacrifice its freedom and individuality. Nor is there any need for such a sacrifice. Dialogue can be concentrated—reduced to a number of essential statements—as effectively as action, just as it is done now in the dialogue titles of silent pictures. Then, the talking picture will also develop the specifically cinematic method of "close up." It will be able to focus an individual utterance, and at the same time put out of focus all the other voices—a procedure unquestionably in advance of the method of the "realistic" stage which, in order that certain characters may be heard, enforces a most unrealistic silence among all the other characters. And such being its technique, the spoken drama of the screen will obviously and inevitably develop into something original and non-stagy— something that will be instinct with the dynamic spirit of the movies.

1929

Harry Alan Potamkin

Harry Alan Potamkin (1900–1933), though largely forgotten today, was one of the most respected and serious film critics of his time. He began as something of a formalist, emphasizing the self-conscious employment of cinematic techniques in the service of film art. "The film which does not dwell upon itself, does not realize itself," he asserted. Writing in the transition period between silent and sound film for such vanguard publications as *Hound and Horn*, *Close Up*, and *Experimental Cinema*, he advocated a "compound cinema" that would merge sound and sight in a mutually satisfying, stylized manner. The Great Depression helped convert him to a Marxist position; he became film critic for *New Masses*, and subsequently emphasized the primary importance of a film's content and what it said about the political and social structure of its society. What is surprising, given his ideology (and obvious sympathy for the Soviet experiment), is how honestly he criticized the new Russian films, which he took to task for being didactic, propagandistic, overly abstract, and prone to caricature, just as he criticized Hollywood films for being sentimental, racist, and unconsciously agitprop. At bottom, Potamkin remained a passionately demanding lover of the movies who was perhaps more interested in film becoming deeply "introspective," in a Dreyer-Dostoievsky sense, than in serving the revolutionary cause. Who knows what fruitful critical resolution he might have made of these contradictory tendencies had he not died young of complications from stomach ulcers.

◆

"A" in the Art of the Movie and Kino

Writing in *Monde*, Henri Barbusse's journal, I said: the American movie can be saved by New York. I did not mean to be taken literally. My meaning was: Hollywood redundancies will keep the film rudimentary and lacking in social, philosophic and æsthetic meaning. A new mind is needed to work upon the rudiments and extend them. Hollywood will not supply that new mind. Hollywood is vested interest. Hollywood is uninspired competence —at its best. Hollywood is empty facility. A critical mind is needed. New York is the concentration center of the critical mind. Even in the use of the instruments (putting aside for the moment philosophy), I look to the director who has not imbibed Hollywood.

There's Rouben Mamoulian of the Theatre Guild. He made a first film at the Astoria studios of the Paramount. He put his camera on rubber wheels and glided it to look upon the players from this angle and that. He was given a typical Hollywood story—no more trashy than the others—and a maudlin heroine, annoyingly reminiscent of Pauline Lord and Gladys Brockwell, and one of those mother-themes (my burlesque good-bad mammy) . . . you know the ingredients—a whore, a pimp, a convent daughter, devoted nuns, a genteel sailor-boy looking for a little wife and a Wisconsin dairy, bichloride of mercury . . . another version of *Stella Dallas*. Given these millstones Mamoulian looked for sympathy to his camera. He proved himself more facile, more competent than Hollywood. But the film *Applause* remains sick stuff. Applause for Mr. Mamoulian must he modified by a censure of him for accepting the theme and the players. A movie, like water, never rises above its source. It can fall below it, but it cannot transcend it. Griffith's *The Birth of a Nation* remains a vindictive platitude, despite its grand composition, because of the thematic, human source in Dixon's *The Clansman*. Vidor could not beat the particularization of the theme of man against the mass in the Johnny Weaver scenario of *The Crowd*. So-called film purists will call my statement literary but I'm too old a hand at movie criticism to be scared by that judgment. What is confusedly termed literary is the substance of the film, its original source, which is converted into the final experience. If the substance is shoddy, specious or spurious, the more dexterous the handling of the instruments, the more remote will be the job from the material. The result is either virtuosity or the inflation of the theme. Mamoulian has proved himself as good a virtuoso as we have in America, but of virtuosity we need no more. We need philosophers who seek great themes told with insight and ultimate import. We need artists who build structures. That Mr. Mamoulian has used his camera as a mobile instrument is O.K. But moving a camera, getting angles, weaving together a couple of different sounds—the mother's chant, the daughter's prayer (what a banal sentimentalism!)—do not build a structure. In the first place the talkie (a misnomer) is a compound film. Its basis is the visual-motor graph (the basis of the simple or mute film). The graph must be constructed with the thought of the placements of sound, simultaneous or progressive placement—in relation to the visual image. There is no such preordained construction in *Applause*, no sustained unified rhythm. Speech is still talkie. Speech should be treated for its abstract qualities as much as sound is. Dialogue is anti-cinema, "speech-as-utterance" is not. I cannot here go into detail with this basic principle; the reader can refer to my contributions to *Close Up* for analyses of my point of view. What I can say here is simply this: Mamoulian has shown himself, in his novitiate, of superior craft-intelligence and daring . . . He brings to the film a proper sophistication in the use of the medium. There is a superb moment where the screen is divided diagonally into two distinct scenes, one of which gradually fills over the second to occupy the full screen. This is an active use of the split screen, surprisingly neglected in America. This alone would indicate what a fresh eye can do for the movie.

Whose fault it is I do not know, but a character of importance in the early part of the film—the comique who is the partner of the burlesque-queen and who woos her—is entirely forgotten. I should like to ask Miss Beth Brown, who wrote the story, what happened to him. He was too devoted to Kitty Darling to disappear. Or was it the fault of the master of the continuity? Well, such little things still happen in Hollywood, and Astoria is just Hollywood's other name. But what happened to the clown? This is the first time I have got excited by a "strange disappearance."

I do not think the Russian kino has as yet found a method that suits its profound material. Once I said: *Potemkin* is a film of powerful surface masses. Eisenstein said shortly after in *The Nation* that it was a poster-film. We agreed, I was vindicated. I said the Russians had better find a new method. Pudovkin said before the Filmliga of Amsterdam he had to find a new technique and Eisenstein in *Close Up* wrote: "Whereas in the first case we are striving for a quick emotional *discharge*, the new cinema must *include deep reflective processes* . . ." (the italics are not mine!). This is exactly my statement. The suggestions for this new cinema are to be found in Dreyer's *The Passion of Joan of Arc* and—in the Ukrainian film, *Arsenal* made by Dovzhenko. Here we have a Russian film that is not didactic but suggestive, that is not a perfection and elaboration of the American film of muscular impact (which is exactly the characterization of the Pudovkin kino), but an intensive, agonized, poignant, introspective film, conceived not as realism punctuated by symbols but as sustained symbolism.

Faults this film has, but that is not to be wondered at. I cannot think of a severer task than creating a structure of symbolism with real solid personalities. But Dovzhenko has succeeded, if not in creating an immaculate symbolic structure, in defining an intention which, by studying the workings of the film, the new Russian director will develop into a form. Russia promises to build a kino where at last thought and poetry and philosophic meaning are active. *Arsenal* renders a film like Vertov's *The Man With the Camera* not obsolete but certainly on a primary lesson for the aspirant.

In *Arsenal* propaganda is freed of its bluntness and becomes a penetrating emotional idea. There is none of the arrogance too often felt in the films of Pudovkin and Vertov. Certainly nothing could be stronger than the ghoulish, garish sights of the entombed soldier and the laughter of the gassed soldier.

They are unrelenting as they should be. This is suggestive of the sort of war film F. W. Murnau would make, showing the actual results of the war: cadavers . . . Andreas Latzko's *Men in War*. There can be no pacifistic film which has a central hero, a protagonist—no matter how anti-militaristic its sentiments are. So long as there is participation, as there was in *The Big Parade*, with the soldiers, such a film accentuates military fervor. So long as the ominous rather than the horrible predominates, as in the British film *The Battle of the Colonel and Falkland Islands*, the military passion is enhanced.

Arsenal is not the greatest of films, but it is one of the most important.

There is another Russian film which must not be neglected: *In Old Siberia* (*Katorga*). It is not the best, but it is one of the most sensitive, and also lacking in arrogance—which is a proof of Russia's adulthood. Another cinematic proof of Russia growing up enough to get a perspective upon itself is Alexander Room's *Bed and Sofa* (*Three In a Basement*), not yet shown here. Room's social comedy is Russia laughing at herself, getting a tickle out of her new morality

Russian films are very often too much caricature and not enough of full human experience. Pudovkin defends this by an analogy with Dickens. Ah! but why not Dostoievsky? Dickens served Dostoievsky—see *The Insulted and the Injured* where even the names and the relationships are paralleled to *The Old Curiosity Shop*—as a "source." Dostoievsky's fantasy was something more than caricature or whimsicality—it was the conversion of the ordinary into the extraordinary. And that is exactly the fantasy—in terms of kino—toward which *Arsenal* tends.

1929

Remarks on D. W. Griffith

David Llewellyn Wark Griffith has been called the first genius of the motion picture. This characterization needs to be qualified. When Griffith entered the movies, in the days of AB (American Biograph), the director was a sort of assistant to the cameraman, who was then George William ("Billy") Bitzer. Griffith came into the AB studio as an actor, and remained to direct. The director of a film was absent one day. Griffith had shown an active curiosity in the new medium, and he was told to take the menial task. He did. With that assumption the director—the artist—of the movie was born.

The development of Griffith is the development of the American film. It has not gone beyond D. W. in idea, composition or human interest. That is to say, it remains quite juvenile. Indeed, there has been no director quite as intuitively gifted as Griffith. Thomas Ince was made of sterner, but at the same time, of weaker, stuff. Griffith it must be allowed, and because of his romanticism, has been more devoted to the motion picture than Ince. If grandiose, as his compositions have been in his large attempts, he has not been flamboyant, like Herbert Brenon or George Loane Tucker or Tod Browning. He has been anxious to present the materials of his own literary conscience.

And that is his first limitation. It is the limitation of a man poorly endowed with content-discrimination. He is an American and Southern gentleman of a desiccate aristocracy. This heritage seeps through all his films. He said not long ago: "The maturer motion picture of today has yet to turn its attention seriously to the kind of themes that we used back in 1908." Mr. Griffith referred to his penchant for "Poesie" and classics, not the purest of tendencies. The Southern gentlemen traditionally go through a training in Xenophon and Ovid, in a classical school remote from the progressive centers and uninformed by the new education, and forever wear this dubious learning as a pathetic blossom in the buttonhole of their intellects. In his penchant for "*poésie*" Griffith is the American Gance—or Gance is the French Griffith. But it is true that within the penchant there was the expression of a need for intensely-felt human episodes. Griffith, as an American, mistook platitudes for criticism, but these platitudes were, if only vague, statements of social impurities. Guided by an intuition fed on unplumbed prejudices, Griffith's social history was articulated in *The Birth of a Nation*, the anticipation of the recrudescence of the Ku Klux Klan! When the Negro, threatened by the bad temper provoked by the film, objected to the picture, Griffith, supported by the liberal and white hypocrisy of "free speech," issued a printed tract and a film-tract on *Intolerance*. A Houston, Texas daily was quoted as saying that the white citizen was not yet prepared to accept orders from the black! Griffith's expansive love of mankind, itself a platitude, did not extend to the Negro. Nor did his *Intolerance* educate him in the skepticism of a true lover of mankind, when America entered the war. He went to England and directed the activities of society dames in support of the war, and produced *Hearts of the World*, a sentimental film urging allied sympathy.

His latest film, *Lincoln*, is another bit of "sweetness and light" in patriotism. After spending months and reading 180 books (he will play at being a scholar), Griffith hired Stephen Vincent Benet, prize-winning author of the unimaginative free verse "John Brown's Body," to write the scenario. A child would have been ashamed of such a presentation of the American legend, Abraham Lincoln. American history and folk-ideology are expressed in the terms of the crudest, most flatulent myths. *Lincoln* is an unintelligent Drinkwater chronicle play on the screen, further reduced to innocuousness by an uncritical director and a bad poet. The fact that it draws tears is rather against it than for it. The pathos of a tremendous social occurrence should not be refined or lachrymose, but revealing. The social occurrence seldom gets a chance here. Slogans of spurious manufacture explain the motivations of the Civil War. It would seem that all of America was discovered, developed and directed for the sole purpose of the Lincoln wise-cracks.

The legend of a people may offer as much substance for revelation as the actual unmythical source. But such revelation demands a critical understanding which alone assures a surpassing of the elementary myth. Griffith possesses no critical penetration. The nostalgia of a desiccate aristocracy seeps through this film. In this he is the same old Griffith. His very insistence on Lincoln is a phobia which, as a defense, Southerners, especially one descended from a Confederate Brigadier-General, are cultivating. *Lincoln* submits a questionable penitence in the silly pretense, with music, to toleration of the black, a sort of rococo Americanese "Volga Boatman" with Negroes. The Southern gentleman is forever present, as in the tiresome reiterations of the virtues of the protagonists, those of the Confederate leader, Richard E. Lee, in particular. The whole film waits like an obsessed schoolboy for the crack of a Lincoln witticism known to the ritualized audience. The Struss-Menzies collaboration in the photography and "art" fulfills all the horrid sentimentalism of the conception and treatment. Abe Lincoln's lip-rouge attests to the dwindling care of Griffith for conviction. The finale of Lincoln's monument is a specious bid for patriotism. Who says the American movie is against propaganda? The innovator of the silent film contributes nothing to the improvement of the garrulous. He has no George William ("Billy") Bitzer to realize his needs, nor has he any needs. His days are over.

Lincoln is the epitome of Griffith's sentimentalism. The portrayal of Ann Rutledge is shamefully simpering. One is happy to have her pass away. The sentimentally idyllic cannot be endured in an "Historic" film. It may be tolerated in a film inherently idyllic, like *The Idol Dancer*, one of Griffith's smaller pictures, or even in an excerpt that might, in better hands, have become an epic, *Scarlet Days*, another of his pictures. But Griffith has never been able to escape the sentimentally idyllic, no more than Gance has, even in his broadest films. *The Birth of a Nation* is soaked with it. However, his compositional sense, of repeated motifs (the "out of the cradle endlessly rocking" of *Intolerance*) has made these films important in cinema history. His invention of the "flash-back" or "cut-back"—a directorial device in montage before the establishment of montage—has been perhaps his greatest contribution to the cinema. The first dramatic use of the "close-up"—in *The Mender of Nets* with Mary Pickford—and of the "long distance shot," the "soft focus" (with the rapid close-up in *Broken Blossoms*), the camera angle and mobile camera (of *Intolerance*), etc., may be attributed to Griffith and his collaborator, Bitzer. But neither Griffith nor his successors in America have developed these uses. They were expediences for Griffith, just as were the insertions of titles into films originally graphic only. Even the critics in the U.S.A., like George Jean Nathan and Gilbert Seldes, have called the "close-up" a banality, unable to recognize it for the structural pivot and pictorial beauty it offers.

It is in the handling of mob scenes that Griffith has accomplished his most original and powerful work. Here again he resembles Gance, the Gance of the resilient march in *Napoleon*. *Lincoln* is pathetic in its scrawny manipulation of the soldiers, who appear every bit like a revue chorus of men of feminine persuasion. In the control of the individual player, Griffith has been undoubtedly zealous and stern, as a director should be. But his code of the gentleman, converted into "refinement," has impoverished his actors and his films as dramatic and human experiences. Samuel Goldwyn says that Mary Pickford ran away from Griffith to rescue her identity. Lillian Gish is a puppet, an inactive puppet, in her mincing portrayals. Only a childish idolater and inane quibbler would insist that Gish is Gish and not the part she plays. The actor is a portion of a conception and must yield to it. If it demands understatement, she must provide understatement; if hyperbole, she must provide hyperbole. Elasticity is an essential of the player, but Griffith stretched that quality in his players beyond the point of elasticity. He established a tradition, by now noxious in the American movie: the tradition of "refinement," a mincing innocence, the pout, the petulance that persists in all the cute players, down to the Farrell-Gaynor combination, and most offensively in Dolores del Rio (griefs of the river!). It will not vindicate Lillian Gish to say: "I have often been called a Griffith product. Well, in a way I am, of course. In a great many ways I am not. Nearly all my early pictures were directed by Tony Sullivan and Christy Cabanne . . ." Lillian Gish was brought up in the Biograph studio, the Griffith tradition in its own four walls, and Cabanne was an assistant to Griffith.

Griffith has undoubtedly been the most important director of the American movie. He was less diverted by careerist ambitions, or by the lure of money than all the others. Indirectly, he was responsible for the beginning of American comedy. Sennett, one of Griffith's players, certainly learned much from Griffith's handling of a comique like Billy Quirk. And Sennett's slapstick parodied the refinements of the Griffith troupe. It is a commentary on both of them, and on the American movie, that they never learned to adequately see the grand talents of Mabel Normand.

Griffith was, in his early days, most impressionable. As he saw the movie progress in its capabilities, and able to handle larger themes running longer, he was the first to seize the opportunity, as in *Man's Genesis* and *Judith of Bethulia*. When the spectacle film came from Europe, in particular Italy, he saw the uses of grandeur and scope (although he rendered these platitudinously) in such films as *The Birth of a Nation* and *Intolerance*. No one in America has gone beyond him in this regard, neither Cruze nor Vidor.

The extensions of Griffith are to be found elsewhere, particularly in the Soviet Union. Pudovkin is a direct extension of Griffith, strengthened by a society of profounder and stronger impetus, and by a cinema of firmer analysis and closer scrutiny—as in the selection of authentic types. In the alternation—amounting to a physiological process—of close view and distant "shot" (as in *Storm Over Asia*) Pudovkin creates a form out of neglected devices. The "flash-back" is used in a dramatic and rhythmic process . . . but Pudovkin resembles Griffith in weaknesses of sentimentalism, expressing themselves in poorly chosen similes (the weeping statue in *The End of St. Petersburg*) and in an over-stress of the person as against the social occurrence. The latter fault has been increasingly apparent in Pudovkin since *Mother*. In Griffith we see what Pudovkin might have been in America 1910–30, although we must allow a technical-aesthetic understanding in Pudovkin superior to that of Griffith—in 1930. In Pudovkin we see what Griffith might have been in the U.S.S.R., sustained and urged by a challenging criticism and a relentless discipline. Griffith has been, sadly enough, too much his heritage and environment. He has not risen above them. And now he is through!

1931

Gilbert Seldes

Gilbert Seldes (1893–1970) was one of the first to defend the artistic value of popular culture. In his groundbreaking 1924 book *The 7 Lively Arts*, he ranged appre-
ciatively over Mack Sennett's Keystone Kops comedies, the comic strip *Krazy Kat*,
the circus, and jazz. He argued that the public's tastes were often preferable to the
more "bogus" or "arty" works the critics preferred. His fears about the influence
of legitimate theater corrupting the swift, kinetic sublimity of early movies must
be understood in this context. Nevertheless, Seldes welcomed the innovation of
sound, as can be seen in this excerpt from his second book, *An Hour with the Movies
and the Talkies* (1929). He also gave a rave review to *Citizen Kane* when it first
appeared. Seldes was, according to David Denby, the first modern film critic in this
country: "By 'modern' I mean a writer who embraced the medium without illusions or disdain and who consequently settled into that tone of fond exasperation
which we recognize as the sound of a movie critic."

◆

from
An Hour with the Movies and the Talkies

It ought to have been clear to everyone that the alliance between the stage
and the screen was a mistake. It had actually failed. But its effect persisted.

This muddle-headed idea that because the screen *could* use the material
and the people of the stage, it was at its best when doing so, is responsible for
the retarded development of the movie in America, giving it, at the age of
twenty-five, the mentality of a child of six. It had fed not on mother's milk, but
on chalk and water; it had not been encouraged to exercise its own legs, but
been carried from early childhood on the back of the adult, somewhat decrepit,
stage. Like a child brought up in a dark room, it shrank from the light, like a
cripple it preferred not to move. And light and movement are its life.

It must be remembered that the close-up—a mechanical device for registering emotion by exaggeration—is merely the movie's counterpart of the
bad actor's necessity for taking stage-center when he wants to produce an
effect. That is the one dubious technical trick of the movies and it comes more
or less directly from the stage; whereas all the good devices of the movie (the
flashback, parallel actions, the projection of a scene or person as seen from

different angles, the dissolves, and so on) are impossible on the stage. It must be remembered that the entire series of problem plays, of an unexampled vulgarity, which made the movies ridiculous, were borrowed or imitated from the stage. The whole "vamp" cycle reproduced a stage convention, a stage type of wickedness; superior as it was to the later, more cinematic exploitations of sex as "it" (because it was more honest, simply) the vamp cycle was bad cinema because it was bad drama to begin with. It was the stage which gave the movies those most dangerous of properties: ideas; and the movie tried to project ideas as the stage did, in words, because they were ideas suitable to the wordy stage. The stage even invaded one of the movie's natural domains, that of the spectacle, and only the inherent vigor of the new form and the sheer magnificence of the camera's capacities, kept the cinema spectacle from falling to the low estate of Mr. Morris Gest's *Aphrodite*.

Put the relationship another way: For many years stage people used stage material for the movies; and not one single essential of the movies has ever been favorably affected by the stage; the stage has contributed nothing lasting to the movies; there isn't a single item of cinema technique which requires the experience of the stage; and every good thing in the movies has been accomplished either in profound indifference to the stage, or against the experience of the stage.

What are these accomplishments? The *Keystone* comedies, the work of Charles Chaplin, *The Birth of a Nation*, certain other technical achievements of D. W. Griffith, *Caligari*, *The Big Parade*, the direction of Ernst Lubitsch and the playing of Emil Jannings, a handful of scenes in the work of a few American directors, *The Last Laugh*, the cinematic technique of the Russians, *Nanook* and *Chang*, the contemporary newsreel, recent trick photography, some abstract films. Until we come to the talking films these are the successive nails upon which we hang our wreaths.

In point of time the *Keystone* comes before, and the final triumph of Chaplin comes after, *The Birth of a Nation*, but they have to be considered together, for the surest way to misunderstand the genius of Chaplin is to ignore the *Keystone* comedies in which and out of which he rose.

I use the name *Keystone* for the entire type of slapstick comedy of which it was for years the prime example. Those actually made by Mack Sennett under the trade name of *Keystone* differed from the others in a single important respect, they were always funny; the others were too often Ham and Bud. Until Harold Lloyd and Buster Keaton began making modified slapstick, the only way to be sure that a comedy was going to be funny (to make you laugh without making you sick, as Mr. Edmund Wilson once put it) was to look for the *Keystone* brand. Out of gratitude, and perhaps sentimentality, I preserve the name; when everything else in the type goes, a frantic chase with cops will still be called "Keystone."

Of course their first point of significance was that they were funny. They might have been, as erudite critics suggested, the resurrection of the Italian harlequinade, but if they hadn't been funny, this antiquarian interest would have done them little good. The particular type of fun they made was not popular with intelligent people at the time; it was unrefined; it was vulgar; and only the multitude applauded—and rocked and roared with laughter—until the supreme genius of Chaplin proved itself by effecting a revolution in critical judgment.

This essential point is, regrettably, the one which eludes definition and proof. The crazy situations, the wildly improbable actions, the fury of violence on the slightest provocation, the mad chases annihilating all the canons of time and space and prosecuted in total defiance of the material universe, are all so purely things to be seen, that their essence escapes before they are reduced to analysis and the printed page. In the case of Chaplin we are so familiar with his methods, with his expression and characteristic movements, that we may smile when we read, "he comes late to his work and to mollify his gorilla-like boss, presents him with a lily"; or if we think the typical movement of Lloyd is funny we may be amused to remember that he is acting as a book agent and charges into a broker's office and is thrown out, and returns and is thrown out, and does this a dozen times in succession, with acceleration of pace; or of Keaton that he is chasing butterflies with a net and is so intent on his work that he doesn't notice the savage Indians who have surrounded him. But in all these cases it is the flick of our pictorial imagination which supplies the fun. Of those comedians who did not become so distinguished in our minds, of the *Keystone* comedies as a whole, we can only try to say *why* they were funny; that they *were* funny must be accepted as experience or granted as an assumption, for the sake of argument.

The *Keystone* appeared in an era of quite silly gentility, when even vaudeville tried from time to time to be refined, when Mr. Ziegfeld was putting further distance between his shows and vulgar musical comedies, when hilarity in entertainment was limited to a few acts in the three-a-day, a few survival-comedians in musicals, a few good clowns, and the burlesque wheel. On the credit side, this developing daintiness eventually brought forth the exquisite *Princess* shows and many attractive revues. But heartiness in humor was being drained out. The assertion of the *Keystones* was that the bodies of human beings lent themselves to comic exploitation, that a man sitting down on a red-hot stove and rushing thence to sit on a cake of ice, which promptly melted, could make people laugh. The *Keystone* did not assert that this was the only, or the most desirable, laughter in the world; it merely worked on the assumption that this was the primal, the basic (or as Mr. Nathan puts it) the belly laugh. It then asserted (not as theory, but as ordinary practise) that the lofty sentiments of humanity were also available as material for farce and roared with laughter over love, honesty, perseverance, courage, and marital fidelity, never forgetting its first principle, so that the mockery of these noble virtues was always accomplished through laughter at physical effects. It made fun of pretty girls by showing them languishing for the love of mountainous fat men; it made fun of heroism by showing a cross-eyed explorer surrendering to a stuffed lion; it had no time for the deep peace of domestic bliss which it interrupted with burning toast and babes who put tacks in the soup; it was supremely contemptuous of the American legend of success—its great business men were always shysters and the boy who made good was usually a dolt; and when the hero and the heroine embraced in the final, obligatory close-up, the *Keystone* leered at the new legend of movie love as the hero winked knowingly at the spectators and the heroine pinched his wallet.

In the thousands of slapstick comedies there were many ugly enough to bring odium on the whole class. Just as there were people who believed that there could never be anything funny in seeing a man throw a custard pie into the face of another man, so there were producers who seemed to think that throwing a custard pie was in itself funny—and the success of several tasteless comedies seemed to justify them. The special merit of the *Keystones* was in their immediate creation of the atmosphere of lunatic fantasy. I have seen slapstick comedies done in the method of realism—and am aware of nothing quite so grim and ugly. Sennett had the knack of removing his comedies at once from the level of everyday experience; like creators of fantasy as widely different as Herriman and Lewis Carroll, he presented you with another world, and the moment you accepted this other world, everything was extraordinarily logical and reasonable, even that motor cars should climb houses and revolvers shoot hundreds of bullets without reloading—and without injuring anyone.

This was, in the terms of psychology, an escape from reality. The spectator was not only "carried out of himself" and away from the preoccupations of his routine life; he was translated to a realm in which the categories of human existence ceased to be operative: there was no predictable relation between cause and effect, there were no logical results as logic is known in practise, there was no inevitable. And this non-human structure ran through the emotions as surely as it did through the physical universe. A hundred pound weight on one side of the scale, with a feather on the other, might send the balance up instead of down; and violence involving multitudes of people and furies of physical assault might result from a shy glance at a girl's ankle. From a world where signing on the dotted line brought an instalment collector every month, where violence had vanished from common experience and was the property of criminals and madmen, where people made love cautiously and ate with their minds on calories and weights, where a hundred sanctities were honored without being considered sacred, where habit and custom ruled, where two and two always made four—from this world, the *Keystone* comedy was an escape mechanism.

It occurs to me that those who easily throw about this phrase, which I reluctantly accept, have always been too much engrossed with the question, Escape from what? and not nearly enough with the parallel: Escape *to* what? It is obvious that in any serious sense all the energy we expend in changing, growing, progressing toward sanctity or fulfilment or renunciation, is directed by our desire to escape from the predicament of being the way we are; in a astounding essay Freud himself has suggested that death is what we are seeking every day of our lives. In connection with the movie another psychoanalyst, Barbara Low, has suggested that the escape is from the baffling oppression of those facts which stand between our desires and their satisfaction. Mr. Ramsaye quotes her:

> It is surely clear that the cinema entertainment must gratify this "magic omnipotence wish" more than any fairy tale, any novel, picture or drama can do—and does so independently, to a large extent, of the theme of the film. It is the *method* which brings about so vividly the sense of wish fulfilment. It is the cinema's business to show all problems solved, all doors opened, all questions answered: it must simplify and arbitrarily select, which is one way of making the spectator feel his wishes are fulfilled, since real life is complex, unselective, often baffling our curiosity, and rarely offering solutions to our problems.

That psychologically the theme is secondary, the method primary, is one of the most incisive comments ever made on the film. The people who go every Friday night "to the movies" or who have nothing to do for an evening and telephone to a friend to come "to the movies" prove the point; for although they may eventually reject one offered picture and choose another, they will go to any movie rather than go to none. They escape to the movies, through the movies, and if the movies offer them meretricious moral problems, or dainty sin, or extravagant luxury, these things also are part of the escape. But if the movie offers them instead creative power, a sustained flight of the imagination, an artistic rectitude, a breath of poetry? We cannot forego the question.

For when we come to Chaplin the answer to Escape *to what?* is all-important. Everything that was contrivance and ingenuity in the *Keystone* is with him imagined and created; with him we enter into the only completely realized creation on the screen. The break with the realism of the screen is decisive—and this does not mean that squalor and ugliness, as they so often appear in his masterpieces, are made pretty or sentimentalized: it means only that they are used as circumstances in a new existence, a new life which exists on the screen.

To some people this will seem a reversal of emphasis, an approach to Chaplin by walking backward. I have chosen it because in almost all his other aspects, he is like, although superior to, all the others in the field of movie comedy; in this one thing, in the continuous and complete functioning of his creative power, he is totally unlike them. He is, as we say, in a world apart—the world of his creation. Using more or less the same materials as the others, he is attempting, and achieving, something entirely different.

In material, in incidents, in pace, the early *Chaplins* are, for example, *Keystone* comedies; they were made by *Keystone*, directed by Sennett. The company would set out with a few properties—a mallet, an umbrella, and a dog were often enough—and improvise farcical situations along a roadside or in a park. Twenty-two comedies are officially listed as the result of Chaplin's first (and only) year with *Keystone*, and many of these feature Mabel Normand, as in *Mabel's Busy Day*, *Mabel's Married Life*, and *Mabel's Strange Predicament*. *The Dog-catcher*, *Caught in the Cabaret*, *The Star Boarder*, suggest the typical situations of the *Keystone*: they are predicaments, life's little ironies translated into grotesques, and projected in a ceaseless flow of movement. The population of the *Keystone* world consists of scamps, scoundrels, shysters, fakers, tramps—outcasts in short of our social order—with policemen and pretty girls as foils to their activity; a little later the poor and the oppressed, waiters and barbers and shopgirls appear; but the successful, well-groomed, alert and smart American never enters.

Slowly Chaplin disengages himself, not by opposition to the others, but by superior understanding of what the others are doing. He begins to create that figure of fun and philosophy which he is to develop for fifteen years, broadening, deepening, refining, but never losing hold of the essential character: the gentle anarchist. Between 1915 and 1918 Chaplin gave to the world twenty-six comedies, at least half of them masterpieces, in which this character appears. You see him entering shyly, at odds with life, from one corner of the screen, wondering what the world will do with him; against his will—merely because he lifts his hat to a pretty girl or tries to help a child across the street—he becomes involved in a tempest of other people's emotions; he still fails to understand their furies, their conventional decencies, their shocks, but he is dragged into the center of the screen in a whirlpool of activity; he fights against the world, for his private character, for his perverse sense of righteousness, for his love or his ideal; then as the tempest subsides, he is thrown off from the rim of the circle, and defeated, but not crushed, you see him disappear, with a little mocking dance-step down the irised street. The little figure, whether it is a floorwalker or a porter in a bank or an escaped prisoner or a drunkard or an immigrant or a policeman, is always a complete creation; it is not Chaplin and it is not a new combination of characteristics Chaplin has seen in other comedies; it is a whole, separate thing, living by its own energies.

This process of creating goes on continually and is seen in flashing moments as well as in complete pictures. In *The Gold Rush* Charlie, as the prospector, waits for his guests and impaling two rolls on the ends of forks, begins to make a little dance; it is dexterous, amusing; so much anyone with manual skill could do; the tiny scene is lifted to another level by the movements of Charlie's head as he follows the dance, and by the play of expression on his face; you become suddenly aware of Charlie as ballet-master and as dancer; you see what is going on in his mind and foresee the disaster which awaits his dinner party. To know that Chaplin has always had this creative capacity we need to look only at a single scene in a very old picture: *His Night Out*. In this, Chaplin, with whom Ben Turpin plays almost on terms of equality, plays a drunk; Turpin, the other drunk, is dragging him by the collar along the street. It is very funny to see the seriousness of Turpin's purpose, although he does not know where he is going, contrasted with the supine indifference of his companion. And suddenly, Charlie's hand reaches out and, as idly as a girl in a canoe plucks a water-lily, he picks a daisy from the grass border and sniffs it. The whole scene which has been drunken and grotesque and male, becomes delicate, feminine; the world straightens out for a moment; when it falls back again into its natural distortion, it is infinitely funnier than it was, because of the contrast; because another world has, in a flash, been created before us. The swiftness, the accuracy, the completeness of this new creation can be judged by this: that remembering the scene as you look at the picture a second time, you wonder whether Chaplin will be able to do it again so well. For with Chaplin's great films you do not associate the idea of printed reels;

you think of them as being made before your eyes. When shivering before the wind, in threadbare coat and tattered trousers, he draws a battered tin can from his pocket and, like a detective in fiction, "carefully selects" a cigarette from the half dozen stubs he has collected, he is making a gentleman live and is announcing that the tramp you have seen a moment ago is merely an outward show of the immortal and unconquerable spirit now before you; he works from the core of his being outward to expression.

This period saw also the rise of moving picture criticism. Several types occur: that of the professional journal, which is merely a by-product of paid advertising and is entirely negligible; that of independent professional journals, directed to the exhibitor and offering for the most part criticism of the box-office value of films, which is often combined with "the lowdown" on producers' claims and frequently coincides with the strictest aesthetic criticism— Welford Beaton with his *Film Spectator* and *Harrison's Weekly* are good examples; that of the daily press which was for a long time in the hands of gushing girls or cub reporters, is still ridden by those pests, but is emerging into decent criticism varying only with the intelligence and the independence of the critics; and that of the unattached aesthetes of the film which has recorded some extraordinary errors. Among these errors the greatest is the long contempt of the movie and all its works; when that passed, came the period of praise for whatever was not popular; later the worship of all foreign films and the denigration of all American films.

These are grave mistakes; combine them with the general low esteem in which the pictures were held and you have one of the reasons why the highbrow has been so ineffective on the course of the movies. Another reason is that he did not take particular pains to make himself clear to the director preoccupied with practical matters or to the dull-witted and ignorant owners of movie property. It is rather a pity. *For in almost all practical matters, the theorist has been right about the movies and the practical men, with a few exceptions, have been consistently wrong.*

I have been among the theorists myself, so this statement may sound arrogant; it is certainly not unprejudiced. But two lines of proof are available.

The first is the panic of the businessmen. The scandals of Hollywood were, to be sure, a disgrace which the newspapers played heavily; but the murderous hatred of multitudes of people when the scandals came indicated that the people of the United States were not only ready to believe the worst about the movies, they were not in any way concerned to salvage the good from the bad. They had no godlike inclination to say that if half a dozen good men were to be found there, the place should be saved; because they had ceased to care passionately for the movie. They still went and spent millions to see pictures, because the pictures were the cheapest and most accessible form of entertainment—the radio was still far off. They still had favorites; one does not disrupt the effect of years of publicity in a single day. But they were ready to use any stick to beat the dog which had once been their pet and had turned stupid. In 1921 the heads of all the great producing companies wrote that they were aware of "the necessity for attaining and maintaining the highest possible standards of motion picture film production" and that they were "striving to have the industry accorded the consideration and dignity to which it is justly entitled, and proper representation before the people . . . so that its position, at all times, may be presented in an unbiased and unprejudiced manner." They desired "to have proper contact with the general public and to retain its confidence." There is no sense of security in these words; one feels the bewilderment, the almost childish wonder at what had happened to them, which frightened the movie magnates. The story of a single orgy, a single unproved accusation of murder, was enough to send them scurrying for shelter, because they had no strength to resist attack, no confidence in what they were offering the public, no assurance that the public remained loyal to them. They appealed to a member of President Wilson's cabinet, a man who had won the confidence and respect they so dearly desired; and it is from their letter to Will Hays, asking him to become dictator of their business, that the above confessions are quoted.

As in organized baseball, where the dictator arrived after revelations of shocking dishonesty, the appointment of a Czar is a confession of internal weakness. The motor car industry has faced depressions and inflations and has managed without a dictator; the stage has had dozens of scandals as shocking as those of Hollywood, and has not needed to place a front of respectability as its façade. The metropolitan night clubs, vaudeville, burlesque, the circus have not escaped criticism and have weathered their little storms. The movies alone rushed to cover. They had to hide not their immorality, but their lack of solid substance, of entertainment value, of intelligence.

The second proof is even more salient. The criticism, the demands, the predictions of the theoretical critics have been justified by events—and justified financially. While the producers were over-capitalizing themselves for spectacles and stars, the critics were insisting that the director held the future of the movies in his hand; it needed only a little intelligence to know this, but that little was more than the manufacturers of movies possessed. Eventually stars subsided and directors rose and turned in profits. The critics announced that the movies were paying too much attention to their plots; and movies with simpler plots—*Chang, Moana, Nanook*, and *Grass*—came and were successful. They said that the exclusive preoccupation with fiction was an error and that biographical and historical pictures were desirable; the producers laughed and when *Abraham Lincoln* won a prize but was not brilliantly profitable, thought themselves justified; but in time films of the Spanish-American War and of the Klondike and of the winning of the west held the screen and made money, and they were films in which the first interest was not the love story, but the history. The critics called for a revival of the Western with the newly developed technique and intelligence of the 1920's—and *The Covered Wagon* and *The Iron Horse* appeared. The critics said the historical romance, the costume drama of the movies, was not dead; and it was not dead, it had life and profit in it. They said that works of fantasy could be translated to the screen if the screen could not create its own fantasy—and Mr. Fairbanks proved they were reasonably right with *The Thief of Bagdad*; they said that the more the movie explained itself by movement, the better, and the less it called upon other arts, the better; and in the end the movie magnates had to confess that what they borrowed from the drama had to be reworked and that they had to give to scenarists and directors innocent of the stage the prizes for good work. The critics said that movie playing was not stage acting, and after many years the producers abandoned their high-priced famous players and began to create their own rosters of straight movie players.

Above all, with monotonous insistence, the theoretical critics had the effrontery to say to the producers that they were not using their own material to best advantage and that the secret of good movies lay in the camera. They said that the camera could be made to express more things, more clearly, more effectively, more rapidly. They were told that the public was too intelligent to have much use for trick photography, as if a horse walking into himself was what they meant by the exploitation of the instrument. And it was, finally, brought home to the producers that the camera could be used as the critics had said. The lesson came from the Germans with their camera angles and nearly every director spoiled himself for a time by shooting any and every scene in distortion; but the principle of using the camera survived, of using camera angles with a specific purpose in keeping with the general structure of the picture. The new uses of the camera and a higher conception of the art of cutting distinguish all the good silent pictures of the present.

A good many of the aesthetes of the cinema were opposed to the talking picture. So were nine-tenths of the commercial producers. The former thought the talkies would be bad pictures; the latter that they would not make money.

So far few good talkies have been made and nearly all of them have made money. The balance of prophecy still favors the theorists over the practical men who sat by while technicians created the talking mechanism and rejected it until the Warners having apparently tried everything else and feeling desperately uncertain of their finances, tried the *Vitaphone*—and by their success forced the talkies upon all the other producers.

The theorists, in brief, said, "use the material most appropriate to your medium and exploit it with all the means in your power"; they were fundamentally right. And if anyone says they were ahead of their time, there is at least one commentary which must be made: by 1920 when the theoretical critics were in full swing, the producers of commercial movies had run off so many million feet of rubbish that the public taste was almost hopelessly corrupted. In the following decade the public did reject two or three unusual pictures; but they accepted, with enthusiasm, half a dozen others which in various ways met the demands of the critics, which in various ways were just what the producers said the public would not stand.

1929

Pare Lorentz

Pare Lorentz (1906–1992) wrote movie criticism for the magazines *Judge*, *Scribner's*, *Vanity Fair*, and *McCall's* from 1926 until 1941. As a critic he decried censorship, championed the role of the film director as artistic creator, and urged the making of more independent, honestly realistic American movies. "His blunt, strong, sharp-eyed reviews give vivid first-hand insights into the film years they covered," wrote critic Stanley Kauffmann. Lorentz himself became an important filmmaker, crafting socially-conscious documentaries such as *The Plow That Broke the Plains* (1936) and *The River* (1938). President Franklin D. Roosevelt was so impressed with the latter that he named Lorentz head of the newly created United States Film Service. Lorentz made and oversaw the production of hundreds of informational films during World War II, which did not prevent him from expressing skepticism (see below) that documentaries would ever be embraced as entertainment by the broader American public.

◆

Anna Christie

The advent of Greta Garbo, with sound, was hailed by her owners as an occasion comparable to the second coming of Sarah Bernhardt. The public was persuaded without difficulty, and the tall, monotonous Swedish star, by the more or less childish trick of learning the English language, has brought the box-office receipts piling in. The occasion was celebrated with *Anna Christie*, based on a play of many seasons ago, written by Eugene O'Neill. Some liberty was taken with the manuscript, so that there is little of the harsh but poetic reality of the early O'Neill retained in the new celluloid version. (The play was given a silent treatment with passable success several years ago.) There are not many alterations, but, in the usual movie manner, the plot is explained in words of two syllables by an extraneous thousand feet or so tacked on before the scene that originally opened the play. This scene was, and is, the most effective and simple bit in the manuscript. It is a dialogue between a young and a worn member of the world's oldest profession.

The two movie audiences I sat with chose to regard the show as a comedy, and I believe their reaction was right. The effective buffoonery of Marie Dressler overclouded her genuine and understanding portrayal of a South

Street wharf rat. Charles Bickford tore into his characterization of a simple seaman with so much gusto that he was regarded as a vaudeville Irish comedian.
Miss Garbo gave an original and surprising interpretation of the heroine.
George Marion, as the announcer who steps to the fore and mumbles about the
"ol' davil sea," acted as though he were giving an elaborate bedtime story over
the radio. But it is Miss Garbo who brought the audience to the theatre, and
who, necessarily, is the subject under discussion.

I do not see that there is any other way to discuss most movies except in
terms of personalities. Here you have a story that is an early effort of a master
craftsman. It was adapted for the movies years ago. As is true of a hundred
movies every month, there is nothing deep, profound, or unique enough about
the plot to dig your toes into. Yet I do not see that my own opinion of Greta
Garbo is of any more use to you than a passing comment on the hat-check girl.
I do know that if you insist on calling her an actress, we then have something
to bicker over, even though I would be hard put to give you my definition of
that craft. Before her first talking role, Miss Garbo impressed me as an indolent young lady with an unusual figure and absolutely no warmth or color,
much less any indication of emotional depth or craft. In *Anna Christie*, she produces a deep, monotonous, but humorous voice. And that was surprising. It
dispelled forever the "mysterious lady" personality and left her a young lady
who was seriously trying to understand her job, but who was much too easygoing and goodnatured to get a sweat up over it.

My opinion of her ability is really based on her work in a movie called *Love*,
adapted with little success from "Anna Karenina." Her monkeyshines with
John Gilbert were of no importance, but in one scene she was called upon to
enter, at great loss of pride, the nursery of her son, whom she had forsaken.
The young lady simply came in the room and played with the toys as though
she were passing the time until tea. I am not a director, and I specify no rules,
but she walked in and out of that set with no more expression or concern on
her face than a clam. I don't ask a great deal of calisthenics with my drama, but
I like to get something of a show for my money. As I am not interested in movie
figures or scandal, I have yet to feel even the slightest curiosity in the Swedish
celebrity. Audibility has given her a good humor. But that doesn't make an
actress capable of projecting the hopeless despair of a Minnesota prostitute isolated on a coal barge with a paranoiac father.

The director, Clarence Brown, should share most of the blame for the
weakness of *Anna Christie* in that he cast a girl whose every gesture indicated a
charming school-girl conception of tragedy for a difficult part, and for that reason I suggest that you see Miss Garbo for yourself.

1930

Good Art, Good Propaganda

During the past five years there has been a great deal of sound and fury about the documentary film. There are movie classes being taught in many colleges and universities; the Museum of Modern Art Film Library has a study course in the documentary film which it has sent all over the country. The Rockefeller Foundation has endowed several motion picture groups; it has an association of film library organizations; it has endowed a modern composer to do research in combining music and film; it has established a complete sound department, and put up money for production at the University of Minnesota.

The Carnegie Foundation has produced one film, *The City*, and has set up a course in general functional arts at Princeton; the Alfred P. Sloan, Jr., Foundation has produced two pictures and is engaged in a large epic study of America; and the British have sent over several flights of lecturers to explain to our dumb but patient citizenry the meaning of the documentary film.

I myself produced three motion pictures for the United States Government, which were promptly labeled "documentary," and I also engaged Joris Ivens to direct a picture for the REA and Robert Flaherty to direct a picture for the Department of Agriculture.

Strung out in this manner, like an old minstrel band in a small town, the documentary film sounds fairly important. Personally, I feel that if there ever was a movement, a school, a development, it is practically stopped dead in its tracks.

Harvard, Columbia University, and the University of Chicago have for years been fiddling with schoolroom movies, and there is no question that in a very short time most of the grammar and high schools in the country will be using both radio and motion pictures to supplement textbooks.

Classrooms and college dormitories give me melancholia, and I know nothing about theories of education, so I shall avoid any discussion of "educational" movies. To me all educators who write long essays about educational films forget that the people they are talking about (i.e., their students) go right around the corner from the classroom and look at Hollywood motion pictures; they also listen to Charlie McCarthy and Jack Benny on the radio along with, possibly, the Philharmonic and the Toscanini symphonic broadcasts.

I cannot believe, then, that even a ten-year-old boy willingly would sit through a bumbling, inept, dry amateur movie in a classroom when he's already become accustomed to the finesse, the speed, and the excitement of a *Pinocchio* or of a *Grapes of Wrath*. I also assume that the same boy has sense enough to know that *Union Pacific* has nothing to do with history, nor does *Virginia City* have anything to do with the Civil War. Even if he can't or won't read, the child probably knows by instinct that such productions are spurious either as art, entertainment, or fact.

Good art is good propaganda. And educators, politicians, and little group-thinkers can't produce good art, or they wouldn't be educators, politicians, or little group-thinkers.

In the past twenty years, we have had Robert Flaherty's *Nanook*, *Moana of the South Seas*, *Man of Aran*, *Elephant Boy*, and, with F. W. Murnau, *Tabu*, and to me, the greatest of these was *Tabu* because Murnau was the greatest artist.

Flaherty, a gentle, courageous, lyrical Irishman, undoubtedly started what is the documentary movement. Flaherty is a poetic explorer, who has been at the ends of practically all the continents of the world; he has worked with Esquimaux, Polynesians, Indians, and Irishmen, not because he wanted to start a school, but because he loved what he was doing.

Ten years ago a cameraman went into the Southern Highlands, picked up a college football player working in a sawmill, found a mountain girl, hired some seven-foot mountaineers, and made *Stark Love*, a startling and beautiful picture in its day. Ernest Schoedsack and a wild-eyed but gracious war-time pilot, Merian Cooper, borrowed some money and made a picture in India about elephants, called *Chang*, that was very successful. There are a few others: *The Wave*, by Paul Strand; *The Spanish Earth* and *400,000,000*, by Joris Ivens; *Crisis*, and, the most recent, *Lights Out In Europe*, by Herbert Kline.

What I am concerned with in this critique is whether the documentary, non-fiction, non-profit, or—to coin a final awkward word—the un-Hollywood film, has any importance either to movie makers or to the general public.

Practically all these pictures have been critical successes but have meant very little to the general public simply because Hollywood has had a lock on all the screens in the country and Hollywood is not interested in documentary films. Now, for the first time in years, the theatre circuits are interested in independent pictures—partly because Hollywood can't afford to produce expensive pictures now that it has lost its world markets, partly because there is an anti-monopoly suit in progress against the producer-distributor corporations.

If there ever was a time when the non-fiction film had an open market, this is the year. Yet I feel that the fiction, rather than the non-fiction, picture will be the most important type of movie we will get from the independent, new movie-makers, and for two reasons.

The first is because of the groups interested in documentary films. Just as they have in the theatre, in literature, and in politics, the extreme left-wingers in movies have taken the attitude that because a movie is liberal it therefore is "good." There is no easy way to write a novel or an essay, or to produce a movie. Thus, while I am personally in favor of the Chinese winning their own country away from the Japanese and while I personally was horrified at the Nazi invasion of Poland, I do not feel that just because a man has made a picture dealing with these subjects he has made a "good" movie.

Again—good art is good propaganda. If a man in Kansas City, profoundly uninterested in European politics, paid money to see some of the pictures I mentioned, he probably was bored—and rightfully so, because he saw aimless direction, heard a meaningless score, and viewed some third-rate photography.

Motion picture-making is a craft. There are endless ways in which a man may combine imagery with personalities, landscapes, words, music, and sound, but the rules of dramatic logic hold just as true for a man who is making a picture about unemployment as they do for a man who is directing Garbo.

It, of course, is totally unfair to compare the work of a man who had no money, no huge studio, no chance to remake his work, with that of a man who has half-a-hundred brilliant technicians and all the millions he needs to help him. But that is not my point. The documentary filmmakers for the most part are more interested in theory than in practice; they are more interested in the subject matter than in the tools they are working with; and when they turn out an inept picture they scream "fascist" at anyone who doesn't consider they have turned out masterpieces.

Hollywood has for years closed its doors against new technical talent. For years it has not developed composers, cameramen, sound men, or directors, and for a long time it has been my hope that some financial group would establish an experimental motion picture organization, documentary or otherwise, so that younger men could learn a complex trade—could work with music and sound and photography in an effort to broaden the potentialities of the film medium.

The documentary film groups have schools of theory and groups within groups, and they are always having committee meetings. As I have written before, no committee can edit a magazine, or publish books, or produce plays or movies successfully. It has been tried many times. More than that, there is no such thing as a school of art. There are only men; some have talent and some haven't.

Thus for all the lectures, committee meetings, study courses, and esoteric jargon, I find no documentary movement going on in this country. On the contrary, there are some young men with talent who are willing to work for low salaries as long as they can make motion pictures about facts more important to the commonwealth than whether Irene Dunne will marry Randolph Scott. However, I don't think they or their work will be really important to the public, schoolchildren, or movie men unless they strive to have just as good photography, editing, and music as Hollywood.

Even under normal conditions, most of these groups would be left-footed to me because they argue that their cause justifies their work—their work must be considered important because their faith is the true faith.

My second reason for feeling that whatever documentary movement was under way has stopped dead is a simple one—that is, there is a war going on.

If there is a private, educational, or governmental group with sufficient power and money to produce pictures of our country in our time using the language and the music of the people, if there is any responsible organization not interested in interpreting this life in terms of war, I haven't encountered it. The documentary school will be in uniform by the time it gets out of the faculty meeting.

1940

William Troy

A distinguished literary critic, whose posthumous *Selected Essays* won a National Book Award in 1968, William Troy (1904–1961), married to the poet Leonie Adams, was a much-loved literature professor at Bennington College, The New School, and New York University. He was also film critic of *The Nation* from 1933 to 1935. To that post he brought an educated, almost professorial tone, which he used sometimes for comic effect (see his query about interspecies love and anatomy in the *King Kong* review). Troy also managed to approach each piece of film criticism as the occasion for some larger essayistic rumination. His feeling for the carpentry of the short review piece is superb.

◆

King Kong

At least one of our national characteristics is illustrated in the RKO-Radio production of *King Kong* which loomed over the audiences of both Radio City movie-houses last week. It is a characteristic hard to define except that it is related to that sometimes childish, sometimes magnificent passion for scale that foreigners have remarked in our building of hundred-story skyscrapers, our fondness for hyperbole in myth and popular speech, and our habit of applying superlatives to all our accomplishments. Efforts to explain it have not been very satisfactory; the result is usually a contradiction in which we are represented as a race that is at once too civilized and not civilized enough. If Herr Spengler interprets the extreme gigantism of the American mind and imagination as the sign of an inflated decadence resembling that of Alexandria and the later Roman Empire, others discover in it the simpler expression of a race still unawakened from childhood. At Radio City last week one was able to see the contradiction pretty dramatically borne out; an audience enjoying all the sensations of primitive terror and fascination within the scientifically air-cooled temple of baroque modernism that is Mr. Rockefeller's contribution to contemporary culture.

What is to be seen at work in *King Kong* is the American imagination faithfully adhering to its characteristic process of multiplication. We have had plays and pictures about monsters before, but never one in which the desired effect depended so completely on the increased dimensions of the monster. Kong is a veritable skyscraper among the apes. In his own jungle haunts he rules like a king over the rest of the animal world; and when he is taken to New York to be exhibited before a light-minded human audience he breaks through his chromium-steel handcuffs, hurls down two or three elevated trains that get in his way, and scales the topmost heights of the Empire State Building with the fragile Miss Fay Wray squirming in his hairy paw. The photographic ingenuity that was necessary to make all this seem plausible was considerable, and in places so remarkable as to advance the possibility of a filming of certain other stories depending largely on effects of scale—*Gulliver's Travels*, for example, and possibly even the *Odyssey*. But unfortunately, it was thought necessary to mitigate some of the predominant horror by introducing a human, all-too-human theme. "It was not the guns that got him," says one of the characters at the end, after Kong has been brought to ground by a whole squadron of battle planes. "It was Beauty killed the Beast." By having Beauty, in the person of Miss Wray lure the great monster to his destruction, the scenario writers sought to unite two rather widely separated traditions of the popular cinema—that of the "thriller" and that of the sentimental romance. The only difficulty was that they failed to realize that such a union was possible only by straining our powers of credulity and perhaps also one or two fundamental laws of nature. For if the love that Kong felt for the heroine was sacred, it suggests a weakness that hardly fits in with his other actions; and if it was, after all, merely profane, it proposes problems to the imagination that are not the less real for being crude.

1933

The Invisible Man

There are two very good reasons why the version of H. G. Wells's *Invisible Man* at the old Roxy is so much better than this sort of thing usually turns out to be on the screen. The first is that James Whale, who is responsible for the direction, has taken a great deal of pains with something that is usually either reduced to a minimum or altogether ignored in these attempts to dramatize the more far-fetched hypotheses of science—namely, setting. Ordinarily we are precipitated abruptly and without warning into the strange and violent world of the scientific romancer's imagination. We are given no time to make our adjustment to the logic of this new world which is so different from the world to which we are accustomed. The result is of course that we never truly believe in this new world: it is too abstract, too intellectually conceived, to take us in very successfully through our feelings. For this reason one is always tempted to lay down as a first principle for writers and directors dealing with the extraordinary the principle that to respond to the unusual we must first be reminded of the commonplace. And James Whale's success in observing the principle makes one more convinced than ever that it should be regarded as a general one. He begins with a carefully documented picture of a small country inn in England: the people, the furnishings, the whole atmosphere are not only instantly recognizable but also so particularized as to have an interest in and for themselves. The background is solidly blocked in so that we can have no uncertainty as to the reality of the people and the places with whom we have to deal. Everything is made ready for the invisible man to step in and perform his marvels.

Now the only problem for the director was to make the best possible use of his idea—an idea which happens to be ideally suited to the talking screen in so far as it is impossible to imagine it being equally well treated in any other medium. For the wretched scientist who has made himself invisible still has a voice. A body without a voice we have had on the silent screen, but not until this picture have we had a voice without a body. And in Wells's novel the sight of the printed words on the page cannot be so disturbingly eerie as the actual sound of Claude Rains's voice issuing from empty chairs and unoccupied rooms. The problem for Mr. Whale, then, was to miss none of the opportunities for humor, pathos, and metaphysical horror which this rare notion opened up to the sound-camera. How admirably he has succeeded it is impossible to indicate without reference to the numerous instances in which his ingenuity surprises our habitual sense-patterns. It will be enough to mention the books hurled through space by an invisible hand, the cigarette smoked by invisible lips, the indentation in the snow of the shattered but still invisible body. Also one must point to the effectiveness of not showing the visible features of the scientist until, in the last few feet of the film, death restores them to him. Of Claude Rains's richly suggestive voice it is not too much to say that it is hardly less responsible than the direction for the peculiar quality of the picture as a whole. The preternatural compound of Olympian merriment and human desolation which are its overtones lends a seriousness that would otherwise be lacking. But taken either as a technical exercise or as a sometimes profoundly moving retelling of the Frankenstein fable, *The Invisible Man* is one of the most rewarding of the recent films.

1933

Cecilia Ager

Cecilia Ager (1902–1981) was the first woman film critic to be employed by *Variety*, the show-business weekly. She later reviewed movies for *PM*, the progressive New York newspaper, in the 1940s, and wrote features on the entertainment business for *Vogue*, *Harper's Bazaar*, and other magazines. First reporting on fashion in the movies—what various female stars were wearing and who designed it—she moved on to critiquing the films themselves, without ever quite relinquishing her emphasis on the "women's stuff." With a witty, mocking style, she used fashion as her entry into examining the constricting roles women were asked to play, in real life and onscreen (object of desire, damsel in distress, adoring wife), the hypocrisy of the sexual double standard, and other themes that would later become staples of feminist criticism. Alastair Cooke described Ager as America's outstanding movie critic, though Otis Ferguson thought she "never seemed to get used to the full-time business of reviewing the whole picture." She was married to songwriter Milton Ager ("Happy Days Are Here Again," "Ain't She Sweet ").

◆

Parachute Jumper

Bette Davis in *Parachute Jumper* seems convinced she's become quite a charmer. Slowly she raises her eyelids to sear the hero with her devastating glances, then satisfied, she smiles a crooked little Mona Lisa smile. Unfortunately, this procedure takes place while Miss Davis is wearing a curious pill-box hat that perches on her head at an angle slightly comic. The hat, and her own self-satisfaction, interfere with the effect.

To make matters still more troublesome for her, Miss Davis must keep to the neat but not helpful black-and-white frocks of a job-hunting stenog. Finally she gets work, and an evening dress, too, from a dope-smuggling employer. The dress is black satin swathings about the hips, little more than a drop shouldered ruffle for the completely backless bodice. A bit too-too for Miss Davis's slender figure.

Claire Dodd, the story says, engages her chauffeurs on their biceps appeal, then gets to the point the day they start work. Miss Dodd is too young and pretty to need to be so aggressive, but the story says she is.

1933

Hallelujah I'm a Bum

Madge Evans is a fortunate girl, and that's because she's such a very nice one. She's fortunate in *Hallelujah I'm a Bum*—for not only Frank Morgan, but Al Jolson is mad about her. Because she's such a nice girl, the story arranges for her to have amnesia, so she can return their adoration each in turn. When she's got a memory, she loves Mr. Morgan, when she's lost it, she loves Mr. Jolson. It would never do for a nice girl to be a two-timer, and a nice girl couldn't fail to find both Mr. Morgan and Mr. Jolson charming. If it seems a little mixed up, that's because the rewards of virtue have been absent from the screen for such a long time that hardly anyone recognizes them any more.

Being true blue, regular and wholesome takes up so much of a nice girl's time that she has very little energy left for the less worthy pursuits—of style, for instance. Miss Evans pauses long enough in her devotions to right to fix herself up with a flatteringly expert make-up that realizes what fine, frank eyes she has, but that's all the attention she can spare for vanity.

Her clothes are neat, of course, and ladylike, but flair is the shallow province of hussies. Miss Evans has a couple of decent suits that will do very nicely, and a light satin one-piece dress for times when she's expected to be a little seductive. That satin dress just proves that nice girls really ought to stay in their own backyard. It clings so desperately in several places that it becomes a little embarrassing. Oftentimes nice girls are that way because their figures don't give them any choice.

1933

Ladies They Talk About

Once in every Barbara Stanwyck picture it has become the custom for Miss Stanwyck to blow up in a shattering emotional scene. *Ladies They Talk About* respects tradition.

Miss Stanwyck therefore suffers a continuous series of treacheries from practically everybody in the cast, so that when the time comes for her to do her stuff, she'll have gathered a goodly store of ammunition. Meanwhile, of course, she lets off little sparks along the way, but she takes proper care to save the full punch for the finish. She permits the audience to suspect she has a temper right from the beginning, and then stuns them with what she can do when she's really mad.

Miss Stanwyck is a bad, bad girl in *Ladies They Talk About*. She's sent to San

Quentin for it and meets a lot of other naughty girls there, Lillian Roth, Dorothy Burgess, Maude Eburne, Cecil Cunningham. They're bad all right, but they've got mighty strong personalities.

And San Quentin's not such punishment at that, more like a finishing school for young ladies. Each girl has her own room which she may decorate to suit her individual flair. Portable phonographs are allowed the pretties, Pekinese dogs if they like, plenty of cigarettes and cigars, and though they must all wear cotton dresses, in the privacy of their own rooms they may put on black lace chemises and sheer mesh stockings, the more pleasantly to muse about their sweethearts. Ruth Donnelly, the matron, is just like a house mother, only she has more sense. Helen Ware is no more strict than a Dean. The girls have their little feuds, but no worse than those at boarding school. Sometimes the girls have to work in the prison laundry, which is really a post office with the letters concealed in the clothes they wash instead of in post boxes. Yet girls are just girls. Miss Stanwyck doesn't like it there somehow. She looks very well during the time she spends at San Quentin. Her hair is always neatly waved and coiffed, her make-up never neglected, but she doesn't appreciate it. She just sulks and pouts and wants to get even all the time.

1933

Our Betters

Constance Bennett flings herself into the hoity-toity snobsy-wobsy elegance of *Our Betters* like the prodigal hot-footing it home. Here's a role that says of her though once she was trusting and dewy with good intentions, life had made her relentless, clever, unscrupulous, triumphant. It's an unsympathetic part, but Miss Bennett is always a little unnatural in sympathetic roles. Somebody's got to show the younger generation how to get on in the world, and Miss Bennett's peerless at that. She plays the foresighted, arrogant Pearl with uncanny understanding. She's so sure in her characterization, she makes it practically an autobiography.

Our Betters is terribly smart, violently upper class. Insistently it shrieks toniness, graduation from Hollywood aristocracy. Its houses have not only drawing-rooms and boudoirs, they have libraries, with books in them, too. Some of its rooms are Empire, some Georgian, it even has a Directoire foyer. Positively nothing is modernistic, that's how swell it is. Constance Bennett, Anita Louise, Phoebe Foster, are presented at court and top anybody Their Majesties have seen, that's how utterly ornamental they are. Miss Bennett wears a white Schiaparelli suit with a three-quarter casual coat and a dark high-necked blouse that smart New York shops plan to stun their customers with this spring, that's how fashion-wise it is. Miss Bennett wears ropes of black pearls with a dark crêpe dress, that's how up in really blatant luxury she is. Every detail is so painstakingly indisputable it sets up a positive nostalgia for the other side of the railroad tracks.

Violet Kemble-Cooper is completely authoritative, continuously effective in her richly exaggerated characterization. Phoebe Foster and Anita Louise screen nicely, but in a cast with Miss Bennett and Miss Kemble-Cooper their lack of flair is too apparent, sets them aside as well meaning, but none the less bores.

1933

King Kong

Despite all her experiences with picture beasties, Fay Wray can't seem to condition herself against the horrid old things. She's just as terrified at King Kong, she screams quite as shrilly as if she couldn't remember from her past encounters that she will surely be saved at the end. She won't learn, Miss Wray, she won't learn. All that's come of her former run-ins with monsters is the overnight change of her hair from black to blonde, but it doesn't help. The curious attraction she has for man-beast combos is not to be denied by superficial hair-colour transformation. It's made matters even worse for her. Blonde, she looks even more the part of Beauty in the fable, *Beauty and the Beast*, so what can the beast do but act good and beasty.

In *King Kong* Miss Wray actually puts on the legendary costume of Beauty, a medieval robe of sheer cloth of gold that falls gracefully off her shoulders and clings devotedly about her hips, girdled snugly with gold braid. She wears it presumably the better to rehearse her part in the film she's engaged to make on the mysterious island; but really and truly that costume is a plant, a hint to the audience in case they've forgotten the fable.

Miss Wray's reaction to Kong makes mincemeat of the fearless modern girl theory. She's not only scared to death, but she completely loses her head. She won't learn that Kong is really her friend. No, she screams and writhes and wriggles and kicks every time she's cradled in his love-lorn paw. Even when he scales the Empire State building holding her firmly in one hand, she carries on so vehemently it seems she wants to be let go so she can be dashed to the ground eighty storeys below. She just has no foresight. Strange girl, Miss Wray.

Night Flight

If *Night Flight* were to give you more than a hint, a teenchy-weenchy suggestion as to the kind of gals Helen Hayes and Myrna Loy are (*Night Flight*'s little women who wait at home while their husbands soar the skies), what would become of its restraint, its well-bred artistic economy, it would like to know. *Night Flight* means to be art, Hemingway kind of art. So away with embroidery. Let the facts be bare and brief.

If the audience can't tell that Helen Hayes loves her husband from watching the good housekeeping details of her preparation for his return, if they can't tell that she's a little bird at heart from noting her love for radio music, if they don't get her spirituality from observing the lack of allure of her routine chiffon and lace négligé, if they don't realize that she's a little soldier from heeding her gallant apprehension when she learns her husband's plane is late, if by this time they haven't learned to love her themselves—it's their hard luck. *Night Flight*'s not going to lead an audience by the hand.

And if they can't see that a flyer's mighty fortunate to have Myrna Loy for a wife, the way she asks no questions, the way she accepts his arrivals and departures, the way she looks at him, but, above all, the way she looks, warm, gentle, yielding—but the chances are the audience sees. For one thing, Miss Loy's photographed more tenderly than Miss Hayes. For another, she doesn't have to play any painfully playful little scenes pretending her husband's dining with her when everybody knows he's up in the skies bucking storms.

1933

Camille

Greta Garbo dies beautifully in *Camille*. You can actually see her do it, sense the precise moment when her lovely spirit leaves her fascinating clay. Though it's Robert Taylor himself who's talking awful dramatic at the moment, you pass him up. You don't pay any attention to Taylor. It's Garbo's face that absorbs you. It grabs at you all through *Camille*, but it's got you complete; you're all tied up when she dies. Complete, even though it looks like she's going to take quite a time dying, loping and staggering from bed to chair and back again. It's a magnificent face; death, and canny lighting and photography, revealing its epic bone structure, showing you that its baffling allure has solid foundation—it's structural, architectural and not, as you may have feared, disbelieving, something you just made up.

Garbo in *Camille* shows up Dietrich in anything as a smooth mask with interesting hollows in her cheeks and a low voice that reads "yes" with a rising inflection. Garbo in *Camille* has character and shading and, surprisingly, warmth. You don't just admire her in *Camille*—you like her. You find her human at last. You are actually, actively, sorry for her—nor does she sacrifice any of her natural dignity to win your sympathy. It's that, in *Camille*, she realizes her potentialities as a great actress. She no longer need depend upon a provocative personality; now every nuance has meaning, is felt, is true.

There is fine showmanship in the externals of her portrait. Just as her cough grows progressively more frequent, chilling you the first time you hear it with its portent of doom and reiterating its ominous message each suc-ceeding time, so does the colour of her costumes change from white in the carefree beginning, to grey when the forces of tragedy gather momentum, until at last sable black with all its dark meaning appears. First, in an all-black vel-vet dress and large black hat that she wears for her journey to the country. Then, when it seems that she is to be happy, white again in cannily pic-turesque lawn dresses with only a black cloak to remind you her fate is sealed; black again after her renunciation—shimmering black net with sequins, but black. For her death, so that you are not too miserable and may find solace in something, a white gown, ecclesiastical in feeling with its monk's cowl, sending you to religion, there to take courage to bear it. Adrian has never been more touching, nor, fortuitously, more decorative. Garbo's coiffure also acts: the friv-olous curled bangs that cover her forehead in the beginning are gradually lifted until at the end the whole serenity of her brow is revealed; there is something spiritual about this process too.

Lenore Ulric, new to pictures, shows Laura Hope Crews, who's been in pictures a lot, that an actress can register raucous vitality without becoming a noisy bore. Even Jessie Ralph is toned down in *Camille*, which makes Miss Crews's violently discordant carryings-on the more singular and distressing.

1937

The Last of Mrs. Cheyney

It is comforting to see, in *The Last of Mrs. Cheyney*, that Joan Crawford has at last attained the manner she's been striving for. She put up a good fight, against what to anyone less determined might seem utterly insurmountable odds, and her final victory is an inspiration to us all. Now everybody, Miss Crawford and her audience, can relax. She emerges from the struggle freed of nearly all her feeling of inferiority (though why she should have felt that way the least bit is baffling, since after all she is a picture star, and picture stars are absolutely top aristocracy today); purged of nearly all the little giveaways that used to worry her so and drive her to an enormous and stridently active elegance in her fierce longing to wipe them out.

Now she quietly looks any actor, no matter how English, straight in the eye, confident of the mastered casualness of her own pronunciation. Nobody's coiffure is more cleanly swept-off-the-brow, more intent upon character and therefore disdainful of artificial coquetry, than hers; nobody's wardrobe more starkly simple—but only on the surface, mind. That calm and repose she's now achieved, that feeling of firm ground beneath her feet, must not be mistaken for just pure simplicity. Far from it. It wells from knowledge—from knowledge, at last, gained the hard way. No more do "beans"—for "beens"—jut out from her speech naked and terrified; no more do unresolved trimmings distract from the compact and self-contained silhouette of her clothes. Still self-conscious, but with a new self-assurance that shows her self-consciousness is only an expression of her awareness of her duty of high-class-example-setter to her public—instead of the mark of self-doubt it used to be—now Miss Crawford goes about doing right things, wearing right things, with deafening poise. Now her quality asserts itself from the inside out, instead of insisting on itself with externals; and the whole show is much more convincing, besides being a lot easier on everybody and cosier to watch.

True, she still keeps her eyes open to their widest range, but surely she has been severe enough with herself to warrant indulgence in this small holdover from her old ways. There is enough blackboard correctness in *The Last of Mrs. Cheyney*, enough horror of vulgarity as it is. After all, only one of Miss Crawford's costumes, the hostess dress with the short Persian jacket, fits rather too tightly across the hips; there are no furs; her jewels, if large, are chastely set. There is enough restraint.

1937

Personal Property

It used to be the girls who took the baths in pictures.

It used to be the girls who lolled, tantalizing, in cloaks of delicate soap bubbles. It used to be the girls who, spending the night away from home, stumbled about adorable in borrowed pyjamas, oh so much too big for them. It used to be the girls who fetched the pretty photography, who got the seductive make-up, who drew the glamour lighting, who wore the clothes.

It used to be the girls who laid in bed and drove everybody mad with just the thought of it. It used to be the girls who had the irresistible bedroom doors, who waited deliciously apprehensive and wide-eyed behind them. It used to be the girls who stuck the flower between their teeth.

However, this was before Robert Taylor, before the advent of a manly beauty so overwhelming, all the old traditions tottered before its might. Now in *Personal Property* it's Robert Taylor who takes the bath.

In *Personal Property* one may have Mr. Taylor in a lather or rinsed, one may quiver to the way he wraps his robe close to his splendid chest and beautifully modelled loins, one may sigh as he ties the belt snug to his waist with such dashing disregard of the buckle. One may learn how he achieves his magnificent coiffure, how he coaxes with his own two hands his lustrous black hair into that proud, clean-swept line, one may even watch him clean his nails.

Although it does leave out the method by which Mr. Taylor nurtures the lovely shape of his eyebrows, it is a stirring performance that Mr. Taylor gives in this sequence—natural, confident, and yet deeply hygienic—and it provides the flaps with a high standard for comparison. Nor, while educating the flaps in the details of what to keep on longing for, do Mr. Taylor and *Personal Property* forget the matrons. They can always be a mother to him, *Personal Property* shows them, consoling them with several scenes of Taylor and Henrietta Crossman kissing one another full on the lips with an ardour far more burning, as a matter of fact, than the feeling Taylor puts into the lone fade-out clinch he accords Jean Harlow.

But then, *Personal Property* executes so conscientiously its mission of pandering for Taylor, it can hardly be expected to take full care of Miss Harlow, too. Miss Harlow's already been made. Besides, *Personal Property* knows it can always be sure, for her part, of her own natural gift for conjuring up the illusion of strip-tease without any of the bother of going through the motions.

1937

Another Dawn

Everybody in *Another Dawn* suffers from a stiff upper lip, which may be why everybody in *Another Dawn* is crazy to die. Because, just before they fold up, they see the angels and then their lips relax into a happy smile, which must be terrific relief.

So everybody's so eager to get popped off by Arab snipers, they double-cross each other only for a chance to get in range. Common soldier and officer alike are obsessed with the urge to be targets, though as befits their superior station, the officers' urge has some high-class complications provided by Miss Kay Francis.

Officers Errol Flynn and Ian Hunter are very sensitive, and their natural British yen to stop bullets with their persons may very well be increased by an unconscious desire to be dead before the prophetic fashions Miss Francis wears become universal.

Ardently searching the horizon—because she's supposed to be a deep one—Miss Francis pretends she doesn't know what she's got on, but there aren't many people who have Miss Francis's ability to be unaware of what she chooses not to be aware of. So, while she's having a soul, she's also got a mess of draperies, the very latest thing for desert sand-storms. So late, in fact, that nobody ever thought of them before, figuring, with stodgy practicality, that a sand-storm is enough trouble without a lot of silken stuffs swirling around. But Miss Francis's floating scarves, dervish skirts and feather capes do have a certain merit, ballooning in the sirocco; watching them sort of hypnotizes people, and keeps their minds off the spiritual things she says.

1937

A Day at the Races

There ought to be a statue erected, or a Congressional Medal awarded, or a national holiday proclaimed, to honour that great woman, Margaret Dumont, the dame who takes the raps from the Marx Bros. For she is of the stuff of which our pioneer women were made, combining in her highly indignant person Duse, stalwart oak, and Chief Fall Guy—a lady of epic ability to take it, a lady whose mighty love for Groucho is a saga of devotion, a lady who asks but little and gets it.

Disappointment can't down her, nor perfidy shake her faith. Always she comes back for more though slapsticks have crippled her, custard pies spattered her trusting face. Surrounded by brothers who are surely a little odd, she does not think so. To her, her world of Marx Bros. pictures is rational, comprehensible, secure. Calmly she surveys it, with infinite resource she fights to keep on her feet in it. Equally ready for amorous dalliance or hair-pulling, for Groucho's sudden tender moods, or base betrayal, all her magnificent qualities are on display in *A Day at the Races*, where once again her fortitude is nothing human. It's godlike.

1937

André Sennwald

André Sennwald (1908–1936) was the first daily reviewer at *The New York Times* with a deep grasp of film culture. He joined the newspaper in 1930 and took over the film critic's job in 1934, where for two years he brought enthusiasm and acumen to daily movie reviews. His defense of Josef von Sternberg's *The Devil Is a Woman*, which was roundly attacked at the time for its caviar aestheticism and loose morals, demonstrates a sophisticated awareness of directorial style and a worldly attitude toward the follies of romantic infatuation. Unfortunately he was killed by a gas explosion in his Manhattan terrace apartment at the age of 28. "André Sennwald (the only promisingly honest one of the first-line newspaper reviewers) murdered himself," claimed Otis Ferguson, though there is no evidence that his death was anything but an accident.

◆

The Devil Is a Woman

It is not hard to understand why Hollywood expressed such violent distaste for Josef von Sternberg's new film. For the talented director-photographer, in *The Devil Is a Woman*, makes a cruel and mocking assault upon the romantic sex motif which Hollywood has been gravely celebrating all these years. His success is also his failure. Having composed one of the most sophisticated films ever produced in America, he makes it inevitable that it will be misunderstood and disliked by nine-tenths of the normal motion picture public. The uninformed will be bored by *The Devil Is a Woman*. The cultivated film-goer will be delighted by the sly urbanity which is implicit in Mr. von Sternberg's direction, as well as excited by the striking beauty of his settings and photography.

Based upon Pierre Louys's novel, *The Woman and the Puppet*, the film also is an atmospheric expression of Rimsky-Korsakoff's "Caprice Espagñole," which has been woven into the musical score. On the surface it is the Carmen-esque tale of a Spanish fille de joie who wrecks the life of an influential middle-aged politician. Recited chiefly in flashbacks rather than in a straightforward narrative style, it is revealed against the sensuous background of the Spanish fiesta. Always a master of light and shadow, Mr. von Sternberg achieves a delicate and sinister beauty, shot through with laughter and song and the confetti madness of the festival.

In Mr. von Sternberg's hands a story which is deceptively conventional on the surface becomes a heartless parable of man's eternal humiliation in the sex struggle. As Don Pasqual dances foolishly at the bidding of the young woman who has him biologically trapped, we begin by laughing with the director at the ludicrous spectacle and end by suspecting that the joke has been a grisly one. For Don Pasqual's downfall is complete. An intelligent and self-respecting gentleman, he is always conscious of what is happening to him in this absurd pursuit of a woman who can never give him anything to compensate for what he is losing. Tragically aware of Concha's contempt for him, he is nevertheless helpless to free himself from the narcotic effect of her physical beauty. It is the particular triumph of the picture that Concha, instead of running off finally with the young man who has caught her fancy—the conventional movie fade out—remains a consistent character by returning to her middle-aged lover.

This column regards *The Devil Is a Woman* as the best product of the Sternberg-Dietrich alliance since *The Blue Angel*. Miss Dietrich herself, under the director's knowing guidance, provides, in addition to her vast personal allure, a series of highly affective panels in the career of a talented fancy lady. Lionel Atwill is at his best as the pathetic Pasqual. His performance elicits not only the ironic laughter which Mr. von Sternberg expects you to produce toward him, but also an emotion that almost but never quite becomes sympathy. These two are the symbols of the endless futility of passion. Cesar Romero personifies the third verity as the virile young man who almost defeats the woman at her own game. There are excellent minor performances by Edward Everett Horton as the provincial governor and Alison Skipworth as the girl's scheming guardian.

1935

The Future of Color

To base a judgment of the color film on the success of *Becky Sharp* as a dramatic entertainment is to become the spiritual kinsman of the fellow who predicted that the automobile would never supplant the horse. *Becky Sharp* happens to be a bad picture which will probably assume a position in the history of the cinema as lofty as that occupied by an even worse picture—the first all-talking film, *Lights of New York*. The fact is that the new Technicolor process has been employed here and there in the photoplay so brilliantly as to bludgeon the intelligent spectator into the belief that color will one day become an integral element in the cinema.

Its function on the screen will be equal in importance to the function of music. It may, properly used, become as basic an element in film technique as photography and sound. *Becky Sharp*, from the color standpoint, so far surpasses the ten or twelve films which Warner Brothers produced several years ago in the two-color process as to lift color out of the novelty class and insure *Becky Sharp* a place among the distinguished milestones in the advance of the cinema.

That is approximately how this column feels about the first full-length photoplay in the new Technicolor three-color process. The critical opinion of the town, as represented in the film columns of its daily newspapers, is about evenly divided on the future of color as reflected in *Becky Sharp*. Almost unanimously the reviewers agree that the picture is a dreary film edition of a tedious dramatization of *Vanity Fair*. Thereafter they divide into two camps, consisting of those who see a revolution on the basis of the film's employment of color in the new process, and those who still want to be shown. Here are significant excerpts:

"The most important cinematic experiment since moving shadows first became articulate. As a dramatic entertainment it has its faults, and some of these stem from the experiment itself, but as the first serious step in an uncharted field it is a considerable triumph."—*The Herald Tribune*.

"Not that the black and white film is to vanish overnight, but it is in the death throes, and the knell was sounded with the arrival in glorious raiment of *Becky Sharp*. A finger pointing dramatically toward hitherto unrealized possibilities in the motion-picture art."—*The Post*.

"It is safe to say that when it is perfected further and if used with well-written stories, it will be of great help to the cinema. If not it will always remain a novelty. But if it is skillfully blended with story, acting, direction and dialogue, it can bring a tempo and an excitement to films that are missing in black and white photography."—*The World-Telegram*.

"Color photography is still in the experimental stage, but *Becky Sharp* shows the strides that have been made in the Technicolor laboratories."—*The Daily News*.

"The picture, as drama, is both helped and hindered by color. Color photography, of course, will some day be taken for granted. That day does not seem to be yet upon us. Hollywood, cautiously watching the opening of *Becky Sharp*, need not hysterically throw away its reliable black-and-white cameras."—*The Sun*.

"This department enthusiastically contributes its vote to the assured success of *Becky Sharp*. Further, it predicts that it will be henceforth as important to the cinema as *The Jazz Singer*."—*The American*.

"A handsome production that, technically, is a great improvement over the earlier experiments in color photography. But color is still a novelty, and it is still too early to say whether, as its sponsors hope, it can replace the black and white of the screen."—*The Evening Journal*.

"The color is exquisite. Subtle olive greens, turquoises, flames, pearls are captured by the camera with accurate fidelity. No previous color picture compares with *Becky Sharp*."—*The Daily Mirror*.

Here we discover enthusiasm, uncertainty and confusion among the town's professional film-goers. Although many brief scenes in *Becky Sharp* have been pigmented with extraordinary cunning and beauty, it seems to me that the problem which faces us is that of using color not as a novelty or as an extra-curricular thrill, but as a constructive and integral element in film-making. The answer, I think, may be found in Rouben Mamoulian's magnificent employment of color, emotionally and dramatically, in the British ball in Brussels when the merry-makers are thrown into confusion and terror by the rumble of Napoleon's cannon in the distance. Here Mr. Mamoulian uses his colors, not as a merely decorative scheme, but as an authentic element in building the scene to its crisis, the hues mounting in excitement in great waves of color emotion and achieving an overwhelming climax in the angry blues and scarlets of the British officers as they rush to their posts.

The major hazard is that this precious new element may fall into the hands of the unlettered and cause such a rape of the laws of harmony and contrast, such a blare of outrageous pigmentations, that only the color-blind will consider it safe to venture inside a motion picture theatre. While men possessed of the artistic conscience of Rouben Mamoulian and Robert Edmond Jones are engaged in charting the unknown for the future use of color on the screen, we can feel reasonably safe. All of us can recall the aural bombardment which plagued us when the screen learned to talk. *Becky Sharp*, coloristically, is further advanced in this fascinating new domain than the early talkies were in their grasp of the principles of sound on film.

Becky Sharp, experimentally, is of enormous interest. Perhaps it was because of its experimental usefulness that this particular story was selected in the first place. As a testing ground for the new process, with its great variety of color blends, the early nineteenth century no doubt impressed the Technicolor sponsors as ideal in its opportunities for symphonic arrangements of brilliant colorings.

The next step, if it is to be an advance over *Becky Sharp*, must be to repress color deliberately to the needs of our modern literature and to recite films in grays and pastels and the subdued colorings of the life which we live in these

1930's. The color in *Becky Sharp* was not natural in any sense except the obvious one that it was an accurate representation of the colorings arranged by Mr. Mamoulian and Mr. Jones for the settings and characters of this particular film. On that basis it would be safe to say that color in its present stage of development is almost ideally suited to the production of screen fantasy and highly sentimental romance. But I believe it is fated to be more than that. The next great step forward must be in the direction of realism.

Meanwhile, we can thrill to *Becky Sharp* as another momentous advance in an art form which has progressed at unbelievable speed during the last thirty years. Perhaps Aldous Huxley was not jesting when he predicted that the cinema would ultimately progress beyond the talkies, and become feelies and smellies.

1935

Rudolf Arnheim

The psychologist, aesthetician, and film critic Rudolf Arnheim (1904–2007) was born in Berlin. There he studied with the founders of gestalt psychology a theory of perception that stressed "visual thinking," and he became one of the first to apply its principles to the visual arts. Later, fleeing Nazi Germany, he immigrated to the United States and spent the rest of his life refining his thought in books about the psychology of art, architecture, and film. At the core of his ideas was the conviction that we think as much, if not more, in images than in words. Infatuated in his youth with silent movies, he wrote one of the first important theories of cinema, *Film* (later expanded into *Film As Art*). In it he took the position that the very lack of sound, color, and three-dimensional depth, "the very properties that make photography and film fall short of perfect reproduction," spurred silent-film artists to develop a powerfully expressive new medium, while the later introductions of these technologies led to artistic dilution. Arnheim's disenchantment may seem premature and even wrong-headed from our present perspective, but some of the assertions he made in the following essay are less easy to dismiss. For instance, his insights about the "commodity" nature of commercial movies, the compromised role of the film critic, and the necessity to regard film "not so much as the expression of individual opinion as it is the expression of political and moral views" constitute challenges that many thoughtful film critics of today have gone back to confronting.

◆

The Film Critic of Tomorrow

It has taken a long time for film criticism to stop functioning as a second-rate job for local reporters and theater and book critics. Newspaper publishers never imagined that film criticism might be anything more than an editorial favor in return for cinema advertisements. Just when film criticism finally worked with its own filmic terms and reached a satisfactory intellectual level— as well as a position on the page that was comparable to that of theater and art criticism—just after its sudden blossoming, the art of film began to wilt away. Today the film critic's main failing is that he judges films in the same manner that his colleagues judge paintings, novels, and theater pieces.

It is true that a genuinely pure work of art (even in conception) emerged only seldom during the course of film art's approximately fifteen years of development. The film critic would have had the opportunity at the time to observe, record, and comment upon a process so rare and exciting in its individual stages that his colleagues would have envied him—even though in their own faculties, a long tradition of art made for works of a purer intent and a higher standard. For here was an emerging art form! Here, from a process of documentation which was initially purely mechanical, the means were gradually being acquired to allow it to present reality in an artistic manner. And this first experiment was so valuable from an aesthetic point of view that, at least initially, it became much more important than the question that would press decisive in the final judgement of the phenomenon—namely, to what heights would the new art eventually develop? (To us the question of whether film is art or not seems misplaced, and ought to be replaced by one regarding the degree to which it might become art.)

If, as we said, it was rare for a pure work of art to appear, as judged by its success and its intentions, at least at that earlier point in time nearly every new film represented a stage in the formation of the new visual language (with some script motif, some point of view, or lighting effect), and the establishment of this fact should have been the task of the film critic of the day.

But film criticism was for the most part not mature enough for this, and thus the opportunity passed without its being taken advantage of.

Artistic creation is not a luxury, is not an embellishment or an accessory, but rather serves to express the theme and the plot. Thus, due to limitations caused by the lack of the word, early film developed artistic means to make the plot, the characters, and the background visually comprehensible. People had thus made use of a certain silent pantomime, of the transformation of the "internal" into visible plot motifs, of the creative means of the film camera, and of montage. With the advent of the talking film, the necessity of using all these tools disappeared.

Yes, not only the necessity, but also to a great extent the possibility of using them. Although it seemed as though there was now a more convenient, direct means of describing plot, character, and background on a purely external and practical level, word and image were each unto themselves such all-encompassing means of representation that they could not supplement each other artistically when applied simultaneously, but could only impair and distort each other.

The resulting development—the decay of the art of expression in film— has not yet been brought to a close. It, too, is quite interesting from an aesthetic point of view, and deserves more attention from film critics. Points worth considering would be, how, under the influence of dialogue, camera angles are devalued and individual scenes are lengthened, thus also doing away with montage; how the travelling shot predominates; how the actor usurps the space in the image; and how the exterior plot atrophies in favor of the spoken word. What sound film has begun, color, three-dimensional, and large format film, as well as the "direct broadcast" of real scenes via television, will complete.

Unfortunately the majority of critics are unaware of this state of things. They see that cinema is not artistically productive but not that this is inevitable. They shift the blame onto the individual producers or director, as though the possibility of good talking films existed.

One of the tasks of the film critic of tomorrow—perhaps he will even be called a "television critic"—will be to rid the world of the comic figure the average film critic and film theorist of today represents: he lives from the glory of his memories like the seventy-year-old ex-court actresses, rummages about as they do in yellowing photographs, speaks of names that are long gone. He discusses films no one has been able to see for ten years or more (and about which they can therefore say everything and nothing) with people of his own ilk; he argues about montage like medieval scholars discussed the existence of God, believing all these things could still exist today. In the evening, he sits with rapt attention in the cinema, a critical art lover, as though we still lived in the days of Griffith, Stroheim, Murnau, and Eisenstein. He thinks he is seeing bad films instead of understanding that what he sees is no longer film at all.

All these theoretical studies would be splendid if they were conducted consciously, as historical, or purely theoretical, research. They are laughable as soon as they are presented to modern film producers as models, as generally happens. We know very well that occasionally—and this will also be true in the future—in the hands of an avant-gardist, a narrow-gauge film amateur, or a documentary hunter, a true film is still made, but the work of a critic cannot be concerned with such exceptional cases. It must instead deal with everyday production, which can only be subjected to aesthetic criticism when a production falls into the realm of aesthetics in principle; that is, when it has the possibility of creating works of art. Formerly, good films differed from mediocre ones only insofar as their quality was concerned; today they are the outsiders, remnants, things of a basically different nature from that which normally passes through the cinemas.

Many a critic today takes refuge in irony, since he has to write something. He is satisfied with more or less good jokes and with detailed criticism of the actors—but is there nothing better for him to do? Doubtless there is. The film critic of today ought to bear in mind his second great task, one which has always been put to him (he used to offer the excuse that his neglect of it was due to the fact that aesthetic criticism required a great deal of space and interest being devoted to it). We mean the consideration of film as an economic product, and as an expression of political and moral viewpoints.

Films are fabricated by manufacturers as commodities which are supposed to make much more money, if possible, than they cost; that is, they are to be made so that as many people as possible consume them. Nevertheless, there used to be frequent cases in which the manufacturer left the artist in his employ a certain freedom in the selection of material and execution, in the hope that, because of, or in spite of this, the film would bring financial success. But every business organization endeavors to perfect itself, to shut out uncontrollable factors, and thus film production has in the meantime consistently made the artist into a mere machine for producing that which the "producer" assigns him, on the basis of his refined feeling for "what the public wants." We are thinking here of the most pronounced type of contemporary commercial film production, primarily American, and take exception with those cases in which authoritarian offices, governments, organizations, etc., attempt to impose some other impulse on the commercial one. In industrialized production, a film today is characterized far more by the company who makes it than by the director. The new directors are less and less distinguishable from one another, as are the new actors.

The typical contemporary film critic quite probably recognizes this situation in theory, but in practice he critiques George Cukor's style and immerses himself in the psychological peculiarities of Joan Crawford, without realizing that these creations, even if nature did endow them with some artistic individuality, are damned, at least in practice, to total dependency. The director is accused of not working out the background's characteristic elements in "his" script; the meeting of a particular director with a particular actor is taken to be an artistically motivated event, so that the reasons for the meeting must be investigated and assessed. In an essay that appeared in these pages recently— and that also contained definite hints of genuine causal relationships—no less than the director Mamoulian was accused of having allowed himself to be influenced by the "innocent vanity" of Greta Garbo. At about the same time, an interview appeared in a German paper in which Greta Garbo said, "Am I satisfied with the Christina film? No, not at all: how can you think that? If I had had anything to say about it, it would have turned out completely differently. But what one wants for oneself never happens. I'll never play the role I've been dreaming of." We are not concerned here with defending Garbo, but rather with the fact that such a film could only have been made the way it was made by that director and that actress, whether they were in agreement and enthusiastic or repelled and forced into it. An artist can generally at most be accused of selling himself to such production methods. Thus, the judgment of a film as the free work of artists, like a novel or a painting, conceals the true state of affairs—that nowadays even a queen among actresses cannot so much as decide which corner of her eyebrows is to be plucked.

The critical approach to historical films is similarly inadequate. Divergences from historical fact are established, and the script author, the director, or the producer is then judged as though he had failed to study the sources correctly, or as though he had diverged from the truth out of pure caprice, owing to a lack of understanding or objectivity, or even due to his wish to further a particular artistic or academic idea—just as one would criticize the author of a historical novel or drama, or of an academic historical study. In reality, the producer, advised by experts and furnished with marvellous archives, probably knows the historical facts better than the critic, and would not think of venting his moods, his lack of judgment, his personal interpretation in the construction of the film. A factory is no place for such passions. Every alteration of history is, far more, a sharply calculated, economic measure designed to make the film more sympathetic, more attractive, exciting, splendid, thrilling for the public—in the same way that every film version of a novel or theater piece is changed. There is much less caprice in these films than in the works of many an artist or scientist. They are prepared according to proven rules, and everything serves the same purpose, from the outline of the plot to the gestures of the hero.

So long as the critic does not know that, or does not say it, his criticism is worthless. It is worthless so long as he metes out praise and blame to individuals and in individual cases without understanding that films turn out the way they do in accordance with basic rules.

First rule: The talking film as a means of representation precludes artistic creation.

Second rule: The film is manufactured as a commodity so that it can be sold as easily as possible.

Third rule: The film is not so much the expression of individual opinions as it is the expression of general political and moral views.

Regarding the third point, it must be said that, in those countries governed by a particular doctrine, governments today point to the political-moral content of film in a very useful manner. Unfortunately, the film critic still does not adequately support them in this. He does not see, for instance, that an average American film, which seems to him merely artistically insignificant and silly, becomes very interesting as soon as it is seen as being characteristic of that which appeals to the masses over there. Whether a film is geared by the producer to the popular psyche, or whether it is used under the influence of a political authority as a means of propaganda and education—it must always, today and tomorrow, be the task of the film critic to analyze these contents and to evaluate them, positively or negatively.

Film is one of the most characteristic means of expression, and one of the most effective means of influence in our time. Not just individuals, but also peoples, classes, and forms of government play a part in it. The film critic of tomorrow will have to take this into account. The one of today, unfortunately, acts all too frequently as though the cinema were a little luxury theater in which a few independent artists act for a few art lovers. This critic of today unfortunately belongs to yesterday.

1935

Lincoln Kirstein

Lincoln Kirstein (1907–1996) was a prolific author of dance and movie criticism, poetry, and fiction, but his greatest contribution to American culture was probably as an impresario. He co-founded the New York City Ballet with George Balanchine in 1948 and ran that company successfully for almost fifty years. He also helped establish *Hound and Horn*, an influential quarterly where he wrote about the movies and other cultural subjects, and was a founding editor of the quarterly *Films* and *Dance Index* magazine. The piece below addresses two of his greatest passions, dance and film, in a knowledgeable assessment of what happens when the two get combined.

◆

Dancing in Films

The films have frequently employed dancing for one reason or another, and even increasingly in the last two years. But from any objective point of view it cannot be said Hollywood has enhanced either the vocabulary of dancing in general or created an idiom for its particular use. While theatrical dancing in all forms has created great interest in the legitimate areas, Hollywood has done its best to capitalize on this rise in prestige without involving itself in any danger of creative pioneering. The more one investigates Hollywood possibilities for dancing, the more hopeless they seem. The treatment of dancing in films is just another piece of testimony corroborating an almost complete impasse.

There are, however, some special considerations to be investigated in the problem of adapting dancing to camera. There is a curious change effected in the carryover of human movement from the stage to the screen. In the theater we see directly whatever image the proscenium focuses. In a film our eye is controlled by the range of the camera's eye. In this transposition something vital is often lost. It is lost even in acting, but in dancing, which is so much more the electric essence of physicality, the loss seems proportionately greater.

In film, as in the theater, the problem of a dance-director is to project soloists against a choral or mass background. There is usually one soloist, and the chorus is further complicated by elaborate scenic "presentation" wherein the ingenuity of the studio engineers ekes out the poverty of the dance-director's imagination. The human scale is, of course, wholly lost.

The movies have developed a few simple tricks to cover transitions from an intimate or naturalistic scale to a cinematic or gigantic one. For example, in the Astaire film *Follow the Fleet* there was a "Riviera" sequence in an im-promptu revue set on an old schooner. The scene opened as it might have on any Hudson River show boat, but almost before one could realize it, another enormously amplified set was being used to accommodate the necessary regi-ment of dancers. Similarly in "opera" sequences, an "opera-house" set of an Italian square will suddenly give place to the square itself. But with music dominating such a scene the visual shift is less of a wrench than in sequences where physical movement is foremost.

Dancing must appeal to movie audiences or it would not be added to pro-duction costs. What kind of dancing has the greatest appeal? Largely, the kind that exploits a personality pleasing for reasons quite apart from dancing. It would hardly help Garbo to dance well (though on several occasions she has), but it is very hard for even first-rate dancers to be effective from the Hollywood standpoint if they haven't sex appeal. Virtuosity is of course compulsory, but many virtuosi exist who can never face a camera. Virtuosity, for film audiences, usually means excessive capability in any one field, as for example, the feet in tap-dancing. It's hard to see how a precision troupe like the Rockettes would have film value except as background since they are so anonymous. And one can even imagine, from the opposite point of view, Fred Astaire being almost as valuable without his taps since he has so much practical charm and so good a vocal delivery. He is surely the best that dancing has to say for itself in our films. Plus his natural elegance and musical instinct, he seems to use more than one part of his body and he makes his camera follow him, seemingly for miles, so that in more inspired moments a very dramatic tension is built up over a large terrain. He is lucky in having such an able partner as Ginger Rogers, and in his dance-director, whoever Hermes Pan may be. But even in such a well-studied genre as the musical, Hollywood is only beginning to make use of dancing as inherent part of dramatic action instead of as interpolated "relief" as in most of the Eddie Cantor works.

There are other good music-hall dancers who have done films. Ray Bolger, a distinguished tap-dancer who, judging from "Slaughter on Tenth Avenue" in *On Your Toes*, would seem to be able to give to his medium a tragic quality it has never enjoyed, was seen briefly in *The Great Ziegfeld*. Paul Draper to a large extent redeemed *Colleen*, in spite of Ruby Keeler, and he also contributed a very imaginative "wedding" sequence which survived the cutters. Eleanor Powell has some box office draw. She is accomplished, monotonous, and comforts many nice people inasmuch as she is so patently a "nice" girl. "Isn't it nice that such a nice girl dances so nicely." Bill Robinson, appearing with Shirley Temple in *The Littlest Rebel*, was superbly himself, the old master. His brilliant style, clear in its unostentatious but transparent theatricality, showed the best that a personal manner in taps can give. Tap-dancing in the films, as on the stage, is a very limited, undramatic form of dancing. It appeals chiefly to the ear, not to the eye, and if a drummer beat out the same rhythms with his hands it would cause little comment. Taps are often badly synchronized. On the stage there is a sharp but delicate sonority to the beats. Frequently on the screen a dancer's feet detonate like a machine gun. Chaplin may be said to use his whole body better than any other dancer in Hollywood, but this usage would probably fall strictly under the category of pantomime. His movements, highly stylized for the sake of instantaneous legibility, are frequently a parody of the five classic ballet positions, which speaks well for his apprenticeship as an English music-hall comedian schooled in the tradition of the old Alhambra. As for ballet-dancers in the classic genre, few have left any imprint. Harriet Hoctor can be counted on for her pastiche of a ballerina, and Gambarelli is less than a mediocrity. Tap has fared comparatively well at the hands of the film in spite of its inexpressive silhouette and its repetitious noise. Audiences like it because, for the most part, it's all they've been given, and since the only dance-directors of influence in Hollywood have been brought over directly from the musical-comedy stage.

Although it has little enough to do with dancing proper, Hollywood has created a type of spectacular diversion employing dancers which has not been seen previously, at least on the same scale. This is the Babylonian vision sponsored by Busby Berkeley and culminating in *The Great Ziegfeld*. He may use forty crystal pianos, seven intercircular ramps, a baby Niagara, and the U.S. Marines, but the result is, more often than not, too big for camera lens, too much to see, and only awe inspiring for its multiplicity of effects. But such evidence that a picture costs money to produce does something mysterious in selling it. Berkeley used to employ overhead symmetrical shots which reduced eighty dancers to an opening eight-petal bud or an American flag. Hermes Pan is far more clever with his tracking shots because he is not interested in making his girls look like flags or flowers but merely like girls dancing in various places on various levels threaded together by the continuity of music and plot. Bobby Connolly does average work-a-day musical-comedy stuff transferred more or less modestly to the screen. Albertina Rasch is distinguished for an operetta-style, in contradistinction to the revue-style of the above. Her dance arrangements for *The Merry Widow* were really imaginative with waltzers floating in doors and out of doors with corresponding pretty shifts in the color values of the costumes. Her sequences seem impersonal and well rehearsed, but she is not free from the general Hollywood elephantiasis and if she can get two more dozen girls in a frame, she'll do it. Chester Hale staged a good pastiche of a ballroom mazurka for *Anna Karenina* in which Garbo's dance-steps coincided with her dialogue. It was not an original achievement, but in its good taste, a model for a kind of choreographic underscoring which is perhaps the most that can be hoped for dancing in our films. In *David Copperfield* there was a quaintly executed ballet sequence of mid-nineteenth century London with the dancers hauled up to heaven on wires. In *Operator 13* there was a similar decorative old-Southern ball with flashes of square-dance figures that had genuine charm and usefully contributed to the atmosphere of a silly story. Margarete Wallman, the ballet-mistress of the Vienna *Staatsoper* did a ridiculous and inappropriate ballet of Russian peasants for *Anna Karenina*. She is without talent, and fondly imagines that she has solved all cinematic problems by photographing everything from two angles directly above her stage. But she is the type of European reputation which represents "Art" and "Class" to the spenders of million-dollar budgets. Agnes de Mille did some splendid work for MGM's *Romeo and Juliet*. Her scholarly research in Renaissance music and dancing produced some touching and vivid backgrounds, particularly the lovely masque in the spirit of Botticelli, framing Juliet at the Ball. It is difficult to say how much will survive in the cutting, since the scenes were shot simultaneously from numerous angles with little intelligence. Benjamin Zemach's dances for *She* in the modern idiom made a ridiculous production funnier. The naïve and calisthenic quality of contemporary concert-dance is eminently unsuitable to the vast technical possibilities of films.

The ballet has much to give to the films, and were the directors wiser they would study classical dancing for its spectacular richness with which a well-handled camera could work wonders. Eisenstein has written well on film technique as applied to dancing, and he had in mind certain choreographic conditionings which must be respected parallel to, but not necessarily overlapping, cinematic conditioning. The ballet is an encyclopedic tradition and it can be pilfered with reward if any Hollywood director has the patience and sense to spend a week on it. Diaghilev had a superstition about films, and he would never permit his ballet to come before a camera, although as early as 1910 a French company was eager to shoot *Scheherezade*. Perhaps he was aware of the limited technical facilities that the epoch offered. *Prince Igor*, or some version of it, has been filmed, however. It appears, weirdly enough, as the ballet given to entertain the Congress of Vienna in *Congress Dances*. When Nijinsky was in Hollywood in 1916, Chaplin took him through his studios, and he was very much interested in the medium, although he said at the time that it would be unwise to film ballets head-on, the way one sees them in the theater. He knew a separate technique would have to be worked out. Douglas Fairbanks and Mary Pickford lent Pavlova a studio, and there are extant records of some of her more famous divertissements such as *The Swan* and *The California Poppy*, but these are documents and not examples of dance made expressly for film. Every classic choreographer of our time has had a little to do with films. Adolf Bolm's *Mechanical Ballet* for Barrymore's *Mad Genius*, based vaguely on Diaghilev, was a great waste. Massine created dances for an unreleased French film, *Le Roi Pausole*, in which his work alone was impressive. Nijinska's sequences in *A Midsummer Night's Dream* have been universally condemned. But, nevertheless, they possessed ideas of film and dance interplay that were not wholly negligible. Reinhardt, as usual, crippled one more collaborator, even had it not been difficult to master an unfamiliar medium as well as create a major work in six weeks. As is frequently the case, a director thought it might be a good idea to have ballets somewhere in the picture, but just where and how he could not be sure. Surely the last thing to be done was to consult the choreographer. When a good choreographer designs, mounts, and rehearses dances for films that is usually considered enough. It is inconceivable that they should also have a hand in pointing the camera-eye at the express angle needed for their preconceived pattern. Frederick Ashton did an agreeable ballet for Bergner's *Escape Me Never*, and in general the English dance sequences in serious films have been far better than the American. Anthony Asquith has an extremely stimulating technical article on "Ballet and the Film" in *Footnotes on the Ballet* (Lovat Dickson, 1936) in which he projects a very free treatment of combined theatrical dancing and atmospheric landscape. Many of René Clair's earlier films had excellently woven dance sequences, notably the scenes in the opera house of *Le Million* where the insanity of backstage life in a superannuated theater floated madly in and out on some fine dancing. Aside from documents of national dances, the Russians have not been lucky in filming dancing. In *Moscow Laughs*, Alexandroff followed super-Hollywood to an unfortunate degree. But perhaps the greatest dance sequence ever filmed was the Xandunga of the Tehuantepec Indians shot by Eisenstein and Tissé and never recovered from the wreck of *Que Viva Mejico!* It is Eisenstein above all others who understands the moving human body in its stylized lyricism, even when he uses skeletons or puppets as in the "Days of the Dead" from the same heroic and disastrous picture.

Jean Cocteau, from his association with Diaghilev and the Russians, achieved an almost perfect synthesis of pantomimic-plastic gesture which was almost dancing in his *Sang d'un poète*. As in the *Cabinet of Dr. Caligari*, the camera was at all times the mind's eye, not the eye of a second-hand audience. His film with Chaplin, if ever achieved, will be of the greatest interest.

Is the idiom of classic theatrical dancing suited to films? In its most extended uses it most surely is. However, there is little to be gained by photographing the Basil Ballet in *Scheherezade* in Technicolor, or *Sylphides* with a group of Chester Hale girls. Aside from a good musician, or at least good music, a choreographer educated not only in ballet but in all the fullest possibilities of the film is needed. By the fullest possibilities one means a treatment of human bodies comparable to the way Disney treats his puppets. *Cock o' the Walk* was an inspired satire on a Busby Berkeley super-super, but its color and fantasy were incidentally beautiful in themselves. The camera can diminish and enlarge, accentuate and subdue, not only tone-values but actual shapes. The retarded camera can be studied for slow-motion emphasis. In Mrs. Frank Tuttle's short film *Spring Night*, two of the dancers from the Monte Carlo Ballet were used. Their plastic pantomime was less rewarding than the use made of certain ballet gestures emphasized by the camera. A leap, for example, was indefinitely prolonged in space, almost an idealization of the mythical leap of Nijinsky in *Spectre de la Rose* in which no one any longer believes. Ballet plus camera would be something not seen before, but a valid something.

What has already been done with the dance in films has been, all things considered, very little. The camera as an eye for dancing is as yet more unstudied than misunderstood. The dance sections of travelogues or news reels are generally carelessly shot and stupidly edited with no sense of climax and with music far from authentic dubbed in. Dancing in feature-length films has little or nothing to do with dramatic continuity, and is introduced as incidental divertissement similar to ballet in nineteenth-century opera. Even in revues or "Parade" pictures the sequences have little interest except as build-ups for stars. This is not always the fault of the dance directors. A sequence involving many well-trained and long-rehearsed dancers and much ingenuity must be shot in about one hour and a half of actual camera clicking. Hollywood insists on a shiny dancing surface, a floor of composition board covered with layers of baked enamel. This gives the effect of a super varnish or halation, a glow of richness that reflects the dancers. But this softens with only a little use. The sequences are cut by editors who have no more idea than their stop-watches and no more policy than to accommodate a pre-indicated direction from on top: "We gotta have eight minutes of dancing." The use of the dance bears intense technical research, but this is never considered as rewarding as the investigation of some new commercial gadget like sound-allocation, the three-dimensional screen, or a super Technicolor. It is difficult to see why a dancer of intelligence would hope much from the present set-up in Hollywood. Much could be done, but from the point of cash there is slight impulse to do it.

1936

Meyer Levin

The novelist, film critic, reporter, and moviemaker Meyer Levin (1905–1981) had a most adventurous if beleaguered life. He was a puppeteer, hung out with Hemingway and the Lost Generation in Paris, wrote novels about immigrant life in Chicago (*Citizens*, *The Old Bunch*), covered the Spanish Civil War and the collapse of the Third Reich as a war correspondent, was among the first to report the full horror of the concentration camps, made documentaries about Jewish settlers in Israel, wrote a sensational best seller (*Compulsion*) on the thrill killers Leopold and Loeb, and got entangled in a long, bitter lawsuit over the dramatization of *The Diary of Anne Frank*. Somewhere in the midst of all that activity he worked from 1933 to 1939 as an associate editor and film critic for *Esquire*. Here Levin attempts to resolve his affection for *The Charge of the Light Brigade*: why, as a left-wing intellectual, he might deplore its imperialist clichés, but as a movie-mad escapist he ate it up.

◆

The Charge of the Light Brigade

I rarely walk out on a picture, and never want to walk out on a simple programme picture. It is only the more pretentious cinema efforts, the ones that try to be something besides just another movie, that may stimulate me to walking out. Such pictures attain a kind of individuality, and if it happens to be the kind of individuality that rubs me the wrong way, the spell is broken and I want to walk out. But even in the most obnoxious picture, I can feel the basic, physical hypnosis of the medium. I want to sit and let the thing roll on and on, but there is the conflicting desire to get up and out of the room invaded by the personality of some actor, or by some idea I dislike.

Now, I know I'm not alone in feeling this hypnotic, habit-forming need for the movie. Sociologists, through the activity of social service workers, have in the past few years secured a fairly wide acceptance of the idea that the motion picture is a necessity, rather than a luxury, to the population. It is no longer a shock when a relief client confesses that a quarter out of the minimum-standard-food-budget allowance for the week is devoted to the purchase of movie tickets.

We are all familiar with the escape-mechanism theory as an explanation for this strange need. Perhaps it is the complete, and the proper explanation. An escape once a week into the other-world of the films, and the heart is able to go on. I think there is something more involved than simple escape; I think the need for congregation is there, the need to feel one's self in a room with other folks, sharing a common experience; and also a kind of religious experience in confronting the unnatural together with other folks. Something primitive, like what makes a bunch of savages gather together and watch a witch-doctor.

Too, there is the factor which those who have recently looked at Veblen will call conspicuous consumption. The need to show one's self spending money for something that is not as obviously necessary as food. This is a secondary factor, for it cannot be operative in the screening room, to which we are admitted free; so below this spending factor must be some really elemental, sensory effect of the moving picture.

Maybe it is simple hypnotism. The hypnotist holds an object before the eye—some shining object, that flickers, reflecting light. The willing subject keeps his eye fixed in this single focus. And the hypnotist drones out something simple, something familiar. There is no element of surprise. The subject knows exactly what is coming next. The hypnotist is going to repeat the same phrase, over and over—go to sleep, sleep, sleep—or he is going to repeat it in established, progressive variation, as in counting. He is not going to skip any numbers.

And presently, the subject is in a trance state, freed of responsibility, freed of himself, happily guided by an outside force. He is often disappointed when the spell is broken.

Maybe that is why people want to sit in the theatre and see two pictures instead of one. Periodically, this craze for dual programmes returns to plague the theatre exhibitors. And as the dual-craze progresses, more and more pictures are made in the secondary category, fill-time pictures which exemplify the trance factor most perfectly. Pictures like *The Luckiest Girl in the World*, or *Adventure in Manhattan*, or *Without Orders*, or *The Isle of Fury*, or what's that little picture I saw yesterday. They roll along, and you would be really shocked if they should roll out of the routine. It would be like a pulp story turning Faulkner.

Sometimes this trance-factor is distilled with super-perfection, and the result is a picture that isn't really a dualler, but a super-special. It has stars, and mob scenes, and is promoted big, and it is *The Charge of the Light Brigade*.

Here, a confusion is likely to ensue. The confusion is in the group of movie-goers who correspond to the group of people who read the slick magazines. Now, it is well known that presidents and geniuses read pulp fiction for relaxation; but this same type of critical mind will most likely skip the slick fiction field, and go to the literary magazines for edification. Thus, there are people who are choosey about their movies; they can stand punk movies, Westerns, and they can get a sort of critical enjoyment from the higher type of movie, from *Dodsworth*, or *Fury*, or *Romeo and Juliet*. But they don't know how to take the slick movie. Maybe the way to take it is to see it in a second-run theatre, where the expectant mood raised by the advance promotion is no longer in effect.

For instance, in what is perhaps the most highly intellectualized precinct in New York, Greenwich Village, there is a neighbourhood movie called the Sheridan Square. On almost any evening, you can run into some of the nation's highest thinkers, standing in line at the box-office, to get their weekly, or bi-weekly dosage. I know some writers who, when they are in the heat of creation, go almost daily.

That's the proper atmosphere for a picture like *The Charge of the Light Brigade*. The hypnotic effect is perfect. You find yourself saying each character's speeches just before he opens his mouth. "We must tell him," the girl will say, when she falls in love with the hero's brother. The next shot will be a close-up of the brother's woodenly agonized face saying, "I can't tell him." The next shot will be of this brother trying to tell the hero that he has stolen his girl away, while the hero doesn't give him a chance to finish his speech, because he's impatient to go to his girl. And later, when the messenger creeps out of the besieged guardhouse, sneaking over the walls, to get aid, you know that the next shot will show him killed, and you know that the following shot will show the people in the guard-house, hopeful of relief, unaware of their messenger's death. It all follows and leads as beautifully, and comforting, as secure as logic, as certain as, 1, 2, 3, 4, 5. It is as satisfying as *Bengal Lancer*, as faithful as *Under Two Flags*. You are willingly hypnotized, and each time the trance is deeper, because you have comfortably given up suspicion, you know the litany, you know the ritual will never be betrayed. That's the movie in its most essential form; it's just a punk picture and I like it.

1936

II

◆

Masters and Moonlighters

The Late 1930s, World War II,
and the Postwar Era

Otis Ferguson

Of the five greatest American film critics—Otis Ferguson, James Agee, Manny Farber, Pauline Kael, and Andrew Sarris—Ferguson (1907–1943) had the distinction of being the first. He began reviewing movies for *The New Republic* in 1934, when many critics and intellectuals were still condescending to the medium, bemoaning the death of silent film, and preferring Russian films to Hollywood's. Ferguson, who loved music and especially jazz, grasped that sound would expand the rhythmic, expressive, and realistic possibilities of the movies. He was ever on the lookout for original performers who embodied the tough, sassy, can-do American temperament—Jimmy Cagney, Mae West, the Marx Brothers, Humphrey Bogart, W. C. Fields, Katharine Hepburn. Today, the 1930s and early 40s look like a golden age of dynamic, entertaining moviemaking, with their lean gangster pictures, screwball comedies, musicals with audacious dance numbers by Busby Berkeley or Fred Astaire, Walt Disney's first animated features. Ferguson's contribution was to chronicle all this, and to register as somehow miraculous the way Hollywood studio craftsmen were perfecting an almost seamless storytelling technique. A humming little charmer like *Stage Door* or *Hands across the Table* might "indicate a wisdom of procedure that is good to find in pictures, where careless use of camera devices, the didactic cutting-in of wheels, clocks, calendar leaves and what not, and all the march-of-timing and Eisensteining in general, are often confused with intelligent and true exploitation of the medium. . . . It is encouraging to remember that anything which is delightful is never old in any real sense of the term, because delight is a fragile and immediate thing, and new always." His preference for invisible craft may explain why he took exception to the great, show-offy self-consciousness of *Citizen Kane*.

Ferguson's own writing took on an improvised, jazzy quality, the sentences speedy, conversational, the words juggled and kept in motion and never allowed to stagnate. His judgments were keen and unsentimental; he could pack three movie reviews in a column and make you feel none had been slighted. He also had a rugged appreciation for the spectacle of work, such as army movies, where "men do the impossible sometimes, doing and enduring in common." After Pearl Harbor, he joined the Merchant Marines as an able-bodied seaman; he was killed in 1943 when his ship was bombed in the Bay of Salerno. Manny Farber wrote, "Americans seem to have a special aptitude for allowing History to bury the toughest, most authentic native talents," and listed Otis Ferguson as a prime example. Though Ferguson has seemed at times the forgotten man of American film criticism, a collection called *The Film Criticism of Otis Ferguson* was published in 1971, and since then his importance has been more widely acknowledged.

◆

It's Up to the Kiddies

My modest system of cataloguing has got to be extended, I see, because it is impossible to sit through a film like *Stand Up and Cheer* and then just file it away in the ordinary drawer labeled Stinkers. This one is extra, it is super, and more, it butters itself very thickly with the most obvious sort of topical significance. In body it is half on the vaudeville side and half in the lap of whatever maternal instinct it is that responds with little cries to the spectacle of diapers in art. But like all musicals it also has a story, and that is where the significance comes in. From the story "suggested" by Will Rogers and Philip Klein it seems there was once a depression, no matter where. Well, the President of the country where this depression was heard about it and decided not to have any. So he called to him and appointed as Secretary of Amusement some flash promoter from the Broadway district, the idea being that any people as ruggedly fibered as that country's citizens could laugh off a depression if they just got to feeling snickery about it. So the promoter (Warner Baxter) appointed an office building and divided his time among his Director of the Kiddies' Hour (Miss Madge Evans), wholesale auditions, and a coast-to-coast trunk line: Yeah, yeah. Twenty male choirs and a gross of trombones. Yeah. . . . Then you begin to see the country singing—sweatshop women, cops, kiddies, brakemen, typists—all singing something about "If I can smile, why can't you?" So pretty soon everybody was smiling and everything. But some bankers and reformers didn't like this smiling promoter, and started a whispering campaign to disconcert him. However, he kept ordering trombones and stroking Miss Evans and then, flash, he quit, and then, flash, he didn't quit after all, and then, flush, he decided to purge the system of such extravagances as Departments of Kiddies' Hours—and then, pitter patter of little feet, what should come but word that the kiddies had made the country laugh and the depression was over. And the way this last was made clear to the reapers and the sowers, to the drivers of trucks and sweatshop help, was by a horseman larruping along at an altitude of about 2,000 feet, looking from his mount and coattails like George Washington and from his aerial Americanism like Charles A. Lindbergh, but from his face, which showed finally in the close-up, exceedingly like a waffle— tearing up the sky until, in a state of complete suspension, he led all the country (which had by now assembled in columns of fours directly underneath) in a community song composed expressly for the occasion with all three of its notes entirely new and different. "We're out of the Red," the song with notes, is the work of the man who composed "Brother, Can You Spare a Dime. . . ." And as this later effort seemed to relieve the people of that country immensely, I suggest that those several million Americans to whom its fine optimism is directed be if possible a little ruggeder, and hock their relief tickets or panhandle some dimes, and go stand up and hear it.

1934

Stars and Garters

Occasionally the question comes up, in connection with the art of the screen, whether much attention should be paid to its actors. There is of course no doubt on this score in the fan magazines or the daily press. There is not really cause for much doubt anyway. But because of the peculiar thoroughness of publicity in this country (where surely more people could be found with a knowledge of the likes and dislikes of Mr. Gary Cooper than with the simplest idea of the main precepts of, say, Jesus Christ), there are those who get so sick of drinking Gary Cooper with their morning coffee that they will turn about and say, If you're going to chat about the stars, you're no kind of critic and to hell with you.

In their reaction against the nationwide puffing of Hollywood favorites these stern friends certainly have a case: it is an awful thing not to be able to go into a theater without the fear that it may be Fredric March again. But in denying the part that a cast plays in any given film, they are merely being silly. Because the most immediate and touching thing about any fiction is the sense of character it manages to build up and because, in the movies, the combination of actor and director is the final means of giving expression to this. Such a sense of real people is not written into the average script; it is never conjured out of a camera. It may be aided or marred by cutting, title writing, technical manipulations one way or another. But in the end it comes across to us from the people whose illusory life is taking place on the screen. A film story without people is like a novel without a character, music without a sound. And all you need for proof is a criticism of *Belle of the Nineties* without mention of Mae West.

Miss West, as a matter of fact, makes her own personality such a focus for a whole picture that its merits become to some extent its defects as well. Her latest film has very few good things outside her, its story is poor, it comes to nothing. Miss West, who is credited with having written it, evidently felt that here was no need of its coming to anything, so long as it gave her a setting, which it does. It is about how the Belle fell out with her slugger and fell in with the bad man of old New Orleans. Plots, double-crossings, and revenge, with Mae West sailing along, as tall and handsome as a ship, serene, full-rigged, setting off broadsides of wisecracks with fine timing and authority. She blows them all down. She sings a song about Her Old Flame and what an experience *he* was (she can't quite remember his name), and the treatment she and Duke Ellington's band (fine accompanists) give the "St. Louis Blues" is the strongest and most appropriate I've heard. As always, she shows a fine grasp of the American idiom and some sense of tradition; her film has some delightful flashes of hoofers in checkerboard suits and a Floradora chorus that would average at least 187 pounds. She has all these things and a great deal more that can't be described: charm, a fine sense of what will be appropriate to her. She not only gives more and better publicity to the chief erogenous zones than any five Godwin authors: she has moments in this picture of clear loveliness. She has the most honest and outrageous and lovable vulgarity that ever was seen on the screen (where, incidentally, she is not the archetype of American womanhood on the make, or the archetype of anything else but Mae West), and enough other qualities so that she can get by with it. They made her change this picture all around, but they have probably found since that if you want to censor Miss West, you have got to lock her in a plaster cast.

But in Mae West we have the case of a performer who is her own manager, knows what is her own good and how to bring it out. Not everyone in the business is so fortunate, and so we have a whole hinterland of people whom a story or a bad director can make foolish, who are cast in lead roles regardless of their aptitudes. They are made over into someone's idea of what would be a money-making type, perhaps, or tweezed and painted until they have the superficial resemblance of some type that has already proved to be a money-maker.

1934

Artists Among the Flickers

In Vertov's *Three Songs about Lenin* the Soviets come forward to bury the great leader in Westminster Abbey, with something of the atmosphere of Patriots' Day. Objectively, it is an attempt to idolize, not so much a man as his concepts; it is thus rather limited in appeal. Washington in boats with his ragged army, Lincoln freeing the slaves—these things could be dramatized in some fashion. But when Lenin tots up a column of figures to give some of the Eastern peoples economic freedom, what are you going to do about it in terms of pictures? Near the end of the film there is a moving section of Lenin's Russia today, with men working, tractors, forges, the dams, etc.; but on the whole it seems poorly melted newsreel material with a poetic cast. I would not have brought it up except that it has gone the way of many foreign films in its reception here, and got its most honorable citation on the grounds of its being pure cinema.

And this suggests the subject of film criticism in general, which is really the subject of this piece. The appreciation of pictures is much like all other forms; but there is the sad fact of its having thus far got so little intelligent consideration that intelligence, when it appears, tends to become the high priest guarding marvels. Everyone goes to the movies, to laugh or to delight his heart: they are a part of common experience and very common at that, usually. Now and then one is good, but in thinking of it we do not think of art. It's just a movie; we only went for the fun. So when someone comes along and says down his nose, Art in the cinema is largely in the hands of artists in cinematographic experimentation, we think, Mm, fancy such a thing, I wonder what *that* is like. When someone, almost holding his breath, says, Well, there is surely no better *montage* (or *régisseur*) than this *montage* (or *régisseur*), we are apt to be discouraged: Oh damn, I missed it again, all I saw was a story with people and action. And when someone says of *Three Songs about Lenin,* This is pure cinema, implying that you couldn't say more for it, we think, Well, well, can't miss that surely.

The pay-off is that *régisseurs* are in ordinary life directors, that *montage* is simply the day-in-day-out (in Hollywood) business of cutting: all you need, except for the higher technical reaches, is a pair of shears and a good sense of timing. As for pure cinema, we would not praise a novel (in which field by this time you must, to be intelligent, be intelligible, or perish) by saying merely that it was pure *roman.* I do not wish to pull rabbits out of the hat, but here is a fact: you too can make pure cinema.

Given the proper facilities and scientific advice, anyone can, me for instance. Out of my window I can see a rather mean-looking tenement. Doors, windows, a sidewalk. Just above it, rising over it, is a tall very recent building, elevator apts. electrolux, 1, 2, 3, 4, 5 rooms, etc., but wait, we'll not open there. We will catch the meanness of the mean street by opening on pages 18–19 of *The New York Times* for last week, dirty and blowing along the mean sidewalk in the morning wind. Dust, desolation. The paper blowing and on the soundtrack a high piccolo note—wheeeeeeee—and the street empty, deserted, it is morning. Now (take the shots separately; cut and paste them together afterward): the sky (gray), the house (sleeping), the paper, the sky, the house, the paper (whee). Follow the paper down to, suddenly, the wheel of a milk truck (Ha! truck—life, the city stirs; throw in a tympani under the piccolo for the city stirring) which goes down to the mean house, stops, the driver gets out:

follow him with one bottle of Grade B up three flights of mean stairs to a mean door where—stop.

Down in the street the driver comes out, yawns. Up the house front slowly to a top-floor window where a man, touseled, yawns. As the truck drives off its wheels turn, gains speed, and suddenly there are other wheels (the city awakes): trucks pounding down the Concourse, the subway, the "El," street-cars and the trucks pounding, the "Els," the subways, and now (on the sound-track, the piccolo goes a fifth higher) you cut in the big dynamo wheels, all the wheels, all the power houses, wheels and wheels. Rah, *montage*. Then from the dynamo out (space, motion, speed) to—what do you think? An electric grill in the big stinking apartment house, with a colored servant in white, frying bacon and looking at the dumbwaiter. Title: WHERE ALL IS THAT MILKMAN NOHOW. Now down to the milkman, taking in a bottle of heavy cream (flash: SERVANTS' ENTRANCE) to the dumbwaiter; now back to the poor house, and out over the city and up over the high, proud bulge of the apartment house to the high gray clouds, over the city, over the rich and poor getting up, getting their separate service from the milkman. And on into a great dither of wheels, clouds, gaping windows, yawns, men walking—into plush elevators, on the hard, mean side-walk, faster, faster, everybody getting into motion, the same city, the same sky, the two remote worlds rich and poor. For special effect, let us say, a kid coming out of the door of the mean house, with pennies for a loaf of whole-wheat, and running past the feet and in front of the wheels, and tripping on the broken cement, falling, smack. Close-up of the head showing a splash of blood spreading on the mean stones, and flash to the apartment house, up, up, to a window, in through the window to the cream being poured into the coffee, being drunk in bed, in silk pyjamas, spilling, a splash of coffee spreading on the silk pyjamas.

Any good? I'm afraid not. But it is pure cinema. Pure cinema can be any-thing: the important thing always is whether it is done well, whether you can pile one thing on another in a clear beautiful moving line. The wonderful and humbling thing about the movies in general is the skill and sure judgment behind this mechanical transfer of images to strips of celluloid, of a certain number of feet of celluloid into a moving series of images that will have a cer-tain effect on those who watch. It doesn't matter whether the result is a story of a Significant Experiment: what we have got to single out is the difference between a picture that catches you up in its own movement, and a picture that stammers, stands doubtfully, hammers at a few obvious meanings, and leaves you with a feeling of all the mechanism used to capture emotion, without the emotion. *Three Songs about Lenin* may have been attacked with a new attack, may be an awesome experiment. My point is that it is not a good picture, and my quarrel with movie criticism is simply that if it was, those who thought so have not done one thing to show why, in so many simple honest words.

1934

Arms and Men

I can see at the start that this film, *Lives of a Bengal Lancer*, is going to cause me a lot of grief, first, because from a social point of view it is execrable, second, because it is a dashing sweat-and-leather sort of thing and I like it. The story is one of men in a frontier division of lancers, and does what *The Lost Patrol* did more strongly last year, substituting for the customary emotional pull of boy and girl the emotions of the service. Kipling stuff. We're in it and it's pretty hot, but we'll take it off neat if it kills us, going down like men. (That is, like Englishmen, because, in fiction at least, a Britisher who catches himself being a man invariably figures that qualities so unusual must be home products.) The colonel's raw cub of a son is brought out to India straight from military school, to carry on the family traditions, and he can't keep his diapers on and eventually gets popped into a bag by the natives (this, you feel, is a fine young squirt for grown men to chase after and lose their lives for). In the end he is shielded by surviving friends, so that it won't break old armorplate's heart, and there is a lot of stuff about this handful of iron men holding up the millions of India and the like. Every attempt to give it mouthfuls of meaning is either silly or a fine glorification of empire and the wars of empire; but somehow these drawbacks don't get in the way as much as it would seem.

The good part of the picture comes in its subsidiary business. There are stock situations, of course, such as rubbing a little nut oil on the face and passing for a native, the imminent Union of the Tribes, etc. There is the business of cavalry drills and formations, really done with great flourish and dash, and there are the life in quarters, the long file riding up to the fort, and the well-managed skirmish scenes, with machine guns spattering around and all. But occupying the best part of the footage is the main situation of men living together and getting in each other's hair, tied together by the strange bond of work and discipline, by the common pride of doing the job.

The execution of all this is what makes it effective. Franchot Tone and Gary Cooper make a convincing relationship by the solid types they build up, with their horseplay and nagging and rough loyalty. You would not have conceived how well they show up when there is no longer need for them to be draped around Miss Shearer's gown for sequence 28, night shot. The scene, for example, where one of them grubs a cigarette from the other, after both have just got through with having burning splinters driven under their nails, their hands fumbling and grotesque, is really strong enough not to be in pictures. The dialogue is laconic and good (when it is not in one of its declamatory moods), and Sir Guy Standing does a good version of the colonel, and C. Aubrey Smith is a fine man for these parts: he has a wide deliberate voice, and presence, and a face appropriately like an old army boot. The direction (Henry Hathaway) seems to show a high amount of skill, for there are not only difficult matters handled very well, but a lot of minor points where missing the beat would have soured whole stretches of the film.

And so I am taken by the show, imperialism and all. After all this fustian of Hollywood romance, I may be a pushover for scenes from the lives of men who live and work together, but I imagine that the glamor will get over generally, and I suspect we can't any more combat by detracting the dangers of having such stuff around than we could save the victims of a handsome woman by tipping them off that she was ugly as sin. And anyway, the important point here is not the glorification of the army *per se*. You see the same thing in shops and in a city room and on farms—men with their minds not on the money, like merchants, nor on just what interests they are serving, like Senators, but on hitting a good lick, on the rough satisfaction of combining finely with all the others to make the thing work, go off smoothly. And in a thing like this the real emotional pinch is not what ideal the men are going down for, but in the suggestion of how men do the impossible sometimes, doing and enduring in common.

1935

Words and Music

In pictures, it would be natural to expect that the best thing this country could turn out would be the musicals. We have a first-class body of popular song writers, the best jazz bands (marvelous enough in themselves), literally millions to squander on choruses, singers, hoofers, and people like Busby Berkeley and Hermes Pan, who live apparently for nothing else but to turn these things into production numbers. And in Hollywood we have a tradition of flash comedy that isn't to be equaled.

But what comes of all this? Something like *Roberta* or *Flying Down to Rio*; something that is colorful or vibrant in this or that part, but as a whole pretty vacuous and dull. So that when a picture like *Broadway Melody of 1936* happens along, with a consistent brightness about it, the show is so much more than was expected as to seem enough. And when there is a picture that is splendid with the presence of Mr. Fred Astaire, people will get violent and say to stop grousing—what do you expect from a musical anyway?

And that is the main trouble: you can't expect anything. A musical rarely attempts to be more than a ragbag of various show tricks; and even when it does, there is no relation between its comedy, which is mostly wisecracks, and its songs, which are mostly sugar. As for possible plots, there are two in use: the Hymie-the-Hoofer type, where the boy makes the grade with his act; the My-Gal-Daisy-She-Durrives-Me-Crazy type, where the boy makes the girl. These are naturally followed with no conviction, the chief problem in any given picture being, how to bring in the first number. Somehow, before the film has gone many feet, somebody has got to take off from perfectly normal conversation into full voice, something about he won't take the train he'll walk in the rain (there is suddenly a twenty-piece band in the room), leaving everybody else in the piece to look attentive and as though they liked it, and as though such a business were the most normal of procedures.

From this first number it is customary to push on to the second. The boy, for instance, refuses to meet the girl, who refuses to meet him. So they fall in love. Singing together in close harmony for the first time without knowing it, they sing:

> How sweet to meet
> My pet unmet
> I kiss your feet
> Madame.

And the band has got five more pieces, including marimba and steel guitar, and a chorus of forty voices resolves one of the spare seventh chords downward, *piano, pianissimo*:

> We kiss your feet'n fite'n fotum. We
> kiss. We—e—e kissyourfeetmadame—

and the line spills out into formations that would cover a four-acre lot.

In short, the second number. Having reached this point, anybody can ad-lib the rest, there being nothing to do now but keep the girl from falling into the boy's lap, by many ingenious devices—such, for example, as having him misremember where he put it. If the picture is R.K.O., the chances are the lap will have been mislaid in the butler's panty, which is the clue for some good and funny business with Eric Blore; and just as you go out of the room, there is E. E. Horton, a nervous wreck; and there can possibly be another touch of comedy before the girl slaps his face and takes off for Lucerne, thus introducing the lonesome, or I-Yearn-for-Lucerne, number.

This business of the comedy element in musical comedy, incidentally, is a ticklish business, because often there seems to be none. *The Gay Divorcée* was a musical built and directed primarily as comedy. *Top Hat*, an attempt to repeat on it, throws in practically the same stock company (Horton, Blore, Erik Rhodes, etc.); but it goes back to the old hit-or-miss method of letting the cast get as many laughs as it can and throwing in a two-line gag whenever anybody thinks about it. *Broadway Melody of 1936* is more in the tradition of the stage revue, and by far the funniest show around. It has, for example, made a place for such charming and individual drollery as that of Robert Wildhack, professor of soft-palate calisthenics, or the snore—austerely scientific in procedure and powers of research, rich with illustration, *e.g.*, the varieties of the labial, or ah-pooh, type, the thin or blonde snore, and the various expirational classes: the whistle, the wow, the straight plop, etc. This is an absolutely star performance and worth the price of the show by itself, although the story derives a lot of meaning from the parts of Jack Benny and Sid Silvers, and some brightness from the tap dancing of Buddy Ebsen and Eleanor Powell. As music, its numbers are flat and stereotyped, lacking even the tailored verve of the several pieces Mr. Berlin wrote for *Top Hat*.

But when we come to the subject of music in the musicals, we come to the first consistent expression of popular songs and rhythms that this medium has seen, namely Fred Astaire. From the crowds he draws, I should say that Astaire must mean many things to many people—as, for example, glamor to married ladies in for the day from Mamaroneck, real elegance to telephone girls whose boys suck their teeth and wear pinstripe suits, etc. But one thing he manages above all others, and that is the best visual expression that has been generally seen in this country, of what is called the jazz. As an actor he is too much of a dancer, tending toward pantomime; and as a dancer he is occasionally too ballroomy. But as a man who can create figures, intricate, unpredictable, constantly varied and yet simple, seemingly effortless, on such occasions as those when the band gathers together its brasses and rhythm section and begins to beat it out—in this capacity he is not to be equaled anywhere: he brings the strange high quality of genius to one of the baser and more common arts. Some of the aspects of jazz—its husky sadness, its occasional brawling strength—do not appear in Astaire; but its best points are sharp in such of his steps as those of the soft-shoe sandman number and in the number where the lights go down, just before the line of men, with top hats and sticks, swings up the steps, over the rim of the stage. Fred Astaire, whatever he may do in whatever picture he is in, has the beat, the swing, the debonair and damn-your-eyes violence of rhythm, all the gay contradiction and irresponsibility, of the best thing this country can contribute to musical history, which is the best American jazz.

1935

In a Dry Month

Hands across the Table is the new Paramount picture, a smooth but natural job, a happy mixture of brainwork and horseplay and a reminder that when intelligence goes for a walk among even the oldest props, the props may come to life. The plot here is Group A, Subtype 11-C: (A) he falls for her at the start yet remains in a state of falling all through the picture, suspended in midair like the floating-hat trick; (11-C) he is a rich young scion and she is a poor young shoot. Add complications AX2 and BOP: he has to marry the society page, she is loved by kindly gent with a million, who would take her under the wing of his yacht for life. Originally a story by Viña Delmar.

But the film people have somehow beveled and canted and trued it up at just the right places until it is a natural, airy structure, mostly well founded. The girl was hardboiled, suspected this business of love (where did it get her mother?); the boy was the son of big money but did not have any ("Maybe you, uh, heard about the Big Crash? Well that was, uh, us") and was also hardboiled, out to make a living and marry it. They met, decided they were of no use to each other, and proceeded to hang around together for awhile, having fun. And most of the picture develops out of that, moving along from give-and-take to tenderness at an easy, smart clip. And without plugging sentiment too hard or taking too seriously the thesis of love triumphant in spite of itself, it is able to wind up still doing nothing in particular, very plausibly.

The trouble and the danger with light comedy as a rule is that it is self-conscious over its lack of weight and either leaves reality altogether in an attempt to be capricious and unexpected about everything, or fastens on each excuse for feeling with a hollow and forced semblance of deep emotion. That *Hands across the Table* keeps the delicate and hard balance between these two courses of procedure is partly the work of direction, cutting, dialogue writing; but considerably the work of Carole Lombard and Fred MacMurray.

In this picture these two make an all-time copybook example of how to play a movie for what it is worth, with subtlety, much resource in the matter of visual expression, and the open, sustained kind of charm that can be projected through the shadows of a mile of celluloid. They are, after all, the deciding factor in whether the whole business of dinner for two, with hiccups, the evening with its last lap in the taxi, shall end up as a collection of comedy ideas or as smooth development of the situation, a successful piece of fancy; and whether the faked call from Bermuda shall be a mere crutch for the plot or straight comedy in itself; and whether roofs, stars, etc. are mere stage properties or what makes the world go around.

But it would be unfortunate if we got too much stress on acting here, because *Hands across the Table* is a first-rate piece of film management. Some stretches are handled pretty much as vaudeville blackouts (especially the part where MacMurray answers the girl's door in his drawers and scares the dumb gentleman friend out of his candy and plenty else, the whole ending in a merry pratfall down the stairs), there is an occasional heavy touch, and the whole idea of getting Ralph Bellamy in to sound his hollow changes on the role of old Mr. Sweetly-kindly is about as germane as a saucerful of warm milk in a glass of beer.

But these are instances merely; in the run of the film there is a shrewd genius for effect through understatement—all sorts of touches like the action when MacMurray leaves the apartment after a sleepless night and you see him stop to look after the milk wagon on the block, the camera looking down through the morning air from over the girl's shoulder. No comment, no superfluous footage. But the hint has been planted, and will later underline the scene where he says he is going to get a job if it kills him, he could deliver milk, couldn't he. Or take the summing-up of that first night, when they had hiccups at dinner, such a lovely time only it had to be the last, and she sits on the edge of the bed after it is all over, all played out, catches suddenly on a hiccup in her throat, and breaks down crying like a kid.

These things taken by themselves are not much, but they indicate a wisdom of procedure that it is good to find in pictures, where careless use of camera devices, the didactic cutting in of wheels, clocks, calendar leaves and what not, and all march-of-timing and Eisensteining in general, are often confused with intelligent and true exploitation of the medium. And the picture itself is not much (builds no Dnieperstroys), except that it is a good one, a rain in a dry month, and incidentally a certain advance in film treatment. Whatever its label may indicate in the way of old stuff to those who count on reading the label, it is encouraging to remember that anything which is delightful is never old in any real sense of the term, because delight is a fragile and immediate thing, and new always.

1935

Cagney: Great Guy

It was just four years ago, when I hadn't been going to the movies very much, that I stopped around to see *Footlight Parade* and made the happy discovery of James Cagney. He had been known to almost everybody else before that in heavier roles (*Public Enemy*, for instance), and before he was well known at all he had been doing bits in pictures. But in this one he happened to be cast as the original Cagney, the hoofer and general vaudeville knockabout. The story had him drilling a line of girls, stomping out the routines and cracking around like the end of a whip, and even the presence of Dick Powell could not dim that vitality and flow of motion, and a grace before the camera that puts him in the company of the few who seem born for pictures.

It was a sunny introduction: seeing him you couldn't help feeling better about the industry—or the state of the nation for that matter. Because through this countrywide medium and in spite of whatever its story was about, this half-pint of East Side Irish somehow managed to be a lot of what a typical American might be, nobody's fool and nobody's clever ape, quick and cocky but not too wise for his own goodness, frankly vulgar in the best sense, with the dignity of the genuine worn as easily as his skin.

Since that time it has come out plainly that his character was no delusion of the flickers, that there was conscious purpose behind it. Once he was a star, Cagney used a star's privilege to tell them what was in character and what wasn't—gently, though, and with tactful stratagems, for he is no sea-lawyer (you will remember from the screen his trick of speaking more softly the more violent he gets). They wanted him to enounce with measure and dignity, now that he's got to be a star on them; so he had to explain that the characters he was portraying never knew anything about this enounce, measure, etc.; and an actor should be in character, shouldn't he? So they finally had to skip that. For *Jimmy the Gent* he got his head shaved and reported for work. The director was scared to death of shooting him that way (Ah, he kept saying with a slight accent, my main love interest should open with a head like a pig's knuckle?); and lord knows what the office would do. But Cagney gentled them and squared it with everybody—and anyway they couldn't hold up work while his hair grew—and managed to bring out a story about a thug who chased ambulances or sneaked up on dead horses or something, giving it the works. And if this wasn't the fastest little whirlwind of true life on the raw fringe, then I missed the other. When the picture *Here Comes the Navy* came out, the New York heavy lads naturally placed it for an incentive to imperialist war—Cagney had been so neat on his feet that only the common citizens got the obvious point of this bantamweight taking his blithe falls out of the stooge tradition of the United States Navy itself.

In such seemingly little ways he has managed to ad-lib, shift emphasis, and bring out his own relief. But behind that is the basic appeal he has for the audience as a person—under all that tough surface and fast talk people glimpse a sweet clarity of nature, a fellow feeling and rightness and transparent personal honesty. It makes all the difference in the world, and when he rips out a statement you sense without stopping to question that it is the living truth spoken through him, and not a line rehearsed and spoken on the set any longer. His screen life is not a natural autobiography, not something he just fell into. He is not a mug but one of the intelligent few; he isn't a perpetual handspring but a man with a troubling illness; his conversation is more a subdued questioning than a bright explosion of syllables; and while he swings all the punches in his stories he has been taking plenty on the chin in all these actual years, from down-under to up-on-top (no one can help wondering if the ship isn't sinking when Jimmie Fiddler creeps over ratguards to write a patronizing Open Letter from awfully safe ground). Don't think because he didn't produce *Hamlet* on Broadway last year that Cagney is automatically himself; and therefore no actor. His art is in an intense projection of those qualities within himself which he feels to be honestly representative of something, and in the fact that while all that rapid fire and assurance and open charm are enough to take the audience anywhere he wants to go, he has a guiding notion of where he's going.

Since blowing up on the Warners more than a year ago, he has made two modest semi-independent pictures. *Great Guy* was all right, but all right for a Class-B picture only, and it is hard to think of Cagney except on top. The new one, *Something to Sing About* is a different thing and about the happiest experience we've got in the last few months, what with all the lavish splashes and worthy wordage.

It's just about Cagney as a performing band leader who goes to the Coast on contract for one film. If I told the whole story I'm sure anyone could stop me because he'd heard it—they don't dare tell the boy how good he is, which he only finds out when the girl he's left behind him comes out for a honeymoon, and then his marriage has to be covered up for publicity purposes, which leads to domestic misery and a final happy finale with the band back home. But this story is less story than business, and the business is subtle, pointed, and meaty. For the producer and press agent (respectively) they have a couple of my favorite seasoned troupers, Gene Lockhart and William Frawley, who either catch the spirit of the thing or had the spirit bred in their bones. There are also the director, who is able to act like a director, the three fates from the department of elocution, make-up, and tailoring, and the Jap valet who speaks better English than any of us and originally had the acting ambition, now hidden behind a prop accent (Sank you, please).

The romance element is not helped by the girl Jimmie is supposed to go for like pups for biscuit, played by Evelyn Daw, a "find" who would be a mild sensation as typist on a WPA project but is fazed by the camera (not that she is afraid of it: there are times when she seems about to chew the hood), with a cute twitter of walking knock-kneed and a jaw always there ahead of her, the little-girl's voice pinched up under her nose, etc. (oh, it isn't her fault, poor girl, but neither is it ours). But in the way the rest of it is worked out there is enough snap and good fun about the movies to make it go.

It is likely that Cagney was responsible for a lot of the spoofing ("I've heard all I want to about Robert Taylor") and someone with union experience was certainly behind that comeback to the four-weeks-vacation offer: "Four weeks *successively?*"—and the Goldwyn producer answers with majesty, "Successively and positively." The fight is one of his favorite subjects: how to set the camera and throw a punch that will miss by millimeters, the precautions to take with green actors. Then his line about, Do these heavies understand this swing-to-miss stuff? You know him—Johnny Come Lately; he just doesn't want to be the only one around there playing house. And the business of the Hollywood double-take, the triple-take, the triple-take with a slow burn and the one-eye fadeaway, is brilliant.

Except for the scenes of the gang around the camera and boom, the actor on the set, the jam in the cutting room—the most quietly natural I've seen—and for bits like the cut in rhythm from the rushing minor thirds of the band to the westbound limited, the direction was run-of-the-mill and sometimes ham—Victor Schertzinger being still punch-drunk no doubt from the film he did with the great Grace ("Moo-Moo") Moore. The good time comes from the feeling that they had a good time making it, that Cagney said, Let's put this in and everybody said, Why not, and they worked it out, a black eye for authority here, a bit of fun at their own expense there. The independence and small budget gives them more leeway and genial leisure, and perhaps we ought to have more of the same (though it is true that Cagney's best film was made in the mass-production pattern: *Ceiling Zero*, still one of the finest).

I think much can be done by good people who break away and bring the industry up short by independent accomplishment. But when all is said and wherever he is, Jim Cagney is bound to shape up as a regular great guy you'd like to have around the house or on any job you're doing. Would anyone argue that in the sacred fields of art there is no room for such?

1937

Through the Looking Glass

Idon't know where you will find so much delight and unspoiled entertainment as in the RKO picture *Stage Door*. The title, which they have scrupulously kept intact, once belonged to a chore Edna Ferber and George Kaufman did for Broadway. The play had some stage people for characters and a moral about how, for a *real* actress, Hollywood was a fate worse than death. It had quite a run and so the movies were happy to buy it. Then apparently they read it, and some smart producer put Morrie Ryskind and Anthony Veiller to work writing a picture around the title and Gregory La Cava to work directing the finished script. And the result is one of those miracles in celluloid.

The outline is simple: a school for girls with a theatrical boarding-house background. There is the little hoyden with the stout warm heart; there are the girl with a sensitive talent on the downgrade and the girl with the rich poppa riding her high horse; there are comradeship, cat fights, and the subsidiary play of gossip, rivalry, boy friends, meals, openings for work—in short the process of life going on. In the relationships of four or five of the girls and the producer, the main story is carried forward simply to the point where the one who should have the big part goes weak and deranged from hunger and walks through the window on opening night, and the smug one who actually got the part makes her entrance through a sudden knowledge of her own wooden deficiency and the sight behind her eyes of that wronged, crumpled figure lying in the alleyway.

The story as written belongs in the department of the true and trite; but I think most of us are agreed by now that the difference between the bound book and the experience is precisely the vital stuff the theater is made of, that even the simplest story can be so presented by actors and direction and living background that the emotional experience of those who follow could not be duplicated by anything short of some great long novel. As the girls sit around in the boarding-house parlor, swapping thrust and riposte and grousing about the stew, their lines and habit of living are undoubtedly both more brilliant and more warmly generous than life. But these reservations are not a part of the theater experience. All that counts is that while this picture is being reeled off it is humanly lovely, bright and sad and true, that any overdose of either brilliance or easy simplicity is carried off in the happy stream of the thing before your eyes. It is temperate with wisdom or perfectly ripping, at its own discretion.

What with Katharine Hepburn, Ginger Rogers, Andrea Leeds, Constance Collier, Gail Patrick, Lucille Ball, and all the others, it is a long time since we have seen so much feminine talent so deftly handled. When you think of Miss Rogers' former song-and-dance appearances, it seems as though this is the first chance she has had to be something more than a camera object and stand forth in her own right, pert and charming and just plain nice, her personality flexible in the actor's expression.

Andrea Leeds as the girl who starves has an arriving talent and a persistent gentle sweetness that puts the story much in her debt; and all around, from Constance Collier's veteran job on the elocutionary biddie to the singing housemaid and the dancing partner with the comeback and the little unsung heroine who marries men from Seattle, and Grady Sutton, and Adolphe Menjou, who drives the meaning and effect of the Broadway-producer part right down through the wood, countersunk.

About Katharine Hepburn, it has been recently fashionable to wink, pull a face, and *poor* Kitty and tsk, tsk, tsk, Hollywood has ruined her and of course she never was more than a couple of mannerisms and a hank of hair to start with, poor *Kate*. As the spoiled rich girl she comes into this story cold, playing across the grain of audience sympathy. But she is the girl of that awful first night, and there is felt through her as she comes on that tension of the inexorable rising curtain and first cue, when the actor is isolated within the range of his own devices and inner terror. And the effect in the audience is one of difficulties falling way in a command, faith, and purity of feeling that leave no room for a doubt or question anywhere.

The point of the story (oh wide and subtle revenge on tailormade wisecrackers) is the bias, cruel ignorance, and commercialism working behind stage productions, as it works in any art. But mainly it is just happy in its story and boarding-house routine—the girl with the cat, for example, wearing it draped around her neck and telling it (when the Perfect Lady shows up in a gorgeous fur): "Get a load of that, Henry; that's where *you'll* wind up," or (at the dinner bell): "Let's go in to the stew, Henry; you might find a mouse in it." And the direction is sometimes inspired, for even leaving out scenes of climax, you get a really first-class play of motion in such scenes as the one where the two girls are at each other's throats in the producer's penthouse, and he trying to square it with each of them, and poor Franklin Pangborn in and out and across corners like a bobbin, doors slammed in his face and harsh words spoken, the most baffling moment of his career. But although memory plays around the words and scenes of these minutes in the theater like blue flames around a Christmas pudding, quotation in example is misleading, the bare words of a report robbing the natural freshness of the actual thing in its context and film pace.

The people in action are the living matter of this piece; yet the idea and fulfillment of it, the direction, camera, and cutting had to come first. And however we analyze, the sum of its parts is one of those things we have to catalogue

under the term Miracle, so little we know of it. The miracle happens when
everybody concerned seems in sympathy with everybody else's intention and
gives it play, each gaining in personal achievement from the common inspiration. Between its extremes of making you laugh and tearing your heart out and
altogether beside what meaning it has, this picture is in touch with its audience
at every point, it seems to grow along with them and they with it. And in this
easy proximity the mechanical voice and flat halftone screen drop away like the
dimensions in a stereopticon; and an audience of millions leaves its private life
to take part in this hour or so of life recreated, passing as though through the
looking glass.

1937

Walt Disney's Grimm Reality

To say of *Snow White and the Seven Dwarfs* that it is among the genuine
artistic achievements of this country takes no great daring. In fact, outside of Chaplin, Disney's is the one Hollywood name that any corn doctor of
art and culture dare mention without fear of losing face, or on the other hand
of having to know too much about the subject. There is this to be said of
Disney, however: he is appreciated by all ages, but he is granted the license
and simplification of those who tell tales for children, because that is his
elected medium to start with. It is not easy to do amusing things for children,
but the more complex field of adult relations is far severer in its demands.

Snow White is a fairy-tale, surely the most vivid and gay and sweet in the
world; it is done in color, photographed on different planes to give depth, and
it runs almost an hour and a half. Some of the short cartoons have been more
of a riot, some have been more tender even. But this is sustained fantasy, the
animated cartoon grown up. The fairy-tale princess is just what you would
have her; the witch is a perfect ringer for Lionel Barrymore (not by accident,
I take it); and the seven dwarfs have been perfectly humanized by somewhat
the same technique, though each is more a composite of types, not quite identifiable. The animals of course are as uncannily studied and set in motion as
they have always been.

The Disney artists and animators are practically zoological, nearer to the
actual life of animals than any who have endowed it with human traits for purposes of fable. Take the young deer in the little scene where the forest life first
gathers around Snow White: shy but sniffing forward, then as she starts to pat
it, the head going down, ears back, the body shrinking and tense, ready to
bound clear; then reassurance, body and head coming up and forward to push

against the hand—half a dozen motions shrewdly carried over from the common cat. Or take the way (later) the same deer moves awkward and unsteady on its long pins in the crush of animals milling about, as it should, but presently is graceful in flight, out in front like a flash. Disney has animals that are played up for comedy, like the turtle here, the lecherous vultures, the baby bird whose musical attempts are a source of alternate pride and embarrassment to his parents (on a finale he will get as high as eight inches straight up from the limb); but even in these cases, the exaggeration is based on typical form and trait.

The story is familiar in its simple fantasy. The castle, the stepmother with her black arts, Snow White escaping in the forest and keeping house for the little men; the witch seeking her out with the apple of living death; finally the young prince coming to break the charm. But all of Disney's fantasy starts out with a simple frame of story: the main body of the thing is incident. And the incidents start from a firm base in the realism of the everyday, serving to steady the fantastic (dwarfs, witches, alchemy) either by complementing it with the matter-of-fact, or by becoming fantastic through a seemingly logical progression from their common shape and function. Thus the fairy-tale dwarfs, in their diamond mine and home, go about their business in a highly natural manner, digging, appraising, grading, leaving the dirty dishes and going to bed. And thus the birds and animals, invading the empty house with the shy fits and starts appropriate to them as real birds and animals, fall to helping the girl clean up with highly unnatural abilities (the squirrel's tail for a bottle brush, other tails for brooms and dusters; the birds winding up cobwebs, flying with sheets).

I was disappointed to see the comedy faltering at times here. Such things as running into doors and trees on the dignified exit, the jumbled consonant (bood goy, I mean goob doy, I mean . . .), headers into various liquids, etc., are short of good Disney. For the most part, the thing is as ingenious as ever, the idiosyncrasies of each dwarf quickly established and made capital of— Grumpy, Dopey, and Sneezy in particular—the flow of comedy through animism still on that level at which Disney's men have never been equaled. Witness the organ pipes in that wonderful music-hour sequence, made of penguins, the vent holes being choked off with little clappers, Grumpy frequently losing patience with his stop and whacking them shut by hand.

It is not all comic and quaint. The imaginative transformation of the stepmother, her mission, flight, and death (the vultures banking slowly down in the dark air), make a suspense and chase interval that will put your heart back a few seconds; and there is something not mawkish but gentle and nice about the little girl, her face and singing and adventures in friendliness with every living thing. Something beautiful about all of it, I think, because it does not try to be wise about fairy-tales, or fairy-talish about its birds, rabbits, people. And all of it, the whole feature-length true motion picture, is nothing but a hundred-odd thousand colored drawings, photographed, and set to music.

The art work is fine, particularly the castle at night, the scenes in the woods, the march home of the little men. The color is the best ever, though it is true that its pastels would be up against more difficulty in a film less deliberately imaginative. And music is as much a part of the picture as it always is in the Disney scorings, with nice songs and a rollicking chant and swell background stuff for the moods of the story.

Disney gives credit to his directors, animators, musicians in a way that is heartening to see and a list as long as your arm; but while it is true that his pictures are built on the conference method, good ideas being kicked around until they suggest others, there is the fact that he apparently has known how to pick his men, train them, and give them free rein to contribute their individual best. A film is a collective enterprise anyway and should be made that way; but in general there are too few men of talent at the top who have the leadership and patience, the exaltation of job over ego, to do it. Walt Disney is a pioneer in more things than his conception of and tireless experiment with the animated cartoon as a reflection of life. Now that the best picture of 1937 has been adjudicated, awarded, etc., the best and most important picture for 1938 is called *Snow White and the Seven Dwarfs*.

1938

Hitchcock in Hollywood

A lfred Hitchcock seemed to be fooling around where he didn't belong in his last two pictures (*Jamaica Inn* and *Rebecca*), but in *Foreign Correspondent* the man has done it again. The plot is bare enough, a routine Oppenheimer about an American reporter who gets caught up in international intrigue between peacemakers and warmongers as of about a year ago—the better part of the action lying in Holland and England. But with Hitchcock it isn't ever so much what was done as what it was done with. He has explored the range of the modern story-film farther than any other man; and if you have any interest in the true motion and sweep of pictures, watching that man work is like listening to music.

Taking the picture for what it is, however—basically spy melodrama with more emphasis on keeping going than on where—there are still awkward bits.

Joel McCrea is an awkward bit—at least when he figures that the part requires acting. The meeting of the peace society has prominently ham elements; the terrific secret is pretty meaningless; and the speechification is sometimes over-done, especially toward the end. Otherwise it goes like the night mail, from the home office to London to The Hague and a shooting in the rain. Then a won-derful sequence out in the flat country and inside the sinister windmill, the chase to London and the murderous practices uncovered there, evil closing in, the flight in the Clipper, the wreck (this last, with its eerie sensation of being fired upon and magnificent water shots, is one of the big dramatic effects in pictures).

Whatever the framework, a detective story with Hitchcock is no longer a detective story—though he's after the same action and suspense, and gets it. He loves details like a Dutch painter, and crowds his set with them, whether they are the wonderful mechanics of the windmill (a Hitchcock interior if you ever saw one) or the Great Dane lumbering around, or the Lett with the blue-plate eyes, or the silly dame, or the local constabulary all speaking Dutch. He loads his set with them without loading down his action; and because every-thing and everybody aren't direct accessories to the plot, so many mechanical aids, you get the effect of life, which also has its dogs and casual passers-by who are real without having anything to do with any plot you know about. He makes a character out of every extra.

Another of his tricks is to show you the little birdie—*i.e.*, he likes to have a bland face or a sweet old lady personify evil, and the tricky-looking fellow turn out to be a right one all along. Even here he shuffles the types around so there is still no rule-of-thumb, for Mr. Ciannelli and his mobsters are sinister enough, and the scene in the torture room is enough to leave you with the creeps. Another trick is the strange-mechanical, like the reversing windmill, the assassin's camera, the disappearing car. And he likes to scare you with high and precarious places.

Above everything there is a feeling of how to use sound and things and people for suspensive effect that is like a painter's sense of color or like a musi-cian's sense—if you haven't got it you can't buy one, and you can copy every last trick in a Hitchcock picture without having anything but Boris Karloff left. He likes to play with wind and rain, with natural music (as opposed to atmos-pheric scores, though there is too much of one here) and a natural background murmur of people talking without the words coming out, of street-noises or machinery or just the wind and rain by themselves. He knows where to set the microphone and camera to catch the effect he has figured out, and with all the devices of this complex art completely under his fingers, you may he sure a person never enters a deserted building or a dark alley without your wondering actively if he will ever come out.

Group scenes too, in action or repose. One of the hardest things film men have had to learn is not to spot one thing out of many by rubbing your nose in it; another, more often achieved, is how to keep a lot of people milling around desperately without the focus getting lost and the end confused.

Add humor. Hitchcock knows suspense should not get too tight, so there is always some absurd side-talk going on, often with edge to it. Robert Benchley is the principal funny man here—though others keep popping up—and the mixture of his feverish ride on the water wagon and his comments on the practice of foreign correspondence is a nice thing to have around. He apparently wrote his own part, and if he didn't have a hand in the general dialogue, somebody did who was good and witty.

In short, if you would like a seminar in how to make a movie travel the lightest and fastest way, in a kind of beauty that is peculiar to movies alone, you can see this once, and then again to see what you missed, and then study it twice. If all you're out for is an evening you'll have that too—or what do you want for 35–75 cents?

1940

For Better, For Worse

You may soon get a chance to see what somebody else thinks are the great parts of the great picture nobody ever saw—the miles of film Sergei Eisenstein exposed down in Mexico, some thousands of feet of which were released as *Thunder over Mexico* in 1933. Marie Seton has resurrected the original and edited from it about an hour of film that is supposed to follow the master's original idea, under the title *Time in the Sun*. It makes an interesting travelogue with pageantry, social overtones, self-conscious mugging natives, and fine though trick photography (Tissé). It was not taken or edited with imagination and moves heavily when it moves at all. The plain truth of the matter is that Eisenstein went to Mexico for some documentary stuff and there got drunk partly on his own reputation and partly on the million different things that could be photographed if you spent the rest of your life at it on subsidy; and that Upton Sinclair took a villainous drubbing for pulling him away in the end and trying to salvage some of that naïve investment. A way to be a film critic for years was to holler about this rape of great art, though it should have taken no more critical equipment than common sense to see that whatever was cut out, its clumping repetitions and lack of film motion could not have been cut *in*. The greatness of that heavy hoax was never left on the cutting-room floor; it was left where it started—inside a lot of very suggestible but not very good heads.

1940

Handsome Is . . .

S ince *High Sierra* seems to meet with some difference of critical opinion, I must caution you that all expressions of praise here are purely coincidental and not to be confused with any living persons. It has faults; but it is fine and exciting and it is a moving picture. It is about a gangster—which, far from putting it in any easy category, is one of the things that make it go so well. The inevitable outcome of the profession of shooting your way places is getting shot yourself, and in this there is an almost perfect nemesis pattern whose state of preservation in movie stories is probably the only gift to pictures conferred by the Decency Code. So when Humphrey Bogart is sprung from a life sentence here in order to take charge of a big underworld project, you need not fear the ending will find him with a radio contract, a cottage, and kids. To keep up with himself as an outlaw from the whole world though living in it, he must go faster and faster toward an end that is precise and inescapable and dramatically right.

Mr. Bogart is a very cool number at his job, but you will not need a recounting of the plot. It is enough that this is one of the rare times a good action story has had naturally within it some of the elements of the fates and the furies which are the material of tragedy, in which death can be neither a bluebird nor a mere pool of blood. Of course the pantywaist moralists will be saying that we are glorifying the gangster again, which will of course be as true a statement of this instance as it would be of whole lashings of the world's art, with its romantic brigands, highwaymen, pirates, dictators, Napoleons, vigilantes, cops and robbers generally. And as little to any purpose.

But no picture may live by its point or civic purpose alone, and this is a picture that lives on the screen. In the middle of it is Humphrey Bogart, whose conception and rock-bound maintenance of the hard-handed, graying, and bitter ex-con is not only one of the finest projections of character in any story of men in action, but the whole vertebrate structure of this one. A good part of the telling time is given to his human side and—particularly in the case of the crippled girl he can help but not marry—is slugged a little too hard. But this is a logical part of his life, and it is his life we must be concerned with. He was not betrayed by the spare few he helped and trusted, and it is absurd to suppose that a man who makes his living with an unlicensed gun may not like dogs or need women.

In the end it is Bogart who makes it true anyway, for there is not one minute in this picture when the intensity of his presence is not felt, or when he is false or foolish. He is a man you are gradually allowed to hear tick and would not monkey with, a man you feel must be obeyed instinctively, and remembered. There are of course the others—good character actors, down to the dog and up to the rather difficult and well done part of Ida Lupino; writing and direction gauged to the stern demands of the true movie (John Huston, W. R. Burnett, Raoul Walsh); and a setting that is as much a tribute to the original conception as to the eloquent, flexible camera setups of Tony Gaudio, with their contained action and high Sierras too.

Except for the tire-patch quality of the crippled-girl theme, and a wet three minutes of putting hearts through the wringer at the end, this is what I should call a film worth exposing negative for, and comes almost as a valedictory, in both dialogue interpolations and its position in a cycle. As I say, it's a divided-response business and perhaps will take more imagination, awe, and pity than you are willing to spare. But like it or not, I'll be damned if you leave before the end or go to sleep; and in the way of movies, that's what I'm talking about.

1941

Citizen Welles

Citizen Kane can be approached in several ways: as a film, as an event, as a topic of the times, etc. The outline of the story is simplicity itself, almost like saying, "Once upon a time there was a man of whom certain things are remembered." But its presentation is managed in complex ways and its conclusions are so vague with the shadows of meaning that it is easy to read almost anything into it, including what was actually put there. The things to be said are that it is the boldest free hand stroke in a major screen production since Griffith and Bitzer were running wild to unshackle the camera; that it has the excitement of all surprises without stirring emotions much more enduring; and that in the line of the narrative film, as developed in all countries but most highly on the West Coast of America, it holds no great place.

The picture starts right in with the death of Citizen Kane alone with his crates of priceless art treasures in his fabulous castle on a mountain, where he has ruled for a time at least a miniature of the world. He said a thing when he died and the March of Time wants to make a story out of it, so we start combing the file of old acquaintance, with episode by episode told in flashbacks, and eventually we get the answer through the efforts of the inquiring reporter, who tracks down documents, the man's oldest friend, his newspaper manager, the girl, the butler of the castle. Some of the points are made by the people questioned: some are made in what there is of story as it moves over the years from back to front; but the main point is that Citizen Kane wanted love from the world and went to most of his fantastic extremes to get it, yet never had any love of his own to give. And the thing the searchers have been after, the dying apostrophe which assumes the importance of a mystery-story clue in the last sequence, develops as no more than a memory of the self of his childhood.

There has been so much snarling and blowing on the subject of what this picture is about that it won't hurt to clear the issue: most of the surface facts parallel incidents in the career of one W. R. Hearst; some traits are borrowed from other figures; some are pure ad-libbing. But any resemblance is distinctly coincidental; I could, and would if the editor were not afraid of libel, give you quite a list of Hearst's undesirable characteristics not possessed by Kane. As for the importance of the figure as an element of society, I don't think you can make that stick either. Kane started a war to get circulation for his paper; we hear in casual reference that he is a yellow journalist, and we see in a three-for-a-nickel montage clip that he fought graft and some corrupt trusts; there is a prophecy, not followed up, that when the workingman becomes organized labor he will not love the workingman; he is interviewed by the press and makes wild statements with gravity; when anyone gets in his way he calls him an anarchist. Otherwise his troubles are personal, and his death is that of a domineering and lonely man, known to all for his money, loved by none. The only possible moral of the picture is, don't be that way or you'll be sorry.

Beyond the facts of the career there is the man himself, and this man is Orson Welles, young, older, middle-aged, and in the last decrepit years, dominant throughout. Here perhaps, not so much spoken as expressed in the figure and bearing, is the ruthless force, the self-will, the restless-acquisitive that we feel the story should express if it is to tell of these things at all. This man in these circumstances should be our twentieth-century brand of a figure out of Gustavus Myers: he did not roll up that fortune to start with, but he is no second generation gone to seed, for he turned the nonworking capital into influence and public excitement and a sort of twisted splendor. It is as though Welles, as the man who conceived and produced this film story, had little enough grasp of the issues involved; but Welles as the actor somehow managed, by the genius that is in actors when they have it, to be more of the thing than he could realize. His presence in the picture is always a vital thing, an object of fascination to the beholder. In fact, without him the picture would have fallen all into its various component pieces of effect, allusion, and display. He is the big part and no one will say he is not worth it.

Of his actors, you can say that there are good jobs done and also that there are better ones still to be done. Dorothy Comingore is forced to be too shrill as the shrill wife (the audience ear will absorb only so much) and too ham as the opera singer (subtlety never hurt anyone, and those of us who aren't gaping yokels are not alone, Mr. Orson Citizen). Joseph Cotten had a part that was possibly short on savor because when he was with the great man he had to be something of a chump and when he was talking of him afterward he had to be something of a Mr. Chips, with twinkle and lip-smacking. Ray Collins did a good piece of work with a stock part, and so did all the other stock parts; but to me the man to remember was Everett Sloane, who seemed to understand and seemed to represent it, the little man with the big mind, the projection without the face motion and flapping of arms. You may be surprised when you take the film apart, and find that his relations to any analysis of Kane were as much as anything else the things that made him real.

Now I believe we can look at the picture, and of course we have been told to wait for that. The picture. The new art. The camera unbound. The picture is very exciting to anyone who gets excited about how things can be done in the movies; and the many places where it takes off like the Wright brothers should be credited to Welles first and his cameraman second (Herman J. Mankiewicz as writing collaborator should come in too). The Kubla Khan setting, the electioneering stage, the end of the rough-cut in the Marsh of Thyme projection room, the kid outside the window in the legacy scene, the opera stage, the dramatics of the review copy on opening night—the whole idea of a man in these attitudes must be credited to Welles himself.

And in these things there is no doubt the picture is dramatic. But what goes on between the dramatic high points, the story? No. What goes on is talk and more talk. And while the stage may stand for this, the movies don't. And where a cameraman like Gregg Toland can be every sort of help to a director, in showing him what will pick up, in getting this effect or that, in achieving some lifting trick the guy has thought up, the cameraman still can't teach him how to shoot and cut a picture, even if he knows how himself. It is a thing that takes years and practice to learn. And its main problem always is story, story, story—or, How can we do it to them so they don't know beforehand that it's being done? Low-key photography won't help, except in the case of critics. Crane shots and pan shots, funny angles like showing the guy as though you are lying down at his feet, or moving in over him on the wings of an angel, won't help. Partial lighting won't help, or even blacking out a face or figure won't help, though it may keep people puzzled. Tricks and symbols never really come to much. The real art of movies concentrates on getting the right story and the right actors, the right kind of production and their smoothing everything out. And after that, in figuring how each idea can be made true, how each action can be made to happen, how you cut and reverse-camera and remake each minute of action, and run it into a line afterward, like the motion in the ocean. Does this picture do this? See some future issue when I have the time to say it doesn't, quite. Right now I have to hurry to catch a boat back to New York.

1941

Welles and His Wonders: II 1941 – written when "CK" came out

To make any sense about technical innovations in any one movie, one should, in an ideal state at least, have some idea of the general technique of making every movie. Before coming to the wonders of *Citizen Kane*, therefore, we will just run over a few fundamentals (we will, that is, if anyone is still around when these wandering messages of mine catch up with themselves).

The first thing necessary to a movie is a story, and the first thing necessary to stories for the screen is a writer who understands the screen and works along the line the director will take later, preferably with the director. But the most important thing in the technique of a motion picture—and here director and writer are in varying degrees interdependent—is its construction shot by shot, not for the effect or punch line of any one fragment, but for such devising and spacing as avoid monotony, hold the interest, and lead easily from one thing into another, *the devices for illusion being always and necessarily hidden in the natural emergence of the illusion itself.* One scene may be broken down into six or twenty camera positions, yet these shifts you are not conscious of: you follow the actor across the room and pick him up coming through the door; you may not see him when he is speaking; you may see only his face when someone else is speaking; he turns to look through a window and suddenly you are looking out the window. These are the smallest things, but they make for pace and variety—which will be the biggest things before you are through.

A scene is made, another to fit with it; there may be interscenes, or long shots covering action, establishing atmosphere; later there will be inserts, titles, the transitional devices of trick or straight cutting, dissolves, montages. At the end of maybe five, maybe ten days' work you will have a sequence, that is, an essential incident in the story carried through from start to finish. And the next sequence should take up without jar, without confusion, and lead on again, shot by shot and scene by scene, in the right way of the story. Finally when all the sequences have been made and assembled in a rough-cut, you must study over and over this familiar work of weeks to inquire whether what you put in it is there, to study it for continuity of mood, for how well the sequences match and balance—and for where to cut, where to remake. Does it move, does it complete its circle, do characters and ideas and the express meaning come alive in action? Maybe you've got a picture, but it won't be by chance.

It is true that of all the arts, movies are farthest from being one-man shows. Actors are the most important in the public eye, and indeed they are the dramatic exposition, the writing hand, of stories on the screen; without good ones you are lost. The music and scenic departments are important, and the cutting room is the watchtower of unsung heroes who have brought a thousand bungling messes out of the hopeless into something that at least moves and has coherence. Technically, the most indispensable is the cameraman, with his crew of assistants and batteries of lights; he is a high man indeed. But it is also true that without writing and direction of intelligence, taste, and actual mastery of the craft, you just won't get a picture that is a good picture. It comes down to this: writer and director (much more the director) tell a story in movie terms, and the way they do it is the prime technique of pictures.

Citizen Kane in its story uses the cut-back method—which is convenient but has its drawbacks in the constant interruption of a steady line; it is quite common and I wish it were less so. For dramatic action, it shows its one big character in four main situations, supplemented by newsreel interludes here and there. This makes a pretty weak structure dramatically, so it has to be surrounded with a great deal of stationary talk, as Kane is described, analyzed, asked about, remembered, talked into existence and practically out of it. This is different from many good movies but it is not new, technically or otherwise. The mood is established or heightened by an occasional symbol: the sled and the falling-snow toy, the curtain-warning light on the stage, the bird screaming in escape, etc. Symbols are a dime a dozen and justify their use in the result achieved. I thought the fading light filament and dying sound-track at the end of the singer's career very effective; also the opening and close on the iron fence around the castle. The smoke rising to heaven at the end was trite to start with and dragged out absurdly.

As you can see, there is nothing startling in these component parts. The outstanding technical effect in the picture is in the conception of settings and the use of the camera. Gregg Toland is a trained cameraman and ace-high in his profession, and it is apparent that Welles himself was fascinated most of all by this department in movies—that many of the things done were first sketched in with the bold freehand of his dramatic imagination. (It shouldn't be forgotten that a screen-mood is more than just "photography," that it results from the collaboration, in this order, of director, cameraman, art director.)

The camera here loves deep perspectives, long rooms, rooms seen through doors and giving onto rooms through other doors, rooms lengthened out by low ceilings or made immense by high-angle shots where the ceiling seems to be the sky. Figures are widely spaced down this perspective, moving far off at will, yet kept in focus. The camera loves partial lighting or underlighting, with faces or figures blacked out, features emphasized or thrown into shadow, with one point of high light in an area of gloom or foreground figures black against brightness, with the key shifting according to mood, with every scene modeled for special effects with light batteries of varying function and power, gobos, barndoors, screens, and what not. These things are all written into the accomplished cameraman's book. There is nothing newer about shooting into lights than shooting into the sun, but there is, I suppose, something new in having the whole book thrown at you at once. Certainly there has not been such use of darkness in masses since the Russians, who simply didn't have any lights.

Sometimes all this is fine and really does the job it is put to. Along with the wide action range, it is a relief from too much closeness and light, an effect of stretching. But at other times it appears just willful dabbling: figures are in the dark for no reason—reading without the light to see, for example; or they are kept in darkness right among other clearly lighted figures (the idea is supposed to be that this shows they aren't important; the effect is to draw attention to them, as being maybe the Masked Marvel). Half real and half fish, as in the case of mermaids, is always a thing to cause vague frustration; and too often here it seems as though they were working up a feeling of omen just for the ride.

This camera also likes many of the angles so thoroughly kicked around by the experimental films—floor shots, especially, where the camera gives figures height and takes away width, makes them ominous, or at least portentous in their motions. Crane shots, too, some of them breathtaking as you move down and forward from heights or rise straight up—some of them overdone, as in the last Cook's tour of Kane's boxed accumulations. Add undercranking, to make the people in the "newsreel" clips jerk and scuttle. Add mirrors. And add the usual working tools of long, medium, and two-shots, close-ups, dolly shots, panoramas.

In the cutting there are several things noticeable. One is the long easy sweep you can get when a scene of action is covered in one long-range setup. Another lies partly in the method of treatment and partly in lack of care, and that is the time-and-place confusion which arises when you go smack from the first two-thirds of a sentence to the last third of the same sentence, spoken elsewhere years later. This is done time and again, and you might call it jump-cutting or you might call it the old shell game as far as the audience is concerned.

Another thing about the cutting that goes altogether to the fault of direction is the monotony and amateurism of handling simple dialogue. Over and over there are the two faces talking, talk, talk, talk, then close-up of the right speaker asking, then close-up of the left speaker answering, then back to two. Outside of getting your name in large letters, being a director consists exactly in knowing how to break this up, to keep interest shifting, to stress the *reaction* to a line more sharply than the face saying it. This is what gives a picture life, and it isn't done by camera ructions, however clever.

Orson Welles was naturally entranced with the marvelous things the moving camera could do for him; and while much has resulted from this pre-occupation, I think his neglect of what the camera could do *to* him is the main reason why the picture somehow leaves you cold even while your mouth is still open at its excitements. There may have been the heart and belief to put into it, but there wasn't the time to learn how this might be done, or much regard for any such humdrum skill. I'll tell you about a picture which was the story of a man's life told by the cut-back method after his death, and which had the real life in it, the skill and the heart too. It was *A Man to Remember*, made in a little over two weeks for a little over $100,000 by an ex-Broadway director who was learning about pictures the hard way, and his name was Garson Kanin. And if you want to read into a story some comment on the modern man of predacious industrial power, how he got that way and what it did to him, I'll remind you of a film that told the story and made it stick, its people full-length and alive. It was made some five years ago for Sam Goldwyn and called *Come and Get It*, and the better part of its direction was done by William Wyler.

As for the contributing departments in *Citizen Kane*, Bernard Herrman's music is an active aid; the sets are made right, both for the fantastic and for use or living; it is an all-round class-A production. But the most effective things in it are the creation of Orson Welles's drawing board, not only in whole story ideas but in plausible and adult dialogue (witty, sardonic, knowledgeable), the impression of life as it actually goes on in the big world, the ready dramatic vigor. You remember things like the kid in the snow outside the window as the hard business is transacted within; the newspaper office at night; the understatement of successive breakfasts in Kane's first marriage; the wonderful campaign-hall scene; the opera-opening (there was too much ham in some of this); the trick approach through the night-club skylight and ensuing scenes; the newsreel projection-room conference as a sendoff for the story; and the newsreels themselves—excellent naturalism here.

This stuff is fine theater, technically or any other way, and along with them the film is exciting for the recklessness of its independence, even if it seems to have little to be free *for.* There is surely nothing against it as a dramatic venture that it is no advance in screen technique at all, but a retrogression. The movies could use Orson Welles. But so could Orson Welles use the movies, that is, if he wants to make pictures. Hollywood is a great field for fanfare, but it is also a field in which even Genius has to do it the hard way; and *Citizen Kane* rather makes me doubt that Orson Welles really wants to make pictures.

1941

Melvin B. Tolson

Known today principally as a poet whose modernist, experimental epic *Harlem Gallery* displayed erudition, quirky syntax, and formal rigor, Melvin B. Tolson (1898–1966) also wrote movie criticism in his lively feature column "Caviar and Cabbage," which appeared in the weekly African-American newspaper *Washington Tribune*. He was particularly incensed with the public's (even the black public's) enthusiasm for *Gone with the Wind*, which he reviewed as a thinly disguised apology for racism and the Ku Klux Klan. In a follow-up article about *GWTW*, entitled "The Philosophy of the Big House," Tolson argued that the plantation house was the one obligatory element in the movie. As Anna Everett put it in her study *Returning the Gaze: A Genealogy of Black Film Criticism*: "Tolson knew that mythological estates on sprawling southern plantations such as *Gone with the Wind*'s Tara and *Jezebel*'s Halcyon housed the nation's escapist fantasies and authorized these films' antiblack and antidemocratic themes." In retrospect, it is enlightening to see how one of the most beloved classics Hollywood ever made might have struck a sardonic black film critic such as Tolson so differently at the time.

◆

Gone with the Wind Is More Dangerous Than *Birth of a Nation*

The acting in *Gone with the Wind* is excellent. The photography is marvelous, Miss Hattie McDaniel registered the nuances of emotion, from tragedy to comedy, with the sincerity and artistry of a great actor. Some of my friends declare that the picture is fine entertainment. So were the tricks of Houdini. So is a circus for children.

But *Gone with the Wind* was announced in the movie magazines, in billboard advertisements, and in the film itself as more than entertainment. It was billed as the story of the Old South—not a story of the Old South. That difference is important for us truth-seekers. Remember—the novel is a historical picture. Both the novelist and the producer say that.

Therefore, the first question is this: Does *Gone with the Wind* falsify history?

Take other historical pictures that came out of Hollywood. *A Tale of Two Cities*, *Zola*, *Abe Lincoln in Illinois*, *Juarez*, *Henry VIII*, *The Life of Louis Pasteur*. Historians were consulted and libraries ransacked to get the HISTORICAL truth for these pictures. A HISTORICAL picture is more than entertainment. Let us get that straight.

The Birth of a Nation was such a barefaced lie that a moron could see through it. *Gone with the Wind* is such a subtle lie that it will be swallowed as the truth by millions of whites and blacks alike. Dr. Stephenson Smith calls the moving picture the greatest molder of public opinion. And the Chinese say a picture is worth a thousand words. I believe it after listening to the comments of some of my friends on this movie, *Gone with the Wind*.

The fact that this movie caused a red-letter day in the South should have warned Negroes. The fact that it was acclaimed by Confederate veterans who fought to keep Negroes enslaved should have warned us. From Key West, Fla., to El Paso, Texas, the White South rejoiced. Margaret Mitchell, who wrote the novel, is the Joan of Arc of Dixie.

Why? Why? Because she told the story from the viewpoint of the South. The picture was praised extravagantly in Darkest Mississippi where Negro children are not permitted to read the Constitution in school. The commendation of the White South means the condemnation of the Negro.

The story of the Old South can be told from the viewpoint of the poor whites, the Negro slaves, the Yankees, or the white masters. Miss Mitchell took the viewpoint of the white masters. That's the reason the White South rejoices over the picture. Be not deceived, if you love your race. I am sure you would not ask an enemy to recommend you for a position.

If you put poison in certain kinds of foods, you can't tell it. If you beat a man long enough with your fists, you can slap him and he'll appreciate the slap.

The poor Negro has been kicked so often that he considers a slap a bit of white courtesy. Since *Gone with the Wind* didn't have a big black brute raping a white virgin in a flowing white gown, most Negroes went into ecstasies. Poor Sambo!

Negroes are like the poor husband who caught his wife in the bedroom necking the iceman and sighed, "Well, it might've been worse!"

I must give that Southern novelist and the white producer credit for one thing: they certainly fooled the Negro and at the same time put over their anti-Negro, anti-Yankee, KKK propaganda.

The tragedy is this: Negroes went to see one thing: whites went to see another. Negroes asked: "Were there any direct insults to the race?" The white folk wanted to know: "Was the North justified in freeing black men?"

Both questions were answered in this picture. Negroes were not directly insulted. The North was wrong in freeing the Negroes. For seventy years Negro-hating white men have tried to prove with arguments and lynchings that the North was wrong in freeing the Negroes. And some Negro fools have agreed with the white Negro-haters. If the North was wrong, then old Frederick Douglass and the Abolitionists were idiots.

Gone with the Wind pretends to show historically the Old South. It fails to do this. It falsifies by leaving out important facts. *Gone with the Wind* is what a description of Washington would be like without the Capitol, the White House, the Federal buildings, Howard University, and other landmarks.

Half of the picture deals with the Civil War. But the Civil War comes like a spontaneous combustion. It appears like a rabbit out of a magician's hat. Every critic in America will tell you that a truthful work of art must have motivation—causation. *Gone with the Wind* shows not a single economic or social or political cause that led to the Civil War. How could a civilization be "gone with the wind" unless there was something to MAKE it go?

According to the picture, slavery was a blessed institution. (Stick to the picture.) The Negroes were well fed and happy. Last summer I stood in the slave market of Charleston. In the picture there were no slave markets tearing husbands and wives, mothers and children apart. As a young man, Abe Lincoln saw a slave market and cried: "If the chance comes, I'll hit this thing a hard blow."

Read Tourgée's historical accounts of his trips through the South. Read Dr. Frank's historical documents on the Old South. See Dr. Reddick's documents on slavery in the famous Schomburg Collection. Read what Thomas Jefferson said about the South. The Civil War was the inevitable culmination of economic, social, political, and psychological events spreading over a period of two hundred years.

It was like water piled up behind a dam finally breaking through. In dealing with history, leave the "if's" out.

The picture, then, lacked the motivation of historical truth, although it was supposed to be a historical picture. The Civil War was inevitable. It had to come because of definite economic causes. Slavery was a bloody institution. Of course, there were good masters. But the institution was built on the rape of Negro women, the hellish exploitation of black men, the brutalities of overseers, and bloodhounds that tore human beings to pieces. Read the documents of Dr. Frank, a white Southerner, in his book, *Americans*.

These are the reasons why the Old South is "gone with the wind." The picture does not show that. Therefore, millions of white men, women, and children will believe that the North was wrong in freeing the Negro.

The picture aims to create sympathy for the white South. We see thousands of dying and dead Confederate soldiers. The only Yankee who dies (in the picture) is a blue-coated soldier trying to rob and rape a Southern white woman. Yet General Sherman ordered the Yankees to protect women and children! When they didn't he had them shot. Atlanta burns. But the picture does not tell us that the Confederates set it afire! We get the impression that the damned Yankees did it.

We see a Union shell crash through a window of a church containing a painting of Christ; wounded Confederate soldiers are in the church. We are not told that white churches defended slavery in the South. These tricks will hoodwink millions of people.

Even the Ku Klux Klan is idolized. We see white gentlemen of the KKK returning home at night, while a big burly Yankee officer questions the innocent while ladies. Nothing is said about the brutalities of the KKK that stank to high heaven. Hitler's persecution of the Jews is nothing compared to the KKK's hellish treatment of our black forefathers!

The happy Negroes (in the picture, of course) go out to dig trenches for the Confederates, to keep themselves and their wives and children in slavery! The historical truth is this: When the Yankees marched through Georgia, the slaves, like sensible people, deserted the plantations by the tens of thousands. Some fell upon their knees and kissed the feet of their Yankee deliverers. General Sherman had to make thousands of them go back to their good (?) masters.

When old Abe Lincoln entered Savannah, he had to chastise the mammy slaves for kissing his boots.

"You should bow to no one but God," said the Great Emancipator.

The picture did not show the poor crackers, who outnumbered the white masters ten to one. These poor white men were degraded by pellagra, illiteracy, and the opium of poverty. That was a lie of omission in the picture.

Plato said 2,000 years ago that aristocracy is built on either chattel slavery or wage slavery. *Gone with the Wind* did not show that Southern aristocracy was built on both. I sat for four long hours waiting for that gigantic historical truth to appear—and all I saw was the heartless action of Scarlett O'Hara.

I am not bothered much with what Negroes think about *Gone with the Wind*. Most of them won't think. They have bridge, and the Strutters' Ball, and the fraternity powwow, and church politics, and fornications to think about.

What, then, will be the effect on millions and millions of whites from the Atlantic to the Pacific? What will be the effect when the picture is shown in South America, France, England, Germany, and the islands of the sea?

It will be this: The North was wrong in fighting to free black men. The grand old Abolitionists were lunatics. Negroes didn't want to be free anyway. Slaves were happy. The greatest pleasure of the slave was to serve massa.

Southern whites understand Negroes; that's the reason they treat them as they do. You need the Ku Klux Klan to keep Negroes in their place. All slaves were black; no white men had any mulatto children. There were no slave markets. Yankee soldiers went through Georgia raping white virgins. Negroes loved (with an undying love) the white masters, and hated the poor whites because they didn't own Negroes. Dixie was a heaven on earth until the damned Yankees and carpetbaggers came.

The Negroes were so dumb that they hated the very Yankees who wanted to free them. All masters were gentlemen—without high-yellah mistresses. Southern gentlemen were so honorable that they didn't yield to temptation when hussies, like Scarlett, threw their passionate bodies at them.

These are the untruthful things white people, all over the world, will believe when they see *Gone with the Wind*. Yes, some Negroes will believe these lies also.

And now, dear readers, to see what I have seen, you will have to put yourself in the place of a white man. Can you do that? I hope you can.

1939

Paul Goodman

Essayist, novelist, poet, playwright, social critic, political gadfly, Paul Goodman (1911–1972) was the last of the generalists. Intellectual curiosity combined in him with the responsibilities of the good citizen, and nothing was beyond his purview, from the philosophy of education (his *Growing Up Absurd* had a strong influence on the counterculture) to city planning, Kafka, gestalt therapy, linguistics—to movies, which he wrote about, off and on, from 1934 to the mid-1960s in such periodicals as *Partisan Review*, *Trend*, and *Moviegoer*. His other connection to movies was a free-lance job he once held writing plot synopses of French novels for the MGM story department at $5 per story.

◆

Griffith and the Technical Innovations

A season of typical blanks gives the usual opportunity to talk in a genetic way about why American films of 1940–41 don't hang together. Restricting myself to merely formal considerations, I'd like to make 2 points: 1. Especially after Griffith, the technique has developed ahead of the art; 2. the atmosphere and style have a meaning apart from the action and thought. These failings have, of course, been obvious for 20 years, but perhaps I can enliven the discussion of them by reporting some current events in New York.

1.

An important difference between the history of cinema and all the other arts is that in other arts the technical innovations were mostly invented one at a time and as part of the total expression that the artist was to achieve; in an incorrect teleological formula we could almost say: "To express something new he invented a new means." In cinema, on the contrary, it seems *as if* a unique technique was available all at once but with nothing unique to express. (The falseness of this "as if" in the case of D. W. Griffith is what I here want to demonstrate.) The only similar outstripping of total expression by technical means that comes ready to my mind is the introduction of steel-construction and, again, of mass-production into modern architecture; and this is an important reason, surely, why most skyscrapers and most Hollywood movies vie with each other in esthetic blankness. (I do not mean in esthetic "badness," as e.g. a painting by Benton is bad because it is inflated, etc.; but rather that you cannot approach these things formally, their parts have so little formal relation.)

Recently (Fall 1940) the Film Library of the Museum of Modern Art gave a Griffith Festival, accompanied by a little volume by Iris Barry: *D. W. Griffith: American Film Master.* The relation between these films and this book is most interesting. On the one hand we have a series of art works, ranging from 1909 short filmed-dramas like *Edgar Allan Poe,* thru such a remarkable combination of cinema and drama as *The Musketeers of Pig Alley* (1912), up to such fine, almost great cinema as *Broken Blossoms* (1919) and *Isn't Life Wonderful* (1924); in all of these, under whatever conditions of story or manner, we have integrated works concentrated to a total effect, often to a single effect; indeed, Griffith is so insistent on this unity, whether of mood, climax, or idea, that the film often seems schematic. On the other hand we have the description of an artist's work as if it were a series of introductions of novel technical means, such as moving the camera, trick-lighting, vignetting, plunging *in medias res,* and cross-cutting; or of novel categories of content, such as realism, psychology, social significance, or the Civil War. But to see these films in this light is to see them all wrong. Let me illustrate.

"Early in 1909 they"—Griffith and Bitzer his cameraman—"together contrived a strikingly novel effect of light and shade in *Edgar Allan Poe,* and a firelight effect which was widely remarked in the otherwise primitive and stilted *A Drunkard's Reformation.*" (p. 16) But this "novel effect of light and shade" is the *whole* of *Poe,* which is nothing but the fusion into this chiaroscuro of the misunderstood poet, his suddenly appearing Raven, his wife dying of starvation, as against the callous publishers in their ordinary light; in fact this sad little picture is almost comic because it concentrates so powerful an expression into such a tiny magnitude. Again, that "widely remarked firelight effect" happens to be the *summation* of the drunkard's reformation: his home rather than his vice, etc. To conceive of these expressions as "technical innovations" or, to use another of the author's phrases, as "the development of screen syntax" is to make of D. W. Griffith a tramp like, say, Mark Sandrich, who is also a great innovator. For before illustrating further, let me draw the moral: How can Miss Barry make such a silly error? *It is precisely because she is thinking, when she thinks of cinema, of all the Hollywood output which employs such a warehouse of technical devices—yes, "introduced" by Griffith and others—with nothing whatever to say.*

Let me cite one or two of her favorite phrases: "Here he hit upon a new way of handling a tried device—the last-minute rescue—which was to serve him well for the rest of his career." (16) "It was a device which had seldom failed Griffith in the past and stood him in good stead now." (30) "Whether as a study in realism, as an ancestor of the gangster films of later decades, or as an exercise [sic!] in motion-picture composition *The Musketeers of Pig Alley* is a remarkable piece. The photography is extraordinary and the whole film predicts what was to come in the modern section of *Intolerance*." (19) As if, that is, the documentary photography, the carefully contrived chaos of the slum-alley, the gangster subject, and the wonderful montage of the man-hunt sequence (= "an exercise in composition") had no intrinsic connection, but were a congeries of "beauties"; but if you imagine you are to hear of the intrinsic connection in the remarks on *Intolerance* of which this was a "forecast," you are sadly deceived. In general, that is, the mode of criticism here is like those books which tell of The Legacy of Egypt, as if the Egyptian culture consisted in the invention of the sun-dial for English country gardens.

Broken Blossoms is almost great; to my taste it is Griffith's most complete work. Miss Barry's remarks on it are in her usual vein and of no account, but let me indicate a few isolated appreciations of the picture itself in order to bring out my main point, which is *the difference between a film where every technical means is in intimate relation with the whole expression, and our films where a bit of technique is a distracting short-cut to convey indirectly some picayune information by the way.* Consider, for instance, Griffith's persistent vertical masking of half of the screen in this film; this is not a "special effect" but *comes to be expected*; thus our attention is centered on each character in his separateness and loneliness; when several come together on the whole screen, it is these isolated persons who come together. Recall, on the other hand, the numerous vignettes and arc-masks in *Birth of a Nation*, which generate the sentiment of being an onlooker at a panoramic spectacle, first distant (telescope), then filling the scene (arc). Such masking and vignetting has been called a mannerism of Griffith's! Yes, used as Ford would use it, it would be a mannerism. Again, consider the employment of color in *Broken Blossoms*; Griffith uses 3 or 4 tints (not technicolor, of course); these are introduced from the very outset to express dominant mood, and they come to be expected; then what a triumph, by what simple means, when the awakening of the Chinese boy to the beauty in his chamber is fortified by the change from a darker hue to the strange pink-violet which had appeared (if my memory serves) in the earlier scene of his peaceful homeland. And the green fog at the climax. But a director 1941 has all the rainbow of technicolor at hand and says nothing. Again, when a character, e.g. the pugilist, is introduced, it is with the following action: he is restrained from pleasure by his manager and does not dare revolt, *therefore* he tyrannizes over the girl; the psychology is schematic (tho sufficient for the story), but it *is* a psychology, it gives depth and pity to the action, and humanity to the catastrophe;—whereas the characters in so "psychological" a film as *The Long Voyage Home* are in the end nothing but faces, without human interest. Again, since so much has been said against Griffith's colorful subtitles, what of the remarkable rhapsodic titles in this film? The characters are again and again shown at their most meaningful moments, no footage is spent on merely expository matters: the poetic, often imagistic title fixes this moment as if in a different dimension; indeed, no higher praise can be given to *Broken Blossoms* than to say that the scene of the catharsis, where the Chinaman brings home the dead girl, is great enough and sufficiently well prepared to carry the famous title "All the tears of the world washed over his heart." Lastly, in the face of the trivial bits of hectic synthetic montage that ornament current movies (for instance, the Extras rolling off the presses to loud music), I would point to those strokes of lightning cunningly withheld by Griffith till the climax, where the wildly bowing young Chinaman suddenly bows at infinite speed and where rushing thru the fog he rushes into the camera at infinite speed.

2.

These are random examples of "technical innovations" as part of the art. In an appendix on photography to *American Film Master*, however, Beaumont Newhall concludes: "During the last 25 years the scope of cinematography has broadened enormously. Bitzer's experiments have been universally adopted and refined. Yet, looking back at the photographic beauty of the epic Griffith-Bitzer films, one is amazed that the quality of cinematography has not kept pace with its technical growth." I should think that there is nothing amazing about it, considering the institutionalizing of cinema as a business, the kind of success aimed at, and the kind of talent attracted. Further, where a medium has an important mechanical part, non-esthetic laboratory researches will produce innovations beyond the contemporary requirements of either expression or communication—e.g., technicolor. Then further, the commercial appeal of sensational innovations will introduce them into the expression anyway. But it is not these causes I am here discussing, but rather the formal effect: What is the formal effect of such an independent development of technique?

The answer is simple: it is the streamlined professional "Style" in which all stories are indirectly communicated—one can hardly say "cinematically presented." By professional I mean such an attitude toward the technique as makes it impossible to overhaul it afresh for each problem. But this uniform "Style" is not a chaos of effects, but a unified complex of: brightly reflected lighting; photogenic make-up; spacious interiors obviously without 4 walls; the ritual series of facial close-up—cut from face to face—*pan* of the interior (nothing is still for a moment)—and the follow-shot of the angelic person moving down halls and thru walls, freed from the laws of matter; the music that sounds from nowhere; the continuity of fades; the scrambling montage in which all dissolves into kaleidoscopy. Etc., etc., for it is worked out in all details. And make no mistake, this Style is itself a realized work of art with an unmistakable total expression: here is freedom, ease, domination of obstacles, evaporation of solidity, speed, super-humanity, day-dream (surely not night-dream!), and the pleasant destruction of the universe.

Well! what objection can even a critic have to so admittedly successful an expression of the abundant life? I confess that my bother is again a merely formal one. It is that the actions, thoughts, and virtues, the conversation, acting, and even beauty of the persons in these films is incommensurate with the prodigious lighting, scenery, camera-work, and cutting. Even the happiest ending (a skip of *two* grades up the economic scale) is not so liberating as the follow-shot thru the solid walls; the most brilliant beauties cannot people this clear space; and the wit and insight of the best Californian poets is not so clever as the montage. To put it another way, we have already seen these plots, this wit and philosophy, in literary romances of even an earlier day; but this world of the cinema style we have never seen on land or sea or in books. Therefore, it seems to me, the esthetic problem of Hollywood is as follows: *To find an action and a system of philosophy and ethics, and to construct out of aluminum a cast of characters, that will fit into an integrated pattern with the professional style of the camera-man and scene-designer.*

1941

James Agee

James Agee (1909–1955) was probably unique among this anthology's contributors in sustaining dual reputations as a major American film critic and a major American writer. His nonfiction classic about Depression sharecroppers, *Let Us Now Praise Famous Men* (with photographer Walker Evans), his novels and poetry (*A Death in the Family, The Morning Watch, Permit Me Voyage*), and his screenplays (including *The Night of the Hunter* and *The African Queen*) all continue to be highly esteemed. Agee's literary reputation helped grant him the freedom to employ a high style in his film criticism. That prose style—syntactically complex, baroque in diction, flamboyant, witty—was a high-wire act that delighted his readers, first in *The Nation*, then at *Time*, from 1942 to 1948. Part of the "joke" or pleasure involved was that one would not have expected to see such linguistic contortions in a movie review.

Agee began his column in wartime, an atmosphere of crisis and communal sacrifice that certainly colored his take on films (see his annual wrap-up of 1944 movies). Unlike Otis Ferguson, he was dissatisfied with the well-oiled Hollywood fantasy or entertainment picture, and looked at first to documentaries, then to Italian neo-realism for a screen art that would mirror the ragged, turbulent world around him. He favored real locations over studio sets, and sometimes nonprofessionals (witness his review of *Shoeshine*) over professional actors. Agee's critical balancing acts often involved a dizzying set of "on-the-one-hand/on-the-other-hand" adjustments. He aimed, above all, to be "stimulating," and that he was. He left off writing criticism when he went to Hollywood to pursue a screenwriting career. Like Edmund Wilson, Agee also wrote an unproduced scenario for Charlie Chaplin. He helped make two classic documentaries with Helen Levitt, *In the Street* and *The Quiet One*. Agee died of a massive heart attack at 46.

◆

The Song of Bernadette

January 29, 1944

Since nothing is more repugnant to me than the pseudo-religious, I went to *The Song of Bernadette* gritting my teeth against my advance loathing. But since, also, many of the deepest resonances of my childhood are Catholic; and since I intensely suspect and fear the implacable pieties of those who deny the rationally inexplicable even when they are being beaten over the head with it; and since, accordingly, I feel a triumphant pride in the work or mere existence of true artists and of the truly experienced in religion, I was unexpectedly and greatly moved by a great many things in the film. I owe this somewhat indecently subjective preface because I doubt that the film can be strongly recommended to anyone whose mind and emotions lack some similar shape. I can add only that the picture is unusually well made—within limits.

The limits are those of middle-class twentieth-century genteelism, a fungus which by now all but chokes the life out of any hope from Hollywood and which threatens any vivid appetite in Hollywood's audience. In proportion to the excellence any given film achieves within these limits—which can be considerable—I suppose it is the more pernicious. If that is so, *Bernadette* is a champion enemy. For within those genteel limits I have seldom seen so tender and exact an attention to mood, to over-all tone, to cutting, to the edging of an emotion, and to giving vitality, sometimes radiance, in terms of the image and the sound more than of the character, the story, the line, the music. Jennifer Jones especially, as Bernadette, whether through Henry King's direction or her own ability, impossibly combines the waxen circumspections of a convent school with abrupt salients of emotion of which Dostoevski himself need not have been ashamed.

But Bernadette Soubirous and the cruel, ridiculous, and unfathomable concentrics which spread from her naive ecstasy composed one of the most appalling and instructive events of our time; to the reproduction of which only an almost unimaginably brilliant film could have been adequate. What you have here, instead, is a tamed and pretty image, highly varnished, sensitively lighted, and exhibited behind immaculate glass, the window at once of a shrine and of a box-office.

Annual Wrap-Up of 1944

January 20, 1945

If you compare the moving pictures released during a given period with the books published during the same period—or with the plays produced or the pictures painted or the music composed—you may or may not be surprised to find that they stand up rather well. I can think of very few contemporary books that are worth the jackets they are wrapped in; I can think of very few movies, contemporary or otherwise, which fail to show that somebody who has worked on them, in front of the camera or in any one of many places behind it, has real life or energy or intensity or intelligence or talent.

But you have only to compare the best of last year's films with the best that have been made or in your conception could be made, and the best that have been made with the best work you have known in any other art you choose, to know that those who make or care for moving pictures have great reason to be angry, for all that is frustrated, and still greater reason to be humble, for all that is fallen short of, frustration or no. And if you foresee how few years remain before the grandest prospect for a major popular art since Shakespeare's time dissolves into the ghastly gelatinous nirvana of television, I think you will find the work of this last or any recent year, and the chance of any sufficiently radical improvement within the tragically short future, enough to shrivel the heart. If moving pictures are ever going to realize their potentialities, they are going to have to do it very soon indeed. Aware of that, and aware also of all the works of genius which have been already achieved in films, I have no patience with the patient and patronizing who remind us mellowly that it took centuries to evolve an Aeschylus or a Joyce.

The sickening thing is that nearly everything that has virtue or hope at all is lukewarm or worse. We are learning better and better all the time, for instance, how to make films beautifully, elegantly, patiently, perfectly—so long as nobody severely questions the nature of the beauty, the quality of the elegance, the focus and result of the patience, the meaning and value of the perfection. In this sense I suppose *The Song of Bernadette* is a nearly perfect picture. I would about as soon see all that kind of skill and devotion used in embroidering the complete text of the Solemnization of Matrimony on a pair of nylon drawers. It is as if all the power and resource of the English language were to culminate in the prose of Donald Culross Peattie.

This suffocating genteelism, this suicidal love for and pride in the utterly controlled and utterly worthless effect, has become as grim a threat to movies as the rankest commercialism that could ever be reputed of Hollywood. Needless, perhaps, to add, it is the one aesthetic logically available to the commercial mind; such minds can hardly be blamed for indorsing a kind of beauty they genuinely care for, to the detriment of kinds they have to accept or indorse, if at all, on faith.

Or consider *With the Marines at Tarawa*, the best of the four or five film records of war which I consider the best films of the year. I profoundly respect their craftsmanship, which is not only good but well used, and their good taste. And I grant that short of a tremendously forceful, daring, and sure creative intelligence, craftsmanship and taste are the best available two hands with which to work at such material. Yet it seems a sorry year in which decent grammar and a modest sense of one's subject, honorable as these are, have earned higher honor than any other achievement.

The best fiction films of the year, *The Curse of the Cat People* and *Youth Runs Wild*, were made by Val Lewton and his associates. I esteem them so highly because for all their unevenness their achievements are so consistently alive, limber, poetic, humane, so eager toward the possibilities of the screen, and so resolutely against the grain of all we have learned to expect from the big studios. But I am afraid there is no reason to believe that the makers of these films, under the best of circumstances, would be equipped to make the great, and probably very vulgar, and certainly very forceful revolutionary pictures that are so desperately needed. Indeed, I suspect that their rather gentle, pleasing, resourceful kind of talent is about the strongest sort we can hope to see working in Hollywood with any consistent, useful purity of purpose; and the pictures themselves indicate to what extent that is frustrated.

If only a half-dozen properly placed men in Hollywood realized and knew how to apply the lessons in *Going My Way*, they might he assured of almost any number of hits, and we might be assured of an equal number of more or less good films. The lessons, if I read them right, are that leisureliness can be excellent, that if you take a genuine delight in character the universe is opened to you, and perhaps above all that a movie, like any other work of art, must be made for love. But I am ready to bet that the chief discernible result, if any, of *Going My Way* will be an anxiety-ridden set of vaudeville sketches about Pat and Mike in cassocks; and on that bet, with enough takers, I could set up a studio of my own.

It seems to me that when an intelligent director and an intelligent boss work smoothly together, you can expect pictures like *Double Indemnity*. It is a neat picture, and it brings back into movies a lot of acid things which ought to be there. But it brings no new ones, and it does not handle the old ones, I would say, with any notable ingenuity or interest in taking a risk. Rather, it is strictly expert—a good thing of itself perhaps; but it looks to me as if the expertness were always as sharply controlled by what is dead sure at the box-office as by what is right. I imagine that in this limited sense we can hope for more from Billy Wilder, in the immediate future, than from anybody else around.

But is it anywhere near enough? I feel more hope, on the whole, in the climate of such a studio as Metro, which gave us last year the very generous and pretty *Meet Me in St. Louis* and the very likably earnest, dogged *30 Seconds Over*

Tokyo. But I would hardly say that either of these films gave me any hope that next year, or the year after, their makers might bring out one that you could never forget; indeed, both were rich in guaranties that nothing of the sort will happen.

As for the films of Preston Sturges, which are of course among the best and most gifted of the year, I will be more at rest in my liking for them when I am thoroughly convinced that Sturges is not rejecting half his talents; or that there is nothing on earth he is temperamentally able to do about it. I will probably always like the films of David Selznick better than reputedly condescending aesthetes like me are allowed to like such things; for I think that more than most things that come out of Hollywood they show both genuine talent, as distinct from mere professionalism, and a genuine love for movies, as distinct from mere executive concentration on them. But I am afraid they also show, and probably always will, an equally genuine love for commercial success, and a weakness for emotional and aesthetic and philosophical attitudes which belong, if anywhere, to soap opera.

In some respects I admire Arthur Ripley more than anyone else who released a picture during the past year—for his *Voice in the Wind*, which was made relatively far outside the mill, on very little money, in very little time. His film showed unequivocal and reckless passion for saving the best things possible in the best way possible. In nearly every other respect, I must admit, I thought it poor. But it is only in that kind of passion and disinterestedness, joined with adequate talent, that I see any hope. Name five men who have or have ever had it, and their position in Hollywood. And try to conceive what difficulties they would encounter, in raising the capital, in making the films, in getting them distributed, if they or any men of their order tried to do the work outside.

When an art is in good health, mediocrity and amorphous energy and commercialism and hostility toward disinterested men become more than forgivable, as lubricants and as stimulants, and the men of skill, or of affable or gentle or charming or for that matter venal talent, are more than welcome to exist, and to be liked and rewarded. When an art is sick unto death, only men of the most murderous creative passion can hope to save it. In either condition it is generally, if by no means always, this dangerous sort of man who does the great work. I wonder whether it is any longer possible, anywhere on earth, for such a man to work in films. I am almost certain it is not possible, and is not ever going to be, in this country.

A Great Film

September 15, 1945

W illiam Wellman and the others who are responsible for *Story of G.I. Joe* obviously did not regard their job as an ordinary one. They undertook a great subject. It is clear that they undertook it in a determination to handle it honestly and to make a masterpiece. A wonderful amount of their achievement measures up to their intention. If their picture had been made under the best of circumstances, in a time when everyone who had the heart and the talent was free to make the best pictures possible, it would still be among the best. Coming as it does out of a world in which even the best work is nearly always compromised, and into a world which is generally assumed to dread honesty and courage and to despise artistic integrity, it is an act of heroism, and I cannot suggest my regard for it without using such words as veneration and love. Many things in the film itself move me to tears—and in none of them do I feel that I have been deceived, or cynically seduced or manipulated, as one usually has to feel about movies. But not even the finest of the picture's achievements are more moving than the angry, bitter nobility of the intention which is implied behind the whole of it.

The authors of the screen play, Leopold Atlas and Guy Endore and Philip Stevenson, have not only avoided writing a story, in any traditional sense; they have also developed a rather original narrative style, dry, keen, sober, and visually very imaginative. This style seems to be based to some extent on that of Hemingway; but it is freer than some of Hemingway's less good writing of self-pity, over-insistent masculinity, and the musical gift which sometimes blurs even the most beautiful things Hemingway observes into one kind of Irish croon. Many of the scenes end abruptly; some are deliberately deflated or interrupted or made to end flat or tonelessly. All these devices are artful or, if you like, artificial, but on one seeing, anyhow, not one seemed dishonest either aesthetically or morally. It is about as taciturn a picture as I have seen; but not a verbal or speechless stretch in it seems forced or ineffective. Much use is made of a commonplace of good movie making which most American studios reject: that you can show a wave of action, even very complex and cryptic action, more excitingly and instructively rather than less if you don't pause continually to explain it to the audience, and if you don't delete the inexplicable. There is a wonderfully discreet and powerful use, for that matter, of purely "meaningless" bits—such as a shot in which Ernie Pyle (Burgess Meredith) sits by the road while some soldiers straggle past—which have as great meaning as anything could have, being as immediate and as unlimited by thought or prejudice as what the eye might see on the spot, in a casual glance. And visually there are some of the most eloquent and simple things ever put into a movie—the scene, for instance, in which the worn-out captain and the wretched young replacement private, silently and in great tension and shyness, watch and approach each other, and are interrupted by the sudden violent mental breakdown of a third soldier.

Many of the best things in the film are done just as exactly and unemphatically. With a slight shift of time and scene, men whose faces have become familiar simply aren't around anymore. The fact is not commented on or in any way pointed; their absence merely creates its gradual vacuum and realization in the pit of the stomach. Things which seem at first tiresome, then to have become too much of a running gag, like the lascivious tongue-clacking of the professional stallion among the soldiers (Wally Cassell) or the Sergeant's continual effort to play the record of his son's voice, are allowed to run their risks without tip-off or apology. In the course of many repetitions they take on full obsessional power and do as much as anything could to communicate the terrific weight of time, fatigue, and half-craziness which the picture is trying so successfully to make you live through. The characters are just as unobtrusively introduced and developed—so quietly, in fact, that it is misleading to speak of "development" in any traditional sense. One of the most terrible things in the movie is the silent uninsistent notice of the change in the face of the youngest of the soldiers, after his first battle, from that of a lonely, brave, frightened boy to something shriveled and poisoned beyond suggesting by words. And the development of the character of the Captain is so imperceptible and so beautifully done that, without ability to wonder why, you accept him as a great man in his one open attempt to talk about himself and the war, and as a virtual divinity in the magnificent scene which focuses on his dead body. This closing scene seems to me a war poem as great and as beautiful as any of Whitman's. One of the glories of the over-all style and tone of the film is its ability to keep itself stopped down so low and so lucid, like a particularly strong and modest kind of prose, and to build a long gently rising arch of increasing purity and intensity, which, without a single concession to "poetic" device, culminates in the absoluteness of that scene.

In a film so excellent there are so many things to honor, and to comment on, that I feel incapable of clearness even on a few, much less of completeness or order. The picture contains, for instance, the first great triumphs of the kind of anti-histrionic casting and acting which I believe is indispensable to most, though by no means all, kinds of greatness possible to movies. It would be impossible in that connection to say enough in praise of the performance of Bob Mitchum as the Captain and Freddie Steele as the Sergeant, or of Wellman for his directing and, I suppose, casting of them. It is also the first great triumph in the effort to combine "fiction" and "documentary" film. That is, it not only makes most of its fiction look and sound like fact—and far more intimate and expressive fact than it is possible to record on the spot; it also, without ever inflating or even disturbing the factual quality, as Eisenstein used to, gives fact the constant power and meaning beyond its own which most "documentors"— and most imaginative artists as well—totally lack feeling for. I don't insist on the word if you feel it is misleading, but most of this film is good poetry, and some of it is great poetry, and all of its achievements, and even most of its fail- ures, are earned in terms purely of moving pictures. The sudden close-up, for instance, of a soldier's loaded back, coldly intricate with the life-and-death implements of his trade, as he marches away from his dead captain, is as com- plete, moving, satisfying, and enduring as the finest lines of poetry I know.

This is not a faultless movie. Most of its scenes are perfectly and often orig- inally fitted together, but one of the major transitions—between Africa and Italy—is diffuse, generalized, and conventional, and another—the fight for Cassino—remains rather a disappointing and somewhat leaky transition, not the climactic release of energy that was needed and I believe intended. Indeed, though I am aware of my limited right to an opinion, it seems to me that the movie does fail in one important thing: to give adequate direct impressions—indirectly, it gives any number—of the individual's experience of combat. Even when shots from *San Pietro* are used, in the last fight, the real- ity to the individual does not come through; and when the Captain and the Sergeant outwit German snipers in a ruined church, the episode seems bril- liant, highly specialized, and almost literary, rather than something common to the experience of many infantrymen. If people as good as these can't commu- nicate that experience, I am about ready to believe it has been proved inex- pressible; but I still wonder what might have been done if during one combat sequence the camera had worked inside some individual as well as outside. Much of the picture is very somber in lighting and slow in movement—it has drawn as intelligently on Mauldin as on Pyle—but some of this darkness seems a little sumptuous and studioesque; and some of the outdoor sets, dili- gent and good as they are, seem over-prepared, with nothing left to chance, like the groundwork of a first-rate diorama—as if the mud had been churned up inch by inch by union labor, before the actors took over. But these are about the only faults worth mentioning; and if by any chance *Story of G.I. Joe* is not a masterpiece, then however stupid my feeling is, I cannot help resenting those films which are.

I imagine that some people, better educated than the infantrymen in *Story of G.I. Joe*, will wish to point out that for all its courage and intelligence "as far as it goes," the film is not, in the sense they understand it, "an indictment of war." Nobody is accused, not even the enemy; no remedy is indicated; and though every foot of the film is as full an indictment of war as I ever expect to see, it is clearly also demonstrating the fact that in war many men go well beyond anything which any sort of peace we have known, or are likely to know, makes possible for them. It seems to me a tragic and eternal work of art, concerned with matters which I know are tragic and which I suspect are as eternal, anyhow, as our use of recent scientific triumphs will permit. Both the film and I may be wrong about this, but I am afraid the burden of proof rests with the optimists.

The Lost Weekend

December 22, 1945

While I watched the movie which Billy Wilder and Charles Brackett have made out of Charles Jackson's story about alcoholism, *The Lost Weekend*, I was pretty consistently gratified and excited. When I began to try to review it, I could not forget what Eisentein said, years ago, when he was asked what he thought of Lewis Milestone's *All Quiet on the Western Front*. He said he thought it was a good Ph.D. thesis. I am afraid that applies to *The Lost Weekend*, too. I don't mean that it is stuffy: it is unusually hard, tense, cruel, intelligent, and straightforward. But I see nothing in it that is new, sharply individual, or strongly creative. It is, rather, a skillful restatement, satisfying and easy to overrate in a time of general dereliction and fatuousness, of some sound basic commonplaces.

On that scale, of course, excellent things can be done. I don't see how the drunkard's first experience of the d.t.'s could be improved on by any means except possibly a dragging-out and brutalization of its climax. Frank Faylen's performance as a male nurse is fully as right and powerful; so is a shrieking free-for-all in an alcoholic ward—which is fought, however, by an incredibly mistaken use of "background" music. Ray Milland's performance as the alcoholic Don Birnam is debatable at first, but so absorbed and persuasive as the picture moves along that he all but wins the picture and the doubters over. There are also some first-rate re-creations of place and atmosphere—a soft-leather, soft-noised cocktail lounge, and a perfect setting of the Birnam apartment, and some shots of New York streets and times of day. At best there is a purity of tone and an acuteness about a city and the people in it which belong high in the movies' great classical strain of unforced, naturalistic poetry. While you watch it, it entirely holds you.

Thinking it over, though, there are curious and disappointing things about the picture. Good as he is, Milland is too robust for the best interests of his role; and in the earlier reels, when he is still sober enough to be assessed as a normal human being, it seems clear that neither he nor the director happens to know very much about the particular kind of provincially born, genteelly bred failed-artist Milland is supposed to be playing. None of the other players seem thoroughly at home, either, in the commonplace yet extremely specialized kind of apartment they use, though Philip Terry's gentle performance as the brother is of itself good, and Jane Wyman is knowingly cast as a *Time* researcher. Howard de Silva plays the ambiguous bartender well and with force, but the force and his face, in this context, turn it into ambiguity for little tots. The players miscast as Miss Wyman's ultra-bourgeois parents are probably not to blame, but they turn a sequence where intelligence and restraint would have been particularly gratifying into heavy caricature.

The causes of Don Birnam's alcoholism were not thoroughly controlled or understood, I thought, in the novel. In the movie they hardly exist. It may have been the better part of valor not to try to tackle them, and not to dabble in streams of consciousness, but when you add to this the fact that Mr. Milland cannot convincingly put before you this particular kind of thirsty man, you can see that the picture is bound to lack certain important kinds of depth, warmth, and intensity, not to mention plain dramatic interest. It becomes, too much of the time, just a virtuoso piece about a handsome, practically unidentified maniac. In one or two scenes you get with some force the terrible humiliation which is one of the drunkard's experiences; but considering the over-all quality of the film, it is remarkable how much you seem to have been given, and how little you actually get. There is very little appreciation, for instance, of the many and subtle moods possible in drunkenness; almost no registration of the workings of the several minds inside a drinker's brain; hardly a trace of the narcissism and self-deceit which are so indispensable or of the self-loathing and self-pity which are so invariable; hardly a hint, except through abrupt action, of the desperation of thirst; no hint at all of the many colorings possible in the desperation. The hangovers lack the weakness, sickness, and horrible distortions of time-sense which they need.

It is irrevelant to the carefully developed, finely photographed, wholly objective scheme of the movie, but I cannot help suggesting that many of these failures might have been avoided if the work had been done from a little farther inside. In some respects the method would still have been objective. A few minutes of dead-silent pantomime (*without music, please!*) of deadly weakness, in hangover, for instance, might have made definitive a good deal that is here only sketched; it should be the kind of weakness in which it is virtually unbearable to lift a hand, and for some reason necessary to do much more than that. Much of the wrestling of minds and moods too, I suspect, could have been registered from outside, through lines, business, mere close-up, and posture: Chaplin, after all, has made incredibly complicated things articulate in pantomime. Surely, for one simple instance—most obviously perhaps after the dawn escape from the hospital—it would have been possible to show the abject shattering coldness to which even temperate men are liable; and perhaps also to capture, through it, the sudden annihilating loneliness and fear of God—or whatever more terrifying it may be—which are so common, if peculiar, an experience. For certain other things you would have to take your camera and soundtrack part way inside the mind. Not to mention the curious enhancements and dilations which the outside world takes on for a drunken man—and I don't mean distortions in any "artistic" or "fantastic" sense but only such qualities as withering, euphoria, and tumescence. In the aftermath of drunkenness one is liable to be excruciatingly oversensitive to things touched, and to sound, and to light. Touch would have had to be carried by business—and might surely have been used to convey feverishness as well. Sound and light peculiarities could have been impacted in the film and track by appropriate, dry exaggerations. A knocking radiator, an abrupt auto horn, coupled with the right kind of playing, might have told the audience as much in an instant as an hour of pure objectivity could. The light equivalents of flashing traffic on a sunny autumn day, as Birnam would experience them, might drive an audience moaning from the theater, unless their exact realism were modified into art.

I undershtand that liquor interesh: innerish: intereshtsh are rather worried about thish film. Thash tough.

Shoeshine

October 11, 1947

The elementary beginning of true reason, that is, of reason which involves not merely the forebrain but the entire being, resides, I should think, in the ability to recognize oneself, and others, primarily as human beings, and to recognize the ultimate absoluteness of responsibility of each human being. (I can most briefly suggest what I mean by a genuine recognition of human beings as such by recommending that you see the Italian movie *Shoeshine* and that you compare it in this respect with almost any other movie you care to name.) I am none too sure of my vocabulary, but would suppose this can be called the humanistic attitude. It is still held, no doubt, by scattered individuals all over the world, is still nominally the germinal force of Western civilization, and must still sleep as a potential among almost unimaginably large numbers and varieties of people; but no attitude is more generally subject to disadvantage, dishonor, and misuse today, and no other is so nearly guaranteed extinction. Even among those who preserve a living devotion to it, moreover, few seem to have come by it naturally, as a physical and sensuous fact, as well as a philosophical one; and fewer still give any evidence of enjoying or applying it with any of the enormous primordial energy which, one would suppose, the living fact would inevitably liberate in a living being. I realize that I must be exaggerating when I think of it as hardly existing in a pure and vigorous form anywhere in contemporary art or living, but I doubt that I am exaggerating much: I know, in any case, that *Shoeshine*, because it furnishes really abundant evidence of the vitality of this attitude, seems to stand almost alone in the world, and to be as restoring and jubilant a piece of news as if one had learned that a great hero whom one had thought to be murdered or exiled or corrupted still lives in all his valor.

This is one of the few fully alive, fully rational films ever made. And one of the beauties of it is that its best intelligence seems to have operated chiefly on an instinctual level, forcing the men who made the film, who are I gather no more than very sincere and quite talented, to do better than the best their talents alone might promise them and better, I imagine, than they planned or foresaw. I suspect that all they intended in this story of two street boys who are caught almost by accident into the corrective machinery of the state, and are destroyed, was an effective work of protest, a work of social art; and that it was more out of the aroused natural honesty of their souls, and their complete devotion to their subject, that they went so much deeper. *Shoeshine* is all that a work of social art ought to be, would have to be to have any worth whatever, and almost never is. It is remarkably perceptive and compassionate in its study of authority and of those who embody authority, serve it, and suffer in and under it. It is also the rarest thing in contemporary art—a true tragedy. This tragedy is cross-lighted by pathos, by the youthfulness and innocence of the heroes, and I suspect that the makers of the film were themselves confused by pathos, but it is stern, unmistakable tragedy as well. The heroes would presumably not have been destroyed unless they had been caught into an imposed predicament; but they are destroyed not by the predicament but by their inability under absolutely difficult circumstances to preserve faith and reason toward themselves and toward each other, and by their best traits and noblest needs as well as by their worst traits and ignoblest needs. Moreover, the film is in no sense a despairing or "defeatist" work, as some people feel it is. I have seldom seen the more ardent and virile of the rational and Christian values more firmly defended, or the effects of their absence or misuse more pitifully and terribly demonstrated.

The film is almost uniquely moving and heartening for still another reason. Almost every minute of it has a kind of rashness, magnanimity, and deep, wise emotional directness which, I am convinced, can hardly if at all exist in a piece of work unless those who make it are sure they are at one with a large, eager, realistic general audience: in other words, very large parts of a whole people must have been moved, for a while at least, by the particular kind of aliveness which gives this film its peculiar radiance. When that is the case, men of any talent whatever can hardly help surpassing themselves. But when most of a people are in apathy, or sufficient anxiety to stun the spirit, every talent or hope, no matter in what spirit or attitude it may operate, is reduced to a fraction of its potentiality.

Great works of art, and the best hopes of good living, could come out of this quality of spirit, as out of no other. This film is not a great or for that matter a wholly well-realized work of art. It has some very considerable virtues besides those already mentioned: one of the few poignant and maturely perceived "love stories" ever to reach the screen; beautifully directed playing by all the boys, who are all amateurs, and by several naturalistic and a few well-chosen florid professionals; and an illusion of spontaneity which, considering that the director, Vittorio da Sica, had to put his amateurs through as many as thirty-nine takes for one scene, is one of the pure miracles of fifty years of movies. And in spite of some near-stock characterizations and situations, everyone in the film bulges with a depth and complexity of realness that is immeasurably beyond the hope of mere naturalism; because everybody is perceived as a complete human being, one feels at every moment that almost anything could happen, and that the reasons why any given thing happens are exceedingly complex and constantly shifting their weight. In playwriting, however, and camera work, and cutting, and sound, though it is eloquent, supple, unaffected, and uninhibited, even the very fine best of the film is seldom sharply inventive; one is very frequently moved and pleased, very seldom convinced that anything has been done definitively. Such feeling for form as there is, is more literary than cinematic. But the quality and energy of spirit are so compelling, pervasive, and valiant that I never felt, and cannot feel now, the pain or anger that is almost inevitable in seeing a good thing fall short of its best possibilities.

I gather that this spirit is already fading in Italy; that audiences are wanting and movie people are preparing costume dramas and screen operas. I suppose that it seldom holds a people strongly in focus, for long; it is a terrible pity that no men of genius were able to take advantage of this moment. But a moment which has made it possible for good, less gifted men to make such films as *Open City*, the still better *Shoeshine*, and a few others which, by their reputation, I hope we shall see soon has been by no means completely lost.

Day of Wrath

May 22, 1948

By the time John McCarten's very favorable review of Carl Dreyer's *Day of Wrath* appeared in the *New Yorker*, the picture was through, at the Little Carnegie. It quite possibly wasn't liked during its short run; but it appears to have been killed at the outset by the daily reviewers. Only two of them, Rose Pelswick and Archer Winsten, reviewed it favorably; the next day Winsten—who also stood practically alone for *Monsieur Verdoux* last year—wrote a valiant, sore article in the film's defense, and in contempt for the degenerate taste of most of his colleagues. In the Sunday *Times* for May 9 Bosley Crowther took a swing, in turn, at Winsten, and wrote of the film: "The tax of [Dreyer's] slow and ponderous tempo upon the average person's time is a rather presumptuous imposition for any motion-picture artist to make. Maybe the cultists can take it. But is it justified? Is it art?"

Hearing the slow movement of Beethoven's "Archduke" Trio, Mr. Crowther might find the tax of Beethoven's slow and ponderous tempo upon the average person's time—meaning, one supposes, *his* time—an equally presumptuous imposition, and might dismiss those who don't agree with him as "cultists," into the bargain; but he still would have said nothing which justified him in asking the rhetorical questions, "Is it justified? Is it art?" It is, after all, possible to use slowness as artfully as speed, in moving pictures as well as in music, and the reactions of the average person are seldom a good indication of how well or ill it has been used; and not even reviewers are necessarily any better qualified.

Winsten wrote me that he felt sure that if some exhibitor with a small overhead would reopen the picture, he could make a go of it. Crowther wrote much the same thing in his column: "Skeptics and outraged art lovers will have to catch it in the tea-spots"—by no chance, of course, to be confused with the Itsy-Bitsy Carnegie—"later on." No doubt they will go, and lap up the tea; meanwhile I suspect that a sustaining number of intelligent and unaffected human beings will wander in and enjoy the show. Winsten and McCarten think it is one of the best ever made. I don't care quite that much for it, but of the movies made during the past twenty years I think it is unquestionably one of the dozen or so best worth seeing. I'll write further of it, in the hope that *enough* favorable reviews may prompt some people to ask small-theater exhibitors about it, and may encourage some exhibitors to risk a few days of it, anyhow. I can at least guarantee them, and any prospective customers, that it is a hundred times better than the run of stuff that shows in the art theaters, genially indorsed by the reviewers who flick this one off their cuffs.

Day of Wrath, which is set in seventeenth-century Denmark, is a study of the struggle between good and evil as waged among—and within—witches, those who burned them, and the members of an old man–young wife–stepson triangle. Movies seldom contain any material, except by inadvertence or head-on outrage, which can interest the morally curious; this one contains a good deal, and none of it is inadvertent or outrageous. I particularly respect the film's interest in the deeply entangled interproductiveness of good and evil among several people and within single people; its steep, Lutheran kind of probity—that is, its absolute recognition of the responsibility of the individual, regardless of extenuating or compulsive circumstances; its compassion; and its detachment.

Originally this was a novel. As I watched it I had to realize that it could still as easily be a novel, or a play; nevertheless, Carl Dreyer has done a very hard job beautifully. He has not only preserved an amount of psychological and moral complexity which isn't popularly supposed to be possible in movies; he has also made them very clear visually, as a rule by very simple means. I don't ordinarily like stuff that is shot in the dark or that depends on very slow movement, because these are ordinarily the first resources of the merely solemn, or pretentious, or arty, when they have nothing of what it takes except ambition. Even less do I ordinarily care for "art" references in camera work—approximations, or reproductions, of famous paintings, or a style derived from painting. I'm not sure I can entirely take this in Dreyer's film, though in general his sense of how and why to use what he wants to take from Rembrandt and others seems very just, modest, useful, clear of "culturalism" or mere weakness of personal style; and his one conspicuous derivation—from Rembrandt's "Lesson in Anatomy"—lends more than mere ironic vitality to the watching clergymen in a torture scene.

Dreyer's lighting, and pace, and sound—including his use of dialogue—I wholly respect. My impression is that, short of absurdity, he wants to work close to their respective absolutes of darkness, stasis, and silence, and never to deviate from these absolutes beyond the minimum that is justified. I don't think this is the only good way to work or necessarily the best; but I suspect for instance that Gluck, and Beethoven, in some of their finest music, were acutely aware of silence. I'm not implying that Dreyer has done anything here to approach their work; I do mean that the style he has worked out for this film has a severe, noble purity which very little else in movies or, so far as I know, in contemporary art can approach, or even tries to. By one seeing, anyhow, I don't think there is a single excess in word or lighting or motion, or a single excessive stopping-down of any of these. Dreyer appears to know and to care more about faces than about anything else; it seems to me a sound preference; and since he is served at worst by very good actors and faces and at best by wonderful ones, the finest things in this film are his close-ups. They are held longer than anyone else except Chaplin could dare or afford to hold them; and as a rule they convey the kind of intricate subtlety, mental and spiritual, which one can ordinarily expect to find only in certain kinds of writing.

In these long close-ups, as in much else that he does, Dreyer goes against most of the "rules" that are laid down, even by good people, for making genuine and good motion pictures. In a sense I have to admit that he is far out at the edge rather than close to the center of all that I think might be most productive and original. But there is only one rule for movies that I finally care about: that the film interest the eyes, and do its job through the eyes. Few movie-makers do that, few even of those who are generally well esteemed. Dreyer has never failed to, and I cannot imagine that he ever will. For that reason alone, even if I did not also respect him as one of the few moralists, and classicists, and incorruptible artists, in movies, I would regard him as a master and this film as a quiet masterpiece.

Siegfried Kracauer

Siegfried Kracauer (1889–1966) established himself as one of the most respected cultural critics in the German-speaking world with his articles for the newspaper *Frankfurter Zeitung*, where he worked from 1920 to 1933 alongside Walter Benjamin, Ernst Bloch, and others, and with his book *Ornaments of the Masses* (1927), about cinema, photography, architecture, tourism, and city planning. He was forced to flee the Nazis in 1933 and immigrated to Paris, then in 1939 to the United States. Here, with the help of Guggenheim Foundation grants, he undertook his influential study *From Caligari to Hitler: A Psychological History of the German Film*, on the correspondences between a public's movie fantasies and its subsequent political nightmare. He taught sociology and film and wrote a further study of the movies, *Theory of Film* (1960), which claimed that the medium's strength resided in its capacity to capture "photographic reality."

◆

Introduction to
From Caligari to Hitler

I

When, from 1920 on, German films began to break the boycott established by the Allies against the former enemy, they struck New York, London and Paris audiences as achievements that were as puzzling as they were fascinating.[1] Archetype of all forthcoming postwar films, *The Cabinet of Dr. Caligari* aroused passionate discussions. While one critic called it "the first significant attempt at the expression of a creative mind in the medium of cinematography,"[2] another stated: "It has the odor of tainted food. It leaves a taste of cinders in the mouth."[3] In exposing the German soul, the postwar films seemed to make even more of a riddle of it. Macabre, sinister, morbid: these were the favorite adjectives used in describing them.

With the passage of time the German movies changed themes and modes

---

[1]Lubitsch's historical costume film *Passion*—the first German production to be brought to this country—was shown at New York late in 1920. In April 1921, there followed the New York release of *The Cabinet of Dr. Caligari*.

[2]Rotha, *Film Till Now*, p. 178.

[3]Amiguet, *Cinéma! Cinéma!*, p. 87.

of representation. But despite all changes they preserved certain traits typical of their sensational start—even after 1924, a year considered the beginning of a long period of decline. In the appraisal of these traits complete unanimity has been reached among American and European observers. What they most admire is the talent with which, from the time of *Caligari*, German film directors marshaled the whole visual sphere: their outspoken feeling for impressive settings, their virtuosity in developing action through appropriate lighting. Connoisseurs also appreciate the conspicuous part played in German films by a camera which the Germans were the first to render completely mobile. In addition, there is no expert who would not acknowledge the organizational power operative in these films—a collective discipline which accounts for the unity of narrative as well as for the perfect integration of lights, settings and actors.[4] Owing to such unique values, the German screen exerted world-wide influence, especially after the total evolution of its studio and camera devices in *The Last Laugh* (1924) and *Variety* (1925). "It was the German camera-work (in the fullest sense of that term) which most deeply impressed Hollywood."[5] In a characteristic expression of respect, Hollywood hired all the German film directors, actors and technicians it could get is hands on. France, too, proved susceptible to screen manners on the other side of the Rhine. And the classic Russian films benefited by the German science of lighting.[6]

Admiration and imitation, however, need not be based on intrinsic understanding. Much has been written about the German cinema, in a continual attempt to analyze its exceptional qualities and, if possible, to solve the disquieting problems bound up with its existence. But this literature, essentially aesthetic, deals with films as if they were autonomous structures. For example, the question as to why it was in Germany that the camera first reached complete mobility has not even been raised. Nor has the evolution of the German cinema been grasped. Paul Rotha, who along with the collaborators of the English film magazine *Close Up* early recognized the artistic merits of German films, confines himself to a merely chronological scheme. "In surveying the German cinema from the end of the war until the coming of the American dialogue film," he says, "the output may roughly be divided into three groups. Firstly, the theatrical costume picture; secondly, the big middle period of the studio art films; and thirdly, the decline of the German film in

[4]Rotha, *Film Till Now*, pp. 177–78; Barry, *Program Notes*, Series I, program 4, and Series III, program 2; Potamkin, "Kino and Lichtspiel," *Close Up*, Nov. 1929, p. 388; Vincent, *Histoire de l'Art Cinématographique*, pp. 139–40.

[5]Barry, *Program Notes*, Series I, program 4.

[6]Jahier, "42 Ans de Cinéma," *Le Rôle intellectuel du Cinéma*, p. 86.

order to fall into line with the American 'picture-sense' output."[7] Why these three groups of films were bound to follow each other, Rotha does not try to explain. Such external accounts are the rule. They lead straight into dangerous misconceptions. Attributing the decline after 1924 to the exodus of important German film people and American interference in German film business, most authors dispose of the German pictures of the time by qualifying them as "Americanized" or "internationalized" products.[8] It will be seen that these allegedly "Americanized" films were in fact true expressions of contemporaneous German life. And, in general, it will be seen that the technique, the story content, and the evolution of the films of a nation are fully understandable only in relation to the actual psychological pattern of this nation.

II

The films of a nation reflect its mentality in a more direct way than other artistic media for two reasons:

First, films are never the product of an individual. The Russian film director Pudovkin emphasizes the collective character of film production by identifying it with industrial production: "The technical manager can achieve nothing without foremen and workmen and their collective effort will lead to no good result if every collaborator limits himself only to a mechanical performance of his narrow function. Team work is that which makes every, even the most insignificant, task a part of the living work and organically connects it to the general task."[9] Prominent German film directors shared these views and acted accordingly. Watching the shooting of a film directed by G. W. Pabst in the French Joinville studios, I noticed that he readily followed the suggestions of his technicians as to details of the settings and the distribution of lights. Pabst told me that he considered contributions of that kind invaluable. Since any film production unit embodies a mixture of heterogeneous interests and inclinations, teamwork in this field tends to exclude arbitrary handling of screen material, suppressing individual peculiarities in favor of traits common to many people.[10]

Second, films address themselves, and appeal, to the anonymous multi-

---

[7]Rotha, *Film Till Now*, p. 177.—It should be noted that Rotha expresses the views then held of the German movies by French and English film aesthetes, although his book is more vigorous and perceptive than those which had preceded it.

[8]Bardèche and Brasillach, *History of Motion Pictures*, p. 258 ff.; Vincent, *Histoire de l'Art Cinématographique*, pp. 161–62; Rotha, *Film Till Now*, pp. 176–77; Jeanne, "Le Cinéma Allemand," *L'Art Cinématographique*, VIII, 42 ff.; etc.

[9]Pudovkin, *Film Technique*, p. 136.

[10]Balázs, *Der Geist des Films*, pp. 187–88.

tude. Popular films—or, to be more precise, popular screen motifs—can therefore be supposed to satisfy existing mass desires. It has occasionally been remarked that Hollywood manages to sell films which do not give the masses what they really want. In this opinion Hollywood films more often than not stultify and misdirect a public persuaded by its own passivity and by overwhelming publicity into accepting them. However, the distorting influence of Hollywood mass entertainment should not be overrated. The manipulator depends upon the inherent qualities of his material; even the official Nazi war films, pure propaganda products as they were, mirrored certain national characteristics which could not be fabricated.[11] What holds true of them applies all the more to the films of a competitive society. Hollywood cannot afford to ignore spontaneity on the part of the public. General discontent becomes apparent in waning box-office receipts, and the film industry, vitally interested in profit, is bound to adjust itself, so far as possible, to the changes of mental climate.[12] To be sure, American audiences receive what Hollywood wants them to want; but in the long run public desires determine the nature of Hollywood films.[13]

III

What films reflect are not so much explicit credos as psychological dispositions—those deep layers of collective mentality which extend more or less below the dimension of consciousness. Of course, popular magazines and broadcasts, bestsellers, ads, fashions in language and other sedimentary products of a people's cultural life also yield valuable information about predominant attitudes, widespread inner tendencies. But the medium of the screen exceeds these sources in inclusiveness.

Owing to diverse camera activities, cutting and many special devices, films are able, and therefore obliged, to scan the whole visible world. This effort results in what Erwin Panofsky in a memorable lecture defined as the "dynamization of space": "In a movie theater . . . the spectator has a fixed seat, but only physically. . . . Aesthetically, he is in permanent motion, as his eye identifies itself with the lens of the camera which permanently shifts in distance and direction. And the space presented to the spectator is as movable

---

[11]See the analyses of these films in the Supplement.

[12]Cf. Farrell, "Will the Commercialization of Publishing Destroy Good Writing?" *New Directions*, 9, 1946, p. 26.

[13]In pre-Hitler Germany, the film industry was less concentrated than in this country. Ufa was preponderant without being omnipotent, and smaller companies carried on beside the bigger ones. This led to a diversity of products, which intensified the reflective function of the German screen.

as the spectator is himself. Not only do solid bodies move in space, but space itself moves, changing, turning, dissolving and recrystallizing. . . ."[14]

In the course of their spatial conquests, films of fiction and films of fact alike capture innumerable components of the world they mirror: huge mass displays, casual configurations of human bodies and inanimate objects, and an endless succession of unobtrusive phenomena. As a matter of fact, the screen shows itself particularly concerned with the unobtrusive, the normally neglected. Preceding all other cinematic devices, close-ups appeared at the very beginning of the cinema and continued to assert themselves throughout its history. "When I got to directing films," Erich von Stroheim told an interviewer, "I would work day and night, without food, without sleeping sometimes, to have every detail perfect, even to descriptions of how facial expressions should change."[15] Films seem to fulfill an innate mission in ferreting out minutiae.

Inner life manifests itself in various elements and conglomerations of external life, especially in those almost imperceptible surface data which form an essential part of screen treatment. In recording the visible world—whether current reality or an imaginary universe—films therefore provide clues to hidden mental processes. Surveying the era of silent films, Horace M. Kallen points to the revealing function of close-ups: "Slight actions, such as the incidental play of the fingers, the opening or clenching of a hand, dropping a handkerchief, playing with some apparently irrelevant object, stumbling, falling, seeking and not finding and the like, became the visible hieroglyphs of the unseen dynamics of human relations. . . ."[16] Films are particularly inclusive because their "visible hieroglyphs" supplement the testimony of their stories proper. And permeating both the stories and the visuals, the "unseen dynamics of human relations" are more or less characteristic of the inner life of the nation from which the films emerge.

That films particularly suggestive of mass desires coincide with outstanding box-office successes would seem a matter of course. But a hit may cater only to one of many coexisting demands, and not even to a very specific one. In her paper on the methods of selection of films to be preserved by the Library of Congress, Barbara Deming elaborates upon this point: "Even if one could figure out . . . which were the most popular films, it might turn out that in saving those at the top, one would be saving the same dream over and over again . . . and losing other dreams which did not happen to appear in the

[14]Panofsky, "Style and Medium in the Moving Pictures," *transition*, 1937, pp. 124–25.
[15]Lewis, "Erich von Stroheim . . . ," *New York Times*, June 22, 1941.
[16]Kallen, *Art and Freedom*, II, 809.

most popular individual pictures but did appear over and over again in a great number of cheaper, less popular pictures."[17] What counts is not so much the statistically measurable popularity of films as the popularity of their pictorial and narrative motifs. Persistent reiteration of these motifs marks them as outward projections of inner urges. And they obviously carry most symptomatic weight when they occur in both popular and unpopular films, in grade B pictures as well as in superproductions. This history of the German screen is a history of motifs pervading films of all levels.

IV

To speak of the peculiar mentality of a nation by no means implies the concept of a fixed national character. The interest here lies exclusively in such collective dispositions or tendencies as prevail within a nation at a certain stage of its development. What fears and hopes swept Germany immediately after World War I? Questions of this kind are legitimate because of their limited range; incidentally, they are the only ones which can be answered by an appropriate analysis of the films of the time. In other words, this book is not concerned with establishing some national character pattern allegedly elevated above history, but it is concerned with the psychological pattern of a people at a particular time. There is no lack of studies covering the political, social, economic and cultural history of the great nations. I propose to add to these well-known types that of a psychological history.

It is always possible that certain screen motifs are relevant only to part of the nation, but caution in this respect should not prejudice one against the existence of tendencies affecting the nation as a whole. They are the less questionable as common traditions and permanent interrelationship between the different strata of the population exert a unifying influence in the depths of collective life. In pre-Nazi Germany, middle-class penchants penetrated all strata; they competed with the political aspirations of the Left and also filled the voids of the upper-class mind. This accounts for the nation-wide appeal of the German cinema—a cinema firmly rooted in middle-class mentality. From 1930 to 1933, the actor Hans Albers played the heroes of films in which typically bourgeois daydreams found outright fulfillment; his exploits gladdened the hearts of worker audiences, and in *Mädchen in Uniform* we see his photograph worshiped by the daughters of aristocratic families.

Scientific convention has it that in the chain of motivations national

---

[17]Deming, "The Library of Congress Film Project: Exposition of a Method," *Library of Congress Quarterly*, 1944, p. 20.

characteristics are effects rather than causes—effects of natural surroundings, historic experiences, economic and social conditions. And since we are all human beings, similar external factors can be expected to provoke analogous psychological reactions everywhere. The paralysis of minds spreading throughout Germany between 1924 and 1929 was not at all specifically German. It would be easy to show that under the influence of analogous circumstances a similar collective paralysis occurs—and has occurred—in other countries as well.[18] However, the dependence of a people's mental attitudes upon external factors does not justify the frequent disregard of these attitudes. Effects may at any time turn into spontaneous causes. Notwithstanding their derivative character, psychological tendencies often assume independent life, and, instead of automatically changing with ever-changing circumstances, become themselves essential springs of historical evolution. In the course of its history every nation develops dispositions which survive their primary causes and undergo a metamorphosis of their own. They cannot simply be inferred from current external factors, but, conversely, help determine reactions to such factors. We are all human beings, if sometimes in different ways. These collective dispositions gain momentum in cases of extreme political change. The dissolution of political systems results in the decomposition of psychological systems, and in the ensuing turmoil traditional inner attitudes, now released, are bound to become conspicuous, whether they are challenged or endorsed.

V

That most historians neglect the psychological factor is demonstrated by striking gaps in our knowledge of German history from World War I to Hitler's ultimate triumph—the period covered in this book. And yet the dimensions of event, milieu and ideology have been thoroughly investigated. It is well known that the German "Revolution" of November 1918 failed to revolutionize Germany; that the then omnipotent Social Democratic Party proved omnipotent only in breaking the backbone of the revolutionary forces, but was incapable of liquidating the army, the bureaucracy, the big-estate owners and the moneyed classes; that these traditional powers actually continued to govern the Weimar Republic which came into shadowy being after 1919. It is also known how hard the young Republic was pressed by the political consequences of the defeat and the stratagems of the leading German industrialists and financiers who unrestrainedly upheld inflation, impoverishing the old middle class.

---

[18]Of course, such similarities never amount to more than surface resemblances. External circumstances are nowhere strictly identical, and whatever psychological tendency they entail comes true within a texture of other tendencies which color its meaning.

Finally, one knows that after the five years of the Dawes Plan—that blessed era of foreign loans so advantageous to big business—the economic world crisis dissolved the mirage of stabilization, destroyed what was still left of middle-class background and democracy, and completed the general despair by adding mass unemployment. It was in the ruins of "the system" which had never been a true structure that the Nazi spirit flourished.[19]

But these economic, social and political factors do not suffice to explain the tremendous impact of Hitlerism and the chronic inertia in the opposite camp. Significantly, many observant Germans refused until the last moment to take Hitler seriously, and even after his rise to power considered the new regime a transitory adventure. Such opinions at least indicate that there was something unaccountable in the domestic situation, something not to be inferred from circumstances within the normal field of vision.

Only a few analyses of the Weimar Republic hint at the psychological mechanisms behind the inherent weakness of the Social Democrats, the inadequate conduct of the communists and the strange reactions of the German masses.[20] Franz Neumann is forced to explain the failure of the communists partly in terms of "their inability to evaluate correctly the psychological factors and sociological trends operating among German workers. . . ." Then he adds to a statement on the Reichstag's limited political power the revealing remark: "Democracy might have survived none the less—but only if the democratic value system had been firmly rooted in the society. . . ."[21] Erich Fromm amplifies this by contending that the German workers' psychological tendencies neutralized their political tenets, thus precipitating the collapse of the socialist parties and the trade-unions.[22]

The behavior of broad middle-class strata also seemed to be determined by overwhelming compulsions. In a study published in 1930 I pointed out the pronounced "white-collar" pretensions of the bulk of German employees, whose economic and social status in reality bordered on that of the workers, or was even inferior to it.[23] Although these lower middle-class people could no longer hope for bourgeois security, they scorned all doctrines and ideals more in harmony with their plight, maintaining attitudes that had lost any basis in reality. The consequence was mental forlornness: they persisted in a kind of

[19]Cf. Rosenberg, *Geschichte der Deutschen Republik*; Schwarzschild, *World in Trance*; etc.
[20]Outstanding among these analyses is Horkheimer, ed., *Studien über Autorität und Familie*; see especially Horkheimer, "Theoretische Entwürfe über Autorität und Familie," pp. 3–76.
[21]Neumann, *Behemoth*, pp. 18–19, 25.
[22]Fromm, *Escape from Freedom*, p. 281.
[23]Cf. Kracauer, *Die Angestellten*.

vacuum which added further to their psychological obduracy. The conduct of the petty bourgeoisie proper was particularly striking. Small shopkeepers, tradesmen and artisans were so full of resentments that they shrank from adjusting themselves. Instead of realizing that it might be in their practical interest to side with democracy, they preferred, like the employees, to listen to Nazi promises. Their surrender to the Nazis was based on emotional fixations rather than on any facing of facts.

Thus, behind the overt history of economic shifts, social exigencies and political machinations runs a secret history involving the inner dispositions of the German people. The disclosure of these dispositions through the medium of the German screen may help in the understanding of Hitler's ascent and ascendancy.

1947

Robert Warshow

Robert Warshow (1917–1955) brought a new note of moral and intellectual seriousness to the practice of American film criticism—not so much by dwelling on the heights of film art as by dissecting the average or artistically mixed motion picture with a clarity and probity that unveiled its soul. Warshow was a consummate essayist, structuring his pieces with through-lines of suspense by putting hard questions to himself and attempting to answer them. As with another great essayist of the time, George Orwell, Warshow comes across as a fundamentally decent, honest man who will sift through his conscience and excavate ambivalences toward a public figure or aspect of popular culture (Orwell on Gandhi and detective stories, Warshow on Chaplin and comic books). That Warshow was indeed a decent man in his personal life seems evident; but beyond that he fashioned a persona composed of candor and reticence that skillfully conveyed this Humane Everyman impression in print. It helped to have written in the postwar years of 1946–1955, a highwater period for literary journals such as *Partisan Review* and *Commentary*, which provided Warshow with the kind of cultivated (though not necessarily film-cultured) readers to whom and for whom he spoke directly, and who would most appreciate his scrupulous examination of American popular culture. His "The Gangster as Tragic Hero" is a classic prose statement, saying a great deal in a small space about both the screen genre and the national characteristics it illuminates. Here, as elsewhere, Warshow's underlying theme was the specific character of American loneliness, a variation of what sociologist David Reisman called "the lonely crowd." In addition to Warshow's sociological grasp of American myths, he also had an astute understanding of film aesthetics. He died at age 37 of a heart attack; later his writings were collected in *The Immediate Experience*, a much-treasured, unavoidably slender, posthumous volume still in print.

◆

The Gangster as Tragic Hero

America, as a social and political organization, is committed to a cheerful view of life. It could not be otherwise. The sense of tragedy is a luxury of aristocratic societies, where the fate of the individual is not conceived of as having a direct and legitimate political importance, being determined by a fixed and supra-political—that is, non-controversial—moral order or fate. Modern equalitarian societies, however, whether democratic or authoritarian in their political forms, always base themselves on the claim that they are making life happier; the avowed function of the modern state, at least in its ultimate terms, is not only to regulate social relations, but also to determine the quality and the possibilities of human life in general. Happiness thus becomes the chief political issue—in a sense, the only political issue—and for that reason it can never be treated as an issue at all. If an American or a Russian is unhappy, it implies a certain reprobation of his society, and therefore, by a logic of which we can all recognize the necessity, it becomes an obligation of citizenship to be cheerful; if the authorities find it necessary, the citizen may even be compelled to make a public display of his cheerfulness on important occasions, just as he may be conscripted into the army in time of war.

Naturally, this civic responsibility rests most strongly upon the organs of mass culture. The individual citizen may still be permitted his private unhappiness so long as it does not take on political significance, the extent of this tolerance being determined by how large an area of private life the society can accommodate. But every production of mass culture is a public act and must conform with accepted notions of the public good. Nobody seriously questions the principle that it is the function of mass culture to maintain public morale, and certainly nobody in the mass audience objects to having his morale maintained.[1] At a time when the normal condition of the citizen is a state of anxiety, euphoria spreads over our culture like the broad smile of an idiot. In terms of attitudes towards life, there is very little difference between a "happy" movie like *Good News*, which ignores death and suffering, and a "sad" movie like *A Tree Grows in Brooklyn*, which uses death and suffering as incidents in the service of a higher optimism.

But, whatever its effectiveness as a source of consolation and a means of pressure for maintaining "positive" social attitudes, this optimism is fundamentally satisfying to no one, not even to those who would be most disoriented without its support. Even within the area of mass culture, there always exists a current of opposition, seeking to express by whatever means are available to it that sense of desperation and inevitable failure which optimism itself helps to create. Most often, this opposition is confined to rudimentary or semiliterate forms: in mob politics and journalism, for example, or in certain kinds of religious enthusiasm. When it does enter the field of art, it is likely to be dis-

[1] In her testimony before the House Committee on Un-American Activities, Mrs. Leila Rogers said that the movie *None But the Lonely Heart* was un-American because it was gloomy. Like so much else that was said during the unhappy investigation of Hollywood, this statement was at once stupid and illuminating. One knew immediately what Mrs. Rogers was talking about; she had simply been insensitive enough to carry her philistinism to its conclusion.

guised or attenuated: in an unspecific form of expression like jazz, in the basically harmless nihilism of the Marx Brothers, in the continually reasserted strain of hopelessness that often seems to be the real meaning of the soap opera. The gangster film is remarkable in that it fills the need for disguise (though not sufficiently to avoid arousing uneasiness) without requiring any serious distortion. From its beginnings, it has been a consistent and astonishingly complete presentation of the modern sense of tragedy.[2]

In its initial character, the gangster film is simply one example of the movies' constant tendency to create fixed dramatic patterns that can be repeated indefinitely with a reasonable expectation of profit. One gangster film follows another as one musical or one Western follows another. But this rigidity is not necessarily opposed to the requirements of art. There have been very successful types of art in the past which developed such specific and detailed conventions as almost to make individual examples of the type interchangeable. This is true, for example, of Elizabethan revenge tragedy and Restoration comedy.

For such a type to be successful means that its conventions have imposed themselves upon the general consciousness and become the accepted vehicles of a particular set of attitudes and a particular aesthetic effect. One goes to any individual example of the type with very definite expectations, and originality is to be welcomed only in the degree that it intensifies the expected experience without fundamentally altering it. Moreover, the relationship between the conventions which go to make up such a type and the real experience of its audience or the real facts of whatever situation it pretends to describe is of only secondary importance and does not determine its aesthetic force. It is only in an ultimate sense that the type appeals to its audience's experience of reality; much more immediately, it appeals to previous experience of the type itself: it creates its own field of reference.

Thus the importance of the gangster film, and the nature and intensity of its emotional and aesthetic impact, cannot be measured in terms of the place of the gangster himself or the importance of the problem of crime in American life. Those European movie-goers who think there is a gangster on every corner in New York are certainly deceived, but defenders of the "positive" side of American culture are equally deceived if they think it relevant to point out that most Americans have never seen a gangster. What matters is that the

---

[2]Efforts have been made from time to time to bring the gangster film into line with the prevailing optimism and social constructiveness of our culture; *Kiss of Death* is a recent example. These efforts are usually unsuccessful; the reasons for their lack of success are interesting in themselves, but I shall not be able to discuss them here.

experience of the gangster *as an experience of art* is universal to Americans. There is almost nothing we understand better or react to more readily or with quicker intelligence. The Western film, though it seems never to diminish in popularity, is for most of us no more than the folklore of the past, familiar and understandable only because it has been repeated so often. The gangster film comes much closer. In ways that we do not easily or willingly define, the gangster speaks for us, expressing that part of the American psyche which rejects the qualities and the demands of modern life, which rejects "Americanism" itself.

The gangster is the man of the city, with the city's language and knowledge, with its queer and dishonest skills and its terrible daring, carrying his life in his hands like a placard, like a club. For everyone else, there is at least the theoretical possibility of another world—in that happier American culture which the gangster denies, the city does not really exist; it is only a more crowded and more brightly lit country—but for the gangster there is only the city; he must inhabit it in order to personify it: not the real city, but that dangerous and sad city of the imagination which is so much more important, which is the modern world. And the gangster—though there are real gangsters —is also, and primarily, a creature of the imagination. The real city, one might say, produces only criminals; the imaginary city produces the gangster: <u>he is what we want to be and what we are afraid we may become.</u>

Thrown into the crowd without background or advantages, with only those ambiguous skills which the rest of us—the real people of the real city—can only pretend to have, the gangster is required to make his way, to make his life and impose it on others. Usually, when we come upon him, he has already made his choice or the choice has already been made for him, it doesn't matter which: we are not permitted to ask whether at some point he could have chosen to be something else than what he is.

The gangster's activity is actually a form of rational enterprise, involving fairly definite goals and various techniques for achieving them. But this rationality is usually no more than a vague background; we know, perhaps, that the gangster sells liquor or that he operates a numbers racket; often we are not given even that much information. So his activity becomes a kind of pure criminality: he hurts people. Certainly our response to the gangster film is most consistently and most universally a response to sadism; we gain the double satisfaction of participating vicariously in the gangster's sadism and then seeing it turned against the gangster himself.

But on another level the quality of irrational brutality and the quality of rational enterprise become one. Since we do not see the rational and routine aspects of the gangster's behavior, the practice of brutality—the quality of unmixed criminality—becomes the totality of his career. At the same time, we are always conscious that the whole meaning of this career is a drive for success: the typical gangster film presents a steady upward progress followed by a very precipitate fall. Thus brutality itself becomes at once the means to success and the content of success—a success that is defined in its most general terms, not as accomplishment or specific gain, but simply as the unlimited possibility of aggression. (In the same way, film presentations of businessmen tend to make it appear that they achieve their success by talking on the telephone and holding conferences and that success *is* talking on the telephone and holding conferences.)

From this point of view, the initial contact between the film and its audience is an agreed conception of human life: that man is a being with the possibilities of success or failure. This principle, too, belongs to the city; one must emerge from the crowd or else one is nothing. On that basis the necessity of the action is established, and it progresses by inalterable paths to the point where the gangster lies dead and the principle has been modified: there is really only one possibility—failure. The final meaning of the city is anonymity and death.

In the opening scene of *Scarface*, we are shown a successful man; we know he is successful because he has just given a party of opulent proportions and because he is called Big Louie. Through some monstrous lack of caution, he permits himself to be alone for a few moments. We understand from this immediately that he is about to be killed. No convention of the gangster film is more strongly established than this: it is dangerous to be alone. And yet the very conditions of success make it impossible not to be alone, for success is always the establishment of an *individual* pre-eminence that must be imposed on others, in whom it automatically arouses hatred; the successful man is an outlaw. The gangster's whole life is an effort to assert himself as an individual, to draw himself out of the crowd, and he always dies *because* he is an individual; the final bullet thrusts him back, makes him, after all, a failure. "Mother of God," says the dying Little Caesar, "is this the end of Rico?"—speaking of himself thus in the third person because what has been brought low is not the undifferentiated *man*, but the individual with a name, the gangster, the success; even to himself he is a creature of the imagination. (T. S. Eliot has pointed out that a number of Shakespeare's tragic heroes have this trick of looking at themselves dramatically; their true identity, the thing that is destroyed when they die, is something outside themselves—not a man, but a style of life, a kind of meaning.)

At bottom, the gangster is doomed because he is under the obligation to succeed, not because the means he employs are unlawful. In the deeper layers of the modern consciousness, *all* means are unlawful, every attempt to succeed is an act of aggression, leaving one alone and guilty and defenseless among enemies: one is *punished* for success. This is our intolerable dilemma: that failure is a kind of death and success is evil and dangerous, is—ultimately—impossible. The effect of the gangster film is to embody this dilemma in the person of the gangster and resolve it by his death. The dilemma is resolved because it is *his* death, not ours. We are safe; for the moment, we can acquiesce in our failure, we can choose to fail.

1948

A Feeling of Sad Dignity

Beneath all the social meanings of Chaplin's art there is one insistent personal message that he is conveying to us all the time. It is the message of most entertainers, maybe, but his especially because he is so great an entertainer. "Love me"—he has asked this from the beginning, buttering us up with his sweet ways and his calculated graceful misadventures, with those exquisite manners so perfectly beside the point, with that honeyed glance he casts at us so often, lips pursed in an outrageous simper, eyebrows and mustache moving in frantic invitation. Love me. And we have, apparently, loved him, though with such undercurrents of revulsion as might be expected in response to so naked a demand.

Does he love us? This is a strange question to ask of an artist. But it is Chaplin himself who puts it in our mouths, harping on love until we are forced almost in self-defense to say: what about *you*? He does not love us; and maybe he doesn't love anything. Even in his most genial moments we get now and then a glimpse of how cold a heart has gone into his great blaze. Consider the scene in *City Lights* when he tactfully permits the blind girl to unravel his underwear in the belief that she is rolling up her knitting wool; the delicacy of feeling is wonderful, all right—who else could have conceived the need for this particular kindness? —but it is he, that contriving artist there, who has created the occasion for the delicacy in the first place. No, the warmth that comes from his image on the screen is only our happy opportunity to love him. He has no love to spare, he is too busy pushing his own demand: love *me*, love *me*, poor

Charlie, sweet Charlie. Probably he even despises us because we have responded so readily to his blandishments, and also because we can never respond enough.

If there was any doubt before, surely *Monsieur Verdoux* made things clear. It gives us the Tramp no longer defeated by his graces but suddenly turning them to account, master of himself and all around him. And what is this mastery? —Verdoux is a murderer. I know very well that Verdoux is not the Tramp, but he rises from the ashes of the Tramp. In their separate ways they both represent the private life of cultivation and sensibility in its opposition to society with its crowds and wars and policemen. If the Tramp had an unconscious (which is not possible), it might make him dream of being Verdoux, for Verdoux's murders are committed so that he can carry on his own idyll with his own Blind Girl; it is true that the idyll is utterly overshadowed by the murders, but this may tell us as much about idylls as it does about murder. *Monsieur Verdoux* is a cold and brilliant movie, perhaps more brilliant than anything else ever done in the movies, but we must make a certain effort of will to like it, for it gives us no clear moral framework, no simple opportunities for sentiment, and not even, despite Verdoux's continual "philosophical" pronouncements, any discernible "message," but most of all an unremitting sensation of the absence of love. The effort should be made. It is no part of Chaplin's function as an artist to love us or anyone, and I do not offer these observations as a complaint.

But if *Monsieur Verdoux* was a disturbing experience for Chaplin's audience, it must have been a truly painful one for Chaplin himself. Sweet Charlie had changed his public personality, or at any rate had thrown off its more agreeable disguises, revealing what he must have thought a more serious and in that sense more "real" aspect of himself. And the experiment was apparently disastrous; nobody loved him any more: the "true" Chaplin was repulsive. There was even an organized campaign against the movie, which, though it ostensibly concentrated its fire on Chaplin's personal and political behavior, could be successful only because *Monsieur Verdoux* was so forbidding. When this campaign culminated some years later in the Attorney General's suggestion that Chaplin, then in Europe, might not be permitted to re-enter this country, there were surprisingly few Americans who cared. We can say easily enough that this is a national shame: once again America has rejected one of her great artists. And Chaplin, no doubt, is only too ready to say the same thing; he has said it, in fact, as crudely and stupidly as possible, by his recent acceptance of the "World Peace Prize." But for him, who has asked so insistently for our love, there must be more to it than that; there must be the possibility that he has given himself away.

Limelight, made during these years of the great comedian's disgrace and completed just before his departure for Europe, is his apology and, so far as he is capable of such a thing, his self-examination. "The story of a clown who has lost his funny-bone," he called it while it was being made, and he has tried to live up to the candor of this description, presenting himself to us from the "inside" so that we may understand what has happened to him and perhaps give him again the love he has forfeited. Of course it remains a question, with him as with any artist, whether there *is* an "inside"; candor is one of the tools of art. Certainly he does not confess to anything, nor can one imagine what he might confess to if he did. But it is clear at any rate that he asks for clemency. He even brings his five children into court to sway the jury (the three youngest, though they appear for only a moment, would go far with any jury I was on). He makes little mocking references to his personal fortunes: "I've had five wives already; one more or less doesn't bother me." And he smiles at us sweetly as he has done so often in the past, but more gently now as fits his years; only once, in some "imitations" of flowers and trees, does he fully recall the archaic elfishness of the Tramp.

Now and then, it is true, he shows his teeth: as individuals, he tells us, we may possibly be lovable, but in the mass we are "a monster without a head"; Chaplin has the gift of stating such "insights" as if they have occurred to him for the first time, thus somehow redeeming them from banality. But most of the time he is rather humble, acknowledging at least the main point: that he cares for our applause. "What a sad business it is, being funny!" says the Blind Girl of this movie, and Calvero replies with a wry smile: "Yes, it is—when they don't laugh." Then he tries to explain more profoundly: "As a man gets on, he wants to live deeply. A feeling of sad dignity comes over him, and that's fatal for a comic." There is a moment when Calvero, in a dream of his past greatness, stands receiving the applause of an audience; then the smile fades, giving place to a fixed mask of the most extreme sorrow, the applause dies, the theater is empty. Again we are aware of a banality that somehow does not matter. The scene is false—how often we have been asked to believe that the sorrows of a clown are deeper than all other sorows! —but Chaplin has lived with the falsehood and is committed to it. Besides, the statements of a clown are always false, his gestures excessive, his mask painted out of all credibility. *After all*, we are supposed to say, there is something very real in all this—but only "after all."

Perhaps, then, if Chaplin is actually trying to tell the truth, he is trying what is not possible to him, and that is why we find ourselves uneasy in his altered presence. But I don't think he has made that mistake. He is only trying to tell a clown's truth, and the "inside" of a clown, if it exists, must be as distorted as the outside—at any rate if he is a thorough clown. Chaplin is among the subtlest of artists, but he is not corrupted by subtlety. His gestures remain broad, his statements marvelously simple and clear, his ideas self-confidently crude. When Calvero smells gas on entering his house, he looks first at the soles of his shoes to see whether he has stepped into dog's excrement. Even while he lectures on the Spirit of Life to the young girl he has saved from suicide, he remains primarily concerned with such distractions as the smell of kippered herring that has got onto his fingers—not exactly to underline what he is saying, though it has this effect, but simply because he knows a smell is always more arresting than an idea. And after all these past years of developing cinematic "art," Chaplin remains the most innocent of film technicians, using his camera only to seek the most direct means of exposition and his lighting only to illuminate; a clown's first task is to make his point unmistakably: if there is subtlety, it will come. What a world of sophistication has had to pass over Chaplin's head so that he may open this film with the epigraph, "The glamour of limelight, from which age must pass as youth enters. . . ."

Of course we would be wrong to take this epigraph entirely at face value. Chaplin often turns out to be more conscious of what he is doing than we suspect, and he has chosen to preserve the archaic tone. But with whatever reservations, he does certainly believe in what it expresses, in the "glamour of limelight"—which must mean the glamour of his own personality. It is true, perhaps, that he ought to be beyond that by now: we all know, don't we, that applause and "glamour" are not what really matter. But he is willing to admit he is not beyond it, just as he is willing to admit he can't keep his mind on the deeper questions of existence because of the smell of herring that clings to his hands. The joke is, of course, that we can't either: nobody ever gets "beyond" anything; that's probably the one joke there is in the world, and all the clowns have nothing to do but tell it to us over and over—no wonder they see no point in being anything but clear.

But though Calvero can never quite get away from the kippered herring, he keeps trying. Once awakened to the advantages of talking pictures, Chaplin in his last two movies has found it almost impossible to stop talking; it seems to have come upon him that he must bring forth all at once the stored-up wisdom of a lifetime. And like many who have thought to save their deepest statements for the last (Mark Twain is another example), Chaplin turns out to have nothing very illuminating to say; his true profundity is still in his silences. Verdoux, having discovered that men do not really live up to their moral ideas, not only drew the logical conclusion by becoming a murderer, but could not resist making little speeches about his discovery, continually poking us in the ribs for fear we might miss the point. In the end Verdoux turned out to be personally as vulnerable as his logic, and that saved the comedy, though one couldn't be sure how much of Chaplin had gone down with Verdoux. Calvero, quite as much a man of the world as Verdoux and sharing his slightly questionable elegance and half-baked independence of mind, is a more agreeable philosopher, preaching not murder but tolerance, vitality, and love. Yet his tone is not very different; like Verdoux, he is over-impressed with his ideas and must be always laboring the point. Now and then he strikes a real spark: "That's all any of us are—amateurs. We don't live long enough to be anything else." More often he can only make a good try: "Life is a desire, not a meaning." Dying, Calvero can leave us only with this: "The heart and the mind—what an enigma!" Is it this kind of thing the Tramp might have been wanting to say during those years of his silence?

I suppose it is, and I suppose it might have been better if we had never found out. But now that Chaplin has broken the silence, I confess I do not find these platitudes of his quite so distressing or inappropriate as, perhaps, I ought to. To be a clown is not an art of detachment. With whatever deliberation he may contrive his effects, in the end the clown must submit *personally* to humiliation, receiving a custard pie in his own face, falling on his own behind. Even though the fall is not so painful as it looks, it is still a real fall. Every clown, no doubt, dreams that because he has practiced the fall in advance it will not truly touch him, his essential being will remain upright; this is the source of that "tragedy" of a clown's life that we have heard so much about. But if he is a true clown, then his essential being is precisely what consents to the fall, and we who refuse to separate him from his role are more right than he is.

In *Limelight*, as in *Monsieur Verdoux*, Chaplin has got caught in this paradox. He has grown reluctant to submit directly to humiliation and is anxious to be accepted as something "more" than a clown; this is the "feeling of sad dignity" that he speaks of. It is true he also takes great pride in being a clown, but pride itself he uses as a means to deny his identity: we become aware of him suddenly as belonging to a "tradition." Of course there *is* a "tradition" and Chaplin is its highest embodiment, but when he presents himself in that role he has to that extent violated it. He is never more dignified, never less a clown, than in the scenes where he appears as a street singer, dressed handsomely in motley, passing a hat for pennies, thoroughly at ease because he has come back to his roots. "This is the only true theater," he says gesturing at the street and the world; the statement is true as it has always been, and he makes it with the authority that belongs to him, but there is something questionable in his making such a statement at all: it would come better from us who watch him.

Verdoux, despite his pretensions, was still basically a figure of absurdity, clearly unable to understand how one must get along; in his way he was just as "innocent" as the Tramp. Calvero, on the other hand, is not supposed to be in himself a clownish figure, he is just a clown by profession. In fact there must be such a division in Chaplin's personality; if there weren't, he would be insane. But his function as an artist is to demonstrate that in some fundamental sense the division is a false one; when he succeeds in obliterating it, as he was able to do entirely in the character of the Tramp and very largely even as Verdoux, he is closest to the kind of truth that most intimately belongs to him and most deeply implicates his audience. In *Limelight* he makes it very clear that he knows this. But, again, his knowledge is not what counts; a clown knows nothing, he only exists. Finding it necessary to make a direct examination of his problem as an artist, Chaplin is forced to repeat in the structure of the movie itself that division between reality and comedy, between dignity and drunkenness, which is the problem the movie deals with. The scenes of actual clowning are presented simply as stage performances, a kind of documentation of the case of the clown Calvero who has "lost his funny-bone," whereas the movie proper, so to speak, is only occasionally funny, and never very much.

The most disturbing thing about Verdoux was that one did not always know how much he was supposed to be accepted on his own terms, how much Chaplin himself was implicated in Verdoux's murders. With Calvero we are left in no such uncertainty: he is Charles Chaplin "in person" presiding at the telling of his own story and not for a moment relinquishing control. If Chaplin is willing in the role of Calvero to acknowledge his own sense of failure, it is only while making it plain that he will be the one to define what is meant by failure. If he has Calvero die breathing that lame little sentence about the enigma of the heart and the mind, it is not because he sees the sentence as dramatically appropriate, but because he thinks it expresses in itself a profound philosophical and poetic truth. The trouble is that it undeniably does, and there seems to be nothing in Chaplin's education or sensibility to tell him what the sentence lacks. And yet, whatever might be true of his education, has he not shown us over and over a sensibility a hundred times more delicate than our own?

*

Here we come back to that coldness of heart which seems to belong inextricably to Chaplin's genius. It must often have been said of him that he is an embodiment of childhood, and it is perfectly true. His perceptions have the eccentricity of viewpoint and the almost dazzling detailed clarity of a child's perceptions, and carry similar suggestions of unspecific and perhaps unintended depth. His feelings are as definite and as strong as a child's, and as irresistibly appealing. But like a child he is also imprisoned within the limits of his own needs and understanding, and can express no true relation with others. Precisely the lack of such a relation is what makes him a clown—the most childish kind of entertainer—and gives him his clown's subject matter. What is the Tramp but the greatest of all egotists?—an outcast by choice refusing to take the least trouble to understand his fellow men, and yet contriving by his unshakable detachment to put everyone else in the wrong, transforming his rejection of society into society's rejection of him. The Tramp can draw close only to those who are outsiders like him: children, animals, the Blind Girl—the maimed and the innocent. And in the end he is always walking away into the depths of the screen with his back turned. Verdoux, instead of protecting the lonely and innocent, preys on them, though the difference is not so absolute as it might seem: he is just as much a sentimentalist as the Tramp, as he demonstrates in sparing the life of one woman merely because he is touched by her history and because she has read Schopenhauer; and even for his victims he has a kind of icy kindness which might be one of the things that attract them.

Calvero, combining Verdoux's doubtful *savoir faire* with the Tramp's sweetness, is neither the victim of his world nor its victimizer, but a kind of benevolent observer with all the threads of life held loose in his hands. Though we come upon him when he is no longer successful as a performer, he has failed by becoming too good for his audience, too "dignified," not by falling below it. Besides, he is the only one who understands his failure, or if he doesn't exactly understand it, at least his tolerant acceptance of it takes the place of understanding. There has been a significant change in the role of the Blind Girl—this time not blind, of course, but lonely, defeated, and suffering from a functional paralysis of the legs. Having saved her from suicide and reluctantly taken her into his lodgings, Calvero in a few minutes of psychoanalysis discovers the cause of her paralysis and proceeds to cure it. Soon she becomes a ballet star. This moment of her success is when the Tramp would have found himself rejected. But now the girl makes a declaration of love—that declaration which the Tramp never had the courage to make for himself—and though Calvero lets himself be persuaded for a time, it is he who eventually refuses;

he must be the one to decide who loves whom, and he has settled it that she belongs to the young composer (a part played by Chaplin's son). This is no very great renunciation, nor indeed is it presented as one. Calvero has simply avoided an entanglement as the Tramp always did, and he has bettered the Tramp by accomplishing this in such a way as to emphasize his own attractiveness. When he has gone away and the girl after many months finds him again to say she still loves him, he replies with magnificent candor: "Of course you do. You always will."

It is easy to believe him, too, for no one else in the movie is allowed to rival his charm and the mature strength of his presence, or even to become real. The girl herself, though she takes her place readily enough in the gallery of Chaplin's heroines, has less independent power than any who have preceded her. Chiefly, her function is to listen attentively, to offer herself as a passive object for his benevolence, and, since she is not actually blind, to look at him with adoration as once the Tramp would have looked at her; the looks Calvero casts back at her are looks of kindness. As for the young man, his function is to be young and nothing more. Calvero will give way to him because age must give way to youth, fathers must give way to sons, the "glamour of limelight" cannot last forever; that is the theme of the movie. But again Chaplin sets his own terms, and if he yields, it is only in principle: between the young man's stiff, undifferentiated "youth" and Calvero's lively and self-assured "age," there can be no real contest. It is Calvero whom the girl will always love—"of course."

Only among the minor characters is the color of reality allowed to emerge: in the frowzy, small-minded landlady, and in her dreadful friend who appears for just a few seconds and says nothing; in an armless music-hall performer encountered in a bar (later cut out of the film); and most of all in the self-contained, almost grotesquely prosaic street musicians who keep reappearing through the movie as representatives both of the hard everyday world where one must make a living as one can and of the "universal" world of art. In his treatment of these marginal figures Chaplin comes closest to a free and disinterested feeling for others; he could not have made such honest and simple use of them without a certain kind of love, even if this love is expressed sometimes only in the pitilessness of his observation.

The peculiarly stilted quality that troubles one in *Limelight* comes, then, not from any failure of sensibility but from a further narrowing of the field of associations and sympathies in which Chaplin's sensibility can operate, and from a consequent suppression of drama. The Tramp, despite his ultimate frigidity, at least maintained an active flirtation with the world, always escaping in the end but keeping up the excitement of the chase and even hinting strongly that he might like to be caught if only he did not like more to get away. Verdoux, having turned his frigidity into a means of making a living, is necessarily involved with the world from the start, though he tries hard to claim he is not; and he does get caught, to have his head cut off—which is possibly the kind of thing the Tramp was afraid might happen. Calvero is too self-contained either to commit murder like Verdoux or to run away like the Tramp; it would be undignified. He simply does not let anyone approach him. Certainly the five wives have left no traces; the pictures on Calvero's walls are pictures of himself. When the girl is practically forced on him, he hastens to proclaim his detachment (". . . one more or less doesn't bother me") and to lay down the terms of their relation, which is to be "platonic." It does not appear that this prescription is ever violated.

Thus Calvero stands alone on the stage—in the fading "limelight"—and does not so much play out his personal drama as expound it. In the very tones of his voice one can feel his refusal to communicate dramatically. The girl, to whom he does most of his talking, is often little more than a point in space toward which he may orient himself; his words pass over and beyond her— they are not really intended for her at all. At bottom they are probably not even intended for us in the audience—the "monster without a head"—though, like the girl, we are allowed to listen and expected to admire. It is as if the whole movie were one of those dreams in which Calvero, trying to reassert his identity, dreams not of *being* on the stage but of *seeing* himself on the stage. He is his own audience, and his "inside," even to him, is only a mirror image of the outside. When he speaks, it is to hear his voice re-echoing within the isolation of his own being. How could he possibly have learned to sense when his words and postures begin to be false?—he has never watched the faces of those he has pretended to be talking to.

But I am not willing to leave it at that. It is not at all necessary that a clown should be in a true relation with others, or even that he should always be funny; the only necessity is that he should fail and that there should be moments when we are able to imagine that his failure is, "after all," a kind of success. Calvero's failure is clear enough: he cannot get us to take him seriously in the way he wants to be taken. We believe as much as he does in "Life" and the "miracle of consciousness"; it is an impertinence for him to lecture us about these things unless he can be eloquent, and eloquence is beyond him: all he can do is suggest the need for eloquence without ever really attaining it. Even his jokes are too often labored and stuffy. "What can the stars do?" he asks in

his discourse on consciousness. "Nothing!—sit around on their axes." To hear
this from the greatest comedian in the world!

But is his failure also a kind of success? I can only say it is possible to see
it that way. I have no convincing argument to advance against those who see
Limelight as no more than a crude structure of self-pity and banal "philosophy"
interspersed here and there with glimpses of a past greatness. But the crudi-
ties of a great artist always have an extra dimension; Chaplin cannot so easily
divest himself of his talent no matter how he may blunder. Nor can we divest
ourselves of the sense of his presence, perhaps one might say his "tradition":
the face and body that move before us on the screen have belonged also for all
these years to the Tramp, and then to Verdoux; even the voice and the words
come somehow not unexpected. This is an extra-aesthetic element, maybe,
but there it is. One way or another, the movies are always forcing us outside
the boundaries of art; this is one source of their special power. And of Chaplin
perhaps it could even be said that in some sense he has never been an artist at
all—though he is full of arts—but always and only a presence.

Calvero's failure has at least this in common with the Tramp's failure and
Verdoux's: he fails in dead earnest and with a straight face, intelligently prepared for failure, it is true, but not for the particular kind of failure that comes
to him, and never dreaming that his essential worth can be called into doubt.
He is an honest bankrupt, so to speak, doing his best to the very end and concealing no assets; it just happens that the money in his vault is in some way
devalued—not exactly counterfeit, but not altogether sound either. And yet
there is something in the confidence with which he hands it over that makes
one hesitate to examine it closely, at least in his presence. Suppose he should
demand to see what money *we* are paying our debts with? "We're all grubbing
for a living, the best of us," Calvero says once, and he is right as usual, though
uninspired. For he does manage in spite of everything to implicate us in his
failure. He does it not by detachment and true insight—as he might do if he
were the projection of a "real" artist instead of a clown—but, on the contrary,
by the hopeless depth of his own involvement; by his suspicious eagerness to
have us look into his messy, unilluminating, and amateurishly doctored
account books; and above all by the irresistible, brilliant purity of his egotism.

Nothing escapes the deflecting force of this uncompromising self-
absorption. When Calvero philosophizes, he puts all philosophy under a cloud.
Falling miles short of the kind of profundity he wants, he achieves instead a
clown's profundity: we are moved not by what he says, but by his desire to
speak. If he ends up with nothing but a wornout "enigma"—well, so do the

real philosophers. Supposing he were to ask us how one enigma can be better than another, could we give him a clear answer? The gap between Calvero and the philosophers is enormous, but in such gaps a clown has his victories: as Calvero gropes confidently in his darkness, it occurs to one finally that this gap between him and the philosophers is nothing compared to the gap between the philosophers and the truth. Again, when Calvero rhapsodizes on the "miracle of consciousness," he manages to suggest not only that we are all responding to life inadequately, but at the same time, by his aggressive "sincerity," that consciousness may be some kind of fake—and also that the possibility of its being a fake does not matter. And when he speaks with his most genuine emotion about love while demonstrating his own impenetrable isolation, and in his "secondary" role as a performer deflates his own sentiment with a savage little song consisting only of a meaningless repetition of the word "love," then he is striking at us very deeply, for at bottom we all fear we are incapable of love, and that what we call love is only something we wish to receive from others. That Chaplin himself is as much a "victim" in all this as we who watch him is only the completion of the irony. A clown's function is to be ridiculous and to make the world ridiculous with him. In this, Calvero has his success.

It remains to be said, nevertheless, that the famous scene near the end of the movie when Calvero performs on the stage as a comic violinist, with Buster Keaton as his accompanist, represents a kind of success far beyond the complex and unsteady ironies of the earlier parts. In this there is no longer any problem of interpretation and choice, no "victims" and no victories, no shifting of involvements back and forth between the performer and his role and his audience, no society, no egotism, no love or not-love, no ideas—only a perfect unity of the absolutely ridiculous. Perhaps the Tramp's adventure with the automatic feeding machine in *Modern Times* is as funny, but there it is still possible to say that something is being satirized and something else, therefore, upheld. The difficulties that confront Calvero and Keaton in their gentle attempt to give a concert are beyond satire. The universe stands in their way, and not because the universe is imperfect, either, but just because it exists; God himself could not conceive a universe in which these two could accomplish the simplest thing without mishap. It is not enough that the music will not stay on its rack, that the violin cannot be tuned, that the piano develops a kind of malignant disease—the violinist cannot even depend on a minimal consistency in the behavior of his own body. When, on top of all the other misfortunes that can possibly come upon a performer humbly anxious to make an impression, it can happen also that one or both of his legs may capriciously grow shorter while he is on the stage, then he is at the last extreme: nothing is left. Nothing except the deep, sweet patience with which the two unhappy musicians accept these difficulties, somehow confident—out of God knows what reservoir of awful experience—that the moment will come at last when they will be able to play their piece. When that moment does come, it is as happy a moment as one can hope for in the theater. And it comes to us out of that profundity where art, having become perfect, seems no longer to have any implications. The scene is unendurably funny, but the analogies that occur to me are tragic: Lear's "Never, never, never, never, never!" or Kafka's "It is enough that the arrows fit exactly in the wounds they have made."

1954

Ralph Ellison

Ralph Ellison (1914–1994) will always be principally remembered for his great first novel, *Invisible Man* (1952), which won the National Book Award and has since become an unchallenged American classic. He was also a fine essayist and published two collections, *Shadow and Act* (1964) and *Going to the Territory* (1986). As the most honored African-American novelist of his day, he was often called upon to pronounce on social issues, a summons that he both chafed under and accepted in his own restrained, dignified way. The essay below, about Hollywood's awkward treatment of racial themes and black characters in the postwar period, demonstrates Ellison's measured tone, thoughtful subtlety, and immense literary skill in approaching these potentially incendiary matters. He would never compromise for a second or a sentence his commitment to racial justice, but neither would he weaken an argument's eloquence with angry bombast.

◆

The Shadow and the Act

Faulkner has given us a metaphor. When, in the film *Intruder in the Dust*, the young Mississippian Chick Mallison falls into an ice-coated creek on a Negro's farm, he finds that he has plunged into the depth of a reality which constantly reveals itself as the reverse of what it had appeared before his plunge. Here the ice—white, brittle and eggshell-thin—symbolizes Chick's inherited views of the world, especially his Southern conception of Negroes. Emerging more shocked by the air than by the water, he finds himself locked in a moral struggle with the owner of the land, Lucas Beauchamp, the son of a slave who, while aiding the boy, angers him by refusing to act toward him as Southern Negroes are expected to act.

To Lucas, Chick is not only a child but his guest. Thus he not only dries the boy's clothes, but insists that he eat the only food in the house, Lucas's own dinner. When Chick (whose white standards won't allow him to accept the hospitality of a Negro) attempts to pay him, Lucas refuses to accept the money. What follows is one of the most sharply amusing studies of Southern racial ethics to be seen anywhere. Asserting his whiteness, Chick throws the money on the floor, ordering Lucas to pick it up; Lucas, disdaining to quarrel with a child, has Chick's young Negro companion, Aleck Sander, return the coins.

Defeated but still determined, Chick later seeks to discharge his debt by sending Lucas and his wife a gift. Lucas replies by sending Chick a gallon of molasses by—outrage of all Southern Negro outrages!—a white boy on a mule. This is too much, and from that moment it becomes Chick's passion to repay his debt and to see Lucas for once "act like a nigger." The opportunity has come, he thinks, when Lucas is charged with shooting a white man in the back. But instead of humbling himself, Lucas (from his cell) tells, almost orders, Chick to prove him innocent by violating the white man's grave.

In the end we see Chick recognizing Lucas as the representative of those virtues of courage, pride, independence and patience that are usually attributed only to white men—and, in his uncle's words, accepting the Negro as "the keeper of our [the whites'] consciences." This bit of dialogue, coming after the real murderer is revealed as the slain man's own brother, is, when viewed historically, about the most remarkable concerning a Negro ever to come out of Hollywood.

With this conversation, the falling into creeks, the digging up of corpses and the confronting of lynch mobs that mark the plot, all take on a new significance: not only have we been watching the consciousness of a young Southerner grow through the stages of a superb mystery drama, but we have participated in a process by which the role of Negroes in American life has been given what, for the movies, is a startling new definition.

To appreciate fully the significance of *Intruder in the Dust* in the history of Hollywood we must go back to the film that is regarded as the archetype of the modern American motion picture, *The Birth of a Nation*.

Originally entitled *The Clansman*, the film was inspired by another Southern novel, the Reverend Thomas Dixon's work of that title, which also inspired Joseph Simmons to found the Knights of the Ku Klux Klan. (What a role these malignant clergymen have played in our lives!) Retitled *The Birth of a Nation* as an afterthought, it was this film that forged the twin screen image of the Negro as bestial rapist and grinning, eye-rolling clown—stereotypes that are still with us today. Released during 1915, it resulted in controversy, riots, heavy profits and the growth of the Klan. Of it Terry Ramsaye, a historian of the American motion-picture industry writes: "The picture . . . and the K.K.K. secret society, which was the afterbirth of a nation, were sprouted from the same root. In subsequent years they reacted upon each other to the large profit of both. The film presented predigested dramatic experience and thrills. The society made the customers all actors in costume."

Usually *The Birth of a Nation* is discussed in terms of its contributions to cinema technique, but as with every other technical advance since the oceanic

sailing ship, it became a further instrument in the dehumanization of the
Negro. And while few films have gone so far in projecting Negroes in a malignant light, few before the 1940s showed any concern with depicting their
humanity. Just the opposite. In the struggle against Negro freedom, motion
pictures have been one of the strongest instruments for justifying some white
Americans' anti-Negro attitudes and practices. Thus the South, through D. W.
Griffith's genius, captured the enormous myth-making potential of the film
form almost from the beginning. While the Negro stereotypes by no means
made all white men Klansmen, the cinema did, to the extent that audiences
accepted its image of Negroes, make them participants in the South's racial ritual of keeping the Negro "in his place."

After Reconstruction the political question of what was to be done with
Negroes, "solved" by the Hayes-Tilden deal of 1876, came down to the psychological question: "How can the Negro's humanity be evaded?" The problem, arising in a democracy that holds all men as created equal, was a highly
moral one; democratic ideals had to be squared with anti-Negro practices. One
answer was to *deny* the Negro's humanity, a pattern set long before 1915. But
with the release of *The Birth of a Nation* the propagation of subhuman images
of Negroes became financially and dramatically profitable. The Negro as
scapegoat could be sold as entertainment; it could even be exported. If the film
became the main manipulator of the American dream, for Negroes that dream
contained a strong dose of such stuff as nightmares are made of.

We are recalling all this not so much as a means of indicting Hollywood as
by way of placing *Intruder in the Dust*, and such recent films as *Home of the Brave*,
Lost Boundaries and *Pinky*, in perspective. To direct an attack upon Hollywood
would indeed be to confuse portrayal with action, image with reality. In the
beginning was not the shadow but the act, and the province of Hollywood is
not action, but illusion. Actually, the anti-Negro images of the films were (and
are) acceptable because of the existence throughout the United States of an
audience obsessed with an inner psychological need to view Negroes as less
than men. Thus, psychologically and ethically, these negative images constitute justifications for all those acts, legal, emotional, economic and political,
which we label Jim Crow. The anti-Negro image is a ritual object of which
Hollywood is not the creator, but the manipulator. Its role has been that of
justifying the widely held myth of Negro unhumanness and inferiority by
offering entertaining rituals through which that myth could be reaffirmed.

The great significance of the definition of Lucas Beauchamp's role in
Intruder in the Dust is that it makes explicit the nature of Hollywood's changed
attitude toward Negroes. Form being, in the words of Kenneth Burke, "the

psychology of the audience," what is taking place in the American movie patron's mind? Why these new attempts to redefine the Negro's role? What has happened to the audience's mode of thinking?

For one thing, there was the war; for another, there is the fact that the United States' position as a leader in world affairs is shaken by its treatment of Negroes. Thus the thinking of white Americans is undergoing a process of change, and reflecting that change, we find that each of the films mentioned above deals with some basic and unusually negative assumption about Negroes: are Negroes cowardly soldiers? (*Home of the Brave*); are Negroes the real polluters of the South? (*Intruder in the Dust*); have mulatto Negroes the right to pass as white, at the risk of having black babies, or if they have white-skinned children, of having to kill off their "white" identities by revealing to them that they are, alas, Negroes? (*Lost Boundaries*); and, finally, should Negro girls marry white men or—wonderful non sequitur—should they help their race? (*Pinky*).

Obviously these films are not *about* Negroes at all; they are about what whites think and feel about Negroes. And if they are taken as accurate reflectors of that thinking, it becomes apparent that there is much confusion. To make use of Faulkner's metaphor again, the film makers fell upon the eggshell ice but, unlike the child, weren't heavy enough to break it. And being unable to break it, they were unable to discover the real direction of their film narratives. In varying degree, they were unwilling to dig into the grave to expose the culprit, and thus we find them using ingenious devices for evading the full human rights of their Negroes. The result represents a defeat not only of drama, but of purpose.

In *Home of the Brave*, for instance, a psychiatrist tells the Negro soldier that his hysterical paralysis is like that of any other soldier who has lived when his friends have died, and we hear the soldier pronounced cured; indeed, we see him walk away prepared to open a bar and restaurant with a white veteran. But here there is an evasion (and by *evasion* I refer to the manipulation of the audience's attention away from reality to focus it upon false issues), because the guilt from which the Negro is supposed to suffer springs from an incident in which, immediately after his friend has called him a "yellowbelly nigger," he has wished the friend dead—only to see the wish granted by a sniper's bullet.

What happens to this racial element in the motivation of his guilt? The psychiatrist ignores it and becomes a sleight-of-hand artist who makes it vanish by repeating again that the Negro is like everybody else. Nor, I believe, is this accidental, for it is here exactly that we come to the question of whether Negroes can rightfully be expected to risk their lives in an army in which they are slandered and discriminated against. Psychiatry is not, I'm afraid, the answer. The soldier suffers from concrete acts, not hallucinations.

And so with the others. In *Lost Boundaries* the question evaded is whether a mulatto Negro has the right to practice the old American pragmatic philosophy of capitalizing upon one's assets. For after all, whiteness *has* been given an economic and social value in our culture, and for the doctor upon whose life the film is based, "passing" was the quickest and most certain means to success.

Yet Hollywood is uncertain about his right to do this. The film does not render the true circumstances. In real life Dr. Albert Johnson, the Negro doctor who "passed" as white, purchased the thriving practice of a deceased physician in Gorham, New Hampshire, for a thousand dollars. Instead, a fiction is introduced in the film wherein Dr. Carter's initial motivation for "passing" arises after he is refused an internship by dark Negroes in an Atlanta hospital because of his color! It just isn't real, since there are thousands of mulattoes living as Negroes in the South, many of them Negro leaders. The only functional purpose served by this fiction is to gain sympathy for Carter by placing part of the blame for his predicament upon black Negroes. Nor should the irony be missed that part of the sentiment evoked when the Carters are welcomed back into the community is gained by painting Negro life as horrible, a fate worse than a living death. It would seem that in the eyes of Hollywood it is only "white" Negroes who ever suffer—or is it merely the "white" corpuscles of their blood?

Pinky, for instance, is the story of another suffering mulatto, and the suffering grows out of a confusion between race and love. If we attempt to reduce the heroine's problem to sentence form we'd get something like this: "Should white-skinned Negro girls marry white men, or should they inherit the plantations of old white aristocrats (provided they can find any old aristocrats to will them their plantations), or should they live in the South and open nursery schools for black Negroes?" It doesn't follow, but neither does the action. After sitting through a film concerned with interracial marriage, we see it suddenly become a courtroom battle over whether Negroes have the right to inherit property.

Pinky wins the plantation, and her lover, who has read of the fight in the Negro press, arrives and still loves her, race be hanged. But now Pinky decides that to marry him would "violate the race" and that she had better remain a Negro. Ironically, nothing is said about the fact that her racial integrity, whatever that is, was violated before she was born. Her parents are never mentioned in the film. Following the will of the white aristocrat, who, before dying, advises her to "be true to herself," she opens a school for darker Negroes.

But in real life the choice is not between loving or denying one's race. Many couples manage to intermarry without violating their integrity, and indeed their marriage becomes the concrete expression of their integrity. In the film Jeanne Crain floats about like a sleepwalker, which seems to me to be exactly the way a girl so full of unreality would act. One thing is certain: no one is apt to mistake her for a Negro, not even a white one.

And yet despite the absurdities with which these films are laden, they are all worth seeing, and if seen, capable of involving us emotionally. That they do is testimony to the deep centers of American emotion that they touch. Dealing with matters which, over the years, have been slowly charging up with guilt, they all display a vitality which escapes their slickest devices. And naturally enough, one of the most interesting experiences connected with viewing them in predominantly white audiences is the profuse flow of tears and sighs of profound emotional catharsis heard on all sides. It is as though there were some deep relief to be gained merely from seeing these subjects projected upon the screen.

It is here precisely that a danger lies. For the temptation toward self-congratulation which comes from seeing these films and sharing in their emotional release is apt to blind us to the true nature of what is unfolding—or failing to unfold—before our eyes. As an antidote to the sentimentality of these films, I suggest that they be seen in predominantly Negro audiences, for here, when the action goes phony, one will hear derisive laughter, not sobs. (Perhaps this is what Faulkner means about Negroes keeping the white man's conscience.) Seriously, *Intruder in the Dust* is the only film that could be shown in Harlem without arousing unintended laughter, for it is the only one of the four in which Negroes can make complete identification with their screen image. Interestingly, the factors that make this identification possible lie in its depiction not of racial but of human qualities.

Yet in the end, turning from art to life, we must even break with the definition of the Negro's role given us by Faulkner. For when it comes to conscience, we know that in this world each of us, black and white alike, must become the keeper of his own. This, in the deepest sense, is what these four films, taken as a group, should help us realize.

Faulkner himself seems to realize it. In the book *Intruder in the Dust*, Lucas attempts not so much to be the keeper of anyone else's conscience as to preserve his own life. Chick, in aiding Lucas, achieves that view of truth on which his own conscience depends.

1949

Martha Wolfenstein
and Nathan Leites

Given their backgrounds, Martha Wolfenstein (1911–1976) and Nathan Leites (1912–1987) would seem an unlikely pair of film critics. Wolfenstein was a professor of psychiatry and a specialist in child psychology who did important work on the ways children process grief and who collaborated on research studies with the anthropologists Margaret Mead and Ruth Benedict. Leites was an authority on the Soviet Union, best known for applying psychoanalytic principles to the study of world figures such as Stalin. Together, while married, they wrote *Movies: A Psychological Study* (1950), which put Hollywood and the American movie-going public on the couch. This trailblazing (for America; Kracauer had already done it for Germany) inquiry into national character and collective mentality, rather than critiquing individual movies as film art, looked for recurring patterns onscreen that might signal more or less unconscious shifts in contemporary behavior. The pair coolly dissected the narrative contradictions a Hollywood picture might stir up in order to have its cake and eat it too: for instance, arousing deep anxiety for the sake of plot tension and then magically whisking it away with a final kiss.

◆

Got a Match?

When Lauren Bacall appeared in the doorway of a shabby hotel room, gave Humphrey Bogart a long level look and asked in a deliberate throaty voice: Got a match?—when in a later episode she kissed him, and commenting on his impassive reaction, taunted: It's even better when you help— she became a new type of movie heroine (*To Have and Have Not*). She is a woman who approaches men with a man's technique. She presents the man with a provocative, slightly mocking mirror image of himself. Her attraction derives from her combination of masculine and feminine. A man can feel at home with her; she talks his language. In relation to her he experiences none of the discomfort or uncertainty of moving into alien territory, of being required to understand whims, susceptibilities and expectations of a creature different from himself. She does not have the organdy-ruffled femininity of the girl who can be shocked, who must be approached with an artificial delicacy, who holds a man at arm's length while awaiting expressions of fine sentiments. On the other hand, she does not have the equally alien satin couch female quality of the woman who expects elaborate boudoir etiquette and eventual transportation into ecstasy. In contrast to both of these, the masculine-feminine girl has the blunt familiar honesty of the man's world. She provides an answer to the old song, "I'd rather have a buddy than a sweetheart": you can have a sweetheart who's a buddy. Unlike the good girl she admits without euphemisms that she is interested in sex. Unlike the vamp she does not carry an unrelieved aura of it. In her masculine aspect, she is free from the mannishness of women who wanted to be equal to men in a competitive way, felt solidarity with other women, and denied the importance of sex difference. Here a masculine attitude is assumed as an approach to men, and with a constant pleasurable awareness of the difference of sex. This type expresses the stock sentiment of *vive la différence* not by adopting distinctively feminine behavior, but rather by assuming what has been characteristically masculine. It is this combination that we mean to express by calling this type masculine-feminine.

The masculine-feminine girl frequently takes more initiative than the man, both in establishing the initial contact and in sexual approach. This may at first sight look like a reversal of the traditional roles of the sexes. But in effect it rather rectifies the older situation, in which the man was required to assume the initiative, so that an atmosphere of equality results. The girl must prove that she has a masculine attitude; the man is assumed to have it. Another apparent reversal of the usual roles occurs when the girl mockingly reproaches the man for holding out on her (It's even better when you help). Just as a man may, without loss of self-esteem, make repeated overtures to a highly attractive woman though he receives only slight encouragement, this type of heroine continues her approaches to the highly attractive man whom she has chosen even though he maintains for some time an appearance of detachment. While she has announced her readiness, she also maintains a coolly humorous attitude; the man need not feel under pressure from her. She embodies perhaps a man's idealized image of his own courtship behavior.

In *The Strange Love of Martha Ivers*, the heroine assumes the initiative throughout the opening phase of her acquaintance with the hero. She picks him up, using in part stock masculine pick-up lines, in part responses to such lines, without requiring him to give the opening for the response. She is sitting on the steps of her rooming house waiting for a taxi when the hero first appears. She asks him for a match and for the time. Later she offers him a lift in her taxi, and afterwards offers to buy him a drink. She confesses to him that she is lonely, thus giving the reply to the stock male pick-up line (not voiced by the hero): Aren't you lonely? When she learns that the hero is driving to the West

Coast, she asks him to take her with him, again giving a positive response to an unexpressed pick-up intention of the man. When the two have installed themselves in adjacent hotel rooms for the night, she comes to his room to trade a Gideon Bible for a cigarette. Her approach represents the characteristic pretense of maintaining contact with the man for the sake of various incidental services to be obtained or offered. This manifest concern with impersonal matters relieves the relationship of the pressure of sexual or sentimental urgency.

In *The Blue Dahlia*, the hero and heroine first meet when she offers him a lift in her car. In *Notorious*, the hero has crashed the gate at a wild party of the heroine's. She, rather drunk, comes up to him, looks him over, and says: I like you. In *Till the End of Time*, the hero and heroine are dancing together at a juke joint where they have just met. She announces: I'm driving you home. When he asks who told her so, she replies: You did, when you sat down beside me. These heroines repeat the most direct masculine line: I like you; and I know you like me—lines whose impact depends on their being used at first meeting, and whose intention is to dispense with preliminaries. A similar taking-things-for-granted line is used at a more advanced stage by the heroine of *The Dark Corner*. In the final scene she announces to various acquaintances that she and the hero have a date at City Hall tomorrow: He hasn't asked me yet, but I always told him I was playing for keeps. This coercion of success, by the brazen assumption that nothing else is possible, is also common to movie heroes.

The masculine-feminine girl is one with whom business and pleasure can be combined without any change of tone. The heroine in *The Dark Corner* is the hero's secretary, and a resourceful ally in his detective work. She is not like the older movie secretary who had to take off her glasses before the boss would notice her. It is clear throughout that she is an attractive girl and she does not conceal the fact that she is making a play for him. Their personal relation is carried on with the same tough, humorous and cagey banter which they use in discussing business. Occasional love-making distracts neither of them from their work. *Tomorrow is Forever* presents a contrasting picture of a boss wooing his secretary in 1918. There is a shift in their relationship when he becomes her suitor, changing from impersonal friendliness to tender protectiveness.

Love is not the whole existence of the masculine-feminine girl. Her approach is casual, deliberate, and knowing. She is not likely to be overwhelmed by unexpected feelings or to have her whole life changed by the coming of a man. All this is a relief to the man, since he does not have to live up to exorbitant expectations, and does not have the guilty feeling that he matters more to the woman than she does to him. The girl conveys this in her attitude that a kiss is just a kiss. Instead of making the man feel that he is taking a fateful step, she assures him that she is mainly interested in appraising the pleasure of the moment. "It's even better when you help" expresses a non-urgent suggestion for having fun, with no strings attached. In *The Big Sleep*, the heroine initiates love-making by asking the hero if he likes her. When he says yes, she taunts him: You haven't done much about it. He kisses her and she responds with: I liked that; I'd like some more. She gets another kiss. Similarly in *Till the End of Time*, the heroine, when the hero first kisses her, remarks appraisingly: I liked that.

In the close-up kisses of the late '20's the screen was filled with two merging profiles. The blanking out of all other sights and sounds expressed the overwhelmingness of the experience. What was probably the most famous kiss of the '46 season, that of Cary Grant and Ingrid Bergman in *Notorious*, showed the couple sauntering through her apartment, interspersing a continuous series of kisses with elated dialogue in such a smooth way that neither seemed to interrupt the other. When he had to talk on the telephone, they still kept on with the intermittent but seemingly continuous kiss. There is less loss of consciousness, less of a break with other activities than in the older style. Talk tends to be increasingly prominent in connection with kissing; the kiss itself, as we have seen, can be discussed. Semi-involuntary movements, such as formerly expressed the melting of the woman, tend to disappear. The heroine being kissed used to begin with her hands braced against the hero's chest, and ended with her hands clasped around his neck. The kiss worked a transformation, revealing to the woman feelings of which she had been unaware. This transforming kiss has now been relegated to comedy. The resistant heroine of *She Wouldn't Say Yes* first begins to love the hero when he kisses her, but her reaction is pictured in a comic light as she looks dazed and staggers slightly. In *The Kid from Brooklyn*, a disgruntled boxer, who wants to pick a fight with the hero, abruptly grabs the hero's sister and kisses her. To everyone's surprise this kiss prolongs itself and produces unanticipated reactions in both partners. It marks the beginning of love, but again the situation is comic.

In the mid-thirties the kiss reaction as an indicator of the rightness of the partner received a romantic comedy treatment in *Tom, Dick, and Harry*. The heroine married the one of her three suitors who made her hear bells ring when he kissed her. The kiss as indicator appears in a more farcical way when the heroine gets hiccoughs (an idiosyncratic reaction to excitement) after the right man kisses her, in *For the Love of Mary*. The indicative function of the kiss remains a recurrent comedy device, thought mainly associated with rather immature and simple-minded heroines. For more worldly-wise girls a kiss means less. The heroine of *One More Tomorrow*, for instance, engages in considerable friendly kissing with the hero, but turns down his first proposal of marriage, unaware until much later that she really loves him. The kiss, having become casual for the woman too, brings no revelation and involves no commitment.

The good-bad girl and the girl with the masculine approach, while they are frequently combined in a single prize package, satisfy to some extent different needs. The good-bad girl fulfils the wish of enjoying what is forbidden and at the same time meeting the demands of what we may call (with only apparent redundance) goodness morality. The good-bad girl is what the man thinks he wants when he is told by society and conscience that he must be good. The girl with the masculine approach satisfies a different need. She is related to what we may call (with only apparent contradiction) fun morality. You ought to have fun. If you are not having fun, something is the matter with you. Fun morality, widely current in America today, makes one feel guilty for not having fun. It imposes a new burden, expressed in the stock complaint attributed to the progressive school child: Do we have to do whatever we like again today? The difficulty of meeting the demands of fun morality may be due to the persistent operation of goodness morality on deeper levels. Fun morality threatens to reveal that we have less strength of impulse than we feel we have when confronted with goodness morality on the conscious level. The masculine-feminine girl helps to solve this problem. With an air of authority she indicates how much intensity is required. Casual and deliberate, she teases the man but does not condemn him when he is not carried away by a kiss. If behind the laconic appraisal of pleasant sensations ("I liked that; I'd like some more") there is passion or deep love, it is all to the good; but it is not compulsory. A pretended lack of emotion is a protection against impermanence from outer or inner causes. (This type of girl appears mainly in melodrama where the future of any relationship is made uncertain by a dangerous world.) The masculine-feminine girl not only reduces the demand for overwhelming feeling, but in a humorous, reasonable way permits recesses from sex. She is a pal with whom it is possible to have fun apart from sex, maintaining an awareness that she is a woman, but making few special demands on this score. The vamp, as a woman not only accessible but demanding, is perhaps a danger which has never been successfully faced and overcome. She has been defensively laughed off, but before she became comic, she was frightening because of her insistence on a passion-dominated and woman-centered existence, in which men were help-less before her unpredictable whims. The masculine-feminine girl has the vamp's readiness for love-making without the emotional hazards. Besides reas-suring the man about the adequacy of his impulses by not raising too high a demand, she helps him to release feelings which too much femininity tended to inhibit. Her active initiative helps him along, and incidentally relieves him of the apprehension that his advances may be unwelcome.

Since goodness morality and fun morality both operate in contempo-rary American culture, we frequently find a movie heroine using a mascu-line approach and appearing as a good-bad girl. The heroine of *The Big Sleep* approaches the hero in the direct manner which we have described, and also appears suspiciously involved with a shady night-club owner. The hero's unhurried reaction to her inducements is rationalized by the necessity of regarding her as a suspect. The heroine of *The Strange Love of Martha Ivers* sim-ilarly combines a masculine approach to the hero with an apparent involve-ment in shady dealings. The good-bad aspect counteracts the tendency for the masculine girl to become too much of a buddy. It demonstrates her attractive-ness to other men. At the same time this association with other men satisfies in another way the wish to invest the girl with a masculine aura. In both the good-bad and the masculine aspect it is essential to demonstrate that the girl loves only the hero. We have already seen how this is proof of her goodness. In relation to her masculine approach it is important to establish that this girl who offers herself so freely to the hero has been less free with other men. It is usu-ally conveyed that she has chosen the hero by an act of infallible choice, not impulsively but knowingly, having appraised at a glance his rare qualities. The hero receives the announcement of his election by her easy approach, which is thus not a sign that she is easy to get, but a special compliment to him.

Since this type of heroine assures the man that she accepts him from the start, she relieves him of the necessity of having to prove his worth. He proves it anyhow, but she does not meanwhile suspend judgment. This image of a woman who immediately gives the man assurance that she thinks he is good may compensate for the real-life mother who brought him up on what Mar-garet Mead has called "conditional love." American children are often weighed and measured, and awarded Mother's love to the extent that they compare favorably with others. The fantasy of the immediate and unconditional award of love by the movie heroine seems related to the suspense and uncertainties of this childhood experience. The occasional taunt of the masculine-feminine girl (It's better when you help. You haven't done much about it.) does not express any doubt about the man's capacities, but rather teases him for not using them.

The masculine-feminine girl may also appear without an admixture of seeming badness. The hero's secretary in *The Dark Corner* is an instance, and even more so the tailored professional woman heroine of *Uncle Harry*. In other cases, for instance in *Gilda*, the good-bad girl may appear without a masculine approach. The heroine lacking the detachment we described is preoccupied with love, demands that the hero love her, and suffers because his suspicions of her postspone their getting together. The hero is saved by these apparently well-founded suspicions from being enveloped by this emotionally demanding woman before the end of the film.

The heroine may, especially in comedies, repeat the mode of amorous approach which the hero has used earlier, either with her or with another girl. Here the girl's taking over the man's technique is spelled out. At the beginning of *Easter Parade*, the hero brings flowers, a bunny, and an Easter bonnet as gifts for the sulky and resistant glamor girl he is courting. In the end, at Easter a year later, the heroine brings flowers, a bunny, and a beribboned top-hat to the hero. The intervening plot details the hero's conversion from the glamor girl to the pal type as represented by the heroine. This is expressed in the style of dance which he performs with each of them. The glamor girl is at first his dancing partner; they perform a ball-room routine in which complementary masculine and feminine roles are expressed. When the glamor girl leaves him, the hero takes the heroine as his partner. After a false start in which she proves clumsy in ball-room dancing, he discovers that she has great talent for tap dancing in which they develop a parallel and interchangeable technique, both performing the same steps. In their most successful number they appear dressed exactly alike as two hoboes. In their off-stage relations, the hero also learns progressively to appreciate the girl who is more like himself.

A type contrasting with the masculine-feminine girl is the bitch, the most dangerous woman to appear since the decline of the vamp. As presented in *Scarlet Street*, she is solely preoccupied with sex. Lounging on an untidy couch, she asks drawlingly, "What else is there?" when her pimp and lover, concerned with business, demands impatiently whether she cannot think of anything else. She is ready to heap contempt on any man who, like the hero, seems inadequate to her demands. Similarly, Mrs. Macomber, in *The Macomber Affair*, takes every opportunity to underscore her husband's weaknesses. A mocking and gleeful witness of his humiliation when he runs away from the lion he has wounded, she ostentatiously bestows her favors on the guide who has been the hero of the hunt. She is a disturbing influence in the man's world, resenting the friendship which later develops between her husband and the guide. When her husband overcomes his fear, she is so piqued at the loss of her dominating and contemptuous position that she shoots him. She is not only intensely demanding, but her demands are impossible to meet. She is the opposite of the masculine-feminine girl who always makes her man feel he is doing all right.

1950

III

◆

The Golden Age of Movie Criticism

The 1950s through the 70s

Barbara Deming

Barbara Deming (1917–1984) was a critic, novelist, and anti-war activist, perhaps best known as a theorist of nonviolence, whose book *Prison Notes* detailed her experience as a civil-rights marcher incarcerated in an Atlanta jail. Deming had earlier worked as a film analyst for the Library of Congress, from 1942 to 1944, where she saw one-quarter of the feature films produced during those years. At that time she began writing the narrative analyses, parts of which appeared in the magazine *City Lights* during the early 1950s, that would ultimately be collected in book form as *Running Away From Myself: A Dream Portrait of America Drawn from the Films of the 40's*. Though this fascinatingly obstinate book appeared in 1969, at the height of auteurism, it steered clear of any commentary on directorial style or nostalgia about the stars and their glamour. Deming's stated purpose was to reveal how most American films, by giving the public "what it wants" in the form of wish-fulfillment dreams, end up reflecting our anxieties rather than our inner strengths, including our capacity for social change. "Through them we can read with a peculiar accuracy the fears and confusions that assail us—we can read, in caricature, the Hell in which we are bound. But we cannot read the best hopes of the time."

◆

The Reluctant War Hero

What is this pumpkin pie Americans are fighting for?" cries a youth just arrived in this country (in *They Live in Fear*, 1944). "Gosh," he is very soon writing to his mother, "people are quite willing to die for it, and I too!"

At a casual glance, our films about the Second World War would seem well summarized in this child's cry of delight. Listen to the voices which join themselves to his: "In other wars, men haven't always known why they were fighting; in this war we are all fighting for the same thing—our lives!" (*Cry Havoc*); "We all see eye to eye!" (*The Yanks Are Coming*); "This has been a happy home" (*Cross of Lorraine*); "When it's all over . . . just think . . . being able to settle down . . . raise your children . . . and never be in doubt about anything!" (*Thirty Seconds over Tokyo*). I could go on quoting from film after film.

My warning in the past chapter would seem a curious one. Where is the unhappy portrait of ourselves of which I spoke? Men die in these films, for this is war, but they fall on a battlefield bright with visions of the life they "almost

happily" die to secure; each with his family photograph, his letter from sweetheart, wife or Mom, with news of the home town he is proud of, tucked in his
pocket; or the page he has torn from a magazine—"Your Ideal Home." "We
shall utterly defeat the enemy," the government film *A Prelude to War* quotes
General Marshall. And at his words, a bright bright globe eclipses a dark.

A few songs in the musicals of those years announce that the soldiers look
forward to "a world that is new." But the words only mean that, through this
war, the rest of the world will come to know some of the happiness that we
already know. After the war, "the people of the whole world will meet together
at one big table" (*Three Russian Girls*), and there the whole world will come to
know the taste of—"What did you call it?" the Russian girl asks the American
aviator. "Pumpkin pie!" he tells her again. When an American in one of these
films wants to explain American life to a stranger, pumpkin pie comes most
readily to mind: we set it out for all who want to gather round, and everybody
gets an equal share. "One big family—that is America," someone sums up
(*They Live in Fear*).

On the field of battle, clear evidence of this happy family meets the eye
wherever it turns. *Guadalcanal Diary* (1943): Here is Catholic side by side with
Jew; here is Brooklyn cabbie next to philosophy teacher; here is—briefly—
black man next to white. *The Purple Heart* (1944): Here are artist, laborer,
lawyer, football player, arm in arm; one of Italian extraction, one Irish, one—
again—Catholic, one a Jew. *Eve of St. Mark* (1944): Here on the one team are
a boy from a small New England farm; a poor city boy, Irish Catholic, who is a
Dodgers fan; a rich southerner from an aristocratic family, who likes to quote
poetry. Again I could continue for pages. Slight tensions are sometimes dramatized, but they are always quickly resolved. In *A Wing and a Prayer* (1944),
there is a little bit of tension between officers and men; but before long the
men come to understand why the officer had to behave as he did. In *Cry Havoc*
(1943), there is a little bit of tension between rich girl and poor; but their differences vanish. In *Destination Tokyo* (1943), there is a little tension between the
doctor, who claims to be a materialist, and one of the men who is deeply religious; but events soon prove just how serious this difference is. After the usual
operation at sea such films feature, the doctor, to the boys muttered prayer,
mutters a fervent "Amen!" Fundamentally "we all see eye to eye." "This is
America!" confident voices chorus.

The voices are always just a little too confident; the tableaux are too carefully composed, one-of-each-of-us placed too punctually in the happy group.
There is another invariable that one can note, also. In film after film there
erupts some really harrowing moment of violence. One could put it down to

realism and pass on. But this is not the mere documentation of reality. The jugular vein, pierced, spurts its blood directly at us, spurts, it almost seems, straight from the screen (*Cross of Lorraine*). As the "Jap" screams, the armored tank charges right over us, as if we were its victims (*Guadalcanal Diary*). The hand-to-hand fight between the "Yank" and the "Jap" is protracted endlessly. We suffer in close-up each killing blow (*Behind the Rising Sun*). The emergency operation will never end. The camera cannot take its fill of that face, where teeth bite lips, eyes suddenly roll in a swoon (for this, name at random almost any film). Here is no controlled rendering of the facts of war. The camera voluptuously involves us in the destructive moment, moves in too close and dwells overlong, inviting us to suffer the ecstasy of dissolution, the thrill of giving it all up.

This compulsion, betraying itself in film after film, belies the bright tableaux arranged, the bright words carefully mouthed, and hints at some very different sense of the actuality of things, repressed but secretly insistent. And a long look confirms just this. The figure of the clear-browed soldier with the dream in his eyes turns insubstantial, and another figure claims attention, member of no happy clan, a figure of bitter aspect, withdrawn upon himself, who cries, *"Don't you ever wonder if it's worth all this—I mean what you're fighting for?"*—who cries, *"I stick my neck out for nobody . . . I'm not fighting for anything any more, except myself! . . . All hail the happy days when faith was something all in one piece!"*

These particular words are taken verbatim from one of the most popular films of 1942—*Casablanca*. They might seem blunt enough to catch one's attention at once. One might ask why some official ear did not note them and have the film withdrawn. But the truth is that the film is one of the last a censor would notice. It is one of the last that would shake up self-questioning and doubt in an audience. The reverse is its very design: to relieve any such agitations. At the film's beginning, the hint is dropped that the hero may be speaking words he does not mean. He is presented as a cipher, a man behind a mask, and the film poses the question: if it should come to a trial, might he not be shown to possess a fighting faith more real than all the rest? Just such a trial is gradually framed, and the film delivers its answer in the affirmative. The very nature of the drama here—the very nature of the question which makes the wheels of the film turn—might still seem to give much away. And here on paper, I believe it does; but not on the screen itself. This is the film's real magic: not only does it bring to the question the right answer; it brings the right answer without letting the audience become fully aware of what the question is; it drowns out the bitter cries without letting the audience become fully aware of what the cries have been all about. (I repeat that all this is likely to have been unconscious on the part of the producers.) But here is the film itself, in synopsis:

It is set abroad, and just before Pearl Harbor, the fight in question not yet our fight. (This, to begin with, makes the tale seem more innocent.) The hero, Rick (Humphrey Bogart), runs a café in Casablanca. Next to his café lies the airfield from which planes take off to Lisbon—and from there to America; so Casablanca is crowded with people trying to flee occupied Europe. Visas are pitifully hard to obtain, legally or illegally, and while they seek, and wait, "everybody goes to Rick's." Among all these displaced people, Rick himself is marked out for us, a homeless one among the homeless, exile in some special degree; and in this case alone the nature of the exile is not an apparent one. Our curiosity about Rick is provoked long before we are allowed to see him. The manner in which we are finally introduced to him carefully prolongs the suspense: a waiter has just informed an eager newcomer that Rick never drinks with customers; we see a check handed across a table; a hand puts an okay to it; the camera draws very slowly off to take Rick in—and we are left more curious than when we started; our introduction is to the very figuration of that question on which the film turns: Rick's glooming deadpan. He sits alone, staring at a drink, "no expression in his eyes."

As the drama unfolds, various facts about Rick's background are provided for us by the characters who press upon him, each, for his own purposes, seeking to guess him right. But always the sense is conveyed that the key to the puzzle, that which would make all the other pieces fall into place, remains to be found. Almost everyone wants something from Rick, starting with poor little Yvonne, "fool to fall in love with a man like" him; but there are two characters who most particularly strain themselves to decipher him. They are Renault (Claude Rains), French prefect of police, and the Nazi Major Strasser, who is in Casablanca to prevent the escape to America of underground leader Victor Lazslo. Two German couriers have been murdered, and letters of transit have been taken from them. Strasser is concerned to see that these letters do not get into Lazslo's hands. He and Renault both come to suspect that Rick knows where they are hidden. We know that he knows. We have seen the little "rat," Ugarte, leave them in his keeping ("Just because you despise me, you're the only one I trust"). And Rick may do what he wants with the letters, for Ugarte, who had his own plans—he helps those who are desperate, at a price—is promptly arrested for murder. We first see Renault trying to figure out how Rick will behave in relation to this arrest, for he plans to take Ugarte at Rick's place. "I stick my neck out for nobody," says Rick. And when the time comes and Ugarte goes scrambling to him, he *doesn't* move to help. This tells us nothing, for why should Rick risk anything for one like Ugarte? The episode—with several others in the film—is a teaser, keeps the guessing going. But Renault has also tried to sound out Rick about Victor Lazslo. In the process, he has provided us with our first tangible facts about Rick's background. A flicker of interest has crossed his face at Lazslo's name, and he has bet Renault ten thousand francs that Lazslo will manage a get-away; but what makes Renault think that he, Rick, might do anything to help? "I know your record," Renault brings out, watching him. "In 1935 you ran guns for Ethiopia, in 1936 you fought in Spain on the Loyalist side." "And got well paid for it on both occasions," Rick returns, deadpan.

Another note out of his past is sounded for us, but this more vague. Rick has run into the interview with Renault by wandering onto the terrace of the café. From here the airfield is visible. The sound of a plane warming up pulls Rick's eyes in that direction and he watches mesmerized as, caught in the glare of the floodlights, the plane speeds down the runway and turns to a speck. "You would like to be on it?" Renault probes. "I have often speculated on why you do not return to America. Did you abscond with the church funds? Did you run off with the President's wife? I should like to think you killed a man." "It was a combination of all three," Rick grunts, eyes still captive of the speck of plane.

Renault introduces Rick to Strasser, and Strasser in his turn tries to get some rise out of Rick with Lazslo's name. Rick lightly comments that his interest in Lazslo is a sporting one (he refers to his bet)—"Your business is politics, mine is running a saloon." But "You weren't always so carefully neutral," says Strasser. He has a dossier on him. "Cannot return to his country," he reads, watching him; "the reason is a little vague." His words fail to disturb the expressionless mask.

And then, suddenly, the film takes a turn. Suddenly we sit up, expectant. Enter Ingrid Bergman—(Mrs. Victor Lazslo). She walks into the café with her husband, and from their table she spots Sam, the Negro pianist, Rick's only intimate. Sam spots Ingrid too, and his glance is nervous. When Lazslo leaves the room for a moment, he crosses to her quickly. "Leave him alone!" he begs. "Leave him alone, Miss Ilse!" And we hold our breath.

We are at the point at last, we feel, of finding Rick out. When they come face to face, this feeling is confirmed. She has insisted on the music that brought him: "Play it once, for old time's sake. Play it, Sam. Play 'As Time Goes By.'" Sam, mumbling words of resistance, has played it, and Rick has come storming in: "I thought I told you never—" his face at last registering an emotion. In the few tense sentences they now exchange, it is obvious that Rick's past confronts us right here, in Ilse's person. We cut to a later hour and Rick alone over his drink, the lights out, the customers all gone, everyone gone but Sam, who pleads, "Don't just sit and stare a hole in that drink, boss." But "Tonight I've got a date with the heebie jeebies," Rick announces. "You know what I want to hear. If she can stand it, I can. Play it!" So Sam, at the piano, fingers out the song. The veil is about to be torn. The music, we know, will softly rend it. "The fundamental things apply, as time goes by . . ." Sam murmurs out the words. "Woman needs man, and man must have his mate, that nobody can deny . . ." We move up on Rick, on the drink before him, and dissolve—into a day in 1940.

An idyl: Rick and Ilse in Paris, in love. They have met only recently, we gather; know nothing about each other's pasts. "Who are you really?" he asks, gazing, love-struck. But she: "We said no questions." Love-struck, he acquiesces. In the background, Sam plays their theme song; they drink the last champagne. For the Germans are advancing on Paris; they will have to flee; but they will flee together. They name the train at which they will meet; Ilse has one thing first to which she must attend. But then we cut to Rick waiting at the station, in the rain; and Ilse does not come. He waits; she does not come; the train is about to pull out—the last train out of Paris. Suddenly Sam arrives with a note: she cannot see him ever again, she writes—but believe believe that she loves him. The raindrops pour down upon the letter, smudging the writing; the train utters its baleful departing whistle, and we dissolve back to Rick over his drink. He looks up and there is Ilse standing in the door, come after all these months to explain. Rick doesn't give her a chance. He mimics her words back there in Paris: "'Rick dear, I'll go with you any place. We'll get on a train together and we'll never stop. All my life, forevermore!' . . . How long was it we had, honey? . . . All hail the happy days," he lashes out, "when there were no questions asked, and faith was something all in one piece!" She gives up and leaves. Rick, giving it all up too, sags over the table; his drink tips, spilling over the cloth; the scene fades out.

So we know him now. The veil has been torn aside for us. He has had his "insides kicked out by a pair of French heels." This is his secret. And this, note, is the context in which he utters that cry: "All hail the happy days when faith was something all in one piece!" As uttered here, this is not the cry at all I seemed originally to report. It is a wounded lover's cry—nothing more.

Actually, a veil has been subtly drawn before our eyes—not parted for us. Look again and see the sleight of hand. Review the puzzle pieces which supposedly assemble for us into the portrait of a man betrayed in love. He never drinks with the customers and is cold to poor little Yvonne—this will fit. The man who fought in Spain and ran guns for Ethiopia will now stick his neck out for nobody—claims to have done what he's done only because he got well paid for it. One who is embittered in love, of course, will often extend that bitterness to life in general. But note too: for reasons unknown he cannot return to his own country. Here is a piece that refuses to be fitted into the place assigned.

It refuses, that is, on paper; but not upon the screen. Rick's "date with the heebie jeebies" is worth going over again, this time in full detail. In this scene, all the variant notes I have just mentioned are introduced again—but in the instant are gathered up, and blur into the one note. As one *watches*, it is persuasive.

When we see Rick sitting there at his bitter drink, he is lit through the café window by a circling finger of light from the airfield—which dramatically enough recalls that trip to America he can never make, an exile quite distinct from the exile he suffers because of Ilse. And listen, now, to a more complete text of what passes between him and Sam. "Don't just stare a hole in that drink," Sam pleads, but Rick answers that this night he has a date with the heebie jeebies. Then he breaks out—"strangely," comments the script— "They grab Ugarte, then she walks in. That's the way it goes. One in and one out. Sam, if it's December 1941 in Casablanca, what time is it in New York? . . . I bet they're asleep in New York. I bet they're asleep all over America. Of all the gin joints in all the towns in all the world, she walks into mine!" Then "Play it!" Look at all the notes that are casually woven in together here. "One in and one out" of Ugarte and Ilse. Ugarte is an opportunist who serves a good cause for a price—as Rick claims to have done, himself. Rick's cold familiarity with this sort of betrayal of a faith here blurs in one split second with his cynicism about love's promises. Note, next, the date, "December 1941"— making this just pre-Pearl Harbor. "I bet they're asleep," in the light of this date, takes on, automatically, political overtones—and Rick's cynicism about the state of his country too is blurred with the very special cynicism of the jilted lover. Finally, when at the fading of the flashback, Ilse appears at the door, it is the circling finger of light from the airfield that picks her out for us, materializes her; so even *that* variant note, with which we began, is gathered in— visually confounded, in a moment, with the other, the lover's bitter loss.

As Ilse stands there now, all bitterness can be said to have been focused on her person. From here on, Rick can come out with whatever cry he wants; it will be harmless. And note: if the film can somehow dispel that very particular disillusion of his, in this girl—by subtle act of substitution, all other harsh notes that have been introduced and blurred into this note will be dispelled.

As the film proceeds, Rick does come forth with ever more cynical outcries. The way to listen to them, as I quote them, is to forget his characterization as the jilted lover, to abstract the cries from this context, and listen to them in themselves. The film proceeds:

After Ugarte's arrest, Lazslo is advised that Rick may have the letters of transit. But when he goes to Rick, Rick turns him aside coldly—"The problems of the world are not in my department. I'm a saloon keeper." When Lazslo retorts that once, he's been told, he was a man who fought for the underdog, Rick comments, "Yes, I found that a very expensive hobby." The characterization of sulking lover is quickly reanimated for us; we are quickly reminded that it is love Rick found to be expensive. He goes on to say that he may not ever use the visas himself, but he won't give them to Lazslo; and when Lazslo mutters, "There must be some reason . . ." replies, "There is. I suggest that you ask your wife."

Then Ilse herself goes to see Rick for her husband. "Richard!" she begs. "So I'm Richard again?" he mocks her. "We're back in Paris. I've recovered my lost identity." But in this interview too, one can, if one wants, listen to his words in terms of a lost identity not simply that of the happy lover. "Do I have to hear again what a great man your husband is and what an important Cause he's fighting for?" "It was your Cause too . . ." "Well, I'm not fighting for anything any more, except myself. I'm the only Cause I'm interested in now." In desperation Ilse pulls a gun. "You'll have to kill me to get them," he tells her. "If Lazslo, if the Cause means so much to you, go ahead!"—with this equation again safely reducing all to a wounded lover's terms.

She cannot shoot, of course; she breaks, she drops the pistol—and flings herself into his arms. "I tried to stay away . . . If you knew . . . how much I loved you . . . still love you!" And the film fades in on them a little later as she explains at last what happened on that fateful day. She had been married to Lazslo already when she met Rick, but she had heard that he had been murdered in a concentration camp. Then that day she had learned that he was alive, had escaped, was waiting for her. She had had to go. But now, she cries, she'll never have the strength to leave Rick again. "I can't fight it any more. I don't know what's right any longer. You'll have to think for both of us, for all of us."

"I've already made up our minds," Rick answers her. But he does not reveal his decision. The question of how he will act is stretched out to the very end. Rick continues inscrutable. The script notes with regularity, "His expression reveals nothing of his feelings." And he continues to utter the most cynical statements. Of course we more and more tend to suspect that such utterances mask his real intentions. We suspect this, even, with some anguish.

Lazslo ducks into Rick's to elude the police, who have broken up an underground meeting, and Rick, sending Ilse off by a back way, gives Lazslo a drink to settle his nerves. Here it is that Rick demands, "Don't you ever wonder if it's worth all this? I mean what you're fighting for?" Lazslo retorts that he sounds like a man "trying to convince himself of something that in his heart he doesn't believe." And we in the audience at this point would gladly be convinced, ourselves, if we could. There is only one level of meaning at which we would think of taking his words, and the price asked does seem a dreadful one.

As Lazslo and Rick stand there, Renault's men burst in and declare Lazslo under arrest on suspicion of having been at that meeting. Rick grimaces at Lazslo, a dark smile: "It seems destiny has taken a hand." And now he takes his most seemingly cynical step. He calls on Renault and suggests a deal. If he'll release Lazslo, Rick will give Renault a real charge against him. He, Rick, does have those visas. He'll pretend to give them to Lazslo, and this will give Renault the chance to walk in and arrest Lazslo for complicity in the murder of the couriers. Under cover of the excitement—if Renault will help—he, Rick, will make use of the visas himself, to leave for America with Ilse. Which should put Renault's mind to rest about his desire to help Lazslo escape. He's the last man he'd want to meet in America. "I'll miss you," Renault tells him. "Apparently you're the only one in Casablanca who has even fewer scruples than I." So Rick goes to Lazslo and offers him the visas for a hundred thousand francs. He tells him to come down to the café with Ilse, a few minutes before the Lisbon plane is to leave. When Lazslo tries to thank him, he cuts him short: "Skip it. This is strictly a matter of business." One cynical gesture is here wrapped within another.

This particular gesture is soon enough annulled, in a little sequence all to itself. When Lazslo does try to hand Rick the money, he refuses it gruffly: "Keep it; you'll need it." In this small instance, at any rate, his cynicism has been proved insubstantial. But we wait to see how he will act in the main matter. Ilse thinks that what he intends to do is send Lazslo off on the plane alone. But nobody at this point really knows how anybody else is going to act. Rick is not at all sure about Renault. The film has been building him up as a minor puzzle. "Rick, have you got those letters of transit?" Renault has asked. "Louis, are you pro Vichy or Free French?" Rick has retorted. "I have no convictions . . . I take what comes," Renault has declared; but on his face too the camera has dwelt teasingly, the smile there ambiguous.

Suddenly everything begins to happen fast—though in a manner, still, that keeps us guessing. Renault walks in and—Lazslo and Ilse stare—declares Lazslo under arrest again. "You are surprised about my friend Rick?" At which

Rick pulls a gun and informs Renault that there will be no arrests—"yet." And he orders him to check with the airport that there will be no trouble. Renault pulls a fast one and, pretending to call the airport, really calls Strasser, who races for the field.

At the field, at last, all our questions are answered. While Lazslo is off somewhere checking arrangements, Rick tells Renault to fill out the names on the visas. They are: Mr. and Mrs. Victor Lazslo. Ilse, dazed, protests, but Rick tells her: she knows and he knows that the Cause needs Lazslo, and Lazslo needs her—she is part of his work, "the thing that keeps him going." "What about us?" she cries, but he answers her, "We'll always have Paris. We didn't have it. We'd lost it . . . We got it back last night." And "I've got a job to do," he tells her. "Where I'm going, you can't follow." Lazslo returns—"Everything is in order." "All except one thing," Rick adds, and he tells him of Ilse's visit. She did it to try to get the visas, he tells him. To get them, she tried to convince him that she was still in love with him. And he let her pretend. "But that was long ago." "Welcome back to the fight," Lazslo salutes Rick. "Now I know our side will win!" And he and Ilse walk off toward the plane.

Strasser bursts in. Further decisions are called for. Renault cries out that Lazslo is on the plane. Rick has Strasser at gun point, but Strasser calls his bluff: he jumps to the phone and asks for the radio tower. Rick shoots Strasser. The French police burst in; and the next move is Renault's. There is an extensive pause as he and Rick exchange stares—faces, to the last, expressionless. Then: "Round up the usual suspects!" Renault barks, and the police dash off. The roar of the ascending plane is heard. The two men turn their eyes. The beacon light sweeps them. The plane roars up over their heads. It might be a good idea to leave Casablanca for a while, says Renault. There is a Free French garrison at Brazzaville. The ten thousand francs he owes Rick—"that should pay our expenses." "*Our* expenses, Louis?" says Rick. "I think this is the beginning of a beautiful friendship." Arms linked, they walk off into the dark.

Look where the film has brought us out: the embittered one, who would stick his neck out for nobody, steps briskly into battle. Look what has been accomplished: the final note here is the very one documented at this chapter's beginning. Arm in arm with comrade, he steps forth, to music, the dream in his heart intact. "Everything is" indeed "in order," magically. The film has permitted a most disturbing figure to take shape, and there before our eyes has comfortably recruited him. Lazslo may well cry out, "Now I know our side will win!"

What is more, the dream has recruited this unlikely warrior without even leaving us with the sense that we have witnessed a remarkable translation. The love story has borne the brunt of the work: it is the guise of the jilted lover that has allowed the figure to take shape at all and utter his bitter cries; and it is the scene in which he regains his lost faith in the beloved that enables us to cancel out those cries and believe in his entry into the fight. But note a further magic: the impression we are left with at the end of the film is that even if Ilse had never returned to explain her leaving him, if it had come right down to it, Rick, for all his gloominess, would of course have rallied to the Cause. This the dream accomplishes by having him continue his bitter gesturing to the end. When we are given proof of how insubstantial is the cynicism about "the problems of the world" that he professes after Ilse has returned to him, automatically we extend even to his original bitter aspect the same judgment; retroactively we dismiss it too. Thus, as the film ends, that glum mask, shaped there before our eyes, has been interpreted as no disturbing sign but sign, rather, of a faith deeper than other faiths. "Just because you despise me, you're the only one I trust," Ugarte has blurted to Rick. The film, in effect, manages the tour de force of defining Rick's relation to the Cause analogously. It leaves us with this half-conscious feeling: just because he wears the aspect of utter cynicism, one can be sure that he is the real man of faith. Precisely by this contradictory sign, one can spot the man who really cares, the man to be relied upon. And so, in the dark, the shadow of our dim disquiet is dispelled.

Some readers will perhaps protest at this point: why cannot the film be taken at face value? Here is a love story, and it is complicated by the fact that the bitterness the hero feels toward his beloved he transfers to life as a whole; but that, they may protest, covers the matter; to read any more into it is artificial. Even at a strictly literal level, however, the label of jilted lover cannot be made to adequately cover Rick's case. At the end of the film one thing remains altogether unexplained: why it was that he could never return to his country. For the purposes of the dream, this stray end is gathered up neatly enough with Ilse's final departure. As Rick's eyes turn this last time to follow the plane's flight, the one exile is fused forever with the other; an audience is unlikely to remember that they are actually separate matters. For our purposes, though, the distinction stands and—even to be altogether literal—does raise the whole question of a wider reference for the drama enacted than any love alone provides. In that last cry of Lazslo's—"Now I know our side will win!"—the producers of the film themselves unconsciously acknowledge the more crucial identity of the hero, the more general nature of the crisis of faith he suffers.

But it is in unison that films most clearly yield up their secrets. It is the joint evidence of other war films that above all exposes the drama of Rick as something more than a drama of love in a war setting. I can name film after film about the war which raises dramatically the question of the hero's faith, then moves forward to confirm that faith and steps him briskly into battle. Among these films, the hero is by no means always a disillusioned lover—though this note too is repeated. He may be any one of a variety of figures. Of any of these figures, viewed individually, one could say, as of Rick: this is a very special case, or a case, at any rate, without any general application for the American public. The hero very often is not even a citizen of this country. But line them all up and the question one has to ask is: why do the American film makers so persistently seek out remote cases of just this sort with which to satisfy their public—unless the identification made is actually one that is not remote at all?

1969

Manny Farber

Manny Farber (b. 1917) is a film critics' film critic—one they often go to when they want to be surprised and replenished. Susan Sontag called him "the liveliest, smartest, most original film critic this country ever produced." Another admirer, Pauline Kael, remarked, "It's his analysis of the film frame as if it were a painter's canvas that's a real contribution." Farber is himself a painter, a very good one, whose canvases are filled with busy incidents and objects but without a pivotal center, so that the viewer gets happily lost poring over them inch by inch. So, too, his criticism, where the process of following out his quirky, dense mind as it roams over a film's surface, rather than any centrally organizing, law-giving judgment, is what counts. Jonathan Rosenbaum once observed that in Farber's criticism "you can't always be sure whether he's praising or ridiculing the subject before him. Maybe he's doing both." His tendency to weld oxymoronic, contradictory adjectives together helps produce that ambiguous effect. Farber's prose style, so rewarding once you surrender to it, is not easy. What makes it dangerous or queasy is that you never quite know where he's going. He doesn't build sustained arguments so much as pursue hunches through convoluted paths, like an ant—or a termite. In a famous formulation, Farber distinguished between what he called "white elephant art" (pompous, message-y, ambitious for "gilt culture," masterpiece status) and "termite art," about which he wrote: "A peculiar fact about termite-tapeworm-fungus-moss art is that it goes always forward eating its own boundaries, and, likely as not, leaves nothing in its path other than the signs of eager, industrious, unkempt activity." Farber could have been talking about his own writing.

He began doing film criticism in the early 1940s, taking over at *The New Republic* when Otis Ferguson's ship was torpedoed, then moved over to *The Nation*, before inheriting his friend James Agee's column at *Time* (where he lasted for six months). Many of his reviews challenged the Academy Award Best Picture syndrome; he found more to admire in the lean, masculine, action-genre pictures that formed the focus of his essay "Underground Films," the fruit of a three-year study. He was among the first to praise the movies of Howard Hawks, Anthony Mann, Samuel Fuller, and Robert Aldrich. Later he became intrigued by the work of avant-garde filmmakers such as Michael Snow, the Straubs, and Chantal Akerman. His seminal piece on films of the 1970s (which he wrote with his wife, painter Patricia Patterson) characteristically attempts to pin down a dramatic but elusive aesthetic shift that he sensed was changing the nature of the screen image, and to link movies with the larger context of modern art.

◆

Underground Films

The saddest thing in current films is watching the long neglected action directors fade away as the less talented De Sicas and Zinnemanns continue to fascinate the critics. Because they played an anti-art role in Hollywood, the true masters of the male action film—such soldier-cowboy-gangster directors as Raoul Walsh, Howard Hawks, William Wellman, William Keighley, the early, pre-*Stagecoach* John Ford, Anthony Mann—have turned out a huge amount of unprized second-gear celluloid. Their neglect becomes more painful to behold now that the action directors are in decline, many of them having abandoned the dry, economic, life-worn movie style that made their observations of the American he-man so rewarding. Americans seem to have a special aptitude for allowing History to bury the toughest, most authentic native talents. The same tide that has swept away Otis Ferguson, Walker Evans, Val Lewton, Clarence Williams, and J. R. Williams into near oblivion is now in the process of burying a group that kept an endless flow of interesting roughneck film passing through the theaters from the depression onward. The tragedy of these film-makers lies in their having been consigned to a Sargasso Sea of unmentioned talent by film reviewers whose sole concern is not continuous flow of quality but the momentary novelties of the particular film they are reviewing.

Howard Hawks is the key figure in the male action film because he shows a maximum speed, inner life, and view, with the least amount of flat foot. His best films which have the swallowed-up intricacy of a good soft-shoe dance, are *Ceiling Zero, Only Angels Have Wings, The Big Sleep*, and *The Thing*. Raoul Walsh's films are melancholy masterpieces of flexibility and detailing inside a lower-middle-class locale. Walsh's victories, which make use of tense broken-field journeys and nostalgic background detail, include *They Drive By Night, White Heat*, and *Roaring Twenties*. In any Bill Wellman operation, there are at least four directors—a sentimentalist, deep thinker, hooey vaudevillian, and an expedient short-cut artist whose special love is for mulish toughs expressing themselves in drop-kicking heads and somber standing around. Wellman is at his best in stiff, vulgar, low-pulp material. In that set-up, he has a low-budget ingenuity which creates flashes of ferocious brassiness, an authentic practical joke violence (as in the frenzied inadequacy of Ben Blue in *Roxie Hart*) and a brainless hell-raising. Anthony Mann's inhumanity to man, in which cold mortal intentness is the trademark effect, can be studied best in *The Tall Target, Winchester 77, Border Incident*, and *Railroaded*. The films of this tin-can de Sade have a Germanic rigor, caterpillar intimacy, and an original dictionary of ways in which to punish the human body. Mann has done interesting work with scissors, a cigarette lighter, and steam, but his most bizarre effect takes place in a taxidermist's shop. By intricate manipulation of athletes' bodies, Mann tries to ram the eyes of his combatants on the horns of a stuffed deer stuck on the wall.

The film directors mentioned above did their best work over a decade ago when it was possible to be a factory of unpretentious picture-making without frightening the front office. During the same period and later, less prolific directors also appear in the uncompromising action film. Of these, the most important is John Farrow, an urbane vaudevillian whose forte, in films like *The Big Clock* and *His Kind of Woman*, is putting a fine motoring system beneath the veering slapstick of his eccentric characterizations. Though he has tangled with such heavyweights as Book of the Month and Hemingway, Zoltan Korda is an authentic hard-grain cheapster telling his stories through unscrubbed action, masculine characterization, and violent explorations inside a fascinating locale. Korda's best films—*Sahara, Counterattack, Cry the Beloved Country*—are strangely active films in which terrain, jobs, and people get curiously interwoven in a ravening tactility. William Keighley, in *G Men* and *Each Dawn I Die*, is the least sentimental director of gangster careers. After the bloated philosophical safecrackers in Huston's *Asphalt Jungle*, the smallish cops and robbers in Keighley's work seem life size. Keighley's handling is so right in emphasis, timing, and shrewdness that there is no feeling of the director breathing, gasping, snoring over the film.

The tight-lipped creators whose films are mentioned above comprise the most interesting group to appear in American culture since the various groupings that made the 1920's an explosive era in jazz, literature, silent films. Hawks and his group are perfect examples of the anonymous artist, who is seemingly afraid of the polishing, hypocrisy, bragging, fake educating that goes on in serious art. To go at his most expedient gait, the Hawks type must take a withdrawn, almost hidden stance in the industry. Thus, his films seem to come from the most neutral, humdrum, monotonous corner of the movie lot. The fascinating thing about these veiled operators is that they are able to spring the leanest, shrewdest, sprightliest notes from material that looks like junk, and from a creative position that on the surface seems totally uncommitted and disinterested. With striking photography, a good ear for natural dialogue, an eye for realistic detail, a skilled inside-action approach to composition, and the most politic hand in the movie field, the action directors have done a forbidding stenography on the hard-boiled American handyman as he progresses through the years.

It is not too remarkable that the underground films, with their twelve-year-old's adventure story plot and endless palpitating movement, have lost out in the film system. Their dismissal has been caused by the construction of solid confidence built by daily and weekly reviewers. Operating with this wall, the critic can pick and discard without the slightest worry about looking silly. His choice of best salami is a picture backed by studio build-up, agreement amongst his colleagues, a layout in *Life* Mag. (which makes it officially reasonable for an American award), and a list of ingredients that anyone's unsophisticated aunt in Oakland can spot as a distinguished film. This prize picture, which has philosophical undertones, pan-fried domestic sights, risqué crevices, sporty actors and actresses, circus-like gymnastics, a bit of tragedy like the main fall at Niagara, has every reason to be successful. It has been made for that purpose. Thus, the year's winner is a perfect film made up solely of holes and evasions, covered up by all types of padding and plush. The cavity filling varies from one prize work to another, from *High Noon* (cross-eyed artistic views of a clock, silhouettes against a vaulting sky, legend-toned walking, a big song), through *From Here to Eternity* (Sinatra's private scene-chewing, pretty trumpeting, tense shots in the dark and at twilight, necking near the water, a threatening hand with a broken bottle), to next year's winner which will probably be a huge ball of cotton candy containing either Audrey Hepburn's cavernous grin and stiff behind or more of Zinnemann's glacéed picture-making. In terms of imaginative photography, honest acting, and insight into American life there is no comparison between an average underground triumph (*The Tall Target*) and the trivia that causes a critical salaam across the land. The trouble is that no one asks the critics' alliance to look straight backward at its "choices," i.e. a horse-drawn truckload of liberal schmaltz called *The Best Years of Our Lives*. These ridiculously maltreated films sustain their place in the halls of fame simply because they bear the label of ART in every inch of their reelage. Praising these solemn goiters has produced a climate in which the underground picture-maker, with his modest entry and soft shoe approach, can barely survive.

However, any day now, Americans may realize that scrambling after the obvious in art is a losing game. The sharpest work of the last thirty years is to be found by studying the most unlikely, self-destroying, uncompromising, roundabout artists. When the day comes for praising infamous men of art, some great talent will be shown in true light: people like Weldon Kees, the early

Robert DeNiro, James Agee, Isaac Rosenfeld, Otis Ferguson, Val Lewton, a dozen comic-strip geniuses like the creator of "Harold Teen," and finally a half dozen directors, such as the master of the ambulance-speedboat, flying-saucer movie: Howard Hawks.

The films of the Hawks-Wellman group are *underground* for more reasons than the fact that the director hides out in the sub-surface reaches of his work. The hard-bitten action film finds its natural home in caves; the murky, congested theaters, looking like glorified tattoo parlors on the outside and located near bus terminals in big cities. These theaters roll action films in what, at first, seems like a nightmarish atmosphere of guzzling, snoring, clicking flashlights, ice-cream vending, and amazing restlessness. After a while, the clatter and congested tinniness is swallowed by the atmosphere of shabby transience, prints that seem overgrown with jungle moss, soundtracks infected with hiccups. The spectator watches two or three action films go by, and leaves feeling as though he were a pirate discharged from a giant sponge.

The cut-throat atmosphere in the itch house is reproduced in the movies shown there. Hawks's *The Big Sleep* not only has a slightly gaseous, sub-surface, Baghdad-ish background, but its gangster action is engineered with a suave, cutting efficacy. Walsh's *Roaring Twenties* is a jangling barrelhouse film which starts with a top gun bouncing downhill, and, at the end, he is seen slowly pushing his way through a lot of Campbell's Scotch broth. Wellman's favorite scene is a group of hard-visaged ball bearings standing around—for no damned reason and with no indication of how long or for what reason they have been standing. His worst pictures are made up simply of this moody, wooden standing around. All that saves the films are the little flurries of bullet-like acting that give the men an inner look of credible orneriness and somewhat stupid mulishness. Mann likes to stretch his victims in crucifix poses against the wall or ground, and then peer intently at their demise with an icy surgeon's eye. Just as the harrowing machine is about to run over the wetback on a moonlit night, the camera catches him sprawled out in a harrowing image. At heart, the best action films are slicing journeys into the lower depths of American life: dregs, castouts, lonely hard wanderers caught in a buzz-saw of niggardly intricate devious movement.

The projects of the underground directors are neither experimental, liberal, slick, spectacular, low-budget, epical, improving, or flagrantly commercial like Sam Katzman two-bitters. They are faceless movies taken from a type of half-polished trash writing that seems like a mixture of Burt L. Standish, Max Brand, and Raymond Chandler. Tight, cliché-ridden melodramas about stock musclemen. A stool pigeon gurgling with a scissors in his back; a fat, nasal-voiced gang leader, escaped convicts, power-mad ranch owners with vengeful siblings, a mean gun with an Oedipus complex and migraine headaches, a crooked gambler trading guns to the red-skins, exhausted GI's, an incompetent kid hoodlum hiding out in an East Side building, a sickly-elegant Italian barber in a plot to kill Lincoln, an underpaid shamus signing up to stop the blackmailing of a tough millionaire's depraved thumb-sucking daughter.

The action directors accept the role of hack so that they can involve themselves with expedience and tough-guy insight in all types of action: barnstorming, driving, bulldogging. The important thing is not so much the banal-seeming journeys to nowhere that make up the stories, but the tunneling that goes on inside the classic Western-gangster incidents and stock hoodlum-dogface-cowboy types. For instance, Wellman's lean elliptical talents for creating brassy cheapsters and making gloved references to death, patriotism, masturbation, suggest that he uses private runways to the truth, while more famous directors take a slow, embalming surface route.

The virtues of action films expand as the pictures take on the outer appearance of junk jewelry. The underground's greatest mishaps have occurred in art-infected projects where there is unlimited cash, studio freedom, an expansive story, message, heart, and a lot of prestige to be gained. Their flattest, most sentimental works are incidentally the only ones that have attained the almond paste-flavored eminence of Museum of Modern Art's film library, i.e. *GI Joe*, *Public Enemy*, and *Scarface*. Both Hawks and Wellman, who made these overweighted mistakes, are like basketball's corner man: their best shooting is done from the deepest, worst angle. With material that is hopelessly worn-out and childish (*Only Angels Have Wings*), the underground director becomes beautifully graphic and modestly human in his flexible detailing. When the material is like drab concrete, these directors become great on-the-spot inventors, using their curiously niggling, reaming style for adding background detail (Walsh), suave grace (Hawks), crawling mechanized tension (Mann), veiled gravity (Wellman), svelte semi-caricature (John Farrow), modern Gothic vehemence (Phil Karlson), and dark, modish vaudeville (Robert Aldrich).

In the films of these hard-edged directors can be found the unheralded ripple of physical experience, the tiny morbidly life-word detail which the visitor to a strange city finds springing out at every step. The Hawks film is as good on the mellifluous grace of the impudent American hard rock as can be found in any art work; the Mann films use American objects and terrain—guns, cliffs, boulders, an 1865 locomotive, telephone wires—with more cruel intimacy than any other film-maker; the Wellman film is the only clear shot at the mean, brassy, claw-like soul of the lone American wolf that has been taken in films. In other words, these actioneers—Mann and Hawks and Keighley and, in recent times, Aldrich and Karlson—go completely underground before proving themselves more honest and subtle than the water buffaloes of film art: George Stevens, Billy Wilder, Vittorio De Sica, Georges Clouzot. (Clouzot's most successful work, *Wages of Fear*, is a wholesale steal of the mean physicality and acrid highway inventions in such Walsh-Wellman films as *They Drive by Night*. Also, the latter film is a more flexible, adroitly ad-libbed, worked-in creation than Clouzot's eclectic money-maker.)

Unfortunately, the action directors suffer from presentation problems. Their work is now seen repeatedly on the blurred, chopped, worn, darkened, commercial-ridden movie programs on TV. Even in the impossible conditions of the "Late Show," where the lighting is four shades too dark and the porthole-shaped screen defeats the movie's action, the deep skill of Hawks and his tribe shows itself. Time has dated and thinned out the story excitement, but the ability to capture the exact homely-manly character of forgotten locales and misanthropic figures is still in the pictures, along with pictorial compositions (Ford's *Last of the Mohicans*) that occasionally seem as lovely as anything that came out of the camera box of Billy Bitzer and Mathew Brady. The conditions in the outcast theaters—the Lyric on Times Square, the Liberty on Market Street, the Victory on Chestnut—are not as bad as TV, but bad enough. The screen image is often out of plumb, the house lights are half left on during the picture, the broken seats are only a minor annoyance in the unpredictable terrain. Yet, these action film homes are the places to study Hawks, Wellman, Mann, as well as their near and distant cousins.

The underground directors have been saving the American male on the screen for three decades without receiving the slightest credit from critics and prize committees. The hard, exact defining of male action, completely lacking in acting fat, is a common item *only* in underground films. The cream on the top of a *Framed* or *Appointment with Danger* (directed by two first cousins of the Hawks-Walsh strain) is the eye-flicking action that shows the American body—arms, elbow, legs, mouths, the tension profile line—being used expediently, with grace and the suggestion of jolting hardness. Otherwise, the Hollywood talkie seems to have been invented to give an embarrassingly phony impression of the virile action man. The performance is always fattened either by coyness (early Robert Taylor), unction (Anthony Quinn), histrionic conceit (Gene Kelly), liberal knowingness (Brando), angelic stylishness (Mel Ferrer), oily hamming (Jose Ferrer), Mother's Boy passivity (Rock Hudson), or languor

(Montgomery Clift). Unless the actor lands in the hands of an underground director, he causes a candy-coated effect that is misery for any spectator who likes a bit of male truth in films.

After a steady diet of undergrounders, the spectator realizes that these are the only films that show the tension of an individual intelligence posing itself against the possibilities of monotony, bathos, or sheer cliché. Though the action film is filled with heroism or its absence, the real hero is the small detail which has arisen from a stormy competition between lively color and credibility. The hardness of these films arises from the aesthetic give-and-go with banality. Thus, the philosophical idea in underground films seems to be that nothing is easy in life or the making of films. Jobs are difficult, even the act of watching a humdrum bookstore scene from across the street has to be done with care and modesty to evade the type of butter-slicing glibness that rots the Zinnemann films. In the Walsh film, a gangster walks through a saloon with so much tight-roped ad-libbing and muscularity that he seems to be walking backward through the situation. Hawks's achievement of moderate toughness in *Red River*, using Clift's delicate languor and Wayne's clay-like acting, is remarkable. As usual, he steers Clift through a series of cornball fetishes (like the Barney Google Ozark hat and the trick handling of same) and graceful, semi-collegiate business: stances and kneelings and snake-quick gunmanship. The beauty of the job is the way the cliché business is needled, strained against without breaking the naturalistic surface. One feels that his is the first and last hard, clamped-down, imaginative job Clift does in Hollywood—his one non-mush performance. Afterward, he goes to work for Zinnemann, Stevens, Hitchcock.

The small buried attempt to pierce the banal pulp of underground stories with fanciful grace notes is one of the important feats of the underground director. Usually, the piercing consists in renovating a cheap rusty trick that has been slumbering in the "thriller" director's handbook—pushing a "color" effect against the most resistant type of unshowy, hard-bitten direction. A mean butterball flicks a gunman's ear with a cigarette lighter. A night-frozen cowboy shudders over a swig of whiskey. A gorilla gang leader makes a cannonaded exit from a barber chair. All these bits of congestion are like the lines of a hand to a good gun movie; they are the tracings of difficulty that make the films seem uniquely hard and formful. In each case, the director is taking a great chance with clichés and forcing them into a hard natural shape.

People don't notice the absence of this hard combat with low, commonplace ideas in the Zinnemann and Huston epics, wherein the action is a game in which the stars take part with confidence and glee as though nothing can stop them. They roll in parts of drug addicts, tortured sheriffs; success depending on how much sentimental bloop and artistic japery can be packed in without encountering the demands of a natural act or character. Looking back on a Sinatra film, one has the feeling of a private whirligig performance in the center of a frame rather than a picture. On the other hand, a Cagney performance under the hands of a Keighley is ingrained in a tight, malignant story. One remembers it as a sinewy, life-marred exactness that is as quietly laid down as the smaller jobs played by the Barton MacLanes and Frankie Darros.

A constant attendance at the Lyric-Pix-Victory theaters soon impresses the spectator with the coverage of locales in action films. The average gun film travels like a shamus who knows his city and likes his private knowledges. Instead of the picture-postcard sights, the underground film finds the most idiosyncratic spot of a city and then locates the niceties within the large nicety. The California Street hill in San Francisco (*Woman in Hiding*) with its old-style mansions played in perfect night photography against a deadened domestic bitching. A YMCA scene that emphasizes the wonderful fat-waisted-middle-aged-physicality of people putting on tennis shoes and playing handball (*Appointment with Danger*). The terrorizing of a dowdy middle-aged, frog-faced woman (*Born to Kill*) that starts in a decrepit hotel and ends in a bumbling, screeching, crawling murder at midnight on the shore. For his big shock effect, director Robert Wise (a sometime member of the underground) uses the angle going down to the water to create a middle-class mediocrity that out-horrors anything Graham Greene attempted in his early books on small-time gunsels.

Another fine thing about the coverage is its topographic grimness, the fact that the terrain looks worked over. From Walsh's *What Price Glory* to Mann's *Men at War*, the terrain is special in that it is used, kicked, grappled, worried, sweated up, burrowed into, stomped on. The land is marched across in dark threading lines at twilight, or the effect is reversed with foot soldiers in white parkas (*Fixed Bayonets*) curving along a snowed-in battleground as they watch troops moving back—in either case the cliché effect is worked credibly inward until it creates a haunting note like the army diagonals in *Birth of a Nation*. Rooms are boxed, crossed, opened up as they are in few other films. The spectator gets to know these rooms as well as his own hand. Years after seeing the film, he remembers the way a dulled waitress sat on the edge of a hotel bed, the weird elongated adobe in which ranch hands congregate before a Chisholm Trail drive. The rooms in big shot directors' films look curiously bulbous, as though inflated with hot air and turned toward the audience, like the high school operetta of the 1920's.

Of all these poet-builders, Wellman is the most interesting, particularly with Hopper-type scenery. It is a matter of drawing store fronts, heavy bedroom boudoirs, the heisting of a lonely service station, with light furious strokes. Also, in mixing jolting vulgarity (Mae Clarke's face being smashed with a grapefruit) with a space composition dance in which the scene seems to be constructed before your eyes. It may be a minor achievement but when Wellman finishes with a service station or the wooden stairs in front of an ancient saloon, there is no reason for any movie realist to handle the subject again. The scene is kept light, textural, and as though it is being built from the outside in. There is no sentiment of the type that spreads lugubrious shadows (Kazan), builds tensions of perspective (Huston), or inflates with golden sunlight and finicky hot air (Stevens).

Easily the best part of underground films are the excavations of exciting-familiar scenery. The opening up of a scene is more concerted in these films than in other Hollywood efforts, but the most important thing is that the opening is done by road-mapped strategies that play movement against space in a cunning way, building the environment and event before your eyes. In every underground film, these vigorous ramifications within a sharply seen terrain are the big attraction, the main tent. No one does this anatomization of action and scene better than Hawks, who probably invented it—at least, the smooth version—in such 1930's gunblasts as *The Crowd Roars*. The control of Hawks's strategies is so ingenious that when a person kneels or walks down the hallway, the movement seems to click into a predetermined slot. It is an uncanny accomplishment that carries the spectator across the very ground of a giant ranch, into rooms and out again, over to the wall to look at some faded fight pictures on a hotel wall—as though he were in the grip of a spectacular, mobile "eye." When Hawks landscapes action—the cutting between light tower and storm-caught plane in *Ceiling Zero*, the vegetalizing in *The Thing*, the shamus sweating in a greenhouse in *The Big Sleep*—the feeling is of a clever human tunneling just under the surface of terrain. It is as though the film has a life of its own that goes on beneath the story action.

However, there have been many great examples of such veining by human interactions over a wide plane. One of the special shockers, in *Each Dawn I Die*, has to do with the scissoring of a stooly during the movie shown at the penitentiary. This Keighley-Cagney effort is a wonder of excitement as it moves in great leaps from screen to the rear of a crowded auditorium: crossing contrasts of movement in three points of the hall, all of it done in a sinking cavernous gloom. One of the more ironic criss-crossings has to do with the coughings of the stuck victim played against the screen image of zooming airplanes over the Pacific.

In the great virtuoso films, there is something vaguely resembling this underground maneuvering, only it goes on above the story. Egocentric padding that builds a great bonfire of pyrotechnics over a gapingly empty film. The perfect example is a pumped-up fist fight that almost closes the three-hour *Giant* film. This ballroom shuffle between a reforming rancher and a Mexican-hating luncheonette owner is an entertaining creation in spectacular tumbling, swinging, back-arching, bending. However, the endless masturbatory "building" of excitement—beautiful haymakers, room-covering falls, thunderous sounds—is more than slightly silly. Even if the room were valid, which it isn't (a studio-built chromium horror plopped too close to the edge of a lonely highway), the room goes unexplored because of the jumbled timing. The excess that is so noticeable in Stevens's brawl is absent in the least serious undergrounder, which attains most of its crisp, angular character from the modesty of a director working skillfully far within the earthworks of the story.

Underground films have almost ceased to be a part of the movie scene. The founders of the action film have gone into awkward, big-scaled productions involving pyramid-building, a passenger plane in trouble over the Pacific, and postcard Westerns with Jimmy Stewart and his harassed Adam's apple approach to gutty acting. The last drainings of the underground film show a tendency toward moving from the plain guttural approach of *G Men* to a Germanically splashed type of film. Of these newcomers, Robert Aldrich is certainly the most exciting—a lurid psychiatric stormer who gets an overflow of vitality and sheer love for movie-making into the film. This enthusiasm is the rarest item in a dried, decayed-lemon type of movie period. Aldrich makes viciously anti-Something movies—*Attack* stomps on Southern rascalism and the officer sect in war, *The Big Knife* impales the Zanuck-Goldwyn big shot in Hollywood. The Aldrich films are filled with exciting characterizations—by Lee Marvin, Rod Steiger, Jack Palance—of highly psyched-up, marred, and bothered men. Phil Karlson has done some surprising modern Gothic treatments of the Brinks' hold-up (*Kansas City Confidential*) and the vice-ridden Southern town (*The Phenix City Story*). His movies are remarkable for their endless outlay of scary cheapness in detailing the modern underworld. Also, Karlson's work has a chilling documentary exactness and an exciting shot-scattering belligerence.

There is no longer a literate audience for the masculine picture-making that Hawks and Wellman exploited, as there was in the 1930's. In those exciting movie years, a smart audience waited around each week for the next Hawks, Preston Sturges, or Ford film—shoe-stringers that were far to the side of the expensive Hollywood film. That underground audience, with its expert voice in Ferguson and its ability to choose between perceptive trash and the Thalberg pepsin-flavored sloshing with Tracy and Gable, has now oozed away. It seems ridiculous, but the Fergusonite went into fast decline during the mid-1940's when the movie market was flooded with fake underground films—plushy thrillers with neo-Chandler scripts and a romantic style that seemed to pour the gore, histrionics, décor out of a giant catsup bottle. The nadir of these films: an item called *Singapore* with Fred MacMurray and Ava Gardner.

The straw that finally breaks the back of the underground film tradition is the dilettante behavior of intellectuals on the subject of oaters. Aesthetes and upper bohemians now favor horse operas almost as wildly as they like the cute, little-guy worshipings of De Sica and the pedantic, interpretive reading of Alec Guinness. This fad for Western films shows itself in the inevitable little magazine review which finds an affinity between the subject matter of cowboy films and the inner aesthetics of Cinemah. The Hawks-Wellman tradition, which is basically a subterranean delight that looks like a cheap penny candy on the outside, hasn't a chance of reviving when intellectuals enthuse in equal amounts over Westerns by Ford, Nunnally Johnson, J. Sturges, Stevens, Delmar Daves. In Ferguson's day, the intellectual could differentiate between a stolid genre painter (Ford), a long-winded cuteness expert with a rotogravure movie sense (Johnson), a scene painter with a notions-counter eye and a primly naive manner with sun-hardened bruisers (John Sturges), and a *Boys Life* nature lover who intelligently half prettifies adolescents and backwoods primitives (Daves). Today, the audience for Westerns and gangster careers is a sickeningly frivolous one that does little more than play the garbage collector or make a night court of films. With this highbrow audience, that loves banality and pomp more than the tourists at Radio City Music Hall, there is little reason to expect any stray director to try for a hidden, meager-looking work that is directly against the serious art grain.

1957

White Elephant Art vs. Termite Art

Most of the feckless, listless quality of today's art can be blamed on its drive to break out of a tradition while, irrationally, hewing to the square, boxed-in shape and gemlike inertia of an old, densely wrought European masterpiece.

Advanced painting has long been suffering from this burntout notion of a masterpiece—breaking away from its imprisoning conditions toward a suicidal improvisation, threatening to move nowhere and everywhere, niggling, omnivorous, ambitionless; yet, within the same picture, paying strict obeisance to the canvas edge and, without favoritism, the precious nature of every inch of allowable space. A classic example of this inertia is the Cézanne painting: in his indoorish works of the woods around Aix-en-Provence, a few spots of tingling, jarring excitement occur where he nibbles away at what he calls his "small sensation," the shifting of a tree trunk, the infinitesimal contests of complementary colors in a light accent on farmhouse wall. The rest of each canvas is a clogging weight-density-structure-polish amalgam associated with self-aggrandizing masterwork. As he moves away from the unique, personal vision that interests him, his painting turns ungiving and puzzling: a matter of balancing curves for his bunched-in composition, laminating the color, working the painting to the edge. Cézanne ironically left an exposé of his dreary finishing work in terrifyingly honest watercolors, an occasional unfinished oil (the pinkish portrait of his wife in sunny, leafed-in patio), where he foregoes everything but his spotting fascination with minute interactions.

The idea of art as an expensive hunk of well-regulated area, both logical and magical, sits heavily over the talent of every modern painter, from Motherwell to Andy Warhol. The private voice of Motherwell (the exciting drama in the meeting places between ambivalent shapes, the aromatic sensuality that comes from laying down thin sheets of cold, artfully clichéish, hedonistic color) is inevitably ruined by having to spread these small pleasures into great contained works. Thrown back constantly on unrewarding endeavors (filling vast egglike shapes, organizing a ten-foot rectangle with its empty corners suggesting Siberian steppes in the coldest time of the year), Motherwell ends up with appalling amounts of plasterish grandeur, a composition so huge and questionably painted that the delicate, electric contours seem to be crushing the shalelike matter inside. The special delight of each painting tycoon (De Kooning's sabrelike lancing of forms; Warhol's minute embrace with the path of illustrator's pen line and block-print tone; James Dine's slog-footed brio, filling a stylized shape from stem to stern with one ungiving color) is usually squandered in pursuit of the continuity, harmony, involved in constructing a masterpiece. The painting, sculpture, assemblage becomes a yawning production of overripe technique shrieking with preciosity, fame, ambition; far inside are tiny pillows holding up the artist's signature, now turned into mannerism by the padding, lechery, faking required to combine today's esthetics with the components of traditional Great Art.

Movies have always been suspiciously addicted to termite-art tendencies. Good work usually arises where the creators (Laurel and Hardy, the team of Howard Hawks and William Faulkner operating on the first half of Raymond Chandler's *The Big Sleep*) seem to have no ambitions towards gilt culture but are involved in a kind of squandering-beaverish endeavor that isn't anywhere or for anything. A peculiar fact about termite-tapeworm-fungus-moss art is that it goes always forward eating its own boundaries, and, likely as not, leaves nothing in its path other than the signs of eager, industrious, unkempt activity.

The most inclusive description of the art is that, termite-like, it feels its way through walls of particularization, with no sign that the artist has any object in mind other than eating away the immediate boundaries of his art, and turning these boundaries into conditions of the next achievement. Laurel and Hardy, in fact, in some of their most dyspeptic and funniest movies, like *Hog Wild*, contributed some fine parody of men who had read every "How to Succeed" book available; but, when it came to applying their knowledge, reverted instinctively to termite behavior.

One of the good termite performances (John Wayne's bemused cowboy in an unreal stage town inhabited by pallid repetitious actors whose chief trait is a powdered make-up) occurs in John Ford's *The Man Who Shot Liberty Valance*. Better Ford films than this have been marred by a phlegmatically solemn Irish personality that goes for rounded declamatory acting, silhouetted riders along the rim of a mountain with a golden sunset behind them, and repetitions in which big bodies are scrambled together in a rhythmically curving Rosa Bonheurish composition. Wayne's acting is infected by a kind of hoboish spirit, sitting back on its haunches doing a bitter-amused counterpoint to the pale, neutral film life around him. In an Arizona town that is too placid, where the cactus was planted last night and nostalgically cast actors do a generalized drunkenness, cowardice, voraciousness, Wayne is the termite actor focusing only on a tiny present area, nibbling at it with engaging professionalism and a hipster sense of how to sit in a chair leaned against the wall, eye a flogging over-actor (Lee Marvin). As he moves along at the pace of a tapeworm, Wayne leaves a path that is only bits of shrewd intramural acting—a craggy face filled with bitterness, jealousy, a big body that idles luxuriantly, having long grown tired with roughhouse games played by old wrangler types like John Ford.

The best examples of termite art appear in places other than films, where the spotlight of culture is nowhere in evidence, so that the craftsman can be ornery, wasteful, stubbornly self-involved, doing go-for-broke art and not caring what comes of it. The occasional newspaper column by a hard-work specialist caught up by an exciting event (Joe Alsop or Ted Lewis, during a presidential election), or a fireball technician reawakened during a pennant playoff that brings on stage his favorite villains (Dick Young); the TV production of *The Iceman Cometh*, with its great examples of slothful-buzzing acting by Myron McCormack, Jason Robards, et al.; the last few detective novels of Ross Macdonald and most of Raymond Chandler's ant-crawling verbosity and sober fact-pointing in the letters compiled years back in a slightly noticed book that is a fine running example of popular criticism; the TV debating of William Buckley, before he relinquished his tangential, counterattacking skill and took to flying into propeller blades of issues, like James Meredith's Ole Miss-adventures.

In movies, nontermite art is too much in command of writers and directors to permit the omnivorous termite artist to scuttle along for more than a few scenes. Even Wayne's cowboy job peters out in a gun duel that is overwrought with conflicting camera angles, plays of light and dark, ritualized movement and posture. In *The Loneliness of the Long Distance Runner*, the writer (Alan Sillitoe) feels the fragments of a delinquent's career have to be united in a conventional story. The design on which Sillitoe settles—a spokelike affair with each fragment shown as a memory experienced on practice runs—leads to repetitious scenes of a boy running. Even a gaudily individual track star—a Peter Snell—would have trouble making these practice runs worth the moviegoer's time, though a cheap ton of pseudo-Bunny Berigan jazz trumpet is thrown on the film's sound track to hop up the neutral dullness of these up-down-around spins through vibrant English countryside.

Masterpiece art, reminiscent of the enameled tobacco humidors and wooden lawn ponies bought at white elephant auctions decades ago, has come to dominate the overpopulated arts of TV and movies. The three sins of white elephant art (1) frame the action with an all-over pattern, (2) install every event, character, situation in a frieze of continuities, and (3) treat every inch of the screen and film as a potential area for prizeworthy creativity. *Requiem for a Heavyweight* is so heavily inlaid with ravishing technique that only one scene— an employment office with a nearly illiterate fighter (Anthony Quinn) falling into the hands of an impossibly kind job clerk—can be acted by Quinn's slag blanket type of expendable art, which crawls along using fair insight and a total immersion in the materials of acting. Antonioni's *La Notte* is a good example of the evils of continuity, from its opening scene of a deathly sick noble critic being visited by two dear friends. The scene gets off well, but the director carries the thread of it to agonizing length, embarrassing the viewer with dialogue about art that is sophomorically one dimensional, interweaving an arty shot of a helicopter to fill the time interval, continuing with impossible-to-act effects of sadness by Moreau and Mastroianni outside the hospital, and, finally, reels later, a laughable postscript conversation by Moreau-Mastroianni detailing the critic's "meaning" as a friend, as well as a few other very mystifying details about the poor bloke. Tony Richardson's films, beloved by art theater patrons, are surpassing examples of the sin of framing, boxing in an action with a noble idea or camera effect picked from High Art.

In Richardson's films (*A Taste of Honey*, *The Long Distance Runner*), a natural directing touch on domesticity involving losers is the main dish (even the air in Richardson's whitish rooms seems to be fighting the ragamuffin type who infests Richardson's young or old characters). With his "warm" liking for the materials of direction, a patient staying with confusion, holding to a cop's lead-footed pacelessness that doesn't crawl over details so much as back sluggishly into them. Richardson can stage his remarkable seconds-ticking sedentary act in almost any setup—at night, in front of a glarey department store window, or in a train coach with two pairs of kid lovers settling in with surprising, hopped-up animalism. Richardson's ability to give a spectator the feeling of being There, with time to spend, arrives at its peak in homes, apartments, art garrets, a stable-like apartment, where he turns into an academic neighbor of Walker Evans, steering the spectator's eyes on hidden rails, into arm patterns, worn wood, inclement feeling hovering in tiny marble eyes, occasionally even making a room appear to take shape as he introduces it to a puffy-faced detective or an expectant girl on her first search for a room of her own. In a kitchen scene with kid thief and job-worn detective irritably gnawing at each other, Richardson's talent for angular disclosures takes the scene apart without pointing or a nearly habitual underlining; nagging through various types of bone-worn, dishrag-gray material with a fine windup of two unlikable opponents still scraping at each other in a situation, that is one of the first to credibly turn the overattempted movie act—showing hard, agonizing existence in the wettest rain and slush.

Richardson's ability with deeply lived-in incident is, nevertheless, invariably dovetailed with his trick of settling a horse collar of gentility around the neck of a scene, giving the image a pattern that suggests practice, skill, guaranteed safe humor. His highly rated stars (from Richard Burton through Tom Courtenay) fall into mock emotion and studied turns, which suggest they are caught up in the enameled sequence of a vaudeville act: Rita Tushingham's sighting over a gun barrel at an amusement park (standard movie place for displaying types who are closer to the plow than the library card) does a broadly familiar comic arrangement of jaw muscle and eyebrow that has the gaiety and almost the size of a dinosaur bone. Another gentility Richardson picked up from fine *objêts d'art* (Dubuffet, Larry Rivers, Dick Tracy's creator) consists of setting a network of marring effects to prove his people are ill placed in life. Tom Courtenay (the last angry boy in *Runner*) gets carried away by this cult, belittling, elongating, turning himself into a dervish with a case of Saint Vitus dance, which localizes in his jaw muscles, eyelids. As Richardson gilds his near vagrants with sawtooth mop coiffures and a way of walking on high heels so that each heel seems a different size and both appear to be plunged through the worn flooring, the traits look increasingly elegant and put on (the worst trait: angry eyes that suggest the empty orbs in "Orphan Annie" comic strips). Most of his actors become crashing, unbelievable bores, though there is one nearly likable actor, a chubby Dreiserian girl friend in *Long Distance Runner* who, termite-fashion, almost acts into a state of grace. Package artist Richardson has other boxing-in ploys, running scenes together as Beautiful Travelogue, placing a cosmic symbol around the cross-country running event, which incidentally crushes Michael Redgrave, a headmaster in the fantastic gambol of throwing an entire Borstal community into a swivet over one track event.

The common denominator of these laborious ploys is, actually, the need of the director and writer to overfamiliarize the audience with the picture it's watching: to blow up every situation and character like an affable inner tube with recognizable details and smarmy compassion. Actually, this overfamiliarization serves to reconcile these supposed long-time enemies—academic and Madison Avenue art.

An exemplar of white elephant art, particularly the critic-devouring virtue of filling every pore of a work with glinting, darting Style and creative Vivacity, is François Truffaut. Truffaut's *Shoot the Piano Player* and *Jules et Jim*, two ratchety perpetual-motion machines devised by a French Rube Goldberg, leave behind the more obvious gadgetries of *Requiem for a Heavyweight* and even the cleaner, bladelike journalism of *The 400 Blows*.

Truffaut's concealed message, given away in his Henry Miller-ish, adolescent two-reeler of kids spying on a pair of lovers (one unforgettably daring image: kids sniffing the bicycle seat just vacated by the girl in the typical fashion of voyeuristic pornographic art) is a kind of reversal of growth, in which people grow backward into childhood. Suicide becomes a game, the houses look like toy boxes—laughter, death, putting out a fire—all seem reduced to some unreal innocence of childhood myths. The real innocence of *Jules et Jim* is in the writing, which depends on the spectator sharing the same wide-eyed or adolescent view of the wickedness of sex that is implicit in the vicious gamesmanship going on between two men and a girl.

Truffaut's stories (all women are villains; the schoolteacher seen through the eyes of a sniveling schoolboy; all heroes are unbelievably innocent, unbelievably persecuted) and characters convey the sense of being attached to a rubber band, although he makes a feint at reproducing the films of the 1930's with their linear freedom and independent veering. From *The 400 Blows* onward, his films are bound in and embarrassed by his having made up his mind what the film is to be about. This decisiveness converts the people and incidents into flat, jiggling mannikins (*400 Blows*, *Mischief Makers*) in a Mickey Mouse comic book, which is animated by thumbing the pages rapidly. This approach eliminates any stress or challenge, most of all any sense of the film locating an independent shape.

Jules et Jim, the one Truffaut film that seems held down to a gliding motion, is also cartoonlike but in a decorous, suspended way. Again most of the visual effect is an illustration for the current of the sentimental narrative. Truffaut's concentration on making his movie fluent and comprehensible flattens out all complexity and reduces his scenes to scraps of pornography—like someone quoting just the punchline of a well-known dirty joke. So unmotivated is the leapfrogging around beds of the three-way lovers that it leads to endless bits of burlesque. Why does she suddenly pull a gun? (See "villainy of women," above.) Why does she drive her car off a bridge? (Villains need to be punished.) Etc.

Jules et Jim seems to have been shot through a scrim which has filtered out everything except Truffaut's dry vivacity with dialogue and his diminutive stippling sensibility. Probably the high point in this love-is-time's-fool film: a languorous afternoon in a chalet (what's become of chalets?) with Jeanne Moreau teasing her two lovers with an endless folksong. Truffaut's lyrics—a patter of vivacious small talk that is supposed to exhibit the writer's sophistication, never mind about what—provides most of the scene's friction, along with an idiot concentration on meaningless details of faces or even furniture (the degree that a rocking chair isn't rocking becomes an impressive substitute for psychology). The point is that, divested of this meaningless vivacity, the scenes themselves are without tension, dramatic or psychological.

The boredom aroused by Truffaut—to say nothing of the irritation—comes from his peculiar methods of dehydrating all the life out of his scenes (instant movies?). Thanks to his fondness for doused lighting and for the kind of long shots which hold his actors at thirty paces, especially in bad weather, it's not only the people who are blanked out; the scene itself threatens to evaporate off the edge of the screen. Adding to the effect of evaporation, disappearing: Truffaut's imagery is limited to traveling (running through meadows, walking in Paris streets, etc.), setups and dialogue scenes where the voices, disembodied and like the freakish chirps in Mel Blanc's *Porky Pig* cartoons, take care of the flying out effect. Truffaut's system holds art at a distance without any actual muscularity or propulsion to peg the film down. As the spectator leans forward to grab the film, it disappears like a released kite.

Antonioni's specialty, the effect of moving as in a chess game, becomes an autocratic kind of direction that robs an actor of his motive powers and most of his spine. A documentarist at heart and one who often suggests both Paul Klee and the cool, deftly neat, "intellectual" Fred Zinnemann in his early *Act of Violence* phase, Antonioni gets his odd, clarity-is-all effects from his taste for chic mannerist art that results in a screen that is glassy, has a side-sliding motion, the feeling of people plastered against stripes or divided by verticals and horizontals; his incapacity with interpersonal relationships turns crowds into stiff waves, lovers into lonely appendages, hanging stiffly from each other, occasionally coming together like clanking sheets of metal but seldom giving the effect of being in communion.

At his best, he turns this mental creeping into an effect of modern misery, loneliness, cavernous guilt-ridden yearning. It often seems that details, a gesture, an ironic wife making a circle in the air with her finger as a thought circles toward her brain, become corroded by solitariness. A pop jazz band appearing at a millionaire's fête becomes the unintentional heart of *La Notte*, pulling together the inchoate center of the film—a vast endless party. Antonioni handles this combo as though it were a vile mess dumped on the lawn of a huge estate. He has his film inhale and exhale, returning for a glimpse of the four-piece outfit playing the same unmodified kitsch music—stupidly immobile, totally detached from the party swimming around the music. The film's most affecting shot is one of Jeanne Moreau making tentative stabs with her somber, alienated eyes and mouth, a bit of a dance step, at rapport and friendship with the musicians. Moreau's facial mask, a signature worn by all Antonioni players, seems about to crack from so much sudden uninhibited effort.

The common quality or defect which unites apparently divergent artists like Antonioni, Truffaut, Richardson is fear, a fear of the potential life, rudeness, and outrageousness of a film. Coupled with their storage vault of self-awareness and knowledge of film history, this fear produces an incessant wakefulness. In Truffaut's films, this wakefulness shows up as dry, fluttering inanity. In Antonioni's films, the mica-schist appearance of the movies, their linear patterns, are hulked into obscurity by Antonioni's own fund of sentimentalism, the need to get a mural-like thinness and interminableness out of his mean patterns.

The absurdity of *La Notte* and *L'Avventura* is that its director is an authentically interesting oddball who doesn't recognize the fact. His talent is for small eccentric microscope studies, like Paul Klee's, of people and things pinned in their grotesquerie to an oppressive social backdrop. Unlike Klee, who stayed small and thus almost evaded affectation, Antonioni's aspiration is to pin the viewer to the wall and slug him with wet towels of artiness and significance. At one point in *La Notte*, the unhappy wife, taking the director's patented walk through a continent of scenery, stops in a rubbled section to peel a large piece of rusted tin. This ikon close-up of minuscule desolation is probably the most overworked cliché in still photography, but Antonioni, to keep his stories and events moving like great novels through significant material, never stops throwing his Sunday punch. There is an interestingly acted nymphomaniac girl at wit's end trying to rape the dish-rag hero; this is a big event, particularly for the first five minutes of a film. Antonioni overweights this terrorized girl and her interesting mop of straggly hair by pinning her into a typical Band-aid composition—the girl, like a tiny tormented animal, backed against a large horizontal stripe of white wall. It is a pretentiously handsome image that compromises the harrowing effect of the scene.

Whatever the professed theme in these films, the one that dominates in unspoken thought is that the film business is finished with museum art or pastiche art. The best evidence of this disenchantment is the anachronistic slackness of *Jules et Jim, Billy Budd, Two Weeks in Another Town*. They seem to have been dropped into the present from a past which has become useless. This chasm between white-elephant reflexes and termite performances shows itself in an inertia and tight defensiveness which informs the acting of Mickey Rooney in *Requiem for a Heavyweight*, Julie Harris in the same film, and the spiritless survey of a deserted church in *L'Avventura*. Such scenes and actors seem as numb and uninspired by the emotions they are supposed to animate, as hobos trying to draw warmth from an antiquated coal stove. This chasm of inertia seems to testify that the Past of heavily insured, enclosed film art has become unintelligible to contemporary performers, even including those who lived through its period of relevance.

Citizen Kane, in 1941, antedated by several years a crucial change in films from the old flowing naturalistic story, bringing in an iceberg film of hidden meanings. Now the revolution wrought by the exciting but hammy Orson Welles film, reaching its zenith in the 1950's, has run its course and been superceded by a new film technique that turns up like an ugly shrub even in the midst of films that are preponderantly old gems. Oddly enough the film that starts the breaking away is a middle-1950's film, that seems on the surface to be as traditional as *Greed*. Kurosawa's *Ikiru* is a giveaway landmark, suggesting a new self-centering approach. It sums up much of what a termite art aims at: buglike immersion in a small area without point or aim, and, over all, concentration on nailing down one moment without glamorizing it, but forgetting this accomplishment as soon as it has been passed; the feeling that all is expendable, that it can be chopped up and flung down in a different arrangement without ruin.

1962

Kitchen Without Kitsch
(with Patricia Patterson)

The lay of the land, in the Seventies film, is that there are two types of structure being practiced: dispersal and shallow-boxed space. *Rameau's Nephew, McCabe and Mrs. Miller, Celine and Julie Go Boating, Beware of the Holy Whore* are films that believe implicitly in the idea of non-solidity, that everything is a mass of energy particles, and the aim, structurally, is a flux-like space to go with the atomized content and the idea of keeping the freshness and energy of a real world within the movie's frame. Inconclusiveness is a big quality in the Seventies: never give the whole picture, the last word. A distinctly different structure and intellectual set—used in films as various as *In the Realm of the Senses, Katzelmacher, Nostalgia* (the Hollis Frampton film in which a set of awful photos are presented and destroyed on a one-burner hot plate), the various short films of minimalist sculptors and painters—is to present a shallow stage with the ritualized, low-population image squared to the edges of the frame. Facing a fairly close camera, the formal-abstract-intellectualized content evolves at right angles to the camera, and usually signifies a filmmaker who has intellectually surrounded the material. In both cases, the strategy is often encasing a strikingly petty event: a nonviolinist scrapes away on a violin in a Richard Serra film; the limp Laurel-and-Hardy high jinks beginning Rivette's *Celine and Julie* has one mugging charmer chasing another through Paris to return a book left on a park bench; *Rameau's Nephew* creates linguistic/filmic systems using avant-garde types in low comic dress; and in Fassbinder's *Katzel-macher*, two indolents gossip their way toward a reverse tracking camera—a startlingly handsome image encasing absurd, inane conversations. Each film picks up the current fascination with keeping things a little bit amateurish, as though that were an automatic connection to drollery and wit. In all the above-mentioned films, grandness and pettiness are blended in skeptical visions that significantly go against heroic careers.

The thing that strikes one about the early-Seventies Fassbinder *Beware of the Holy Whore* is the movement of both camera and actors, a kind of lurching serpentine of petulant drawling sounds, inside jokes, and minute-long temper tantrums. They're all like flicks within a flux of sexual liaisons. Everyone is distracted, anxious: they're weeping, betraying, at the level of two cents. Kurt Raab collapses onto the bar, exaggerated and whining, very melodramatic, "I can't bear it!" The circular, 360-degree pan of a hotel lobby picks up bits of decadence from strays around the room: one girl saying she likes a Spanish light technician sitting nearby, another member of this desultory film crew saying to his new acquaintance, "I could help you if you came to Rome."

Central to the Seventies dispersed movie is the lack of big statement (as there is in *Citizen Kane*, *L'Avventura*). It is a profoundly rhythmic filmmaking, with a lot of lower-case observations, a brusque, ragged movement in *Mean Streets* and a ballad-like rhythm in Altman's *McCabe* with its clutter of ideas about frontier life, starting with the individual-vs.-the-corporation problem, the bewildered love of a foolhardy romantic for a practical down-to-earther, etc. etc. What is picked up about the trudging, muttering McCabe character, with his derby and long overcoat, is a half sentence ("got poetry in me—ain't gonna put it down"), a suspicious and balky glance. Centering upon a person or event is not involved. *Celine and Julie Go Boating* is a new organism, the atomization of a character, an event, a space, as though all of its small spaces have been de-solidified to allow air to move amongst the tiny spaces. A bit like a Cézanne watercolor, where more than half the event is elided to allow energy to move in and out of vague landscape notations, Rivette's slaphappy duo in a musical without music can't be defined. Each is a series of coy and narcissistic actions. They appear out of nowhere, no past profession or character traits: at one moment Celine is a sober librarian, and at another she is a stage magician, suddenly a fantastic extrovert. Who are those people in the large Gothic establishment? A shaft of air encircles each bit of information about the two mysteries; things are deliberately kept uncircled.

The Straubs—Danièle Huillet and her husband—are the penultimate exponents of shallow space filming: a very hard presentation of minimal visual information with the one major difference, that the composition is angled diagonally into the shallow space. While they move back and forth between grand spatiality (*Moses and Aaron*) and movies in which the subject matter is tight to the surface (*History Lessons*), the Straubs are always major spade-and-shovel workers in framing that places the material close to the surface, whether they are doing classical theater on a sun-baked Roman terrrace or a long tracking on the Landsbergerstrasse in Munich's red-light district, or staging a telescoped filmed play. Their Bach film is a breakthrough in filming an undramatized act: underlining the editing rhythm, a very programmed camera, and the geometry of groups: adding a documentarian's respect for the subjects and asserting the most rigorous respect for a movie's text ever perpetrated. The Straubs' upfront framing is interesting in that it creates both a feeling of cement blocks and extraordinary poetry at the same time.

It's also interesting here to mention Ozu's far-earlier-than Seventies work with shallow-boxed frame innovations, using still-life interstices to do the work of an establishing shot, framing the most jagged husband-mistress conflict across railroad tracks as a two-dimensional emblematic design, playing out entire episodes in bars and modern "project" rooms so that every door frame, every crossover move by a snotty six-year-old, is schematized and abstracted into a perfectly poised, becalmed world view. Ozu, without drawing a heavy breath, predicted many of the conditions in upfront boxed movies: a limited cast, very domestic situations, abstract placements, the sense of people trying to break-out of or living within the rules, super-controlled direction.

The images of the wife and daughter waiting at the dinner table for Hans to come home in Fassbinder's *Merchant of the Four Seasons* had the same visual stillness and handsomeness containing suppressed nerves at the dinner table as the scenes with mother and son in Chantal Akerman's *Jeanne Dielman, 23 Quai de Commerce—1080 Bruxelles*: the same sparsity of dialogue, phrases like "Isn't the beef better this week than last, I added less water this time" or "Don't read at the table" or "I've received a letter from Aunt Fernande in Canada." Each of Jeanne's isolated remarks is responded to by a *oui*, a grunt, a nod, and each one preceded and followed by an uneasy but unaccented silence. This is Bressonian territory. But unlike the dinner-table scenes in *Merchant*, in this film one gets the entire meal: its purchase, preparation, consumption, the cleaning up of the table and washing of the dishes, all this conveyed through images of terrific clarity. Each step in this meal's progress necessitates passages from kitchen to hallway, through doorway rectangles of flower-printed wallpaper and painted woodwork, the figure of Jeanne framed over and over as she moves from room to room, putting lights on and off, changing into and out of her work smock, her cardigan sweaters, her street coat.

A marginal life away from the progressing mainstream, with all the traditional forms and strictures, is chronicled with a static wide-angled lens, using structural traits first found in Warhol's fixed-frame film (early Sixties) and developed in other repetitive films (Ernie Gehr, Michael Snow, *et al.*) in which the space becomes spiritualized and proliferates ideas. The Dielman film—in which the spectator peculiarly becomes a coolly curious voyeur and jurist watching a case history—is often a breathtaking, crisp, and luminous example of shallow-boxed framing.

The drily pugnacious title (*Jeanne Dielman, 23 Quai de Commerce—1080 Bruxelles*) is a give away on the movie's politics and mental set. It suggests that Chantal Akerman, a shrewd young Belgian who is bridging the gap between the commercial film and the structural (every part, every shot is representative of the movie's shape), has a passion for the factual, is not going to make the heroine, a field marshall of the kitchen (Delphine Seyrig), any more or less than what she is; has a contemporary yen for a blunt presentation of objects, spaces, proper names, and geography; and is concerned with defining a puritanistic and routinized woman in her space, describing her existence, how she moves from sink to table, her daily rounds in a one-bedroom, fusty flat. There is a definite respect for surfaces; a lot of this is Babette Mangolte, whose dead-straight cinematography, impeccably framed, is responsive to the cool hardness of a tile wall, the flat light cast by one ceiling fixture, the crisp whiteness of bed linen, light changing on a casement window. The movie is thoroughly a product of Seventies sensibility: the integrity of things as they already stand, the presentation of a text as a concrete object, and out-front admission of the means of production.

This still-life film—a genre painting by a Seventies Chardin (to quote Babette Mangolte: "a Forties story shot by a Seventies camera")—is vivified by a welter of louder than natural noises on the sound track. What an inspired idea, to treat the sounds of the kitchen as music: sounds of pot covers, ladling, a kettle hissing, water running, splashing, sponge against pot, sponge against plate, plate against table. And in the image, there is the incessant turning on and off of lights by the penny-conscious Jeanne, the small intricacies of housekeeping, opening and shutting drawers, handing up scrub brushes, returning dish towels to their place, and replacing lids on pots. It's a movie in which neither the heroine nor the director cuts any corners, except on dialogue. The only line spoken in the kitchen: "Did you wash your hands?"

She's a logician who turns firm material into brilliantly sound equations: an industrious loner living a static existence is equaled by a space filled with noises; a life of routines going right, clicking, turn midway in the film into the same life of routines misfiring in little ways. The perfect symmetry of Akerman's constructions operates also in the plot, in which an everywoman's life is glued to a flashy red-light-herring idea.

A forty-year-old widow, mother of a dour son (obedient but pampered, like a fifteen-year-old De Gaulle) runs a matriarchal household without a wrinkle on the few bucks she makes from turning one trick a day. One might think that the luridness of the Simenon-like plot—that Jeanne Dielman is a prostitute, conducting her business in her tidy uptight bedroom once each afternoon, and that she scissors to death one of her clients on a mysterious postcoital impulse—came out of a pragmatic desire for more audience by a director whose heart belongs to the structural film but who wants more audience than a Gehr-Frampton-Sharits film gets at stray film clubs and college dates. But it's just as likely that the sex-gore material is an extreme expression of the director's radical feminism. Analysis of the luridness issue is further complicated by the fact there is an off-screen murder in which a near-corpse staggers into the frame in *Wavelength*, which has to be a big item in any structuralist's background.

Jeanne Dielman is the persevering woman's film, a conscientious mom forced into "the life" for the sake of son and s-income (before Seyrig's performance: Ruth Chatterton, Dietrich, Bankhead, Constance Bennett, and Garbo), reconsidered by three sophisticated women of the Seventies. The three pronged effort: a purified performance (Delphine Seyrig's) sustaining one suppressed note; a mesmerizing colored image (Babette Mangolte's) that uses the troublesome wide angle lens to suggest the entirety of Seyrig inside each frame, from her chaste pumps to the flat lighting of a single ceiling fixture; and, using some of its heroine's obsessive control on traditional detail, a feat of recall and engineering (Chantal Akerman's) which rearranges this second-by-second tragedy so that it has a bold, electric frontality, very close to the effect in Mike Snow's *The Central Region*.

Whatever image one has of Delphine Seyrig is bound to be involved with her haute-couture sinuosity, her graceful undulating body and voice. But the Seyrig of *Last Year at Marienbad* and *India Song* doesn't even resemble the straight-up-and-down puritan, Jeanne Dielman: seduction is out here. The A-1 intent of this fugue-like movie is to divulge the molecules of moment-to-moment existence, the repetitive conditions of life: eating, sleeping, cleaning. Both Seyrig and Akerman nail this single-track woman into her condition of doing and redoing; her elevator trips, dishwashing, rising from bed in cold pre-dawn are magnificently fulfilled by a performance that doesn't obfuscate the movie's routinized, repetitious *mise-en-scène*.

It's a resolute film that knows exactly what it wants. Its three makers are seemingly in perfect accord as to what they want to say about a tradition-bound treadmill whose back-forth, up-down existence is the phenomenological stuff of this movie, what other movies leave out. The hallway scenes—which take on a shoving force and awkward angularity as Seyrig's one-track woman goes over the same tasks, errands, exits, and entrances—convey her driven state of mind. With its sculptural capture of hallway surfaces and the unchanging gaze of the factual camera, Seyrig's force as a human metronome hits the spectator with the monotony and poignance of such a life. When this movie's going right, it makes the spectator aware not only of repetitiousness but of the actual duration of a commonplace act. What's wonderful is that we are made to *feel* the length of time it takes water to filter through in coffee-making, the length of time a sponge bath consumes, the number of spoonfuls it takes to eat soup, the number of steps from the kitchen stove to dining-room table, how many floors it takes the elevator to move Jeanne from her flat to the ground.

In the morning Seyrig-Dielman awakes to the alarm. She is buried inside the voluminous, white, linen-encased comforter which is like a tidal wave across the entire lower half of the screen. Next to this arctic white mass is a dark-looming wardrobe, and at the foot of the bed a window opens up into the room. Jeanne throws off the covers in one gesture, gets up and stands at the open window, looking out as she puts on her pale-blue flannel robe. She stands abstracted, still groggy, buttoning her robe. A hard, minimal space, with early-morning air wafting through a modern composition, thrusts each shape at the audience as though the surface of the form had been flattened and weighted.

Within this sharp, cold dampness (it is one of the few moments of distinct climate in a largely indoor film), Jeanne moves to the kitchen, beginning the elaborate start of the daily ritual, grinding the coffee, putting on the kettle, polishing her son Sylvain's shoes, setting the kitchen table for his breakfast. The kitchen is like a shallow stage of black and white tiles and green curtains, a stage that has a peculiar still-shot-shallowness and seems estranged, cut off from neighbors, the rest of the city. As in Vermeer's equally bounded painting, pettiness and grandness are blended in a seamless domesticity in which every item carries precise information and registers within a color that looks both slow and full.

Her traits are those of a monumentally efficient housewife, totally routinized, detail-obsessed. (A great example: she searches all over Brussels to match a button for a jacket.) Jeanne Dielman is brought up to a certain point of portrayal and then left an abstraction, a symbol of the repressed woman. Repressed in many ways: she can't express herself in anything but formularized paths. She doesn't know how to use language personally, and can only say things like "My son is a wonderful boy. I don't know what I would do without him." She serves the same meals in the same sequence each week.

Jeanne D., locked within her three-room flat existence, fits the conditions of a structural film to a T or a D. Her life unfolds in perfect mathematical inhale-exhale clarity, first running well and then at midpoint falling apart over the same routines. The conditions of a minimal underground classic—that the shape of a film be discernible in any single frame; that a single-camera strategy be the basis for the movie's metaphysic and any situation within the film; that the repetitions of the camera, which is always obviously present, creates a spirituality; and that the field of examination be more or less static, durational, and un-romanticized—couldn't have found a better narrative than the one in which a life dedicated to perfection breeds its opposite, an apocalypse of sinister results.

The movie's key is that it presents one full day as the handy heroine's norm, and then shows it spinning out of control midway in the tragedy when the wooden Jeanne is jolted. Her attention, which till now has been exclusively focused on timing (her paid coital encounters are timed to fit into the act of boiling potatoes for her momma-regulated son's dinner), is distracted by a new bedroom experience with her second day's customer. Only after having seen a normal twenty four-hour cycle does a spectator discern the signals of Seyrig's distress. The potatoes burn because she's washed the tub before taking the spuds off the fire; her hair is allowed to escape from its helmet-like perfection ("Your hair's all tousled" is her son's flat, Bressonian remark); she forgets to turn on the radio after dinner, and can't concentrate on a letter to her sister Fernande. "No inspiration," asks Sylvain from the couch.

With its still-shot vision and durational attitude toward recording chores in full, Seyrig's ladylike stylization stimulates speculations of all types. Akerman's probable reaction to such spectator psychology work would probably be boredom: "O.K., if you want to find a polemic against the nuclear family, go right ahead." But the fact is that the movie proves itself by generating intellectual action. It is no minor plus, the wealth of questions that are thrown up (Is this a diatribe against housework? Is it a Marxian examination of the isolated individual in an every-man-for-himself society?) to keep earnest eggheads ruminating long after its handsome image and flat sculpted shapes have disappeared.

In the background of its three artists are such prestigious Manhattanites as Robert Frank, Annette Michelson, Yvonne Rainer, Mike Snow, P. Adams

Sitney, ad infinitum. These and other voices echo through this acute and impressive work: the look of the film, its geometric clarity (Ozu, Straub, Snow), the heroine's psychology and behavior (Buñuel and Bresson), the script's co-existence of respectability and prostitution (*Belle de Jour* and Godard's *Two or Three Things*): As in Buñuel's *El*, the fetishistic handling of items that resonate sexuality gives a movie that is closemouthed and dour a lot of humor, intentional or not. Basically, three women are insisting that the conventional world of a woman be seen straight in a film that is stylistically somewhat domesticated, being a delta of the most influential style-content movies in the less straight film world—the one called variously as radical, visionary, avant-garde, or underground.

Partly it is the early Warhol gig: almost like a silent movie, no music, very little dialogue, a self-willed woman's working is pinned by one unbudging four-to-five feet high camera. As in Warhol's *Nude Kitchen* or *Bike Boy*, a movie that is stylized from first to last moment makes a theater of the mundane act of Jeanne's every chore. The final long extended glimpse of a staring Jeanne seated at the dining-room table suggests the final Warhol shot freezing an image of his sleeper.

The same strategy which presents Gustav Leonhardt playing an entire harpsichord piece within one diagonal camera setup in Straub's *Chronicle of Anna Magdalena Bach* is used to present Delphine Seyrig making a meat loaf. In both cases what is presented has complete documentary integrity within a self-contained frame. A virtuoso of the harpsichord or mixing bowl is being allowed a full imprint or registration without types of filmic spicing (fancy mimicry, seductive camera shots, editing for impact or psychology).

Though somewhat pat in comparison to its fiercer influences, the Akerman revelation is a political thrust against the box-office hype of the straight press, which has convinced audiences that it needs Vito Corleones, Johnny Guitars, or Carries, constant juicing, dramatic rises and falls for its satisfaction. The audience has been brainwashed to believe it can't stand certain experiences, thanks to the Mekas propaganda wheel as well as the media hypesters. Watching the luminously magical space of a washing-smoothing-cooking-slicing-kneading near-peasant is particularly provocative in that it suggests a workable parlance between the structural and commercial film.

1977

Parker Tyler

It was the conviction of Parker Tyler (1904–1974) that popular movies, while mainly intended as entertainment, also transmitted unconscious meanings that formed the symbolic bases of our modern myths. In his book *Magic and Myth in the Movies*, he turned film plots inside-out and interrogated them for hidden, underlying patterns, blithely explaining that he was merely following the lead of psychoanalysis and the law courts in showing how *things are not always what they seem*. In the analysis of *Double Indemnity* below, he found surprising undercurrents by tracking the relationship between the characters played by Fred MacMurray and Edward G. Robinson. It is important to realize that Tyler wrote this critique in the 1940s, when *Double Indemnity* first appeared and long before it had attained its current status as a *film noir* classic. His uncovering of homoerotic content was provocative at the time; later, in the 1960s, he wrote the pioneering study *Screening the Sexes: Homosexuality in the Movies*, in which he put forward more explicitly his vision of human beings as taken by multiple longings, or what might be called pan-sexuality. Movies, so physically attentive to the human body and its gestures, were uniquely suited to capture these nuances. "In sexual matters, more than other matters, the movies become profound," wrote Tyler. Though there had long been an underground market in picture books about Eros and the cinema, Tyler never relinquished his high critical criteria while discussing these matters—never stooped to prurience or artistic over-valuation. His cultivated, restrained tone and formal diction barely concealed a mischievous smile at the regular triumph of unconscious desire over rational sense. In his other movie criticism, such as *Classics of the Foreign Film*, he displayed wide-ranging discernment and appreciation of film as art. Parker Tyler's major achievement was summarized by fellow critic Andrew Sarris: "He was the first American film critic and scholar to explore the subject [of sex] in depth with wit, taste, and high cultural standards."

◆

Double into Quadruple Indemnity

In the misty, before-dawn streets of a city a roadster races, barely missing other vehicles but apparently not pursued, therefore bent on some destination. It pulls up before an office building, and the tall, rather hunched figure of a man alights and rings the night bell. One arm seems to be stiff as the elderly, chatty custodian takes him up in the elevator. He stalks onto the mezzanine of the spacious quarters of a life-insurance firm, seeks an inner office, and falling awkwardly into a chair, removes his coat, worn cloak fashion, and reveals a dark, wet hole—blood—in the shoulder of his jacket. Breathing heavily and sweating, he reaches for a dictaphone, starts the mechanism, and settles back, gasping, to begin his message. It is a confession of murder . . . addressed to the head claim adjuster of the firm for which he is a salesman.

This is the bravura and effective manner in which the bravura and effective *Double Indemnity* opens, a story that emerges from film hands as a thing considerably different from the novel by James Cain on which it was based. However tight and attention-holding the telling—and it is that—there are momentary interims when one wonders why the culprit, who has murdered a man with the man's wife as accomplice in order to collect his life insurance, should be confessing in this manner when he might be attempting a getaway over the near-by border. The cinema specialists would hardly create the device merely in order to be mechanically effective. There is a most interesting reason for it, however, when all the elements of this melo-melo are correlated.

From top to bottom and from side to side the pattern is one of dualism, both intentional and unintentional. Indeed what would Hollywood do without its supplementary automatism? Thus the title, *Double Indemnity*, has a basic symbolism. Murdering the gentleman in question without being aware that he has been the object of previous solicitude entails payment of a sum to his widow, who, as it happens, is to share it with her lover and co-criminal, the insurance agent. But Neff, the agent, quite familiar with the double-indemnity clause, has planned a doubly lucrative death, since, according to the statistics of mortality, falling off a train is a most out-of-the-way accident. Both the lady, Phyllis Didriksen, and her colleague, Neff, might be supposed subject to mere greed—well and good. But considering the saturative dualism in the movie, too much in the way of ambiguous motivation is present to make such a simple premise seem valid. We must skeptically investigate the possible claim of Hollywood and common sense in this respect.

To start back even before the insurance agent happens upon Phyllis, with her exposed legs and her anklet, one hot afternoon when he calls about accident insurance on the Didriksen car—and finds the master of the house absent—it is plain that Neff's relation with the claim adjuster, Keyes, contains the dualism of subtle business hostility and personal friendship. Keyes's job is to determine if insurance claims are valid; in other words, he is the guardian angel of occasions when Neff's policy sales have their most unfortunate and anticlimactic aspect; that is, when their logic of possibility, death or accident, becomes a factual certainty and the firm groans and has to pay up. Thus Keyes stands by, always alert, as an internal corrective, from the firm's viewpoint, for fraudulent representations of deaths and accidents. Keyes in Neff's eyes is ever present to validate the myth of his daily sales talks, which is that human wisdom has provided a method of safeguarding against certain consequences of accident or death. On the other hand, Keyes is also waiting to *invalidate* this myth by sometimes assuming and on notable occasions proving its falsity. If a client of Neff's burns down his own truck and wants to collect, he is willy-nilly realizing the *logic* of Neff's sales talk, but Keyes in rooting out the fraud mocks the ideal logic, the mythological charm, of Neff's sales talk by calling attention to the unpleasantness involved in its consequences—not to the mere fact of destruction but to the causation of destruction as in the case of the burned truck. The would-be beneficiary is no ideal victim of fate but a low cheater of insurance firms.

Let us examine more thoroughly the reasons why the invalidation of insurance claims might bother a policy salesman. As we know, the insurance company is a profit-making organization, and the logical basis of its profit is that in the great percentage of cases the emotional logic of the sales talk—the scientific possibility of the insured party's death or accident to property or self converted into emotional probability—is false. It is on this type of falsity that a salesman's earnings are based, for, as is well known, he has to overcome the psychological aversion from the emotional probability of death as the nucleus of resistance in his prospective client. It is the client's ordinary prejudice against formal psychological consent to the possibility of his death that spoils many a policy sale. The salesman's persuasiveness overcomes this prejudice, only perhaps to be followed later with a claim for accident indemnity that the claim adjuster believes invalid. So claim validation stands as an ethical corrective to possible fraudulent consequences flowing from the policy sale.

We are well aware that insurance firms are not torn asunder by such an ethically obscure and rather abstract sort of dichotomy. But here we are involved with a particular salesman and a particular claim adjuster, the structure of whose personal relationship is an extension, partly symbolic and partly material, of the moral elements contained in their business relationship and its overtones of human ethics. In view of the plot itself, we have to assume a special sensitivity of conscience on Neff's part, a special recognition of Keyes's claims on him, both business and personal. His climactic confession into the dictaphone is a convincing symptom of this situation. Moreover, as Keyes's last speech, uttered over the wounded and trapped Neff, effectively clinches, Keyes takes a personal, neo-paternal interest in Neff, a concern to whose warmth Neff most belatedly and ironically responds by confessing the murder; in doing this, however, he proves that Keyes has cleverly penetrated the fraud concocted by himself and Phyllis and so gives the claim adjuster his deserved triumph as an expert. But on the face of it why should Neff, who seems a rather typical hard-boiled sort, appear as the self-immolative instrument of tragic irony? Some obscure fate must dominate him, one related to but by no means wholly defined by a desire to redeem his conventional honesty before the firm and its claim adjuster. In seeking out the nature of this fate I mean to indicate the more or less unconscious rightness of the author's and movie-maker's instinct in supplying a double symmetry, business and personal, for the relations between Keyes and Neff.

At a crucial point of the tension preceding the carefully planned crime Keyes offers Neff a job as claim adjuster, and after Neff responds with an uninterested negative and Keyes gives Neff's self-esteem a pep talk, Phyllis interrupts by phoning to say the moment has come for the crime; her husband is making a train trip. Neff calls her Margie and successfully disguises the meaning of the conversation. But the blunt Keyes scoffs at this Margie and rather directly blames women and carousing for Neff's indifference to the honor offered him—since at first he would have to take a reduction in salary. "I'll bet she drinks from the bottle!" Keyes exclaims of Margie. Neff's habitual treatment of Keyes's friendly feelings, which are obvious enough beneath the claim adjuster's hard-shelled exterior, is laconic and grinning, touched, moreover, with quaint irony by an often repeated and, I think, symbolic incident.

Keyes is always smoking cigars but is just as consistently without matches with which to light them. With an ironic little grin Neff ritually pulls out a matchbox, strikes a match, and lights Keyes's cigar. This may have been a bit of routine invention by busy studio scribes, or they may have borrowed it in characteristic blind haste—but blind haste may be most intuitive. From the mellow tenets of psychology we know that very small habits of this sort become rituals through the deliberate, even if veiled-from-self cultivation of the person who receives the favor. A master at his job and a poised individual, having made his moral peace with life, Keyes, extremely well played by Edward G. Robinson, may especially enjoy this tiny bit of moral dependence on Neff, whom he likes and whose liking he solicits. Emotional liking—there is no evidence that Keyes is married or has women—may be the only thing lacking to his daily satisfactions. Neff is not responsive, but in his good-natured yielding to the ritual of providing Keyes with a light he is submitting to an etiquette of friendliness that he performs in no other way. On the surface it is an empty form, and it may be as a mere symbolic form that Keyes accepts it—just as a lady secretly in love with the doorman of her hotel may derive a subtle, withal empty, satisfaction from his touch as he hands her into a cab.

It seems to me that the presence of the little ritual between Neff and Keyes is no accident and that its graphic nature is highly suggestive. Keyes has reason to be envious of Neff in those very sexual relations at which he scoffs, for Keyes is short and homely, and Neff is tall, younger, attractive, and obviously lusty. But if Keyes is always completely well balanced, Neff is subtly unbalanced; and we take for granted that Keyes, explicitly a psychologist, cannot help noting albeit subconsciously the accentuated signs of nervousness in Neff during the period when the crime is planned and after it occurs. But the very fact that the alertly intuitive Keyes, with his interior "little man" who informs him whenever a claim is fraudulent, does not register the pertinence of Neff's tense manner during the Didriksen case may indicate that *he has already interpreted the cause of Neff's habitual manner and the basis of his own interest in it*. Therefore added tension in Neff would not be especially striking to Keyes.

Neff's personality has undoubtedly been doped out by the friendly psychologist Keyes as sexually promiscuous, uncomfortably so, entailing the sort of irresponsibility and lack of serious intention that makes a man drink too much, carouse too hard, and eventually fall down on his job. Therefore Keyes's offer of another job seems an effort to reorientate Neff psychologically to a position where he does not have to make himself so persuasive with people; it is in order to impersonalize him and make him a more objective judge of people that Keyes wants him to become the impersonal, objective, and justice-minded claim adjuster. According to this assumption, it is plausible that, subtly envious of Neff's success with women and having an incoherent affection for him, Keyes aims basically with the job offer at a specific reorientation of Neff's attitude toward women—a curbing of sexual promiscuity by the suggestion of the curbed promiscuity of his sales personality. So the pattern of Keyes's interest in Neff divines and repeats that of the very extension of Neff's salesmanship, which leads to his doom, for Neff virtually sells Mrs. Didriksen a sex policy on himself at the moment he literally sells her a death policy on her husband. Now if the primary relations between the men, Neff and Keyes, have this sexual underpattern, the nature of the match-striking ritual has its sexual interpretation. Neff is demonstrating to Keyes his successful sexual "spark" and *symbolically* communicating this capacity, which Keyes lacks and of which he is envious no less than suspicious.

The congruence of the sexual motivation of the crime with this pattern is self-evident. Since it turns out, however, that Phyllis asserts she was never in love with Neff but was coldly and cruelly using him all the time, we must analyze the limitations of the involved sexual motives. This is the story's climax: since the insurance company, inspired by Keyes's supposed though actually mistaken identification of Phyllis' accomplice, refuses to recognize the claim, Neff—under much tension—turns tail and thinks only of saving his own hide; one night he and Phyllis meet secretly in her darkened house, each planning the other's murder as the only way out. After he mockingly betrays his own purpose, Phyllis quietly plugs him with a revolver shot but does not fire again when she has wounded him in the shoulder, because, although she confesses her love has been insincere, "something stops her." They move into each other's arms, yet Neff does not kiss her upraised lips; he has taken the revolver from her hand, and now he puts it to her side, pulling the trigger. She falls dead. Neff then goes on his mad ride to the insurance company's office and confesses fully and pictorially into Keyes's dictaphone.

Here the version of a sexual motive for a criminal act is so cynical, and Barbara Stanwyck in the rôle of Phyllis is so unrelieved by any frill of nice femininity, that the wiseacres of Hollywood have provided the movie with a subplot, a romance between Phyllis' stepdaughter and a misunderstood youth, which turns out to be the real thing. Yet the muscle tone of this highly diverting fable of modern sex does not yield to the drug of romance thus cutely administered while apparently the story wasn't looking. Phyllis' sexuality and Neff's are obviously more genuine and convincing than the other pair's so far as modern mores go. Insofar as personal sincerity is concerned, it is only a most unsophisticated version of it that, now or in the previous history of the human race, is not considered subject to possible self-deception and the objective dangers of moral and legal conventions. The indemnity involved in this movie is not only double but quadruple. For the lovers start out on a declaration that is not only life insurance for Didriksen (money) but life insurance for Mrs. Didriksen's adulterous affair with the insurance salesman. It is true that the original inspiration for the crime, emanating from Phyllis, occurs in the form of opportunism; she sees the salesman is smitten with her, and the idea bursts into bloom. But this does not mean that she herself is not sexually moved. Indeed, although apparently the motivation of the money-making crime is only mechanically sexual, the true objective being the selfish one of money, why may it not be just the reverse? The crime against her despised husband's life may function for Phyllis as the logical mechanism to involve her in a purely sensual, and this time honest, sex affair. The inducing of Neff to commit the crime to win her would then be merely a vulgarly morbid method of binding him to her, since she might threaten exposure if he ever wanted to leave her. Thus the crime may be Phyllis' own accident insurance against Neff's insincerity or the possible eventuality of his sometime desertion.

Certainly this is sex without conventional idealism, and in baring so morally base a mechanism, so calculating a form of sexual psychology, Hollywood has provided a chunk of truth hard for sentimental patrons of the movies to digest. But really sentimental or at least militantly sentimental movie-goers are growing scarcer, I believe, all the time. Of course they exist in large numbers in the great outlying wastes, but Hollywood has plenty of antidotes for such a dose of sex poison as this one. Neff himself, his motivation, is of course the crux of the plot and its controlling mechanism. It is Neff who mediates between the highly explicit form of sex in Phyllis and the highly implicit form in Keyes and thus balances these forces of the plot.

As yet we have not looked directly at Neff, played with a certain grotesque aptitude by Fred MacMurray. If the movie makes one thing obvious, it is the genuineness of Phyllis' attraction for him. So in a sense he is rooked into the crime. And yet, when it seems that the only way to clear himself of the whole mess is to rid her of life, he unhesitatingly sets out to murder her. He is abetted in this objective by the information from her stepdaughter that her marriage to Didriksen may have occurred because Phyllis had hastened the former Mrs. Didriksen's death when she was her nurse. This motivates Neff's desire to murder her; he is completely disillusioned with her, and lust, under the pressure of fear, turns into hatred. But the point is that both Phyllis and Neff are psychologically licked and capitulate to the shrewd maneuvering of Keyes. Yet there is small basis for assuming that they would be panicked by mere threats from Keyes. Why are they?

As a matter of fact, if Phyllis had had time in which to push her suit against the firm and if she had kept the superb nerve she had all along, Keyes, having wrongly picked the stepdaughter's sweetheart as Phyllis' accomplice, would have been baffled in court. It is true that if her sweetheart had been involved, the stepdaughter would have talked; but even if she had, not only would she have sworn an alibi for her boy friend, but there was no iota of evidence to prove that he or any other man colluded with Phyllis or even that there was a murder. Yet both Neff and Phyllis, adult, experienced, and hard-boiled, are thrown utterly off balance. Why? Evidently they do not trust each other. And why do they not trust each other? Because, I hazard, both know that one of them does not get or give satisfaction in sexual relations. Regardless of the ambiguity of Phyllis' motivations, I believe the over-all pattern of the story makes it inevitable that Neff is the sexually handicapped party and wishes to be done with the affair irrespective of the crime factor.

In the course of their plotting Phyllis has surreptitiously visited Neff several times in his apartment. We must not forget that Neff is the master hand in the affair. Provided he has a clear sexual conscience, he has every reason to be confident of ultimate success. Indeed, given assurance of sexual prowess, both subjectively and objectively effective, he is the sort of man to be misled by overconfidence rather than lack of confidence. It is too absurd to believe that the stepdaughter's hysteria stirs his conscience and unmans him. At the same time it may be true that the rumor of Phyllis' previous technique with Didriksen's wife may convince him that she intends deserting him if not killing him. She would do so only if she did not care for him. But Neff on the surface has every reason to believe he is the type of man to make her care. He has little cause to calculate that she intends the same fate for him as for Didriksen, especially because a dead Neff would considerably complicate her claim for the indemnity. Even if Neff imagines he will be humiliated later by Phyllis' desertion, he is certainly much overestimating such a humiliation in view of the fact that he is counting on half the money with which to console himself—*unless* this sexual slap in the face should be the climax of previous less crucial humiliations, casual ones that Keyes is always hinting at even though blindly in his little lectures to Neff. The general psychological situation is such that Neff may have placed some supreme hope on Phyllis as a sexual partner who would inspire him to get and give satisfaction—a hope that is crushed.

Moreover, when Neff first meets Phyllis and hears her daring, scarcely veiled suggestion, he may grasp at the deed as a way of finally ridding himself of Keyes, *who presides over his life as the hidden judge of his sexual claims as well as the insurance claims of his clients.* Neff, let us assume, wants permanent insurance against Keyes's subtle inquisition into the ostensible claims of his sexual life; to murder a man for his wife appeals to Neff therefore as an ideal method of refuting Keyes's moralism and defying him as a sexual claim adjuster. If we do not accept this pattern, there is no stable foundation for Neff's panic, capitulation, and irrational murder of Phyllis—nor, to sum it up, for his voluntary confession of guilt rather than an immediate attempt at a getaway over the near-by border into Mexico. Yet all tallies perfectly if we accept the present supposition.

The elevator operator reports blood on the floor of the car after Neff has entered the office, and as a result Neff has barely completed his confession into the dictaphone when Keyes appears. Previously Keyes has vouched for Neff to the insurance company and prevented the salesman's being put under surveillance in the case. At the last Neff wants to vindicate Keyes and his professional reputation, for in doing this he is vindicating Keyes's over-all conception of fraud—including the technical fraud in invalid *sexual* claims as well as the technical fraud in invalid *insurance* claims.

Neff asks Keyes for a chance at a getaway and staggers out, after Keyes, realizing that Neff has lost much blood, says he can't get as far as the door on his own feet. Neff slumps in the outer doorway and, as Keyes overtakes him and kneels beside him, fumbles for a cigarette; he has no match. This time it is Keyes who has the match—the answer, the symbolic instrument of power. He strikes it for the supine Neff, now convicted of his double fraud. Trying to grin, pulling on the cigarette, Neff makes a remark to the effect that no longer will they see each other daily across the desk. Keyes replies that Neff has been, to him, "closer than that." I don't know what other evidence is needed to show that Keyes himself is obscurely aware that he symbolizes Neff's sexual conscience and that the plot demonstrates that the double-indemnity clause in the insurance policy symbolizes Neff's last desperate and doomed effort to prove the latent efficacy of his *sexual salesmanship.*

The lugubrious face of the movie is provided by the fact that to the Phyllises and Neffs of this world there seems available no other form of compensation for sexual inadequacy but money. Despite its barbarously Zolaesque quality—and a little because of it—this movie is one of the most psychologically cogent ever to emerge from the developing studios of Hollywood—presenting, as it does so ingeniously, the insurance company's judgment of sexual problems. Neff's pathological illusion is one of the diseases of American culture: that salesmanship can be an esthetic value. The larger truth may be that, analogously to those who adopt and cultivate a war psychology, Neff desperately sells himself the idea of murderous violence as an aid to moral enthusiasm—in his case an enthusiasm for sex.

1947

Warhol's New Sex Film

The one mistake most dangerous to make about Andy Warhol's films is to assume that their basilisk stare is directed at *reality* in any widely or historically accepted sense of that word. Warhol's inspiration was to decide to be literal toward attitudes *about reality*, or more specifically, attitudes inventing reality before our eyes. First of all, reality (today anyway) is largely the invention of journalism and is based on the formula of the neat, transmissible word-summary of action past. Visual media simply convert this formula into sight terms. In both fiction and so-called fact media, or a fusion of them, the same banal process always takes place: the technicians invent a plausible simulacrum of what is supposed to happen or have happened in life. A newsreel or documentary film is supposed (a) to represent accomplished fact or (b) typical and/or current and continuous fact. Each is an item, more or less edited, detached from the whole continuum of reality yet presumed to stand for reality—reality in an ontological sense, the "world," and so on.

Sex happens to be the "real" subject of Warhol's new film titled by the four-letter word that still tends to burn a hole in the paper it's printed on. But the important thing about *Fuck*—indeed, the *only* important thing about it—is that it does not deal in any familiar reality-formulas. It is neo-Kinsey, one might say, or better, neo-"human sexual response," and yet it has all scientific interest and scientific preparation pressed out of it beforehand. Even those couples who went to bed in order to be observed by sociologists with ideas of scientific investigation were attempting to achieve a one-shot summary of their regular sexual relations. One might term the whole reality-myth of film (and journalism for that matter) a rational effort to formally summarize "normal" behavior.

If we take, for example, any of the fiction films nowadays exploiting sex by showing erotically occupied nudes, we see professional actors (more or less skilled as the case may be) providing a simulacrum of something deemed plausible and typical of the human race. Sometimes the photography and the direction make the action look arty, sometimes the photography and direction make it look deliberately coarse, shocking. In any case there is an avowed plan, a script of some sort, which the actors learn by heart and then proceed to demonstrate in person. On the other hand, the peculiar interest of Warhol's blatantly artless films—any aesthetic interest in them is purely coincidental and does not refer to any individual living or dead—lies in the fact that they are direct, technically primitive records of improvised human behavior, quite unconcerned with "reality."

True, some of these films have had scripts of a sort. For commercial reasons (as in the Broadway run of *My Hustler*) some have also been edited, given an altered or augmented shape after being made. Yet, by and large, they are unarranged reports on what certain people who desire camera publicity, or consent to it, are willing to do while enjoying that publicity. In one case, the film was simply an anthology of couples doing nothing but kissing. This is not to say that the usually offbeat characters who work for Warhol's cameras (by now their names are fairly well-known) are either innerly depraved, morbid exhibitionists or simple frauds. What we see in *Fuck* is not what might happen (certainly not yet) in broad daylight on Times Square. No! This episode in sexual conjugation is something the couple here "did for Andy." Such obligingness gets one automatic prestige in the underground set.

Inevitably, to think à la "human sexual response," what we see must resemble, to some extent, this man's and this woman's ordinary behavior in bed. But this information is not at all (here I think all sensitive spectators will agree) the true point of interest in *Fuck*. Rather, starting from scratch, i.e., the first physical point of contact, this couple invent bed-reality bit by bit, rub by rub, word by word, toss by toss, posture by posture. During the tiresome action—boredom is an essential ingredient of warholism: by design left *out* of entertainment, by design left *in* Warhol films—it may occur to some to wonder what the sexual partners are thinking or feeling, how much they are enjoying themselves, how quickly, and so on; for example: do they stall during preliminaries in order to expand the camera time? This, all the same, does not affect the impression that in exploring each other's body, reacting to different parts and getting down to the business of copulating, the two actors are witnessing that perfectly true kind of lazy leisure which is born of the freedom to act as one pleases. We are watching "reality" in the instance of two organic human bodies on a bed, and elsewhere, intent on doing something, but doing it only as they are prompted by some inner impulse to do it; part of which, as I say, is doing it for Andy.

I daresay that when the couple, the man's entry finally achieved, shift their position to show us their profile (we have been seeing them at rather oblique eye-level from the back), Warhol may have directed the shift either by plan or some spontaneous sign of which we are unaware; on the other hand, it may merely have been the impulse of the man to give the camera a more articulated view. Here is, anyway, *Fuck*'s most dramatic moment: one of those crucial shifts of action that are all-important but manage, like great art, to come as a surprise because they utterly conceal their nature as "devices." In other words, there is no difference here between "reality" and "device" whereas in both fiction and fact representation, including journalism, the device can never quite conceal its mediation between us and reality.

Or take an early Warhol film such as *Empire* or *Eat*. True, we know the Empire State Building is always there (we also know that during a day and night, it wears an everchanging chiaroscuro) but it would not occur to us to watch it for eight or even six hours, not to mention one hour. Time is of immense importance in Warhol's mesmerically boring films simply because the watcher, submissively or rebelliously, is being forced to participate in the actual *durée* of an object—and not, note well, because that is what "reality" is, but rather because this is what reality (as human consciousness) is *not*. The literalism of Warhol is, first and last, supremely artificial—a calculated impertinence, even an insult. In *Eat*, the modern painter, Robert Indiana, eats a large mushroom in unchanging and unchanged position for a time which begins to make the spectator wonder if really some of the previous mastication is not cleverly being re-run. How could anyone in the world, even purposely, take so long to eat a single mushroom? There is no "normal" reason for it unless we wish to admit Warhol's kind of film-making into the realm of normality.

It is not normal to *re*live the life which we—that is, all people—live from minute to minute of absolutely continuous time. Even our own subjective consciousness *qua* consciousness is quite incapable of registering everything that passes or rests before our eyes, passes or stays in our minds, because in the twinkle of a clock's second, some distinct train of thought may be utterly obliterated, probably never to return in precisely the same form. Time, as it is lived in consciousness, is of the essence of changefulness. Take the commonplace view of indifferent landscape gazed at from the window of a moving train. Do we not become hypnotized by the way nearer things seem to pass more quickly, farther things more slowly—regardless of what things they may be? Inversely, Warhol attains the same hypnotic abstract effect by the moveless camera eye directed at a relatively moveless point in space. Only actors within the moveless or almost moveless space change and usually they change only at an exasperatingly slow rate. The logical result is for us to be hypnotized by the slow rate of movement and its extremely narrow scope, which (like the eating of the mushroom) is basically repetitious.

What we know as narrative time in fiction (film or otherwise) is strictly formal, selective and summative; it is representation by the memoranda of signs. Nor does it have to be fiction, i.e., imaginary action, for the identical process takes place in reporting a riot or a diplomatic conference on the front page of the New York *Times*. The media regularly give us the gist of a past event in the world, the gist of its human consciousness, without regard to the physical quantity of experience that is literally measured by the clock, and no matter what aspect or aspects of it are handled or for what purpose (documentary or imaginative). This technique results from the *device* of compressing actions of diverse kinds, spread through lengthy clock time perhaps, into a conveniently communicative form (narrative, expository, etc.). Life in Warhol films (as he likes them to remain, unedited, with nothing whatever on the cutting-room floor) is a sort of dead-eye dick when it comes to such accepted formal transmutation. Values, take note, are *not* involved; that is, even here in *Fuck*, the process of fucking is not calculated to depict sexual sensations in a way to illustrate what supposedly is their chief charm: a real excitement, mounting steadily to orgasmic climax. What we know as "blue films," however much faked or however real the feelings of those sexually involved, would normally seek to represent a certain palpable excitement, to grow "hot," to mount tantalizingly to the climax. If the result be hollow or obviously phony, it is the fault of carelessness or ineptitude or some "plausible" sort of faking. But all this is not at all the point in Warhol's (actually cool) *Fuck*.

This film is not meant *to represent*; it is meant *to be*. And therein, like it or leave it, lies its great, really cool distinction. Are the performers here self-conscious; do they look at the camera—or the camera man? They certainly do the latter, and if they are also self-conscious at times, it is because they wish to give no version, however artificial, of "reality." Actually, the woman seems listless, perhaps narcissistic, not especially man-prone (". . . disgusting!" she says archly, perhaps not insincerely, of his suddenly exposed genitals); the man seems overcasual, moodily exhibitionistic and routine. When the sex-act is being accomplished, it is he who provides all or nearly all the copulative movement, the woman doing very little to help promote orgasm. They do not kiss passionately meanwhile; they hardly kiss at all. What could be more "unnatural" than neglecting to kiss so as to "represent" sexual passion? Yet the negligence has a certain artificial necessity, or "naturalness," precisely because it feels no obligation to represent "reality." Even passion, here, is left to take care of itself.

Thus, no matter how much this pair show signs of being watched, everything they do is eminently natural in the sense of being self-initiated. They may not, either of them, have particularly wanted to go to bed together. But they did so—for the camera, for Andy. And doing so, being fairly cool types, they do not trouble to pretend they feel something when they don't. Or if, for some invisible reason, they force their words, their expressions, their postures, there is no canon presupposed by which we can blame them, or even measure, plausibly, how much of what they do is a good-natured put-on. A Warhol film promises or presupposes nothing and achieves, therefore, everything. The everything is "all too much" according to your taste.

Fuck (especially when peripheral doings are performed) is an action where, strictly speaking, feelings do not matter, so that any feeling which does appear (the man becomes mildly excited and wilfully seeks orgasm) is bound to be perfectly genuine, whatever its degree. Above all, *Fuck* is not a sexploitational film of the kind being profusely shown on 42nd Street in New York. In those, everything is calculated, however gauchely, to provide an illusion of erotic pleasure or lust, whether by innuendo or supposed actual copulation. All *blue films* thus begin by wishing to present that domain of reality we know as sexual excitement, which according to its destiny as a pleasure-giving spectacle must be as exciting as possible to the emotions. *Fuck* is definitely not as exciting as possible to the emotions. Which is the sole reason why it is so exciting to the intelligence. . . . It just won't pretend that fucking is Heaven—or Hell. It *may* involve a trip—who knows if the couple are on one?—but if so, it means the dish has an invisible source, and this makes *Fuck* all the more artificial: unreal as a reality-formula. Fucking, it says, *is*. And this is it. *Is it?*

1969

Eugene Archer

Eugene Archer (1931–1973) lived a double life: as a second-string film reporter-reviewer for *The New York Times* in the late 1950s and early 1960s (during the inglorious reign of Bosley Crowther) and as an informed film critic for more underground film journals such as *Film Culture* (which published his thoughtful appraisals of Elia Kazan and Chaplin's *A King in New York*, among others). The Texas-born Archer, who served in the Air Force, had an encyclopedic knowledge of film history; he and his friend Andrew Sarris helped develop an auteurist approach to American movies, compiling lists together and collaborating on various writing projects before they went their separate ways. Archer also was instrumental in getting the New York Film Festival started. He quit the *Times* and moved to Paris—co-authoring Claude Chabrol's film *Ten Days Wonder*, and acting in Eric Rohmer's *La Collectionneuse*—but his life was cut short by ill health in 1973.

◆

A King in New York

The works of genius are frequently difficult to understand, and the films of Charles Chaplin, operating simultaneously on several levels of meaning, present a critical problem of particular complexity. As the density of Chaplin's work has increased, the volumes of analysis have multiplied, and the task of attempting an initial appraisal of a new Chaplin release has assumed formidable proportions.

Even when the difficulties are taken into consideration, however, the record of critical evaluations of Chaplin has not been good. *The Circus*, at the time of its first appearance, was reviewed merely as a farce. *City Lights* was considered too tragic, *Modern Times* too consciously political, *The Great Dictator* both too jocular in its attitude toward a serious subject and far too grave in its final resolution. *Monsieur Verdoux* and *Limelight*, two of Chaplin's most important works and certainly the most complex, were denounced for their outmoded technique and derided for their content, *Verdoux* as a bitter and isolated attack on war and *Limelight* as a maudlin outcry of self-pity. Such controversies were appropriate enough, for none of these highly original creations conformed to advance expectations and all possessed significant qualities which were not readily apparent to the superficial observer. Eventually, after the initial outcries of excitement and disappointment had diminished, each of these films assumed its proper place in the uninterrupted sequence of Chaplin masterpieces.

The case of Chaplin is complicated by the intrusion of elements from his personal life into his work. As in the works of any creative artist, there were traces of Chaplin's individual story even in his earliest films. It is an ironic contradiction that the character of the little tramp, the greatest modern symbol of Universal Man, was personified by an eccentric genius whose egocentric peculiarities have been widely publicized. The criticism of Chaplin the man—his morals, his politics, his failure to become an American citizen or to fight in World War I—began early in his career and eventually, inevitably, had its effect upon his work. Nevertheless, as long as Chaplin played the tramp, his artistic achievements could be divorced from his private personality, in spite of the connotations evoked by sequences in *City Lights* (the rich man who loved the tramp when drunk but rejected him when sober) and *Modern Times* (the tramp as an extreme individualist, confused and rebellious in his relationship to mechanized society). Since the demise of the tramp in *The Great Dictator*, however, the increasingly autobiographical nature of Chaplin's work has been impossible to ignore. In *Monsieur Verdoux*, Chaplin no longer pretended to symbolize the modern man and attacked contemporary society with the attitude of the complete non-conformist. In *Limelight*, he denounced a public which chose to admire him only for the wrong reasons. *A King in New York* refers all too clearly to the unfortunate recent events in Chaplin's relations with the United States. While the modern tendency toward universal conformity has increased, the screen image of Chaplin has become the symbol of the rabid individualist.

A Chaplin who refuses to conform to contemporary social standards, who criticizes the society which has fostered him, can hardly be expected to retain his popularity. This, however, is not a unique position for a man of his stature; history is full of similar examples of artists rejected by their contemporaries. The situation presents an ancient social problem: can the genius be expected to conform to society, or is it the responsibility of that society to provide a place for its geniuses? By rejecting Chaplin, America must ask if the gain can compensate for the loss.

This is the underlying theme of *A King in New York*. It would have been much easier for his detractors if Chaplin had actually made the "hate America" film which was rumored long before the film had been completed, but Chaplin has not chosen to simplify the problem for anyone. Working for posterity, as always, he has made a film which is neither bitter nor vindictive, as might have been expected, but is instead comic, pensive, and ultimately sad.

A qualitative judgment of *A King in New York* is impossible, since this film, like all of Chaplin's, depends for its final effect on the responses of the individual observer. The rewards correspond in direct ratio to the amount of intellectual effort which the spectator is willing to expend. Such early works as *The Gold Rush* and *City Lights* were more immediately gratifying: to the casual observer, unwilling to search for deeper meanings, the hilarious comedy of these films made them satisfactory on the most elementary level. *Monsieur Verdoux* and *Limelight* were another matter; these films were serious even on the surface and most displeasing to observers disinclined to think about their content. On a superficial level, without considering its intellectual meanings, *A King in New York* is much more amusing. Its proportions are approximately three parts farce to one part drama. Most of the comedy is successful (although never as hilarious as, for example, *Modern Times*); at least half of the dramatic scenes obtain the proper emotional effect. The remaining scenes—constituting about a fourth of the film—aim at comic or emotional effects which they fail, for various reasons, to achieve. These are not bad proportions for a comedy, particularly since the film is logically constructed and skillfully edited, although the weak moments and the serious ending are qualifications which must inevitably limit its popular appeal. If the subject were non-political and the creator someone other than a world celebrity, the film could be critically evaluated as a clever comedy with a number of defects, and consequently, a moderate success.

For Chaplin, however, a superficial examination is never enough; and the subject of *A King in New York* can hardly be dismissed. The artist is consciously referring to recent events in his life which have aroused universal controversy; the setting is America, the topic McCarthyism, and Chaplin has much to say about both. The first half of the film chronicles the experiences of a deposed European monarch in satirizing various aspects of modern civilization: immigration red-tape, press conferences, the garish carnival of Times Square, a rock-and-roll stage show at the Paramount, Cinemascope, Hollywood movies, progressive schools, professional hostesses, the cult of youth (in a long plastic-surgery sequence), and—with particular emphasis—television commercials. Much of the old Chaplin is visible here, in farcical moments reminiscent of his best works. Not all of the jokes are original, but neither were the jokes in *The Gold Rush*. These sequences are rapid, inventive, and consistently funny, representing a welcome return of the artist to the area of his original achievements. The mockery is healthy and remarkably tolerant. Chaplin has never harmed America by laughter; in these scenes, he is jibing at conventions, as he always has. His creation of King Shadow provides the perfect focus for the humor—a naive and engaging old man, incurably optimistic, never discouraged by his tribulations, and full of *joie de vivre*. There are occasional disturbing moments.

His speech extolling American freedom while being fingerprinted jars the spectator, but Chaplin reads the speech with apparent sincerity. When he watches teen-agers dancing wildly in a theater aisle, he pauses to ask if this is really healthy. The king's mission in America—to promote a plan for the peaceful use of atomic energy—has enigmatic connotations. The specter of a man whose idealistic objectives are ignored while his dinner-party antics make him a television celebrity evokes the memory of Chaplin's bitterness in *Limelight* toward a public which appreciated him for the wrong reasons. Most notably, perhaps, the king's age has its effect upon the spectator: lively and animated as Chaplin is, he is now an old man, and the lonely and deposed old king is essentially a figure of pathos. The animated display of *joie de vivre* plays against this image, to good tragi-comic effect.

These questionable moments, however, are fleeting. The only really troublesome sequence in the early reels occurs in the plastic-surgery episode. The king, his face lifted for television purposes, goes to a night club to watch a low-comedy team play an ancient vaudeville act. Although the blasé night club audience is convulsed, the spectator is not, and the spectacle of the king struggling to keep from laughing (he is afraid his stitches will burst) provokes only moderate amusement. The scene presents an interesting theoretical question: did Chaplin expect the audience to laugh at the vaudeville? The routine is one of Chaplin's old ones (he employed it in *Work*), but the rendition is inept. A similar problem occurs in *Limelight*, when one of Chaplin's long vaudeville acts evokes no applause; later, before a sympathetic audience at a benefit, the same act is received with wild approval. Whether or not Chaplin intended the routine to be funny is problematical; the presentation provides no clues. In *A King in New York*, the observer's indifference to the vaudeville predicament and the mediocrity of the act may easily be intentional; but in any event, the scene is too long.

It is in the progressive school episode that the political theme is first introduced, and the treatment of this scene amplifies its automatically controversial elements. The entire sequence is played for a grim kind of humor. Visiting the school merely as a public relations gesture, without any real sympathy for the children or for this type of education, the king is first appalled and then increasingly terrified by these ferocious modern *enfants terribles*. The school director is embarrassingly effeminate; the children, encouraged to "express themselves" without inhibitions, do so in the most repellent manner available. The king views them with distaste, but retains his royal politeness and sits down for a friendly chat with a twelve-year-old boy described as the school prodigy (Michael Chaplin). The boy promptly begins lecturing him vehemently about politics, in an oratorical manner which is immediately ridiculous. Although the king repeatedly tries to argue against this tireless stream of Marxist invective, he is unable to interrupt the excited child; and his difficulties are increased by the simultaneous activities of the other children, who continue to annoy the king in every way until, in an elaborate slapstick climax, he sits on a huge layer cake. Most of the critics unsympathetic to Chaplin have disregarded the comic treatment of this scene and described the boy's rhetoric as the "heart" of the film. This verdict is obviously inaccurate (if Chaplin wished to emphasize the boy's oratory, why should he go to such extravagant lengths to distract the observer's attention from the speech?) and recalls the Marxist criticism of *Modern Times*, which interpreted Chaplin as a symbol of the "oppressed masses" because of the sequence in which the tramp waves a red flag at the head of a Communist procession. A study of the context of that scene reveals that the flag had dropped from the rear of a truck; the tramp picked it up and ran after the truck to return it, quite oblivious to the parade which was approaching behind him, and although an innocent bystander, he was subsequently arrested for inciting a riot. Clearly, in Chaplin's work, nothing can he overlooked. The slapstick surrounding the child's oratory in *A King in New York* suggests that the speech is not to be taken seriously, and observers searching for anti-Russian propaganda could easily interpret the entire sequence as a mockery of Communist rhetoric. Neither interpretation, however, is completely satisfactory, and the scene as a whole is curiously ill-defined. Although the slapstick accompaniment seems obviously designed to distract attention from the context of the speech, the sequence is not entirely successful as comedy. Chaplin made Hitler's speeches in *The Great Dictator* seem ridiculous, not only by surrounding them with slapstick, but by delivering them in Esperanto. In *A King in New York*, however, the boy's arguments are entirely too audible, and observers who listen to them carefully will discern certain comments concerning passport regulations and governmental restrictions which disturbingly echo Chaplin's own sentiments as quoted in his interviews with the press.

If the final meaning of this sequence is unclear, the king's reaction to the boy's argument is equally ambiguous. He later describes the boy as "the most obnoxious child I ever met—but a genius." The comment is never amplified, and Chaplin leaves the audience to wonder whether the boy is to be considered a genius because of the merits of his argument, or merely because, at his age, he is able to argue at all.

The king, in any event, is never persuaded by the boy's rhetoric. His later affection for the child is entirely emotional and divorced from political motivations. When the boy is next encountered, he is presented as a lonely waif shivering in the snow, an image vividly recalling Jackie Coogan in *The Kid*. The boy has run away from the school because his parents, former Communists, have been subpoenaed by a Congressional investigating committee, and the boy does not want to be questioned about their activities; but this history is unimportant to the king. To Chaplin, any child shivering in the snow is automatically a figure of pathos, and the king befriends him as a gesture of simple humanity. "Suppose his parents are Communists." the king argues, "is that any reason for me to let him freeze to death?" Nevertheless, disturbed by the political connotations, the king asks the boy if he is a Communist himself, and to his surprise the boy, formerly an anarchist, says that he is. His reason is emotional: he is tired of being asked to defend his position and now calls himself a Communist simply because society makes it an advantage not to be one. (This reply is reminiscent of the scene in Kazan's *Gentleman's Agreement* in which Sam Jaffe, as a renowned Jewish scientist, proves scientifically that there is no such thing as a "Jewish race" but ironically suggests that the Jews cling to the title as an act of pride because it remains a handicap in the modern world.)

After this briefly serious passage, the film returns to a comedy vein in a mordant satire on McCarthyism. Three blustering congressmen encounter the boy in the king's rooms and are appalled by the apparition of infant Communism. A cynical news commentator uses the link between the king and the child to begin a rumor about an international espionage ring. "Who ever heard of a king being a Communist?" Chaplin scoffs. "It's a contradiction in terms." Nevertheless, he is frightened by the incomprehensible situation and, in a farcical chase passage, vainly attempts to avoid a process-server. The running motif continues through the next sequence, when the king, anxious not to be late for his appearance before the Congressional committee, becomes entangled in a fire hose and ultimately drenches the congressmen, reporters, and his terrified lawyer. The rapid pacing of these scenes captures much of the hectic mood of this particular period in American political affairs, and the satirical thrusts at McCarthyism recall the many similar parodies at the time of the televised McCarthy hearings by such popular American comedians as Bob Hope. If the underlying mood of worried urgency tends to reduce the comic effectiveness of these scenes, it is perhaps surprising that Chaplin was able to find any humor in the situation at all.

In contrast to the generally humorous treatment of the climax, Chaplin provides a reflective conclusion which is entirely serious. (The poignant ending, it will be recalled, has been a consistent Chaplin device since *The Circus*.) The king is cleared of Communist affiliations by the committee, and he is assured that the fire-hose episode has made him more popular than ever with the

American public. If his plans for the peaceful use of atomic energy have been rejected, it is only because Washington has similar plans of its own. The McCarthy hysteria, he is told, is only a passing phase and is representative of only a part of the American population. Hopefully, he agrees; the king has not lost his optimism. But he has grown tired and feels too old to continue the battle. A quiet life in Europe beckons, and a wife who has grown to love him; he prefers to retire to the sidelines and wait for the hysteria to end. A younger man, one feels, would perhaps have remained; and there are traces of regret in this sad departure. The conclusion sharply reminds the audience of Chaplin's age and of the autobiographical circumstances which dictate this resigned retreat. Only in the epilogue with the boy does a sign of bitterness betray itself, in his attitude toward a matter which has not affected Chaplin personally. The boy has cooperated with the committee and "revealed names" to save his stubborn parents from prison, in a childish but human betrayal of his own convictions, and Chaplin presents the child as a pathetic figure, spiritually broken by circumstance of which the author sharply disapproves. Yet the king's words to the child are kind and comforting, a repetition of the king's own decision: all this will pass, we must make the best of it, the boy also must retire from the battle and quietly retreat with the king. As always in Chaplin's films, life is difficult and the human condition is essentially depressing: one must simply try to make the best of things. If his present message advocates retirement from the battle, it is a decision which has been forced upon him after a long lifetime of engagement.

Chaplin has told this unusual story in his usual manner, with a cinematic technique most often conspicuous by its absence. His direction concentrates on effects of the utmost simplicity; the camera is present merely to observe the action, without searching for its own meanings, and the actors are left to create their own effects within the frame. This method, as usual, is far more congenial to Chaplin the actor than to his supporting players, who are no more than adequate and, in the case of a number of British players pretending to be Americans, frequently less. Although sometimes awkward as the flippant modern ingenue, Dawn Addams has an appealing quality which Chaplin has employed to great advantage. Michael Chaplin is shrill in scenes of invective, but properly pathetic in quieter moments. The sets are obviously studio-manufactured, and several exteriors are recognizably British rather than American. Chaplin's musical score, as always, is simple and effective. Throughout the film, Chaplin's individual performance is brilliant, alternately reflecting the inventive ingenuity of the old Charlie and the later tragic pathos of the aging clown in *Limelight*.

If *A King in New York* finally lacks the significance of Chaplin's great masterpieces of the past, it is neither because he has chosen to satirize certain aspects of American society nor because he has substantially declined as an artist. Although the film is neither as funny as *Modern Times* nor as moving as *Limelight*, it is comic and emotional enough to satisfy most critical requirements. American audiences, who are accustomed to self-criticism but sensitive, naturally enough, to criticism from abroad, can hardly be expected to regard the film with complete objectivity. Although Parisian critics have correctly observed that the film is hardly as critical of America as Kazan's recent *A Face in the Crowd*, it is inevitable that Chaplin's comedy, coming from a man who must now he considered an alien, should arouse a more defensive reaction. *A King in New York* was primarily designed for European audiences, and America should perhaps be relieved that Chaplin, who has apparently tried to be fair, has not chosen to criticize the country more severely.

It is nonetheless significant that Chaplin, who began as the symbol of Universal Man, should now present a film on a theme which is automatically destined to arouse hostility from a large segment of the world's population. Although Chaplin obviously considers himself a great humanitarian, above such matters as politics and social mores, his audiences can hardly be expected to share this point of view. By regarding America from outside her boundaries and by selecting a subject as intellectually and historically limited as McCarthyism, Chaplin has adopted a specialized role which contradicts his original aspirations toward universality. As an alien who observes isolated aspects of a particular social framework without actually understanding or actively engaging himself in that society, Chaplin suddenly becomes the symbol of the individualist in an ivory tower, an image very different from the tramp who once represented all things to all men.

Provocative as this image is in the light of Chaplin's personal drama, it is the antithesis of the proper position for a creative artist. It is because of this basic alienation that *A King in New York* emerges as a tentative film, rather than a complete artistic achievement. After the fine, affirmative personal statement of *Limelight*, the new film assumes the aspect of an unhappy afterthought, an interim work in the long chronology of Chaplin's career. More than in any of his other films, the concluding moments—a plane carrying the tired but still optimistic old king to semi-retirement and exile in Europe—seem designed, not as an ending, but as a bridge to Chaplin's next great film, perhaps the final summary of his achievements which every admirer of Chaplin's artistry, and of the cinematic medium itself, must hopefully anticipate.

1958

Arlene Croce

Arlene Croce (b. 1934) is one of America's greatest dance critics. For 25 years, as a columnist for *The New Yorker*, she educated readers to the highest standards of ballet, modern dance, tap, and folk in a remarkable prose style that conveyed her vast knowledge of the subtle technicalities of movement and gesture through pane-clear, conversational language and readily graspable images. Her dance writings have been compared in quality to the criticism of James Agee in film, Randall Jarrell in poetry, and Bernard Shaw in the theater. In her early career Croce wrote excellent movie criticism for *Film Culture* and other magazines, including the Satyajit Ray review that follows. But it is her first book, *The Fred Astaire–Ginger Rogers Book*, that remains her lasting contribution to American film criticism. In it she analyzed the ten films that the pair made together and the meaning of their partnership. Croce, a champion of George Balanchine's pure, non-narrative ballets, has stated that art should be about beauty, not ideas, and that belief factors into her discussion of *Shall We Dance*, as she explains her preference for Fred Astaire's over Gene Kelly's choreography: "Where Kelly has ideas, Astaire has steps."

◆

Pather Panchali and *Aparajito*

The arrival of *Pather Panchali* was attended by presentiments of doom. Despite its mantle of honors from the European festivals, word had somehow got abroad that it was a long dull Indian film all about nothing—an untouchable, therefore, from the standpoint of American distributors. Mr. Edward Harrison, however, took his chances, and the film is now well into its fifth month at the Fifth Avenue Cinema in New York.

In the matter of quality imports, what we see or don't see depends largely on the courage and good will of our distributors and, apparently, on their ability to sense propitious shifts in audience taste. None of the formulas seems to work. One might come right out and admit, for example, that we don't favor the sternly intellectual or the coldly theological; Bresson has always flopped here and so has Dreyer. (After an initially substantial run, *A Man Escaped* escaped indeed, though it turned up once recently on a double bill with a solid winner, *Gervaise. Ordet* vanished.) Ingmar Bergman received respectful notices in the New York dailies for *The Seventh Seal*, but it died at the Paris. On the other hand, while we are dwelling on cold theology, *Symphonie Pastorale* was one of the greatest hits in the history of foreign importations, and *Celui Qui Doit Mourir* may well repeat its success. The somewhat hotter theology of Fellini scores with *La Strada* but fails with *Cabiria*, and *The Flowers of St. Francis* (in many ways more Fellini's film than Rossellini's) is a fading memory for the few. More often than not, for those who must keep up with foreign films, the price of attendance is eternal vigilance. The two Bardem films that have been shown here (ignominiously retitled *The Age of Infidelity* and *The Lovemaker*) opened and shut like traps. I don't know anyone who managed to catch *Raices* while it was playing, but then, I don't know anyone who hasn't seen *Pather Panchali*.

And the reviews, if they were ever a reliable index, were on the whole ominous. "Time," to be sure, was tremulous in its appreciation, and the "New Yorker" considered it of more than routine interest. But Mr. Crowther, predictably, was upset by its "listless" tempo and, while he approved, rather grudgingly, of its simplicity, led us to expect the worst, technically. Even the two weeklies longest associated with responsible coverage, the "New Republic" and the "Nation," were not impressed: the one thought it an exotic documentary, while the other was dismayed that none of the people in it "fought back."

Pather Panchali has its exotic charms. As a close-range examination of the habits and poverty of Bengali life, it is undoubtedly instructive. But it is no grinding recital of economic desperation (what if it were?), nor is it merely a sensuous montage of saris, veils, pottery and naked feet. The two deaths that mark its highest drama occur because of (1) old age and (2) a whimsical overexposure to the elements resulting in pneumonia. What is the theme of *Pather Panchali*? It is "about" the human struggle against extinction in the same way that "The Iliad" is "about" war. It is not a tragedy because it does not invade those metaphysical reaches, and it is never literary in the sense that *The Bicycle Thief* is literary because cause and effect are more closely joined—its hero fought back. *Pather Panchali* has no protagonists, none of the arching conflicts or proud confrontations of which fiction is usually made, nothing to surprise us again and again. Even *The Childhood of Maxim Gorki*, the film it most closely resembles in spirit, surprises us, somewhat literarily, with its fine eccentricity. *Pather Panchali* shows the creative imagination in its humblest involvement with the pathos of the commonplace. As if to emphasize the limits which it sets itself, some of the most affecting moments in the last reel have the dumb stun, the galling heaviness of only partially assimilated impressions. For all its tranquillity and orderly selection, the film seems intuitively, rather than philosophically, informed. But so intimate are its revelations, so innocent is its embrace of casual experience that, without ever seeming to concern itself with "Man", it succeeds in evoking gestures of universal credence. The large, legible rendering of common fatality which it finally achieves is wrought most purely and precisely in its own language. The film makes no generalized Esperanto appeal to other lives and customs; by choosing to remain most patiently true to its subject, it ends by coming true for us as well. Its credentials aren't faked; we are referred to our own family albums. The one hundred and twelve minutes of *Pather Panchali* are a celebration of the utterly familiar, of the mysterious drone of life as it passes. In this, it is one of the beauties of our time.

The story is so simple we cannot understand what makes it great. In a peculiar vertical perspective of high forests and tall crumbling stone walls which constitute the rural outskirts of Bengal, a family lives. There are two lively children, a boy and a girl; an aged great aunt, bent, half blind, with the shrewd head of a buzzard and the childish good cheer of the very old; a mother, alternately shrill and becalmed with disappointment, who forms the film's moral center; and a father, a bad provider with a good heart, who goes away on business toward the beginning of the film and returns toward the end. The film is shaped by a series of divertissements: the visit of the candy man, of some strolling players, a local wedding. The little girl is suspected of theft and is punished by her mother; the aunt, rejected for the burden she has become, crawls into the woods to die alone; the mother pawns the family silver for more rice and potatoes. When the rains come at last to the fevered earth, the girl dances for joy in the downpour and catches a chill. In the night the storm rages; in the morning the mother sits numbly by her dead child. The father returns to his wasted property and wracked family. He gathers them up in an oxcart and they set out for Benares. In the end a snake slithers into the deserted house as they leave in the rolling cart, the three heads held in a single frame for an enduring close shot, a quiet tribute of almost Biblical eloquence.

On the strength of this sweet, sorrowful film alone, it is possible to place Satyajit Ray among the great humanists of the cinema—Flaherty, de Sica, Donskoi, Renoir. Though he has Renoir's eye and de Sica's caressive feeling for detail, his method, already in this first film, is unique and completely formed. It is a method of poetic understatement and poetic linkage. Very little in the film is insisted upon, still less seems to say, Look you, and weep. The film is both sober and gay. But its sobriety isn't down-in-the-mouth and there is none of that baleful "behold-my-people" condescension that can lie like a stone in the guilty Western heart. The intelligence behind this film is one of gentility and sophistication. The humor is graciously ironic, as when a local rag-tag band wheezes "It's a Long Way to Tipperary."

Unlike some of the self-styled primitive realists, Ray's camera is articulate, highly mobile. The scene in which the mother nurses her dying child in the darkness of the stormed hut is almost wholly composed of dolly shots—slow, dread-laden approaches in a panicky light. He has placed great trust in his actors, most of them non-professionals, and their beauty and complete absorption make possible the relentless portraiture, the brimming close shots that carry and dignify the film. There is a passage illustrating a break in the weather and the play of the rain on the riled surface of the lake that brings the film dangerously close to auto-intoxication, and there are a few *longueurs* in the incidental action that don't seem wholly justified. But the genuinely spellbound camera is no small achievement. I wonder what the bug-eyed Bausch and Lomb lenses that shoot our supermovies would make of the lowering skies and fading lights of Bengal—probably Georgia in a mist.

Ray's control of his material reveals a cinematic instinct that need take lessons from nobody. The one occasion where rhetoric is openly used is the scene where the father learns of his daughter's death. Ray attempts, and achieves, a heroic effect, both in the frame and on the sound track. It begins with the mother's outburst, replaced in the sound track by the rising wail of a sitar. As realization dawns in the husband, he rises half out of the frame, then, stupified, collapses back into it, the camera bearing in upon a face stretched like a tragic mask; immediately the sitar is cut off and we hear his choking sobs. It is the film's emotional peak, a delayed spasm that, when it is over, is like a ritual purgation. After this, there is one scene of great justice wherein the boy finds the necklace his dead sister had stolen. He heaves it into a stagnant pool and the scum closes officially over the secret. The final shot, with its sober, unpitying affirmation, rings with the cleansing power of an apotheosis.

There is also in this film the pleasure of a narrative scheme which advances its incidents two by two, in a sort of sped time, conveying the impression that nothing happens singly and that everything is significant. As much emphasis is laid upon the adventure of the children in the white field of *kaash* flowers where they go to see the trains, as upon the death of the old aunt. The two sequences, as they mount, are intercut in the intense, poetic manner of Dovzhenko, and they come together in a profound silence when the children discover the old lady's crouching corpse. Countless moments in the film overlap, for irony or for some deeper revelation, and the boldest and most logical link is made between this film and its sequel, *Aparajito*.

When the boy Apu puts his ear to the humming telegraph pole and watches his first train rush by in *Panchali*, there is the first hint of the divisive loyalties that form the subject of the sequel. Trains are the leit-motif of *Aparajito*. Symbol of the boy's passage from country to city, from childhood to young manhood, from the ancestral world of obligations to the modern world of opportunity, the shunting trains darken the landscape of the second film as their full meaning comes, finally, to weight its hero's conscience. *Aparajito* is in every sense a transitional film. It doesn't have the self-contained, mute grandeur of *Panchali*, nor does it have anything to match the poetic, motion-less evolution of the former film. It is instead a conventional story-skim that never wholly cuts free from its literary source, a popular novel of Bengali life. The freshness of insight that distinguished the first film, and the irresistible physical delight it took in its people and their pursuits, are now replaced by a smooth, page-turning professionalism that may possibly indicate technical advance at the expense of an original expression. The delicacy is still there, and the great sweetness and affection, but there is also a suggestion of creeping Esperanto, and the suspicion arises that what we are going to get is an Indian *version* of an autobiographical stereotype instead of a whole new personal con-tribution. There isn't anything wrong with what happens in *Aparajito* or with what seems to be going to happen later. The boy grows up and makes deci-sions and sets forth. What counts is whether he turns into a Bengali David Cop-perfield or someone more like himself, whom we haven't met before in books or movies.

In the second film, the grand design of Ray's trilogy comes quietly into view: the emergence, through a painful sequence of trial and sacrifice, of Apu as a "social being." The dimensions of the material are thus dramatically enlarged, and the narrative line proceeds in a somewhat cautious chronology. The family is caught up in the crush of life in Benares. The father dies early in the film, gasping for Ganges water, and at this point Ray cuts swiftly to a dark shot of startled, crazily wheeling birds. The mother obtains work as a cook for a privileged family and they move back to the country where Apu, now about 12, takes up his father's priestly duties. Revolt comes when Apu insists on going first to the local school and later on pursuing his studies in Calcutta. The mother ineffectually resists, and the film settles down to a silent struggle between the lonely, slowly withering woman and her ambitious son, who has now grown into a disturbingly beautiful, slightly callow young intellectual. The poignancy of this situation isn't developed in its full complexity. The coun-tering values are taken somewhat for granted; and so there is a curiously null, pared down quality about the final episode, which compasses the death of the mother and Apu's decision to return to the city. Despite the bleak melancholy which shrouds these scenes, and the brilliantly expressive shots of the black trains creeping along the horizon of the flat country like bugs on a shelf, a final emotional consolidation is missing: the film doesn't end, it simply ceases to be. And when the mother dies, she does so in a vague trail of ellipses, very narrowly, instead of in circumstances of cumulative tension and despair. I wouldn't substitute a bang for a whimper, but it is strange that the death of the most perfectly realized and sustained character in the work thus far should not have elicited some imaginative discovery, some conclusive union of sympathy and meaning beyond the hammily atmospheric giveaway which the director elects. But this is less an error of taste than of dramatic comprehension, and it is failures of this sort that make *Aparajito* a not-quite-worthy sequel to *Panchali*.

The film has its most rewarding feature in the playing of a large cast. The schoolmasters, every one of them, are delightful, and the acting or, rather, the consistently appropriate presence of Karuna Banerji as Apu's mother is one of Ray's proudest accomplishments. If *Aparajito* falls somewhat short of its goal, it nevertheless discloses a lengthening talent, and one refreshingly free from specialization.

Those who took *Pather Panchali* for a gloss on alien folkways will perhaps be comforted by the more domesticated concerns of *Aparajito*—by the recognition that it is, after all, about "people like us." Those for whom *Panchali* sprang as from some long-buried primordial experience of selfhood will be disappointed by the generalizations of its sequel, but they will follow it with the pleasure and commitment of charter subscribers.

It is impossible to guess what the third installment will be like. Ray has composed one major movement and an interesting, but underdeveloped, *Andante*. Whatever else he may achieve, he has give the world cinema one of its monuments. In one leap, with *Panchali*, he left the field of competition far behind. One awaits *The World of Apu* with the cruelest excitement, for we now ask of Satyajit Ray what we ask only of great artists—that he surpass himself.

1959

A Note on La Belle, La Perfectly Swell, Romance

About four minutes into the movie *Shall We Dance*, Fred Astaire shows Edward Everett Horton a flip book of Ginger Rogers dancing and says, "I haven't even met her, but I'd kinda like to marry her," which is exactly what a movie audience of 1937 would have expected him to say. He's not just a man who has fallen in love with a picture of a girl, he's a man who has fallen in love with a girl who dances like *that*. From that moment on, the audience waits for them to dance together, knowing that Fred's feeling for Ginger can't be expressed in conventional love scenes—that until he dances with her he hasn't possessed her.

This very simple but very specialized form of love story was the basis of the series of Astaire–Rogers musicals that RKO produced in the Thirties and that many people regard as the greatest musicals in movie history. Certainly no greater dance musicals exist. Oddly enough, the dance emphasis that made them unusual also made them popular. Although Astaire and Rogers did many things in their movies besides dance—the way they looked and read their lines and wore their clothes and sang in their funny voices has become legendary, too, and they could make a song a hit without dancing to it—it was through their dancing that the public grew to love them and to identify their moods, the depth of their involvement, and the exquisite sexual harmony that made them not only the ideal dancing couple but the ideal romantic team. No dancers ever reached a wider public, and the stunning fact is that Astaire and Rogers, whose love scenes were their dances, became the most popular team the movies have ever known. In the three middle years of their partnership, they were listed among the top ten box office attractions in the poll of exhibitors conducted by *Motion Picture Herald*. In 1936, their peak year, they were in third place (after Shirley Temple and Clark Gable). It probably isn't a coincidence that their two films for 1936, *Follow the Fleet* and *Swing Time*, contain the best dances they ever did together. One can say of them, as of few performers in any art, that at their greatest they were most loved.

"Fred and Ginger," as we speak of them, are the characters created by Fred Astaire and Ginger Rogers while they are dancing. In their dance they grow suddenly large and important in a way that isn't given to Fred alone or to Fred with someone else. When Fred dances alone, he's perfect. For as long as we have known him he has been simply Astaire, *the* dancing man, self-defined. He is his own form of theater and we ask nothing more. But when he dances with Ginger we suddenly realize what further revelations that theater can produce: it can encompass the principle of complementarity. That principle has been missing from every Astaire film since his partnership with Rogers ended. He never ceased to dance wonderfully and he has had some good dancing partners. But it is a world of sun without a moon.

Ginger Rogers was, as a partner, a faithful reflection of everything that Astaire intended. She could even shed her own light. All of their great romantic duets took place, so to speak, in the light of the moon, and one of the pleasures of the RKO series is watching that lunar radiance increase. Rogers could never have won an international tap-dancing contest, but then she never tried. Her technique became exactly what she needed in order to dance with Fred Astaire, and, as no other woman in movies ever did, she created the feeling that stirs us so deeply when we see them together: Fred need not be alone.

Nor could Astaire have won an international tap-dancing contest, but who looks for mere technique from him? His "peerlessness" is a legend; it means, not that there were no other tap-dancers, but that there were no other Astaires. Above everything else, he was a master dramatist. Drama clings to every move he makes and to every move that Rogers makes with him. And yet they do not act, they dance. They had that kind of professional attitude toward, and respect for, dancing that comes from doing the work of it. At the core of their professionalism was a concentration upon dance as dance, not as acrobatics or sexy poses or self-expression. Their absorption gave plausible life and seriousness to what remained generically lyric fantasy—the continuing lyric fantasy of which all their numbers were a part. Their confidence was such as to breed an almost mischievous gaiety. When they watch each other throughout the two duets in the "Continental" sequence of *The Gay Divorcee*, it seems impossible that the screen will ever again capture such a delicious *entre nous* sparkle of fun. To some observers the fun is a bit coldly technical; the dancing looks intricate and too objective, like the challenge of a competition ("Beautiful music . . . dangerous rhythm . . ."). Just as it should look, for in an Astaire–Rogers film the dancing is often the only real, the only serious business. Their way of dancing up to a song, rather than down to a plot, is what takes you by surprise; that, and the way they give each song all the emotion that belongs to it, even if it is deeper than the plot and characterization allow for.

Yet the dances are not about nothing. Frequently they have the most intimate connection with literal plot action. The finale of *Shall We Dance* combines all the elements, symbolic as well as dramatic, of the plot. In "I'll Be Hard to Handle" in *Roberta*, they start the dance as casual friends and end it as soulmates on their way to love. The great "Never Gonna Dance" sequence recapitulates all the important action of *Swing Time* and sweeps it forward to a heart-rending climax as, in a spasm of clenched anger, she whirls out of his life. But while there is a great deal being said in these dances, Astaire never once changes his choreographic style. It stays very dry. Nor do he and Rogers ever press meanings upon us. Their smooth, informal, light objectivity continues straight across the lines of reference, and since the weight of gesture seems no more than what the music of the moment deserves, we are free to enjoy dancing unpressured by extraneousness, as audiences of the Thirties were free. And we may even feel like raising a silent toast to those audiences who could take their dancing, as it were, neat.

Those of us who were brought up on the movie musicals of the Forties and Fifties had much to enjoy: we had Astaire still, we had Garland, we had Gene Kelly, but we didn't have anything like the essential seriousness of the Astaire–Rogers movies. The major difference between Astaire and Kelly is a difference, not of talent or technique, but of levels of sophistication. On the face of it, Kelly looks the more sophisticated. Where Kelly has ideas, Astaire has steps. Where Kelly has smartly tailored, dramatically apt Comden and Green scripts, Astaire in the Thirties made do with formulas derived from nineteenth-century French farce. But the Kelly film is no longer a dance film. It's a story film with dances, as distinguished from a dance film with a story. When Fred and Ginger go into their dance, you see it as a distinct formal entity, even if it's been elaborately built up to in the script. In a Kelly film, the plot action and the musical set pieces preserve a smooth continuity of high spirits, so that the pressure in a dance number will often seem too low, the dance itself plebeian or folksy in order to "match up" with the rest of the picture. Wonderful as *Singin' in the Rain* is, the fun of it hasn't much to do with dancing.

The Astaire–Rogers dance films were romances, or rather, chapters in a single epic romance. In a line from *Swing Time*, Dorothy Fields called it "la belle, la perfectly swell, romance." From *The Gay Divorcee*'s "Night and Day," the true beginning of the partnership, to "Never Gonna Dance," the last of the great romantic duets, it is only two years. But in those years dancing was transformed into a vehicle of serious emotion between a man and a woman. It never happened in movies again.

1972

Jonas Mekas

Jonas Mekas (b. 1922) was born in Lithuania, spent several years in a Nazi forced-labor camp and subsequently five years more in Displaced Persons camps, then immigrated at age 22 to New York City (experiences he detailed in his poignant memoir *I Had Nowhere to Go*). There he wrote poetry and became chief advocate for the New American Cinema, a group of experimental filmmakers that included Stan Brakhage, Kenneth Anger, Andy Warhol, and Mekas himself. He also started the magazine *Film Culture*. In his weekly *Village Voice* column "Movie Journal," Mekas sought to present on-the-fly, soulful, scrappily partisan, countercultural alternatives to the measured film reviews of the establishment press. Mekas's is above all a poet's film criticism, with the license to use visionary, charged language that that term implies. His films (*Lost Lost Lost, As I Was Moving Ahead Occasionally I Saw Brief Glimpses of Beauty*, among others) are personal epics, composed of lyrical fragments and home movies, complexly edited.

◆

The Creative Joy of the Independent Film-Maker

January 12, 1961

Newspapers and critics are looking for waves. Let them look for them, goodby, goodby! There is a new cinema, and there was, for a good fifteen years, the experimental cinema, but critics did not see it. The reason is simple: They do not know what to look for. As in that Zen tale:

> It's too clear and so it's hard to see:
> The man once searched for a fire
> with a lighted lantern;
> had he known what fire was,
> he could have cooked his rice sooner.

The French *nouvelle vague* is really not so new—and not so different from the rest of the commercial French or any cinema. If they are so conventional at twenty, imagine what they will be at forty!

The most original new American movies never even intended to compete with the commercial cinema. Beginning with *The Quiet One* and all the way down the line through *On the Bowery* and *The Sin of Jesus*, this cinema is an outcast, an "outsider" cinema, and its authors know it. They are not after another Hollywood; Hollywood is doing its job well without them.

I have often spoken against professionalism. *Next Stop 28th Street* is a good example of what I mean. In this film the bleak, sad poetry of the subway is caught as nobody has caught it before (except Peter Orlovski), as no Hollywood with no ten tons of lights and studio sets could ever catch it. Oh, the helplessness of the professionals, and the creative joy of the independent film artist, roaming the streets of New York, free, with his 16 mm. camera, on the Bowery, in Harlem, in Times Square, and in the Lower East Side apartments—the new American film poet, not giving a damn about Hollywood, art, critics, or anybody.

Renoir and Plotless Cinema

January 26, 1961

There is a new book by Ezra Goodman, *The Fifty-Year Decline and Fall of Hollywood* (Simon & Schuster). Goodman quotes D. W. Griffith as saying: "The simple things, the human things are important in pictures. There are supposed to be only seven or eight plots. They are relatively unimportant. The most important thing is humanity." The old man of cinema knew it all the time.

It is an important point, this plot business. It almost makes the whole difference between entertainment and art, between purely commercial cinema and author's cinema. Crazed about the plot, the critics almost killed *Picnic on the Grass* and *Another Sky*, two of the best movies to come to town in a long time. Kurosawa's *Drunken Angel* they did not even notice. Now they are trying to kill Buñuel. The critics prefer plot, the artist prefers the regions beyond plot.

The masterpiece of the personal, "plotless" cinema is Jean Renoir's *Rules of the Game* (at the 8th Street Playhouse). And it is in *Rules of the Game* that we see the superiority of Renoir over Bergman. Cinema vs. theatre. Whereas Bergman sustains his scenes through the dramatic climaxes, Renoir avoids any such dramatizations. Renoir's people look like people, act like people, and are confused like people, vague and unclear. They are moved not by the plot, not by theatrical dramatic climaxes, but by something that one could even call the stream of life itself, by their own irrationality, their sporadic, unpredictable behavior. Bergman's people do not have a choice of free movement because of the imposed dramatic construction; Renoir's people have no choice because of the laws of life itself. Bergman's hero is the contrived 19th-century hero;

Renoir's hero is the unanimous hero of the 20th century. And it is not through the conclusions of the plot (the fake wisdom of pompous men) that we learn anything from Renoir; it is not who killed whom that is important; it is not through the hidden or open symbolism of the lines, situations, or compositions that Renoir's truth comes to us; but through the details, characterizations, reactions, relationships, movements of his people, the *mise-en-scène*. Gradually, as the film progresses, plotless as it is, the whole nerve system of the pre-World War II French aristocracy is revealed to us, sickening as it is.

And that is the secret of the art of Buñuel and Renoir. The very last image of *The Young One*, with Zachary Scott standing there alone by the water's edge, the burning patch of sun behind the trees, and the overgrowth of the trees—this in itself is worth more than all the New York film critics and their papers put together. Our film critics are butchers of the human and the beautiful. And so are their papers.

Marilyn Monroe and the Loveless World

February 9, 1961

Marilyn Monroe, the saint of Nevada Desert. When everything has been said about *The Misfits*, how bad the film is and all that, she still remains there, MM, the saint. And she haunts you, you'll not forget her.

It is MM that is the film. A woman who has known love, has known life, has known men, has been betrayed by all three, but has retained her dream of man, love, and life.

She meets these tough men, Gable, Clift, Wallach, in her search for love and life; she finds love everywhere and she cries for everyone. She is the only beautiful thing in the whole ugly desert, in the whole world, in this whole dump of toughness, atom bomb, death.

Everybody has given up their dreams, all the tough men of the world have become cynics, except MM. And she fights for her dream—for the beautiful, innocent, and free. It is she who fights for love in the world, when the men fight only wars and act tough. Men gave up the world. It is MM that tells the truth in this movie, who accuses, judges, reveals. And it is MM who runs into the middle of the desert and in her helplessness shouts: *"You are all dead, you are all dead!"*—in the most powerful image of the film—and one doesn't know if she is saying those words to Gable and Wallach or to the whole loveless world.

Is MM playing herself or creating a part? Did Miller and Huston create a character or simply re-create MM? Maybe she is even talking her own thoughts, her own life? Doesn't matter much. There is so much truth in her little details, in her reactions to cruelty, to false manliness, nature, life, death, that she is overpowering, one of the most tragic and contemporary characters of modern cinema, and another contribution to The Woman as a Modern Hero in Search of Love (see *Another Sky*, *The Lovers*, *Hiroshima, Mon Amour*, *The Savage Eye*, etc., etc.).

It's strange how cinema, bit by bit, can piece together a character. Cinema is not only beautiful compositions or well-knit stories; cinema is not only visual patterns or play of light. Cinema also creates human characters.

We are always looking for "art," or for good stories, drama, ideas, content in movies—as we are accustomed to in books. Why don't we forget literature and drama and Aristotle! Let's watch the face of man on the screen, the face of MM, as it changes, reacts. No drama, no ideas, but a human face in all its nakedness—something that no other art can do. Let's watch this face, its movements, its shades; it is this face, the face of MM, that is the content and story and idea of the film, that is the whole world, in fact.

On Andy Warhol's *Sleep*

Cool piece: Not answering questions. Just asking them.

January 30, 1964

What does Warhol's *Sleep* do? What doesn't it do? Is it cinema? Is this the ultimate extension of Pop Art? The slowing down, stretching a detail to its limit, to what maximum effect? Using the screen as a sounding board for the viewer's dreams, fantasies, thoughts? An exercise in hypnosis? Test of patience? A Zen Joke? If it makes you angry, why? Can't you relax and take a good joke? Running? Where to? Searching for Art in *Sleep*, doesn't it betray our own pompousness? Why do we go to cinema? It abandons the usual movie experience for what? Pure cinema, no fake entertainment, no fake stories, isn't that something worth trying? Does this bringing down to absurdum mean that we have to start from scratch, to forget all previous movie experiences? Doesn't it remind us that there is not much sense in rushing? Doesn't it remind us of the secret, almost unnoticeable motions, variations? What was wrong with those few who sat through all the six hours of the movie? Were they sick, or were they capable of satoris and delights which we are not capable of enjoying? What did it do to them, what did it really destroy or start in them, what did it germinate during those six hours which we missed—an experience which we missed in our silly (and/or sick) haste? All these questions and many more you could hear in the lobby of the Gramercy Arts Theatre last weekend, during the screening of Andy Warhol's <u>monumental</u> *Sleep*.

Not Everything That Is Fun Is Cinema

September 10, 1964

A *Hard Day's Night* took our movie reviewers by surprise. Reviewers liked it. The Beatle fans liked it. Crowther liked it. Sarris said it shook his film aesthetics. The movie will make millions. The Beatles sing sweetly. They behave like nuts. There is something beat about the Beatles.

The movie is beautifully photographed. It uses underground cinema techniques, it swings. It's not locked to one spot, it moves freely.

But neither good acting nor good photography can make a good movie. There must be an artist behind it. There must be a madness of a different kind. Two or three inspired shots remain two or three inspired shots. There is no movie. *A Hard Day's Night* is a sufficiently well-made melodrama about the Beatles.

The Maysles brothers made a film about the Beatles. You have to see the Maysles film to realize what really good photography is, or what cinema is, or what really the Beatles are.

Only one who is completely ignorant of the work of the New American Cinema film-makers during the past three years can call *A Hard Day's Night*, even jokingly, the *Citizen Kane* of the hand-held cinema (Sarris did it).

But why should I argue about it? There are so many people who like *A Hard Day's Night* for so many different reasons. I have said often enough that art is not the only thing in life.

But I haven't said strongly enough, and I may as well say it right now, that art exists. Aesthetic experience exists. *A Hard Day's Night* has nothing to do with it. At best, it is fun. But "fun" is not an aesthetic experience: Fun remains on the surface. I have nothing against the surface. But it belongs where it is and shouldn't be taken for anything else.

On Bresson and *Une Femme Douce*

October 2, 1969

Here is what I thought, walking home from *Une Femme Douce. Une Femme Douce* is a film about diagonals. Diagonal angles, diagonal glances. About eyes that never really meet. A film without a single frontal shot. A film about three-quarter spaces. About the sound of closing doors. About the sound of footsteps. About the sound of things. About the sound of water. About shy glances. About unfinished glances. About the sound of glass. About death in our midst. About light falling on faces. About lights in the dark, falling on faces. About blood on forehead. About unfinished playing records. About a white crepe blouse. About blue. About flowers picked and never taken home. About the roaring of cars. About the roaring of animals. About the roaring of motor-cycles. About green. About how life and death intercut with each other. About hands giving and taking. About hands. About bourgeois pride. About pride. About lights on the door. About lights behind the door. About doors opening and closing. About bourgeois jealousy. About jealousy. About lamps turned out. About brown and yellow. About yellow. About indirect glances. About glances. About one peaceful glance (in the gallery, Schaeffer?). About unfinished records. About doors opening and closing. About doors opening very gently. About a half-opened door. About people standing behind glass doors and looking in. About fool's hopes. About hopes. About a window which doesn't lead into life. About a red car seat. About a red shop window. About standing behind the door, looking in. About a green bed and green curtains. About one happy smile in the mirror, at oneself. About eyes which do not look even when asked. About the sound of metal. About sleep. About two diagonal lives.

Stanley Kauffmann

Stanley Kauffmann (b. 1916) has achieved the remarkable feat of writing regular film criticism (mostly in *The New Republic*) for over half a century. Even more remarkable is that each column of his continues to be a model of moral intelligence, crafted language, compositional balance, measured judgment, and enthusiastic openness to innovation. A playwright, novelist, and teacher as well as a critic, he started with a deep understanding of the theater and its potential for complex character roles, insights he has transported naturally to his cinematic assessments. Kauffmann's analysis of a movie's weaknesses (see review of *The Misfits*) is invariably delivered "more in sorrow than in anger"; he is honest but never mean-spirited. His determination to consider one film at a time, and his resistance to the systematic adoration of "pantheon" directors which was being promoted by auteurist criticism, may be seen in his credo-like critique of *Lola Montes*.

◆

The Misfits

Arthur Miller, in his plays, has done some representative worrying for all of us about certain defects and defeats in contemporary life. Now he has broken a five-year silence with a screenplay called *The Misfits* in which he expresses further concern.

The premise is promising: a Chicago girl goes to Reno for a divorce, and there meets three Western men. She is desperate for reliable human relationships, they are in a last-ditch fight against the diminution of large-scale life. She lives with one of them, then the other two pursue her; after a mustang-hunting expedition which acts as a touchstone, she elects to remain with the first man.

It is pointless, if not offensive, to underscore that this screenplay is, in idea and much of its execution, several universes above most American films. But *The Misfits* is finally unsuccessful both in its treatment of its subject and as a use of the film form, and it is a cheerless task, because of respect for Miller and agreement with his concerns, to examine the reasons.

The film moves with Roslyn, the girl: she is one of the two chief searchers for truth and she is the cause of the revelation of truth to Gay, her lover. But what does her search consist of? In the beginning we are shown a highly insecure, neurotic girl. ("The trouble is I'm always back where I started". . . . "Maybe you're not supposed to believe anything people say. Maybe it's not even fair to them," etc.) Then, although she has just told Gay she doesn't feel "that way" about him, she moves in with him; and the first time they are visited by their friends, one of them tells her "You found yourself, haven't you?", and the other says, "You have the gift of life." Where did she get it? From then on this girl, but lately nervous and restless, is treated as the Eternal Feminine, in tune with the universe ("hooked in" with the stars). What produced this fantastic change? A few weeks of bliss with Gay? Can Miller seriously believe that?

And how does she effect a resolution in Gay? Through her extreme revulsion against pain—specifically against hunting. She won't let him kill a rabbit (although she never bats an eye when he tells her that their friend Guido goes eagle-killing in his plane); and on the horse-hunting trip, when she learns that the mustangs are to be killed for dog-food, she becomes so frenzied that Gay gives up the hunt and hunting and decides to change his mode of living. But how has this made him realize that the straitening of contemporary life is inevitable? He has known for some time that mustang-hunting is less than it was when he first did it to get stock for breeding and riding. Her hysteria is not persuasive as a reason for his seeing these facts more clearly. She would presumably have been equally hysterical in 1850 if he had been killing deer to feed himself and her. Her outburst is unrelated to the modern debasement of his mustanging as such.

The author seems bemused by Roslyn, rather than perceptive about her. She is a night-club performer, who had an unsettled childhood and now makes her living by scantily clad "interpretive" dancing. We have no reason to believe her more than a good-hearted, highly sentimental showgirl, like hundreds of others, but the longer Miller looks at her, the more rich and mysterious qualities he sees in her. It is something like a man becoming infatuated with an attractive but undistinguished girl and, out of a sense of guilt, investing her with qualities which the world simply doesn't see.

This infatuation leads to some embarrassingly bathetic instances in her dialogue. "Birds must be brave to live out here. Especially at night. . . ." Or when the drunken Guido starts working on his unfinished house in the middle of the night: "He's just trying to say hello. . . ." Or, after an emotional scene, looking at the sky, "Help."

Miller has often had surprising lumps in his generally true dialogue. (In *Death of a Salesman* the vernacular Biff apologizes to his mother: "I've been remiss.") Here the mixture is as before. There is much acute and vivid writing;

a phone-call to his mother by Perce, the third man, is a brilliant character sketch. Then we get literary utterances like Guido's "We're all blind bombardiers . . . Droppin' a bomb is like tellin' a lie—makes everything so quiet afterwards."

In form this screenplay is basically uncomfortable because Miller is a theater-writer who has a generally orthodox and socially utilitarian view of theatrical art. Dialectical dialogue is its bloodstream. It is an honorable tradition, and *The Crucible* ornaments it; but it is not film-writing. Miller knows this and has tried to compensate for the verbal quality of this film by including some graphic visual elements, like the rodeo and the hunt. But essentially the story is "talked out." Indeed, these uncommonly loquacious Westerners almost seem to be competing for the girl by offering her their troubled souls. And when Gay and Roslyn go off together at the end, we get a fast, almost synoptic talking-into-final-shape of the theme. And this ending, after all the candid confrontation of harsh facts in our world, is as suddenly and incredibly "upbeat" as anything by the late Oscar Hammerstein.

John Huston's direction is his best in years, well-knit and hard, at times even recalling *The Treasure of Sierra Madre*. Too bad that his camera occasionally peers lubriciously down the girl's bodice or elsewhere to remind us that Roslyn is really Marilyn Monroe.

Miss Monroe, complete with hushed, monotonous voice and with eye makeup even after a night in the mountains, copes more successfully with the neurotic than with the "elemental" qualities in her part. But at her best we sense that she has been coached and primed in thirty-second segments, which wouldn't matter if we weren't aware of it. Her hysterical scene near the end will seem virtuoso acting to those who are overwhelmed by the fact that she has been induced to shout.

In his last film Clark Gable has his best part since Rhett Butler and demonstrates why, although he was a transparently mechanical actor, he was a world-bestriding star. He radiates likeable, decent-roguish masculinity.

Eli Wallach, as Guido the ex-Army pilot, sounds less bronco-hunter than Bronx. There is something vulgar in this gifted actor's reliance on vulgarity as a *métier*. Montgomery Clift, who was last seen as a Westerner (unconvincingly) in *Red River*, here brings moving life to Perce, the battered young exile, who has nothing to live on but his willingness to get thrown off bucking horses.

1961

L'Avventura

A t last. Michelangelo Antonioni is an Italian director who has just made his seventh film and who is so highly esteemed abroad that there has already been an Antonioni Festival in London. For the eleven years of his career no Antonioni film has been released here. Now at last comes *L'Avventura*, which is the sixth of his works.

The first ten minutes make it clear that this is the work of a discerning, troubled, uniquely gifted artist who speaks to us through the refined center of his art. We may even "like" this film, but those first ten minutes indicate that liking is not the primary point. We "like" Maurice Chevalier, but do we "like" *Wozzeck* or *No Exit*? If so, all the better, but we know from the start that it is irrelevant to their effective being.

This is not to say that *L'Avventura* is an unpleasant or uninteresting experience: simply that it does not come out of the wings like a chorus girl with a grin on her face to make a hit fast.

The setting is contemporary Italy. Anna, a wealthy Roman girl, is having an affair with Sandro, a fortyish architect. They go off on a yachting weekend—together with Claudia, a close friend of Anna's—as guests of a dissolute princess. The party lands on a small island north of Sicily to bathe, and Anna, who has been moody and depressed, disappears. The island is searched without success; Claudia and Sandro stay overnight with a shepherd while the others go for the police.

And now the focus shifts. As in *Madame Bovary* (for example), we see that the prominent figure of the opening has been used merely to take us to the heart of the situation and, having delivered us, recedes. We never see Anna again. Sandro has increasingly to force himself to look distraught and to search; Claudia is increasingly disturbed because her genuine anxiety for her friend is being elbowed by her latent desire for Sandro and her subconscious realization that now she can have him. Before they have left the island—less than twenty-four hours later—Sandro has kissed her and has made her realize that she is glad of Anna's disappearance.

However, motions must still be gone through. They all go to Sicily following a sketchy clue that Anna may have fled with some fishermen, and Sandro, accompanied by Claudia, spends some days in more and more desultory search. During the search Sandro and Claudia become lovers, and criss-cross the path of the pleasure-seeking princess and her party as they make their way to the south of Sicily. The film ends in a palatial hotel in Taormina; Sandro has already been unfaithful to Claudia and she has already forgiven him. Or rather she accepts what they must accept in order not to spend all of life in tears, fights, futile beating against the facts of their natures and the moral temper of their time. They settle for what they are.

Over this slow, divagating search for the lost girl, which is really Claudia's discovery of herself, Antonioni hovers with his camera: peering, following, lingering to savor a place after the people have left it. He is more interested in personality, mood, and the physical world than in drama; and it is this—if we apply conventional standards—that at times makes his picture seem to have lost its way. But Antonioni is trying to exploit the unique powers of the film as distinct from the theater. Many superb film directors (like De Sica) are oriented theatrically; Antonioni is not. He attempts to get from film the same utility of the medium itself as a novelist whose point is not a story but mood and character and for whom the texture of the prose is as relevant as what he says in the prose.

By purely theatrical standards, this film could easily be condensed by any skilled cutter—the search on the island, the visit to the deserted town, the kisses of Sandro and Claudia in the field. But when it is all over, you see that this condensation would sharpen the pace at the expense of the purpose. Antonioni wants the discoveries of this pair to occur in something more like real time than theatrical time. Obviously it is not real time or we would all have to bring along sandwiches and blankets; but a difference of ten seconds in a scene is a tremendous step toward veristic reproduction rather than theatrical abstraction.

The story is Antonioni's. The theme is upper-middle-class morality—not low enough to be corseted by suburban respectability, not high enough to be subject to *noblesse oblige*. These are Chekhov's people in Italy today; and, like Chekhov's people, we see them overripening before they drop. It is no accident that much of this film takes its indolent way across Sicily (Danilo Dolci's Sicily!—with disease and rooted poverty screaming just off-stage). It is an important part of the design that Sandro is disgusted with his professional success, which has betrayed his youthful plans. In profligate harmony with Sandro's resolve to get as much mundane compensation as he can, there are the princess and her *ami*, who wearily puts his hand in her bodice to flatter himself and her; and the frantic wife of a jaded husband hungrily devouring a nineteen-year-old admirer.

It is part of this design that makes Sandro spill ink on a young artist's sketch, deliberately hurting this reminder of his own youth in order to provoke a fight, then hurrying back to the hotel to make love with Claudia in order to substitute a little of the present for the lost past.

I wish that a few loose threads had been omitted (the mysterious boat we never see, the hint that the smugglers know where Anna is). And I wish I could expand on more of the fine touches like the blaring sound truck whose popular song carries us and the immanence of contemporary vulgarity into Claudia's bedroom; and do more than note the beautiful melancholy of Lea Massari (Anna), the sense of life in a sexual ambience conveyed by Monica Vitti (Claudia), the attractive but slightly shallow resignation of Gabrielle Ferzetti (Sandro).

In this film Antonioni stands quite apart from the Italian neorealists. He does not try to show life "as it is" but as he sees it. In the sense that his films are intensely personal in viewpoint and style and poetic rather than naturalistic, he is more comparable to Bergman than to his fellow Italians. But there is a great difference. The fountainhead of Bergman's films is mysticism: is the God-man relation still viable? Antonioni seems to have answered that question in the negative; thinks men have to learn self-reliance or crumble; is hoping for the possibility of hope.

1961

Lola Montes

Max Ophuls' *Lola Montes* was made in 1955, in France and Bavaria, and, except for some festival showings, is now seen here for the first time in unmutilated form. (A butchered, dubbed version was released in 1959.) This is an important event both because of what the film is and is not, and because of what it crystallizes in critical approaches.

Lola Montes was Ophuls' last work; he died in 1957. He was a German Jew, born Max Oppenheimer, who changed his name because his family objected to his becoming an actor. By the time he was twenty-two, in 1924, he had become a theater director and by 1930 is said to have directed almost two hundred productions, including some work at the Burgtheater in Vienna. He began directing films in 1930 and, for obvious reasons, began directing elsewhere in 1932—France, Italy, Holland, Switzerland. By 1941 he was in Hollywood but did not get his first American film until 1947. He did four pictures in the U.S.; probably the best known is *Letter from an Unknown Woman*. He returned to France in 1949 and made four more pictures. Preceding *Lola Montes* were *La Ronde*, *Le Plaisir*, and *The Earrings of Madame de.* . . .

Some critics consider *Lola Montes* to be "the greatest film of all time." To say that I disagree is not merely to quibble with the phrase "all time" as applied to a seventy-five-year-old art; not merely to deplore the facileness with which the accolade of greatness is broadcast in film criticism; it is to differ thoroughly and fundamentally about the means and potentials of film. Some *Lola* lovers concur about some of the flaws I'll describe; but they give different weight to those flaws. That is the heart of the argument.

The film tells the story—a version of it, anyway—of the famous nineteenth-century dancer-courtesan. It begins with the older Lola, playing in a circus in New Orleans. She sits in the center of the ring, as the ringmaster narrates her life, and the bulk of the film is in flashback. We see the end of her affair with Franz Liszt, her (earlier) marriage to her mother's lover, some other embroilments, and her affair with King Ludwig of Bavaria. Throughout, we keep returning to the circus, and it ends there, with people streaming forward to pay a dollar to kiss the hand of Lola, seated in a cage. Thus the structure is cyclical. The cyclical had always appealed to Ophuls: the idea and very title of *La Ronde* (made from Schnitzler's *Reigen*); the reappearance of the earrings in *Madame de* . . . ; the recurrence of the lover in *Letter from an Unknown Woman*. In *Lola* the circus ring itself underscores the cyclical motif.

From first moment to last, *Lola Montes* is treasure for the eye, abundant, exciting in its abundance, rich in what Ophuls includes and in the way he handles it. The first things we see are two gorgeous chandeliers descending from a height. (Suggested to Ophuls by the Josefstadt Theater in Vienna?) The chandeliers pass a circus band whose leader is in Uncle Sam costume; and the camera, ever moving, then picks up the ringmaster as he enters. He walks past a multi-leveled swirl of activity to the center the ring, in front of two parallel lines of girls who proceed to juggle ninepins and comment in chorus on the tale the ringmaster is telling in flamboyant style. Soon Lola makes her entrance in a gorgeous carriage and is borne to the center. All this to a counterpoint of changing lights and bizarre costumes. (The film is in color and Cinemascope.) The effect—of glittering chaos falling marvelously into order—is precisely the same as in the opera-house sequence of *Citizen Kane* and for the same reason, I would guess: both Ophuls and Welles had large theatrical experience. The changes of light within a scene—dimmings, swellings, pinpointings, falls of color—and the knowing use of *entrances*, these are marks of stage experience.

The most noted hallmark of Ophuls' film style is his moving camera and his cuts from one moving shot to another. Here in the beginning it is used to create a sense of overture, partly by the way the camera grandly ignores the richness of what is happening behind or in passing. The combination of swirl and prodigality promises us largesse: we needn't bother about that dwarf or those splendid horses or that bevy of girls; a great deal is going to spill on the screen.

And it does spill. This is not a matter of purchased Hollywood extravagance. It is Ophuls' gift for selecting the right element of decor, like the low Gothic arch in Liszt's room; for layering every scene with planes of detail ("Details make art," he said) so that the characters are always moving through a world that just happens to tell us something relevant or characteristic about itself at the moment they pass. Examples: the hens roosting all the way up the narrow inn steps; the maimed soldier in Ludwig's castle, past whom the servants have to run when they are on a trifling errand for the king in whose service this man lost his leg; the clown, with whom Lola's doctor waits, who has the voice and demeanor of a prime minister. And, always, these excellent touches are *ignored*.

The visual virtuosity is also in what is done, as well as in the materials included: Lieutenant James chasing Lola crisscross through the descending galleries of the theater; the rope that swings from the stage flies in the foreground as, behind it, Ludwig expresses interest in Lola; the students running toward us down a long ramp to meet Lola's carriage at an angle near the camera; the very last shot, in which the camera pulls back over the hordes advancing on Lola until we are far from her. No fadeout; in the theatrical vein of the film, the curtains close.

All this is superb. There is not a flaw in the *mise en scène*, not a dull frame for the eye. (Well, one reservation: Ophuls either detested or feared Cinemascope and, in some intimate scenes, he puts arbitrary shadows at the edges to narrow the picture.) But after it's all over—*before* then—we are faced with the Chesterton comment. The first time G. K. Chesterton walked down Broadway at night past the flashing electric advertisements, he said, "What a wonderful experience this must be for someone who can't read." In the case of *Lola*, one might add: "Or for those who want to pretend that they can't read."

For the script of *Lola* is just one more teary version of the Prostitute with the Heart of Gold, the whore ennobled by whoring, whom all her friends adore. The matters that made the real Lola an extraordinary woman are omitted completely; we are given only the picture of a woman turned to sexual adventuring by her mother's callousness; who makes her way with her loins; who dramatizes farewells a bit and can develop a little tenderness if the man is a king who gives her a palace; but is only an adventuress, with a touch of Carmen deviltry. To see this Lola as a mythopoeic figure of romance or a figure of the Eternal Feminine, to posit that her story is related to our culture's concepts of romance, is to me a quasi-adolescent insistence on glorifying whores. The difference between, say, Dumas's Marguerite Gauthier and Ophuls' Lola is one between an early attempt to show the particularized humanity of a type and the luxuriant exploitation of the type itself.

The acting of most of the principals is very bad. The late Martine Carol, who is Lola, never could act, and here she doesn't even look pretty. Ophuls spent little time on making her face attractive, even in her younger scenes. Oskar Werner, as her German-student lover, is waxen-faced and cutesy (miscast as a twenty-year-old). Will Quadflieg and Ivan Desny as Liszt and James are sticks. Peter Ustinov, the ringmaster, has merely a fraction of the modulation and shading that he showed in his recent pastry *Hot Millions*. Only Anton Walbrook as Ludwig is substantial.

Some of the *Lola* admirers might agree with all of this; all of them might agree with some of it. Together they reject its relevance. Why? Because they subscribe, with passionate and unquestionable conviction, to a theory of the hierarchy of film values. They believe in selecting and exalting sheerly cinematic values, like the matters I praised earlier, and in subordinating or discounting such matters as those I objected to. To them, this is exultation in the true glory of cinema.

To me, it is a derogation and patronization of cinema. To me, this hierarchy says: "This is what film can do and we mustn't really expect it to do any more, mustn't be disappointed if this is all it does." A chief motive behind the hierarchy is to avoid discussion of the strictured elements forced on film making by the ever-present money men. *Lola* was commissioned as an expensive showcase for Martine Carol. The money men foisted Miss Carol and a cheap novel—by the author of *Caroline Cherie*—on Ophuls, so let's not criticize those elements, let's concentrate on Ophuls' marvelous décor, detail, and camera movement and, by the simple act of appropriate omission, presto, we have a masterpiece.

I disbelieve in this hierarchy. There are money men involved in every art. No one would dream of praising an architect because he designed his interiors well, if he had debased his overall form to please his client's pocketbook. Why a special leniency for film?

Why indeed—in the face of the fact that film has proved it doesn't need it, has achieved *thoroughly* fine work? The worst aspect of this approach is that it crimps the film out of its cultural heritage—the cinematic *and* the literary and theatrical and psychological and social-political—and says to it, "Just go and be cinematic. If anything else is achieved, good. It not, no great matter." It is an esthetic equivalent of the Victorian ethic of "knowing your place."

This concentration on part of a work leads to inflation of the value of that part. Ophuls, who in some ways was masterly, is extolled as a master of romance. To speak only of *Lola*, I see him sheerly as cynic, burdened with this trumpery novel and this mammary star and deciding to give it back to the world in spades. One critic envisions Lola in the circus as a presence "redeeming all men both as a woman and as an artistic creation." *This* woman? *This* artistic creation? The last scene, in which the crowd presses forward to buy kisses of the caged Lola, gave me a vision of Ophuls himself chuckling at the Yahoos who are wonder-struck by this earlier Zsa Zsa Gabor, this "celebrity" in the word's synthetic present-day sense, a crowd scrabbling to pay for a touch of this scandal-sheet goddess. And I also had a concentric vision of Ophuls chuckling at his film audiences, as they press forward to pay for a chance to adulate his caged talent.

Let me give the last word, on this matter of exalting a medium in itself, to the German poet Hans Magnus Enzensberger. Writing about McLuhan in the latest *Partisan Review*, Enzensberger says:

It is all too easy to see why the slogan "The medium is the message" has met with unbounded enthusiasm on the part of the media, since it does away, by a quick fix worthy of a card-sharp, with the question of truth. Whether the message is a lie or not has become irrelevant, since in the light of McLuhanism truth itself resides in the very existence of the medium, no matter what it may convey. . . .

1969

Andrew Sarris

For Andrew Sarris (b. 1928), to write criticism is to engage in a lifelong act of rumination and reconsideration. A regular movie reviewer since 1955, first for *Film Culture* and the weekly *Village Voice*, now for *The New York Observer*, a professor of Cinema Studies at Columbia, he has written books on John Ford, Josef von Sternberg, and the Talkies, while never relinquishing his responsibility to see and respond in print to the latest releases. Sarris first gained national attention with *The American Cinema*, one of the most influential books of film criticism, which mapped the entire canon of American movies by assessing and rating directors. In doing so he creatively adapted the *auteur* outlook of André Bazin and the *Cahiers du cinéma* circle to his native soil. Sarris once wrote that "a long sojourn in Paris in 1961 reassured me that film not only demanded but deserved as much faith as did any other cultural discipline. . . . I have never really recovered from the Parisian heresy (in New York eyes) concerning the sacred importance of the cinema." Sarris's ancestor-worship for the great old directors whom he placed in his pantheon shows up in his appreciation of Hitchcock's *The Birds* and his willingness to give an aging Orson Welles and Charlie Chaplin the benefit of the doubt (see below). Having made the case for formalist visual analysis over social-conscious film criticism, he then reversed field and wrote one of his best collections on *Politics and Cinema*. Sarris's willingness to change direction, admit mistakes, and re-evaluate former positions (as he famously did with Billy Wilder, for instance, or *2001*), is unusual among film critics, for whom the general rule has usually been Don't Look Back. A law-giver in his younger days, he gained the confidence to be more self-skeptical and uncertain as he grew older.

Sarris's approach to a film, rather than burrowing methodically into it scene by scene (as Pauline Kael often did), is to glance off it through a mixture of personal disclaimers and confessions of initial prejudice, quick plot summary, aperçus about the human condition, puns, doubts, digressions into film history, and career assessments. One is never left in doubt about his overall feeling toward a picture, but his vast knowledge of film history (as much a scholar's as a critic's) can generate a free-fall of association. A most appealing aspect of Sarris's writing is his humanity; he is remarkably self-mocking, undefensive, and vulnerable, especially for a critic, and seems always on the side of compassion and wisdom. In an era given over to special effects and teen demographics, he remains devoted to psychologically mature films for adults (see his review of *La Guerre est Finie*, which conveys, too, his lifelong passion for French cinema).

◆

The Birds

The Birds is here (at the Palace and Sutton), and what a joy to behold a self-contained movie which does not feed parasitically on outside cultural references, Chekhov, Synge, O'Neill, Genet, Behan, Melville, or what have you. Drawing from the relatively invisible literary talents of Daphne DuMaurier and Evan Hunter, Alfred Hitchcock has fashioned a major work of cinematic art, and "cinematic" is the operative term here, not "literary" or "sociological." There is one sequence, for example, where the heroine is in an outboard motor boat churning across the bay while the hero's car is racing around the shore road to intercept her on the other side. This race, in itself pure cinema, is seen entirely from the girl's point of view. We see only what she can see from the rowboat. Suddenly, near shore, the camera picks up a sea gull swooping down on our heroine. For just a second, the point of view is shifted, and we are permitted to see the bird before its victim does. The director has apparently broken an aesthetic rule for the sake of a shock effect gull pecks girl. Yet this momentary incursion of the objective on the subjective is remarkably consistent with the meaning of the film.

The theme, after all, is complacency, as the director has stated on innumerable occasions. When we first meet each of the major characters, their infinite capacity for self-absorption is emphasized. Tippi Hedren's bored socialite is addicted to elaborately time-consuming practical jokes. Rod Taylor's self-righteous lawyer flaunts his arrogant sensuality. Suzanne Pleshette, his ex-fiancee, wallows in self-pity, and Jessica Tandy, his possessive mother, cringes from her fear of loneliness. With such complex, unsympathetic characters to contend with, the audience quite naturally begins to identify with the point of view of the birds, actually the inhuman point of view. As in *Psycho*, Hitchcock succeeds in implicating his audience to such an extent that the much-criticized, apparently anticlimactic ending of the film finds the audience more blood-thirsty than the birds. Although three people are killed and many others assaulted by man's fine feathered friends, critics and spectators have demanded more gore and more victims.

In *Psycho*, if you recall, there is a moment after Tony Perkins has run Janet Leigh's car into a swamp when the car stops sinking. One could almost hear the audience holding its breath until the car resumed its descent below the surface. At that first intake of breath, the audience became implicated in the fantasy of the perfect crime. In *The Birds*, the audience is similarly implicated, but this time in the fantasy of annihilation. The point Hitchcock seems to be making is that morality is not a function of sympathy, but a rigorous test of principles. If we can become even momentarily indifferent to the fate of a promiscuous blonde (Janet Leigh in *Psycho*) or a spoiled playgirl (Tippi Hedren in *The Birds*), we have clearly failed the test.

As symbols of evil and disorder, Hitchcock's winged bipeds lend themselves to many possible interpretations—Freudian, Thomistic, Existential, among others—but the imaginative spectator can draw his own analogies. What is beyond speculation is the strikingly visual potential of the subject. One penultimate shot of a row of blackbirds perched magisterially above the fearfully departing humans is worth a thousand words on man's unworthiness. Hitchcock's dark humor is as impressive as ever on both human and ornithological planes. There is something indescribably funny in the familiar gesture of a man winding up to throw a rock at some crows before being deterred by his prudent girl friend. Her "let sleeping birds perch" philosophy explodes its grotesque context into half-fragmented memories of human presumption.

Yet, in the midst of all the human guilt, the idea of innocence survives. When the survivors of the bird attacks venture past thousands of their erstwhile enemies, now ominously passive, the hero's eleven-year-old sister asks him to return to the house for her caged love birds. "They did no harm," she insists. The audience fears and anticipates the worst, but nothing happens. The caged love birds do not arouse the free hordes of the species. Instead, these two guiltless creatures seem to clear the path to the car as if the rediscovery of innocence were yet the only hope of the world.

The Birds finds Hitchcock at the summit of his artistic powers. His is the only contemporary style which unites the divergent classical traditions of Murnau (camera movement) and Eisenstein (montage). (Welles, for example, owes more to Murnau, while Resnais is closer to Eisenstein.) If formal excellence is still a valid criterion for film criticism, and there are those who will argue that it is not, then *The Birds* is probably the picture of the year.

1963

La Guerre Est Finie

Alain Resnais' *La Guerre est finie* (at the Beekman) embellished the 1966 New York Film Festival with its extraordinary excellence. It's a long way from the Abraham Lincoln Brigade to Lincoln Center but memory and nostalgia have a way of preserving lost causes as the conscience of history. Thus simply for its subject *La Guerre est finie* should regain for Resnais most of the admirers he lost somewhere on the tracks between Hiroshima and Marienbad. The almost irresistible temptation to insult the Idiot Left must be resisted at all costs. Who is to say that people should not admire the right films for the wrong reasons? It is for the critic to register the right reasons. The creator prefers profitable misunderstandings and confusions so that he can find the funds to continue his career.

If *La Guerre est finie* is in some ways the most satisfying movie Resnais has made, credit is due largely to the lucidity and integrity of Yves Montand's characterization of Diego, a revolutionary engulfed by fears, fantasies, and futilities. However fragmented the director's feelings may be, Montand remains a rock of commitment, and with Montand's solidity as an actor serving as an anchor of style, a sea of images can be unified into a mental characterization. Whereas the awesome majesty of the late Nikolai Cherkassov obliterated montage in the late Sergei Eisenstein's *Ivan the Terrible*, the humanity of Montand domesticates montage in *La Guerre est finie*. We are no longer concerned with the pretentious counterpoint of Love and the Bomb, Past and Present, Illusion and Reality, Society and the Individual, etc. We are obsessed instead with the doubts of Diego, even the fantasies of Diego. Through his mind passes what we are to know and feel about the heritage of the Old Left, that last, desperate camaraderie commemorated in kitchens and cemeteries as old comrades grapple with the old rhetoric they are doomed never to forget and the new reality they are doomed never to understand.

For Resnais, it is enough to celebrate remembrance and mourn forgetfulness as fragments of personality and politics disintegrate in the void of time. Civilization is the process of trying to remember, and Resnais once did a documentary on the Paris Library as the supreme ornament of civilization. Cinema, however, is more than remembering and forgetting. It is also acting, doing, resolving, indeed being. Cinema, like life, is a process of creating memories for the future. Resnais has always drawn on the past without paying for the future. His cinema has been hauntingly beautiful if dramatically improvident in its ghostliness. His characters have been paralyzed by the sheer pastness of their sensibilities. Montand's Diego is no exception, but a marvelous thing has happened. Montand's dignity and bearing have broken through the formal shell of Resnais' art to dramatize the doubts and hesitations of the director. Diego has become a hero of prudence and inaction. He has shown what it is to be a man without the obvious flourishes of virility so fashionable today. (Even the stately explicitness of the love-making is a measure of the hero's stature.) To be a man, it is above all necessary to be patient as one's life dribbles away on the back

streets, blind alleys, and dead ends of political impotence. The at times agonizing slowness of *La Guerre est finie* achieves the pathos of patience by
expressing a devotion to detail common to both Diego and Resnais. It has
always seemed that Resnais was more suited to documentary than fiction
because of a preoccupation with facts rather than truths. The parts in Resnais
always seem superior to the whole, and if *La Guerre est finie* is an exception, it
is because the integral behaviorism of a performer has buttressed the analytical style of a director. It is as if Resnais were dropping things all over the screen,
and Montand walking around picking them up. That *La Guerre est finie* finally
makes us weep is a tribute to Montand's tenacity.

As for what the film actually "says," Jorge Semprun's script is explicit
enough for the least sophisticated audiences. The meaning is in the title. The
War is Over, and Resnais, unlike Zinnemann in the grotesquely unfeeling
Behold a Pale Horse, makes no attempt to reconstruct the agonies of antiquity
with old newsreels. The ultimate tragedy of the Spanish Civil War is that all
its participants are either dead or 30 years older. Spain still exists as a geographical entity, but it has been repopulated with an indifferent generation.
Tourists swarm through Madrid and Barcelona while old Bolsheviks haul pam-
phlets into Seville. The New Left sneers at the Old Left. But it doesn't matter
as long as one man can keep the faith in the midst of uncertainty.

1967

Falstaff and *A Countess from Hong Kong*

Orson Welles' *Falstaff* (at the Little Carnegie) and Charles Chaplin's *A
Countess from Hong Kong* (at the Sutton) deserve the support of every
serious moviegoer. Bosley Crowther has panned both films in no uncertain
terms, but Mr. Crowther panned *Citizen Kane* and *Monsieur Verdoux* in their
time. I don't wish to single out Mr. Crowther as a critic, only as an awesome
power on the New York film scene. He is certainly not alone in panning *A
Countess from Hong Kong*. To my knowledge, only William Wolf of *Cue* has rallied to Chaplin's defense. Happily, *Falstaff* has found powerful defenders in
Joseph Morgenstern of *Newsweek*, Judith Crist of the *World Journal Tribune*, and
Archer Winsten of the *Post*. Even so, Mr. Crowther is entitled to his opinion,
and he is scarcely the least enlightened of American film critics. Henry Hart of
Films in Review has earned that dubious distinction with ease. The problem
with Crowther is power. Not only can he still make or break most "art" films
in New York. He can dictate to distributors what films they may or may not

import. Lately he has been credited even with determining what will or will not be produced. In a letter to the *Times*, the producer of *Dutchman* whined that Crowther had seemed to encourage the project at a pre-production dinner. The producer in question is not the first person in the industry to learn that Crowther cannot be had for a free meal. I'll say that much for Bos. He is not corruptible in the vulgar way most of his detractors suspect. He is affable, urbane, polite, genial, and easy to misunderstand in personal relationships. The industry is full of glad-handers and promoters who claim to have Crowther's ear but who only get the back of his hand when the early editions of the *Times* hit the stands. This kind of unpredictability is all to Crowther's credit. United Artists planned a Bond-like promotion of Sergio Leone's *A Fistful of Dollars* and the sequels largely because Crowther seemed to have been impressed by the Italian Western cycle on his European jaunt for the *Times* last year. When it turned out there was too much pasta in them than oats, Crowther back-tracked and UA had to dump the project.

Power must always be fought, however, because power itself tends to corrupt. The moviegoer should think for himself to the point that he would find it unthinkable to miss a Welles or Chaplin work simply because a critic, any critic, said it was not worth seeing. What I object to in Crowther's review of *Falstaff* is the implication that he is going to punish the distributors for bringing *Falstaff* to America against his express wishes announced in a dispatch from Cannes last year. We in America can thank Mr. Crowther for having waited almost a year to see *Falstaff*. The distributors even changed the film's title from *Chimes at Midnight* to *Falstaff* in a naive attempt to confuse the readers of the *Times*. The distributors should have known better. While I was reading Crowther's review of *Falstaff*, I suddenly understood what the real issue had become. The cyclical pattern of regular reviewers made more sense than even Truffaut had realized when he discovered it many years ago. The reason a Crowther will pan a Welles or Chaplin, the reason a Crist will complain about "cultists," the reason the daily reviewers loathe the New York Film Festival, is simply power. Crowther and Crist and all the critics combined cannot keep a so-called "cultist" from seeing *Falstaff* or *A Countess from Hong Kong*. Consciously or unconsciously, the power-oriented critic tries to keep these cults under control by giving every director a certain quota of pans so that he doesn't get too uppity. With Welles and Chaplin, there are additional incentives. The critic can call them old-fashioned and dated and used up as if critics stayed young forever and only directors became senile. I would expect old critics, particularly, to understand what *Falstaff* and *Countess from Hong Kong* are all about.

But no, the older the critic, the more up-to-date he must pretend to be even though anything genuinely modern from *Citizen Kane* to *Masculine Feminine* has always filled him with revulsion.

The great sin of Welles and Chaplin is their failure to abandon their own personal visions of the world to current fashions. Welles is still Humpty-Dumpty from Wisconsin, and all the king's lenses and all the king's screens can't put Humpty together again. *Citizen Kane* was made by an old man of 25. Welles seems to have been rehearsing for Falstaff and Lear all his life. Welles the actor now sounds like a muffled echo of everything he once wanted to be. Welles the mountainous man is a monument to compulsive self-destructiveness. The important thing is that Welles feels Falstaff from the inside out, and that he is enough of an artist to look at himself with ironic detachment. He is enough of an intellectual to give Shakespeare a distinctive shape and size. The production is Gothic and Pastoral at the same time, towers above and mud below. Prince Hal, the Shakespearean hero who most resembles Dick Nixon, resembles in Keith Baxter's interpretation Welles himself. Welles, like Hal, is cursed with the ability of seeing even the present as some future past. For Hal, Falstaff is life as it endures. Hal's real father, John Gielgud's death's head Henry IV, is life as preparation for death. Welles' *Falstaff* dramatizes the conflict of two fathers, or two aspects of fatherhood. Falstaff is gross, warm animal affection, but also genuine love. Henry is pride and authority. Falstaff's world is horizontal, Henry's vertical. The final renunciation scene is thus inevitably shaped by the geometry of the setting.

Welles displays here a sensibility from the '30s and '40s when choices, however anguished, still seemed morally meaningful. Despite his ironic humor, Welles is not in tune with current mannerisms of cruelty and absurdity. His *Falstaff* is graced with dramatic grandeur of an intelligent sobriety we have almost forgotten in our search for new sensations. Welles's battle scenes are especially noteworthy for not blinking at the brutal spectacle of war, and yet not winking at the audience for its satiric indulgence. Consequently, the spectacle of the fat knight in glorious retreat becomes a beautiful piece of mise-en-scène.

Chaplin's *A Countess from Hong Kong* had me hooked from the pre-credit sequence when a sailor in Hong Kong struts into a dance hall where all the girls are "countesses." Chaplin's sentimental music closes in on a succession of medium shots of not particularly attractive, not particularly unattractive girls, and Charlie loves them all, and everyone begins dancing awkwardly in silent-movie style, and we are back in a world Chaplin both inhabited and invented a long time ago. Few reviewers have bothered to observe Chaplin's role is being played by Sophia Loren, the tramp with oversized men's pajamas and a heart of gold. Chaplin had problems with both Loren and Brando simply because neither is Chaplin, but the movie still generates a surprising amount of charm and wit. Chaplin's writing still strains for many of its ironic effects, and the plot is almost too sentimental to synopsize safely, but the lines are underplayed almost to a whisper, and one particularly sticky scene is brilliantly redeemed by the slap-stick of sea-sickness.

Attacks on Chaplin for his sentimentality and/or vulgarity date back almost to the beginning of his career. John Grierson wrote learnedly on why Chaplin should not have wound up with the girl in *The Gold Rush*. People who attack *A Countess from Hong Kong* in the name of the Chaplin they once allegedly loved have probably forgotten what Chaplin was like in the past. If you ever liked Chaplin, you will probably like *A Countess from Hong Kong*. It is the quintessence of everything Chaplin has ever felt. One reviewer complained about the doubling up of sets, but Chaplin has never worried that much about sets. His is too much of a one-man sensibility for nuanced detail. Nor has Chaplin ever achieved his effects through camera movement, montage, or Rembrandt lighting. His basic axiom has been that comedy is long-shot and tragedy is close-up, and most of *Countess* is long-shot. Chaplin's genius resides in that secret passageway from the physical to the emotional through which bodies and faces are transformed by grace and expressiveness into universal metaphors.

A Countess from Hong Kong is far from Chaplin's past peaks, but one scene with a momentarily irrepressible butler (Patrick Cargill) in Sophia's bedroom is as comically exhilarating as anything Chaplin has ever done. Chaplin might have been more modern of course. He might have read selections from *Lady Chatterley's Lover* at $5 a throw. Better still, he might have displayed the footage featuring Chaplin directing Loren and Brando in *A Countess from Hong Kong* and called the whole shebang *80½*. Unfortunately, Chaplin will die as he has lived, an unregenerate classicist who believes in making movies he can feel in his frayed lace valentine heart.

1967

Science Fiction: *The Forbin Project*

The Forbin Project represents the most up-to-date variation of the old monster movies, particularly *Frankenstein* (actually mentioned in the script as the key to the spiritually presumptuous scientist-protagonist Forbin), *King Kong* (in which sympathy is sentimentally transferred from man and his infernal machines to a beast innocently enraptured by beauty) and *The Golem* (an unearthly creature that served as the avenging conscience and creation of the Jewish ghetto). Other aspects of *The Forbin Project* may remind you of *The Sorcerer's Apprentice* from *Fantasia*, the Doomsday Machine from *Dr. Strangelove*, the computerized voice from *Alphaville* and, most strikingly of all, the harried HAL from *2001: A Space Odyssey*.

Nonetheless, the screenplay by James Bridges from the novel *Colossus* by D. F. Jones comes up with some wrinkles of its own as it postulates a world suddenly dominated by two autonomous computers, one American (Colossus) and one Russian (Guardian). For a time Forbin (Eric Braeden) and his Russian counterpart Kuprin (Alex Rodine) attempt to control the computers they have created, but no human being is a match for the monsters in tandem, and mere people are reduced to being victims or slaves of a superior though inhuman intelligence. Joseph Sargent directs all the actors in that dull, deadpan, repressed, ho-hum Houston style that Stanley Kubrick brilliantly anticipated in *2001*. Gordon Pinsent's President of the U.S.A. and Leonid Rostoff's First Chairman of the U.S.S.R. are so colorlessly cool on the hot line that they make the computers seem bubbly by comparison.

The horrible thing about *The Forbin Project* is how casually inevitable it all seems. Why *not* turn the world over to the computers? I'd much rather listen to Colossus croaking out its instructions than have to listen to Nixon and Agnew explaining the subtler points of the Cambodian campaign. We have now entered a new era not only in our politics but also in the context of our political satire. Through the Kennedy–Johnson years there was a kind of simplistic intolerance of the gap between what politicians practiced and what they preached, even between what they practiced and what they really felt. Hence, Lenny Bruce built a popular comedy routine around Lyndon Johnson's laborious effort to learn to say "nigra" instead of "nigger," as if Johnson's regional heritage were more important than his political actions. As it happened, Johnson put through more civil-rights legislation than the more charismatic FDR and JFK put together. But that didn't really matter. Now we have a President who has probably never said "nigger" in his life but who enjoys listening to "Welfare Cadillac" and calls college protesters "bums." And perhaps Spiro Agnew *is* funny, but it is beginning to hurt too much to laugh. It was much better in the old days when the liberals in power were too insecure in their position to strike back at the professional purists and innocents of the Left. Even now in this hour of dire Constitutional peril, Jerry Rubin links arms with Spiro Agnew to denounce Kingman Brewster, and it isn't really funny or even deliciously ironic anymore but just plain desperate. The world as we know it may be dying before our eyes, and we seem completely helpless. It's not just one particular system that is collapsing but every social contract man has ever conceived. No version of Marxism or anarchism can halt the deterioration of our environment and the brutalization of our culture by the sheer mass of mankind. And it doesn't seem to matter who pretends to be President—Nixon, Johnson or Liberace. Events cast a larger shadow than can be attributed to the follies of those in high places, and politics has become as much a decadently bourgeois luxury as aesthetics.

Consequently, my traditionally humanistic arguments against *The Forbin Project* (and Kubrick's *2001*) now seem increasingly irrelevant. I have always tended to sniff suspiciously at the sentimentalization of brutish innocence at the expense of human irascibility. I have always been turned off by so-called "humane" types who actually prefer dogs to other human beings. Indeed, a recent poll of humane-society members in England showed that the great majority favored the retention of the death penalty for human beings.

But now alienation and anomie are taking such a psychic toll of our social instincts that we may indeed become indistinguishable from the mechanisms we monitor. This seems to be one of the subsidiary points of *The Forbin Project*, especially when Forbin and his comely assistant Cleo (Susan Clark) try to fool Colossus by pretending to be lovers, and then actually become lovers in very stiffly performed scenes that resemble nothing so much as the shy, excessively self-aware exhibitionism of computer dating. But when Colossus "tells" Forbin that he has poured too much vermouth into a martini, the audience is conditioned (in the most charming way imaginable) to surrender to a mechanistic world of pure reason on the screen if only as a respite from the increasingly mindless chaos everywhere else. Moviegoers of the world, surrender yourself to *The Forbin Project*! You have nothing to lose but your *Angst*! Forget Cambodia, and leave the driving to Colossus!

And while we remain in this mood of apocalyptic anguish, I must report that I recently paid another visit to Stanley Kubrick's *2001* while under the influence of a smoked substance that I was assured by my contact was somewhat stronger and more authentic than oregano on a King Sano base. (For myself, I must confess that I soar infinitely higher on vermouth cassis, but enough of this generation rap.) Anyway, I prepared to watch *2001* under what I have always been assured were optimum conditions, and surprisingly (for me) I find myself reversing my original opinion. *2001* is indeed a major work by a major artist. For what it is, and I am still not exactly enchanted by what it is, *2001* is beautifully modulated and controlled to express its director's vision of a world to come seen through the sensibility of a world past. Even the dull, expressionless acting seems perfectly attuned to settings in which human feelings are diffused by inhuman distances.

However, I don't think that *2001* is exclusively or even especially a head movie (and I now speak with the halting voice of authority). For once, the cuts in the movie helped it by making it seem less perversely boring for its own sake. The cuts also emphasized that the greatness of the movie is not in its joints and connections (the literary factor) but in the expressive slowness of its camera movements (the plastic factor) and the distended expansiveness of its environment (the visual factor). I am still dissatisfied by the open-ended abstractness of the allegory, not to mention the relatively conventional sojourn in psychedelia. Nonetheless, *2001* now works for me as Kubrick's parable of a future toward which metaphysical dread and mordant amusement tiptoe side by side. Even on first viewing, I admired all the stuff about HAL literally losing his mind. On second viewing, I was deeply moved by HAL as a metaphor of reason afflicted by the assaults of neurotic doubt. And when his rectangular brain cells were being pulled out one by one, I could almost feel the buzzing in my own brain cells as they clung ever more precariously to that psychic cluster I call (quite automatically) ME. I have never seen the death of the mind rendered more profoundly or more poetically than it is rendered by Kubrick in *2001*.

I believe also that *2001* gains immeasurably by being projected on a flat wide screen rather than on the distorted curve of Cinerama. On a flat screen, *2001* is seen more clearly as Kubrick's personally designed tableau. On a curved screen, the miniatures and the simulations seem more trivially illusionist and cartoonish. *2001* is concerned ultimately not so much with the outer experiences of space as with the inner fears of Kubrick's mind as it contemplates infinity and eternity. As the moon shots should have demonstrated by now, there is absolutely nowhere we can go to escape our selves.

1970

Billy Wilder

Billy Wilder is too cynical to believe even his own cynicism. Toward the end of *Stalag 17*, William Holden bids a properly cynical adieu to his prison-camp buddies. He ducks into the escape tunnel for a second, then quickly pops up, out of character, with a boyish smile and a friendly wave, and then ducks down for good. Holden's sentimental waste motion in a tensely timed melodrama demonstrates the cancellation principle in Wilder's cinema. For example, the director's irresponsible Berlin films—*A Foreign Affair* and *One, Two, Three*—have been wrongly criticized for social irresponsibility. This is too serious a charge to level at a series of tasteless gags, half anti-Left and half anti-

Right, adding up to Wilder's conception of political sophistication. Even his best films—*The Major and the Minor, Sunset Boulevard, Stalag 17*, and *Some Like It Hot*—are marred by the director's penchant for gross caricature, especially with peripheral characters. All of Wilder's films decline in retrospect because of visual and structural deficiencies. Only Laughton's owlish performance makes *Witness for the Prosecution* look like the tour de force it was intended to be, and only Jack Lemmon keeps *The Apartment* from collapsing into the cellar of morbid psychology. Wilder deserves full credit for these performances, and for many of the other felicities that redeem his films from the superficial nastiness of his personality. He has failed only to the extent that he has been proved inadequate for the more serious demands of middle-class tragedy (*Double Indemnity*) and social allegory (*Ace in the Hole*). A director who can crack jokes about suicide attempts (*Sabrina* and *The Apartment*) and thoughtlessly brutalize charming actresses like Jean Arthur (*Foreign Affair*) and Audrey Hepburn (*Sabrina*) is hardly likely to make a coherent film on the human condition.

If Billy Wilder's stock has risen slightly in recent years with the escalation of satiric savagery in *Kiss Me Stupid* and *The Fortune Cookie*, it is not so much because of the films themselves, but rather because Wilder has chosen to remain himself while almost everyone else has been straining to go mod. Curiously, Wilder seems to have completely abandoned the Lubitsch tradition he upheld ever so briefly with *Love in the Afternoon*, an Audrey Hepburn vehicle not without its cruelties toward agingly jaded Gary Cooper, but not without its beauties as well.

1968

Billy Wilder Reconsidered

People often ask if I have any regrets over my rankings of directors in *The American Cinema*. Actually, there have been shifts and slides, rises and falls, all along the line. Film history is always in the process of revision, and some of our earliest masters are still alive. *The American Cinema* was a very tentative probe designed mainly to establish the existence of a subject worthy of study. The rest is refinement and elaboration.

To go back to the question, however, at this time, I must concede that seemingly I have grossly under-rated Billy Wilder, perhaps more so than any other American director. His twilight resurgence in the seventies with such mellow masterpieces as *The Private Life of Sherlock Holmes* (1969), *Avanti!* (1972), and even the very flawed *The Front Page* (1974) made me rethink Wilder, but, mostly, I have been motivated by rueful memories of how somehow I managed to let people talk me out of my instinctive enthusiasm for his films. Whereas the moviegoer in me traipsed back again and again to see *The Major and the Minor* (1942), *Double Indemnity* (1944), *The Lost Weekend* (1945), *Sunset Boulevard* (1950), *Stalag 17* (1953), *Love in the Afternoon* (1959), *Some Like It Hot* (1959), and *The Apartment* (1960), the film critic in me was always heard clucking that Wilder was too clever and cynical for his own and everyone else's good. Somehow his clinkers always did double duty to discredit his classics. With other directors, the classics were credited to them, and the clinkers to the "system." But Wilder was thought of as the system personified with all its serpentine wiles and crass commercialism.

The year 1950 was very crucial in the evolution of my conflicting responses toward Wilder. I must have seen *Sunset Boulevard* about twenty-five times during its first run at the Radio City Music Hall. I was working then in a very menial position at David O. Selznick's New York office, and for the first time began meeting industry-wise film buffs. One such chap and I argued through most of the latter part of 1950 the relative merits of *Sunset Boulevard* and *All About Eve*. I stuck to *Sunset* through thick and thin, but I was defensive. I did not know how to counter arguments about Wilder's excessive morbidity, and about the facile pathology of the Norma Desmond character, played with unmodulated bravura by Gloria Swanson.

Perhaps the most damning bit of critical analysis of Wilder was put forth by François Truffaut in a *Cahiers* essay at about the same time of *Sabrina* (1954). The thrust of Truffaut's remarks was that while Wilder had a minor flair for comedy inherited from Lubitsch (also minor in Truffaut's *politique),* Wilder lacked the structural capability for more serious films (like *Double Indemnity* and *The Lost Weekend*). This was one of Truffaut's more cryptic essays, and though it would not in itself have been decisive, it helped drive the final nail in the coffin. For their part, the *Sight and Sound* and *Sequence* people had always doubted the depth of Wilder's commitment, and Agee himself had expressed strong reservations about both *Double Indemnity* and *The Lost Weekend*.

Certainly, there are flaws in almost all of Wilder's output but what is more important is the value we attach to Wilder's virtues. In *Double Indemnity*, for example, I was never able to perceive the motivational moment when Fred MacMurray's breezy insurance investigator and devil-may-care womanizer is transformed into a purposeful murderer. That is a weakness of characterization even in terms of the violent expectations of the genre, and yet it is also a reflection of Wilder's tendency to jump the gap between motivation and action by using very personal feelings of guilt and corruption. In *The Lost Weekend* there is a sketchy rendering of the psychological problems behind Ray Milland's alcoholism. The author Charles Jackson's intimations of homosexual conflicts in the film have been replaced by showy delusions of glassy-eyed grandeur. But in our concern with what Wilder was not about, we have neglected to explore the director's own feelings of perpetual insecurity. More important, we have always interpreted, or misinterpreted, the flamboyant glibness of Wilder's characters as proof of the director's insincerity. Hence, Wilder's brightness was too often seen as mere brashness. Now that dialogue in general is duller and more "sincere" than ever, Wilder's quick-wittedness seems more charming than ever.

If we trace the trajectory of Billy Wilder's directorial career in the forties, we find that he made a sparkling debut with *The Major and the Minor* in 1942, did his bit for the war effort and Erich von Stroheim with *Five Graves to Cairo* in 1943, fashioned a classic of the *film noir* with *Double Indemnity* in 1944, hit his peak of social significance and establishment eminence with *The Lost Weekend* in 1945, and then receded in a haze of respectability with an overly fluffy Franz Josef conceit out of the cuisine of Chez Ernst (*The Emperor Waltz*) (1948) and a cynical view of war-ravaged and Nazi-tainted Berlin (*A Foreign Affair*) in 1948.

Still, as the Paramount director par excellence he had outlasted Preston Sturges and outlived Ernst Lubitsch, and the very tasteful Mitchell Leisen, who had previously profited from scripts by Sturges and the Brackett and Wilder team, saw his career decline. By contrast, Wilder went on to a long and productive career, and was still employable, if only intermittently, in the seventies. But he never caught the brass ring of absolute auteurist pre-eminence. For too long he was linked with the very well-liked Charles Brackett, who, it was whispered in industry circles, exercised a restraining, civilizing influence on Billy Wilder's cynical, callous, morbid tendencies. Hence, when a Wilder movie seemed particularly heartless, Wilder got all the blame; and when a Wilder movie proved particularly compassionate, Wilder had to share the credit with Brackett.

Nonetheless, Wilder was always credited with a lively intelligence in revamping old narrative formulas. He was seen as particularly adept at switch-casting, notably in persuading Ginger Rogers to endure little-girl (not to mention Lolita) drag for *The Major and the Minor*, Fred MacMurray to abandon his likable persona for the part of a calculating murderer in *Double Indemnity*, and Ray Milland to make the switch from lounge lizard to lush in *The Lost Weekend*. In all instances, the players in question reportedly resisted playing against type at first, but eventually were to see their careers being given a new lease on life. Brackett and Wilder, who had been well publicized as a sterling script-writing team in the late thirties, by the mid-forties were being lionized as a film-making unit.

Wilder in one interview was adamant about his opposition to such Kris Kringle camera effects as shooting a scene from behind the fire in the fireplace, an impossible angle in terms of any personal point of view. Wilder may have been thinking of the showy shot of Jennifer Jones's being illuminated by the flames in *Love Letters*, which had been photographed somewhat in the old Germanic style by director William Dieterle and cinematographer Lee Garmes. The subtlety of the point Wilder was making was not fully perceived in that primitive period of stylistic analysis, but what he was suggesting was that photographic embellishment was no substitute for truly restructured narrative.

Even later, however, most of Wilder's critics failed to realize that his apparent cynicism was the only way he could make his raging romanticism palatable. The same problem had plagued Ernst Lubitsch before Wilder, and has plagued Richard Lester after Wilder. Cynicism and sophistication, relatively rare in movies at any time, are apt to be seized upon as indicators of the full register of a director's personality. The passion beneath the polish is thereby overlooked. In Wilder's case, the seemingly facile reversals in his films obscured the deep sentiments of his characters. For all its gimmicks, *The Major and the Minor* is one of the most enchanting love stories ever told on the screen, and for all its deadpan stoicism *Double Indemnity* strikes uncommonly sweet chords of male camaraderie in its final confrontation between Fred MacMurray and Edward G. Robinson.

Wilder managed to step on a few toes politically as well with such films as *Five Graves to Cairo* (1943) and *A Foreign Affair* (1948), being denounced for the former as anti-French by the influential French Marxist film historian Georges Sadoul, and as irredeemably irresponsible for the latter by just about every single solemn film critic. Sadoul was particularly outraged by Anne Baxter's personification of France as a soft-hearted whore at the beck and call of Nazi supermen played by Erich von Stroheim and Peter Van Eyck. Sadoul's is a bizarre analysis, indeed, but in a way it is symptomatic of Wilder's bad luck in getting penalized for being more honest and more open about the realities of human sexuality than most of his Hollywood colleagues. Similarly, Marlene Dietrich's unrepentant Nazi siren in *A Foreign Affair* is a more daring characterization than most that emerged after World War II. Indeed, Wilder came closer to anticipating the bitter cross-purposes of the post-war world than his more idealistic One World-oriented contemporaries. But with Lubitsch having been condemned for *To Be or Not To Be* in 1942, and Hitchcock for *Lifeboat* in 1943, for Wilder it almost could have been an honor to be condemned for

A Foreign Affair had it not been for his needless brutalization of Jean Arthur—for which I attacked him in *The American Cinema* and for which I have yet to forgive him.

Yet, am I blaming Wilder too much, and the devastating Dietrich too little, for what happened to Miss Arthur in *A Foreign Affair?* After all, Hitchcock once told me that Jane Wyman burst into tears when she saw how she looked next to Dietrich in *Stage Fright,* and yet I never condemned Hitch for his cruelty. Why then condemn Wilder? I suppose because of having been conditioned for many years to attribute the worst motives to his movies, and even to suspect the ultimate source of their undeniable charms, it is time at long last to come to terms with my most primal moviegoing instincts. For me as a critic, Wilder has served in the same manner Hitchcock has served so many of my colleagues: as a filmmaker one likes too much and too easily to respect properly.

1968

John Wayne's Strange Legacy

There was always more to the legend of John Wayne than met the eye. To judge by most of the obituaries, the unifying effect of his long war against cancer had transcended the divisive effect of his long war against communism. His illness was thus regarded as a metaphor for all the problems that plague Western man in his descent from power. With Wayne's passing, we were told by solemn editorialists, the last simplistic American Hero had bitten the dust. This meant that there would be no more Vietnams on the American horizon. Of course, a bemused bystander might observe that Vietnam had more to do with John Kennedy than with John Wayne, and that the newest crop of crotch-thrusting rock stars do not necessarily make more exemplary or more complex heroes than an old gunfighter. But to argue Wayne's politics, pro or con, is to ignore the considerable achievement of his poetics. Wayne was, after all, a movie actor, not a politician, and his great feat was not to play "himself," whatever that means, but to fashion a new self from his screen image.

The squint, the rolling walk, the roundhouse right, the clipped cadences of his speech were not granted to Marion Michael Morrison at his birth on May 26, 1907 in Winterset, Iowa. They were industriously assembled, mannerism by mannerism, through an unusually long apprenticeship on the Hollywood sound stages in the 1930s. Unlike many of his stellar contemporaries, Wayne was far from an overnight sensation. From his walk-on in a Richard Barthelmess vehicle entitled *Drop Kick* (1927) to his grand entrance as the Ringo Kid in John Ford's *Stagecoach* (1939), Wayne toiled away in 65 movies, most of which were produced on poverty row for the boondocks and kiddie matinee audiences.

Having obtained his big chance and the screen name "John Wayne" in 1930 with Raoul Walsh's superwestern *The Big Trail*, Wayne saw his opportunity for stardom sidetracked for almost a decade. His youth was gone by the time Ford dragged him off to Monument Valley for a second chance. His biographers have written that Wayne was on the screen for almost 50 years, but it would be a mistake to say that his iconic flame burned with equal brightness throughout that period. Ultimately, Wayne appeared in some of the best films ever made in Hollywood—*Stagecoach, The Long Voyage Home, They Were Expendable, Fort Apache, Red River, She Wore a Yellow Ribbon, The Quiet Man, The Searchers, The Wings of Eagles, Rio Bravo, The Man Who Shot Liberty Valance, El Dorado*—and some of the worst—*Tycoon, The Fighting Kentuckian, Big Jim McLain, The Conqueror, The Alamo, The Green Berets*. But his overall reputation with the public depended less on the classics and the disasters than upon a steady stream of routine but robust romances from the 1940s through the 1970s. I happened to have grown up on the John Wayne of *Dark Command, Seven Sinners, The Shepherd of the Hills, Lady for a Night, Reap the Wild Wind, The Spoilers, Flying Tigers, In Old Oklahoma, Tall in the Saddle*, and *Angel and the Badman*. I remember responding to him in a relatively uncomplicated way though he seldom functioned as a conventional hero. He could be accursed or obsessed. In *Wake of the Red Witch* he drowns at the bottom of the deep so that he can sail forever on the ghostly high seas with his dead sweetheart (Gail Russell). He dies also in *Reap the Wild Wind, Sands of Iwo Jima, The Man Who Shot Liberty Valance, The Cowboys*, and *The Shootist*—an unusually high number of fatalities for a supposedly optimistic genre figure. And on many other occasions the characters he played faced a twilight existence of loneliness and dependency.

An appreciation of the complete John Wayne depends therefore upon a perceptive familiarity with the varieties and paradoxes of his career. The Goldwaters and the Nixons among his admirers have merely appropriated snapshots of Wayne as the Rugged Individualist to promote their own political fantasies. Wayne's most enduring image, however, is that of the displaced loner vaguely uncomfortable with the very civilization he is helping to establish and preserve. He is not a Wild Man of the West seeking ever new frontiers, but he wanders much of the time nonetheless. At his first appearance we usually sense a very private person with some wound, loss, or grievance from the past. At his best he is much closer to a tragic vision of life than to a comic one. Shortly before Wayne's death Ralph Richardson remarked in an interview that the "Duke" projected the kind of mystery one associated with great acting. Jean-

Luc Godard once observed that as much as he despised the reactionary politics of John Wayne, he could never help but be moved in John Ford's *The Searchers* by the emotional sweep of the awesomely avuncular gesture with which Wayne gathers up Natalie Wood, after having given every indication that he wished to kill her for defiling his sacred memories of a little girl accepting his medal as a token of his chivalric devotion to her mother. In this, his greatest film, Wayne acts out the mystery of what passes through the soul of Ethan Edwards in that fearsome moment when he discovers the mutilated bodies of his brother, his beloved sister-in-law, and his nephew. Surly, cryptic, almost menacing even before the slaughter, he is invested afterward with the implacability of a figure too much larger than life for any genre but the Western.

Still, the notion of John Wayne as a great actor sits strangely with most people. Wayne himself would have scoffed at the suggestion that he belonged in the same category with, say, Laurence Olivier, whom he greatly admired. Toward the end of his life Wayne acknowledged the high-brow veneration accorded him by serious cineastes here and abroad. "I was just the paint for the palettes of Ford and Hawks," he once remarked with rueful modesty. This may have been true at the time of Ford's *Stagecoach* (1939) and Hawks's *Red River* (1948), but by the time of Ford's *The Man Who Shot Liberty Valance* (1962), and Hawks's *El Dorado* (1967), they needed him more than he needed them. To a great extent he had become his own *auteur*.

There is another factor to be considered, however, in Wayne's apparent self-denigration as an actor. The supposed authenticity of his personality could have been compromised by the stigma of self-consciousness. Carole Lombard once noted disapprovingly that Gary Cooper had become "feminine" in his narcissistic absorption with his own looks. A noted ballet critic once spoke approvingly of the rollicking sensuality of Wayne's posterior wiggle. The suspicion that such a maneuver might have been contrived with the actor's full awareness of its effect could do much to destroy the Duke's credibility with the mass of moviegoers on five continents. Yet when we recall Wayne's long career on the screen without any cultural preconceptions we are reminded of a long dance across disconcertingly natural backgrounds. As with Buster Keaton and Alfred Hitchcock, the kinetic and dynamic qualities of the medium itself have coalesced with a determined talent to produce images of genius.

Many theater people still believe that the only truly "serious" acting is performed on a stage, and within this circle Wayne is of course artistically nonexistent. Certainly no one ever suggested that Wayne's acting range extended to Restoration fops and Elizabethan fools. (Dustin Hoffman got a big laugh at a *Village Voice* Off-Broadway "Obie" award ceremony a few years back with his imitation of Wayne's undertaking a stage performance of *Hamlet* in London.) But as Olivier himself has demonstrated on too many occasions, the assumption of an infinite "range" contains its own pitfalls. A trick accent, a beard, an eye-patch, old-age make-up—these are the accoutrements of acting to many people. And that is why the worst acting is so often mistaken for the best, particularly on the screen, where being transcends pretending, and just standing there can often be more effective than doing something.

Wayne was dismissed not only because he lacked the wide classical range of the great British actors, but also because he lacked the emotional depth of the great method actors. Wayne was thus less than Olivier on one level, and less than Brando on another. Indeed, nothing could be more alien to Wayne's temperament and upbringing than the Freudian-Stanislavskian mix of the method. Instead of reaching back into his past to dredge up the feelings that would bring his characters to life, Wayne followed a relatively Jungian process of building up a new persona into which he gradually grew. He had never been a real-life Western hero like Tom Mix, nor even a real-life cowboy like Gary Cooper, but rather, a druggist's son in pinched middle-class surroundings. From an early age he found a more satisfying existence on the movie screen, and he labored long and hard to paint himself on that magical canvas so that it would seem that he had always inhabited it. In the end Wayne himself was just about all that was left of the Old West in our imagination.

The discretion of graveyard etiquette aside, there remain strong, influential, and even understandable pockets of resistance to the Wayne legend on grounds other than the obvious political ones. Women, Easterners, Intellectuals, Gentle Souls Dedicated to Non-Violence, and even Scholars of the Real West were never the strongest champions of either Wayne or the Westerns in which he appeared. Many of his detractors have never seen his best films; many have never patronized Westerns as a matter of course. Much that has been written casually about the Western is remarkably ill-informed with respect to the almost dialectical diversity within the genre. Take weapons, for example. Relatively "liberal" types like Henry Fonda and Paul Newman have been considerably more conspicuous than Wayne in the manner of flaunting virility and swaggering about with six-shooters at the ready. Newman in particular exploited the Western to express his own anarchic spirit. By contrast, Wayne embodied the brutal, implacable order of the West less with personal flair than with archetypal endurance. He was more likely to outlast his opponents than to outdraw them, and from *Stagecoach* on he never hesitated to use the rifle, an instrument more efficient and more realistic, if less phallic, than the six-shooter.

Apart from appreciative essays by Joan Didion and Molly Haskell, there is little evidence to suggest that Wayne was as well-liked by women as by men. He lacked the curiously calculating little-boy-lost quality of a Gable or a Cooper, and his clumsy exasperation was often mistaken for bullying. From time to time in his career he ventured into relatively straight boy-girl projects in order to broaden his appeal. The results seemed discouraging at first glance. Wayne clearly lacked finesse, subtlety, and patience, the indispensable tools of womanizing on the screen. Of his performance opposite Jean Arthur in *A Lady Takes a Chance* (1943), James Agee wrote: ". . . John Wayne suggests how sensational he might be in a sufficiently evil story about a Reno gigolo. . . ." And on his playing opposite Claudette Colbert in *Without Reservations* (1946), Agee was similarly clear-eyed: "Messrs. Wayne and Defore have kinds of hardness and conceit, in their relations with women, which are a good deal nearer the real thing than movies usually get."

Marlene Dietrich, his co-star and reported flame in *Seven Sinners* (1940), *The Spoilers* (1942), and *Pittsburgh* (1942), recently complained in print that Wayne had never read a book in his life. And despite his having been married to three Spanish-speaking women, he never learned more than a few words of Spanish. "I guess I never listened to what they were saying," he once confessed candidly, but not without a trace of self-mockery. Yet warmth and devotion are amply present in his screen liaisons with Maureen O'Hara in *The Quiet Man* and *Wings of Eagles*, with Angie Dickinson in *Rio Bravo*, and with Patricia Neal in *In Harm's Way*. Like Faulkner's hero in *Knight's Gambit*, he improved with age, and he learned before our eyes both how to feel and how to project a deep and abiding love.

But there is no getting away from it. John Wayne was not one of us, if by "us," we stipulate the kind of people who read and contribute to *The New Republic*. John Wayne was the Other. He had graduated by 1939 from the trivial pulp Westerns and adventure romances in which cardboard heroes wrestled with stock villains. In the grown-up Westerns of subsequent decades villainy was supplanted by evil, and Wayne confronted evil directly with ruthless, unblinking violence. The liberal imagination steadfastly resists the idea of incorrigible evil, and the absolute and vengeful morality it spawns in the persona of John Wayne. For my own part, I am not in the habit of socking my enemies in the jaw. I snipe at them in print instead, and feel singularly unheroic in the process. John Wayne was therefore something of a graceful and beautiful fantasy figure for me, but he was also and remains still the test of my own negative capability as a film critic. It took me a long time to appreciate him as an actor, and now I hope to make amends by explaining his subtler virtues to the stubbornly unbelieving.

1979

Susan Sontag

Susan Sontag (1933–2004) was one of America's most distinguished contemporary writers, an essayist and novelist of international stature. In her nonfiction books, such as *Against Interpretation*, *Styles of Radical Will*, *Under the Sign of Saturn*, *On Photography*, and *Regarding the Pain of Others*, she meditated steadfastly on the modern condition, which often included the aesthetic and ethical dimensions of the photographed image. Though Sontag never held a regular reviewer's post, she wrote impressive, informed film criticism throughout her career. (Her knowledge of the medium derived in part from having directed four features herself.) Typically, Sontag wrote about serious, challenging foreign directors such as Godard, Bresson, Bergman, Fassbinder, and Syberberg; but she also defended the pleasures of camp and pop culture. In "The Imagination of Disaster" she brought her formidable powers of analysis to bear on the sci-fi genre, and produced a classic piece of film criticism.

By establishing a parallel she is elevating the B-movie sci-fi genre — To a greater established genre

The Imagination of Disaster

The typical science fiction film has a form as predictable as a Western, and is made up of elements which, to a practiced eye, are as classic as the saloon brawl, the blonde schoolteacher from the East, and the gun duel on the deserted main street.

One model scenario proceeds through five phases.

(1) The arrival of the thing. (Emergence of the monsters, landing of the alien spaceship, etc.) This is usually witnessed or suspected by just one person, a young scientist on a field trip. Nobody, neither his neighbors nor his colleagues, will believe him for some time. The hero is not married, but has a sympathetic though also incredulous girl friend.

(2) Confirmation of the hero's report by a host of witnesses to a great act of destruction. (If the invaders are beings from another planet, a fruitless attempt to parley with them and get them to leave peacefully.) The local police are summoned to deal with the situation and massacred.

(3) In the capital of the country, conferences between scientists and the military take place, with the hero lecturing before a chart, map, or blackboard. A national emergency is declared. Reports of further destruction. Authorities

from other countries arrive in black limousines. All international tensions are suspended in view of the planetary emergency. This stage often includes a rapid montage of news broadcasts in various languages, a meeting at the UN, and more conferences between the military and the scientists. Plans are made for destroying the enemy.

(4) Further atrocities. At some point the hero's girl friend is in grave danger. Massive counter-attacks by international forces, with brilliant displays of rocketry, rays, and other advanced weapons, are all unsuccessful. Enormous military casualties, usually by incineration. Cities are destroyed and/or evacuated. There is an obligatory scene here of panicked crowds stampeding along a highway or a big bridge, being waved on by numerous policemen who, if the film is Japanese, are immaculately white-gloved, preternaturally calm, and call out in dubbed English, "Keep moving. There is no need to be alarmed."

(5) More conferences, whose motif is: "They must be vulnerable to something." Throughout the hero has been working in his lab to this end. The final strategy, upon which all hopes depend, is drawn up; the ultimate weapon—often a super-powerful, as yet untested, nuclear device—is mounted. Countdown. Final repulse of the monster or invaders. Mutual congratulations, while the hero and girl friend embrace cheek to cheek and scan the skies sturdily. "But have we seen the last of them?"

The film I have just described should be in color and on a wide screen. Another typical scenario, which follows, is simpler and suited to black-and-white films with a lower budget. It has four phases.

(1) The hero (usually, but not always, a scientist) and his girl friend, or his wife and two children, are disporting themselves in some innocent ultra-normal middle-class surroundings—their house in a small town, or on vacation (camping, boating). Suddenly, someone starts behaving strangely; or some innocent form of vegetation becomes monstrously enlarged and ambulatory. If a character is pictured driving an automobile, something gruesome looms up in the middle of the road. If it is night, strange lights hurtle across the sky.

(2) After following the thing's tracks, or determining that It is radioactive, or poking around a huge crater—in short, conducting some sort of crude investigation—the hero tries to warn the local authorities, without effect; nobody believes anything is amiss. The hero knows better. If the thing is tangible, the house is elaborately barricaded. If the invading alien is an invisible parasite, a doctor or friend is called in, who is himself rather quickly killed or "taken possession of" by the thing.

(3) The advice of whoever further is consulted proves useless. Meanwhile,

318 ◆ SUSAN SONTAG

It continues to claim other victims in the town, which remains implausibly isolated from the rest of the world. General helplessness.

(4) One of two possibilities. Either the hero prepares to do battle alone, accidentally discovers the thing's one vulnerable point, and destroys it. Or, he somehow manages to get out of town and succeeds in laying his case before competent authorities. They, along the lines of the first script but abridged, deploy a complex technology which (after initial setbacks) finally prevails against the invaders.

Another version of the second script opens with the scientist-hero in his laboratory, which is located in the basement or on the grounds of his tasteful, prosperous house. Through his experiments, he unwittingly causes a frightful metamorphosis in some class of plants or animals which turn carnivorous and go on a rampage. Or else, his experiments have caused him to be injured (sometimes irrevocably) or "invaded" himself. Perhaps he has been experimenting with radiation, or has built a machine to communicate with beings from other planets or transport him to other places or times.

Another version of the first script involves the discovery of some fundamental alteration in the conditions of existence of our planet, brought about by nuclear testing, which will lead to the extinction in a few months of all human life. For example: the temperature of the earth is becoming too high or too low to support life, or the earth is cracking in two, or it is gradually being blanketed by lethal fallout.

A third script, somewhat but not altogether different from the first two, concerns a journey through space—to the moon, or some other planet. What the space-voyagers discover commonly is that the alien terrain is in a state of dire emergency, itself threatened by extra-planetary invaders or nearing extinction through the practice of nuclear warfare. The terminal dramas of the first and second scripts are played out there, to which is added the problem of getting away from the doomed and/or hostile planet and back to Earth.

I am aware, of course, that there are thousands of science fiction novels (their heyday was the late 1940s), not to mention the transcriptions of science fiction themes which, more and more, provide the principal subject-matter of comic books. But I propose to discuss science fiction films (the present period began in 1950 and continues, considerably abated, to this day) as an independent subgenre, without reference to other media—and, most particularly, without reference to the novels from which, in many cases, they were adapted. For, while novel and film may share the same plot, the fundamental difference between the resources of the novel and the film makes them quite dissimilar.

Certainly, compared with the science fiction novels, their film counterparts have unique strengths, one of which is the immediate representation of the extraordinary: physical deformity and mutation, missile and rocket combat, toppling skyscrapers. The movies are, naturally, weak just where the science fiction novels (some of them) are strong—on science. But in place of an intellectual workout, they can supply something the novels can never provide— sensuous elaboration. In the films it is by means of images and sounds, not words that have to be translated by the imagination, that one can participate in the fantasy of living through one's own death and more, the death of cities, the destruction of humanity itself.

Science fiction films are not about science. They are about disaster, which is one of the oldest subjects of art. In science fiction films disaster is rarely viewed intensively; it is always extensive. It is a matter of quantity and ingenuity. If you will, it is a question of scale. But the scale, particularly in the widescreen color films (of which the ones by the Japanese director Inoshiro Honda and the American director George Pal are technically the most convincing and visually the most exciting), does raise the matter to another level.

Thus, the science fiction film (like that of a very different contemporary genre, the Happening) is concerned with the aesthetics of destruction, with the peculiar beauties to be found in wreaking havoc, making a mess. And it is in the imagery of destruction that the core of a good science fiction film lies. Hence, the disadvantage of the cheap film—in which the monster appears or the rocket lands in a small dull-looking town. (Hollywood budget needs usually dictate that the town be in the Arizona or California desert. In *The Thing From Another World* [1951] the rather sleazy and confined set is supposed to be an encampment near the North Pole.) Still, good black-and-white science fiction films have been made. But a bigger budget, which usually means color, allows a much greater play back and forth among several model environments. There is the populous city. There is the lavish but ascetic interior of the spaceship—either the invaders' or ours—replete with streamlined chromium fixtures and dials and machines whose complexity is indicated by the number of colored lights they flash and strange noises they emit. There is the laboratory crowded with formidable boxes and scientific apparatus. There is a comparatively old-fashioned-looking conference room, where the scientists unfurl charts to explain the desperate state of things to the military. And each of these standard locales or backgrounds is subject to two modalities—intact and destroyed. We may, if we are lucky, be treated to a panorama of melting tanks, flying bodies, crashing walls, awesome craters and fissures in the earth, plummeting spacecraft, colorful deadly rays; and to a symphony of screams, weird electronic signals, the noisiest military hardware going, and the leaden tones of the laconic denizens of alien planets and their subjugated earthlings.

Certain of the primitive gratifications of science fiction films—for instance, the depiction of urban disaster on a colossally magnified scale—are shared with other types of films. Visually there is little difference between mass havoc as represented in the old horror and monster films and what we find in science fiction films, except (again) scale. In the old monster films, the monster always headed for the great city, where he had to do a fair bit of rampaging, hurling busses off bridges, crumpling trains in his bare hands, toppling buildings, and so forth. The archetype is King Kong, in Schoedsack and Cooper's great film of 1933, running amok, first in the native village (trampling babies, a bit of footage excised from most prints), then in New York. This is really no different in spirit from the scene in Inoshiro Honda's *Rodan* (1957) in which two giant reptiles—with a wingspan of 500 feet and supersonic speeds—by flapping their wings whip up a cyclone that blows most of Tokyo to smithereens. Or the destruction of half of Japan by the gigantic robot with the great incinerating ray that shoots forth from his eyes, at the beginning of Honda's *The Mysterians* (1959). Or, the devastation by the rays from a fleet of flying saucers of New York, Paris, and Tokyo, in *Battle in Outer Space* (1960). Or, the inundation of New York in *When Worlds Collide* (1951). Or, the end of London in 1966 depicted in George Pal's *The Time Machine* (1960). Neither do these sequences differ in aesthetic intention from the destruction scenes in the big sword, sandal, and orgy color spectaculars set in Biblical and Roman times—the end of Sodom in Aldrich's *Sodom and Gomorrah*, of Gaza in De Mille's *Samson and Delilah*, of Rhodes in *The Colossus of Rhodes*, and of Rome in a dozen Nero movies. Griffith began it with the Babylon sequence in *Intolerance*, and to this day there is nothing like the thrill of watching all those expensive sets come tumbling down.

In other respects as well, the science fiction films of the 1950s take up familiar themes. The famous 1930s movie serials and comics of the adventures of Flash Gordon and Buck Rogers, as well as the more recent spate of comic book super-heroes with extraterrestrial origins (the most famous is Superman, a foundling from the planet Krypton, currently described as having been exploded by a nuclear blast), share motifs with more recent science fiction movies. But there is an important difference. The old science fiction films, and most of the comics, still have an essentially innocent relation to disaster. Mainly they offer new versions of the oldest romance of all—of the strong invulnerable hero with a mysterious lineage come to do battle on behalf of good and against evil. Recent science fiction films have a decided grimness, bolstered by their much greater degree of visual credibility, which contrasts strongly with the older films. Modern historical reality has greatly enlarged the imagination of disaster, and the protagonists—perhaps by the very nature of what is visited upon them—no longer seem wholly innocent.

The lure of such generalized disaster as a fantasy is that it releases one from normal obligations. The trump card of the end-of-the-world movies—like *The Day the Earth Caught Fire* (1962)—is that great scene with New York or London or Tokyo discovered empty, its entire population annihilated. Or, as in *The World, The Flesh, and The Devil* (1957), the whole movie can be devoted to the fantasy of occupying the deserted metropolis and starting all over again, a world Robinson Crusoe.

Another kind of satisfaction these films supply is extreme moral simplification—that is to say, a morally acceptable fantasy where one can give outlet to cruel or at least amoral feelings. In this respect, science fiction films partly overlap with horror films. This is the undeniable pleasure we derive from looking at freaks, beings excluded from the category of the human. The sense of superiority over the freak conjoined in varying proportions with the titillation of fear and aversion makes it possible for moral scruples to be lifted, for cruelty to be enjoyed. The same thing happens in science fiction films. In the figure of the monster from outer space, the freakish, the ugly, and the predatory all converge—and provide a fantasy target for righteous bellicosity to discharge itself, and for the aesthetic enjoyment of suffering and disaster. Science fiction films are one of the purest forms of spectacle; that is, we are rarely inside anyone's feelings. (An exception is Jack Arnold's *The Incredible Shrinking Man* [1957].) We are merely spectators; we watch.

But in science fiction films, unlike horror films, there is not much horror. Suspense, shocks, surprises are mostly abjured in favor of a steady, inexorable plot. Science fiction films invite a dispassionate, aesthetic view of destruction and violence—a *technological* view. Things, objects, machinery play a major role in these films. A greater range of ethical values is embodied in the décor of these films than in the people. Things, rather than the helpless humans, are the locus of values because we experience them, rather than people, as the sources of power. According to science fiction films, man is naked without his artifacts. *They* stand for different values, they are potent, they are what get destroyed, and they are the indispensable tools for the repulse of the alien invaders or the repair of the damaged environment.

The science fiction films are strongly moralistic. The standard message is the one about the proper, or humane, use of science, versus the mad, obsessional use of science. This message the science fiction films share in common with the classic horror films of the 1930s, like *Frankenstein, The Mummy, Island of Lost Souls, Dr. Jekyll and Mr. Hyde.* (Georges Franju's brilliant *Les Yeux Sans Visage* [1959], called here *The Horror Chamber of Doctor Faustus*, is a more recent example.) In the horror films, we have the mad or obsessed or misguided scientist who pursues his experiments against good advice to the contrary, creates a monster or monsters, and is himself destroyed—often recognizing his folly himself, and dying in the successful effort to destroy his own creation. One science fiction equivalent of this is the scientist, usually a member of a team, who defects to the planetary invaders because "their" science is more advanced than "ours."

This is the case in *The Mysterians*, and, true to form, the renegade sees his error in the end, and from within the Mysterian spaceship destroys it and himself. In *This Island Earth* (1955), the inhabitants of the beleaguered planet Metaluna propose to conquer earth, but their project is foiled by a Metalunan scientist named Exeter who, having lived on earth a while and learned to love Mozart, cannot abide such viciousness. Exeter plunges his spaceship into the ocean after returning a glamorous pair (male and female) of American physicists to earth. Metaluna dies. In *The Fly* (1958), the hero, engrossed in his basement-laboratory experiments on a matter-transmitting machine, uses himself as a subject, exchanges head and one arm with a housefly which had accidentally gotten into the machine, becomes a monster, and with his last shred of human will destroys his laboratory and orders his wife to kill him. His discovery, for the good of mankind, is lost.

Being a clearly labeled species of intellectual, scientists in science fiction films are always liable to crack up or go off the deep end. In *Conquest of Space* (1955), the scientist-commander of an international expedition to Mars suddenly acquires scruples about the blasphemy involved in the undertaking, and begins reading the Bible mid-journey instead of attending to his duties. The commander's son, who is his junior officer and always addresses his father as "General," is forced to kill the old man when he tries to prevent the ship from landing on Mars. In this film, both sides of the ambivalence toward scientists are given voice. Generally, for a scientific enterprise to be treated entirely sympathetically in these films, it needs the certificate of utility. Science, viewed without ambivalence, means an efficacious response to danger. Disinterested intellectual curiosity rarely appears in any form other than caricature, as a maniacal dementia that cuts one off from normal human relations. But this suspicion is usually directed at the scientist rather than his work. The creative scientist may become a martyr to his own discovery, through an accident or by pushing things too far. But the implication remains that other men, less imaginative—in short, technicians—could have administered the same discovery better and more safely. The most ingrained contemporary mistrust of the intellect is visited, in these movies, upon the scientist-as-intellectual.

The message that the scientist is one who releases forces which, if not controlled for good, could destroy man himself seems innocuous enough. One of the oldest images of the scientist is Shakespeare's Prospero, the overdetached scholar forcibly retired from society to a desert island, only partly in control of the magic forces in which he dabbles. Equally classic is the figure of the scientist as satanist (*Doctor Faustus*, and stories of Poe and Hawthorne). Science is magic, and man has always known that there is black magic as well as white. But it is not enough to remark that contemporary attitudes—as reflected in science fiction films—remain ambivalent, that the scientist is treated as both satanist and savior. The proportions have changed, because of the new context [*Local →*] in which the old admiration and fear of the scientist are located. For his sphere [*Global*] of influence is no longer local, himself or his immediate community. It is planetary, cosmic.

One gets the feeling, particularly in the Japanese films but not only there, [*Nuclear*] that a mass trauma exists over the use of nuclear weapons and the possibility [*War*] of future nuclear wars. Most of the science fiction films bear witness to this trauma, and, in a way, attempt to exorcise it.

The accidental awakening of the super-destructive monster who has slept in the earth since prehistory is, often, an obvious metaphor for the Bomb. But there are many explicit references as well. In *The Mysterians*, a probe ship from the planet Mysteroid has landed on earth, near Tokyo. Nuclear warfare having been practiced on Mysteroid for centuries (their civilization is "more advanced than ours"), ninety percent of those now born on the planet have to be destroyed at birth, because of defects caused by the huge amounts of Strontium 90 in their diet. The Mysterians have come to earth to marry earth women, and possibly to take over our relatively uncontaminated planet . . . In *The Incredible Shrinking Man*, the John Doe hero is the victim of a gust of radiation which blows over the water, while he is out boating with his wife; the radiation causes him to grow smaller and smaller, until at the end of the movie he steps through the fine mesh of a window screen to become "the infinitely small." . . . In *Rodan*, a horde of monstrous carnivorous prehistoric insects, and finally a pair of giant flying reptiles (the prehistoric Archeopteryx), are hatched from dormant eggs in the depths of a mine shaft by the impact of nuclear test explosions, and go on to destroy a good part of the world before they are felled by the molten lava of a volcanic eruption. . . . In the English film, *The Day the Earth Caught Fire*, two simultaneous hydrogen bomb tests by the United States and Russia change by 11 degrees the tilt of the earth on its axis and alter the earth's orbit so that it begins to approach the sun.

Radiation casualties—ultimately, the conception of the whole world as a casualty of nuclear testing and nuclear warfare—is the most ominous of all the notions with which science fiction films deal. Universes become expendable. Worlds become contaminated, burnt out, exhausted, obsolete. In *Rocketship X-M* (1950) explorers from the earth land on Mars, where they learn that atomic warfare has destroyed Martian civilization. In George Pal's *The War of the Worlds* (1953), reddish spindly alligator-skinned creatures from Mars invade the earth because their planet is becoming too cold to be inhabitable. In *This Island Earth*, also American, the planet Metaluna, whose population has long ago been driven underground by warfare, is dying under the missile attacks of an enemy planet. Stocks of uranium, which power the force field shielding Metaluna, have been used up; and an unsuccessful expedition is sent to earth to enlist earth scientists to devise new sources for nuclear power. In Joseph Losey's *The Damned* (1961), nine icy-cold radioactive children are being reared by a fanatical scientist in a dark cave on the English coast to be the only survivors of the inevitable nuclear Armageddon.

There is a vast amount of wishful thinking in science fiction films, some of it touching, some of it depressing. Again and again, one detects the hunger for a "good war," which poses no moral problems, admits of no moral qualifications. The imagery of science fiction films will satisfy the most bellicose addict of war films, for a lot of the satisfactions of war films pass, untransformed, into science fiction films. Examples: the dogfights between earth "fighter rockets" and alien spacecraft in the *Battle in Outer Space* (1960); the escalating firepower in the successive assaults upon the invaders in *The Mysterians*, which Dan Talbot correctly described as a non-stop holocaust; the spectacular bombardment of the underground fortress of Metaluna in *This Island Earth*.

Yet at the same time the bellicosity of science fiction films is neatly channeled into the yearning for peace, or for at least peaceful coexistence. Some scientist generally takes sententious note of the fact that it took the planetary invasion to make the warring nations of the earth come to their senses and suspend their own conflicts. One of the main themes of many science fiction films—the color ones usually, because they have the budget and resources to develop the military spectacle—is this UN fantasy, a fantasy of united warfare. (The same wishful UN theme cropped up in a recent spectacular which is not science fiction, *Fifty-Five Days in Peking* [1963]. There, topically enough, the Chinese, the Boxers, play the role of Martian invaders who unite the earthmen, in this case the United States, England, Russia, France, Germany, Italy, and Japan.) A great enough disaster cancels all enmities and calls upon the utmost concentration of earth resources.

Science—technology—is conceived of as the great unifier. Thus the science fiction films also project a Utopian fantasy. In the classic models of Utopian thinking—Plato's Republic, Campanella's City of the Sun, More's Utopia, Swift's land of the Houyhnhnms, Voltaire's Eldorado—society had worked out a perfect consensus. In these societies reasonableness had achieved an unbreakable supremacy over the emotions. Since no disagreement or social conflict was intellectually plausible, none was possible. As in Melville's *Typee*, "they all think the same." The universal rule of reason meant universal agreement. It is interesting, too, that societies in which reason was pictured as totally ascendant were also traditionally pictured as having an ascetic or materially frugal and economically simple mode of life. But in the Utopian world community projected by science fiction films, totally pacified and ruled by scientific consensus, the demand for simplicity of material existence would be absurd.

Yet alongside the hopeful fantasy of moral simplification and international unity embodied in the science fiction films lurk the deepest anxieties about contemporary existence. I don't mean only the very real trauma of the Bomb—that it has been used, that there are enough now to kill everyone on earth many times over, that those new bombs may very well be used. Besides these new anxieties about physical disaster, the prospect of universal mutilation and even annihilation, the science fiction films reflect powerful anxieties about the condition of the individual psyche.

For science fiction films may also be described as a popular mythology for the contemporary *negative* imagination about the impersonal. The other-world creatures that seek to take "us" over are an "it," not a "they." The planetary invaders are usually zombie-like. Their movements are either cool, mechanical, or lumbering, blobby. But it amounts to the same thing. If they are non-human in form, they proceed with an absolutely regular, unalterable movement (unalterable save by destruction). If they are human in form—dressed in space suits, etc.—then they obey the most rigid military discipline, and display no personal characteristics whatsoever. And it is this regime of emotionlessness, of impersonality, of regimentation, which they will impose on the earth if they are successful. "No more love, no more beauty, no more pain," boasts a converted earthling in *The Invasion of the Body Snatchers* (1956). The half-earthling, half-alien children in *The Children of the Damned* (1960) are absolutely emotionless, move as a group and understand each others' thoughts, and are all prodigious intellects. They are the wave of the future, man in his next stage of development.

These alien invaders practice a crime which is worse than murder. They do not simply kill the person. They obliterate him. In *The War of the Worlds*, the ray which issues from the rocket ship disintegrates all persons and objects in its path, leaving no trace of them but a light ash. In Honda's *The H-Man* (1959), the creeping blob melts all flesh with which it comes in contact. If the blob, which looks like a huge hunk of red Jello and can crawl across floors and up and down walls, so much as touches your bare foot, all that is left of you is a heap of clothes on the floor. (A more articulated, size-multiplying blob is the villain in the English film *The Creeping Unknown* [1956].) In another version of this fantasy, the body is preserved but the person is entirely reconstituted as the automatized servant or agent of the alien powers. This is, of course, the vampire fantasy in new dress. The person is really dead, but he doesn't know it. He is "undead," he has become an "unperson." It happens to a whole California town in *The Invasion of the Body Snatchers*, to several earth scientists in *This Island Earth*, and to assorted innocents in *It Came From Outer Space, Attack of the Puppet People* (1958), and *The Brain Eaters* (1958). As the victim always backs away from the vampire's horrifying embrace, so in science fiction films the person always fights being "taken over"; he wants to retain his humanity. But once the deed has been done, the victim is eminently satisfied with his condition. He has not been converted from human amiability to monstrous "animal" bloodlust (a metaphoric exaggeration of sexual desire), as in the old vampire fantasy. No, he has simply become far more efficient—the very model of technocratic man, purged of emotions, volitionless, tranquil, obedient to all orders. (The dark secret behind human nature used to be the upsurge of the animal—as in *King Kong*. The threat to man, his availability to dehumanization, lay in his own animality. Now the danger is understood as residing in man's ability to be turned into a machine.)

The rule, of course, is that this horrible and irremediable form of murder can strike anyone in the film except the hero. The hero and his family, while greatly threatened, always escape this fate and by the end of the film the invaders have been repulsed or destroyed. I know of only one exception, *The Day That Mars Invaded Earth* (1963), in which after all the standard struggles the scientist-hero, his wife, and their two children are "taken over" by the alien invaders—and that's that. (The last minutes of the film show them being incinerated by the Martians' rays and their ash silhouettes flushed down their empty swimming pool, while their simulacra drive off in the family car.) Another variant but upbeat switch on the rule occurs in *The Creation of the Humanoids* (1964), where the hero discovers at the end of the film that he, too, has been turned into a metal robot, complete with highly efficient and virtually indestructible mechanical insides, although he didn't know it and detected no difference in himself. He learns, however, that he will shortly be upgraded into a "humanoid" having all the properties of a real man.

Of all the standard motifs of science fiction films, this theme of dehumanization is perhaps the most fascinating. For, as I have indicated, it is scarcely a black-and-white situation, as in the old vampire films. The attitude of the science fiction films toward depersonalization is mixed. On the one hand, they deplore it as the ultimate horror. On the other hand, certain characteristics of the dehumanized invaders, modulated and disguised—such as the ascendancy of reason over feelings, the idealization of teamwork and the consensus-creating activities of science, a marked degree of moral simplification—are precisely traits of the savior-scientist. It is interesting that when the scientist in these films is treated negatively, it is usually done through the portrayal of an individual scientist who holes up in his laboratory and neglects his fiancée or his loving wife and children, obsessed by his daring and dangerous experiments. The scientist as a loyal member of a team, and therefore considerably less individualized, is treated quite respectfully.

There is absolutely no social criticism, of even the most implicit kind, in science fiction films. No criticism, for example, of the conditions of our society which create the impersonality and dehumanization which science fiction fantasies displace onto the influence of an alien It. Also, the notion of science as a social activity, interlocking with social and political interests, is unacknowledged. Science is simply either adventure (for good or evil) or a technical response to danger. And, typically, when the fear of science is paramount—when science is conceived of as black magic rather than white—the evil has no attribution beyond that of the perverse will of an individual scientist. In science fiction films the antithesis of black magic and white is drawn as a split between technology, which is beneficent, and the errant individual will of a lone intellectual.

Thus, science fiction films can be looked at as thematically central allegory, replete with standard modern attitudes. The theme of depersonalization (being "taken over") which I have been talking about is a new allegory reflecting the age-old awareness of man that, sane, he is always perilously close to insanity and unreason. But there is something more here than just a recent, popular image which expresses man's perennial, but largely unconscious, anxiety about his sanity. The image derives most of its power from a supplementary and historical anxiety, also not experienced *consciously* by most people, about the depersonalizing conditions of modern urban life. Similarly, it is not enough to note that science fiction allegories are one of the new myths about—that is, one of the ways of accommodating to and negating—the perennial human anxiety about death. (Myths of heaven and hell, and of ghosts, had the same function.) For, again, there is a historically specifiable twist which intensifies the anxiety. I mean, the trauma suffered by everyone in the middle of the 20th century when it became clear that, from now on to the end of human history, every person would spend his individual life under the threat not only of individual death, which is certain, but of something almost insupportable psychologically —collective incineration and extinction which could come at any time, virtually without warning.

From a psychological point of view, the imagination of disaster does not greatly differ from one period in history to another. But from a political and moral point of view, it does. The expectation of the apocalypse may be the occasion for a radical disaffiliation from society, as when thousands of Eastern European Jews in the 17th century, hearing that Sabbatai Zevi had been proclaimed the Messiah and that the end of the world was imminent, gave up their homes and businesses and began the trek to Palestine. But people take the news of their doom in diverse ways. It is reported that in 1945 the populace of Berlin received without great agitation the news that Hitler had decided to kill them all, before the Allies arrived, because they had not been worthy enough to win the war. We are, alas, more in the position of the Berliners of 1945 than of the Jews of 17th century Eastern Europe; and our response is closer to theirs, too. What I am suggesting is that the imagery of disaster in science fiction is above all the emblem of an *inadequate response*. I don't mean to bear down on the films for this. They themselves are only a sampling, stripped of sophistication, of the inadequacy of most people's response to the unassimilable terrors that infect their consciousness. The interest of the films, aside from their considerable amount of cinematic charm, consists in this intersection between a naïve and largely debased commercial art product and the most profound dilemmas of the contemporary situation.

Ours is indeed an age of extremity. For we live under continual threat of two equally fearful, but seemingly opposed, destinies: unremitting banality and inconceivable terror. It is fantasy, served out in large rations by the popular arts, which allows most people to cope with these twin specters. For one job that fantasy can do is to lift us out of the unbearably humdrum and to distract us from terrors—real or anticipated—by an escape into exotic, dangerous situations which have last-minute happy endings. But another of the things that fantasy can do is to normalize what is psychologically unbearable, thereby inuring us to it. In one case, fantasy beautifies the world. In the other, it neutralizes it.

The fantasy in science fiction films does both jobs. The films reflect worldwide anxieties, and they serve to allay them. They inculcate a strange apathy concerning the processes of radiation, contamination, and destruction which I for one find haunting and depressing. The naïve level of the films neatly tempers the sense of otherness, of alien-ness, with the grossly familiar. In particular, the dialogue of most science fiction films, which is of a monumental but often touching banality, makes them wonderfully, unintentionally funny. Lines like "Come quickly, there's a monster in my bathtub," "We must do something about this," "Wait, Professor. There's someone on the telephone," "But that's incredible," and the old American stand-by, "I hope it works!" are hilarious in the context of picturesque and deafening holocaust. Yet the films also contain something that is painful and in deadly earnest.

There is a sense in which all these movies are in complicity with the abhorrent. They neutralize it, as I have said. It is no more, perhaps, than the way all art draws its audience into a circle of complicity with the thing represented. But in these films we have to do with things which are (quite literally) unthinkable. Here, "thinking about the unthinkable"—not in the way of Herman Kahn, as a subject for calculation, but as a subject for fantasy—becomes, however inadvertently, itself a somewhat questionable act from a moral point of view. The films perpetuate clichés about identity, volition, power, knowledge, happiness, social consensus, guilt, responsibility which are, to say the least, not serviceable in our present extremity. But collective nightmares cannot be banished by demonstrating that they are, intellectually and morally, fallacious. This nightmare—the one reflected, in various registers, in the science fiction films—is too close to our reality.

1965

Pauline Kael

Pauline Kael (1919–2001) made it exciting to go into film criticism as a profession, and her influence on the next generation of film critics has been enormous. A native Californian, she began her critical career in the Bay Area, reviewing for *Film Quarterly* and KPFA and writing program notes for a repertory movie house she helped run, then free-lancing for *Atlantic Monthly*, *The New Republic*, *McCall's*, and *Vogue* before signing on with *The New Yorker* and moving to the East Coast. The marriage between Kael and *The New Yorker* proved to be one of the longest lasting and most mutually beneficial in modern magazine history. They provided her with security and the chance to write at length for a national audience; she helped them to loosen up, to become more street-smart and more youthful.

Among her many critical assets, Kael was a brilliant observer of acting styles and could capture in apt metaphor the look and bounce of a performer. She understood the morality of narrative structure, zeroing in on those plot imbalances brought about through self-satisfaction, hypocrisy, or pandering to the crowd. She had a genius for showing how a film she found suspect was a hit by analyzing the audience's narcissistic investment in some social undercurrent of the moment. No one has written better about the appeal of "trash," or the tangential pleasures we get from movies that aren't very good. Eroticizing the film-going experience, she could speak of "the special aphrodisia of movies—the kinetic responsiveness, the all-out submission to pleasure. . . . What we all sometimes want from the movies [are] sensations we can't control, an excitement that is a great high." Her use of the first-person plural showed the identification she felt with her readers, but which some of Kael's critics found presumptuous. In any case, she always sympathized more with the movie public's hunger for roller-coaster exhilaration than with the coterie critic's search for a restrained, rigorous film art, and wrote: "Vulgarity is not as destructive to an artist as snobbery." She liked to fall in love with movies, and her enthusiasm for one of her favorites would sometimes lead to hyperbole or strategic downplaying of its flaws. But she could also, as in her review of *Funny Girl*, precisely weigh a film's strengths and weaknesses. Her prose was flexible, persuasive, vivid, and dynamic. Her sentence-writing is on a consistently high level, and her criticism belongs with the best American nonfiction prose of the modern era.

Band of Outsiders

Jean-Luc Godard intended to give the public what it wanted. His next film was going to be about a girl and a gun—"A sure-fire story which will sell a lot of tickets." And so, like Henry James's hero in "The Next Time," he proceeded to make a work of art that sold fewer tickets than ever. What was to be a simple commercial movie about a robbery became *Band of Outsiders*.*

The two heroes of *Band of Outsiders* begin by playacting crime and violence movies, then really act them out in their lives. Their girl, wanting to be accepted, tells them there is money in the villa where she lives. And we watch, apprehensive and puzzled, as the three of them act out the robbery they're committing as if it were something going on in a movie—or a fairy tale. The crime does not fit the daydreamers nor their milieu: we half expect to be told it's all a joke, that they can't really be committing an armed robbery. *Band of Outsiders* is like a reverie of a gangster movie as students in an espresso bar might remember it or plan it—a mixture of the gangster film virtues (loyalty, daring) with innocence, amorality, lack of equilibrium.

It's as if a French poet took a banal American crime novel and told it to us in terms of the romance and beauty he read between the lines; that is to say, Godard gives it *his* imagination, re-creating the gangsters and the moll with his world of associations—seeing them as people in a Paris café, mixing them with Rimbaud, Kafka, Alice in Wonderland. Silly? But we know how alien to our lives were those movies that fed our imaginations and have now become part of us. And don't we—as children and perhaps even later—romanticize cheap movie stereotypes, endowing them with the attributes of those figures in the other arts who touch us imaginatively? Don't all our experiences in the arts and popular arts that have more intensity than our ordinary lives tend to merge in another imaginative world? And movies, because they are such an encompassing, eclectic art, are an ideal medium for combining our experiences and fantasies from life, from all the arts, and from our jumbled memories of both. The men who made the stereotypes drew them from their own scrambled experience of history and art—as Howard Hawks and Ben Hecht drew *Scarface* from the Capone family "as if they were the Borgias set down in Chicago."

***Band of Outsiders* (with Anna Karina, Sami Frey, Claude Brasseur) opened and closed in New York in a single week of March 1966.

The distancing of Godard's imagination induces feelings of tenderness and despair which bring us closer to the movie-inspired heroes and to the wide-eyed ingenue than to the more naturalistic characters of ordinary movies. They recall so many other movie lives that flickered for us; and the quick rhythms and shifting moods emphasize transience, impermanence. The fragile existence of the characters becomes poignant, upsetting, nostalgic; we care *more*.

This nostalgia that permeates *Band of Outsiders* may also derive from Godard's sense of the lost possibilities in movies. He has said, "As soon as you can make films, you can no longer make films like the ones that made you want to make them." This we may guess is not merely because the possibilities of making big expensive movies on the American model are almost nonexistent for the French but also because as the youthful film enthusiast grows up, if he grows in intelligence, he can see that the big expensive movies now being made are not worth making. And perhaps they never were: the luxury and wastefulness, that when you are young seem as magical as peeping into the world of the Arabian Nights, become ugly and suffocating when you're older and see what a cheat they really were. The tawdry American Nights of gangster movies that were the magic of Godard's childhood formed his style—the urban poetry of speed and no afterthoughts, fast living and quick death, no padding, no explanations—but the meaning had to change.

An artist may regret that he can no longer experience the artistic pleasures of his childhood and youth, the very pleasures that formed him as an artist. Godard is not, like Hollywood's product producers, naïve (or cynical) enough to remake the movies he grew up on. But, loving the movies that formed his tastes, he uses this nostalgia for old movies as an active element in his own movies. He doesn't, like many artists, deny the past he has outgrown; perhaps he is assured enough not to deny it, perhaps he hasn't quite outgrown it. He reintroduces it, giving it a different quality, using it as shared experience, shared joke. He plays with his belief and disbelief, and this playfulness may make his work seem inconsequential and slighter than it is: it is as if the artist himself were deprecating any large intentions and just playing around in the medium. Reviewers often complain that they can't take him seriously; when you consider what they do manage to take seriously, this is not a serious objection.

Because Godard's movies do not let us forget that we're watching a movie, it's easy to think he's just kidding. Yet his reminders serve an opposite purpose. They tell us that his aim is not simple realism, that the lives of his characters are continuously altered by their fantasies. If I may be deliberately fancy: he aims for the poetry of reality and the reality of poetry. I have put it that way to be either irritatingly pretentious or lyrical—depending on your mood and frame of reference—in order to provide a critical equivalent to Godard's phrases. When the narrator in *Band of Outsiders* says, "Franz did not know whether the world was becoming a dream or a dream becoming the world," we may think that that's too self-consciously loaded with mythic fringe benefits and too rich an echo of the narrators of *Orphée* and *Les Enfants Terribles*, or we may catch our breath at the beauty of it. I think those most responsive to Godard's approach probably do both simultaneously. We do something similar when reading Cervantes. Quixote, his mind confused by tales of Knight Errantry, going out to do battle with imaginary villains, is an ancestor of Godard's heroes, dreaming away at American movies, seeing life in terms of cops and robbers. Perhaps a crucial difference between Cervantes's mock romances and Godard's mock melodramas is that Godard may (as in *Alphaville*) share some of his characters' delusions.

It's the tension between his hard, swift, cool style and the romantic meaning that this style has for him that is peculiarly modern and exciting in his work. It's the casual way he omits mechanical scenes that don't interest him so that the movie is all high points and marvelous "little things." Godard's style, with its nonchalance about the fates of the characters—a style drawn from American movies and refined to an intellectual edge in postwar French philosophy and attitudes—is an American teen-ager's ideal. To be hard and cool as a movie gangster yet not stupid or gross like a gangster—that's the cool grace of the privileged, smart young.

It's always been relatively respectable and sometimes fashionable to respond to our own experience in terms drawn from the arts: to relate a circus scene to Picasso, or to describe the people in a Broadway delicatessen as an Ensor. But until recently people were rather shamefaced or terribly arch about relating their reactions in terms of movies. That was more a confession than a description. Godard brought this way of reacting out into the open of *new* movies at the same time that the pop art movement was giving this kind of experience precedence over responsiveness to the traditional arts. By now— so accelerated has cultural history become—we have those students at colleges who when asked what they're interested in say, "I go to a lot of movies." And some of them are so proud of how compulsively they see everything in terms of movies and how many times they've seen certain movies that there is nothing left for them to relate movies *to*. They have been soaked up by the screen.

Godard's sense of the present is dominated by his movie past. This is what makes his movies (and, to a lesser degree, the movies of Jacques Demy) seem so new: for they are movies made by a generation bred on movies. I don't mean that there haven't been earlier generations of directors who grew up on movies, but that it took the peculiar post-World War II atmosphere to make love of movies a new and semi-intellectualized romanticism. To say it flatly, Godard is the Scott Fitzgerald of the movie world, and movies are for the sixties a synthesis of what the arts were for the post-World War I generation—rebellion, romance, a new style of life.

The world of *Band of Outsiders* is both "real"—the protagonists feel, they may even die—and yet "unreal" because they don't take their own feelings or death very seriously, as if they weren't important to anybody, really. Their only identity is in their relationship with each other. This, however we may feel about it, is a contemporary mood; and Godard, who expresses it, is part of it. At times it seems as if the movie had no points of reference outside itself. When this imagined world is as exquisite as in *Band of Outsiders*, we may begin to feel that this indifference or inability to connect with other worlds is a kind of aesthetic expression and a preference. The sadness that pervades the work is romantic regret that you can no longer believe in the kind of movie you once wanted to be enfolded in, becoming part of that marvelous world of beauty and danger with its gangsters who trusted their friends and its whores who never really sold themselves. It's the sadness in frivolity—in the abandonment of efforts to make sense out of life in art. Godard in his films seems to say: only this kind of impossible romance is possible. You play at cops and robbers but the bullets can kill you. His movies themselves become playful gestures, games in which you succeed or fail with a shrug, a smile.

The penalty of Godard's fixation on the movie past is that, as *Alphaville* reveals, old movies may not provide an adequate frame of reference for a view of *this* world. Then we regret that Godard is not the kind of artist who can provide an intellectual structure commensurate with the brilliance of his style and the quality of his details. Because, of course, we think in terms of masterpieces and we feel that here is a man who has the gifts for masterpieces. But maybe he hasn't; maybe he has artistry of a different kind.

1966

Funny Girl

Barbra Streisand arrives on the screen, in *Funny Girl*, when the movies are in desperate need of her. The timing is perfect. There's hardly a star in American movies today, and if we've got so used to the absence of stars that we no longer think about it much, we've also lost one of the great pleasures of moviegoing: watching incandescent people up there, more intense and dazzling than people we ordinarily encounter in life, and far more charming than the extraordinary people we encounter, because the ones on the screen are objects of pure contemplation—like athletes all wound up in the stress of competition—and we don't have to undergo the frenzy or the risks of being involved with them. In life, fantastically gifted people, people who are driven, can be too much to handle; they can be a pain. In plays, in opera, they're divine, and on the screen, where they can be seen in their perfection, and where we're even safer from them, they're *more* divine.

Let's dispose at once of the ugly-duckling myth. It has been commonly said that the musical *Funny Girl* was a comfort to people because it carried the message that you do not need to be pretty to succeed. That is nonsense; the "message" of Barbra Streisand in *Funny Girl* is that talent is beauty. And this isn't some comforting message for plain people; it's what show business is all about. Barbra Streisand is much more beautiful than "pretty" people. This has not always been as true for the movies as for the stage; not handled carefully, some stage stars looked awful on the screen, so the legend developed that movie actors and actresses had to have "perfect" little features, and studio practices kept the legend going. But the banality of mere prettiness is a blight on American movies: Who can tell those faces apart? The Italian actresses, with their big, irregular features, became so popular here because we were starved for a trace of life after all those (usually fake) Wasp stereotypes. It's unfortunate that in this case the (I assume unintentional) demonstration of how uninteresting prettiness is should be at the expense of Omar Sharif, who goes as far as to demonstrate that good looks can be nothing.

Most Broadway musicals are dead before they reach the movies—the routines are so worked out they're stiff, and the jokes are embalmed in old applause. But Streisand has the gift of making old written dialogue sound like inspired improvisation; almost every line she says seems to have just sprung to mind and out. Her inflections are witty and surprising, and, more surprisingly, delicate; she can probably do more for a line than any screen comedienne since Jean Arthur, in the thirties. There hasn't been a funny girl on the screen for so long now that moviegoers have probably also got used to doing without one of the minor, once staple pleasures of moviegoing: the wisecracking heroines, the clever funny girls—Jean Arthur, of course, and Claudette Colbert, and Carole Lombard, and Ginger Rogers, and Rosalind Russell, and Myrna Loy, and all the others who could be counted on to be sassy and sane. They performed a basic comic function—they weren't taken in by sham; they had the restorative good sense of impudence—and in the pre-bunny period they made American women distinctive and marvellous. The story and the situations of *Funny Girl* are even drearier than those of most big musicals, but we know the form is corrupt and we're used to the conventions of rags-to-riches-to-price-of-fame, and it's easy to take all that for granted and ignore it when a performer knows how to deliver a line. The form is corrupt but the spirit of the performer isn't—that's why a big, heavy, silly musical like this can still have some brute force in it. The comedy is the comedy of cutting through the bull, of saying what's really on your mind. Such comedy was usually derived from urban Jewish humor, even in the thirties; now the Midwestern mask has been removed. Though this comedy is often self-deprecating (not hostile or paranoid), it's *lightly* self-mocking, in a way that seems admirably suited to the genre. Here one can see the experience and tact of a good, solid director like William Wyler. Younger, less capable, more anxious directors will permit anything for a laugh, and material like this could easily become raucous and embarrassing; we're never in danger in Wyler's hands, and that sense of security puts us in the right mood for laughter.

It is Streisand's peculiar triumph that in the second half, when the routine heartbreak comes, as it apparently must in all musical biographies, she shows an aptitude for suffering that those clever actresses didn't. Where they became sanctimonious and noble, thereby violating everything we had loved them for, she simply drips as unself-consciously and impersonally as a true tragic muse. And the tears belong to her face; they seem to complete it, as Garbo's suffering in *Camille* seemed to complete her beauty. Much stronger and more dominating than the earlier comediennes, she skirts pathos because her emotions are so openly expressed. She doesn't "touch" us for sympathy in the Chaplinesque way by trying to conceal her hurt. She conceals nothing; she's fiercely, almost frighteningly direct.

Whenever Streisand is not on the screen, the movie is stodgy, advancing the plot and telegraphing information in tedious little scenes of Sharif with servants, Sharif gambling, etc. We know that he's playing Nicky Arnstein, Fanny Brice's husband, but we can't make any sense of him. If shady gamblers are not going to be flashy and entertaining, what good are they as musical-comedy heroes? This Arnstein is too phlegmatic for a playboy and too proper for a gambler, and he seems not only devoid of humor but almost unaware of it. So what is supposed to draw him and a funny girl together? Sharif appears to be some sort of visiting royalty, with a pained professional smile to put the common people at their ease. The result is that no one seems to know how to talk to him. But then there's no one in the movie but Streisand anyway; the world of the movie is a stage full of stooges (with Walter Pidgeon stuck playing Ziegfeld like Mr. Miniver). In all these ways it's a terrible movie, and though Streisand's makeup and costumes are beautiful and sumptuous (she sometimes resembles Monica Vitti), the other girls are not well served—partly, it appears, through a failure to decide whether the Ziegfeld girls should be glorified or parodied. (No definite tone is taken.) And the sets are not elegant and stylized; they're just bad period reconstructions. Sometimes all this gets in the way of enjoyment: the visual affront of square photography and a studio "alley" help to kill the "People" number (it's also strategically ill placed), and the shipboard sequences are damaged by their unappealing look. But one can fault everything else in the movie, too, and it doesn't really matter—not even the fact that the second half has to coast on the good will built up in the first. The crucial thing is that Wyler never makes the kind of mistake that Tony Richardson made in *The Entertainer* when he cut away from Laurence Olivier's great number to give us backstage business. We do not ask of a musical like *Funny Girl* that it give us the life story of Fanny Brice; we know that her story is simply the pretext for a show, a convention of our realistically rooted musical theatre, which seeks protection in great names or big properties from the past. What we do ask is that an actress who plays a star like Fanny Brice be able to live up to the image of a great star; if she isn't, we cannot accept the pretext, and the show is exposed as just an attempt to cash in on past glories. There is no such difficulty with *Funny Girl*. The end of the movie, in a long single take, is a bravura stroke, a gorgeous piece of showing off, that makes one intensely, brilliantly aware of the star as performer and of the star's pride in herself as performer. The pride is justified.

1969

Trash, Art, and the Movies

Like those cynical heroes who were idealists before they discovered that the world was more rotten than they had been led to expect, we're just about all of us displaced persons, "a long way from home." When we feel defeated, when we imagine we could now perhaps settle for home and what it represents, that home no longer exists. But there are movie houses. In whatever city we find ourselves we can duck into a theater and see on the screen our familiars—our old "ideals" aging as we are and no longer looking so ideal. Where could we better stoke the fires of our masochism than at rotten movies in gaudy seedy picture palaces in cities that run together, movies and anonymity a common denominator. Movies—a tawdry corrupt art for a tawdry corrupt world—fit the way we feel. The world doesn't work the way the schoolbooks said it did and we are different from what our parents and teachers expected us to be. Movies are our cheap and easy expression, the sullen art of displaced persons. Because we feel low we sink in the boredom, relax in the irresponsibility, and maybe grin for a minute when the gunman lines up three men and kills them with a single bullet, which is no more "real" to us than the nursery-school story of the brave little tailor.

We don't have to be told those are photographs of actors impersonating characters. We know, and we often know much more about both the actors and the characters they're impersonating and about how and why the movie has been made than is consistent with theatrical illusion. Hitchock teased us by killing off the one marquee-name star early in *Psycho*, a gambit which startled us not just because of the suddenness of the murder or how it was committed but because it broke a box-office convention and so it was a joke played on what audiences have learned to expect. He broke the rules of the movie game and our response demonstrated how aware we are of commercial considerations. When movies are bad (and in the bad parts of good movies) our awareness of the mechanics and our cynicism about the aims and values is peculiarly alienating. The audience talks right back to the phony "outspoken" condescending *The Detective*; there are groans of dejection at *The Legend of Lylah Clare*, with, now and then, a desperate little titter. How well we all know that cheap depression that settles on us when our hopes and expectations are disappointed *again*. Alienation is the most common state of the knowledgeable movie audience, and though it has the peculiar rewards of low connoisseurship, a miser's delight in small favors, we long to be surprised out of it—not to suspension of disbelief nor to a Brechtian kind of alienation, but to pleasure, something a man can call good without self-disgust.

A good movie can take you out of your dull funk and the hopelessness that so often goes with slipping into a theater; a good movie can make you feel alive again, in contact, not just lost in another city. Good movies make you care, make you believe in possibilities again. If somewhere in the Hollywood-entertainment world someone has managed to break through with something that speaks to you, then it isn't *all* corruption. The movie doesn't have to be great; it can be stupid and empty and you can still have the joy of a good performance, or the joy in just a good line. An actor's scowl, a small subversive gesture, a dirty remark that someone tosses off with a mock-innocent face, and the world makes a little bit of sense. Sitting there alone or painfully alone because those with you do not react as you do, you know there must be others perhaps in this very theater or in this city, surely in other theaters in other cities, now, in the past or future, who react as you do. And because movies are the most total and encompassing art form we have, these reactions can seem the most personal and, maybe the most important, imaginable. The romance of movies is not just in those stories and those people on the screen but in the adolescent dream of meeting others who feel as you do about what you've seen. You do meet them, of course, and you know each other at once because you talk less about good movies than about what you love in bad movies.

II

There is so much talk now about the art of the film that we may be in danger of forgetting that most of the movies we enjoy are not works of art. *The Scalphunters*, for example, was one of the few entertaining American movies this past year, but skillful though it was, one could hardly call it a work of art—if such terms are to have any useful meaning. Or, to take a really gross example, a movie that is as crudely made as *Wild in the Streets*—slammed together with spit and hysteria and opportunism—can nevertheless be enjoyable, though it is almost a classic example of an unartistic movie. What makes these movies—that are not works of art—enjoyable? *The Scalphunters* was more entertaining than most Westerns largely because Burt Lancaster and Ossie Davis were peculiarly funny together; part of the pleasure of the movie was trying to figure out what made them so funny. Burt Lancaster is an odd kind of comedian: what's distinctive about him is that his comedy seems to come out of his physicality. In serious roles an undistinguished and too obviously hard-working actor, he has an apparently effortless flair for comedy and nothing is more infectious than an actor who can relax in front of the camera as if he were having a good time. (George Segal sometimes seems to have this gift of a wonderful amiability, and Brigitte Bardot was radiant with it in *Viva Maria!*) Somehow the alchemy of personality in the pairing of Lancaster and Ossie Davis—another powerfully funny actor of tremendous physical presence—worked, and the director Sydney Pollack kept tight control so that it wasn't overdone.

And *Wild in the Streets*? It's a blatantly crummy-looking picture, but that somehow works for it instead of against it because it's smart in a lot of ways that better-made pictures aren't. It looks like other recent products from American International Pictures but it's as if one were reading a comic strip that looked just like the strip of the day before, and yet on this new one there are surprising expressions on the faces and some of the balloons are really witty. There's not a trace of sensitivity in the drawing or in the ideas, and there's something rather specially funny about wit without *any* grace at all; it can be enjoyed in a particularly crude way—as Pop wit. The basic idea is corny—*It Can't Happen Here* with the freaked-out young as a new breed of fascists—but it's treated in the paranoid style of editorials about youth (it even begins by blaming everything on the parents). And a cheap idea that is this current and widespread has an almost lunatic charm, a nightmare gaiety. There's a relish that people have for the idea of drug-taking kids as monsters threatening them—the daily papers merging into *Village of the Damned*. Tapping and exploiting this kind of hysteria for a satirical fantasy, the writer Robert Thom has used what is available and obvious but he's done it with just enough mockery and style to make it funny. He throws in touches of characterization and occasional lines that are not there just to further the plot, and these throwaways make odd connections so that the movie becomes almost frolicsome in its paranoia (and in its delight in its own cleverness).

If you went to *Wild in the Streets* expecting a good movie, you'd probably be appalled because the directing is unskilled and the music is banal and many of the ideas in the script are scarcely even carried out, and almost every detail is messed up (the casting director has used bit players and extras who are decades too old for their roles). It's a paste-up job of cheap moviemaking, but it has genuinely funny performers who seize their opportunities and throw their good lines like boomerangs—Diane Varsi (like an even more zonked-out Geraldine Page) doing a perfectly quietly convincing freak-out as if it were truly a put-on of the whole straight world; Hal Holbrook with his inexpressive actorish face that is opaque and uninteresting in long shot but in close-up reveals tiny little shifts of expression, slight tightenings of the features that are like the movement of thought; and Shelley Winters, of course, and Christopher Jones. It's not so terrible—it may even be a relief—for a movie to be without the look of art; there are much worse things aesthetically than the crude good-natured crumminess, the undisguised reach for a fast buck, of movies without art. From *I Was a Teen-Age Werewolf* through the beach parties to *Wild in the Streets* and *The Savage Seven*, American International Pictures has sold a cheap commodity, which in its lack of artistry and in its blatant and sometimes funny way of delivering action serves to remind us that one of the great appeals of movies is that we don't have to take them too seriously.

Wild in the Streets is a fluke—a borderline, special case of a movie that is entertaining because some talented people got a chance to do something at American International that the more respectable companies were too nervous to try. But though I don't enjoy a movie so obvious and badly done as the big American International hit, *The Wild Angels*, it's easy to see why kids do and why many people in other countries do. Their reasons are basically why we all started going to the movies. After a time, we may want more, but audiences who have been forced to wade through the thick middle-class padding of more expensively made movies to get to the action enjoy the nose-thumbing at "good taste" of cheap movies that stick to the raw materials. At some basic level they *like* the pictures to be cheaply done, they enjoy the crudeness; it's a breather, a vacation from proper behavior and good taste and required responses. Patrons of burlesque applaud politely for the graceful erotic dancer but go wild for the lewd lummox who bangs her big hips around. That's what they go to burlesque for. Personally, I hope for a reasonable minimum of finesse, and movies like *Planet of the Apes* or *The Scalphunters* or *The Thomas Crown Affair* seem to me minimal entertainment for a relaxed evening's pleasure. These are, to use traditional common-sense language, "good movies" or "good bad movies"—slick, reasonably inventive, well-crafted. They are not art. But they are almost the maximum of what we're now getting from American movies, and not only these but much worse movies are talked about as "art"—and are beginning to be taken seriously in our schools.

It's preposterously egocentric to call anything we enjoy art—as if we could not be entertained by it if it were not; it's just as preposterous to let prestigious, expensive advertising snow us into thinking we're getting art for our money when we haven't even had a good time. I did have a good time at *Wild in the Streets*, which is more than I can say for *Petulia* or *2001* or a lot of other highly praised pictures. *Wild in the Streets* is not a work of art, but then I don't think *Petulia* or *2001* is either, though *Petulia* has that kaleidoscopic hip look and *2001* that new-techniques look which combined with "swinging" or "serious" ideas often pass for motion picture art.

III

Let's clear away a few misconceptions. Movies make hash of the school-marm's approach of how well the artist fulfilled his intentions. Whatever the original intention of the writers and director, it is usually supplanted, as the production gets under way, by the intention to make money—and the industry judges the film by how well it fulfills that intention. But if you could see the "artist's intentions" you'd probably wish you couldn't anyway. Nothing is so deathly to enjoyment as the relentless march of a movie to fulfill its obvious purpose. This is, indeed, almost a defining characteristic of the hack director, as distinguished from an artist.

The intention to make money is generally all too obvious. One of the excruciating comedies of our time is attending the new classes in cinema at the high schools where the students may quite shrewdly and accurately interpret the plot developments in a mediocre movie in terms of manipulation for a desired response while the teacher tries to explain everything in terms of the creative artist working out his theme—as if the conditions under which a movie is made and the market for which it is designed were irrelevant, as if the latest product from Warners or Universal should be analyzed like a lyric poem.

People who are just getting "seriously interested" in film always ask a critic, "Why don't you talk about technique and 'the visuals' more?" The answer is that American movie technique is generally more like technology and it usually isn't very interesting. Hollywood movies often have the look of the studio that produced them—they have a studio style. Many current Warner films are noisy and have a bright look of cheerful ugliness, Universal films the cheap blur of money-saving processes, and so forth. Sometimes there is even a *spirit* that seems to belong to the studio. We can speak of the Paramount comedies of the Thirties or the Twentieth Century–Fox family entertainment of the Forties and CinemaScope comedies of the Fifties or the old MGM gloss, pretty much as we speak of Chevvies or Studebakers. These movies look alike, they move the same way, they have just about the same engines because of the studio policies and the *kind* of material the studio heads bought, the ideas they imposed, the way they had the films written, directed, photographed, and the labs where the prints were processed, and, of course, because of the presence of the studio stable of stars for whom the material was often purchased and shaped and who dominated the output of the studio. In some cases, as at Paramount in the Thirties, studio style was plain and rather tacky and the output—those comedies with Mary Boland and Mae West and Alison Skipworth and W. C. Fields—looks the better for it now. Those economical comedies weren't slowed down by a lot of fancy lighting or the adornments of "production values." Simply to be enjoyable, movies don't need a very high level of craftsmanship: wit, imagination, fresh subject matter, skillful performers, a good idea—either alone or in any combination—can more than compensate for lack of technical knowledge or a big budget.

The craftsmanship that Hollywood has always used as a selling point not only doesn't have much to do with art—the expressive use of techniques—it probably doesn't have very much to do with actual box-office appeal, either. A dull movie like Sidney Furie's *The Naked Runner* is technically competent. The appalling *Half a Sixpence* is technically astonishing. Though the large popular audience has generally been respectful of expenditure (so much so that a critic who wasn't impressed by the money and effort that went into a *Dr. Zhivago* might be sharply reprimanded by readers), people who like *The President's Analyst* or *The Producers* or *The Odd Couple* don't seem to be bothered by their technical ineptitude and visual ugliness. And on the other hand, the expensive slick techniques of ornately empty movies like *A Dandy in Aspic* can actually work against one's enjoyment, because such extravagance and waste are morally ugly. If one compares movies one likes to movies one doesn't like, craftsmanship of the big-studio variety is hardly a decisive factor. And if one compares a movie one likes by a competent director such as John Sturges or Franklin Schaffner or John Frankenheimer to a movie one doesn't much like by the same director, his technique is probably not the decisive factor. After directing *The Manchurian Candidate* Frankenheimer directed another political thriller, *Seven Days in May*, which, considered just as a piece of direction, was considerably more confident. While seeing it, one could take pleasure in Frankenheimer's smooth showmanship. But the material (Rod Serling out of Fletcher Knebel and Charles W. Bailey II) was like a straight (*i.e.*, square) version of *The Manchurian Candidate*. I have to chase around the corridors of memory to summon up images from *Seven Days in May*; despite the brilliant technique, all that is clear to mind is the touchingly, desperately anxious face of Ava Gardner—how when she smiled you couldn't be sure if you were seeing dimples or tics. But *The Manchurian Candidate*, despite Frankenheimer's uneven, often barely adequate, staging, is still vivid because of the script. It took off from a political double entendre that everybody had been thinking of ("Why, if Joe McCarthy were working for the Communists, he couldn't be doing them more good!") and carried it to startling absurdity, and the extravagances and conceits and conversational non sequiturs (by George Axelrod out of Richard Condon) were ambivalent and funny in a way that was trashy yet liberating.

Technique is hardly worth talking about unless it's used for something worth doing: that's why most of the theorizing about the new art of television commercials is such nonsense. The effects are impersonal—dexterous, sometimes clever, but empty of art. It's because of their emptiness that commercials call so much attention to their camera angles and quick cutting—which is why people get impressed by "the art" of it. Movies are now often made in terms of what television viewers have learned to settle for. Despite a great deal that is spoken and written about young people responding visually, the influence of TV is to make movies visually less imaginative and complex. Television is a very noisy medium and viewers listen, while getting used to a poor quality of visual reproduction, to the absence of visual detail, to visual obviousness and overemphasis on simple compositions, and to atrociously simplified and distorted color systems. The shifting camera styles, the movement, and the fast cutting of a film like *Finian's Rainbow*—one of the better big productions—are like the "visuals" of TV commercials, a disguise for static material, expressive of nothing so much as the need to keep you from getting bored and leaving. Men are now beginning their careers as directors by working on commercials—which, if one cares to speculate on it, may be almost a one-sentence résumé of the future of American motion pictures.

I don't mean to suggest that there is not such a thing as movie technique or that craftsmanship doesn't contribute to the pleasures of movies, but simply that most audiences, if they enjoy the acting and the "story" or the theme or the funny lines, don't notice or care about how well or how badly the movie is made, and because they don't care, a hit makes a director a "genius" and everybody talks about his brilliant technique (*i.e.*, the technique of grabbing an audience). In the brief history of movies there has probably never been so astonishingly gifted a large group of directors as the current Italians, and not just the famous ones or Pontecorvo (*The Battle of Algiers*) or Francesco Rosi (*The Moment of Truth*) or the young prodigies, Bertolucci and Bellocchio, but dozens of others, men like Elio Petri (*We Still Kill the Old Way*) and Carlo Lizzani (*The Violent Four*). *The Violent Four* shows more understanding of visual movement and more talent for moviemaking than anything that's been made in America this year. But could one tell people who are not crazy, dedicated moviegoers to go see it? I'm not sure, although I enjoyed the film enormously, because *The Violent Four* is a gangster genre picture. And it may be a form of aestheticism—losing sight of what people go to movies for, and particularly what they go to foreign movies for—for a critic to say, "His handling of crowds and street scenes is superb," or, "It has a great semi-documentary chase sequence." It does, but the movie is basically derived from our old gangster movies, and beautifully made as it is, one would have a hard time convincing educated people to go see a movie that features a stunning performance by Gian Maria Volonte which is based on Paul Muni and James Cagney. Presumably they want something different from movies than a genre picture that offers images of modern urban decay and is smashingly directed. If a movie is interesting primarily in terms of technique then it isn't worth talking about except to students who can learn from seeing how a good director works. And to talk about a movie like *The Graduate* in terms of movie technique is really a bad joke. Technique at this level is not of any aesthetic importance; it's not the ability to achieve what you're after but the skill to find something acceptable. One must talk about a film like this in terms of what audiences enjoy it for or one is talking gibberish—and might as well be analyzing the "art" of commercials. And for the greatest movie artists where there is a unity of technique and subject, one doesn't need to talk about technique much because it has been subsumed in the art. One doesn't want to talk about how Tolstoi got his effects but about the work itself. One doesn't want to talk about how Jean Renoir does it; one wants to talk about what he has done. One can try to separate it all out, of course, distinguish form and content for purposes of analysis. But that is a secondary, analytic function, a scholarly function, and hardly needs to be done explicitly in criticism. Taking it apart is far less important than trying to see it whole. The critic shouldn't need to tear a work apart to demonstrate that he knows how it was put together. The important thing is to convey what is new and beautiful in the work, not how it was made—which is more or less implicit.

Just as there are good actors—possibly potentially great actors—who have never become big stars because they've just never been lucky enough to get the roles they needed (Brian Keith is a striking example) there are good directors who never got the scripts and the casts that could make their reputations. The question people ask when they consider going to a movie is not "How's it made?" but "What's it about?" and that's a perfectly legitimate question. (The next question—sometimes the first—is generally, "Who's in it?" and that's a good, honest question, too.) When you're at a movie, you don't have to believe in it to enjoy it but you do have to be interested. (Just as you have to be interested in the human material, too. Why should you go see *another* picture with James Stewart?) I don't want to see another samurai epic in exactly the same way I never want to read *Kristin Lavransdatter*. Though it's conceivable that a truly great movie director could make any subject interesting, there are few such artists working in movies and if they did work on unpromising subjects I'm not sure we'd really enjoy the results even if we did *admire* their artistry. (I recognize the greatness of sequences in several films by Eisenstein but it's a rather cold admiration.) The many brilliant Italian directors who are working within a commercial framework on crime and action movies are obviously not going to be of any great interest unless they get a chance to work on a subject we care about. Ironically the Czech successes here (*The Shop on Main Street, Loves of a Blonde, Closely Watched Trains*) are acclaimed for their techniques, which are fairly simple and rather limited, when it's obviously their human concerns and the basic modesty and decency of their attitudes plus a little barnyard humor which audiences respond to. They may even respond partly because of the *simplicity* of the techniques.

IV

When we are children, though there are categories of films we don't like—documentaries generally (they're too much like education) and, of course, movies especially designed for children—by the time we can go on our own we have learned to avoid them. Children are often put down by adults when the children say they enjoyed a particular movie; adults who are short on empathy are quick to point out aspects of the plot or theme that the child didn't understand, and it's easy to humiliate a child in this way. But it is one of the glories of eclectic arts like opera and movies that they include so many possible kinds and combinations of pleasure. One may be enthralled by Leontyne Price in *La Forza del Destino* even if one hasn't boned up on the libretto, or entranced by *The Magic Flute* even if one has boned up on the libretto, and a movie may be enjoyed for many reasons that have little to do with the story or the subtleties (if any) of theme or character. Unlike "pure" arts which are often defined in terms of what only they can do, movies are open and unlimited. Probably everything that can be done in movies can be done some other way, but—and this is what's so miraculous and so expedient about them—they can do almost anything any other art can do (alone or in combination) and they can take on some of the functions of exploration, of journalism, of anthropology, of almost any branch of knowledge as well. We go to the movies for the variety of what they can provide, and for their marvelous ability to give us easily and inexpensively (and usually painlessly) what we can get from other arts also. They are a wonderfully *convenient* art.

Movies are used by cultures where they are foreign films in a much more primitive way than in their own; they may be enjoyed as travelogues or as initiations into how others live or in ways we might not even guess. The sophisticated and knowledgeable moviegoer is likely to forget how new and how amazing the different worlds up there once seemed to him, and to forget how much a child reacts to, how many elements he is taking in, often for the first time. And even adults who have seen many movies may think a movie is "great" if it introduces them to unfamiliar subject matter; thus many moviegoers react as naïvely as children to *Portrait of Jason* or *The Queen*. They think they're wonderful. The oldest plots and corniest comedy bits can be full of wonder for a child, just as the freeway traffic in a grade Z melodrama can be magical to a villager who has never seen a car. A child may enjoy even a movie like *Jules and Jim* for its sense of fun, without comprehending it as his parents do, just as we may enjoy an Italian movie as a sex comedy although in Italy it is considered social criticism or political satire. Jean-Luc Godard liked the movie of *Pal Joey*, and I suppose that a miserable American movie musical like *Pal Joey* might look good in France because I can't think of a single good dance number performed by French dancers in a French movie. The French enjoy what they're unable to do and we enjoy the French studies of the pangs of adolescent love that would be corny if made in Hollywood. A movie like *The Young Girls of Rochefort* demonstrates how even a gifted Frenchman who adores American musicals misunderstands their conventions. Yet it would be as stupid to say that the director Jacques Demy couldn't love American musicals because he doesn't understand their conventions as to tell a child he couldn't have liked *Planet of the Apes* because he didn't get the jokey references to the Scopes trial.

Every once in a while I see an anthropologist's report on how some pre-literate tribe reacts to movies; they may, for example, be disturbed about where the actor has gone when he leaves the movie frame, or they may respond with enthusiasm to the noise and congestion of big-city life which in the film story are meant to show the depths of depersonalization to which we are sinking, but which they find funny or very jolly indeed. Different people and different cultures enjoy movies in very different ways. A few years ago the new "tribalists" here responded to the gaudy fantasies of *Juliet of the Spirits* by using the movie to turn on. A few had already made a trip of *8½*, but *Juliet*, which was, conveniently and perhaps not entirely accidentally, in electric, psyche-delic color, caught on because of it. (The color was awful, like in bad MGM musicals—so one may wonder about the quality of the trips.)

The new tribalism in the age of the media is not necessarily the enemy of commercialism; it is a direct outgrowth of commercialism and its ally, perhaps even its instrument. If a movie has enough clout, reviewers and columnists who were bored are likely to give it another chance, until on the second or third viewing, they discover that it affects them "viscerally"—and a big expensive movie is likely to do just that. *2001* is said to have caught on with youth (which can make it happen); and it's said that the movie will stone you—which is meant to be a recommendation. Despite a few dissident voices—I've heard it said, for example, that *2001* "gives you a bad trip because the visuals don't go with the music"—the promotion has been remarkably effective, with students. "The tribes" tune in so fast that college students thousands of miles apart "have heard" what a great trip *2001* is before it has even reached their city.

Using movies to go on a trip has about as much connection with the art of the film as using one of those Doris Day–Rock Hudson jobs for ideas on how to redecorate your home—an earlier way of stoning yourself. But it is relevant to an understanding of movies to try to separate out, for purposes of discussion at least, how we may personally *use* a film—to learn how to dress or how to speak more elegantly or how to make a grand entrance or even what kind of coffee maker we wish to purchase, or to take off from the movie into a roman-tic fantasy or a trip—from what makes it a good movie or a poor one, because, of course, we can *use* poor films as easily as good ones, perhaps *more* easily for such nonaesthetic purposes as shopping guides or aids to tripping.

V

We generally become interested in movies because we *enjoy* them and what we enjoy them for has little to do with what we think of as art. The movies we respond to, even in childhood, don't have the same values as the official culture supported at school and in the middle-class home. At the movies we get low life and high life, while David Susskind and the moralistic reviewers chastise us for not patronizing what they think we should, "realistic" movies that would be good for us—like *A Raisin in the Sun*, where we could learn the lesson that a Negro family can be as dreary as a white family. Movie audiences will take a lot of garbage, but it's pretty hard to make us queue up for pedagogy. At the movies we want a different kind of truth, something that surprises us and registers with us as funny or accurate or maybe amazing, maybe even amazingly beautiful. We get little things even in mediocre and terrible movies—José Ferrer sipping his booze through a straw in *Enter Laughing*, Scott Wilson's hard scary all-American-boy-you-can't-reach face cutting through the pretensions of *In Cold Blood* with all its fancy bleak cinematography. We got, and still have embedded in memory, Tony Randall's surprising depth of feeling in *The Seven Faces of Dr. Lao*, Keenan Wynn and Moyna Macgill in the lunch-counter sequence of *The Clock*, John W. Bubbles on the dance floor in *Cabin in the Sky*, the inflection Gene Kelly gave to the line, "I'm a rising young man" in *DuBarry was a Lady*, Tony Curtis saying "avidly" in *Sweet Smell of Success*. Though the director may have been responsible for releasing it, it's the human material we react to most and remember longest. The art of the performers stays fresh for us, their beauty as beautiful as ever. There are so many kinds of things we get—the hangover sequence wittily designed for the CinemaScope screen in *The Tender Trap*, the atmosphere of the newspaper offices in *The Luck of Ginger Coffey*, the automat gone mad in *Easy Living*. Do we need to lie and shift things to false terms—like those who have to say Sophia Loren is a great actress as if her *acting* had made her a star? Wouldn't we rather watch her than better actresses because she's so incredibly charming and because she's probably the greatest model the world has ever known? There are great moments—Angela Lansbury singing "Little Yellow Bird" in *Dorian Gray*. (I don't think I've ever had a friend who didn't also treasure that girl and that song.) And there are absurdly right little moments—in *Saratoga Trunk* when Curt Bois says to Ingrid Bergman, "You're very beautiful," and she says, "Yes, isn't it lucky?" And those things have closer relationships to art than what the schoolteachers told us was true and beautiful. Not that the works we studied in school weren't often great (as we discovered *later*) but that what the teachers told us to admire them for (and if current texts are any indication, are still telling students to admire them for) was generally so false and prettified and moralistic that what might have been moments of pleasure in them, and what might have been cleansing in them, and subversive, too, had been coated over.

Because of the photographic nature of the medium and the cheap admission prices, movies took their impetus not from the desiccated imitation European high culture, but from the peep show, the Wild West show, the music hall, the comic strip—from what was coarse and common. The early Chaplin two-reelers still look surprisingly lewd, with bathroom jokes and drunkenness and hatred of work and proprieties. And the Western shoot-'em-ups certainly weren't the schoolteachers' notions of art—which in my school days, ran more to didactic poetry and "perfectly proportioned" statues and which over the years have progressed through nice stories to "good taste" and "excellence"— which may be more poisonous than homilies and dainty figurines because then you had a clearer idea of what you were up against and it was easier to fight. And this, of course, is what we were running away from when we went to the movies. All week we longed for Saturday afternoon and sanctuary—the anonymity and impersonality of sitting in a theater, just enjoying ourselves, not having to be responsible, not having to be "good." Maybe you just want to look at people on the screen and know they're not looking back at you, that they're not going to turn on you and criticize you.

Perhaps the single most intense pleasure of moviegoing is this non-aesthetic one of escaping from the responsibilities of having the proper responses required of us in our official (school) culture. And yet this is probably the best and most common basis for developing an aesthetic sense because responsibility to pay attention and to appreciate is anti-art, it makes us too anxious for pleasure, too bored for response. Far from supervision and official culture, in the darkness at the movies where nothing is asked of us and we are left alone, the liberation from duty and constraint allows us to develop our own aesthetic responses. Unsupervised enjoyment is probably not the only kind there is but it may feel like the only kind. Irresponsibility is part of the pleasure of all art; it is the part the schools cannot recognize. I don't like to buy "hard tickets" for a "road show" movie because I hate treating a movie as an occasion. I don't want to be pinned down days in advance; I enjoy the casualness of moviegoing—of going in when I feel like it, when I'm in the mood for a movie. It's the feeling of freedom from respectability we have always enjoyed at the movies that is carried to an extreme by American International Pictures and the Clint Eastwood Italian Westerns; they are stripped of cultural values. We may want more from movies than this negative virtue but we know the feeling from childhood moviegoing when we loved the gamblers and pimps and the cons' suggestions of muttered obscenities as the guards walked by. The appeal of movies was in the details of crime and high living and wicked cities and in the language of toughs and urchins; it was in the dirty smile of the city girl who lured the hero away from Janet Gaynor. What draws us to movies in the first place, the opening into other, forbidden or surprising, kinds of experience, and the vitality and corruption and irreverence of that experience are so direct and immediate and have so little connection with what we have been taught is art that many people feel more secure, feel that their tastes are becoming more cultivated when they begin to *appreciate* foreign films. One foundation executive told me that he was quite upset that his teen-agers had chosen to go to *Bonnie and Clyde* rather than with him to *Closely Watched Trains*. He took it as a sign of lack of maturity. I think his kids made an honest choice, and not only because *Bonnie and Clyde* is the better movie, but because it is closer to us, it has some of the qualities of direct involvement that make us care about movies. But it's understandable that it's easier for us, as Americans, to see *art* in foreign films than in our own, because of how we, as Americans, think of art. Art is still what teachers and ladies and foundations believe in, it's civilized and refined, cultivated and serious, cultural, beautiful, European, Oriental: it's what America isn't, and it's especially what American movies are not. Still, if those kids had chosen *Wild in the Streets* over *Closely Watched Trains* I would think that was a sound and honest choice, too, even though *Wild in the Streets* is in most ways a terrible picture. It connects with their lives in an immediate even if a grossly frivolous way, and if we don't go to movies for excitement, if, even as children, we accept the cultural standards of refined adults, if we have so little drive that we accept "good taste," then we will probably never really begin to care about movies at all. We will become like those people who "may go to American movies sometimes to relax" but when they want "a little more" from a movie, are delighted by how colorful and artistic Franco Zeffirelli's *The Taming of the Shrew* is, just as a couple of decades ago they were impressed by *The Red Shoes*, made by Powell and Pressburger, the Zeffirellis of their day. Or, if they like the cozy feeling of uplift to be had from mildly whimsical movies about timid people, there's generally a *Hot Millions* or something musty and faintly boring from Eastern Europe—one of those movies set in World War II but so remote from our ways of thinking that it seems to be set in World War I. Afterward, the moviegoer can feel as decent and virtuous as if he'd spent an evening visiting a deaf old friend of the family. It's a way of taking movies back into the approved culture of the schoolroom—into gentility—and the voices of schoolteachers and reviewers rise up to ask why America can't make such movies.

VI

Movie art is not the opposite of what we have always enjoyed in movies, it is not to be found in a return to that official high culture, it is what we have always found good in movies only more so. It's the subversive gesture carried further, the moments of excitement sustained longer and extended into new meanings. At best, the movie is totally informed by the kind of pleasure we have been taking from bits and pieces of movies. But we are so used to reaching out to the few good bits in a movie that we don't need formal perfection to be dazzled. There are so many arts and crafts that go into movies and there are so many things that can go wrong that they're not an art for purists. We want to experience that elation we feel when a movie (or even a performer in a movie) goes farther than we had expected and makes the leap successfully. Even a film like Godard's *Les Carabiniers*, hell to watch for the first hour, is exciting to think about after because its one good sequence, the long picture-postcard sequence near the end, is so incredible and so brilliantly prolonged. The picture has been crawling and stumbling along and then it climbs a high wire and walks it and keeps walking it until we're almost dizzy from admiration. The tight rope is rarely stretched so high in movies, but there must be a sense of tension somewhere in the movie, if only in a bit player's face, not just mechanical suspense, or the movie is just more hours down the drain. It's the rare movie we really *go* with, the movie that keeps us tense and attentive. We learn to dread Hollywood "realism" and all that it implies. When, in the dark, we concentrate our attention, we are driven frantic by events on the level of ordinary life that pass at the rhythm of ordinary life. That's the self-conscious striving for integrity of humorless, untalented people. When we go to a play we expect a heightened, stylized language; the dull realism of the streets is unendurably boring, though we may escape from the play to the nearest bar to listen to the same language with relief. Better life than art imitating life.

If we go back and think over the movies we've enjoyed—even the ones we knew were terrible movies while we enjoyed them—what we enjoyed in them, the little part that was good, had, in some rudimentary way, some freshness, some hint of style, some trace of beauty, some audacity, some craziness. It's there in the interplay between Burt Lancaster and Ossie Davis, or, in *Wild in the Streets*, in Diane Varsi rattling her tambourine, in Hal Holbrook's faint twitch when he smells trouble, in a few of Robert Thom's lines; and they have some relation to art though they don't look like what we've been taught is "quality." They have the joy of playfulness. In a mediocre or rotten movie, the good things may give the impression that they come out of nowhere; the better the movie, the more they seem to belong to the world of the movie.

Without this kind of playfulness and the pleasure we take from it, art isn't art at all, it's something punishing, as it so often is in school where even artists' little *jokes* become leaden from explanation.

Keeping in mind that simple, good distinction that all art is entertainment but not all entertainment is art, it might be a good idea to keep in mind also that if a movie is said to be a work of art and you don't enjoy it, the fault may be in you, but it's probably in the movie. Because of the money and advertising pressures involved, many reviewers discover a fresh masterpiece every week, and there's that cultural snobbery, that hunger for respectability that determines the selection of the even bigger annual masterpieces. In foreign movies what is most often mistaken for "quality" is an imitation of earlier movie art or a derivation from respectable, approved work in the other arts—like the demented, suffering painter-hero of *Hour of the Wolf* smearing his lipstick in a facsimile of expressionist anguish. Kicked in the ribs, the press says "art" when "ouch" would be more appropriate. When a director is said to be an artist (generally on the basis of earlier work which the press failed to recognize) and especially when he picks artistic subjects like the pain of creation, there is a tendency to acclaim his new bad work. This way the press, in trying to make up for its past mistakes, manages to be wrong all the time. And so a revenge-of-a-sour-virgin movie like Truffaut's *The Bride Wore Black* is treated respectfully as if it somehow revealed an artist's sensibility in every frame. Reviewers who would laugh at Lana Turner going through her *femme fatale* act in another Ross Hunter movie swoon when Jeanne Moreau casts significant blank looks for Truffaut.

In American movies what is most often mistaken for artistic quality is box-office success, especially if it's combined with a genuflection to importance; then you have "a movie the industry can be proud of" like *To Kill a Mockingbird* or such Academy Award winners as *West Side Story*, *My Fair Lady*, or *A Man for All Seasons*. Fred Zinnemann made a fine modern variant of a Western, *The Sundowners*, and hardly anybody saw it until it got on television; but *A Man for All Seasons* had the look of prestige and the press felt honored to praise it. I'm not sure most movie reviewers consider what they honestly enjoy as being central to criticism. Some at least appear to think that that would be relying too much on their own tastes, being too personal instead of being "objective"— relying on the readymade terms of cultural respectability and on consensus judgment (which, to a rather shocking degree, can be arranged by publicists creating a climate of importance around a movie). Just as movie directors, as they age, hunger for what was meant by respectability in their youth, and aspire to prestigious cultural properties so, too, the movie press longs to be elevated in terms of the cultural values of their old high schools. And so they, along with the industry, applaud ghastly "tour-de-force" performances, movies based on "distinguished" stage successes or prizewinning novels, or movies that are "worthwhile," that make a "contribution"—"serious" messagy movies. This often involves praise of bad movies, of dull movies, or even the praise in good movies of what was worst in them.

This last mechanism can be seen in the honors bestowed on *In the Heat of the Night*. The best thing in the movie is that high comic moment when Poitier says, "I'm a police officer," because it's a reversal of audience expectations and we laugh in delighted relief that the movie is not going to be another self-righteous, self-congratulatory exercise in the gloomy old Stanley Kramer tradition. At that point the audience sparks to life. The movie is fun largely because of the amusing central idea of a black Sherlock Holmes in a Tom and Jerry cartoon of reversals. Poitier's color is used for comedy instead of for that extra dimension of irony and pathos that made movies like *To Sir with Love* unbearably sentimental. He doesn't really play the super sleuth very well: he's much too straight even when spouting the kind of higher scientific nonsense about right-handedness and left-handedness that would have kept Basil Rathbone in an ecstasy of clipped diction, blinking eyes and raised eyebrows. Like Bogart in *Beat the Devil* Poitier doesn't seem to be in on the joke. But Rod Steiger compensated with a comic performance that was even funnier for being so unexpected—not only from Steiger's career which had been going in other directions, but after the apparently serious opening of the film. The movie was, however, praised by the press as if it had been exactly the kind of picture that the audience was so relieved to discover it wasn't going to be (except in its routine melodramatic sequences full of fake courage and the climaxes such as Poitier slapping a rich white Southerner or being attacked by white thugs; except that is, in its worst parts). When I saw it, the audience, both black and white, enjoyed the joke of the fast-witted, hyper-educated black detective explaining matters to the backward, blundering Southern-chief-of-police slob. This racial joke is far more open and inoffensive than the usual "irony" of Poitier being so good and so black. For once it's *funny* (instead of embarrassing) that he's so superior to everybody.

In the Heat of the Night isn't in itself a particularly important movie; amazingly alive photographically, it's an entertaining, somewhat messed-up comedy-thriller. The director Norman Jewison destroys the final joke when Steiger plays redcap to Poitier by infusing it with tender feeling, so it comes out sickly sweet, and it's too bad that a whodunit in which the whole point is the demonstration of the Negro detective's ability to unravel what the white man can't, is never clearly unraveled. Maybe it needed a Negro super director. (The picture might have been more than just a lively whodunit if the detective had proceeded to solve the crime not by "scientific" means but by an understanding of relationships in the South that the white chief of police didn't have.) What makes it interesting for my purposes here is that the audience enjoyed the movie for the vitality of its surprising playfulness, while the industry congratulated itself because the film was "hard-hitting"—that is to say, it flirted with seriousness and spouted warm, worthwhile ideas.

Those who can accept *In the Heat of the Night* as the socially conscious movie that the industry pointed to with pride can probably also go along with the way the press attacked Jewison's subsequent film, *The Thomas Crown Affair*, as trash and a failure. One could even play the same game that was played on *In the Heat of the Night* and convert the *Crown* trifle into a sub-fascist exercise because, of course, Crown, the superman, who turns to crime out of boredom, is the crooked son of *The Fountainhead*, out of Raffles. But that's taking glossy summer-evening fantasies much too seriously: we haven't had a junior executive's fantasy-life movie for a long time and to attack this return of the worldly gentlemen-thieves genre of Ronald Colman and William Powell *politically* is to fail to have a sense of humor about the little romantic-adolescent fascist lurking in most of us. Part of the fun of movies is that they allow us to see how silly many of our fantasies are and how widely they're shared. A light romantic entertainment like *The Thomas Crown Affair*, trash undisguised, is the kind of chic crappy movie which (one would have thought) nobody could be fooled into thinking was art. Seeing it is like lying in the sun flicking through fashion magazines and, as we used to say, feeling rich and beautiful beyond your wildest dreams.

But it isn't easy to come to terms with what one enjoys in films, and if an older generation was persuaded to *dismiss* trash, now a younger generation, with the press and the schools in hot pursuit, has begun to talk about trash as if it were really very serious art. College newspapers and the new press all across the country are full of a hilarious new form of scholasticism, with students using their education to cook up impressive reasons for enjoying very simple, traditional dishes. Here is a communication from Cambridge to a Boston paper:

To the Editor:
The Thomas Crown Affair is fundamentally a film about faith between people. In many ways, it reminds me of a kind of updated old fable, or tale, about an ultimate test of faith. It is a film about a love affair (note the title), with a subplot of a bank robbery, rather than the reverse. The subtlety of the film is in the way the

external plot is used as a matrix to develop serious motifs, much in the same way that the *Heat of the Night* functioned.

Although Thomas Crown is an attractive and fascinating character, Vicki is the protagonist. Crown is consistent, predictable: he courts personal danger to feel superior to the system of which he is a part, and to make his otherwise overly comfortable life more interesting. Vicki is caught between two opposing elements within her, which, for convenience, I would call masculine and feminine. In spite of her glamour, at the outset she is basically masculine, in a man's type of job, ruthless, after prestige and wealth. But Crown looses the female in her. His test is a test of her femininity. The masculine responds to the challenge. Therein lies the pathos of her final revelation. Her egocentrism had not yielded to his.

In this psychic context, the possibility of establishing faith is explored. The movement of the film is towards Vicki's final enigma. Her ambivalence is commensurate with the increasing danger to Crown. The suspense lies in how she will respond to her dilemma, rather than whether Crown will escape.

I find *The Thomas Crown Affair* to be a unique and haunting film, superb in its visual and technical design, and fascinating for the allegorical problem of human faith.

The Thomas Crown Affair is pretty good trash, but we shouldn't convert what we enjoy it for into false terms derived from our study of the other arts. That's being false to what we enjoy. If it was priggish for an older generation of reviewers to be ashamed of what they enjoyed and to feel they had to be contemptuous of popular entertainment, it's even more priggish for a new movie generation to be so proud of what they enjoy that they use their education to try to place trash within the acceptable academic tradition. What the Cambridge boy is doing is a more devious form of that elevating and falsifying of people who talk about Loren as a great actress instead of as a gorgeous, funny woman. Trash doesn't belong to the academic tradition, and that's part of the *fun* of trash—that you know (or *should* know) that you don't have to take it seriously, that it was never meant to be any more than frivolous and trifling and entertaining.

It's appalling to read solemn academic studies of Hitchcock or von Sternberg by people who seem to have lost sight of the primary reason for seeing films like *Notorious* or *Morocco*—which is that they were not intended solemnly, that they were playful and inventive and faintly (often deliberately) absurd. And what's good in them, what relates them to art, is that playfulness and absence of solemnity. There is talk now about von Sternberg's technique—his use of light and decor and detail—and he is, of course, a kitsch master in these areas, a master of studied artfulness and pretty excess. Unfortunately, some students take this technique as proof that his films are works of art, once again, I think, falsifying what they really respond to—the satisfying romantic glamour of his very pretty trash. *Morocco* is great trash, and movies are so rarely great art, that if we cannot appreciate great *trash*, we have very little reason to be interested in them. The kitsch of an earlier era—even the best kitsch—does not become art, though it may become camp. Von Sternberg's movies became camp even while he was still making them, because as the romantic feeling went out of his own trash—when he became so enamored of his own pretty effects that he turned his human material into blank, affectless pieces of decor—his absurd trashy style was all there was. We are now told in respectable museum publications that in 1932 a movie like *Shanghai Express* "was completely misunderstood as a mindless adventure" when indeed it was completely *understood* as a mindless adventure. And enjoyed as a mindless adventure. It's a peculiar form of movie madness crossed with academicism, this lowbrowism masquerading as highbrowism, eating a candy bar and cleaning an "allegorical problem of human faith" out of your teeth. If we always wanted works of complexity and depth we wouldn't be going to movies about glamorous thieves and seductive women who sing in cheap cafés, and if we loved *Shanghai Express* it wasn't for its mind but for the glorious sinfulness of Dietrich informing Clive Brook that, "It took more than one man to change my name to Shanghai Lily" and for the villainous Oriental chieftain (Warner Oland!) delivering the classic howler, "The white woman stays with me."

If we don't deny the pleasures to be had from certain kinds of trash and accept *The Thomas Crown Affair* as a pretty fair example of entertaining trash, then we may ask if a piece of trash like this has any relationship to art. And I think it does. Steve McQueen gives probably his most glamorous, fashionable performance yet, but even enjoying him as much as I do, I wouldn't call his performance art. It's artful, though, which is exactly what is required in this kind of vehicle—and if he had been luckier, if the script had provided what it so embarrassingly lacks, the kind of sophisticated dialogue—the sexy shop-talk—that writers like Jules Furthman and William Faulkner provided for Bogart, if the director Norman Jewison had Lubitsch's lightness of touch, McQueen might be acclaimed as a suave, "polished" artist. Even in this flawed setting, there's a self-awareness in his performance that makes his elegance funny. And Haskell Wexler, the cinematographer, lets go with a whole bag of tricks, flooding the screen with his delight in beauty, shooting all over the place, and sending up the material. And Pablo Ferro's games with the split screen at the beginning are such conscious, clever games designed to draw us in to watch intently what is of no great interest. What gives this trash a lift, what makes it entertaining is clearly that some of those involved, knowing of course that they were working on a silly shallow script and a movie that wasn't about anything of consequence, used the chance to have a good time with it. If the director, Norman Jewison, could have built a movie instead of putting together a patchwork of sequences, *Crown* might have had a chance to be considered a movie in the class and genre of Lubitsch's *Trouble in Paradise*. It doesn't come near that because to transform this kind of kitsch, to make art of it, one needs that unifying grace, that formality and charm that a Lubitsch could sometimes provide. Still, even in this movie we get a few grace notes in McQueen's playfulness, and from Wexler and Ferro. Working on trash, feeling free to play, can loosen up the actors and craftsmen just as seeing trash can liberate the spectator. And as we don't get this playful quality of art much in movies except in trash, we might as well relax and enjoy it freely for what it is. I don't trust anyone who doesn't admit having at some time in his life enjoyed trashy American movies; I don't trust *any* of the tastes of people who were born with such good taste that they didn't need to find their way through trash.

There is a moment in *Children of Paradise* when the rich nobleman (Louis Salou) turns on his mistress, the pearly plebeian Garance (Arletty). He complains that in all their years together he has never had her love, and she replies, "You've got to leave something for the poor." We don't ask much from movies, just a little something that we can call our own. Who at some point hasn't set out dutifully for that fine foreign film and then ducked into the nearest piece of American trash? We're not only educated people of taste, we're also common people with common feelings. And our common feelings are not all *bad*. You hoped for some aliveness in that trash that you were pretty sure you wouldn't get from the respected "art film." You had long since discovered that you wouldn't get it from certain kinds of American movies, either. The industry now is taking a neo-Victorian tone, priding itself on its (few) "good, clean" movies—which are always its worst movies because almost nothing can break through the smug surfaces, and even performers' talents become cute and cloying. The lowest action trash is preferable to wholesome family entertainment. When you clean them up, when you make movies respectable, you kill them. The wellspring of their *art*, their greatness, is in not being respectable.

VII

Does trash corrupt? A nutty Puritanism still flourishes in the arts, not just in the schoolteachers' approach of wanting art to be "worthwhile," but in the higher reaches of the academic life with those ideologues who denounce us for enjoying trash as if this enjoyment took us away from the really disturbing, angry new art of our time and somehow destroyed us. If we had to *justify* our trivial silly pleasures, we'd have a hard time. How could we possibly *justify* the fun of getting to know some people in movie after movie, like Joan Blondell, the brassy girl with the heart of gold, or waiting for the virtuous, tiny, tiny-featured heroine to say her line so we could hear the riposte of her tough, wisecracking girlfriend (Iris Adrian was my favorite). Or, when the picture got too monotonous, there would be the song interlude, introduced "atmospherically" when the cops and crooks were both in the same never-neverland nightclub and everything stopped while a girl sang. Sometimes it would be the most charming thing in the movie, like Dolores Del Rio singing "You Make Me That Way" in *International Settlement;* sometimes it would drip with maudlin meaning, like "Oh Give Me Time for Tenderness" in *Dark Victory* with the dying Bette Davis singing along with the chanteuse. The pleasures of this kind of trash are not intellectually defensible. But why should pleasure need justification? Can one demonstrate that trash desensitizes us, that it prevents people from enjoying something better, that it limits our range of aesthetic response? Nobody I know of has provided such a demonstration. Do even Disney movies or Doris Day movies do us lasting harm? I've never known a person I thought had been harmed by them, though it does seem to me that they affect the tone of a culture, that perhaps—and I don't mean to be facetious— they may poison us collectively though they don't injure us individually. There are women who want to see a world in which everything is pretty and cheerful and in which romance triumphs (*Barefoot in the Park, Any Wednesday*); families who want movies to be an innocuous inspiration, a good example for the children (*The Sound of Music, The Singing Nun*); couples who want the kind of folksy blue humor (*A Guide for the Married Man*) that they still go to Broadway shows for. These people are the reason slick, stale, rotting pictures make money; they're the reason so few pictures are any good. And in that way, this terrible conformist culture does affect us all. It certainly cramps and limits opportunities for artists. But that isn't what generally gets attacked as trash, anyway. I've avoided using the term "harmless trash" for movies like *The Thomas Crown Affair* because that would put me on the side of the angels—against "harmful trash," and I don't honestly know what that is. It's common for the press to call cheaply made, violent action movies "brutalizing" but that tells us less about any actual demonstrable effects than about the finicky tastes of the reviewers —who are often highly appreciative of violence in more expensive and "artistic" settings such as *Petulia.* It's almost a class prejudice, this assumption that crudely made movies, movies without the look of art, are bad for people.

If there's a little art in good trash and sometimes even in poor trash, there may be more trash than is generally recognized in some of the most acclaimed "art" movies. Such movies as *Petulia* and *2001* may be no more than trash in the latest, up-to-the-minute guises, using "artistic techniques" to give trash the look of art. The serious art look may be the latest fashion in *expensive* trash. All that "art" may be what prevents pictures like these from being *enjoyable* trash; they're not honestly crummy, they're very fancy and they take their crummy ideas seriously.

I have rarely seen a more disagreeable, a more dislikable (or a bloodier) movie than *Petulia* and I would guess that its commercial success represents a triumph of publicity—and not the simple kind of just taking ads. It's a very strange movie and people may, of course, like it for all sorts of reasons, but I think many may dislike it as I do and still feel they should be impressed by it; the educated and privileged may now be more susceptible to the mass media than the larger public—they're certainly easier to reach. The publicity about Richard Lester as an artist has been gaining extraordinary momentum ever since *A Hard Day's Night*. A critical success that is also a hit makes the director a genius; he's a magician who made money out of art. The media are in ravenous competition for ever bigger stories, for "trend" pieces and editorial essays, because once the process starts it's considered news. If Lester is "making the scene" a magazine that hasn't helped to build him up feels it's been scooped. *Petulia* is the come-dressed-as-the-sick-soul-of-America-party and in the opening sequence the guests arrive—rich victims of highway accidents in their casts and wheel chairs, like the spirit of '76 coming to opening night at the opera. It's science-horror fiction—a garish new world with charity balls at which you're invited to "Shake for Highway Safety."

Lester picked San Francisco for his attack on America just as in *How I Won the War* he picked World War II to attack war. That is, it looks like a real frontal attack on war itself if you attack the war that many people consider a just war. But then he concentrated not on the issues of that war but on the class hatreds of British officers and men—who were not engaged in defending London or bombing Germany but in building a cricket pitch in Africa. In *Petulia*, his hate letter to America, he relocates the novel, shifting the locale from Los Angeles to San Francisco, presumably, again, to face the big challenge by showing that even the best the country has to offer is rotten. But then he ducks the challenge he sets for himself by making San Francisco look like Los Angeles. And if he must put carnival barkers in Golden Gate Park and invent Sunday excursions for children to Alcatraz, if he must invent such caricatures of epicene expenditure and commercialism as bizarrely automated motels and dummy television sets, if he must provide his own ugliness and hysteria and lunacy and use filters to destroy the city's beautiful light, if, in short, he must falsify America in order to make it appear hateful, what is it he really hates? He's like a crooked cop framing a suspect with trumped-up evidence. We never find out *why*: he's too interested in making a flashy case to examine what he's doing. And reviewers seem unwilling to ask questions which might expose them to the charge that they're *still* looking for meaning instead of, in the new cant, just reacting to images—such questions as why does the movie keep juxtaposing shots of bloody surgery with shots of rock groups like the Grateful Dead or Big Brother and the Holding Company and shots of the war in Vietnam. What are these little montages supposed to do to us—make us feel that even the hero (a hard-working life-saving surgeon) is implicated in the war and that somehow contemporary popular music is also allied to destruction and death? (I thought only the moralists of the Soviet Union believed that.) The images of *Petulia* don't make valid connections, they're joined together for shock and excitement, and I don't believe in the brilliance of a method which equates hippies, war, surgery, wealth, Southern decadents, bullfights, etc. Lester's mix is almost as fraudulent as *Mondo Cane*; *Petulia* exploits any shocking material it can throw together to give false importance to a story about Holly Golightly and The Man in the Gray Flannel Suit. The jagged glittering mosaic style of *Petulia* is an armor protecting Lester from an artist's task; this kind of "style" no longer fools people so much in writing but it knocks them silly in films.

Movie directors in trouble fall back on what they love to call "personal style"—though how impersonal it often is can be illustrated by *Petulia*—which is not edited in the rhythmic, modulations-of-graphics style associated with Lester (and seen most distinctively in his best-edited, though not necessarily best film, *Help!*) but in the style of the movie surgeon, Anthony Gibbs, who acted as chopper on it, and who gave it the same kind of scissoring which he had used on *The Loneliness of the Long Distance Runner* and in his rescue operation on *Tom Jones*. This is, in much of *Petulia*, the most insanely obvious method of cutting film ever devised; keep the audience jumping with cuts, juxtapose startling images, anything for effectiveness, just make it *brilliant*—with the director taking, apparently, no responsibilty for the *implied* connections. (The editing style is derived from Alain Resnais, and though it's a debatable style in his films, he uses it responsibly not just opportunistically.)

Richard Lester, the director of *Petulia*, is a shrill scold in Mod clothes. Consider a sequence like the one in which the beaten-to-a-gruesome-pulp heroine is taken out to an ambulance, to the accompaniment of hippies making stupid, unfeeling remarks. It is embarrassingly reminiscent of the older people's comments about the youthful sub-pre-hippies of *The Knack*. Lester has simply shifted villains. Is he saying that America is so rotten that even our hippies are malignant? I rather suspect he is, but why? Lester has taken a fashionably easy way to attack America, and because of the war in Vietnam some people are willing to accept the bloody montages that make them feel we're all guilty, we're rich, we're violent, we're spoiled, we can't relate to each other, etc. Probably the director who made three celebrations of youth and freedom (*A Hard Day's Night*, *The Knack*, and *Help!*) is now desperate to expand his range and become a "serious" director, and this is the new look in seriousness.

It would be too easy to make fun of the familiar ingredients of trash—the kook heroine who steals a tuba (that's not like the best of Carole Lombard but like the worst of Irene Dunne), the vaguely impotent, meaninglessly handsome rotter husband, Richard Chamberlain (back to the rich, spineless weaklings of David Manners), and Joseph Cotten as one more insanely vicious decadent Southerner spewing out villainous lines. (Even Victor Jory in *The Fugitive Kind* wasn't much meaner.) What's terrible is not so much this feeble conventional trash as the director's attempts to turn it all into scintillating art and burning comment; what is really awful is the trash of his ideas and artistic effects.

Is there any art in this obscenely self-important movie? Yes, but in a format like this the few good ideas don't really shine as they do in simpler trash; we have to go through so much unpleasantness and showing-off to get to them. Lester should trust himself more as a director and stop the cinemagician stuff because there's good, tense direction in a few sequences. He got a good performance from George C. Scott and a sequence of postmarital discord between Scott and Shirley Knight that, although overwrought, is not so glaringly overwrought as the rest of the picture. It begins to suggest something interesting that the picture might have been about. (Shirley Knight should, however, stop fondling her hair like a miser with a golden hoard; it's time for her to get another prop.) And Julie Christie is extraordinary just to look at—lewd and anxious, expressive and empty, brilliantly faceted but with something central missing, almost as if there's no woman inside.

VIII

2001 is a movie that might have been made by the hero of *Blow-Up*, and it's fun to think about Kubrick really doing every dumb thing he wanted to do, building enormous science-fiction sets and equipment, never even bothering to figure out what he was going to do with them. Fellini, too, had gotten carried away with the Erector Set approach to moviemaking, but his big science-fiction construction, exposed to view at the end of *8½*, was abandoned. Kubrick never really made his movie either but he doesn't seem to know it. Some people like the American International Pictures stuff because it's rather idiotic and maybe some people love *2001* just because Kubrick did all that stupid stuff, acted out a kind of super sci-fi nut's fantasy. In some ways it's the biggest amateur movie of them all, complete even to the amateur-movie obligatory scene—the director's little daughter (in curls) telling daddy what kind of present she wants.

There was a little pre-title sequence in *You Only Live Twice* with an astronaut out in space that was in a looser, more free style than *2001*—a daring little moment that I think was more fun than all of *2001*. It had an element of the unexpected, of the shock of finding death in space lyrical. Kubrick is carried away by the idea. The secondary title of *Dr. Strangelove*, which we took to be satiric, *"How I learned to stop worrying and love the bomb,"* was not, it now appears, altogether satiric for Kubrick. *2001* celebrates the invention of tools of death, as an evolutionary route to a higher order of *nonhuman* life. Kubrick literally learned to stop worrying and love the bomb; he's become his own butt—the Herman Kahn of extraterrestrial games theory. The ponderous blurry appeal of the picture may be that it takes its stoned audience out of this world to a consoling vision of a graceful world of space, controlled by superior godlike minds, where the hero is reborn as an angelic baby. It has the dreamy somewhere-over-the-rainbow appeal of a new vision of heaven. *2001* is a celebration of cop-out. It says man is just a tiny nothing on the stairway to paradise, something better is coming, and it's all out of your hands anyway. There's an intelligence out there in space controlling your destiny from ape to angel, so just follow the slab. Drop up.

It's a bad, bad sign when a movie director begins to think of himself as a myth-maker, and this limp myth of a grand plan that justifies slaughter and ends with resurrection has been around before. Kubrick's story line—accounting for evolution by an extraterrestrial intelligence—is probably the most gloriously redundant plot of all time. And although his intentions may have been different, *2001* celebrates the *end of man*; those beautiful mushroom clouds at the end of *Strangelove* were no accident. In *2001, A Space Odyssey* death and life are all the same: no point is made in the movie of Gary Lockwood's death—the moment isn't even defined—and the hero doesn't discover that the hibernating scientists have become corpses. That's unimportant in a movie about the beauties of resurrection. Trip off to join the cosmic intelligence and come back a better mind. And as the trip in the movie is the usual psychedelic light show, the audience doesn't even have to worry about getting to Jupiter. They can go to heaven in Cinerama.

It isn't accidental that we don't care if the characters live or die; if Kubrick has made his people so uninteresting, it is partly because characters and individual fates just aren't big enough for certain kinds of big movie directors. Big movie directors become generals in the arts; and they want subjects to match their new importance. Kubrick has announced that his next project is *Napoleon*—which, for a movie director, is the equivalent of Joan of Arc for an actress. Lester's "savage" comments about affluence and malaise, Kubrick's inspirational banality about how we will become as gods through machinery, are big-shot show-business deep thinking. This isn't a new show-business phenomenon; it belongs to the genius tradition of the theater. Big entrepreneurs, producers, and directors who stage big spectacular shows, even designers of large sets have traditionally begun to play the role of visionaries and thinkers and men with answers. They get too big for art. Is a work of art possible if pseudoscience and the technology of moviemaking become more important to the "artist" than man? This is central to the failure of *2001*. It's a monumentally unimaginative movie: Kubrick, with his $750,000 centrifuge, and in love with gigantic hardware and control panels, is the Belasco of science fiction. The special effects—though straight from the drawing board—are good and big and awesomely, expensively detailed. There's a little more that's good in the movie, when Kubrick doesn't take himself too seriously—like the comic moment when the gliding space vehicles begin their Johann Strauss waltz; that is to say, when the director shows a bit of a sense of proportion about what he's doing, and sees things momentarily as comic—when the movie doesn't take itself with such idiot solemnity. The light-show trip is of no great distinction; compared to the work of experimental filmmakers like Jordan Belson, it's third-rate. If big film directors are to get credit for doing badly what others have been doing brilliantly for years with no money, just because they've put it on a big screen, then businessmen are greater than poets and theft is art.

IX

Part of the fun of movies is in seeing "what everybody's talking about," and if people are flocking to a movie, or if the press can con us into thinking that they are, then ironically, there is a sense in which we want to see it, even if we suspect we won't enjoy it, because we want to know what's going on. Even if it's the worst inflated pompous trash that is the most talked about (and it usually is) and even if that talk is manufactured, we want to see the movies because so many people fall for whatever is talked about that they make the advertisers' lies true. Movies absorb material from the culture and the other arts so fast that some films that have been widely *sold* become culturally and sociologically important whether they are good movies or not. Movies like *Morgan!* or *Georgy Girl* or *The Graduate*—aesthetically trivial movies which, however, because of the ways some people react to them, enter into the national blood-stream—become cultural and psychological equivalents of watching a political convention—to observe what's going on. And though this has little to do with the art of movies, it has a great deal to do with the appeal of movies.

An analyst tells me that when his patients are not talking about their personal hangups and their immediate problems they talk about the situations and characters in movies like *The Graduate* or *Belle de Jour* and they talk about them with as much personal involvement as about their immediate problems. I have elsewhere suggested that this way of reacting to movies as psychodrama used to be considered a pre-literate way of reacting but that now those considered "post-literate" are reacting like pre-literates. The high school and college students identifying with Georgy Girl or Dustin Hoffman's Benjamin are not that different from the stenographer who used to live and breathe with the Joan Crawford-working girl and worry about whether that rich boy would really make her happy—and considered her pictures "great." They don't see the movie as a movie but as part of the soap opera of their lives. The fan magazines used to encourage this kind of identification; now the *advanced* mass media encourage it, and those who want to sell to youth use the language of "just let it flow over you." The person who responds this way does not respond more freely but less freely and less fully than the person who is aware of what is well done and what badly done in a movie, who can accept some things in it and reject others, who uses all his senses in reacting, not just his emotional vulnerabilities.

Still, we care about what other people care about—sometimes because we want to know how far we've gotten from common responses—and if a movie is important to other people we're interested in it because of what it means to them, even if it doesn't mean much to us. *The Graduate*'s small triumph was to have domesticated alienation and the difficulty of communication, by making what Benjamin is alienated from a middle-class comic strip and making it absurdly evident that he has nothing to communicate—which is just what makes him an acceptable hero for the large movie audience. If he said anything or had any ideas, the audience would probably hate him. *The Graduate* isn't a *bad* movie, it's entertaining, though in a fairly slick way (the audience is just about programmed for laughs). What's surprising is that so many people take it so seriously. What's funny about the movie are the laughs on that dumb sincere boy who wants to talk about art in bed when the woman just wants to fornicate. But then the movie begins to pander to youthful narcissism, glorifying his innocence, and making the predatory (and now crazy) woman the villainess.

Commercially this works: the inarticulate dull boy becomes a romantic hero for the audience to project into with all those squishy and now conventional feelings of look, his parents don't communicate with him; look, he wants truth not sham, and so on. But the movie betrays itself and its own expertise, sells out its comic moments that click along with the rhythm of a hit Broadway show, to make the oldest movie pitch of them all—asking the audience to identify with the simpleton who is the latest version of the misunderstood teen-ager and the pure-in-heart boy next door. It's almost painful to tell kids who have gone to see *The Graduate* eight times that once was enough for you because you've already seen it eighty times with Charles Ray and Robert Harron and Richard Barthelmess and Richard Cromwell and Charles Farrell. How could you convince them that a movie that sells innocence is a very commercial piece of work when they're so clearly in the market to buy innocence? When *The Graduate* shifts to the tender awakenings of love, it's just the latest version of *David and Lisa*. *The Graduate* only wants to succeed and that's fundamentally what's the matter with it. There is a pause for a laugh after the mention of "Berkeley" that is an unmistakable sign of hunger for success; this kind of moviemaking shifts values, shifts focus, shifts emphasis, shifts everything for a sure-fire response. Mike Nichols' "gift" is that he lets the audience direct him; this is demagoguery in the arts.

Even the cross-generation fornication is standard for the genre. It goes back to Pauline Frederick in *Smouldering Fires*, and Clara Bow was at it with mama Alice Joyce's boyfriend in *Our Dancing Mothers*, and in the Forties it was *Mildred Pierce*. Even the terms are not different: in these movies the seducing adults are customarily sophisticated, worldly, and corrupt, the kids basically innocent, though not so humorless and blank as Benjamin. In its basic attitudes *The Graduate* is corny American; it takes us back to before *The Game of Love* with Edwige Feuillère as the sympathetic older woman and *A Cold Wind in August* with the sympathetic Lola Albright performance.

What's interesting about the success of *The Graduate* is sociological: the revelation of how emotionally accessible modern youth is to the same old manipulation. The recurrence of certain themes in movies suggests that each generation wants romance restated in slightly new terms, and of course it's one of the pleasures of movies as a popular art that they can answer this need. And yet, and yet—one doesn't expect an *educated* generation to be so soft on itself, much softer than the factory workers of the past who didn't go back over and over to the same movies, mooning away in fixation on themselves and thinking this fixation meant movies had suddenly become an art, and *their* art.

X

When you're young the odds are very good that you'll find something to enjoy in almost any movie. But as you grow more experienced, the odds change. I saw a picture a few years ago that was the sixth version of material that wasn't much to start with. Unless you're feebleminded, the odds get worse and worse. We don't go on reading the same kind of manufactured novels—pulp Westerns or detective thrillers, say—all of our lives, and we don't want to go on and on looking at movies about cute heists by comically assorted gangs. The problem with a popular art form is that those who want something more are in a hopeless minority compared with the millions who are always seeing it for the first time, or for the reassurance and gratification of seeing the conventions fulfilled again. Probably a large part of the older audience gives up movies for this reason—simply that they've seen it before. And probably this is why so many of the best movie critics quit. They're wrong when they blame it on the movies going bad; it's the odds becoming so bad, and they can no longer bear the many tedious movies for the few good moments and the tiny shocks of recognition. Some become too tired, too frozen in fatigue, to respond to what *is* new. Others who *do* stay awake may become too demanding for the young who are seeing it all for the first hundred times. The critical task is necessarily comparative, and younger people do not truly know what is new. And despite all the chatter about the media and how smart the young are, they're incredibly naïve about mass culture—perhaps *more* naïve than earlier generations (though I don't know why). Maybe watching all that television hasn't done so much for them as they seem to think; and when I read a young intellectual's appreciation of *Rachel, Rachel* and come to "the mother's passion for chocolate bars is a superb symbol for the second coming of childhood" I know the writer is still in his first childhood, and I wonder if he's going to come out of it.

One's moviegoing tastes and habits change—I still like in movies what I always liked but now, for example, I really want documentaries. After all the years of stale stupid acted-out stories, with less and less for me in them, I am desperate to know something, desperate for facts, for information, for faces of non-actors and for knowledge of how people live—for revelations, not for the little bits of show-business detail worked up for us by show-business minds who got them from the same movies we're tired of.

But the big change is in our *habits*. If we make any kind of decent, useful life for ourselves we have less need to run from it to those diminishing pleasures of the movies. When we go to the movies we want something good, something sustained, we don't want to settle just for a bit of something, because we have other things to do. If life at home is more interesting, why go to the movies? And the theaters frequented by true moviegoers—those perennial displaced persons in each city, the loners and the losers—depress us. Listening to them—and they are often more audible than the sound track—as they cheer the cons and jeer the cops, we may still share their disaffection, but it's not enough to keep us interested in cops and robbers. A little nose-thumbing isn't enough. If we've grown up at the movies we know that good work is continuous not with the academic, respectable tradition but with the glimpses of something good in trash, but we want the subversive gesture carried to the domain of discovery. Trash has given us an appetite for art.

1969

McCabe & Mrs. Miller

McCabe & Mrs. Miller is a beautiful pipe dream of a movie—a fleeting, almost diaphanous vision of what frontier life might have been. The film, directed by Robert Altman, and starring Warren Beatty as a small-time gambler and Julie Christie as an ambitious madam in the turn-of-the-century Northwest, is so indirect in method that it throws one off base. It's not much like other Westerns; it's not really much like other movies. We are used to movie romances, but this movie is a figment of the romantic imagination. Altman builds a Western town as one might build a castle in the air—and it's inhabited. His stock company of actors turn up quietly in the new location, as if they were part of a floating crap game. Altman's most distinctive quality as a director here, as in *M*A*S*H*, is his gift for creating an atmosphere of living interrelationships and doing it so obliquely that the viewer can't quite believe it—it seems almost a form of effrontery. He has abandoned the theatrical convention that movies have generally clung to of introducing the characters and putting tags on them. Though Altman's method is a step toward a new kind of movie naturalism, the technique may seem mannered to those who are put off by the violation of custom—as if he simply didn't want to be straightforward about his storytelling. There are slight losses in his method—holes that don't get filled and loose ends that we're used to having tied up—but these losses (more like temporary inconveniences, really) are, I think, inseparable from Altman's best qualities and from his innovative style.

There's a classical-enough story, and it's almost (though not quite) all there, yet without the usual emphasis. The fact is that Altman is dumping square conventions that don't work anymore: the spelled-out explanations of motive and character, the rhymed plots, and so on—all those threadbare remnants of the "well-made" play which American movies have clung to. He can't be straightforward in the old way, because he's improvising meanings and connections, trying to find his movie in the course of making it—an incredibly risky procedure under modern union conditions. But when a director has a collaborative team he can count on, and when his instinct and his luck both hold good, the result can be a *McCabe & Mrs. Miller*. The classical story is only a thread in the story that Altman is telling. Like the wartime medical base in *M*A*S*H*, the West here is the life that the characters are part of. The people who drop in and out and the place—a primitive mining town—are not just background for McCabe and Mrs. Miller; McCabe and Mrs. Miller are simply the two most interesting people in the town, and we catch their stories, in glimpses, as they interact with the other characters and each other. But it isn't a slice-of-life method, it's a peculiarly personal one—delicate, elliptical. The picture seems to move in its own quiet time, and the faded beauty of the imagery works a spell. Lives are picked up and let go, and the sense of how little we know about them becomes part of the texture; we generally know little about the characters in movies, but since we're assured that that little is all we need to know and thus all there is to know, we're not bothered by it. Here we seem to be witnesses to a vision of the past—overhearing bits of anecdotes, seeing the irrational start of a fight, recognizing the saloon and the whorehouse as the centers of social life. The movie is so affecting it leaves one rather dazed. At one point, cursing himself for his inability to make Mrs. Miller understand the fullness of his love for her, McCabe mutters. "I got poetry in me. I do. I got poetry in me. Ain't gonna try to put it down on paper . . . got sense enough not to try." What this movie reveals is that there's poetry in Robert Altman and he *is* able to put it on the screen. Emotionally far more complex than *M*A*S*H*, *McCabe & Mrs. Miller* is the work of a more subtle, more deeply gifted—more mysterious—intelligence than might have been guessed at from *M*A*S*H*.

The picture is testimony to the power of stars. Warren Beatty and Julie Christie have never been better, and they *are* the two most interesting people in the town. They seem to take over the screen by natural right—because we want to look at them longer and more closely. Altman brings them into focus so unobtrusively that it's almost as if we had sorted them out from the others by ourselves. Without rigid guidelines, we observe them differently, and as the story unfolds, Beatty and Christie reveal more facets of their personalities than are apparent in those star vehicles that sell selected aspects of the stars to us. Julie Christie is no longer the androgynous starlet of *Darling*, the girl one wanted to see on the screen not for her performances but because she was so great-looking that she was compelling on her own, as an original. She had the profile of a Cocteau drawing—tawdry-classical—and that seemed enough: who could expect her to act? I think this is the first time (except, perhaps, for some of the early scenes in *Doctor Zhivago*) that I've believed in her as an *actress*—a warm and intense one—and become involved in the role she was playing, instead of merely admiring her extraordinary opaque mask. In this movie, the Cocteau girl has her opium. She's a weird, hounded beauty as the junky madam Mrs. Miller—that great, fat underlip the only flesh on her, and her gaunt, emaciated face surrounded by frizzy ringlets. She's like an animal hiding in its own fur. Julie Christie has that gift that beautiful actresses sometimes have of suddenly turning ugly and of being even more fascinating because of the crossover. When her nose practically meets her strong chin and she gets the look of a harpy, the demonstration of the thin line between harpy and beauty makes the beauty more dazzling—it's always threatened. The latent qualities of the one in the other take the character of Mrs. Miller out of the realm of ordinary movie madams. It is the depth in her that makes her too much for the cocky, gullible McCabe; his inexpressible poetry is charming but too simple. An actor probably has to be very smart to play a showoff so sensitively; Beatty never overdoes McCabe's foolishness, the way a foolish actor would. It's hard to know what makes Beatty such a magnetic presence; he was that even early in his screen career, when he used to frown and loiter over a line of dialogue as if he hoped to find his character during the pauses. Now that he has developed pace and control, he has become just about as attractive a screen star as any of the romantic heroes of the past. He has an unusually comic romantic presence; there's a gleefulness in Beatty, a light that comes on when he's onscreen that says "Watch this—it's fun." McCabe pantomimes and talks to himself through much of this movie, complaining of himself to himself; his best lines are between him and us. Beatty carries off this tricky yokel form of soliloquy casually, with good-humored self-mockery. It's a fresh, ingenious performance; we believe McCabe when he says that Mrs. Miller is freezing his soul.

A slightly dazed reaction to the film is, I think, an appropriate one. Right from the start, events don't wait for the viewers' comprehension, as they do in most movies, and it takes a while to realize that if you didn't quite hear someone's words it's all right—that the exact words are often expendable, it's the feeling tone that matters. The movie is inviting, it draws you in, but at the opening it may seem unnecessarily obscure, perhaps too "dark" (at times it suggests a dark version of Sam Peckinpah's genial miss *The Ballad of Cable Hogue*), and later on it may seem insubstantial (the way Max Ophuls's *The Earrings of*

Madame de . . . seemed—to some—insubstantial, or Godard's *Band of Outsiders*). One doesn't quite know what to think of an American movie that doesn't pretend to give more than a partial view of events. The gaslight, the subdued, restful color, and Mrs. Miller's golden opium glow, Leonard Cohen's lovely, fragile, ambiguous songs, and the drifting snow all make the movie hazy and evanescent. Everything is in motion, and yet there is a stillness about the film, as if every element in it were conspiring to tell the same incredibly sad story: that the characters are lost in their separate dreams.

The pipe dreamer is, of course, Robert Altman. *McCabe & Mrs. Miller* seems so strange because, despite a great deal of noise about the art of film, we are unaccustomed to an intuitive, quixotic, essentially impractical approach to moviemaking, and to an exploratory approach to a subject, particularly when the subject is the American past. Improvising as the most gifted Europeans do has been the dream of many American directors, but few have been able to beat the economics of it. In the past few years, there have been breakthroughs, but only on sensational current subjects. Can an American director get by with a movie as personal as this—personal not as in "personal statement" but in the sense of giving form to his own feelings, some not quite defined, just barely suggested? A movie like this isn't made by winging it; to improvise in a period setting takes phenomenal discipline, but *McCabe & Mrs. Miller* doesn't look "disciplined," as movies that lay everything out for the audience do. Will a large enough American public accept American movies that are delicate and understated and searching—movies that don't resolve all the feelings they touch, that don't aim at leaving us *satisfied*, the way a three-ring circus satisfies? Or do we accept such movies only from abroad, and then only a small group of us—enough to make a foreign film a hit but not enough to make an American film, which costs more, a hit? A modest picture like *Claire's Knee* would probably have been a financial disaster if it had been made in this country, because it might have cost more than five times as much and the audience for it is relatively small. Nobody knows whether this is changing—whether we're ready to let American moviemakers grow up to become artists or whether we're doomed to more of those "hard-hitting, ruthlessly honest" American movies that are themselves illustrations of the crudeness they attack. The question is always asked, "Why aren't there American Bergmans and Fellinis?" Here is an American artist who has made a beautiful film. The question now is "Will enough people buy tickets?"

1971

Dwight Macdonald

Dwight Macdonald (1906–1982) was a widely read critic on the Left who edited the progressive magazine *Politics* and wrote political and cultural criticism for *Partisan Review* and *The New Yorker*. (He also popularized the word "middlebrow.") Macdonald exemplified the public intellectual who agrees to be pressed into service as a film critic while remaining dubious about the whole cult of cinema. He had two notable periods as a film critic: the first in his youth, when he was smitten by the silent classics of the 1920s, especially Eisenstein, and trusted wholly in montage as the identifying mark of film art; the second when, a graybeard, he served as *Esquire*'s monthly reviewer from 1960 to 1966 during the art-house, mise-en-scène heyday of Truffaut, Godard, Bergman, Fellini, Antonioni, and Kurosawa. Immensely readable, a true essayist, if overly dismissive at times of innovation, Macdonald was notorious among more zealous colleagues for failing to catch many of the new releases; perhaps he enjoyed too much his semi-amateur film critic status to compromise the pleasure with compulsive overwork. The essay on Fellini's *8½* shows him at his most appreciative and urbane.

8½

I can't say that Fellini has been one of my favorite directors. *The White Sheik* I thought crude compared to Antonioni's comparable tragicomedy about a similar milieu, *The Lady Without the Camellias*. For all its poetic realism, *La Strada* left a sentimental aftertaste, mostly because of the performance of Fellini's wife, Giulietta Masina, which was praised for just the quality that put me off: her miming, which recalled all too faithfully the original creators of the style—Langdon, Keaton and Chaplin. My favorite up to now has been *Cabiria* (1957), a Dickensian mixture of realism, pathos and comedy; Mrs. Fellini also played the lead, this time with more restraint. The much-admired *I Vitelloni* (1953) I've seen only on a tiny 16-millimeter screen; it looked good, but my eye isn't practiced enough to know how it would look full-size.* The also admired *La Dolce Vita* I thought sensationalized, inflated and cinematically conventional,

---

*I have seen it full-size since this was written and it *didn't* look good. I think it one of those historically important films like Visconti's *La Terra Trema*, Godard's *Breathless* and (possibly) Resnais' *Hiroshima, Mon Amour* which haven't worn well because their innovations have become commonplace—too successful, in a sense—while there isn't enough else in them to engage our interest today. The antidramatic naturalism which fifteen years ago was exciting in *I Vitelloni* has become so familiar that the film now looks pedestrian, faded.

despite some brilliant episodes which (like the unbrilliant ones) made their point before they were half over. And Fellini's episode in *Boccaccio 70* was even worse than De Sica's: a stertorous laboring of a theme—censors are secretly prurient—that was probably considered hackneyed by Menander. But now Fellini has made a movie that I can't see any way not to recognize as a masterpiece.

This portrait of the artist as a middle-aged man is the most brilliant, varied and entertaining movie I've seen since *Citizen Kane*. I saw it twice in as many weeks, and the second time I discovered many points that had escaped me in the first viewing, so headlong is its tempo, so fertile its invention. What I had found exciting the first time still seemed so, nor was I conscious of any *longueurs*, with two exceptions: the night visit to the tower (Guido's talk with Rosella merely verbalized what had already been shown to our eyes) and the scene in the car between Guido and Claudia (her "How big will my part be" would have been enough to make the point). A great deal is packed into every scene, like *Kane*: of well-observed detail; of visual pleasure; of fine acting in minor roles (Guido Alberti's The Producer, Edra's La Saraghina, Madeleine Lebeau's Actress). And finally, like *Kane*, it deals with large topics like art, society, sex, money, aging, pretense and hypocrisy—all that Trollope wrote about in *The Way We Live Now*—just the opposite of these cautious little (though not short) art films that lingeringly explore some tiny area of impingement between three undefined characters or, if the director feels in an epic mood, four.

The action, or Argument, is as simple as its development is complex. Guido (played by Marcello Mastroianni with style, humor and delicacy) is a famous director who has retreated to an Italian seaside health resort to avoid a breakdown and to finish the script of a spectacular of stupefying banality about the flight to another planet of the survivors of a nuclear war. The script is long overdue: a huge Canaveral-type launching tower has been erected on the beach—it cost a real $140,000 in the real film, we are told by the Joseph E. Levine handout which is also real, relatively—cast, producer, technicians, everybody is waiting around while costs tick along like a taxi meter as Guido tries to break through his Creative Block, and meanwhile to placate and if possible evade their persistent demands. His mistress arrives (a full-bodied, empty-headed soubrette right out of a Franz Lehar operetta—really wonderful performance by Sandra Milo) and is presently followed by his wife (Anouk Aimée manages to look astringent and attractive simultaneously), necessitating another series of evasions and placations that are all the more difficult because his relation to each is unsatisfactory since he is still, in middle age, trying to square the sexual circle: to possess without being possessed, to take without giving. His personal and professional lives are thus speeding toward catastrophe on parallel tracks. It happens. Mistress and wife finally clash in a scene of irretrievable social horror. The movie comes to smash at a huge publicity party the producer gives to force Guido's hand. Badgered by questions he can't answer, since the script is still hardly begun, Guido crawls under a buffet table and shoots himself. He springs back to life at once and begins to solve all his problems, emotional as well as cinematic, in a happy ending that has been widely deplored.

There are three kinds of reality in *8½*, and the film proceeds with constant shifting of gears between them. (Like *Marienbad*, but a secular version of that hieratic mystery: quick, humorous, jazzy, direct—you always know what gear you're in.) There is Guido's real present, as outlined above. There are his memories of his boyhood and of his dead parents. And there are his Walter Mitty daydreams of a harmonious realm of *luxe, calme, et volupté* in which all his problems are magically solved: the artist's world of creative fantasy. Its symbol is a beautiful young girl in white who keeps materializing and fading away throughout the film, and seems to be a kind of Muse. After his wife and his mistress have disastrously collided, Guido leans back in his café chair, closes his eyes (behind dark glasses), and revises the scene so that the wife compliments the mistress on her dress, and the two are presently waltzing together; since this works so well, Guido's editing goes all the way, and we have the lovely, and witty, harem fantasy, which poeticizes Freudian ideas about the libido even as it parodies them.

Everything flows in this protean movie, constantly shifting between reality, memory, and fantasy. Free association is its structural principle. A description of just what happens in two sequences may give some idea; I make no claim for detailed accuracy for these notes taken in the dark; they are merely what one viewer saw, or thought he saw. The first comes early in the film; the second covers the last half hour or so.

(1) A bedroom in a shabby hotel. Guido asks Carla, his mistress, to make up like a whore and go out into the corridor and come into the room as if to an unknown client. Carla: "Oh, good—we've never tried *that* before!" But she keeps spoiling the mood by chattering about her husband. (She's always trying to get Guido to give him a job: "He's serious, not pushy at all, that's his tragedy," she says in an earlier scene. "He knows more about Roman history than anybody. You'd like him.") Also by remarking, as Guido makes her up: "just like one of your actresses"; and, as she goes out, wrapped in a sheet, "I

don't think I'd like that kind of life, I'm a homebody, really." (Cf. Proust's Charlus trying to get the hard-working youth he's hired to whip him in the male brothel to admit he's really a brutal criminal—the young man is shocked, he's the only support of an invalid mother, he insists, to Charlus's disgust.) She spoils it completely when she comes in, flourishing a bottle of mineral water— "The landlady gave it to me for my stomach." It's a hopeless anticlimax when she flings wide the sheet. . . . Guido sleeps while Carla reads a comic book; both sleep. . . . A black-robed woman, seen from behind, appears; Guido wakes; she gestures to him to follow. . . . He is in a great weedy cemetery bounded by two long lines of high crumbling walls in which are niches and tombs. He talks with his dead father and mother (the woman in black). His father complains, in a reasonable tone and with precise gestures, as one explains why a new flat won't do, that his tomb is uncomfortably cramped; Guido listens sympathetically. . . . The producer and his assistant appear and complain to his parents that Guido is lazy and irresponsible; the parents agree he has always been a problem. . . . Guido helps his father back into his grave, tenderly, a dutiful son. He kisses his mother goodbye, she suddenly embraces him passionately and kisses him on the mouth, turning into a younger woman (his wife, as we find later).

(2) Interior of a movie theatre, empty except for Guido, who is isolated with his contemptuous collaborator; lower down we see his wife with her sister and friends, and the producer with his entourage. Guido must at last choose the cast, from screen tests; no more stalling, the producer warns, I can make it tough for you if you force me to. Wife's party murmur approval, everybody glares at Guido. The critic-collaborator, sitting just behind him, begins again to tell him how stupid his ideas are. Guido listens courteously, as always, then (beginning of shortest fantasy-sequence) raises one finger. Two assistants take the critic by the arms, lead him into the aisle, put a black hood over his face, a rope around his neck, and hang him. Back to reality: shot of Guido with his collaborator, undamaged, still sitting behind him. Producer calls for projectionist to begin; screen is lit by a blazing rectangle of light that is switched off at once. Beginning of longest fantasy, which lasts to the end, with dreams inside dreams inside dreams; from now on, despite some misleading illusions of reality, we are inside Guido's head. The screen tests are not for parts in the science-fiction movie Guido is supposed to be making, but for roles in his own story, i.e., in the movie we have been watching: wife, mistress, La Saraghina, etc. The producer sees nothing strange, since he's now in Guido's head too, and keeps demanding that a choice be made. But Guido says they're all bad.

Only the originals will do, after all, since no matter how talented the massive actress who imitates La Saraghina, she isn't the real thing.

A man whispers to Guido, as he sits dejectedy watching the tests, that Claudia, whom he knew years ago as a young actress, wants to see him about a part. Guido follows him eagerly, is excited to find that Claudia (played by Claudia Cardinale) looks exactly like the Muse (also played by Cardinale) he has already encountered several times in mysterious and frustrating circumstances. He takes her for a night drive in his sports car to talk it over. The first thing she says is, "How big will my part be?" . . . Cut to a provincial town square, old houses facing each other, a baroque gateway closing one end, the whole giving the effect of an oblong room open to the sky: camera peers through the only window that is lit and we see Claudia the Muse, all in white, against white walls, setting a white table with fruit and wine—a lovely, poetic glimpse. (Gianni di Venanzo's photography alone would make *8½* worth seeing.) Guido and the other Claudia drive into the square, but now all the windows are dark—his Muse has fled before her earthly (and earthy) twin. Stopping the car, Guido tries to explain his troubles to Claudia. "It's because you don't know how to make love," she replies, with a smile implying she could teach him. No, you're wrong, he insists, a woman cannot change a man. "Then you brought me here, you cheated me, and there's no part for me?" "Yes, there's no part for you," he replies wearily, "and there's no movie." Suddenly they are blinded by the headlights of three cars that roar into the square, bearing the producer and his aides. The producer tells Guido he has decided to get things started with a big press conference and party at the launching tower tomorrow morning. They all get into the cars and drive off. . . .

The journalists and cast and guests are gathered at the tower on the beach; it is cold and windy. (Someone says, "You kept us waiting so long—look, it's almost winter.") Waiters behind long tables with elaborate foods and drinks. Guido arrives, tries to escape, is seized by the arms and dragged to the speakers' table, past a lineup of reporters shouting questions in various languages. Everybody surges up to the table—more questions, pleas, insults—skirts and tablecloths billow in the wind, which is getting stronger—bedlam, babel, a Mad Hatter's press conference. Guido refuses to say anything since he has not even cast the movie yet. Producer, venomous aside: "I'll break you, I'll see that you never make another picture, you're ruining me." Guido dives under the table, crawls along on hands and knees, people reach down to grab him, he pulls out a pistol, puts it to his temple, a loud report. . . .

Guido alone on the beach except for some workmen on the towers. "Take it down," he shouts up at them, "all of it." Collaborator-critic appears, Guido explains he's decided not to make the picture. "You're absolutely right," says the critic, "I respect you." They get into Guido's car, the critic drones on congratulating Guido on having the courage not to make a mediocre film "that will leave a mark on the sands of time like the deformed footprint of a cripple." As Guido starts to drive away, the magician from an earlier scene—an old friend who seems to have occult powers—appears in front of the car in his top hat and tails, his face made up dead white with red lips and darkened eyes like a clown, smiling his professional smile (manic yet gentle) and pointing with his wand. Guido looks out of the car and sees his father and mother, who wave to him, then Claudia the Muse, smiling and beckoning, then the others from his past and present, all dressed in white. (The critic is still explaining why it's impossible to create in this age—he cannot see these people.) Guido gets out of the car, takes up his director's bullhorn and begins to arrange everybody; he has decided to make an entirely different movie, about himself—his memories, his women, his creative problems—in short, the movie we have just seen. Like Prospero in another drama with a most implausible happy ending, he summons them all: parents, wife, mistress, producer, technicians, actors, the Muse Claudia, even himself as a boy who leads a gay little parade of musical clowns. And they all come, walking up from the sea, pouring down from the steps of the launching tower, linking hands with Guido and his wife in a long line that dances along a seawall to the tinny blare of the circus band. The last shot is of the ten-year-old Guido, dressed in his seminarian's uniform (now white instead of black), strutting along proudly in front of his band.

Most of the critics have objected to this finale as bogus, escapist, sentimental, a specious "solution" that is incongruous with what has gone before, a happy ending arbitrarily tacked on, etc. In a generally favorable review in *Sight and Sound*, for instance, Eric Rhode writes in solemn disapproval: "Both Guido and Fellini show themselves incapable of making a distinction between the truths of the mind and those of behavior. The self-reflective spirit can swiftly turn narcissistic, and although Guido may confront his inner world, he fails to confront his social obligations." Or, as a psychiatrist objected to me: "He has failed to integrate reality and fantasy." This is all true—no confronting of social obligations, no integration of the real and the unreal, and plenty of escapism. I didn't for a minute believe that Guido had changed: the reconciliation with his wife—he asks her if their marriage can't be "saved" and she replies, "I can try if you will help me"—was unintegrated fantasy, as was the affectionate kiss he gives his mistress. On the plane of real behavior, his wife will continue to be censorious, his mistress will continue to be vulgar, and he will continue to betray both of them and will still greedily try to get love without giving love. The most that has happened in the "real" world is that Guido has achieved some insight—"I am what I am and not what I want to be"—which may or may not influence his future behavior; probably not. But he has triumphed in the "unreal" world of fantasy, which for him is the real one, since it is there he creates. In the sphere of the imagination, he *has* faced up to his problems and resolved them, for there he has made a work of art that hangs together and is consistent with itself. (I could never understand why "art for art's sake" is usually sneered at—for what better sake?) All through *8½* Guido (and Fellini) are escaping from one kind of reality, but only in order to rush boldly and recklessly into another kind, the artist's kind. In this sense, the finale is consistent with what has gone before—and, in fact, its logical conclusion.

John Francis Lane wrote in a recent issue of *Sight and Sound*: "I'm afraid that however fond we may be of the director of *I Vitelloni* we are not really deeply concerned about his intellectual and sexual fetishes. Fellini has been too honest, too courageous, too sincere. He has made a film director's notebook, and I am not surprised that directors everywhere (even those who usually hate Fellini's films) love this picture." I think the implication of self-indulgent narcissism in the first sentence is wrong. Granted that, as Fellini was the first to insist ("more than a confession . . . my testament"), Guido is himself and *8½* is his own Life and Hard Times, I think the miracle is how tough-minded his autobiography is, how he has been able to see himself at a distance, neither self-sparing nor self-flagellating, a wonderful Latin moderation throughout, realistic and ironic. Guido's hat, for instance, clerical black but worn at a lady-killing slant and with a worldly twist, is a perfect symbol of Fellini's own ambivalent feelings about the Church. Or there is the clowning he often uses to preserve his humanity in the movie jungle, such as kneeling between the marble lions at the foot of the hotel's grand stairway, salaaming and ululating gibberish salutations to the producer making his stately descent. Nothing duller than someone else's fetishes and neuroses, agreed, but I think in *8½* Fellini has found the objective forms in which to communicate his subjective explorations.

A major theme of the film is aging, which obviously worries Fellini. He expresses it not in Bergmanesque symbols or narcissistic musings, but in episodes that arise naturally out of the drama: the elderly patients lining up for the curative waters; the senile cardinal; Guido's friend, the aging diplomat (who looks very much like him, with a decade or two added) who is divorcing his wife to marry one of his daughter's school friends and whom we see, doggedly jaunty, doing the twist with his nymphet fiancée, sweat pouring from a face set in an agonized grin; the aging actress who desperately cries out to Guido as he tries to escape politely: "I am a very passionate woman—you'll see!"; the magician reading the dowager's thoughts: "You would like to live another hundred years." One of the most sympathetic traits of Guido is the patience, gentleness, humor—the good manners of an old and tolerant culture—with which he responds to the reproaches of everybody around him, reproaches all the more irritating because they are justified. He is less patient, however, when the nerve of old age is touched. He encourages an old stage-hand with acting ambitions to do a soft-shoe dance and croak out a song, then dismisses him brutally. *Memento mori.* So with the half dozen dignified old men his assistant has rounded up for extra parts: "How old are you?" he asks each. "Seventy-one," "sixty-three," "eighty-four," etc. "You're not old enough," he says, turning away contemptuously. The theme is stated most fully in a scene in the corridor outside the production office (where everybody has been working in a Kafkaesque-bureaucratic frenzy at three in the morning) when Guido is waylaid by his elderly assistant director, Conocchia, who begins by weeping into his handkerchief ("You don't trust me, you won't let me help you, you tell me nothing, I was once your friend"), and works himself up into a rage: "I've been in movies thirty years—we used to do things you'd never dare!" Guido, who has been listening with his usual ironical patience, like a man waiting for a thunderstorm to pass, suddenly explodes: "Get out, leave me alone, you . . . old man!" (Two young men from the production office poke their heads out: *"Vecchio? Vecchio?"*) But Conocchia has the last word. "You're not the man you used to be!" he shouts as Guido walks away.

I hazard that *8½* is Fellini's masterpiece precisely because it is about the two subjects he knows the most about: himself and the making of movies. He doesn't have to labor his points, he can move freely, quickly, with the ease of a man walking about his own home. And so much can be suggested in so little footage! That tall, aristocratic blonde, for instance, Guido glimpses several times in the hotel. She fascinates him because she looks like the heroine of an international spy thriller; he never meets her (the closest he comes is to put her into his dream harem), but he does overhear her end of a long-distance tele-phone conversation, which sounds like a bad movie script but which vastly intrigues him. Several kinds of parody are intertwined in this tiny episode: of movie clichés, of Guido's romantic eroticism, and—a feedback—of a man whose job it is to fabricate these glamorous stereotypes, himself falling for them. Successful parody is possible only when the parodist feels "at home with" (significant phrase) his subject. This familiarity also means that Fellini is able to keep *8½* right down to earth, so that what might have been one more labored exercise in fantasy—like De Sica's *Miracle in Milan*, for instance—is spontaneous, lifelike and often very funny. I think Fellini has become the greatest master of social comedy since Lubitsch.

8½ takes us further inside the peculiar world of movie-making than any other film I know. I once asked the Argentine director, Torre Nilsson, why important movie directors seem to lose their creative powers so much more often—and completely—than major artists in other fields. (I was thinking of Welles and Hitchcock.) He replied: "In movies, once you make a success, you become public property; you are overwhelmed with fame, money, women, admirers, promoters, and you can never get away from it. A painter or writer or composer creates by himself, but directors have to have hundreds of other people around all the time. So they burn themselves out early." When I saw *8½*, I saw what he meant. Guido is distracted in the literal sense: "to divide [the mind, attention, etc.] between objects." They're all here: the highbrow journalist who asks about his philosophy, and also the lowbrow one— "Couldn't you tell me something about your love life?"; the producer who bullies him about the production schedule and the accountants who nag him about costs; the property man who begs Guido to take on as extras his giggling teen-age "nieces"; the playboy who wants him to sit up all night drinking; the man who waylays him in the lobby, waving a script: "It shows the necessity of universal disarmament; only a man of your courage and integrity could do it"; the press agents and tourists and mistresses, including his own. All there, and each wants a slice of him.

The reviews of *8½* in the newspapers and in magazines like *Newsweek* and *The New Yorker* have been enthusiastic. The public likes it, too. But the "little-magazine" critics have been cool and wary, as though they felt they were being conned. Their objections, remarkably uniform, suggest to me that the trouble with serious film criticism today is that it is too serious.

All these sequences are so magnificently filmed that the breath is hardly left to voice a query as to what they mean. Gianni di Venanzo's black-and-white photography and Piero Gherardi's sets and costumes provide such visual magic that it seems pointless to make philosophical reservations on the film's content. Yet the sheer beauty of Fellini's film . . . is deceiving us. (John Francis Lane in *Sight and Sound*.)

He goes on to complain of "pretentiousness of subject matter" and "artistic inflation." It's true, beauty and art are deceivers ever. The pea is never under the shell Fellini has given us every reason to believe contains it. In James and Conrad this is called ambiguity.

The trouble seems to come from another quarter—moral and intellectual content. Fellini's last three films seem to me to rank in merit according to the amount of "meaning" in each. *La Dolce Vita* fairly reeked of "meaning," with its Christ symbols, parallels to Dante, moral indictment of a contemporary life style, and what not. [This is not ironical—D.M.] The *Boccaccio '70* episode had its little fabulated moral. But *8½* has little or no intellectual content. The difference shows in the very titles. *La Dolce Vita* evokes a moral tradition of some kind. *The Temptation of Dr. Antonio* (with its echo of "The Temptation of St. Anthony") prepares us for religious allegory. But *8½* drives us right back into Fellini's biography. . . . The artist's promise of a moral or intellectual "point" bribes us (me) to take part in his (my) illicit fantasies. Without an intellectual superstructure, his personal fantasy fails to engage other persons. (Norman N. Holland in *Hudson Review*.)

It would be needlessly cruel to comment on these stiff-jointed lucubrations, though I can't help wondering what the quotes around meaning mean. Does he "mean" it? In addition to his other burdens, Mr. Holland groans under a massive load of primitive Freudianism. Maybe this explains why he dares to express openly a puritan nervousness when confronted by useless beauty that his colleagues express more discreetly.

Since *La Dolce Vita*, Fellini's films have been following a trend that certainly culminates in *8½*. [Briefest trend in cultural history since the only Fellini film between *Vita* and *8½* was the half-hour episode in *Boccaccio 70*—D.M.] It is the triumph of style over content. At the end of *8½* we are excited not because Fellini has told us something significant about the artistic process, but because he has found such a visually exciting metaphor for his idea that it does not matter if this idea is not quite first-rate. . . . Nothing very significant is said about illusion and reality, dream and art. (Gary Carey in *The Seventh Art*.)

True that when it comes to making significant statements about illusion and reality and other high topics, Fellini is "not quite first-rate" compared to, say, Dr. Erwin Panofsky, of the (Princeton) Institute of Advanced Studies, whose 1934 essay, "Style and Medium in the Moving Pictures," is a classic. But I doubt that Dr. Panofsky, a modest and sensible man, would claim he could have made *8½*, any more than Fellini, also sensible if not modest, would aspire to a professorship of, say, Cinematic Philosophy. Mr. Carey ends his review on the usual sub-puritan note: "*8½* is really a visual experience, its only profundity resting there." And what better resting place?

Fellini's latest "autobiographical" oddity. . . . The nicest possible thing one could say is that he had had the guts to try and shove this particular form of lachrymose sexuality into the environs of art. . . . Of course, the result is horrendously pretentious. . . . She [Anouk Aimée as the wife] is where Fellini's vulgarity positively beckons us into attention and in so doing ruins a fantasy. He just can't deal with the grown-up issues she incarnates. But as a cinematic outlet for the imagination—the sort of stuff a director like Fellini *can* cope with . . . the film is extraordinary. . . . *8½* looks marvelous and doesn't matter much of a damn. (John Coleman in the London *New Statesman*.)

No comment.

    The tone is never sure, but falters between irony and self-pity, between shamefaced poeticism and tongue-tied self-mockery. . . . The second failure . . . [is] ignorance. . . . *8½* piles problem upon problem, which is permissible; but sheds no light, which is not. . . . Fellini, apparently afraid of becoming a self-repeater with diminishing returns as so many famous Italian directors have become, tries for something new: symbolism, metaphysics, solid intellectual content. . . . What made Fellini's early films great . . . was their almost total avoidance of intellectualizing. (John Simon in *The New Leader*.)

The first sentence seems to me about as obtuse or perverse or both as you could get in eighteen words: I detected no self-pity, but on the contrary was impressed by the objectivity with which Fellini presented himself and his most personal worries; the poeticism was real poetry, and it was far from shamefaced, in fact it was blatant, exuberant; and any critic who could apply the adjective "tongue-tied" to Fellini, always fluent to the point of garrulity, must have an ax to grind. Mr. Simon's was a polemical one: his review is unique in finding nothing to praise in *8½*. The closest he comes is: "Despite two or three good scenes [not specified] it is a disheartening fiasco." (It pains me to write thus, or should anyway, since I respect Mr. Simon's critical acumen so much that I wrote an introduction to his recent collection of essays, *Acid Test*.) Why "ignorance" is a fault in an artist I don't see, nor why he has to solve any problems except those of constructing a work of art, which are difficult enough. Shakespeare was a bit of an ignoramus—"little Latin and less Greek"—nor do we expect *King Lear* to "shed light" on geriatrics. I agree that Fellini is no thinker, and that he is at his worst when he intellectualizes. I also agree that "all the principal characters . . . are sublimely dichotomous," that "the dialogue bulges with antinomies," and that Fellini isn't in the same league as "the great masters of ambiguity—Pirandello, Brecht, Valéry, Eliot." Compared to that Yankee lineup, he's a busher. But all this is beside the point since, at least as I read *8½*, Fellini is *not* trying for "symbolism, metaphysics [or] solid intellectual content."

    This brings me to the crux of my quarrel with the all-too-serious critics (an exception was Jack Hirschman's jazzy paean in *Film Quarterly*) and indeed to what I see as the crux of the film itself. Because it is technically sophisticated, and because it deals with major areas of experience, these critics look for philosophical depths in a movie which is superficial—I think deliberately—in every way except as a work of art. They call Fellini a phony for not delivering the goods, but I don't see his signature on their bill of lading. On the contrary, some of the best comedy in his film is provided by intellectuals: the affected young beauty who has written a treatise on "The Solitude of Modern Man in the Contemporary Theater"; the highbrow British reporter who pesters Guido with questions like, "Is it that you cannot communicate? Or is that merely a mask?" And above all the collaborator who has been assigned to help Guido complete his script—an eye-glassed, beak-nosed superintellectual whose lean face is fixed in lines of alert, sour suspicion. This personage—listed in the cast credits as The Writer, and played with waspish authority by Jean Rougeul—is endlessly articulate about the script; it's narcissistic ("just another film about your childhood"), romantic, pretentious, tasteless, and mindless: "Your main problem is the film lacks ideas, it has no philosophical base. It's merely a series of senseless episodes. . . . It has none of the merits of the avant-garde film and all the drawbacks." How can a director make more explicit his rationale? Life imitated art, as elsewhere in this strange film* and the actual highbrow critics reacted to *8½* much as The Writer did to Guido's script. Several people I've talked to—and I must admit there is as much conversational as printed opposition to *8½*—have suggested that The Writer is merely a ploy by Fellini to disarm his critics by making all their points in advance; they might have added the American woman who at the end shouts, "He's lost. He hasn't anything to say." Maybe. But he was a good prophet. For the "serious" critics have by now become habituated to profound, difficult films that must be "interpreted" from the language of art (what's on the screen) into the language of philosophy (what what's on the screen "really means"). It began with Bergman (whom I've always thought strongest at his shallowest) and reached a comic climax in the recent efforts of Franco-American *auteur* critics to read *The Birds* as a morality play about Modern Civilization, and a pathetic one in the efforts of almost everybody to make sense out of that triumph of non- and indeed anti-

---

*"Fellini found himself embarked, with costly sets built and stars under contract, on a kind of explanatory sequel to *La Dolce Vita*," reports *The New Statesman*. When he found this didn't work, he did what Guido did—switched to a film about himself, that is, about a famous director who finds himself blocked on a film. Reality came as close to overwhelming Fellini as it did Guido. According to *Sight and Sound*: "Two weeks before *8½* opened in Rome he still hadn't made up his mind how to end it."

sense, *Last Year at Marienbad*—everybody except its creators, who said they themselves disagreed on what it "meant."

The off-putting quality of *8½* for all but the less intellectualized critics (and the public) is that it is nothing but a pleasurable work of art which might have been directed by Mozart—and there were no doubt pundits in his day who deplored the frivolous way he played around with Masonic symbolism in *The Magic Flute*. It is a worldly film, all on the surface: humorous, rhetorical, sensuous, lyrical, witty, satiric, full of sharply realistic detail and also of fantastic scenes like the great one in the steam bath. The essence of *8½* is here: the visual panache of the movie-makers making their way down the stairs, swathed in sheets like Roman senators and wreathed in smoky steam like the damned going down to hell, terrific but also just a touch burlesque on Biblical spectaculars—the loudspeaker, "Guido, Guido: His Eminence will see you now"—the burlesque becoming strident as Guido's colleagues push around him, warning, "Don't hold anything back from His Eminence," while they ask him to put in a word for them, and then turning to satire, as Guido stands before the aged Cardinal (also wrapped in a sheet, bony neck and chest bare, mist swirling about him like God's mantle) and complains, "I'm not happy, Your Eminence." "Why should you be, my son?" the Cardinal replies with unexpected vigor. "That's not your job in life. . . . *Nulla salvatio extra ecclesiam.* . . . That which is not of God is of the Devil." The scene closes with an exterior shot of a small cellar window that swings slowly shut as if excluding the sinner (*extra ecclesiam*) from the heaven within. There is plenty of symbolism here, indeed every shot is a metaphor, but they are all as obvious as the closing window. This is perhaps the difficulty; nothing for the interpretative tooth to mumble, no Antonionian *angst*, no Bergmanesque Godhead, no Truffaut-style existential Absurd to perplex us. Like Baroque art, of which it is a belated golden ray, *8½* is complicated but not obscure. It is more Handel than Beethoven—objective and classical in spirit as against the romantic subjectivism we are accustomed to. It's all there, right on the surface, like a Veronese or a Tiepolo.

One could drop still another name, the greatest of all. Is there not something Shakespearean in this range of human experience expressed in every mode from high lyric to low comic, from the most formal rhetoric to the most personal impressionism? And don't the critics remind one of those all-too-serious students who try to discover "Shakespeare's philosophy" and always fail because Shakespeare hadn't any; his "ideas" were all *ad hoc*; their function was to solve dramatic rather than philosophical problems. As Jack Hirschman writes: "Fellini has . . . come free of that awful psycho-philosophical air which pervades *La Dolce Vita*. . . . In *8½* people are on earth not because they are destined to be trapped by cultural despair, but because they are destined to play out the roles of their individual realities."

Finally, in *8½* Fellini steals from everybody, just like Shakespeare. "Theft" on this scale becomes synthesis: *8½* is an epitome of the history of cinema. His thefts are creative because they are really borrowings, which are returned with the fingerprints of the thief all over them. The childhood episodes are Bergmanesque chiaroscuro, as the great scene on the beach when La Saraghina dances for the schoolboys, which echoes, right down to the brutal beat of the music, an even greater beach scene, that between the soldiers and the clown's wife at the beginning of *Naked Night*: but this is a Latin Bergman, sensuous and dramatic and in no way profound. When Guido and his wife quarrel in the hotel bedroom, the bleak failure to make contact (and the austere photography) recall Antonioni, but *this* alienated couple don't suffer in silence, they yell at each other. The early scene in the rest-cure garden is full of heroic close-ups à la Eisenstein, but they are used (like "The Ride of the Valkyries" thundered out by the hotel band) for satiric counterpoint to the aging, prosaic faces of the invalids. The general structure—a montage of tenses, a mosaic of time blocks—recalls *Intolerance*, *Kane*, and *Marienbad*, but in Fellini's hands it becomes light, fluid, evanescent. And delightfully obvious.

1964

Renata Adler

Renata Adler (b. 1938) has written novels (*Speedboat*, *Pitch Dark*), book-length reportage (*Reckless Disregard*), and essay collections about politics and the media. Having established a reputation with her *New Yorker* pieces, she was invited "as a just-under thirty person then, of fairly contemporary experience," to take over the film critic's post at *The New York Times*, succeeding the long-tenured, incurably fuddy-duddy Bosley Crowther. Adler herself lasted 14 months, an adventure she chronicled in her collection *A Year in the Dark: A Year in the Life of a Film Critic 1968–1969*. She wanted, as she put it, "to review films in earnest (or in fun, depending on the film) with a bit more tension and energy than the traditional paper way." Struggling to find the right pace and form, she often seemed to be trying to fit a round peg (stylish quarterly prose) into a square hole (newspaper deadlines), a feat she accomplished at times through sheer candor, virtuosity, and vocal texture, as in this review of *In Cold Blood*.

◆

Cold Blood: Cheap Fiction

1-28-68

The film *In Cold Blood* is probably as faithful in spirit to its original novel as any movie has ever been. And it reveals by what it finds necessary to explain, and paper over, and underscore, just what sort of book Truman Capote's much publicized non-fiction novel was.

The book's accretions of falsely illuminating detail ("Double-mint, Dick's favorite flavor; Perry preferred Juicy Fruit") are gone. Its two genuine bits of Americana (the little boy and his grandfather living on soda bottle refunds; the fat death-row homicidal prodigy pasting food pictures into his scrapbook) remain. So do the character outlines and the time structure of the book. *In Cold Blood*, in both media—unlike non-fiction novels by the real originators of the form (Gibbs, Ross, Mitchell, McKelway)—does not structure the facts for any truth beyond the scope of conventional journalism. It structures details to arrive at nothing deeper than an elaborate tease.

It begins with two killers converging upon four stereotypes: apple pie daughter, neurasthenic mother, salt of the earth father, fine young son. The Clutters might comfortably inhabit any aspirin or mouthwash commerical.

385

They are set up as coldly and two-dimensionally as in a shooting range, with infinitely less reality than the people of Gasoline Alley. Despite the author's familiarity with the diaries, files, and correspondence of these dead (who could not present themselves to him in person, or, for that matter, sign his releases), one knows virtually nothing about them. On the screen, they are unactable, as in the book they were uninteresting. They are there to die. Perhaps they satisfy some East Coast idea that people in Kansas are two-dimensional. Or perhaps one tends to regard all objects of such a hunt as stereotypes.

For the movie, like the book, is a thriller with a single fact withheld. We know who is going to die. We know who is going to kill them. We know the killers will be caught. And we know what will happen to them. But *In Cold Blood*, in both media, uses every technique of cheap fiction—every cut, every shift, every flashback—to put off the actual murder scene. "I promise you, honey," Dick says early in the film, "we'll blast hair all over them walls." It is a promise to the audience, really. They will be present at the murders, know how they were done, what was said, how it looked and felt. After some delay (in the book it was 263 pages), everyone wants to know.

At Cinema I, where *In Cold Blood* is now playing to sell-out crowds, this is very clear. Throughout the first ninety minutes of the movie, the audience is relaxed, talking, laughing with the killers, waiting. Then, long after the crime has been disclosed, long after the killers have completed their travels and been arrested in Las Vegas—in fact, long after everything but the last pitch of morbid interest has gone by—Detective Alvin Dewey's car stops before the Clutter homestead in the night. The audience perceptibly draws its breath. This is it. They know what is coming. Perry will re-enact the crime.

There is no real reason why it should happen at this moment. With all its "No. No. No's" and "Oh, please don't's," and jerked back heads, and exposed blades, and tied ankles, and twitching feet. It should have occurred—in terms of the movie's actual time sequence—about an hour ago. Not too much blood, after all. No hair. This is not the Grand Guignol, but a serious study of violence in American life that sold over 600,000 copies and now lines them up around the block. There follows an absolutely dead interval of film: the trial, the prison, more homey jokes and delay. After a little rest, the audience is primed again: for the hangings. More twitching, some physiological detail, the drop. Everyone can go home. A serious study of violence, etc., and a treatise on capital punishment. A liberal intellectual double feature.

It is, of course, nothing of the kind. The soundtrack, for one thing, is among the most crudely exacerbating ever put on film. Everything is treble, an inexcusably high volume: guitar squeaks, paper cracklings, knuckle crackings, zipper slides, shotgun checks, sirens, brake squeals, train shrieks, stairs creaking, a scream. The "s's" alone of John Forsythe, who plays detective Alvin Dewey, are so sibilant they amount to a speech impediment; they become excruciating. The sound of a map being folded, an arm entering a sleeve, a cigarette being tamped, an intake of breath, even coffee being poured is tuned so high on the treble that it is a constant irritation, like a man sitting beside you whistling through his nose. When it is not a high-frequency agony. This is the level at which the direction is nervy.

The dialogue, where it diverges from the book, is largely impossible: cheap jokes, an aura of false cool, dime-store philosophy and psychiatry ("I'm glad you don't hate your father any more." "But I do. I hate him and I love him"), dead-ear interviewer's pretensions ("Mr. Jensen, what is your interest in this case?" "A violent, unknown force destroys a decent honorable family . . ."). But it is interesting where the book's own lines are virtually undeliverable. The "yellow bird" of Perry's imagination, never quite realized in the book, sounds in the movie like an advertisement for an airline. The line from the confession, "I thought he was a very nice gentleman. Soft spoken. I thought so right up to the moment I cut his throat," sounds completely false, like an interviewer's plant ("Did you like Mr. Clutter?" "Yes." "Did you think he was a nice man?" "Yes." "And yet you cut his throat," etc.).

It is interesting that the most severe criticism the book *In Cold Blood* received at the time of its publication came from England, where Kenneth Tynan accused the author of not having tried hard enough to keep Perry and Dick from capital punishment. It was a curious criticism. In the first place, Capote did try. In the second, there was no earthly reason why he should. And in the third, if there ever were two persuasive arguments for capital punishment, they were Dick Hickock and Perry Smith. It is true that Dick studied law in his prison cell, and Perry read and drew pictures; but hobbies acquired late in life hardly constitute an atonement for the taking of four lives. True, hanging takes twenty minutes, and the book might be taken to argue that, out of the same fastidiousness which led Perry to put Mr. Clutter out of his misery after his throat was cut, the state ought to do away with people more humanely. But nothing in the book explained that split second when Perry used his knife (the movie tries to paper this over by having his father appear to him). One gets the feeling it might have happened to anyone to be killer or victim at that time. For the rest, one believes in capital punishment or one does not. The book and the film do not constitute an argument either way. (Indeed, if they have any moral at all, it is that it is unwise to hire ex-convicts if they are prospective repeaters and gossips as well.)

What was curious was that it was exploitation of the *killers*, not the victims, that worried the critics. The pacing of the book (and now of the movie) has been set up in such a way that only the killers have any reality at all. The book, the movie, the killers, the audience are stalking the family together. It was not the graves of Hickock and Smith that the Beautiful People—in the party that probably marked their overdue end as an American infatuation—were dancing on. It was the graves of the Clutters. Who, in the book's own terms, were never really alive. And who, in the movie, are set up in two dimensions six times a day, to be killed pointlessly again.

1968

Donald Phelps

An underground critic with a sophisticated following, Donald Phelps (b. 1929) has written on film, art, poetry, and popular culture for many magazines, including *Moviegoer*, *Film Comment*, and *For Now*, a periodical he started. His film criticism specializes in career analyses of less-appreciated directors and actors, often written in a heady, baroque, metaphor-rich prose style, densely packed with ideas. His two books, *Covering the Ground: Essays for Now* and *Reading the Funnies*, have become collector's items for "the happy few." Phelps wrote a beautiful appreciation of Manny Farber's criticism and artwork, and may be seen as working in a similarly idiosyncratic, burrowing critical vein.

◆

The Runners

The heroes of Allan Dwan's best films, I would suggest, are fugitives: people figuratively, or more often actually, on the run. Their terrain (in films like *Tennessee's Partner*, *Montana Belle*, *Slightly Scarlet*, *Silver Lode*, *The Restless Breed*) is a broken field of guilt and suspicion and misunderstanding; which, in tally, suggests Hitchcock. But, unlike Hitchcock, Dwan's interest is in his heroes' resourcefulness, their athletic suppleness, even—especially—their innocence and grace. Unlike Hitchcock, he shows no interest in pummeling or immobilizing them; quite the opposite. Dwan is a former football player with Rockne, a former director of Douglas Fairbanks (*Robin Hood*, *A Modern Musketeer*). The skimmings and skirtings and manipulations of his characters assume—the more space they're given—the double fascination, grace and contest, of a great sporting event.

His concern with movement offers a strong reason, I suspect, why Dwan, in the thirties and early forties, so often seems to have been a clearing-house for some of Hollywood's most formidable brassware. The Ritz Brothers, Shirley Temple— But seeing the Ritzes' *Three Musketeers*, or Shirley's *Heidi*— or a worthier piece of pottery, *Friendly Enemies* (1941) featuring the two Charlies, Winninger and Ruggles, as German Americans floundering among divided loyalties—Dwan surprises me repeatedly by his equalness to the task. My first recollection of *Heidi* is neither Shirley herself, nor even Jean Hersholt's Alm Uncle (with those oddly Santa Claus-like whiskers on the rough old hermit);

but the delightful wooden shoe ballet which Shirley sings and executes, about halfway through the film; its buoyant, arc-ing figures and controlled picture-book backdrop, so far from Johanna Spyri's warm reality, but close to authentic, quite physical fantasy.

But for me, who have seen very little of Dwan's silent work (though its obvious legacies help make his work today lively and original), the pivot of his best films lies with a few brilliant, compact, quite overlooked comedies filmed by him in the middle forties: *Brewster's Millions*, *Up in Mabel's Room*, *Getting Gertie's Garter*, *Rendezvous With Annie*. Three of these—the first three—were free adaptations of decades-old Broadway farces; the second and third were what once were called "bedroom farces." In all of them, however, Dwan reduced the conventions of second-rate stage humor to pure speed: these comedies are fantasies of speed and maneuver, all prurience (except what serves to clock the players) boiled away: seamless, translucent, and not so much funny as exhilirating; the laughter is that of excitement and relief, paired as at a hockey game or horse race. The actors look longer, less heavy, more reed-like than ever before: Dennis O'Keefe, Marie MacDonald, Ruth Hussey, Jerome Cowan. Again, his heroes are eluders and evaders of archetypal kind: entangled by lies and misunderstandings, adding to their number, O'Keefe and Cowan and Eddie Albert keep their films alive by their quick, sinuous navigations; and an incriminating garter or lingerie, an inconvenient million dollars, becomes a marker in an intensely followed paper-chase.

I'm not talking about themes; Dwan's preoccupations are not themes in the sense that they are structured or amplified, or intended to emerge through the films; they are, simply, *preoccupations*, and they are simply there. Nor would consistency of theme matter in the slightest if Dwan were a mediocre artist (many of whom have exhibited thematic consistency). But he is an artist of intense dedication, recurrent freshness (especially in those films made when he was well into his seventies) and acute beauty—and the beauty of finely-executed, well-gauged motion, which he loves in his characters and displays in his visual style. Thus does the content of his films at last become their theme: that the sheer ability to stay on one's feet can be at last self-redemptive and lovely.

Dwan's best films seem to me triumphs of brisk, clear intelligence which can extract the essentials of narrative and character from a shaggy screenplay; an economy which fuses expediency and elegance (so that a high-budgeter like *Suez* and a cheapie like *Silver Lode* show the same urbane fluidity;) and a quiet intensity of storytelling which follows even clichés which their screenwriters have stopped believing in, to their natural conclusions. Thus the vaguenesses of an underwritten script can afford Dwan genuine perceptions about the shiftiness of innocence and worldiness, or evil—qualities which are constantly changing hats in his films. Even in a tacky little Dorothy Lamour reject like *Pearl of the South Pacific*, I got a pleasant start watching Virginia Mayo's hilarious camp of a sea-going doxie impersonating a lady missionary—next to *White Heat*, the best casting I've seen of this second-string Susan Hayward. And in the same picture, the usually-unctuous Basil Ruysdael has been coaxed into giving a cold arrogance to the role of the islanders' benevolent white leader.

A signal specimen of Dwan's talents, though not one of my favorites, is *The Restless Breed*, in which—from a skimpy script and production, and such usual deadweights as Scott Brady and Rhys Williams—Dwan at times elicited a subtly disquieting reversal of *High Noon*–type western values. Here, the entire suspense comes from Dwan's visualization of Brady's zigzag course between opposing moralities. Determined to trap and murder the smuggler who killed his sheriff-father, Brady is argued at by sheriff (a relatively subdued Jay C. Flippen) and minister (Williams, who stands here and there, turning his Toby Jug ogle to the camera to convey piety) who represent morality; and the minister's ward, an all-but-mute Ann Bancroft, who doesn't want him to get killed. Well, after a number of centuries, this remains a promising plot-situation—but only when good writing uses it. Dwan, however, turns the film into a web of sinuous, evasive motion. Brady is kept in the foreground—getting drunk, bullying hangers-on at the bar, snuggling with Miss Bancroft—and, in a stunningly executed sequence, dispatching three or four of the boss heavy's aides in a brilliant synchronization of ambush tactics. Even Brady's beefy petulance is turned to the advantage of the hero's late-adolescent ambiguity. The result frequently suggests an extended pantomime of a man struggling to free himself from obsession.

But my favorite Dwans are complicated jobs like *Passion* and *The Most Dangerous Man Alive* and *Tennessee's Partner*: with their coruscations of plot, their picaresque chains of incident, through which Dwan traces a skein of narrative logic. The dual effect of these films is an overall winding smoothness of the film's movement, counterpointed, scene by scene and frame by frame, with angular, jabbing action and crisply diagrammed imagery. Dwan has carried from his silent period the silent filmmakers' preoccupation with making every shot, every camera set-up do its maximum share, the film taking responsibility for its own world. Thus, in *Passion* every phase of the operetta-like plot— a young *ranchero* hunting down the land-grabbers who have murdered his family, enmiring himself in deception and slaughter—is translucently clear, leaving abundant room for those moral questions which seldom take priority in such melodrama—least of all in the "adult" varieties. The often stale-looking features of Cornel Wilde and Yvonne DeCarlo here seem removed from the contexts of their past films; directed so hard and so fast that no room is left for such associations. In his one science-fiction film, *The Most Dangerous Man Alive*, Dwan produced a masterpiece of rootless bitterness—very parallel to *The Restless Breed*—from the performances of Ron Randell and Debra Paget (excellent as a gangster's dumb, sluttish ex-girl friend) and a typically unpromising story about a dead hoodlum, resurrected—and turned into a potential walking holocaust—by nuclear radiation. The climactic scene of Randell perishing on a mountain top—a fusion of *High Sierra* and Euripidean tragedy—commanded a more genuine awe than a stableful of Godzillas.

Dwan's economy is not simple mechanical expediency, but something closer to courtly austerity. Although he repeatedly holds his camera still, avoiding reverse shots and similar ploys, I almost never get the impression that a set-up was done that way merely for budget's sake. His single takes are often filled with some of the most elaborate sustained tracking shots done by an American director apart from Cukor. His austerity, I say, is a positive trait: not simply the will to deny, but to deny in order to assert—even indulge—himself; wherein he is an artist and, I suspect, a damned near unique one in Hollywood today.

His one sensuosity is that of grace: choreographic movement to which sets, actors and all other components are subordinated. He must have fairly opulent production values, as he must have elaborate plots, in order to subdue them. His films are as textureless as any I can recall: as often as not, the actors seem to have turned in their flesh for something resembling balsa wood. The few erotic moments in his films come and go vaporously: even Rhonda Fleming in an 1870's bathtub seems fully corseted and petticoated.

His handling of violence displays the same austerity. Though he never skimps any necessary violence—the plots of *Tennessee's Partner* and *Slightly Scarlet* are saturated with murders, bombing, bludgeonings—Dwan leaves remarkably little aftertaste of violence. Even when showing violent action detail by detail, he controls the milieu so stringently that the bloodshed seems replaced by urbane, sardonic dispassion. One of the best scenes in *Slightly Scarlet* is a basically routine sequence of a gang-girl being cuffed by hoodlums, whereupon they are raided by the police. Dwan does the whole sequence in what seemed to me, at most two takes; keeping the camera at prudent middle-distance while the slapping gangster delivers his blows with a foolish-sounding "Ah!—*Ah!*" Then, when the police boil in, a slight shove pitches another hoodlum on his face. The control and vivid eccentricity of these businesses pinpoints—in every sense—the violence, so that it becomes as graphic—and remote—as next-door gossip.

Dwan prefers seemingly stolid actors who, at appropriate moments, can deliver schist-like glints of intelligence or vivacity. He uses these performers, often, by turning them into ensembles of arms and legs, which he then deploys according to his perceptions of character and bodily rhythm. Arlene Dahl gives what is possibly the most eloquent performance of her career in *Slightly Scarlet*, where, as an alcoholic nympho, she was given a cursive walk—like a nineteen-twenties fashion model—and oversweeping gestures, as to a secret clock synchronized with no other in the world. Dwan's star performer is John Payne—a one-time Jimmy Stewart surrogate, who, after the wartime forties, returned to films with a look of sour harassment, and bearing of an All-American gone faintly rancid. Dwan—in *Tennessee's Partner* and *Slightly Scarlet* —turned these features to expressions of ironic opportunism and stoic bitterness. Payne's presence, as well as that of not-yet-Governor Reagan— co-operated with Dwan's talent to make *Tennessee's Partner* a melancholy, lyric and quite de-sentimentalized expansion of the Bret Harte tale.

Dwan's pictures repeatedly induce the feeling of one era—that of the twenties silents—being carried over into another, virtually intact. His ability to point and place a shot or scene, enables him to use very old devices with the freshness of combined directness, wit and necessity. In *Slightly Scarlet*, the device of surrounding crime lord Ted DiCorsia with darkness whenever he appears, is plyed with such aptness, control and visual acumen that you don't realize how Dwan—by reverting to the expressionist films of the twenties— has outstripped the similar but more pretentious gimmicks of its near-contemporaries—Wyler's *Detective Story*, or Wilder's *Sunset Boulevard*.

I think, too, that Dwan brought from the twenties—and possibly to the detriment of his career—the personal immersion in craft, prior even to art, which held such premium, then, among the best film-makers. From such immersion, he transmits the sense of the actor, on screen, manufacturing the film from his body, silk-worm-like; the story flowing as inevitably as any non-natural work possibly can. In response to a 1963 interview issued by *Cahiers du Cinéma* to various American directors, Dwan wrote: "I want to keep making films until I die", and "any working conditions are alright for me. Obstacles are merely challenges for me to surmount." Sheer banality in many a mouth, these phrases ring absolutely true in Dwan's. "Keep making films"—"obstacles": a near-Puritanical fusion of self-abnegation, pride and love, by which art itself becomes a set of circumstances to surmount, adjust, transect. Occasions and necessities rebuilt each time. I think it was such devotion—and the lack of that ambition, or vainglory, or sense of gratuity which distinguishes some of the very best, and occasionally destroys them—which made Dwan (this is sheer inference) glad to accept the factotum's role which was flung him for years. And, in turn, that puritan estheticism, I think, induced in many watching his films, an uneasy sense of nothing to grasp, nothing that could be confiscated, no edges or naperies of personality, strangeness, or simple waste. Thus, the grotesque irony of their conclusion: Dwan is a cold, mechanical film-maker; forgetting or never knowing that films are the medium among media where devotion to mechanics can be infused with personal warmth, with passion. And—not knowing this—never recognizing the additional gratuity of bone-clean American narrative art, with which Allan Dwan made pictures for half a century.

1969

Vincent Canby

Vincent Canby (1924–2000) took the practice of newspaper movie reviewing to new heights by composing, almost daily, film criticism of seemingly effortless literary grace, wit, and taste. Canby was as much at home with the quirky American independent or foreign film as with the latest Hollywood blockbuster, and he championed the personal styles of Rainer Werner Fassbinder, Mike Leigh, Woody Allen, and Jane Campion when they first appeared. Beginning his career as a reporter for *The Motion Picture Herald* and *Variety*, he joined *The New York Times* in 1965 and reigned as its senior film critic from 1969 to 1993 before ending his career as that paper's theater critic. Canby also wrote novels and plays, but he never lost his reporter's down-to-earth curiosity, modesty, and respect for facts. Inclined to be amused rather than appalled by a turkey, he could make a very negative review entertaining, stopping well short of sadism. The following examples, taken almost at random (since he never wrote badly) from his early years as a reviewer, demonstrate the flexibility of his responses in an era of social and artistic upheaval, as well as his unwillingness to be flummoxed by a movie's pretensions. Canby did not allow a Selected Reviews to be printed in his lifetime, leaving a serious gap in the record of American film criticism, whose alleviation is long overdue.

◆

Midnight Cowboy

Joe Buck is 6 feet tall and has the kind of innocence that preserves dumb good looks. Joe Buck fancies himself a cowboy, but his spurs were earned while riding a gas range in a Houston hamburger joint. Ratso Rizzo, his buddy and part-time pimp from the Bronx, is short, gimpy and verminous. Although they are a comparatively bizarre couple, they go unnoticed when they arrive at one of those hallucinogenic "Village" parties where the only thing straight is the booze that no one drinks. Everybody is too busy smoking pot, popping pills and being chic. Joe Buck, ever-hopeful stud, drawls: "I think we better find someone an' tell 'em that we're here."

Trying to tell someone that he's there is the story of Joe Buck's life—28 years of anxiety and dispossession fenced off by Priapian conquests that always, somehow, leave him a little lonelier than he was before. Joe is a funny, dim-witted variation on the lonely, homosexual dream-hero who used to wander disguised through so much drama and literature associated with the nineteen-fifties.

Midnight Cowboy, which opened yesterday at the Coronet Theater, is a slick, brutal (but not brutalizing) movie version of James Leo Herlihy's 1965 novel. It is tough and good in important ways, although its style is oddly romantic and at variance with the laconic material. It may be that movies of this sort (like most war movies) automatically celebrate everything they touch. We know they are movies—isolated, simplified reflections of life—and thus we can enjoy the spectacle of degradation and loss while feeling superior to it and safe.

I had something of this same feeling about *Darling*, which was directed by John Schlesinger and in which Julie Christie suffered, more or less upwardly, on her way to fame and fortune in a movie as glossy as the life it satirized. There is nothing obviously glossy in *Midnight Cowboy*, but it contains a lot of superior laughter that has the same softening effect.

Schlesinger is most successful in his use of actors. Dustin Hoffman, as Ratso (his first movie performance since *The Graduate*), is something found under an old door in a vacant lot. With his hair matted back, his ears sticking out and his runty walk, Hoffman looks like a sly, defeated rat and talks with a voice that might have been created by Mel Blanc for a despondent Bugs Bunny. Jon Voight is equally fine as Joe Buck, a tall, handsome young man whose open face somehow manages to register the fuzziest of conflicting emotions within a very dim mind.

Waldo Frank's screenplay follows the Herlihy novel in most of the surface events. Joe Buck, a Texas dishwasher without friend or family, comes to New York to make his fortune as a stud to all the rich ladies who have been deprived of their rights by faggot eastern gentlemen. Instead, he winds up a half-hearted 42d Street hustler whose first and only friend is a lame, largely ineffectual con artist.

As long as the focus is on this world of cafeterias and abandoned tenements, of desperate conjunctions in movie balconies and doorways, of catchup and beans and canned heat, *Midnight Cowboy* is so rough and vivid that it's almost unbearable. Less effective are abbreviated, almost subliminal fantasies and flashbacks. Most of these are designed to fill in the story of the young Joe Buck, a little boy whose knowledge of life was learned in front of a TV set while his grandmother, good-time Sally Buck, ran a Texas beauty parlor and lived with a series of cowboy-father images for Joe.

Schlesinger has given his leads superb support with character actors like Ruth White (Sally Buck), John McGiver, Brenda Vaccaro, Barnard Hughes and Sylvia Miles. Miss Miles is especially good as the aging hooker Joe picks up under the mistaken impression she is a society lady. The one rather wooden performance, oddly, is that of superstar Viva, who plays a "Village" zombie with none of the flair she exhibits in Andy Warhol's improvisations.

Midnight Cowboy often seems to be exploiting its material for sensational or comic effect, but it is ultimately a moving experience that captures the quality of a time and a place. It's not a movie for the ages, but, having seen it, you won't ever again feel detached as you walk down West 42d Street, avoiding the eyes of the drifters, stepping around the little islands of hustlers and closing your nostrils to the smell of rancid griddles.

1969

The Wild Bunch

Sam Peckinpah's *The Wild Bunch* is about the decline and fall of one outlaw gang at what must be the bleeding end of the frontier era, 1913, when Pancho Villa was tormenting a corrupt Mexican Government while the United States watched cautiously from across the border.

The movie, which opened yesterday at the Trans-Lux East and West Theaters, is very beautiful and the first truly interesting, American-made Western in years. It's also so full of violence—of an intensity that can hardly be supported by the story—that it's going to prompt a lot of people who do not know the real effect of movie violence (as I do not) to write automatic condemnations of it.

The Wild Bunch begins on a hot, lazy afternoon as six United States soldiers ride into a small Texas border town with all the aloofness of an army of benign occupation. Under a makeshift awning, the good bourgeoisie of San Rafael is holding a temperance meeting. Gentle spinsters, sweating discreetly, vow to abstain from all spirits.

The "soldiers" pass on to the railroad office, which they quietly proceed to rob of its cash receipts. Down the street, a group of children giggle as they watch a scorpion being eaten alive by a colony of red ants. A moment later, the town literally explodes in the ambush that has been set for the outlaws.

Borrowing a device from *Bonnie and Clyde*, Peckinpah suddenly reduces the camera speed to slow motion, which at first heightens the horror of the mindless slaughter, and then—and this is what really carries horror—makes it beautiful, almost abstract, and finally into terrible parody.

The audience, which earlier was appalled at the cynical detachment with which the camera watched the death fight of the scorpion, is now in the position of the casually cruel children. The face of a temperance parade marcher erupts in a fountain of red. Bodies, struck by bullets, make graceful arcs through the air before falling onto the dusty street, where they seem to bounce, as if on a trampoline.

This sort of choreographed brutality is repeated to excess, but in excess, there is point to a film in which realism would be unbearable. *The Wild Bunch* takes the basic elements of the Western movie myth, which once defined a simple, morally comprehensible world, and by bending them turns them into symbols of futility and aimless corruption.

The screenplay, by Peckinpah and Walon Green, follows the members of the Wild Bunch from their disastrous, profitless experience at San Rafael to Mexico, where they become involved with a smilingly sadistic Mexican general fighting Villa. Although the movie's conventional and poetic action sequences are extraordinarily good and its landscapes beautifully photographed (lots of dark foregrounds and brilliant backgrounds) by Lucien Ballard, who did *Nevada Smith*, it is most interesting in its almost jolly account of chaos, corruption and defeat. All personal relationships in the movie seem somehow perverted in odd mixtures of noble sentimentality, greed and lust.

Never satisfactorily resolved is the conflict between William Holden, as the aging leader of the Wild Bunch, and Robert Ryan, as his former friend who, with disdain, leads the bounty hunters in pursuit of the gang. An awkward flashback shows the two men, looking like characters out of a silent movie, caught in an ambush in a bordello from which only Holden escapes.

The ideals of masculine comradeship are exaggerated and transformed into neuroses. The fraternal bonds of two brothers, members of the Wild Bunch, are so excessive they prefer having their whores in tandem. A feeling of genuine compassion prompts the climactic massacre that some members of the film trade are calling, not without reason, "the blood ballet."

Peckinpah also has a way of employing Hollywood life to dramatize his legend. After years of giving bored performances in boring movies, Holden comes back gallantly in *The Wild Bunch*. He looks older and tired, but he has style, both as a man and as a movie character who persists in doing what he's always done, not because he really wants the money but because there's simply nothing else to do.

Ryan, Ernest Borgnine and Edmond O'Brien add a similar kind of resonance to the film. O'Brien is a special shock, looking like an evil Gabby Hayes, a foul-mouthed, cackling old man who is the only member of the Wild Bunch to survive.

In two earlier Westerns, *Ride the High Country* (1962) and *Major Dundee* (1965), Peckinpah seemed to be creating comparatively gentle variations on the genre about the man who walks alone—a character about as rare in a Western as a panhandler on the Bowery.

In *The Wild Bunch*, which is about men who walk together, but in desperation, he turns the genre inside out. It's a fascinating movie and, I think I should add, when I came out of it, I didn't feel like shooting, knifing or otherwise maiming any of Broadway's often hostile pedestrians.

1969

Easy Rider

Easy *Rider*, which opened yesterday at the Beekman, is a motorcycle drama with decidedly superior airs about it. How else are we to approach a movie that advertises itself: "A man went looking for America. And couldn't find it anywhere"? Right away you know that something superior is up, that somebody is making a statement, and you can bet your boots (cowboy, black leather) that it's going to put down the whole rotten scene. What scene? Whose? Why? Man, I can't tell you if you don't know. What I mean to say is, if you don't groove, you don't groove. You might as well split.

I felt this way during the first half-hour of *Easy Rider*, and then, almost reluctantly, fell into the rhythm of the determinedly inarticulate piece. Two not-so-young cyclists, Wyatt (Peter Fonda) who affects soft leather breeches and a Capt. America jacket, and Billy (Dennis Hopper), who looks like a perpetually stoned Buffalo Bill, are heading east from California toward New Orleans.

They don't communicate with us, or each other, but after a while, it doesn't seem to matter. They simply exist—they are bizarre comic strip characters with occasional balloons over their heads reading: "Like you're doing your thing," or some such. We accept them in their moving isolation, against the magnificent Southwestern landscapes of beige and green and pale blue.

They roll down macadam highways that look like black velvet ribbons, under skies of incredible purity, and the soundtrack rocks with oddly counterpointed emotions of Steppenwolf, the Byrds, the Electric Prunes—dark and smoky cries for liberation. Periodically, like a group taking a break, the cyclists stop (and so does the music) for quiet encounters—with a toothless rancher and his huge, happy family or with a commune of thin hippies, whose idyll seems ringed with unacknowledged desperation.

Suddenly, however, a strange thing happens. There comes on the scene a very real character and everything that has been accepted earlier as a sort of lyrical sense impression suddenly looks flat and foolish.

Wyatt and Billy are in a small Southern town—in jail for having disturbed the peace of a local parade—when they meet fellow-inmate George Hanson (Jack Nicholson), a handsome, alcoholic young lawyer of good family and genially bad habits, a man whose only defense against life is a cheerful but not abject acceptance of it. As played by Nicholson, George Hanson is a marvelously realized character, who talks in a high, squeaky Southern accent and uses a phrase like "Lord have mercy!" the way another man might use a four-letter word.

Hanson gets the cyclists sprung from jail and then promptly joins them. He looks decidedly foolish, sitting on the back of Wyatt's bike, wearing a seersucker jacket and his old football helmet, but he is completely happy and, ironically, the only person in the movie who seems to have a sense of what liberation and freedom are. There is joy and humor and sweetness when he smokes grass for the first time and expounds an elaborate theory as to how the Venutians have already conquered the world.

Nicholson is so good, in fact, that *Easy Rider* never quite recovers from his loss, even though he has had the rather thankless job of spelling out what I take to be the film's statement (upper case). This has to do with the threat that people like the nonconforming Wyatt and Billy represent to the ordinary, self-righteous, inhibited folk that are the Real America. Wyatt and Billy, says the lawyer, represent freedom; ergo, says the film, they must be destroyed.

If there is any irony in this supposition, I was unable to detect it in the screenplay written by Fonda, Hopper and Terry Southern. Wyatt and Billy don't seem particularly free, not if the only way they can face the world is through a grass curtain. As written and played, they are lumps of gentle clay, vacuous, romantic symbols, dressed in cycle drag.

Easy Rider, the first film to be directed by Dennis Hopper, won a special prize at this year's Cannes festival as the best picture by a new director (there was only one other picture competing in that category).

With the exception of Nicholson, its good things are familiar things—the rock score, the lovely, sometimes impressionistic photography by Laszlo Kovacs, the faces of small-town America. These things not only are continually compelling but occasionally they dazzle the senses, if not the mind. Hopper, Fonda and their friends went out into America looking for a movie and found instead a small, pious statement (upper case) about our society (upper case), which is sick (upper case). It's pretty but lower case cinema.

1969

Z

Costa-Gavras's *Z*, the French film that won the Jury Prize (in effect, the third prize) at this year's Cannes Festival, is an immensely entertaining movie—a topical melodrama that manipulates our emotional responses and appeals to our best prejudices in such satisfying ways that it is likely to be mistaken as a work of fine—rather than popular—movie art.

The film, which opened last night at the Beekman, is based on Vassili Vassilikos's novel, which, in turn, is a lightly fictionalized account of the 1963 assassination in Salonika of Gregarios Lambrakis, a professor of medicine at the University of Athens and a leader of the forces opposing the placement of Polaris missiles in Greece. There is a kind of momentum to democratic processes, and the official investigation of that murder, instigated with some reluctance by the Government, eventually uncovered a plot involving high Government officials as well as a secret right-wing organization of patriotic goons.

In the course of the scandal, the Greek Government fell and the men morally and directly responsible for the murder were brought to trial. Within four years, there was a military coup d'état, after which almost everyone connected with the assassination was conveniently "rehabilitated."

The story of the Lambrakis affair is one of national sorrow, of idealism, of bravery, of defeat, of terrible irony. The movie is not one of ideas or ideals, but of sensations—horror, anger, frustration and suspense.

These are communicated—sometimes with all of the subtlety of a hypodermic needle stuck in a nerve—through the extraordinary color camerawork of Raoul Coutard, the man who has photographed just about every important French film of the nineteen-sixties, including Démy's *Lola*, Truffaut's *Jules and Jim* and Godard's *Weekend*.

Coutard may be unique among cinematographers in the manner in which he adapts himself to the individual demands of his directors without losing his own identity. His work on *Z*, shot entirely in an Algiers designed to suggest Salonika, is largely responsible for Costa-Gavras's realization of what is, actually, a dazzling, super-*Dragnet* film, a sort of remarkable newsreel record of events rather than people.

Costa-Gavras, the Greek-born French director (*The Sleeping Car Murder*) collaborated with Jorge Semprun (*La Guerre Est Finie*) on a screen adaptation that quite consciously subordinates characterization to vivid incident. The cast is large and excellent: Yves Montand as the assassinated doctor, Jean-Louis Trintignant (*Ma Nuit Chez Maud*) as the government's investigator, Jacques

Perrin as a totally dispassionate newspaper reporter, Pierre Dux and Julien Guiomar as right-wing leaders, and Renato Salvatori and Marcel Bozzufi as the assassins whose patriotism is for hire.

A small part of me, however, tends to rebel against the film's carefully programed responses, including the sight of Irene Papas, who can be a very fine actress, as the doctor's widow. The film thus employs for easy effect Miss Papas's professional image of perpetual bereavement. Without telling us much of what the assassinated doctor believes (except that he is against missiles and for peace), the film makes us grieve by shocking us with graphic details of brutal beatings and civil disorders.

Just as the fascists in the film appeal to their audiences by oversimplification, by generalities, by fear, so does the film appeal to us by its use of the techniques of rather ordinary suspense drama—a car speeding crazily down a sidewalk in an attempt to run over a witness. Ever since the days of the swastika, I've been leery of symbols designed to elicit automatic emotional responses—even leery of the peace symbol and of Z itself, which, I'm told, stands for the Greek words "he is alive" and is employed by the assassinated doctor's followers in the film.

These are not meant to be major reservations, but I mention them because I think they restrict the film to a genre that is perfectly respectable but incapable of greatness. A lot of people are going to become emotionally unstuck about Z, seeing it as a strong political statement, which is an unnecessary ruse to ennoble sheer entertainment.

1969

They Shoot Horses, Don't They?

Can I get you something for your feet?" the nurse at the dance marathon asks Gloria (Jane Fonda) who, after approximately 700 hours of continuous dancing, looks like an exhausted Little Orphan Annie. Gloria asks in return: "How about a saw?" And, for a brief moment you can almost see Gloria, propped up on a grimy cot during her 10-minute break, purposefully dismembering her feet as an offscreen band plays something cheerful like "Japanese Sandman."

Gloria, a Typhoid Mary of existential despair, is the terrified and terrifying heroine of Sydney Pollack's *They Shoot Horses, Don't They?*, the film adaptation of Horace McCoy's Depression novel that opened yesterday at the Fine Arts Theater. The movie is far from being perfect, but it is so disturbing in such important ways that I won't forget it very easily, which is more than can be said of much better, more consistent films.

McCoy's novel, sometimes called "a minor classic" (a patronizing way of saying that something's good but not great), was written and published in its own time (1935). It's a spare, bleak parable about American life, which McCoy pictured as a Los Angeles dance marathon in the early thirties.

The setting is a shabby ballroom on an amusement pier at the edge of the Pacific. The narrator, Robert Syverton, is a gentle, passive nonentity who, as he is tried for Gloria's murder and then as he awaits execution, recalls the events leading up to the murder. When asked why he did it, he answers simply: "She asked me to," adding: "They shoot horses, don't they?" Robert Syverton is the sort of character who, 15 years later, might have sought his fate in an exotic North Africa created by Paul Bowles.

There is, however, nothing exotic about McCoy's novel, which, although lean, is full of the kind of apocalyptic detail that both he and Nathanael West saw in life as lived on the Hollywood fringe.

Gloria, an Angel of Death who wears ankle socks and favors a marcel permanent wave, is too old, too bitter and too gross even to have gotten registered by Central Casting. Robert, who has fantasies of being a great director like von Sternberg and Mamoulian and Vidor, has only played a few "atmosphere bits." In desperation they enter the dance marathon, set, symbolically, at the edge of the Pacific Ocean, the last, impenetrable frontier.

Without actually changing the structure of the novel, told in flashbacks, the movie takes as its principal setting the marathon itself, and flashes forward to the trial in quick, subliminal, highly stylized cuts. Pollack, and his screenwriters, James Poe and Robert E. Thompson, have, necessarily, taken liberties in fleshing out a movie story. They have added characters, some of which like Red Buttons (as an over-age marathon contestant) and Susannah York (as a would-be Jean Harlow with delusions of grandeur) have their prototypes in the sort of nineteen-thirty B-picture microcosms set on submarines or in sorority houses.

Characters who existed in the book as little more than names have been given histories. Rocky, an aging, tank-town Ben Bernie (beautifully played by a no-longer young Gig Young) who is the marathon's emcee, now has as much of a past (his father was a faithhealer) as either Gloria or Robert (Michael Sarrazin). The effect of this is to blunt the edge of—and to overstate—the novel's single-minded nightmare-like qualities.

Even with all of the quite marvelous period touches—the songs, the settings, the costumes and the jargon—the movie always looks like a 1969 recapitulation of another time and place. The book, conceived as a contemporary tale, was not so encumbered with artifacts.

Nevertheless, the movie is by far the best thing that Pollack has ever directed (with the possible exception of *The Scalphunters*). While the cameras remain, as if they had been sentenced, within the ballroom, picking up the details of the increasing despair of the dancers, the movie becomes an epic of exhaustion and futility. The circular patterns of the dancers, the movement that leads nowhere, are the metaphors of the movie.

All of the performances are fine—Miss Fonda, Sarrazin, Young, Miss York and Bonnie Bedelia (as a little Okie girl who carries on in the seventh month of pregnancy). There are some small anachronisms, including a new Johnny Green song that recalls the 1940's or 1950's, instead of the 1930's. These are not really important, however.

The most disquieting thing is the movie's stated assumption that people are horses (I don't even think horses should be people, as in *Black Beauty*), an assumption that is somehow denied by the physical opulence (which, in some curious way, represents a kind of optimism) of the production itself.

1969

Patton

Patton: *A Salute to a Rebel* looks and sounds like the epic American war movie that the Hollywood establishment has always wanted to make but never had the guts to do before. The film, which is now in its premiere road-show engagement at the Criterion Theater, is 20th Century–Fox's $12-million tribute to the late General George S. Patton Jr., the brilliant, unstable World War II tactician who saw himself as nothing less than the divine instrument for making the world safe for future wars.

It's also an incredible gas, especially in this time and place. *Patton* is a loving, often sentimental, semi-official portrait of a man it characterizes as a near-schizo, a man who admitted that he damn well loved war, was surprised and somewhat taken aback when men near to him were killed, who quoted the Bible, believed in reincarnation, had the political acumen of Marie Antoinette, and, according to the movie, somehow so touched General Omar Bradley with his folksy honesty ("I'm a prima donna—I know it!") that Bradley went through the war looking always as if he were about to weep.

The fact that a supposedly sympathetic character, in a superspectacle such as this, will admit to loving war is, in a negative way, a refreshing change from the sort of conventional big-budget movie claptrap that keeps saying that war is hell, while simultaneously showing how much fun it really is. I don't think that the fact of the existence of a movie like *Patton* necessarily marks an advance in the civilizing processes of our culture, but it's a good deal less hypocritical than most patriotic American war movies. If I sound ambivalent about *Patton*, it's because the movie itself is almost as ambivalent about its hero.

Patton is, I think, a typical example of a movie of which the production company (Fox) is the real auteur. This is not meant to denigrate the very real contributions of its director, Franklin Schaffner (*Planet of the Apes*, *The War Lord*), or of its producer, Frank McCarthy, for whom the film has been something like a 10-year labor of love.

Rather, it's to acknowledge the continuity that, in the good old days, could be detected in the films of an individual studio. In the case of Fox, a large part of that continuity has been provided by the seemingly immortal presence of one man, Darryl F. Zanuck, a founder of the company over 35 years ago (with Joseph Schenck), for many years its production chief, now its board chairman.

Zanuck always has had a soft spot for the military (as did the former Fox president, Spyros P. Skouras), and Fox has often had military brass on its board of directors. During World War II, Zanuck served briefly in the United States Signal Corps and, I'm told, still doesn't mind being addressed as "Colonel." In addition, Zanuck and Fox have always had a strong affection for the quasidocumentary film, the headline film, and the war film, all of which came together in 1962 in Zanuck's last personal production, *The Longest Day*. This was the all-star reenactment of the 1944 Normandy landings, reproduced with all the accuracy that money can buy, but without much cinematic point (which, of course, money cannot buy).

The Longest Day was an extremely successful film financially, and ever since its release Zanuck has dreamed of duplicating the success. This is worth pointing out because it describes the context in which the decisions were made to spend $12-million on *Patton* and even more on *Tora! Tora! Tora!*, the not-yet-released Fox spectacle in which the Japanese attack on Pearl Harbor is reenacted.

I have no idea of the problems that went into writing a script about Patton, but, after seeing the finished film, it seems that at least some of the people working on the project must have had mixed feelings about the man and the film. So much money and so much care have been spent on the physical production that you might not think it would have an idea in its head. It does, and because the ideas are often contradictory, *Patton* is the first $12-million movie ever made that I could imagine seeing twice.

The opening of the film, which is really a kind of overture, comes very close to being conscious Camp. Patton (George C. Scott) stands on a stage addressing us, the people in the movie audience who have become, apparently, his troops. He is a fine, overly virile figure of a man, riding crop in hand and with so many medals on his chest that he could be a member of the chorus of *The Student Prince*. But—and this is important—he is dwarfed by a huge American flag that is pure Rauschenberg, and whose broad red and white stripes form an Op frame around him. He exhorts us, with manic intensity, not simply to kill the enemy, but "to tear his guts out." "All Americans love the sting of battle," he says, and the audience giggles in embarrassment. "That's why we've never lost a war [the giggles stop] . . . We're going to go through [the enemy] like crap through a goose!"

Thus, consciously, I'm sure, the contradictory tone of the film is set. "No bastard ever won a war by dying for his country," he says. "He won it by making some other poor bastard die for his country." Although the military reasoning is sound, the speech is one of astonishing arrogance, a jingoistic tour de force, full of enthusiasm for the butchery to come and reeking with the assumption that there is a God who is, of course, on the side of the Allies. The speech is so wild, in fact, that I'm not completely sure it wasn't written by Robert Downey for use in *Putney Swope*.

The almost three-hour film follows Patton's career in what is essentially a series of magnificently photographed *tableaux vivants* depicting the North African campaign, the assault on Sicily (including the incident in which Patton slapped a shell-shocked soldier for being a coward), climaxing in the brilliant sweep of his Third Army through France some weeks after the D-Day he was not allowed to participate in.

Patton's private life, his relations with his wife and family, are not even hinted at. Instead, the film presents what could be called an intimate portrait of a public figure. The portrait does not really change in the course of the film; it is simply filled in with additional details. Depending on your point of view, these details show Patton as the embodiment of all of one's fears about the rich, white, Protestant military establishment, a man who confidently believed that America and England should rule the world, or, as a ruthlessly dedicated, eccentric genius, described with great affection as "a 16th-century man lost in the 20th century."

The surprise of the film is not that the weight is clearly in favor of the latter interpretation. Any other choice would be unthinkable for the studio that brought us such films as *A Wing and a Prayer* and *The Fighting Sullivans*, along with *The Longest Day*. In spite of *M*A*S*H*, Fox hasn't become so hip that it would spend $12-million debunking one of our most sacred institutions.

Patton is meant, I'm sure, as a completely sincere tribute to a man to whom it simply isn't easy to pay tribute.

The real surprise is that the film, though long (and, from my point of view, appalling), is so consistently fascinating. It isn't just that Scott's performance is full of odd, unexpected details that compel constant attention. Although you pretty much know the way the movie is going, you can never be sure Scott is going in the same direction, quietly. The film is much more than the one performance that dominates it. Shot in a 70-millimeter film process called Dimension-150, it is extraordinarily, almost unrealistically, beautiful—the epitome of Pop movie epic with lots of broad vistas caught in clear, deep focus. The battle scenes, including desert confrontations as well as Patton's dash through France in the deep of winter, are always more spectacular than bloody. In one frame, you might have Patton in foreground, a tank attack group in the middle ground, and a line of fighter planes flying in over the horizon. A sense of the true horror and panic of battle is thus distanced, replaced by the awe one has of such carefully coordinated, logistically complex filmmaking. Schaffner shoots his interior scenes—mostly the cavernous castles and baroque palaces in which Patton was bivouacked—with a similar eye for grandeur. More than one scene opens with a shot of a frescoed ceiling, followed by a slow pan that carries the eye down to the action below. It's almost as if the director, like Patton, were constantly paying his respects to God.

1970

Zabriskie Point

I don't have to prove my revolutionary credentials to you!" an angry young man shouts to—I think—Kathleen Cleaver in the meeting of activists that opens Michelangelo Antonioni's new film, *Zabriskie Point*.

Thereafter, revolutionary credentials—beautiful, shiny and largely bogus —are flashed all over the screen at the Coronet Theater, where the film began its run yesterday. They are also there in the film's advertising, which employs the stars-and-stripes motif so favored these days by movies aspiring to sociopolitical significance. You know the ones—*Medium Cool, Easy Rider, Patton*.

Zabriskie Point is Antonioni's first American film and the 11th feature in a filmography that includes *L'Avventura, La Notte, Red Desert* and *Blow-Up*. Coming to us with those credentials, *Zabriskie Point* demands to be taken seriously, if only by Antonioni buffs for whom no assumption is too outrageous to make in the interests of filling in the blank spaces in the master's plan.

I suspect that for the rest of us—with the possible exception of highway engineers (the film includes a lot of lovely aerial shots of macadam roads snaking into blue distances)—*Zabriskie Point* will remain a movie of stunning superficiality, another example of a noble artistic impulse short-circuited in a foreign land.

The story is a kind of activists' brief encounter. Mark (Mark Frechette), a young man who may or may not have shot a policeman during a strike in Los Angeles, steals a small plane and flies up to Death Valley where he meets Daria (Daria Halprin), a sweet, pot-smoking post-teenybopper of decent inclinations. For several hours they wander through the photogenic Death Valley landscape philosophizing (She: "It's so peaceful." He: "It's dead."), exchanging political views (She: "There are a thousand different sides to every question." He: "You gotta have heroes and villains so you can fix things up."), and finally making love.

Towards the end of a day in which, from the varying lengths of the shadows we've seen, the sun has spun around on a drunken axis, she helps him paint his plane in psychedelic designs. He returns to Los Angeles and certain arrest ("I want to take the risks," he says by way of explanation), and she drives off to Phoenix where her boss (Rod Taylor), who may or may not be her lover, has a desert Berchtesgaden.

This, of course, is not the real story, as *L'Avventura* wasn't really about a girl who got lost on a craggy island, or *Blow-Up* a whodunit. The story of Mark and Daria is one of options faced and taken—in this case by two young people in a world of such grotesqueness that (according to Antonioni) violence is the only rational response.

The main problem with *Zabriskie Point* is that Antonioni has done nothing with his physical production to illuminate in any meaningful way the emotional states of his two principal characters—if, indeed, they have any.

They are completely instinctive people, but their instincts have been imposed upon them by an intellectualizing Antonioni, rather than by God. Everything in the film is calculated, including the prettily-photographed, conventionally-ironic contrasts between the principal locations—Los Angeles (used-car lots, absurd billboards, glass-and-steel office buildings reaching above the smog) and Death Valley, whose barren hills look like the remains of some cataclysmic oatmeal war of prehistory.

Paradoxically, even though everything is calculated, nothing within the film justifies its final, apocalyptic vision of the disintegration of the Western world to the accompaniment of a funky rock tune. It's lovely to look at (books, furniture, food, a copy of *Look* magazine, all hanging suspended in an emulsion of deep blue), but completely absurd in the context.

So too is a giant specialty number that Antonioni inserts within the film when Mark and Daria make love on the side of a sand dune. All of Death Valley erupts with life and love. Bodies (members of Joe Chaikin's Open Theater), most of whom keep their clothes on, writhe in various kinds of desperate couplings and triplings as we watch as if through a sandstorm. The once austere, puritanical Antonioni seems now to have opted for erotica, which becomes unintentionally funny. When Antonioni finally returns the air to its natural state, Mark notes quietly: "I always knew it would be like that."

Because of the fundamental emptiness of his American vision, all sorts of flaws that one might overlook in better Antonioni films become apparent. The two young leads, who have never acted before, are beautiful (he, I'm afraid, has the edge), but they move and talk with all the conviction of the life-sized mannequins who perform in a Sunny Dunes television commercial within the film. Only Rod Taylor, a real actor, seems human.

Various Antonioni mannerisms—the blank screen suddenly filled with a face, the endless tracking shots, the pregnant pauses between unfinished thoughts—are finally only tolerable because you remember the times when they were better used. In *Zabriskie Point*, Antonioni, like Mark and Daria, succumbs to the hostile terrain.

1970

Is *Fiddler* More DeMille Than Sholem Aleichem?

Because a mean spirit, as well as snobbishness, have been imputed to anyone who doesn't find *Fiddler on the Roof* the most powerful movie musical ever made, I'd like to say right off—in a friendly, humble, populist sort of way—that I hope the film, now at the Rivoli, will make pots of money for everyone connected with it. Not only is it a well-meant, if literalized, adaptation of a lovely, stylized show (which can still be seen in something like its original Broadway purity at the Broadway Theater, several blocks north of the Rivoli), but business has been so bad this year that any movie that can possibly keep the creditors away—without insulting its audience—deserves our support.

However, that doesn't necessarily mean that it deserves our blind admiration, if unfelt, or our denial of a fact of history. That is, that the decline in movie attendance over the years, the increase in the costs of production, plus the well-deserved flops of *Star* and *Dr. Dolittle*, have just about finished the once joyful tradition of the original American film musical. It's no accident, I think, that with the possible exception of *Gigi*, none of the great original movie musicals of the 1940s and 1950s (*An American in Paris, Singin' in the Rain, Funny Face*, etc) was conceived as a movie that had to be financially successful if the company that produced it was to survive. In that once-upon-a-time, movie musicals were no big deals. When they were good, they looked free and casual and unafraid.

Today we have what amounts to a new, mostly joyless tradition, that of the safe, artistically solemn, pre-sold musical behemoth adapted from the Broadway hit. It's a tradition that puts a terrible burden on the already reeling Broadway theater (which is now in the position to kill off film musicals forever). It also puts a dreadful strain on the imagination of the filmmaker, who must decide how to preserve the original sensibility, which accounted for the Broadway success, in a medium that can show us hundreds of people, at one time, or the saliva in a man's mouth, but can simulate the excitement of the stage's person-to-person contact only through the recognition of shared emotions.

The movie *Fiddler* is superior in almost every respect to *Hello, Dolly!* and *Paint Your Wagon*, each of which had the intimate charm of the Brooklyn Bridge wired as a sound-and-light show, to *Funny Girl* and *On a Clear Day* (although it lacks their star performances and occasional moments of splendor), and to *Oliver*—largely because the source material—the libretto and the score—is superior. It's not a grossly bad movie, but it left me so untouched that several days after seeing it, I walked up the street to the Broadway Theater to see the original—which meant subjecting myself to more *Fiddler*, in a short space of time, than perhaps any non-addict need sanely do. It was, I realize, an unfair test for the cast of a show that's been running seven years and that's not exactly getting younger with each performance. Yet, miracle of miracles (comparatively speaking, anyway), the show still lives, even though a bit run-down at the heels and a bit automatic in its responses to the live audience. It is very much a Broadway show, employing the sophisticated Broadway technology that is much further removed from the world of Tevye, and the life of the Jews in a Czarist Russian shtetl, than Broadway is removed from Hollywood. Why, then, does the show evoke emotional responses that are left undisturbed by the movie? It should follow that if you are moved by one, then you must be moved by the other. Or does it?

Jerome Robbins, who staged the show, employed the kind of Broadway shorthand that comes close to being—in very unexpected ways—the theatrical equivalent of the Sholem Aleichem prose. The dancers soar and the singers traffic in images and melodies that are Tin Pan Alley cum Jewish folk, but nothing denies the direct simplicity of the narrative, which has a marvelous, woeful modesty to it. The show is a fable told in highly theatrical Broadway terms, and it never makes the mistake of indicating that it knows it's an epic. Such a thought would, I'm sure, make the show's Tevye shrug with a certain embarrassment. He talks directly to God, and to us, but he lets us discover his happinesses and his sorrows discreetly.

To call the movie an epic is really to define what's wrong with it, which is to mistake Sholem Aleichem for Leo Tolstoi, and to substitute for the necessarily limited physical resources of the stage, the vast physical resources of the screen. In literalizing the show, in making a big ethnic thing out of it in real landscapes and real houses, Norman Jewison, the director, and Joseph Stein, who adapted his stage book to the screen, have effectively overwhelmed not only Aleichem, but the best things about the stage production. These include Mr. Robbins' breathtaking choreography, which is mostly seen on the screen in bits and pieces, either from the neck up or from the knees down, and the lovely Sheldon Harnick–Jerry Bock score, which is strong, as Broadway scores go, but which was never designed to meet the grand, operatic requirements of a literal exodus. Thus pushed beyond its limits, the music goes flat and renders banal moments that, on the stage, are immensely moving.

Perhaps because the mannerisms of the New York Yiddish theater have common philosophical roots with Aleichem, I found the single most touching performance in the film to be that of Molly Picon as the matchmaker. She is excessive and outrageous and very dear. Equally fine, though a good deal more legitimate, is Leonard Frey as Motel, the otherwise timid tailor who carries off Tevye's eldest daughter to what promises to be a life of blissful hardship.

The entire show must, however, be shouldered by the actor who plays Tevye, and this is where the movie takes its boldest step, and one that is most distorting. Topol, the Israeli actor, is a fine, vigorous performer, a man with the easy, slightly calculating charm of a matinee idol, and, when he is not being upstaged by the movie's visual and aural grandeur, or by close-ups so huge that you pull back in your seat, he does shoulder the movie. However, he shoulders it as if he were a youngish Moses instead of a rueful Job, which amounts to a kind of theatrical blasphemy. It's difficult, for me, to be very much moved by a Moses figure, since I'm always aware that Moses has a hot-line to God, whereas Job (and Tevye) seem often to be talking into receivers that someone has left off the hook, quite arbitrarily.

Gone—spirited away, so to speak—with the substitution of Moses for Job, is a measure of the magnificence of a certain kind of human indomitability, which is what I take Aleichem to be all about. There are hints of Aleichem throughout the film, but don't be fooled. Deep within it there beats the mechanical heart of Cecil B. DeMille's 1956 *The Ten Commandments*, which may possibly turn out to be a stroke of genius, at least for the box-office success of a very valuable property, but it diminishes *Fiddler on the Roof*.

1971

William S. Pechter

During the 1960s and 70s, writing for such periodicals as *Commentary*, *The Kenyon Review*, *Sight and Sound*, and *Commonweal*, William S. Pechter (b. 1936) epitomized the best qualities of the quarterly film critic. Weighing in with sane intelligence, often after the first hype or controversy had settled, he would consider a movie at length and from angles both formal and ethical. Above all he was a humanist, responding warmly and subjectively, then qualifying these instinctual responses with more dispassionate afterthoughts. As he described the process in the introduction to his collection *Movies Plus One*: "The peculiar and perhaps archetypal moviegoing experience for me has occasionally seemed that of feeling tears well in my eyes at some film's maudlin finale at the same time that I'm saying to myself, 'What crap!'—or, similarly, the experience of watching a pornographic movie and finding myself *both* aroused *and* bored." In the following pieces he dissects Buñuel's art, and answers with grace that impossible parlor-game question (for a film critic): "What is your favorite movie?"

◆

These Are a Few of My Favorite Things

Do I have a favorite movie? Do I have a favorite novel? (I have, perhaps, a favorite novella: Chekhov's *Three Years*.) More important, *should* I have a favorite movie? The question provokes resistance in me even though I recognize it to be intellectually respectable in a way that a similar but (I assume) distinguishable question—What is the greatest movie ever made?—is not. And yet, in some ways, the silly question would be the easier to answer. If for greatness one requires breadth of compass, prodigious range of mood and style—in a word, richness—then it would be hard to think of a richer and, therefore, greater film than *The Rules of the Game*. Is it also my favorite film? Yes—well, yes and no. That is to say, sometimes yes and sometimes no.

The argument that, in a general way, can be used to assert *The Rules of the Game*'s supremacy among films mirrors one that's been used to advance film's supremacy among the arts: that of its nature as a synthetic medium, one incorporating the resources of the other arts and transcending by combining them. Why is it, though I might be inclined to a specific argument in behalf of *The Rules of the Game*'s supreme greatness, that I find the general case for it and for the film medium so uncompelling? Among films, *The Rules of the Game* may well be of incomparable richness—drawing not only on the resources of theater, music, painting, and poetry but on the muses of both tragedy and comedy as well—but do I really prefer it to films one might characterize as *narrow*, like Godard's *Le Petit Soldat* or Buñuel's *El?* And if by favorite film one means the film one's fondest of, do I prefer *The Rules of the Game* even to such films as *Animal Crackers* or *The Fatal Glass of Beer*, which may not be describable as works of art at all?

There is a way in which film can be considered a synthetic (or, perhaps better, eclectic) medium that, for me, has greater meaning than do theoretical speculations on esthetic attributes. *The Rules of the Game* is a great work of art, and there are times when I want the experience of great works of art, but also times when I'm drawn to films such as those of the Marx Brothers, which, in effect (and at their best), spit on art and culture. That I can gratify both impulses in seeing films—my impulse toward art and toward some different but related pleasure—is what most distinguishes my moviegoing experience from my experience of reading and complicates any attempt to decide on my favorite movie; for how can one choose among incomparables? I may be unusual in this, but (apart from some occasional periodical reading) I no longer read with the motivation solely of being entertained, as I do go to some movies. (About as close as I now come to this is in reading Kingsley Amis, by whom I know I'll be entertained even should his novels fail artistically.) Of course, one may contend that Marx Brothers movies *are* works of art despite their esthetic anarchy, and a film such as *Duck Soup* does seem to be (in part) a coherent satire of war and politics—which is one reason why the earlier *Animal Crackers* (at least, in my fond memory of it), which satirizes nothing, seems to me a more perfect vehicle for the Marx Brothers' leveling nihilism: even the earlier film's technical primitivism seems felicitously to enhance its anarchic spirit. The temptation to justify esthetically one's pleasure in a Marx Brothers movie is, of course, understandable; one wants to celebrate what one likes, and film enthusiasts, in particular, have for so long been on the defensive vis-à-vis partisans of the other arts that such justification has been almost a polemical necessity. But the esthetic justification of the Marx Brothers and of a great many other admirable films seems to me finally to falsify the nature of the pleasure to be found in them, as well as to misrepresent one's critical rectitude. Even now, I feel faintly ashamed as a "highbrow" and a professional critic to admit to my fondness for a film such as *Shane*. I think one *can* defend *Shane* esthetically, and I'd like to try someday to do this. But can any such justification completely explain why it is that I find *Shane*, of whose artistic defects I'm fully fully aware, so *thrilling?* Isn't the appeal to me of *Shane* at least in part to something in me that's childish?

If there's a common denominator to the many and disparate films that, at various times (at least, during the times of my seeing them), are my favorite movie, it's the centrality in them of the human figure: the felt presence of a personality, whether that of the character, actor, star, or even director (for, certainly, my one-time hero worship of such film-makers as Huston and Welles was only a highbrow version of the ordinary fan's state of being star-struck, and so, I think, is much of the director adulation of the *auteur* critics today). It seems to me, on reflection, no accident that the intensity of my moviegoing fluctuated—not so much the frequency of my attendance but the intensity of my concentration or fixation on the screen—according to the fluctuations of social and sexual activity in my life. Though my attachment to films has managed to survive the assaults on solitude that becoming a husband and father entail, moviegoing remains, as it's always been for me, an essentially solitary occupation: in part, by choice, because I enjoy it more that way, but also, in part, because films were something gone to as an escape from solitude; and, in the latter aspect, what movies provided for me most of all was the company of another.

Given the complex intermingling of motives that brought me to the movies and the multiplicity of things I found at them, can I really pretend to esthetic rigor or avoid personal confession in attempting to choose a favorite among them? For one fairly long stretch of my life, I probably could have said *The Quiet Man* was my favorite movie, but, though I think now, no less than I did then, that it would be easy to make an esthetic defense of the film, my admiration for it as an artistic achievement was at least equaled by my absorption in the romance of the principal characters and my enchantment by the idyllic picture, so far from the difficult and prosaic life of my own, of a simple and beautiful life into which I longed, in fantasy, to escape. (Though I love *The Quiet Man* still, I've grown a good deal less susceptible to basing fantasies on it; it remains one of my favorite films, as do several others of John Ford, but probably it's no longer even my favorite Ford film.) Nor am I really always sure, as I was in the case of *The Quiet Man* (or in those of the several musicals, *The Band Wagon* chief among them, that I love, and from the elation of whose world I'm always somewhat reluctant to return to the nonsinging, nondancing world of my own), just where the artistic boundaries of a film end and my own fantasizing relation to it begins. On the simplest level, even after having published highbrow criticism of film, I've sat raptly through abysmal movies whose plots and even titles I couldn't have recalled five minutes after leaving the theater, so single-mindedly was my attention focused on an adored actress (discretion forbids my naming the object of the last such infatuation, as she's now the wife of another critic in a marriage any fantast must find inspirational). On a more complex level, after seeing *Force of Evil* for the first time on a television program that consisted of the same movie's being shown several times a day during the course of a week and then seeing the film again some eight or ten times during the course of that week, I hardly knew, by week's end, whether the characters in *Force of Evil* existed only in the film and in my head or whether they were real and really enacting their recurring roles in a drama being played out, now and forever, somewhere in the unknowable reaches of New York City. I've since gone on to get some distance on *Force of Evil* and, after some false starts, even to write something that, I believe, does the film justice without scanting the qualities in it that made it, during that first week and thereafter, one of my favorite movies. But sometimes I feel that the immediate, "uncritical" response to certain films is really the most just criticism of them. At least, I've never come across any criticism of another of my favorite films, *Meet Me in St. Louis*, that improves on someone's saying to me after seeing it, "I'm so glad they didn't have to leave St. Louis."

Increasingly, however, as I sink into middle age, there's another figure whom I go to the movies in search of. Though my recollections of books I've read are no less vivid than my recollections of films I've seen, it's rare that my recollection of a book is situated in a memory of the experience of my having read it: a memory of a particular time and place. Nor does my rereading of a book I read long before usually recapture for me the feelings I had when reading it the first time. Yet when I see now films I saw as a child in the forties, my memories of having seen them the first time—of a theater, a neighborhood, a kind of weather, a congeries of sights and smells, and, most of all, the emotions of that person who once saw them—can flood back over me (I don't mean always, but sometimes) with an almost painful acuity. The experience, for me, is a recognition really of my own mortality, of aging and loss, and, though I seek it out, I also fight it (I tend, for example, to think of all movies from the fifties on as "recent" and am always surprised when others don't regard them likewise). The "eternal return" of films has often been remarked on: there, for as long as the film stock itself is physically preserved, Bogart unwraps a parcel and Belmondo runs dying down a street, the Morgans and Ambersons go on a sleigh ride and Wyatt Earp sits lazily on the veranda, the tramp takes the flower from the now sighted blind girl and Magnani steps before the curtain and replies to the director's asking her if she misses her three lovers, "A little." But preserved for me as well, for as long as my senses and memory survive, are all those past selves I left behind me, sitting and watching, rejecting and devouring, living parts of my life simultaneously with the life unfolding on the screen.

The question was asked: What is my favorite movie? My answer, if it is an answer, is not the defense of any particular film or the elaboration of an esthetic but some discursive remarks on the nature of my moviegoing experience itself, though I hope they suggest why it is that I can't give the question any other kind of answer. Among my favorite films are those I can't defend esthetically but love for extraesthetic reasons, and others I once loved somewhat blindly and whose faults, though I now see them, I don't wish to speak of, preferring to be less a critic rather than unfaithful to enthusiasms past. We're all blind, whether unknowingly or willfully, to the imperfections of our loved ones, and to those we loved in our innocence most of all, and I don't suppose my feelings in this are, in any way, unique; Pauline Kael can't abide the sweetness of *Meet Me in St. Louis* yet is indulgent of the sweetness of Cukor's *Little Women* and D. W. Griffith (I like much of Griffith's sweetness also; it's his bombast that turns me off). If my becoming a film critic had been continuous with my adoption of an esthetic or of a critical method, I might answer *The Rules of the Game* and be done with it. But my writing of film criticism has been continuous rather with my experience of moviegoing in all its esthetic impurity. Relatively early, it became clear to me that I was going to spend a large part of my life at the movies, with or without benefit of any justifying profession. I've heard some film critics making impassioned defenses of their vocation and of film criticism as an art among the others, and I've no reason to doubt their sincerity; probably such critics have their favorite movies and even nominations for the greatest film ever made. But, for me, from early on, becoming a film critic was less the pursuit of an exalted calling than a means of averting social disapproval by justifying unbreakable habit.

1982

Buñuel

On the simplest level, there is Buñuel the foot fetishist. This is the Buñuel who makes films which freely indulge a complex of private obsessions and fantasies—a figure which extends to include Buñuel the sadist, applying razors to the end of literally opening eyes—and, of all the "false Buñuels," it is probably the most persistent. Following close on this is the liberal's Buñuel, scourge of the clergy and bourgeoisie. (In the account of one mindless idolater: "Any child brought up by priests bears some trace of this upbringing. With normal boys, religious education is transformed in time into a healthy reaction *against*. Buñuel was a normal boy."[1]) Frequently in tandem with this appropriation of Buñuel as political ally is the notion of his observational, "documentary" style. ". . . The art of a master like Luis Buñuel lies in his being not only original and radical but also utterly unobtrusive. He simply uses his camera to look at people, plainly, patiently, mostly in mid-shot, without tricks or illusions or expectations. Like a man whose gift of silence makes other people talk more and more anxiously, Buñuel's camera waits for the characters to reveal themselves—their obsessions, their perversions, their corruptions. The director, meanwhile, defines nothing, asserts nothing; he remains detached, accepting, sardonic."[2] From this follows, especially for those who would agree with such a description but put a less sympathetic construction on it, the sense of Buñuel as cold, withdrawn, uncommunicative.

This last Buñuel makes a prominent appearance in a piece by Pauline Kael that is virtually a little anthology of "false Buñuels."[3] (As it is the measure of most of what passes for criticism in the specialist film books and magazines[4] that it seems as worthless when capable of being adduced in support of one's own view as it seems irrelevant as something to take issue with, so also is it true that one can often learn as much in disagreeing with the "mistakes" of a good critic as one can from finding one's own and the critic's views in agreement. And, in many ways, Miss Kael's is the most valuable Buñuel criticism in English; a piece worth taking issue with—as I intend to—and worth appreciating for the clarity and conciseness with which it articulates those issues on which a relevant discussion of Buñuel should take place.) Yet, certainly, Buñuel's films cannot be considered cold in the sense that one may speak of the coldness of, say, the later works of Carl Dreyer, with their wintry refusal to entertain the possibility of any emotional transaction with an audience (an intransigence that can, to be sure, have its own fascination). The coolness of Buñuel's films is not in their relation to their audience, since their aim, above all, is to arouse and disturb that audience, but rather in their relation to their subject. It is that subject—human cruelty and suffering—that is regarded

---

[1]Ado Kyrou, *Luis Buñuel: An Introduction*, New York, Simon and Schuster, 1963. It is ironic that Buñuel, who of all major film-makers has been perhaps the most unfailingly lucid and illuminating in commenting on his own work, should also probably be, of all major film-makers, the object of the greatest amount of dithyrambic nonsense by others.

[2]A. Alvarez, *Beyond All This Fiddle*, New York, Random House, 1969.

[3]"Saintliness," *Going Steady*, Boston, Atlantic–Little, Brown, 1970.

[4]See, for example, *Luis Buñuel* by Raymond Durgnat, Berkeley, University of California Press, 1968, or almost anything on Buñuel in *Sight and Sound*.

coolly, yet *this* coolness, far from bespeaking an absence of feeling, creates tensions which act to intensify the feelings of the spectator, and is at the heart of the films' impact upon their audience. The camera looks coolly at material of a burning agitation; we cannot. But much as a film by De Sica (the De Sica of the neo-realist period, to invoke the artistic model for the critical orthodoxy ascendant in 1950 when, after a silence of fifteen years, *Los Olvidados*, or *The Young and the Damned*, suddenly thrust Buñuel again before an audience's attention) is so completely suffused by the director's own feeling that ours can only be carried along by the tide, so conversely does Buñuel's reticence force us to a response; his reluctance to draw the conclusion presses us to reach ours. And, to the extent that we are aware that we are unable to respond, or to respond adequately, we laugh. It is the laughter of black comedy, and ultimately one may recognize in it the only response a sane person can make.

It is this stylistic reticence that has given rise to the notion of Buñuel's documentary "objectivity," a reticence that does indeed remain intact between *Land Without Bread* (or *Las Hurdes*), his one actual documentary film, and the fictional films which precede and follow it. Yet, if the forgotten wastes of Las Hurdes do actually exist, they are equally a region of Buñuel's mind; if they didn't exist, he would have invented them, and he has, before and after. Buñuel's camera does not "wait . . . without . . . expectations . . . for the characters to reveal themselves" as though these characters were not of his creation, and their revelation not the measured effect of that artistic creation and control. If, in that subjective world which Buñuel's camera "objectively" evokes, some may be disposed to see merely the expression of an antipathy toward the clergy and the bourgeoisie, they must blind themselves both to all that is admirable in Nazarin (displayed most unmistakably in his angry speech to the colonel) and all that is corrupt in Jorge, the "progressive" son in *Viridiana*, with his radio blaring "Shake your cares away," and his games of cards. And if, in that world's ubiquitous fetishism, some can see only the indication of Buñuel's own idiosyncrasies, they must disregard the fact that the fetish is a perfect physical manifestation of the principle of functionless or dislocated energy around which that world revolves and of the harvest of frustration in which that principle has its issue. For what is the foot fetish but an instance of the concentration of the most fundamental human energy and desire on an object in which there can be found no truly satisfactory consummation—unless it is by a kick. It is useless, and the uselessness it exemplifies lies at the very center of the world of Buñuel's films, radiating outward in such variegated forms as the hallucinatory jealousy of Francisco (in *El*, released in the U.S. as *This Strange Passion*) and the saintliness of Simon upon his pillar, and finding what is perhaps its most ambiguously disturbing embodiment in the incident of the exploited dog which Jorge releases from his master only to have yet another dog bound to a cart in identical enslavement follow in its wake. We laugh, but why? What do we laugh at when we laugh at Buñuel's films, and why?

Far from there being, as Pauline Kael contends, "no way to get a hold on what Buñuel believes in," Buñuel's films constitute, with a singleness of purpose as unwavering as any to be found in art, a continually unfolding fiction in the form of an almost scientifically methodical testing of the proposition that we are living in the worst of all possible worlds—a belief if ever there was one. It is a world emblematized by its dislocations, whether inflicted by the folly of institutions, as in the saintliness of Simon and bourgeois "virtue" of Don Francisco, or the cruelties of nature, as in the hopeless passion of the dwarf for his full-grown inamorata in *Nazarin*; or, as in the miseries of the Hurdanos, by the complicity of both.[5] It is a world evoked by an art in which loathing, a Swiftian revulsion and disgust, is a motive force; but an art in which, if one cannot really discover a recognizable sympathy or compassion in the "entomological" interest out of which a Francisco is explored, neither is there misanthropy.[6] Socially refined man may indeed be the monstrous creature which populates Buñuel's *Diary of a Chambermaid*, but the human needs on which society is based are depicted in Buñuel's *Adventures of Robinson Crusoe*, seen there undistorted by social institutions, as endowed with both dignity and a kind of beauty. If then, as Pauline Kael says, "Buñuel makes the charitable the butt of humor," it is not necessarily the impulse toward charity that is being ridiculed. The charitable impulse of Nazarin is never impugned (nor is that of the enlightened reformatory director in *Los Olvidados*, or that of Jorge toward the dog), but the main fact about Nazarin as about them all is that he's ineffectual, irrelevant to the plight of those to whom his charity is directed, *useless*. "You're thoroughly good and I'm thoroughly bad, and neither of us serves any purpose," the thief tells Nazarin in prison. Nazarin is as self-defeating in his charity as Francisco is in his jealousy; he is, like Simon of the desert and Archibaldo de La Cruz, like the young man in *Un Chien Andalou* and the *husband* in *Belle de Jour*, like Don Francisco (and all—church and state—that Don Francisco internalizes and exemplifies), *obsessive*; unyielding in the refusal to compromise with reality.

[5]And, in the words of André Bazin: "It does not matter that they [the Hurdanos] are an exception; what matters is that such a thing can be."

[6]Neither, however, is there always that "impression of incorruptible human dignity" which Bazin speaks of finding in *Las Hurdes* and *Los Olvidados*. Indeed, chief among Buñuel's charges against the world as it is made is precisely its power and propensity to strip man of his dignity and corrupt him.

They are not idealists but (like Cordelier, in Renoir's lone Buñuel-like black comedy) absolutists, and it is absurd, faced with a work so richly ambiguous as *Nazarin*, to say, as does Pauline Kael, that Buñuel is "so enraged by the unfulfillment of ideals that he despises dreamers who can't make their dreams come true," or that Buñuel fails to "give in" to the film's final gesture. For, though the specific effect on Nazarin of the woman's gift of the pineapple following his disillusionment with saintliness may not be knowable, the affective impact that the woman's mundane charity has on him is unmistakable in every detail of the scene's realization, from his stunned bewilderment to the final, shattering roll of drums; indeed, it is a case of the final moment of the film (like the last line of Waugh's *The Ordeal of Gilbert Pinfold*) retrospectively transforming everything that we have experienced before. And, though it may be true that one cannot say with certainty that when Buñuel's obsessed characters "lose their faith" they become any more useful, it certainly would be false to assert that Buñuel is suggesting that human nature doesn't change, or that he holds a Grand Inquisitor's view of man's basic animality; false to the very essence of his films, which are nothing if not a demonstration that we must change human nature and change the institutions that at once distort and reinforce it in its present state; changes to which saintliness is irrelevant. And if it is true that Buñuel's films cannot be made to yield any programmatic definition of what a better human nature might be, it is clearly the implied injunction of his surrealist commitment and of the ribbon of dream which runs through his work that there can be no meaningful change which does not admit and dignify the irrational side of man's nature; this not as a surrender to animality but as a victory for a more whole humanity.

Apart from such things as the mock reformation of Archibaldo and mock damnation of Simon,[7] Nazarin's is the one serious instance of a Buñuel

---

[7]Seldom can any sequence in films as straightforward as the ending of *Simon of the Desert* have been met with such obtuseness as that of most of the film's American critics. For, far from revealing to us Buñuel's vision of hell (and its impoverishment), *Simon* ends with a brilliantly insolent joke on the banality of "sin." Simon, unchanged in his "damnation," sits in a discothèque, sipping Coke, mechanically trading formulae ("Devil behind me!"—"Devil above you!") with Satan, both locked no less than before in their mutual irrelevance; it is, after all, the devil who describes the kids' innocuous dance as "Radioactive flesh . . . the latest and the last," and who earlier remarks to Simon, "We're very similar, you and I." Moreover, anyone reading the ending as originally written (published in *Three Screenplays*, New York, the Orion Press, 1969, with interpretive comments one takes on faith and reason not to be by Buñuel) can see that the ending as filmed has been made to emphasize just this joke, and that no shortage of money can, as has been alleged, be held accountable for the differences. But the strongest argument for one's understanding Buñuel's joke as I have described it is simply this: it, and not the moralistic interpretation of the critics, is totally in character with everything in the film (and in Buñuel's work) that has gone before.

character brought in this world to at least the brink of some fundamental change of nature, though what lies over that brink we cannot know. Yet the importance with which Buñuel invests the critical moment in which that change hangs in the balance, the respect he accords it, is never in doubt. Buñuel's scorn is reserved for such change's substitute and counterfeit: for those anodyne half-measures which serve to make clear consciences, of which the most troubling instance is that of Jorge and the dog. For surely what Buñuel makes us see, and laugh at, in Jorge's act is not the particular kindness but its general inadequacy, and, more specifically, the vastness of its inadequacy in conjunction with Jorge's satisfaction in having acted virtuously. It is not the "saving one Jew from the ovens or one Biafran baby from starvation" that we laugh at, in Pauline Kael's emotionally charged comparison, but ourselves, and our ameliorative checks to the Biafra relief fund, which ameliorate, to be sure, while things go on essentially as before. Is Jorge only a realist who does what he can? But it is just this kind of realism, and the reality that shapes it, which Buñuel exposes to our shamed laughter. Yet Buñuel's scorn for our ameliorist liberalism comes not from the side of a Lawrence or Pound, as Pauline Kael misleadingly suggests, but from that of a surrealist anarchism.[8] And though we may be unable to appropriate him to any congenial reformism, the fact remains that his refusal to make the reformist statements is precisely that quality in his work which, in its denial of feelings to assuage ours, presses us to our own confrontation.[9] Upon our habitual numbness, Buñuel's films exert the terrible pressure of the noncommittal. And we laugh.

We laugh, in black comedy, at a vision of the world so intensely terrible that only our laughter can relieve its pressure; we laugh, at its very extremity, in order to endure it. (And it is no paradox that, but for the unflaggingly witty *Simon of the Desert*, Buñuel's deliberately light or playful films—*The Criminal Life of Archibaldo de La Cruz* or *Belle de Jour* or *The Milky Way*—are actually less funny than the darker ones.) It is the world of Modot in *L'Age d'Or*, the Hurdanos, the forgotten ones of Mexico City, Nazarin, Viridiana and her Uncle Jaime, Celestine the chambermaid and Joseph the fascist brute. It is a world

[8]". . . In a world so badly made, as ours is, there is only one road—rebellion." (Buñuel, quoted in Kyrou, *op. cit.*)

[9]"I will let Friedrich Engels speak for me. He defines the function of the novelist (and here read film maker) thus: 'The novelist will have acquitted himself honorably of his task when, by means of an accurate portrait of authentic social relations, he will have destroyed the conventional view of the nature of those relations, shattered the optimism of the bourgeois world, and forced the reader to question the permanency of the prevailing order, and this even if the author does not offer us any solutions, even if he does not clearly take sides.'" (Buñuel, quoted *ibid.*)

at the very center of which lives Francisco in *El*, like a character out of French bedroom farce except that the farce is being played in his head. Whether prosecuting his paranoid legal suit (whose fortunes are so intertwined with those of his marriage) to redress some ancient grievance, straightening a picture or his wife's shoes, or scurrying around the house in his bathrobe with his queer assortment of implements, he is a figure as preposterous (in his sheer ineffectuality) as he is inescapably disturbing. Francisco is continually creating situations in which all alternatives confirm his suspicions; and it is in our sense of the discrepancy between things as they are, things as he imagines them, and the elaborate, self-defeating stratagems by which he attempts to deal with things as he imagines them, that the film's comedy lies. And yet, recognizably, his world is ours, and he its creation; almost, one might say, its purest creation. For the madman is also the model citizen and perfect Christian gentleman; the product of the institutions which sanction him. "Don't hurt him! He's my friend!" cries the priest, at the end, of the victim of that "friendship," and it is a cry into which Buñuel has managed to infuse not only his icy rage but also something surprisingly like compassion. If, then, we laugh, what is our laughter, the laughter of black comedy, but a strategy for preserving sanity while contemplating the intolerable? And, if the "entomological" interest can yield this, as it yields also the tortured Modot, the miseries of the Hurdanos and *los olvidados*, the agony of Nazarin, the convulsions of innocence in *Viridiana* and decadence in *The Diary of a Chambermaid*, then one must acknowledge that Buñuel's "coolness" is something which may contain passion; that it is, like the "coolness" of a Brecht or Bresson, an instance of the transformation of passion by art. And the sensitizing effect this coolness produces on us is a testimony to the degree of passion Buñuel's art truly contains.

"What can I do against . . . the idiotic multitude which has pronounced as *beautiful* or *poetic* what in essence is only a desperate and passionate appeal to murder?"[10] Unlike the later work of a Welles or von Sternberg, Buñuel's films are marked by an evolution *away* from pictorial beauty, from richness of decor and what newspapermen are given to calling "poetry" in films, and toward a kind of stripped-down bluntness. Probably, *Los Olvidados* is the last of Buñuel's films to be visually striking in a way that immediately connects with the brilliant imagery of *Un Chien Andalou* and *L'Age d'Or*; thereafter, "beauty" is to be found in the autumnal rotting leaves and deliberately revolting, overripe beauty of *The Diary of a Chambermaid* and (to some degree) *Belle de Jour*.

[10]Buñuel, *L'Age d'Or and Un Chien Andalou*, New York, Simon and Schuster, 1969.

(Indeed, it is a tribute to the resolve with which Buñuel has sought this antibeauty that he has been able consistently to impose his own characteristic visual directness on the work of Gabriel Figueroa, Mexico's most famous cinematographer and one notorious for his penchant for lush effects.) The images of Buñuel's films are conceived as those not of a plastic but a dramatic art, and what they lack in beauty they make up in strength, a strength which has its own beauty. Perhaps, Buñuel's "Last Supper" from *Viridiana* may be taken to typify that myriad of indelible images with which his work abounds, from the severed hand in *Un Chien Andalou* to Simon on his column; and to typify also that quality of Buñuel's art which is probably most problematical for an audience bred on a modern aesthetic: its lack of subtlety. Yet is subtlety an inalterably superior virtue in art? I think not, and think that Buñuel's films make what is possibly the most powerful argument in contemporary art for its opposite: one might call it boldness. Yet if, like much that is great in Buñuel, the "Last Supper" is unsubtle, it is, for that, no less complex. Beyond symbol or parody, it fixes itself in our imagination as another Last Supper to set beside Christ's, and to throw open, by its separate existence, the values upon which a world is based. Like Francisco's house, with its mysteriously closed-off, darkened room, and his final zigzagging walk, both exact objectifications of his convoluted psyche, like the crucifix which conceals a blade in *Viridiana*, a common item found throughout Spain,[11] it symbolizes nothing, if, indeed, anything in Buñuel's work can accurately be called symbolic. Rather, they are all a surrealist art's autonomous "found objects"; physical manifestations of the irrational, whose "meaning" lies not in correspondences but in themselves and is to be discovered not behind their disguises but in their juxtapositions.

". . . Technique is no problem for me."[12] Buñuel's technical "indifference" has been remarked on by a number of critics, both those who, like Pauline Kael, seem unsure whether there isn't more to admire in it than to deplore and others, like James Price, who writes:

He has an instinctive gift; but sometimes one wishes he hadn't, and that instead he had to grapple with his equipment to make it answer his purposes, that sometimes a technical difficulty would actually *alter* what it was he wanted to do or say. The art and literature we value most very often exhibits the signs of the artist's struggle with his means. But Buñuel's films never do. . . . Mallarmé fought with language, Michelangelo with stone, and Beethoven with the combinations of

---

[11] "One day my sister, who is very religious, met a nun who was using one of these same little knives to peel apples." (Buñuel, quoted in Kyrou, *op. cit.*)

[12] Buñuel, quoted *ibid*.

sound capable of being produced by a string quartet. In Buñuel's case the sense of creative tension which this kind of struggle produces is absent.[13]

No matter how one chooses to construe "indifference," the common judgment on the "indifference" of the acting in Buñuel's films should not be allowed to go unchallenged, given such extraordinary performances as those of Gaston Modot in *L'Age d'Or*, Dan O'Herlihy in *The Adventures of Robinson Crusoe*, Arturo de Cordova in *El*, Francisco Rabal in *Nazarin*, Jeanne Moreau in *The Diary of a Chambermaid*, and Pierre Clementi in *Belle de Jour*, among others. But there is a sense in which what James Price says is true, and also capable of another construction. Buñuel's art *does* evince a struggle, not so much technical as formal—as in the failures to integrate the nonnaturalistic premise of *The Exterminating Angel* to its realistic mode, or adequately to sustain the parity of plot and theme in *Belle de Jour*; both failures aspects of Buñuel's major problems as an artist: that of reconciling his surrealist perception of the world with his fundamental allegiance to an art of narrative realism. Yet I wouldn't wish to defend Buñuel against Price's comment by instancing these failures. I think, rather, that one must situate Buñuel in a different (antiromantic) artistic "tradition" from that of Beethoven and Mallarmé; in that of, say, Cervantes, Haydn, Picasso, Thelonius Monk; artists who, however disparate their technical resources, nevertheless share the characteristic of seeming always to have possessed all the technical means needed for their expressive ends; and the tradition especially of such artists as Swift, Melville, Dostoyevsky, Strindberg, whose imaginative struggle was not primarily with art but with the world. Such prospect as one can see for the outcome of that struggle which rages through Buñuel's art may indeed appear bleak; it is hard to think of many other artists whose work has offered in such warring combination so dark a pessimism about the world with so great an urgency to remake it. And yet Buñuel's pessimism, far from being depressing, is elating; there is, in films, almost nothing else I can think of which so engages this paradoxical quality save for Kurosawa's *Yojimbo*. In Buñuel's work as in the Kurosawa film, a vision of the world of an almost overpowering blackness is somehow felt to be exhilarating. Our exhilaration is that of watching while someone we sense to be of an exemplary sanity shows us what is, for him, the truth.

[13]"The Andalusian Smile: Reflections on Luis Buñuel," *Evergreen Review*, No. 40, April 1966.

1971

Molly Haskell

For over a quarter century Molly Haskell (b. 1939) has been one of film criticism's most reliable voices of sense, historical balance, and psychological wisdom. In *From Reverence to Rape* (1974), Haskell wrote the classic study on the portrayal of women in American movies. What seems remarkable in retrospect is how non-doctrinaire, worldly, and nuanced this work of film criticism reads today (see the chapter below on "The Woman's Film"), especially compared with much gender theory that followed. Sensitive as Haskell has always been to the injustice of sexist objectification, she is also humorously aware of the way women onscreen have wielded power based on their looks, and how political correctness does not always square with women's secret desires. Haskell (who is married to fellow film critic Andrew Sarris and is the author of a beguiling memoir about their lives together, *Love and Other Infectious Diseases*) has also been a reviewer for *The Village Voice*, *Vogue*, *New York*, and other periodicals, and an inveterate commentator on new and old films.

◆

The Woman's Film

What more damning comment on the relations between men and women in America than the very notion of something called the "woman's film"? And what more telling sign of critical and sexual priorities than the low caste it has among the highbrows? Held at arm's length, it is, indeed, the untouchable of film genres. The concept of a "woman's film" and "women's fiction" as a separate category of art (and/or kitsch), implying a generically shared world of misery and masochism the individual work is designed to indulge, does not exist in Europe. There, affairs of the heart are of importance to both men and women and are the stuff of literature. In England, the woman's film occupies a place somewhere between its positions in France and in America; *Brief Encounter* and *The Seventh Veil* are not without soap opera elements, but they are on a slightly higher plane than their American counterparts.

Among the Anglo-American critical brotherhood (and a few of their sisters as well), the term "woman's film" is used disparagingly to conjure up the image of the pinched-virgin or little-old-lady writer, spilling out her secret longings in wish fulfillment or glorious martyrdom, and transmitting these fantasies to the frustrated housewife. The final image is one of wet, wasted afternoons. And if strong men have also cried their share of tears over the weepies, that is all the more reason (goes the argument) we should be suspicious, be on our guard against the flood of "unearned" feelings released by these assaults, unerringly accurate, on our emotional soft spots.

As a term of critical opprobrium, "woman's film" carries the implication that women, and therefore women's emotional problems, are of minor significance. A film that focuses on male relationships is not pejoratively dubbed a "man's film" (indeed, this term, when it is used, confers—like "a man's man"—an image of brute strength), but a "psychological drama." European films, too, are automatically exempted from the "woman's film" caste; thus, the critical status of *Mayerling* over *Love Affair*, *Le Carnet du Bal* over *Angel*, *Jules and Jim* over *Design for Living*, *My Night at Maud's* over *Petulia*, and *The Passion of Anna* over Bergman's English-language *The Touch*. Also exempted are films with literary prestige, like *Carrie* or *Sunday, Bloody Sunday*.

In the thirties and forties, the heyday of the "woman's film," it was as regular an item in studio production as the crime melodrama or the Western. Like any routine genre, it was subject to its highs and lows, and ranged from films that adhered safely to the formulae of escapist fantasy, films that were subversive only "between the lines" and in retrospect, and the rare few that used the conventions to undermine them. At the lowest level, as soap opera, the "woman's film" fills a masturbatory need, it is soft-core emotional porn for the frustrated housewife. The weepies are founded on a mock-Aristotelian and politically conservative aesthetic whereby women spectators are moved, not by pity and fear but by self-pity and tears, to accept, rather than reject, their lot. That there should be a need and an audience for such an opiate suggests an unholy amount of real misery. And that a term like "woman's film" can be summarily used to dismiss certain films, with no further need on the part of the critic to make distinctions and explore the genre, suggests some of the reasons for this misery.

In the woman's film, the woman—*a* woman—is at the center of the universe. Best friends and suitors, like Bette Davis' satellites (Geraldine Fitzgerald and George Brent) in *Dark Victory*, live only for her pleasure, talk about her constantly, and cease to exist when she dies. In the rare case where a man's point of view creeps in, as screenwriter Howard Koch's did in *No Sad Songs for Me*, it is generally reconciled with the woman's point of view. Thus, after Margaret Sullavan dies, the husband (Wendell Corey) will marry the woman (Viveca Lindfors) he almost had an affair with. But it is with the dead wife's blessing (she has actually chosen the woman who will replace her as wife and mother), and with the knowledge that when the chips were down, he preferred the wife to the "other woman." The result is the same as that of *Dark Victory*: The two loved ones—the remainders—may unite out of loneliness, but always with the shadow and memory of the "great woman" (vivid and in her prime) between them. If woman hogs this universe unrelentingly, it is perhaps her compensation for all the male-dominated universes from which she has been excluded: the gangster film, the Western, the war film, the *policier*, the rodeo film, the adventure film. Basically, the woman's film is no more maudlin and self-pitying than the male adventure film (what British critic Raymond Durgnat calls the "male weepies"), particularly in the male film's recent mood of bronco-busting buddies and bleary-eyed nostalgia. The well of self-pity in both types of films, though only hinted at, is bottomless, and in their sublimation or evasion of adult reality, they reveal, almost by accident, real attitudes toward marriage—disillusionment, frustration, and contempt—beneath the sunny-side-up philosophy congealed in the happy ending.

The underlying mystique of the man's film is that these are (or were) the best of times, roaming the plains, or prowling the city, in old clothes and unshaven, the days before settling down or going home, days spent battling nature or the enemy. In such films, the woman becomes a kind of urban or frontier Xantippe with rather limited options. She can be a meddling moralist who wants the hero to leave off his wandering; or a last resort for him, after his buddies have died or departed; or an uptight socialite to whom the hero can never confess his criminal, or even just shadowy, past; or a nagging nice-girl wife, who pesters the hero to spend more time with her, instead of always working, working, working or killing, killing, killing. The most common pattern is probably the wife competing with her husband's other life—business, crime, or crime detection; and since these activities are the dramatic focus and lifeblood of the film, the wife becomes a killjoy, distracting not only the hero but the audience from the fun and danger.

Marriage becomes the heavy. The implication is clear: All the excitement of life—the passion, the risk—occurs outside marriage rather than within it. Marriage is a deadly bore, made to play the role of the spoilsport, the ugly cousin one has to dance with at the ball. An excruciating example, and they abound, occurs in *The Big Clock*, in the husband-wife relationship of Ray Milland and Maureen O'Sullivan. Milland, an advertising executive, has been framed for murder; he is in life-or-death danger as he tries to track down the real culprit. Meanwhile O'Sullivan—naturally, as the wife, the last to be informed—keeps complaining of Milland's long hours at the office and his failure to take her on a promised wedding trip. Indeed, the murderer (Charles Laughton) is by far a more sympathetic character than the wife. By intruding on and sometimes interfering with the melodrama, such women become harpies even when they aren't meant to—*The Big Clock*, after all, was directed by Maureen O'Sullivan's husband, John Farrow.

That love is woman's stuff is a hoary Anglo-Saxon idea, devolving from the (American) tough guy and (British) public school etiquette that to show emotion is bad form, a sign of effeminacy, and that being tender in love is the equivalent of doing the dishes or darning socks. The association takes. For the housewife, betrayed by her romantic ideals, the path of love leads to, becomes, the dead end of household drudgery. The domestic and the romantic are entwined, one redeeming the other, in the theme of self-sacrifice, which is the mainstay and oceanic force, high tide and low ebb, of the woman's film. The equation of time and Tide is not so risible as it seems, just as the emphasis in the women's movement on domestic arrangements is not a trivializing of "larger issues." Rather, it is an intuitive recognition that the essence of salvation is not in the single leap of the soul, but in the day-to-day struggle to keep the best of oneself afloat—the discovery that perdition is not the moment of Faustian sellout, but the gradual dribbling of self-esteem, and self, down the drain of meaningless activity.

To the view that women's concerns, and the films that depict them, are of minor significance in the drama of life and art, women themselves have acquiesced, and critics have led the way. James Agee was almost alone among critics in not dismissing the woman's film summarily. In a favorable review of *Brief Encounter*, he wrote that when he associated the film with the best of women's magazine fiction, he did not intend a backhand compliment. "For it seems to me that few writers of supposedly more serious talent even undertake themes as simple and important any more: so that, relatively dinky and sentimental as it is—a sort of vanity-sized *Anna Karenina*—*Brief Encounter* is to be thoroughly respected."

But for every Agee, there have been critics whose voices dripped sarcasm and whose pens went lax when they came to review a woman's film. In his 1946 book *On Documentary*, the late John Grierson, the father of the "serious subject" critics, interrupted his anti-Hollywood and prosocial-realism diatribe to deplore Anthony Asquith's waste of time and talent on *Dance, Pretty Lady*. Grierson, admitting the film was "a delight to the eye," nonetheless deplored its subject: "This is it, bless you. Claptrap about a virginity. Why the entire sentiment that makes a plot like that possible went into discard with the good, prosperous, complacent Victoria. It was, relatively, an important matter then. But it is mere infant fodder now when you consider the new problems we carry in our bellies, and think of the new emphases we must in mercy to ourselves create out of our different world." Apparently the way to a socially conscious critic's heart is through his stomach. A woman's virginity (infant fodder, indeed!), and where and how she lost it, is at least as important as the high and mighty manly themes of the films Grierson approved of.

The deprecation of women's films takes a different form among critics who are not socially conscious—the aesthetically open, "movie-movie critics" represented, in the thirties and forties, by Agee, Otis Ferguson, Robert Warshow, and Manny Farber. There, the prejudice is more subtle: It is not that they love women less, but that they admire men more. Even Ferguson and Agee, who were enraptured with certain female presences on the screen, reserved their highest accolades for the films that showed men doing things and that captured the look and feel of down-at-heel losers, criminals, or soldiers, men battling nature or big-city odds. Agee never avoided the emotional or sentimental side of film (in the forties, who could?), but like the others, he had a slight case of Hemingwayitis. This infatuation with the masculine mystique was the pale-face New York intellectual's compensation for life in a cubicle, a *nostalgie de la boue* for the real grit and grime, as opposed to synthetic smudge—the kind that rubs off on your hands from typewriter erasures or newspapers.

There has been a corollary blindness on the part of most film critics to the achievements of the "woman's director," to the mixture of seriousness and high style that Europeans like Max Ophuls, Douglas Sirk, Otto Preminger, and Lubitsch bring to women's subjects, not just enhancing but transforming them; or to the commitment of a John Stahl or Edmund Goulding to material from which other directors withdraw in tasteful disdain (as did Wyler and Stevens, "graduating" as soon as they got the opportunity from the woman's film subjects of their early and best work to the bloated seriousness of their later work); or to the complete identification of a director like George Cukor with the woman's point of view, so that the attitude expressed is not his so much as hers.

Central to the woman's film is the notion of middle-classness, not just as an economic status, but as a state of mind and a relatively rigid moral code. The circumscribed world of the housewife corresponds to the state of woman in general, confronted by a range of options so limited she might as well inhabit a cell. The persistent irony is that she is dependent for her well-being and "fulfillment" on institutions—marriage, motherhood—that by translating the word "woman" into "wife" and "mother," end her independent identity. She then feels bound to adhere to a morality which demands that she stifle her own "illicit" creative or sexual urges in support of a social code that tolerates considerably more deviation on the part of her husband. She is encouraged to follow the lead of her romantic dreams, but when they expire she is stuck.

Beyond this common plight of a generic nature, there are as many kinds of woman's film as there are kinds of women. One division, providing the greatest tension with conventions of the genre, is between the upper-middle-class elite and the rest of the world, between women as models and women as victims. There are the "extraordinary" women—actresses like Marlene Dietrich, Katharine Hepburn, Rosalind Russell, Bette Davis, and characters like Scarlett O'Hara and Jezebel—who are the exceptions to the rule, the aristocrats of their sex. Their point of view is singular, and in calling the shots they transcend the limitations of their sexual identities. But their status as emancipated women, based as it is on the very quality of being exceptional, weakens their political value as demonstration-model victims and makes them, in their independence, unpopular with a majority of men and women.

Then there are the "ordinary" women—women whose options have been foreclosed by marriage or income, by children or age, who are, properly speaking, the subject of women's films at their lowest and largest common denominator. As audience surrogates, their heroines are defined negatively and collectively by their mutual limitations rather than by their talents or aspirations. Their point of view is not singular but plural, political rather than personal. They embrace the audience as victims, through the common myths of rejection and self-sacrifice and martyrdom as purveyed by the mass media. These—the media—have changed over the years, from magazines like *Good Housekeeping, Cosmopolitan, The Saturday Evening Post,* and from novels like those of Fannie Hurst, Edna Ferber, and Kathleen Norris, through the movies of the twenties, thirties, and forties, to television soap opera today. But the myths have not changed, nor has the underlying assumption: that these women are stuck, and would rather be stuck than sorry. The purpose of these fables is not to encourage "woman" to rebel or question her role, but to reconcile her to it, and thus preserve the status quo. The fictions are her defense not only against "man," but against the "extraordinary woman." For the average housewife, who has not quite gotten around to sex therapy or sensitivity training or group grope, prostitution, drugs, or even drink, these matinee myths are her alcoholic afternoons.

Between these two, there is a third category, one to which the better women's films aspire: It is the fiction of the "ordinary woman who becomes extraordinary," the woman who begins as a victim of discriminatory circumstances and rises, through pain, obsession, or defiance, to become mistress of her fate. Between the suds of soap opera we watch her scale the heights of

Stendhalian romance. Her ascent is given stature and conviction not through a discreet contempt for the female sensibility, but through an all-out belief in it, through the faith, expressed in directorial sympathy and style, that the swirling river of a woman's emotions is as important as anything on earth. The difference between the soap opera palliative and the great woman's film (*Angel, Letter from an Unknown Woman*) is like the difference between masturbatory relief and mutually demanding love.

All women begin as victims. Anna Karenina is a victim of the double standard no less than is Laura in *Brief Encounter*; Emma Bovary is as much a casualty of middle-class morality as is Ruby Gentry. Anna and Emma cease to be victims, cease to be easy identification figures, as they become increasingly complex and cruel, as they take fate into their own hands. As with all his characters, Tolstoy kept Anna at arm's length, in "middle shot," finding external correlatives to suggest her inner state. But movie heroines are in close-up; they have a narrower context in which to operate, and they must achieve stature in a different way. They cannot afford to alienate us (if the movie *Madame Bovary* had ended like the novel it would have been more catastrophic than courageous), because there is no wider field of vision, no social context or alternate major characters to claim our attention and absorb the shock. The movie of *Anna Karenina* is not, like the novel, about [Anna + Vronsky + Karenin + Levin + Kitty; country + city; society + art + religion] but about Garbo—or, in the later version, Vivien Leigh. (Sometimes the producers' reluctance to have a star alienate or disappoint the audience goes too far; in the first, silent version of *Anna Karenina* which was called *Love*, and starred Garbo, an alternate happy ending was provided with the print sent to theaters; in it, according to a synopsis, "Anna and Vronsky are happily reunited three years later, after her husband's opportune death.") The movie *Madame Bovary* is not about [Emma + French provincial society + the art form itself] but about Jennifer Jones' rapt romanticism as envisioned by Vincente Minnelli. But in the distinguished women's films, the combination of director and star serve the same function as the complex perspective of the novelist: They take the woman out of the plural into the singular, out of defeat and passivity and collective identity into the radical adventure of the solitary soul, out of the contrivances of puritanical thinking into enlightened self-interest.

It is this unique combination of actress plus director that makes, for example, one version of *Back Street* better or worse than another, even when the plot is identical. There are stars like Garbo and Marie Dressler and Joan Crawford who are their own genres. There are also distinctions to be made between one decade and another. Still, the bare bones remain remarkably similar, like grammatical models from which linguistical examples are formed. The themes of the woman's film can themselves be reduced to four categories, often found overlapping or in combination: sacrifice, affliction, choice, competition.

In the first, the woman must "sacrifice" (1) herself for her children—e.g., *Madame X, The Sin of Madelon Claudet*; (2) her children for their own welfare—e.g., *The Old Maid, Stella Dallas, To Each His Own*; (3) marriage for her lover—e.g., *Back Street*; (4) her lover for marriage or for his own welfare—e.g., *Kitty Foyle* and *Intermezzo*, respectively; (5) her career for love—e.g., *Lady in the Dark, Together Again*; or (6) love for her career—e.g., *The Royal Family of Broadway, Morning Glory*. The sacrifice film may end happily, with the wife/mother reclaiming her husband/child when her rival dies, or tragically, as mother watches daughter's happiness from afar, or sees son or lover only to lose him once again. In either case, the purgative sensations—the joy of suffering, the pain of joy—are very close. But not identical. Indeed, most of the thirties' and forties' woman's films ended tragically, an indication perhaps of the vision women had of themselves.

In the second category, the heroine is struck by some "affliction" which she keeps a secret and eventually either dies unblemished (*Dark Victory*), despite the efforts of her doctor-turned-lover, or is cured (*The Magnificent Obsession*) by the efforts of her lover-turned-doctor.

The third category, "choice," has the heroine pursued by at least two suitors who wait, with undivided attention, her decision; on it, their future happiness depends (*The Seventh Veil, Daisy Kenyon, Lydia*).

In the final category, "competition," the heroine meets and does battle with the woman whose husband (fiancé, lover) she loves (*The Great Lie, When Ladies Meet, Love Story*—the forties' English version; *Old Acquaintance*). While deciding the man's fate, the women will discover, without explicitly acknowledging it, that they prefer each other's company to his. The obtuseness of men generally is implied by their inability to perceive love or (in the case of the second category) disease.*

As patently idiotic as these themes sound, how is one to explain the degree to which some of them enthrall us: the mesmerized absorption, the choking, the welling up of tears over some lugubrious rendition of a famous piano concerto that will haunt us forever afterward with the memory of James Mason rapping Ann Todd's knuckles or Margaret Lockwood banging away in Albert Hall?

The Mason-Todd scene comes, of course, from *The Seventh Veil*, coauthored

---

*Sometimes the categories overlap, as in *No Sad Songs for Me*, in which a dying Margaret Sullavan prepares to turn her husband over to another woman.

by the husband-and-wife team of Muriel and Sydney Box, and directed by Compton Bennett. The title refers, in the pseudo-psychoanalytical idiom of the film, to that last "wall" between a woman and her innermost thoughts. Along with *Daisy Kenyon*, this is a model of the "choice" category, one of the most likable and yet most spurious, the pretense of suffering in a totally pleasurable situation being the height of hypocrisy. It is woman's understandable revenge, and reversal, of the state of affairs in which, as Byron said, "Man's love is of man's life a thing apart/'Tis woman's whole existence." The pattern of such films is to open with a period in which the heroine is spoiled and petted (metaphorically, of course) by several devoted males whose infatuation she either does not notice or is aggrieved by, after which she is given an ultimatum. She has to make a decision. At this point, a pretext will be found whereby the suitors are assembled, like characters in an Agatha Christie mystery—preferably at the bottom of a large staircase—to hear the "solution." This is, staircase and all, the arrangement that concludes *The Seventh Veil*. Ann Todd, resting upstairs, having been cured of her traumatic paralysis by psychiatrist Herbert Lom, will shortly descend and select either Hugh McDermott, the boorish American jazz musician whose wife has just divorced him, leaving him free to return to his first love; Albert Lieven, the world-weary Viennese artist who thought no woman could rekindle his dying passion; or James Mason, the witheringly sardonic guardian who trained and tyrannized her, poured his own pent-up talent into her, and couldn't let her go. (Although Lom, too, is undoubtedly in love with her, we can discount him as a contender, this being the modest era before mutual Oedipal transference and doctor-participation therapy.)

It isn't the list of players that tips us off—this is practically James Mason's first noteworthy movie. Nor is it the dime-store Freudianism that attaches to Mason's character (think of the penis envy potential in Todd's fingers and Mason's sadism). Nor is it just that he retains his dignity while those about him begin to fall apart. The choice has to be Mason, as any Anglo-American woman knows instinctively, because he, with his cultivated, misogynous manner, is the paragon of the English lover, the type most irresistible to the puritan woman. Father figure and mentor, Professor Higgins and Pygmalion, he exacts the best from her artistically, intellectually, spiritually, but makes no sexual demands. He never imposes on her; on the contrary, his indifference is the spur to her attraction. He is for most American women, the male ideal—cultured, genteel, refined, repressed, with a slight antagonism toward women that is not congenital but the result of an earlier wound or disillusionment, and therefore curable. But it is curable only by her. About all other women he continues to be cynical and disbelieving, and thus his fidelity is assured. He is, like the celibate clergyman or "confirmed bachelor," a challenge to a woman, and a relief from the sexually aggressive male.

The delicate, well-bred British hero (Mason, Herbert Marshall, the Howards—Trevor and Leslie) has had far more appeal than such matinee idol stock figures as John Boles, John Lund, George Brent, and all the other pretty profiles. Women's preference for the English gentleman—witty, overrefined, unsexual or apparently misogynous, paternal—is rooted in an instinct for self-preservation that expresses itself in the romantic drive. There is a split in a woman's sensibility, revealed over and over again in literature that expresses a woman's point of view, between her romantic interest—elevated, "total" (that is, not total, but psychological, spiritual)—focusing on a hero who will look into her eyes and embrace her soul and demand nothing sexually, and her sexual drive, brute and impersonal, demanding to be ravished "anonymously," that is, taken without asking, almost unawares, so that she will neither be responsible for her surrender nor bound by it afterward. (Even today, studies show that an amazing number of modern women neglect to prepare themselves for intercourse with contraception, indicating that women still prefer to think of sex as a seduction rather than a partnership. The reluctance of women to take responsibility for sex would seem a prime factor in perpetuating the stereotypes of the dominant, active male and the submissive, passive female.) Hence Scarlett's bliss the morning after her "rape" by Rhett Butler, although—and because—she will never love him the way she loves the unavailable, the undemanding Ashley. Her love for Ashley is passionate, but it is that of a tigress for a kitten; and his resistance and general effeteness assure us that even if he were to succumb she would have the upper hand. She is a diabolically strong woman—deceptively so, in the manner of the southern belle—and she fears the loss of her strength and selfhood that a total, "animal" relationship with Rhett would entail.

The "Ashley" figure, the sexually unthreatening male, whether as romantic lover or friend, crops up repeatedly in fiction written by women. The character of Waldo Lydecker, the acid-tongued columnist in Otto Preminger's *Laura*, is a perfect example. In Preminger's coolly perverse melodrama, made from a novel by Vera Caspary, the beautiful, self-possessed heroine has evaded marriage largely through the ritual savaging of her beaux by Clifton Webb's brilliant Lydecker. They make a dazzling team—Gene Tierney's career woman and the epicene, knife-blade-lean New York intellectual who launched her. Lydecker has a hold on Laura that cannot be explained merely by her indebtedness to him, and he is able to influence her further in the way that she is already predisposed. Not wanting to lose her, and expressing his own ambivalent attraction and repulsion, he ridicules her sexually demanding suitors, of whom Dana Andrews' detective is the crudest and therefore the least vulnerable. By making no claims to the chic and cultivation of the Laura-Lydecker world (by entering the battle of wits without a weapon), he emerges unscathed by Lydecker's sword and proves himself Laura's true knight.

Another Preminger gem and quintessential "choice" film is *Daisy Kenyon*, in which Joan Crawford, as a successful dress designer, has to choose between Dana Andrews, the married man who is her lover, and Henry Fonda, her boat-designing beau. Adapted from a novel by Elizabeth Janeway, it is a movie filled with typical "woman's film" scenes: the jangling telephone; the scene in the bar, when the rivals fruitlessly try to bypass Daisy and reach some sort of agreement on their own; or the climactic image of Joan Crawford, having left the two men at her country cabin to await her decision, driving eighty miles an hour through the woods, her chin jutting, her eyes glaring ahead not at the road but into the middle distance of her own self-absorption, in a narcissistic trance that can only be broken (since she can't change expression) by the crash when she drives off the road.

Strictly speaking, the "sacrifice" film constitutes a separate category, but in a broader sense it is, like the idea of "middle-classness," synonymous with the woman's film. The sacrifice film offers relief in, indeed thrives on, a contravention of its own morality: that "you can't have your cake and eat it too." The narrative impetus is based on an either/or ethic, on the universally accepted existence of fixed, life-and-death, in-or-out social rules which it is the film's precise purpose to circumvent. Doomed heroines, by not dying until the last moment, do not (as far as the experience of the film is concerned) really die. Women with fatal diseases receive all the attention and sympathy of an invalid without actually acting or looking sick. A heroine gets moral credit for not telling anyone of her illness . . . while only divulging it to an audience of millions.

Because the woman's film was designed for and tailored to a certain market, its recurrent themes represent the closest thing to an expression of the collective drives, conscious and unconscious, of American women, of their avowed obligations and their unconscious resistance. Children are an obsession in American movies—sacrifice of and for children, the use of children as justification for all manner of sacrifice—in marked contrast to European films about love and romantic intrigue, where children rarely appear at all and are almost never the instruments of judgment they are in American films. (To compare films made from almost-identical stories, Max Ophuls' *Letter from an Unknown*

Woman introduces the illegitimate child only to kill him off shortly thereafter, while John Stahl's *Only Yesterday* makes his "legitimization" the culmination of the film and the redemption of the mother.)

But in true having-your-cake-and-eating-it-too fashion, the underlying resentment will have its say. In films where the unmarried or poverty-stricken mother sacrifices her children for their advancement, the children are usually such little monsters that their departure provides secret relief. Where a mother holds on to the kids and sacrifices herself for them, they are even more thankless (*Mildred Pierce* is a good example).

The sacrifice of and for children—two sides of the same coin—is a disease passing for a national virtue, and a constant theme in films that preach one thing and, for anyone who is listening, say another. Whether the totem is challenged, as in the woman's films of European directors like Ophuls and Sirk (*Reckless Moment, There's Always Tomorrow, All That Heaven Allows*), or played straight and heartwarmingly, as in *Penny Serenade, Mildred Pierce, To Each His Own*, all three versions of *Madame X, The Old Maid*, and *That Certain Woman*, the spectacle of a woman owned by her children or consumed by her maternal zeal is as much the mainstay of the woman's film as it is of American culture and middle-class marriage.

Like all obsessions, this one betrays a fear of its opposite, of a hatred so intense it must be disguised as love. The obsession is composed of various related elements: a conviction that children are the reason for getting married (*Penny Serenade*) or the only thing holding marriage together (*The Great Lie, The Marrying Kind*), or woman's ultimate *raison d'être*, her only worth-confirming "career." The chain becomes a vicious circle. The woman without a job, without interests, without an absorbing marriage, invests her whole life, her erotic and emotional energy, in the child, who then becomes a divining rod, further drawing off the energy and electricity that should provide a constant current between husband and wife. The child that is seen as the means of shoring up a marriage becomes the wedge that drives a couple apart. But to admit this, to admit any reservations about having children or toward the children themselves, is to commit heresy. The only way to express this hostility is through a noble inversion: the act of sacrifice, of giving them up. Thus, the surrender of the children for their welfare (*Stella Dallas* and *The Old Maid*) is a maneuver for circumventing the sacred taboo, for getting rid of the children in the guise of advancing their welfare. (The sacrifice of oneself for one's children is a more subtle and metaphorical means to the same end: of venting hostility on the children through approved channels.) Both of these transactions represent beautifully masked wish fulfillments, suggesting that the myth of obsession—the love lavished, the attention paid to children, their constant inclusion in narratives where their presence is not required—is compensation for women's guilt, for the deep, inadmissible feelings of not wanting children, or not wanting them unreservedly, in the first place.

This goes some way toward explaining the plot contrivances and emotional excesses to be found in the "sacrifice" film: Martyrdom must be proportionate to guilt, and the greater the aversion to having a child, the greater the sacrifices called for. The inconveniences the child will cause (to an unwed mother, for example) and which are the source of her aversion, become trials actively sought as tests of her mother-love. In *To Each His Own*, Olivia de Havilland has become pregnant as the result of a one-night affair with an aviator who has been killed in the war. She goes to New York to have the child, but instead of staying there, where she could live with the child unquestioned, she returns to the provincial hamlet and gives the baby up to a neighbor, asking only for the privilege of spending one day a week with him. In one sense she "rejects" the child, as her lover, in dying, had "rejected" her; in another sense, the child becomes the object of all her pent-up emotions, a surrogate lover. When an old beau reappears and tries to persuade her to marry him and go away, he mistakes her refusal—and the light in her eyes—for commitment to another. And indeed it is. But it is to her own son, not a suitor, and the misinterpretation which follows revealingly suggests the degree to which an American woman's feelings for son and lover are identical. The loveliest part of the film concerns neither of these passions, but the very touching, adult encounter—the flirtation between two middle-aged air wardens (de Havilland and Roland Culver) in London—that begins and ends the film.

The mother's excessive and covertly erotic attachment to her children leads to a sense of bereavement, of the mistress "spurned," when they grow up and away from her. Once again the "woman's film" provides her with myths to support her sense of betrayal, to give her the sweet taste of revenge. Her sacrifice has spoiled them: When they leave home or "outgrow" their parents, it is not from a child's natural desire to be on his or her own, but because they have adopted "false values." In the materialism with which mothers like Stella Dallas and Mildred Pierce smother their children (a figurative rendering of the cultural advantages, higher education, and "quality" friends, in which the children go beyond their parents), in pushing them to want "more," they are creating monsters who will reject and be "ashamed" of them; simultaneously, the children's heartlessness will vindicate and earn audience sympathy for the mothers.

Less riddled with ambivalence is the "sacrifice-for-lover" film, although it carries a similar sense of pessimism and doom regarding marriage. Love is not lasting under the best of circumstances, such films suggest philosophically, but the best circumstances are not to be found in marriage. Hence the numerous stories of impossible, imaginary, or extra-marital love. In the latter category, *Back Street* is perhaps the most familiar, and offers, in its various remakes, a reflection of changing values.

The woman's film underwent a change between the thirties and forties, affecting—and affected by—the change in the image of women themselves. The forties were more emotional and neurotic, alternating between the self-denying passivity of the waiting war wife and the brittle aggressiveness of heroines like Davis and Crawford; thirties' heroines were spunkier and more stoical than their forties' sisters, the difference perhaps between a stiff and a quivering upper lip. Thirties' films unfolded against a normal society, whose set of standards the heroine automatically accepted. The social structure wavered in the forties, with women moving up the employment ladder and down from the pedestal, paying for one with their fall from the other. There is, as a result, a constant ambivalence in forties' films, a sensibility that is alternately hard and squishy, scathing and sentimental.

In the thirties, most heroines were still content with white-collar jobs or life at home. In the 1932 version of *Back Street*, with John Boles and Irene Dunne, Dunne is merely and merrily the town beauty. Even when she transfers to New York, following a missed rendezvous and Boles' marriage to another woman, her job is vague. The emphasis is on her reunion with Boles, who becomes her lover, and the tiny apartment where she waits and suffers. The supreme suffering, which he inflicts on her, is his refusal to let her have a baby. (Naturally she, who wants a baby and has plenty of occasion to conceive, never becomes pregnant, while Olivia de Havilland, like most movie heroines, gets pregnant from a one-night fling. But even the one-night-stand pregnancy, the seemingly silliest of movie conventions, has a source in real life: indifference on the part of women seems practically to insure pregnancy, while desperate longing seems invariably to forestall it.) In the 1941 remake (with Charles Boyer in the Boles role), Margaret Sullavan is an enterprising woman working in the family dry goods store, a buyer who knows her stuff and trades quips with the men. It is, in fact, her sharp tongue that gets her into trouble and precipitates the missed appointment. But the fact that Sullavan is more independent and self-sufficient than Dunne makes her sacrifice for love that much more humiliating; in Dunne's case, that sacrifice gives point and nobility to a life that would have been at best ordinary and conventional. Love *is* Dunne's career, and obsession is its own justification. This is one of the paradoxes basic to the woman's film, a paradox which is promptly undermined by another: The idea of a woman "giving up all" for Charles Boyer is a lot easier on the pride than the idea of "giving up all" for John Boles. But then, Boyer's delicacy and intelligence make it impossible to believe him capable of the insensitive behavior toward a woman that one can believe of Boles. It is part of the double bind of masochistic rationalization triggering the woman's film that what adds to its conviction on one level subtracts from it on another. The intelligence and chemistry of Sullavan-Boyer make them a more exciting and romantic couple than Dunne-Boles, but the ending (in their separate deaths) seems a waste and a letdown, which the fantasy happy ending—in which they meet instead of missing each other at the dock—does nothing to dispel. On the other hand, John Stahl's direction, and the script, of the earlier version become sublime at just this point. In a stunning final sequence, the appointment at the gazebo (a more felicitous location than the dock) is kept, the lovers are united, and in death they gain a beauty they never had in life.

The third version, an inane, jet-setting remake, stars John Gavin as the contemporary answer to Boles (plastic replacing plastic) and Susan Hayward as a globe-trotting fashion executive. Of all, she is the most exalted professionally and the least convincing emotionally, because her success and mobility (and here paradox dissolves in mere contradiction) undercut the closed system of decisions and consequences on which middle-class tragedy depends.

Women's films, particularly those of the thirties, have a stronger sense of social reality than their glossy-magazine or vacuum-sealed television equivalents. Aside from the portrait of American society they give as a matter of course, there are unconscious reflections of misery "in passing," like the image of a drunk or a prostitute reflected on the shiny surface of a parked limousine. The spectacle of perverted child-love is one such image, as are the American obsession with money, status, social climbing and its epiphenomenon, the *faux pas*. Who can forget the horror, and terrible humor, of the birthday party scene in King Vidor's *Stella Dallas*, when Stanwyck and daughter Anne Shirley wait at the place-marked and overdecorated table as first one, then another and another note of regret arrives.

A growing ambivalence and coyness in films began in the thirties and ran into the forties. (Sometimes it wasn't so ambivalent; for example, a strong antifeminist and philistine sentiment runs through Lubitsch's *That Uncertain Feeling*, with its derisive attitude toward the "cultural evening" that opens the film.) Part of the silliness arose from the fact that sexual passion and desire could not be shown: compare the 1929 version of *The Letter*, in which Jeanne Eagels seems to disintegrate before our eyes with the force of her passion, and the 1941 remake, in which Bette Davis has to give a suppressed and largely psychological performance in conformance with code decorum. There was also a retrenchment from the feminism of the twenties and thirties. Women might have better jobs, largely as a result of the war and a shortage of male personnel, but they would pay more heavily for them in the movies. Naturally. They were more of a threat. Men were nervous not so much about women taking their jobs—the firing of women directly after the war and the reinstatement of protective legislation that had been temporarily suspended would take care of that—but about women leaving the home "untended" as they crept back to work. For it was a fact that once women had savored the taste of work and independence, many didn't want to go back to being "just housewives." And so in films working women (who were statistically older than their prewar counterparts) were given a pseudo-toughness, a facade of steel wool that at a man's touch would turn into cotton candy.

As fixed point of Hollywood and lodestar of the woman's film, managing always to be where it was or vice versa, Joan Crawford provides a running commentary of changing attitudes. In *Susan and God*, her multiple-cause crusading woman, patterned on Eleanor Roosevelt, is subtly mocked for neglecting the home. Professionally, Crawford's roles reflected the American woman's rise up the wage scale: a perfume salesgirl in *The Women*, a chain-restaurateuse in *Mildred Pierce*, a designer in *Daisy Kenyon*; in *The Damned Don't Cry* she goes from being the smalltown wife of a pinchpenny hardhat, to being a "model," to being the rich and powerful "socialite" Lorna Hansen Forbes, and she does it by having more guts than any man ("I wouldn't have had the nerve," says her male protégé; "You don't need it," Crawford snaps back, "I got enough for both of us"). Then as the woman's film began to die, she moved into the neurotic women's roles of off-center *auteurs* like Nicholas Ray and Robert Aldrich. If her move from Mildred of Mildred's franchise to the single saloon-owner, Vienna, of Ray's *Johnny Guitar* was a step down economically, it was something of a leap forward iconographically. Whatever satisfaction Mildred got from Jack Carson's doglike self-abasement, Vienna's prestige was multiplied by that of her employee, Sterling Hayden, as a guitar-playing gunfighter. Vienna's final showdown with malevolent Mercedes McCambridge not only puts Mildred's altercation with her daughter to shame, it rivals such climactic mortal combats as that between Gary Cooper and Walter Huston in *The Virginian*. As the outrageous gun-toting Vienna (a more respectful *reductio ad absurdum* of her persona than Aldrich's *What Ever Happened to Baby Jane?*), Crawford alternates between the masculine and feminine elements of her personality with a bravura that is grand and funny without ever being ludicrous or demeaning.

The all-out perversity and outrageousness of *Johnny Guitar* and *What Ever Happened to Baby Jane?* are to be preferred to the sly, hidden nastiness of a film like *They All Kissed the Bride*. There, Crawford played the head of a trucking firm in conflict with Melvyn Douglas' labor leader. To suggest—leeringly, not openly—that all male-female conflict is sexual and that Crawford is really "just a girl," she goes, literally, weak in the knees every time she sees Douglas and must grab on to something or fall. It would be more humiliating if one believed for a moment that Joan Crawford could really go weak in the knees. But she can't and one doesn't. Her appeal is that she is not "just a girl" underneath; in fact, there is nothing underneath. Her hard-as-nails exterior conceals no heart of gold, or even steel. That's all there is—a sheet-metal facade, intense and glittering.

The unselfconscious luster of the early Joan Crawford hardens into the carefully polished sheen of the star. That she was a woman of many faces and uncommon adaptability is not surprising, perhaps, for a girl who had four names before she was twenty-one. She was christened Billie Cassin by her mother and adoptive father (who, in a curious parallel to Bette Davis' biography, abandoned the family when Joan was seven); she took the name (Lucille) LeSueur from her real father when she learned of his existence; she was rechristened Joan Arden by the M-G-M publicity department when she first got to Hollywood; and finally, when it was discovered that the name Joan Arden had already been assigned, she became Joan Crawford.

Even the leading men she chose to share her life with reflect the evolution of her career. She was the dancing lady of the silents whose marriage to Douglas Fairbanks, Jr., confirmed her as a symbol of flaming youth; the aspiring actress of the thirties whose marriage to Franchot Tone confirmed her seriousness; the businesswoman of the forties whose marriage to Pepsi-Cola chairman Alfred Nu Steele cemented her power and gave her security as a lifetime executive of Pepsi-Cola. The obsessively responsible heroine of *Mildred Pierce* (1945) is a long way from the feckless secretary of *Grand Hotel* (1932), the flapper of the silents, or the beautiful degenerate of *Rain*. Indeed, her performance in *Rain* is one of her loveliest and most appealing, although the 1932 film was poorly received by the press and public, and Crawford herself dislikes it. In her autobiography, she blushes an un-Crawford-like blush over her portrayal of Sadie Thompson, insisting that the critics were indeed right (just this once, is the implication) in accusing her of overacting. But her twisted relationship with the zealous reformer played by Walter Huston—her spiritual conversion, his guilty surrender to the lust against which his whole life's work has been a fortress—is one of those heady, erotic encounters that only the pre-code thirties could produce.

In her transition from the wanton, overly made-up, fluffy-haired Sadie to the severe, self-sacrificing hollow-eyed convert of *Rain*, Crawford curiously prefigured the transition in her own career from the go-go flapper to the glazed icon, from the natural party girl to the star, conscious of the importance of her fan club, of her religious commitment. But in *Rain*, even at her most pious, she has a prodigal luster, the radiance of a woman not yet aware of her powers, or of the fingernail-digging strength she will need to survive.

As she became more of a star, she was less inclined to do anything unpleasant, anything that might antagonize her audience; she thus compounded a weakness already inherent in the woman's film. But it was a paradoxical progression: If she was always morally righteous at the expense of libertine recklessness, it was also a form of security, of self-possession in which she no longer felt the need to flirt with and flatter men. The message behind the progression is not reassuring, for it tells us that a woman can't be both feminine and successful. As Crawford ceases to use her charms, she becomes less "attractive" to men; she becomes tougher and professionally driven. She becomes a "woman's woman," but as such she transgresses the etiquette and basic social laws of woman's dependency; and so her toughness is exaggerated as if to punish her and, in a vicious circle, she becomes even less sexually appealing.

Crawford, in the transition from glamour girl to self-reliant woman, reveals not just what a woman must do once her sexual commodities are no longer in demand, but suggests that a terrible loss is sustained in the process. For a woman trading on her looks, survival and adaptability are gained at a price, the price of the inner self, the core, the continuum that exists in most men unaltered by phases or changes of life. It is something men are born with, or given a sense of almost at birth; it is the bedrock sense of self on which they build. But women, when they gear their lives to men and neglect their own inner resources, are caught short by the aging process and must suddenly develop in ways that could not have been foreseen. Thus the fragmentation of a woman's character, given symbolical and perhaps not altogether witting expression in Crawford's performance in *Possessed*. As a woman obsessed by her love for a callous architect (Van Heflin), a conscientious nurse to a rich man's wife, wife to that man (Raymond Massey) when the wife dies, suspect in the murder of the wife, mistrusted stepmother of Massey's wild daughter (Geraldine Brooks), and finally distraught murderer of Van Heflin, she encompasses vastly more facets than are strictly required by the "split personality" that is the subject of the film, one of the clinically oriented movies about psychoanalysis that were so popular in the forties. For reasons that are partly the fault of script and direction, but not entirely, we begin to wonder which, if any, is the real Crawford, so perfectly does she become each successive role. There finally seems to be no connecting link, and the madwoman roaming the streets in the film's first sequence becomes a perfect expression of the end of the line, the total confusion and centerlessness for a woman in whom existence has replaced essence.

In *Mildred Pierce*, the lower-middle-class, greasy spoon, California milieu of the James Cain novel was upgraded and much of the point was lost. By refusing to muss herself up, physically and psychologically, Crawford took the guts out of the character and the class crunch out of the mother-daughter conflict. She became a dulcifluous housewife, whose only fault, if it could be so designated, was loving her daughter too much. The obsession with the daughter (Ann Blyth), with its erotic implications, is the most fascinating aspect in the movie, since it is a veiled expression of self-love, and takes on the aspect of narcissism that is the ultimate Crawford posture.

Even Mildred's competence in the business world, radical enough, perhaps, for its time, is not a sign of independence sought for its own sake, but of initiative in the service of family (or of self-love pervertedly disguised). Mildred's ambitions are for some "higher purpose" than self-fulfillment. Her words to Pierce, her first husband, elided into one sesquipedalian word, might stand as the motto of the woman's film: "I'lldoanythingforthosekidsdoyou-understandanything," she says, packing another homemade pie into a box for delivery.

Eve Arden's role in *Mildred Pierce* also tells us much. In the film she plays her characteristic role of the smart, cheerfully bitter woman, sidekick to the heroine and running commentary on the cruelties and stupidity of men. In many ways, her character is the most treacherously and heartbreakingly sexist of all. Independent, witty, intelligent, a true friend to her own sex and of all women the most apparently "complete" within herself, she is made to talk constantly and longingly of men, to deprecate her own powers of attraction, to place greater emphasis on sex than all the silly ninny sex objects who have nothing else to live for, in short, constantly to bemoan her "incompleteness." She thus becomes the greatest feather in the cap of male vanity. In what is an obvious contradiction of her true nature—for her relationship with Crawford is close, generous, and satisfying—she confirms the male (and, derivatively, female) idea that a bunch of women together are at best incomplete, if not downright silly.

Even more insidious is her portrayal as being "out of the running" romantically and sexually, while she is the most outspoken and least puritanical of women. There is, by implication, something "improper" in the woman (Aline MacMahon often plays the same type) who actually expresses sexual desire, and an ability to handle it, and a light touch, so that she must be denied getting the man, while the coy, hard-to-get virgin wins the prize. There is something as disheartening as it is brave in her acceptance of the status quo, for she is using her brains to deprecate their importance and downgrading her friendships with women as second-best arrangements.

Generally—and typically—the only films that allowed dignity to working women were those based on historical figures, real-life women, the singularity (and therefore nonapplicability) of whose achievement would not make them a threat to men. Or to other women. Mme Curie and Amelia Earhart would hardly start a rush on women scientists and aviatrixes, or, being dead, intimidate the living with their accomplishments. In *Blossoms in the Dust*, Greer Garson's dedicated woman battling to erase the stigma of illegitimacy from birth certificates (based on a historical case) is no problem. Yet, despite the safety of the nineteenth-century milieu, Katharine Hepburn's feminist in *A Woman Rebels* was too threatening. The film flopped and ushered in her period of "box-office poison."

Hepburn was one of the few, if not the only, actresses allowed to sacrifice love for career, rather than the other way around. The explanation usually offered is that her arrogance and eccentricity exempted her: She was neither a "regular guy" (in fact, she never won any popularity prizes in Hollywood) nor a representative of the American woman. Even in *Morning Glory*, where she gave up love for her theatrical career, the implication was that she would turn into a dried-up, defeminized old lady. And even in the hands of a sympathetic director like George Stevens or Cukor or Hawks, there was a cutting edge to her parts as written, a kind of ruthless, upper-class eccentricity, that was more a revenge on, than an expression of, her personality. In *Woman of the Year*, her cosmopolitan political reporter is pitted against Spencer Tracy's no-nonsense, boys-in-the-back-room sports reporter. Their enchanting interplay (this was their first film together) creates a sense of complementary natures and equality which is gradually eroded, then cruelly and dishonestly shattered, as Hepburn's "weaknesses"—her drive, her lack of interest in creating a home and family—are belabored and blackened while Tracy's faults—his philistinism, his "old-fashioned" American values—are softened and colored as virtues by comparison. In *The Philadelphia Story*, she is attacked from all sides for her supposed coldness (for real coldness, see Grace Kelly in the fifties' musical version, *High Society*), of which there is not a shred of evidence. This is the furtive revenge of mediocrity on excellence; she is being convicted merely for being a superior creature. In *Alice Adams*, she is bitten by the most antipathetic and unattractive bug of them all, social climbing, and she manages to make it seem like the most charming of aspirations. In *Bringing Up Baby*, she is impervious to the havoc she wreaks on poor Cary Grant. But through all these films, she refuses to be humiliated or look ugly. Her combined integrity, intelligence, and proud, frank beauty rise to the surface, making us feel, with her, the difficulty and joy of being such a woman. A scene which is consummate Hepburn in its mingling of pride and vulnerability and the young, still-searching-for-herself woman, occurs during the courtship on the porch in *Alice Adams*, when she asks Fred MacMurray what his impression of her is, what he would like her to be. At this moment, as she looks into his eyes, she would willingly become what he wants, just as every girl is always shaping and reshaping her image according to her reflection in a man's eyes. Here she reveals the terrible, chameleon aspect of a woman's life, the necessity of adapting to others' needs, in constant, cosmetic metamorphosis, rather than finding and remaining true to the hard-core changeless being of the inner self. This is the trembling, smiling readiness Hepburn expresses (the terrified eagerness of a woman for psychological rape, as for her first sexual experience), and yet her entire life and persona suggest exactly the opposite and are a victory over this. She evolved, developed, played different parts, and in remaining true to her intractable self, made some enemies. And she made life difficult for those who believed that a woman could not be brilliant and beautiful, and ambitious and feminine at the same time.

Women have been caught between Scylla and Charybdis. Just as Hepburn was ridiculed in *Woman of the Year* for not paying enough attention to the home, Rosalind Russell, the heroine of *Craig's Wife*, was criticized for devoting too much attention to the home, valuing its contents more than people. In *Roughly Speaking*, the Rosalind Russell wife is more ambiguous—a demoness of energy (childbearing and otherwise) beside whom even her second husband (her first, feeling superfluous, left), an indefatigable entrepreneur, pales.

At the other end of the spouse spectrum, no less monstrous in her way, is Dorothy McGuire as *Claudia*, the helpless and adorably incompetent child-wife. Made from the successful Broadway play by Rose Franken, the film, directed by Edmund Goulding, was a hit and inspired a sequel, *Claudia and David*, also starring Dorothy McGuire and Robert Young. McGuire is the neurotic housewife whose arsenal of charms and eccentricities seems an unconscious device to postpone direct contact with her husband, and whose fixation on her mother is transferred, after the mother's death, to her own son. It is impossible to imagine the husband and wife having any real communion, verbal or sexual, "offstage," and the dynamics of both films spring from the relationship between the women: Dorothy McGuire and Ina Claire in the first, Dorothy McGuire and Mary Astor in the second. Claudia's total and loving dependence on her mother, played by Ina Claire, becomes, like child obsession for other "woman's film" heroines, the relationship which takes all the emotional energy from her marital responsibilities (both sexual and spiritual) and from her own, indefinitely postponed growing up. Dorothy McGuire is irresistible in the part. One hears, in her slightly cracked, desperately pleading voice, the admission, for so many American women, of a complete unpreparedness for married life. And, with the fear of sex that has been inculcated in her, and the pressure to be a perfectionist housekeeper, who can blame her for reverting to a state of childlike helplessness in which she will not have to perform sexually or domestically? But these subterfuges only increase her self-contempt. Seeing that she cannot even perform these trivial chores (while her husband has his interesting work and masters "important" challenges), she is quite ready to believe that he could be lured by another, more interesting woman.

With McGuire, as with so many women's film heroines, what moves—even convulses—us is not her self-pity but, on the contrary, her absolute refusal to feel sorry for herself. We supply what these heroines hold back. Who can help weeping all the tears refused by the laughing-on-the-outside bravura of Bette Davis in *Dark Victory* or Margaret Sullavan in everything; the cheerfully stoical Irene Dunne in *Love Affair* or Susan Hayward in *My Foolish Heart*.

Given the fictional necessity of woman's self-sacrifice—a premise we rightly challenge today—the heroine's attitude was often resolute and brave, an act of strength rather than helplessness. Nor did she deal in the eternal hope and the endless postponements of tragedy provided by soap opera. Rather, hers was a more exacting and fatalistic form of "escape," in which certain steps or nonsteps were decisive and irrevocable. In *When Tomorrow Comes*, Irene Dunne plays a waitress to Charles Boyer's concert pianist. For their last dinner together, wearing a dress on which she has spent six months' wages, she sits conversing cheerfully, knowing she will never see him again. In *Only Yesterday*, John Boles has an affair with Margaret Sullavan and, unbeknownst to him, gets her pregnant. He goes off to war, she brings up the child, and that is the last she hears of him . . . until one day years later, she runs into him at a New Year's Eve party and he doesn't remember her at all. The ultimate nightmare of a man's (husband's, lover's) "forgetfulness." She goes and spends the night with him without reminding him.

A similar situation occurs in *Letter from an Unknown Woman*, Max Ophuls' 1949 masterpiece, in which Joan Fontaine loses her head and heart, first as a young girl, then as an adult, over concert pianist Louis Jourdan. The film, adapted by Howard Koch from a novel by Stefan Zweig, is framed by the letter in which a dying Fontaine informs Jourdan of her love for him, and, in awakening his honor, seals his death. They had an affair—one of many for him—but were separated. She has his child and in order to provide the boy with security, makes a comfortable marriage: Jourdan meanwhile continues his life of women and dissipation. One night a long time later, she encounters him after an opera; he asks her to come to his apartment the following night, and she accepts, knowing that if she goes, she will never be able to return to her husband. She arrives at the appointed time, begins talking to him, and, waiting tremulously for the reconciliation, suddenly realizes that he doesn't recognize her, that she is just another pretty woman and he hasn't the faintest idea who she is.

The exquisite pain of this scene, of her humiliating surrender to a love that is so unreciprocated, is balanced, in Ophuls' vision and sublimely sensitive direction, by the sense of Jourdan's general depletion and decline, but mainly by the counterweight of Fontaine's obsessiveness, the stubbornness of her will to love this one man against all reason and logic, her certainty that she can "save" him; by that total defiance of social rules, she becomes not only the architect of her fate, but the precipitator of her downfall, and thus a tragic heroine. She is radical in her refusal to follow the "normal" path of a woman's destiny—to stop dreaming once she has married the proper man and settled down. Similarly the Danielle Darrieux character in Ophuls' great French film, *Madame de* (note the anonymity of the women in both titles, their exemption from names and social identities) forgoes the duties and pleasures of a normal wife, first out of vanity and lovelessness, finally out of the love for which she dies. In their abrogation of ordinary responsibilities, both women become outlaws, militarists of love, heroic and cruel. From the opening of *Madame de*, when Darrieux is examining her clothes and jewels to determine which she will pawn, to the end in which the earrings are consecrated to God and her soul symbolically redeemed, she undergoes the tortures of love and, through the consequences of her habitual frivolity, the loss of that love, finally to attain the stature of a saint, as the movie attains the stature of great art.

What Ophuls shows is that he, like the ceremonial Boyer-Darrieux marriage, like the woman's film itself, is only superficially superficial. For what greater conflict can there be within woman than that between what she conceives of as a biologically rooted duty and her spiritual wish to be free? And, like the greatest directors, Ophuls reveals this deep conflict through surfaces: through the endless movements of camera, and characters within a fixed society, he captures the inner movement of the soul in its rare, solitary passage to tragedy and grace.

The woman's film reaches its apotheosis under Ophuls and Douglas Sirk in the late forties and fifties, at a time when the genre was losing its mass audience to television soap opera. Eventually women-oriented films, like the women-oriented plays from which many of them were adapted, disappeared from the cultural scene. The derisive attitude of the eastern critical establishment won the day and drove them out of business. But at one time the "matinee audience" had considerable influence on movie production and on the popularity of certain stars. This influence has waned to the point that the only films being made for women are the afternoon soaps, and there is very little attempt to appeal to women in either regular films or nighttime television.

Where are the romantic idols who made their reputations on their appeal to women, the John Barrymores and Leslie Howards to whom women offered themselves in marriage? To Robert Redford and Paul Newman, who might conceivably be thought of as their successors, women, when they bother, send only billet-doux. But like most of their colleagues, Redford and Newman would rather be "real people" than actors, and would rather be "real actors" than romantic leads. So instead of playing opposite beautiful women in love stories of civilized narratives, they play opposite each other in *Butch Cassidy and the Sundance Kid* and romance takes on a whole new twist. They are on their way to becoming the Myrna Loy–William Powell of the seventies.

Women respond to them perhaps because they represent the wine of the old romance in a new bottle. It is the rapport between Newman and Redford in *Butch Cassidy* rather than between either one of them and Katharine Ross, that has all the staples—the love and loyalty, the yearning and spirituality, the eroticism sublimated in action and banter, the futility and fatalism, the willingness to die for someone—of women's fantasies as traditionally celebrated by the woman's film.

The woman's film, its themes appropriated by the man's film, has died out, and with it a whole area of heterosexual feeling and fantasy. For the woman's film, like other art forms, pays tribute at its best (and at its worst) to the power of the imagination, to the mind's ability to picture a perfect love triumphing over the mortal and conditional. Fontaine's and Darrieux's obsessions become leaps into immortality. The lovers in *Back Street* are finally united—in the resurrection of filmed time. In *Peter Ibbetson*, Ann Harding and Gary Cooper, separated by prison walls, live their love in their dreams and in the bowery radiance of Lee Garmes' cinematography. They are transfixed at the sublime moment of their love (denying yet improving on reality) by the power of the imagination, by the screen, and by their permanence in our memories.

1974

Sophisticated Interiors

Even though no less an ex-sexist than Dr. Spock is prepared to see them topple, Eric Erikson's building-block discoveries (girls build houses; boys build towers and the concept of inner space) are borne out by much of world literature, especially the modern American branch. Women writers, to the extent that they are not expatriates from their gender, have been more concerned with interiors, with people, with reality, with the everyday transactions of relationships, whereas male writers have extended themselves further into fantasy, action, myth, allegory. Compare the latest fiction of Joan Didion, Sandra Hochman, Mary McCarthy, Shirley Ann Grau, for example, with John Hawkes, John Gardner, Barth, Gass, *et al*. Men reject authority, are suspicious of reality, and build superstructures to escape the ordinary, while women burrow furiously into the ordinary in search of smaller miracles.

Of course, by now we accept the mixture of male and female properties in all of us, and a writer's sensibility is more androgynous than the ordinary person's, but to the extent that one predominates (female in Proust, male in Gertrude Stein) certain characteristics can be said to follow.

When we talk of women's directors we are often talking about directors who are good with actors in general, directors who are attuned to people, who are sensitive to relationships, to shadows of suggestion and behavior. (In a sense this is what movies are all about and what all directors have to be.)

It is interesting to see what happens when a man directs a woman's screenplay. Frank Perry seems to have done better with Eleanor Perry, finding local exteriors appropriate to her psychological interiors. But Fritz Lang could have done without the services of his screenwriter wife, Thea von Harbou. In that case, Frau von Harbou's unnecessarily complicated love interests cluttered the clean line and momentum of Lang's melodrama. Lately Frank Gilroy has taken Paula Fox's *Desperate Characters* and used them as pawns in an aesthetic chess game, staples of atmosphere in a mood piece.

John Schlesinger, on the other hand, seems to have been perfectly suited to direct Penelope Gilliatt's original screenplay in the film *Sunday, Bloody Sunday* (bloody as in boring and beastly rather than corpses and catsup). He has proved his talent with actors—Julie Christie, Tom Courtenay, Dirk Bogarde, Laurence Harvey, Alan Bates, Peter Finch, Dustin Hoffman and Jon Voigt— and his feeling for a certain kind of sophisticated sensationalism. Here his affinity for the material—a wise and wistful comedy of manners about a woman (Glenda Jackson) and a man (Peter Finch) in love with the same young man— is what makes the film so effective without taking it to that other level (where it doesn't want to go, anyway) of formal complexity or mystery or myth which would make you want to see it again for new revelations. If you do see it a second time, you'll be doubly impressed with certain things: with Schlesinger's tact and subtlety. Except for a few sociological forays into drugs and vandalism, and the overextended bar mitzvah, his direction is the height of tact. He handles the shock of Finch's homosexuality, which lies in his emotional rather than sexual vulnerability, with delicate timing and tenderness. And you'll appreciate more than ever the details—harried, work-filled lives, interrupted by telephones, filled with the small gratifications of human encounters; and the wickedly comical picture of a progressive, children-tyrannized family (friends of both Finch and Glenda Jackson). But you will be disappointed if you expect even these two great performances to yield new insights.

It is a very grown-up screenplay, charged with the kind of impossibly adult common sense I associate with Germaine Greer. And Penelope Gilliatt. (And which sometimes makes me, I'm ashamed to say, want to talk baby talk back.) It's the kind of film that can poke fun at the mother of the precocious, pot-smoking child-monsters who says, "We think it's very important not to pretend," while basically pursuing her philosophy.

Peter Finch, as Dr. Daniel Hirsh, general practitioner with an Orthodox Jewish background, an unorthodox sex life, and a gentle, cultivated, masculine manner, and Glenda Jackson as Alex Greville, a well-brought-up and well-educated, cerebral and searching divorcée, are the picture's brilliant left hand and right hand. Murray Head (Judas on the recording of *Jesus Christ Superstar!*) is perfect as Bob Elkin, the designer of kinetic sculptures as elusive and free-floating and pragmatic as his own young heart. He is the love object of whom neither will ever get enough because "that's all there is." His performance has been underrated, perhaps, for being seamless and unanalyzable. He is like a one-cell creature in this context, a character on a lower rung of the evolutionary ladder.

He is the foil, the occasion for a contrast (or a coming together) of these two wonderfully individualized human beings with detailed existences, who, although they never meet until the very end, seem almost to be playing to each other instead of to Head. Except for one being fastidious (Finch, of course) and one sloppy, one heterosexual and one homosexual, they have more in common than either has with him. In addition to a lover and an answering service (manned, or womaned, with impersonal inefficiency by the remarkable Bessie Love), they share certain generational and intellectual attitudes: a feeling for privacy, possessiveness (people and things), professionalism, humor, and all the clashes of ego and superego by which they have come to define their identities.

Are they not, in a sense, self-fulfilling people, who need only a nominal, sometime partner for the outlet for their romantic feelings, for sex, for the contemplation of their misery, the exercise of regret, for the exquisitely refined understanding that in loving a lesser being on a part-time basis, they are not selling themselves short but reveling in the dual satisfaction of abasement and superiority. Glenda Jackson protests the sharing, the fragments of love. But she reminds me of certain friends in "impossible relationships" who say, "This can't go on," not as a genuine ultimatum but to experience new permutations of agony and create movement within stasis. For the only activity more absorbing than being happy in love is being miserable in love. Whereas happiness graciously takes to the wings for other activities, generously giving them a secret halo, misery insists on center stage, usurping all thoughts and emotions in its useless, selfish, luxurious wastefulness. Its celebration amounts to a quasi-religious experience like the heartbreakingly beautiful Terzettino from *Così fan tutte* which forms the musical theme of the film.

What's missing in *Sunday, Bloody Sunday* is the exploration and discovery which comes from a genuine sense of tragedy. The insights are predigested, the facts of life too well understood. Elkin's departure for America, abandoning both his lovers, is far from being tragic and inevitable. Its timing is arbitrary, and his fate is incidental to the rich reflection of sorrow it occasions.

1972

Melancholy Males or Movies About Men Turning 50

By a curious coincidence I happened to see three great "last chance" films back to back, that is, movies in which aging male stars play has-beens trying to recover some shred of their former luster and self-respect. In a medium relentless in its demand for ever newer and fresher talent, the specter of human obsolescence hovers in the wings, more often subtext than text. So there's something especially moving and exhilarating—not to mention risky—when familiar actors are willing to put their weary features and sagging bones on display, face the music of time in a medium which counts 50 not as midlife opportunity but as career-ending antiquity.

The films—two revivals and one new release—were Jacques Becker's classic *Touchez Pas au Grisbi* with Jean Gabin as an aging gangster; *The Band Wagon*, Minnelli's gloriously moody 1953 musical with Fred Astaire as a song and dance man no longer swift of foot; and Sophia Coppola's haunting *Lost in Translation*, in which Bill Murray as an erstwhile star now making whiskey commercials in Japan hooks up with a similarly disoriented young married woman.

Truffaut wrote that *Touchez Pas au Grisbi*, whose star was 49, whose director 48, was "a movie about turning 50." But the same could be said of the other two films: Astaire (born in 1899) was 54, Bill Murray (b. 1950) is 53. The three are different, of course. Because his image depends on sexual desirability, Gabin, *l'homme dur* of French cinema and magnet for women, feels the pinch of age more acutely. Astaire, the ethereal dandy of musical comedy, was always more romantic than sensual; and Bill Murray, being comic actor rather than traditional leading man, is the least affected by the passage of time. Indeed, his wry mournful pockmarked face and quizzical voice have always seemed to gently mock the vainglorious posturings and blithe, fresh-faced optimism of the stars. He radiates a Zen-like resignation to both the passage of time and its refusal to budge, captured most memorably in the time-stuck comedy *Groundhog Day*.

With unusual frankness, these three offer the spectacle of their own anxieties about aging in one of those unnerving instances, called "doubling" by Bazin, when real and fictional life coincide. Their gallantry is also a gamble. Will we be charmed or repelled by their untouched-up older personae; by their pairing with much younger women? Were the sexes reversed—a 50-year-old woman with a 25-year-old man—the recoil would be automatic, the women seen as grotesque. But even with men whose attraction credentials supposedly improve with age, the viability of the aging star is no sure thing. "Yum" can turn into "yuk" at the whim of an ever-fickle audience.

The Band Wagon, with its wise and urbane script by Betty Comden and Adolph Green, begins with a prolonged humiliation: Astaire is so passé that in an auction of his personal effects, his signature cane only fetches a few dollars. On the train to New York, where he hopes to revive his career in a

Broadway musical, two portly gents in the bar car chortle over his fallen status. One of them betrays the murderous envy of the lay person towards the star when he complains of the way his wife used to see Tony Hunter's films, over and over again—her infatuation a scathing comment on the vacuity of her marriage and husband. A gathering of reporters turns out to be clamoring not for him but for Ava Gardner. And then, defying age and space, he embarks on one of his most magical numbers, "Shine on Your Shoes," in a Times Square arcade.

Touchez Pas au Grisbi is less introspective than *Band Wagon*, but, with its wry domestic touches, unusually realistic for an action *policier*. Gabin's Max is ready to retire with the bourgeois perks he's accumulated when he and his gang are obliged to stage a bloody showdown to retain the loot (*grisbi*) they've stolen. The burned-out kingpin no longer has the energy for the nightclub scene, he prefers a gourmet snack at home with his buddy, and at the end of the film, he actually dons eyeglasses to make a phone call. The glamorous woman at his side is more an accessory than love or sex object. Gabin's career, then in a slump, was given a major boost by the movie, which also featured Lino Ventura (Gabin's discovery) as a rival gangster and Jeanne Moreau, who hadn't yet come into her distinctive brand of intelligent beauty, as a treacherous tart.

Lost in Translation is all about spiritual yearning and the ability of two people at opposite ends of the age spectrum—Scarlett Johansson as the lovely, youthful Yale graduate who is counterpoint to Murray's melancholy has-been—to live with ungratified desire. Staying in the same Tokyo hotel, sleepless and at loose ends, these two come together from pools of mutual lostness, becoming for each other an opportunity for reflection as much as attraction: where is my life going? What should I do? asks this smart yet self-deprecating young woman, whose celebrity-hungry photographer is off on a "shoot." What has my life been, he questions back. His great days are behind him, and how great were they anyway? His wife calls, barraging him with redecorating questions, he's in another mood entirely, they don't connect, yet he accepts such disjunctions as an inevitable part of marriage. It's really the repression of sex (think old love stories like *Brief Encounter* and *Love Affair*) and the acceptance of a carnal boundary that can't be crossed that becomes, in their eloquent silence-filled rapport, a form of love more life-altering than the sexual contortions now monotonously de rigueur. Nothing happens (too little for most audiences), yet everything happens. Johannson is as delectable as Spring, but not conventionally beautiful, and a bit mulish as well. Murray is sublime, funny, both baffled and wise, as agitated as a young lover, as calm as a Buddhist. May and December are equally adrift. Age becomes what you make of it, and a retreat from the pleasures of the flesh is, in this remarkable instance, anything but a defeat.

2003

Paul Schrader

Paul Schrader (b. 1946), best known as both a screenwriter for some of Martin Scorsese's most important films (*Raging Bull, Taxi Driver*) and a film director of considerable distinction in his own right (*American Gigolo, Mishima, Affliction, Auto Focus*), began his career as a film critic, one with a pronounced intellectual bent and a cogent prose style. In addition to his regular movie reviews for *LA Free Press*, Schrader's 1972 book-length study *Transcendental Style in Film: Ozu, Bresson and Dreyer* did a fine job of synthesizing the common elements in a disparate body of film that courted the meditative and the sacred. He also traced shared attributes in action filmmakers he admired, as can be seen in this analysis of *film noir*, which he persuasively insisted on regarding as a style rooted in a specific historical moment rather than as a genre that can keep returning indefinitely.

◆

Notes on Film Noir

In 1946 French critics, seeing the American films they had missed during the war, noticed the new mood of cynicism, pessimism and darkness which had crept into the American cinema. The darkening stain was most evident in routine crime thrillers, but was also apparent in prestigious melodramas.

The French cineastes soon realized they had seen only the tip of the iceberg: as the years went by, Hollywood lighting grew darker, characters more corrupt, themes more fatalistic and the tone more hopeless. By 1949 American movies were in the throes of their deepest and most creative funk. Never before had films dared to take such a harsh uncomplimentary look at American life, and they would not dare to do so again for twenty years.

Hollywood's *film noir* has recently become the subject of renewed interest among moviegoers and critics. The fascination *film noir* holds for today's young filmgoers and film students reflects recent trends in American cinema: American movies are again taking a look at the underside of the American character, but compared to such relentlessly cynical films noir as *Kiss Me Deadly* or *Kiss Tomorrow Goodbye*, the new self-hate cinema of *Easy Rider* and *Medium Cool* seems naïve and romantic. As the current political mood hardens, filmgoers and filmmakers will find the *film noir* of the late Forties increasingly attractive. The Forties may be to the Seventies what the Thirties were to the Sixties.

Film noir is equally interesting to critics. It offers writers a cache of excellent, little-known films (*film noir* is oddly both one of Hollywood's best periods and least known), and gives *auteur*-weary critics an opportunity to apply themselves to the newer questions of classification and transdirectorial style. After all, what is *film noir*?

Film noir is not a genre (as Raymond Durgnat has helpfully pointed out over the objections of Higham and Greenberg's *Hollywood in the Forties*). It is not defined, as are the western and gangster genres, by conventions of setting and conflict, but rather by the more subtle qualities of tone and mood. It is a film "*noir*," as opposed to the possible variants of film gray or film off-white.

Film noir is also a specific period of film history, like German Expressionism or the French New Wave. In general, *film noir* refers to those Hollywood films of the Forties and early Fifties which portrayed the world of dark, slick city streets, crime and corruption.

Film noir is an extremely unwieldy period. It harks back to many previous periods: Warner's Thirties gangster films, the French "poetic realism" of Carné and Duvivier, Sternbergian melodrama, and, farthest back, German Expressionist crime films (Lang's *Mabuse* cycle). *Film noir* can stretch at its outer limits from *The Maltese Falcon* (1941) to *Touch of Evil* (1958) and most every dramatic Hollywood film from 1941 to 1953 contains some *noir* elements. There are also foreign offshoots of *film noir*, such as *The Third Man*, *Breathless* and *Le Doulos*.

Almost every critic has his own definition of *film noir*, and a personal list of film titles and dates to back it up. Personal and descriptive definitions, however, can get a bit sticky. A film of urban nightlife is not necessarily a *film noir*, and a *film noir* need not necessarily concern crime and corruption. Since *film noir* is defined by tone rather than genre, it is almost impossible to argue one critic's descriptive definition against another's. How many *noir* elements does it take to make a *film noir noir*?

Rather than haggle definitions, I would rather attempt to reduce *film noir* to its primary colors (all shades of black), those cultural and stylistic elements to which any definition must return.

At the risk of sounding like Arthur Knight, I would suggest that there were four conditions in Hollywood in the Forties which brought about the *film noir*. (The danger of Knight's *Liveliest Art* method is that it makes film history less a matter of structural analysis, and more a case of artistic and social forces magically interacting and coalescing). Each of the following four catalytic elements, however, can define the film noir; the distinctly *noir* tonality draws from each of these elements.

(1) **War and post-war disillusionment.** The acute downer which hit the U.S. after the Second World War was, in fact, a delayed reaction to the Thirties. All through the Depression, movies were needed to keep people's spirits up, and, for the most part, they did. The crime films of this period were Horatio Alger-ish and socially conscious. Toward the end of the Thirties a darker crime film began to appear (*You Only Live Once*, *The Roaring Twenties*) and, were it not for the War, *film noir* would have been at full steam by the early Forties.

The need to produce Allied propaganda abroad and promote patriotism at home blunted the fledgling moves toward a dark cinema, and the *film noir* thrashed about in the studio system, not quite able to come into full promi-nence. During the War the first uniquely *film noir* appeared: *The Maltese Falcon*, *The Glass Key*, *This Gun for Hire*, *Laura* but these films lacked the distinctly *noir* bite the end of the war would bring.

As soon as the War was over, however, American films became markedly more sardonic—and there was a boom in the crime film. For fifteen years the pressures against America's amelioristic cinema had been building up, and, given the freedom, audiences and artists were now eager to take a less opti-mistic view of things. The disillusionment many soldiers, small businessmen and housewife/factory employees felt in returning to a peacetime economy was directly mirrored in the sordidness of the urban crime film.

This immediate post-war disillusionment was directly demonstrated in films like *Cornered*, *The Blue Dahlia*, *Dead Reckoning* and *Ride a Pink Horse*, in which a serviceman returns from the war to find his sweetheart unfaithful or dead, or his business partner cheating him, or the whole society something less than worth fighting for. The war continues, but now the antagonism turns with a new viciousness toward the American society itself.

(2) **Post-war realism.** Shortly after the War every film-producing country had a resurgence of realism. In America it first took the form of films by such pro-ducers as Louis de Rochemont (*House on 92nd Street*, *Call Northside 777*) and Mark Hellinger (*The Killers*, *Brute Force*), and directors like Henry Hathaway and Jules Dassin. "Every scene was filmed on the actual location depicted," the 1947 de Rochemont–Hathaway *Kiss of Death* proudly proclaimed. Even after de Rochemont's particular "March of Time" authenticity fell from vogue, realistic exteriors remained a permanent fixture of *film noir*.

The realistic movement also suited America's post-war mood; the public's desire for a more honest and harsh view of America would not be satisfied by the same studio streets they had been watching for a dozen years. The post-war realistic trend succeeded in breaking *film noir* away from the domain of the high-class melodrama, placing it where it more properly belonged, in the streets with everyday people. In retrospect, the pre–de Rochemont *film noir* looks definitely tamer than the post-War realistic films. The studio look of films like *The Big Sleep* and *The Mask of Dimitrios* blunts their sting, making them seem polite and conventional in contrast to their later, more realistic counterparts.

(3) **The German influence.** Hollywood played host to an influx of German expatriates in the Twenties and Thirties, and these filmmakers and technicians had, for the most part, integrated themselves into the American film establishment. Hollywood never experienced the "Germanization" some civic-minded natives feared, and there is a danger of over-emphasizing the German influence in Hollywood.

But when, in the late Forties, Hollywood decided to paint it black, there were no greater masters of chiaroscuro than the Germans. The influence of expressionist lighting has always been just beneath the surface of Hollywood films, and it is not surprising, in *film noir*, to find it bursting out full bloom. Neither is it surprising to find a larger number of Germans and East Europeans working in *film noir*; Fritz Lang, Robert Siodmak, Billy Wilder, Franz Waxman, Otto Preminger, John Brahm, Anatole Litvak, Karl Freund, Max Ophuls, John Alton, Douglas Sirk, Fred Zinnemann, William Dieterle, Max Steiner, Edgar G. Ulmer, Curtis Bernhardt, Rudolph Mate.

On the surface the German expressionist influence, with its reliance on artificial studio lighting, seems incompatible with post-war realism, with its harsh unadorned exteriors; but it is the unique quality of *film noir* that it was able to weld seemingly contradictory elements into a uniform style. The best *noir* technicians simply made all the world a sound stage, directing unnatural and expressionistic lighting onto realistic settings. In films like *Union Station*, *They Live by Night*, *The Killers* there is an uneasy, exhilarating combination of realism and expressionism.

Perhaps the greatest master of *noir* was Hungarian-born John Alton, an expressionist cinematographer who could relight Times Square at noon if necessary. No cinematographer better adapted the old expressionist techniques to the new desire for realism, and his black-and-white photography in such gritty *film noir* as *T-Men*, *Raw Deal*, *I the Jury*, *The Big Combo* equals that of such German expressionist masters as Fritz Wagner and Karl Freund.

(4) **The hard-boiled tradition.** Another stylistic influence waiting in the wings was the "hard-boiled" school of writers. In the Thirties, authors such as Ernest Hemingway, Dashiell Hammett, Raymond Chandler, James M. Cain, Horace McCoy and John O'Hara created the "tough," a cynical way of acting, and thinking which separated one from the world of everyday emotions— romanticism with a protective shell. The hard-boiled writers had their roots in

pulp fiction or journalism, and their protagonists lived out a narcissistic, defeatist code. The hard-boiled hero was in reality a soft egg compared to his existential counterpart (Camus is said to have based *The Stranger* on McCoy), but he was a good deal tougher than anything American fiction had seen.

When the movies of the Forties turned to the American "tough" moral understrata, the hard-boiled school was waiting with preset conventions of heroes, minor characters, plots, dialogue and themes. Like the German expatriates, the hard-boiled writers had a style made to order for *film noir*; and, in turn, they influenced *noir* screenwriting as much as the Germans influenced *noir* cinematography.

The most hard-boiled of Hollywood's writers was Raymond Chandler himself, whose script of *Double Indemnity* (from a James M. Cain story) was the best written and most characteristically *noir* of the period. *Double Indemnity* was the first film which played *film noir* for what it essentially was: small-time, unredeemed, unheroic; it made a break from the romantic *noir* cinema of *Mildred Pierce* and *The Big Sleep*.

(In its final stages, however, *film noir* adapted and then bypassed the hardboiled school. Manic, neurotic post-1948 films such as *Kiss Tomorrow Goodbye*, *D.O.A.*, *Where the Sidewalk Ends*, *White Heat*, and *The Big Heat* are all post-hardboiled: the air in these regions was even too thin for old-time cynics like Chandler.)

Stylistics. There is not yet a study of the stylistics of *film noir*, and the task is certainly too large to be attempted here. Like all film movements *film noir* drew upon a reservoir of film techniques, and given the time one could correlate its techniques, themes and casual elements into a stylistic schema. For the present, however, I'd like to point out some of *film noir*'s recurring techniques.

■ The majority of scenes are lit for night. Gangsters sit in the offices at midday with the shades pulled and the lights off. Ceiling lights are hung low and floor lamps are seldom more than five feet high. One always has the suspicion that if the lights were all suddenly flipped on the characters would shriek and shrink from the scene like Count Dracula at sunrise.

■ As in German expressionism, oblique and vertical lines are preferred to horizontal. Obliquity adheres to the choreography of the city, and is in direct opposition to the horizontal American tradition of Griffith and Ford. Oblique lines tend to splinter a screen, making it restless and unstable. Light enters the dingy rooms of *film noir* in such odd shapes—jagged trapezoids, obtuse triangles, vertical slits—that one suspects the windows were cut out with a pen knife. No character can speak authoritatively from a space which is being continually cut into ribbons of light. The Anthony Mann/John Alton *T-Men* is the most dramatic but far from the only example of oblique *noir* choreography.

■ The actors and setting are often given equal lighting emphasis. An actor is often hidden in the realistic tableau of the city at night, and, more obviously, his face is often blacked out by shadow as he speaks. These shadow effects are unlike the famous Warner Brothers lighting of the Thirties in which the central character was accentuated by a heavy shadow; in *film noir,* the central character is likely to be standing *in* the shadow. When the environment is given an equal or greater weight than the actor, it, of course, creates a fatalistic, hopeless mood. There is nothing the protagonist can do; the city will outlast and negate even his best efforts.

■ Compositional tension is preferred to physical action. A typical *film noir* would rather move the scene cinematographically around the actor than have the actor control the scene by physical action. The beating of Robert Ryan in *The Set-Up*, the gunning down of Farley Granger in *They Live by Night*, the execution of the taxi driver in *The Enforcer* and of Brian Donlevy in *The Big Combo* are all marked by measured pacing, restrained anger and oppressive compositions, and seem much closer to the *film noir* spirit than the rat-tat-tat and screeching tires of *Scarface* twenty years before or the violent, expressive actions of *Underworld U.S.A.* ten years later.

■ There seems to be an almost Freudian attachment to water. The empty *noir* streets are almost always glistening with fresh evening rain (even in Los Angeles), and the rainfall tends to increase in direct proportion to the drama. Docks and piers are second only to alleyways as the most popular rendezvous points.

■ There is a love of romantic narration. In such films as *The Postman Always Rings Twice, Laura, Double Indemnity, The Lady from Shanghai, Out of the Past* and *Sunset Boulevard* the narration creates a mood of *temps perdu*: an irretrievable past, a predetermined fate and an all-enveloping hopelessness. In *Out of the Past* Robert Mitchum relates his history with such pathetic relish that it is obvious there is no hope for any future: one can only take pleasure in reliving a doomed past.

■ A complex chronological order is frequently used to reinforce the feelings of hopelessness and lost time. Such films as *The Enforcer, The Killers, Mildred Pierce, The Dark Past, Chicago Deadline, Out of the Past* and *The Killing* use a convoluted time sequence to immerse the viewer in a time-disoriented but highly stylized world. The manipulation of time, whether slight or complex, is often used to reinforce a *noir* principle: the how is always more important than the what.

Themes. Raymond Durgnat has delineated the themes of *film noir* in an excellent article in the British *Cinema* magazine ("The Family Tree of *Film Noir*," August, 1970), and it would be foolish for me to attempt to redo his thorough work in this short space. Durgnat divides *film noir* into eleven thematic categories, and although one might criticize some of his specific groupings, he does cover the whole gamut of *noir* production (thematically categorizing over 300 films).

In each of Durgnat's *noir* themes (whether Black Widow, killers-on-the-run, *dopplegangers*) one finds that the upwardly mobile forces of the Thirties have halted; frontierism has turned to paranoia and claustrophobia. The small-time gangster has now made it big and sits in the mayor's chair, the private eye has quit the police force in disgust, and the young heroine, sick of going along for the ride, is taking others for a ride.

Durgnat, however, does not touch upon what is perhaps the over-riding *noir* theme: a passion for the past and present, but also a fear of the future. The *noir* hero dreads to look ahead, but instead tries to survive by the day, and if unsuccessful at that, he retreats to the past. Thus *film noir*'s techniques emphasize loss, nostalgia, lack of clear priorities, insecurity; then submerge these self-doubts in mannerism and style. In such a world style becomes paramount; it is all that separates one from meaninglessness. Chandler described this fundamental *noir* theme when he described his own fictional world: "It is not a very fragrant world, but it is the world you live in, and certain writers with tough minds and a cool spirit of detachment can make very interesting patterns out of it."

Film noir can be subdivided into three broad phases. The first, the wartime period, 1941–46 approximately, was the phase of the private eye and the lone wolf, of Chandler, Hammett and Greene, of Bogart and Bacall, Ladd and Lake, classy directors like Curtiz and Garnett, studio sets, and, in general, more talk than action. The studio look of this period was reflected in such pictures as *The Maltese Falcon, Casablanca, Gaslight, This Gun for Hire, The Lodger, The Woman in the Window, Mildred Pierce, Spellbound, The Big Sleep, Laura, The Lost Weekend, The Strange Love of Martha Ivers, To Have and Have Not, Fallen Angel, Gilda, Murder My Sweet, The Postman Always Rings Twice, Dark Waters, Scarlet Street, So Dark the Night, The Glass Key, The Mask of Dimitrios,* and *The Dark Mirror.*

The Wilder/Chandler *Double Indemnity* provided a bridge to the post-War phase of *film noir.* The unflinching *noir* vision of *Double Indemnity* came as a shock in 1944, and the film was almost blocked by the combined efforts of Paramount, the Hays Office and star Fred MacMurray. Three years later, however, *Double Indemnity*s were dropping off the studio assembly lines.

The second phase was the post-War realistic period from 1945–49 (the dates overlap and so do the films; these are all approximate phases for which there are many exceptions). These films tended more toward the problems of crime in the streets, political corruption and police routine. Less romantic heroes like Richard Conte, Burt Lancaster and Charles McGraw were more suited to this period, as were proletarian directors like Hathaway, Dassin and Kazan. The realistic urban look of this phase is seen in such films as *The House on 92nd Street, The Killers, Raw Deal, Act of Violence, Union Station, Kiss of Death, Johnny O'Clock, Force of Evil, Dead Reckoning, Ride the Pink Horse, Dark Passage, Cry of the City, The Set-Up, T-Men, Call Northside 777, Brute Force, The Big Clock, Thieves' Highway, Ruthless, Pitfall, Boomerang!* and *The Naked City.*

(3) The third and final phase of *film noir*, from 1949–53, was the period of psy-chotic action and suicidal impulse. The *noir* hero, seemingly under the weight of ten years of despair, started to go bananas. The psychotic killer, who had in the first period been a subject worthy of study (Olivia de Havilland in *The Dark Mirror*), in the second a fringe threat (Richard Widmark in *Kiss of Death*), now became the active protagonist (James Cagney in *Kiss Tomorrow Goodbye*). There were no excuses given for the psychopathy in *Gun Crazy*—it was just "crazy." James Cagney made a neurotic comeback and his instability was matched by that of younger actors like Robert Ryan and Lee Marvin. This was the phase of the "B" *noir* film, and of psychoanalytically-inclined directors like Ray and Walsh. The forces of personal disintegration are reflected in such films as *White Heat, Gun Crazy, D.O.A., Caught, They Live by Night, Where the Sidewalk Ends, Kiss Tomorrow Goodbye, Detective Story, In a Lonely Place, The Jury, Ace in the Hole, Panic in the Streets, The Big Heat, On Dangerous Ground,* and *Sunset Boulevard.*

This third phase is the cream of the *film noir* period. Some critics may pre-fer the early "gray" melodramas, others the post-War "street" films, but *film noir*'s final phase was the most aesthetically and sociologically piercing. After ten years of steadily shedding romantic conventions, the later *noir* films finally got down to the root causes of the period: the loss of public honor, heroic conventions, personal integrity, and, finally, psychic stability. The third-phase films were painfully self-aware; they seemed to know they stood at the end of a long tradition based on despair and disintegration and did not shy away from that fact. The best and most characteristically *noir* films—*Gun Crazy, White Heat, Out of the Past, Kiss Tomorrow Goodbye, D.O.A., They Live by Night,* and *The Big Heat*—stand at the end of the period and are the results of self-awareness. The third phase is rife with end-of-the-line *noir* heroes: *The Big Heat* and *Where the Sidewalk Ends* are the last stops for the urban cop, *Ace in the Hole,* for the newspaper man, the Victor Saville–produced Spillane series (*I the Jury, The Long Wait, Kiss Me Deadly*) for the private eye, *Sunset Boulevard* for the Black Widow, *White*

Heat and *Kiss Tomorrow Goodbye* for the gangster, *D.O.A.* for the John Doe American.

Appropriately, the masterpiece of *film noir* was a straggler, *Kiss Me Deadly*, produced in 1955. Its time delay gives it a sense of detachment and thorough-going seediness—it stands at the end of a long sleazy tradition. The private eye hero, Mike Hammer, undergoes the final stages of degradation. He is a small-time "bedroom dick," and makes no qualms about it because the world around him isn't much better. Ralph Meeker, in his best performance, plays Hammer, a midget among dwarfs. Robert Aldrich's teasing direction carries *noir* to its sleaziest and most perversely erotic. Hammer overturns the underworld in search of the "great whatsit," and when he finally finds it, it turns out to be—joke of jokes—an exploding atomic bomb. The inhumanity and meaningless of the hero are small matters in a world in which The Bomb has the final say.

By the middle Fifties *film noir* had ground to a halt. There were a few notable stragglers, *Kiss Me Deadly*, the Lewis/Alton *The Big Combo*, and *film noir*'s epitaph, *Touch of Evil*, but for the most part a new style of crime film had become popular.

As the rise of McCarthy and Eisenhower demonstrated, Americans were eager to see a more bourgeois view of themselves. Crime had to move to the suburbs. The criminal put on a grey flannel suit and the footsore cop was replaced by the "mobile unit" careening down the expressway. Any attempt at social criticism had to be cloaked in ludicrous affirmations of the American way of life. Technically, television, with its demand for full lighting and close-ups, gradually undercut the German influence, and color cinematography was, of course, the final blow to the *"noir"* look.

New directors like Siegel, Fleischer, Karlson and Fuller, and TV shows like *Dragnet*, *M-Squad*, *Lineup* and *Highway Patrol* stepped in to create the new crime drama. This transition can be seen in Samuel Fuller's 1953 *Pickup on South Street*, a film which blends the black look with the red scare. The water-front scenes with Richard Widmark and Jean Peters are in the best *noir* tradition, but a later, dynamic fight in the subway marks Fuller as a director who would be better suited to the crime school of the middle and late Fifties.

Film noir was an immensely creative period—probably the most creative in Hollywood's history—at least, if this creativity is measured not by its peaks but by its median level of artistry. Picked at random, a *film noir* is likely to be a better made film than a randomly selected silent comedy, musical, western and so on. (A Joseph H. Lewis "B" *film noir* is better than a Lewis "B" west-ern, for example.) Taken as a whole period, *film noir* achieved an unusually high level of artistry.

Film noir seemed to bring out the best in everyone: directors, cameramen, screenwriters, actors. Again and again, a *film noir* will make the high point on an artist's career graph. Some directors, for example, did their best work in *film noir* (Stuart Heisler, Robert Siodmak, Gordon Douglas, Edward Dmytryk, John Brahm, John Cromwell, Raoul Walsh, Henry Hathaway); other directors began in *film noir* and, it seems to me, never regained their original heights (Otto Preminger, Rudolph Mate, Nicholas Ray, Robert Wise, Jules Dassin, Richard Fleischer, John Huston, Andre de Toth, and Robert Aldrich); and other directors who made great films in other molds also made great *film noir* (Orson Welles, Max Ophuls, Fritz Lang, Elia Kazan, Howard Hawks, Robert Rossen, Anthony Mann, Joseph Losey, Alfred Hitchcock, and Stanley Kubrick). Whether or not one agrees with this particular schema, its message is irrefutable: *film noir* was good for practically every director's career. (Two interesting exceptions to prove the case are King Vidor and Jean Renoir.)

Film noir seems to have been a creative release for everyone involved. It gave artists a chance to work with previously forbidden themes, yet had conventions strong enough to protect the mediocre. Cinematographers were allowed to become highly mannered, and actors were sheltered by the cinematographers. It was not until years later that critics were able to distinguish between great directors and great *noir* directors.

Film noir's remarkable creativity makes its long-time neglect the more baffling. The French, of course, have been students of the period for some time (Borde and Chaumenton's *Panorama du Film Noir* was published in 1955), but American critics until recently have preferred the western, the musical or the gangster film to the *film noir*.

Some of the reasons for this neglect are superficial, others strike to the heart of the *noir* style. For a long time *film noir*, with its emphasis on corruption and despair, was considered an aberration of the American character. The western, with its moral primitivism, and the gangster film, with its Horatio Alger values, were considered more American than the *film noir*.

This prejudice was reinforced by the fact that *film noir* was ideally suited to the low budget "B" film, and many of the best *noir* films were "B" films. This odd sort of economic snobbery still lingers on in some critical circles: high-budget trash is considered more worthy of attention than low-budget trash, and to praise a "B" film is somehow to slight (often intentionally) an "A" film.

There has been a critical revival in the U.S. over the last ten years, but *film noir* lost out on that too. The revival was *auteur* (director) oriented, and *film noir* wasn't. *Auteur* criticism is interested in how directors are different; *film noir* criticism is concerned with what they have in common.

The fundamental reason for *film noir*'s neglect, however, is the fact that it depends more on choreography than sociology, and American critics have always been slow on the uptake when it comes to visual style. Like its protagonists, *film noir* is more interested in style than theme, whereas American critics have been traditionally more interested in theme than style.

American film critics have always been sociologists first and scientists second: film is important as it relates to large masses, and if a film goes awry it is often because the theme has been somehow "violated" by the style. *Film noir* operates on opposite principles: the theme is hidden in the style, and bogus themes are often flaunted ("middle-class values are best") which contradict the style. Although, I believe, style determines the theme in *every* film, it was easier for sociological critics to discuss the themes of the western and gangster film apart from stylistic analysis than it was to do for *film noir*.

Not surprisingly it was the gangster film, not the *film noir*, which was canonized in *The Partisan Review* in 1948 by Robert Warshow's famous essay, "The Gangster as Tragic Hero." Although Warshow could be an aesthetic as well as a sociological critic, in this case he was interested in the western and gangster film as "popular" art rather than as style. This sociological orientation blinded Warshow, as it has many subsequent critics, to an aesthetically more important development in the gangster film—*film noir*.

The irony of this neglect is that in retrospect the gangster films Warshow wrote about are inferior to *film noir*. The Thirties gangster was primarily a reflection of what was happening in the country, and Warshow analyzed this. The *film noir*, although it was also a sociological reflection, went further than the gangster film. Toward the end *film noir* was engaged in a life-and-death struggle with the materials it reflected; it tried to make America accept a moral vision of life based on style. That very contradiction—promoting style in a culture which valued themes—forced *film noir* into artistically invigorating twists and turns. *Film noir* attacked and interpreted its sociological conditions, and, by the close of the *noir* period, created a new artistic world which went beyond a simple sociological reflection, a nightmarish world of American mannerism which was by far more a creation than a reflection.

Because *film noir* was first of all a style, because it worked out its conflicts visually rather than thematically, because it was aware of its own identity, it was able to create artistic solutions to sociological problems. And for these reasons films like *Kiss Me Deadly*, *Kiss Tomorrow Goodbye* and *Gun Crazy* can be works of art in a way that gangster films like *Scarface*, *Public Enemy* and *Little Caesar* can never be.

1972

John Simon

John Simon (b. 1925) has written film criticism for *Esquire, The New Leader, New York*, and other publications, as well as copious theater, music, and literary criticism. "The most fundamental thing to remember about film criticism is that it is not fundamentally different from any other kind of criticism," he once stated. Simon, who was born in the former Yugoslavia and moved at age ten with his family to the United States, has retained an émigré's disdain for what he regards as the more childish aspects of American culture. Some have found cruel the relish he takes in pointing out a production's artistic flaws and even its actresses' physical imperfections. Simon has justified his demanding, astringent manner (his favorite filmmaker is Ingmar Bergman) by saying: "But to the critic to whom art is important, sacred, and, ultimately, coextensive with life itself, to produce bad art and to condone it—and thereby give rise to further bad art and finally drive out the good—are the two most heinously dangerous sins imaginable." In any case, no one has ever questioned the superiority of Simon's prose style, which is elegant, poised, and trenchant. Both his caustic review of *The Last Picture Show* by Peter Bogdanovich (once a rival film critic) and his appreciation of the freshness in *Chinatown* demonstrate his conviction that a film must do more than merely please the eye.

◆

The Last Picture Show

Peter Bogdanovich is America's answer to the *Cahiers* phenomenon of film critic turned filmmaker; yet behind every answer there is a question. In this case, how good was he as a critic in the first place? The answer is that he was never a serious critic, only an auteurist hero-worshiper. And how is he as a filmmaker? His first film, *Targets*, handled a valid subject in a trashy way; his new one, *The Last Picture Show*, is a great hit with the reviewers, less so with the audiences, and strikes me as not bad by current standards. Inasmuch as Bogdanovich is in his very early thirties, this may augur well. But there is a "but" here, and quite a big, fat but it is, too.

The Last Picture Show takes place in the two-horse town of Anarene, Texas, in 1951, when the town's only picture show (i.e., movie theater) closed down before the onslaught of television, which brought the dream factory right into the living room. Sonny Crawford, co-captain of the high-school football team, is at the center of this one-year chronicle. We see him go from unsatisfactory pettings with his plain but busty girlfriend in the back of the picture show or in the front seat of his pickup truck, to an affair with Ruth Popper, the neglected middle-aged wife of the crude football coach; thence to an unconsummated affair and promptly annulled wedding with Jacy Farrow, a classmate who is the local pretty and spoiled rich bitch.

Meanwhile Sonny's best friend, Duane Jackson, the backfield captain, goes from being Jacy's platonic boyfriend to becoming, ever so fleetingly, her lover, thence to the army and the Korean War. Two lovable figures around town die: Sam the Lion—owner of the picture show, poolroom, and eatery, the three sole recreational centers of Anarene—a fine remnant of a more romantic West; and Billy, a little idiot boy whom Sam took care of and Sonny, often inadequately, protected.

Jacy goes from fooling around with Duane to getting herself deflowered by him merely to move in on the fast, smart set of Wichita Falls, where virginity would be held against her; thrown over by one of those megalopolitan rich boys, she returns to the local talent and takes on, first, Abilene, her mother's lover, then Sonny himself, only to cast him off. On the sidelines, there are two women watching and commenting: Genevieve, the hardy, good-natured café waitress; and Lois, Jacy's jaded mother, bored and exasperated by her loveless marriage to Anarene's oil millionaire.

All this is framed by an opening shot of the picture show still functioning, and a closing shot of it standing there on the town's main street, deserted. The former shows us a dry, windy, dusty, bleak day, and sets the climate of the film. The latter is a superimposition: Sonny, who has graduated and is already a forgotten outsider at the school football games, has sneaked back to see Ruth Popper, whom he so recklessly abandoned for Jacy. Ruth receives him nicely, gives him coffee, and then has her outburst: Why has she always been so self-effacing, waiting on everyone, Sunny included; why has she never asserted her rights? Sunny is remorseful, Ruth's moment of rebellion passes. Now they sit there, dejected, no longer lovers and not yet friends, holding hands unhopefully as their image dissolves into that of the abandoned movie theater of a godforsaken town.

Though schematic, this doesn't sound half bad. But look at the film more closely. The locale is captured accurately by Robert Surtees's black-and-white cinematography, and the time seems indeed to be 1951, as we are told it is. Told? Clobbered with it. Just about every hit song of the period manages to hit us from radios or jukeboxes; every major television program of the time seems to be watched by someone in the film at some point or other.

Yet this is fairly easy. The lay of the land has not changed much since Larry McMurtry wrote or lived the autobiographical novel on which he and Bogdanovich based this screenplay. I got my air-force basic training near Wichita Falls in 1944, and I can vouch for the area's being of the sort that a decade or two can barely make a dent in. The monochromatic photography is quite good, but in an era when almost everything is filmed in color, you can score easy points just by clinging to black-and-white—whether it is finally called honesty, nostalgia, or an *hommage* to your favorite directors of the period. And, certainly, the general outline of the film convinces: McMurtry lived it, wrote it almost without sentimentality or anger, and Bogdanovich approaches the material reverently—all too reverently, in fact.

McMurtry, who also wrote the novel on which *Hud* was based, considers himself a minor regional novelist, and engagingly mentioned at a symposium that, in working on the script of *The Last Picture Show*, he discovered how much better a novel could have been made from the material—and, by implication, how much better a film, had Bogdanovich not been so enamored of the published text. But as both Pauline Kael and Andrew Sarris (who have, unlike me, read the novel) pointed out, there were some minor yet not wholly insignificant changes made, adding up to a certain romanticizing of the matter. Thus the movies the kids see in the film are better than the ones in the novel (Bogdanovich even anachronistically drags in *Red River*, as a tribute to one of his auteur-heroes, Howard Hawks); Lois is not allowed, in the film, to have sex with Sonny, whom her daughter has just betrayed; Jacy's crude sexual bout with her mother's lover on a pool table, and the young bloods having intercourse with a blind heifer are also excised.

What is kept is not always particularly persuasive, either. I cannot believe the scene where all their classmates watch Jacy's and Duane's sexual initiation from cars parked outside the motel; I do not see the need to make Lester, a two-bit operator (Randy Quaid), seem more idiotic than Billy, the real halfwit. I think it is a bad boiling down of the novel that introduces Sonny's father out of nowhere as an outcast, drops him immediately, and never tells us anything about Sonny's home life; the same goes for Duane and his family, with a mother making a belated, almost subliminal appearance. The character of Abilene, the town stud, is woefully underdeveloped; Sam the Lion is so idealized that we see him only in scenes where he can deploy generosity, righteous indignation, gracious forgiveness, or noble, homespun philosophizing. His basic, quotidian relationship to Genevieve and Billy is left completely unexamined.

The whole last part of the film proceeds by jerky, disparate lurches that do not blend into a balanced narrative, and the conclusion is so ambiguous (my interpretation, given above, is perforce quite arbitrary) as to be close to a mere effect. Worst of all, Sonny is unconvincing—whether in the writing, acting, or directing, or in all three, hardly matters. We are supposedly looking, for the most part, through his eyes, and he is meant to be a reasonable enough young fellow in the process of coming of age. Yet what has he really learned, or taught us, in the end? And how can we take him seriously if he is so stupid that, when Genevieve observes the town is so small that no one can sneeze in it without all the other people holding out a handkerchief, he asks, "What do you mean?"

Indeed, almost all of these people are cloddish. The fact that Anarene is a cultural backwater may explain this, but does not necessarily reconcile us to spending two hours with its essentially dreary denizens. True artists, of course, can illumine the simplest people—in both senses of the verb—and can make plain words take on great resonance. Though McMurtry and Bogdanovich succeed once or twice, that is hardly enough to rouse one's sympathy from its sleep.

Potentially most gripping are those unfulfilled older women: Ruth, Genevieve, Lois Farrow. But none of them quite makes it. Ellen Burstyn is very competent as Lois, yet the part is too skimpy and burdened with drippy lines like "Nothing has really been right since Sam the Lion died." Eileen Brennan's Genevieve captures the essence of the likable tough broad of the old movies, but they, rather than life, seem to be the unfortunate source of the character. As Ruth, Cloris Leachman gives a poor performance: her weeping comes out comic, her shy love for a very young boy lacks genuine warmth and seems almost calculating, her face is usually a rather unattractive blank. She seems to be all nose and sharp bones; even a boy like Sonny might have found her no sexier than a Gillette razor blade.

Above all, Bogdanovich's direction is sheer derivativeness. To put it bluntly, it is cinémathèque direction. A John Ford shot is followed by a George Stevens one; a Welles shot by one out of Raoul Walsh. Even if every sequence is not so patently copied as the funeral is from *Shane*, the feeling is unmistakable that one is watching a film directed not by a young director in 1971, but by a conclave of the bigger Hollywood directors circa 1941. This may give the film visual authenticity, but of what kind? Imagine a present-day composer writing like Haydn, a painter working in the exact style of Vermeer. At best, such men are epigones; at worst, forgers. At its most successful, *The Last Picture Show* rises to the heights of pastiche.

There are also serious minor problems, the most bothersome of them being unsubtlety. When Sonny and Ruth make love for the first time, the springs of the bed do not just squeak, they ululate. If this were intended as deliberate heightening from a subjective point of view, it would have to occur throughout the film, which it doesn't. Sonny has a way of fondly turning around the baseball cap on Billy's head, so that the visor faces backward. He does this some half-dozen times in the film, and when *he* doesn't do it, Duane does. It becomes grating in its predictability. Or take Billy's death; the boy is run over by a truck. The scene is staged stiffly and ploddingly, and the gloom-inducing devices run amuck. Never, on those other windy days, has a shutter been banging in the poolroom; now there is one beating the Devil's tattoo. Never before has a single tumbleweed tumbled down the streets of Anarene; now there is a bunch of them doing enough tumbling for the main ring at Barnum & Bailey's.

At other times, instead of hitting us over the head, Bogdanovich does not make a point at all. When Sonny, after Billy's death, gets into his truck and drives off to leave this horrible town forever, we follow him along the empty road across scarcely less empty country until suddenly, for no visible reason, he makes a U-turn and capitulates. A reliable filmmaker would have taken us inside Sonny as the resolution to escape peters out; if nothing else, he would have found an objective correlative, the tiny external factor that undermines the boy's resolve. Instead, like so many things in the film, the change of mind has to be taken simply on faith.

The acting is far from consistently good. Aside from Cloris Leachman's and Randy Quaid's unpleasant work, there are Clu Gulager's Abilene, Timothy and Sam Bottoms's Sonny and Billy, and Cybill Shepherd's Jacy to leave one unmoved. Miss Shepherd is a model (though how, with that dubious figure, I can't imagine) whose face Bogdanovich found on a teen-age magazine cover. Although her face is absolutely right for Jacy, nothing else is. Ben Johnson does nicely by Sam the Lion, however, and Jeff Bridges is convincingly oxlike as Duane.

1971

Jaundice of the Soul

With *Chinatown*, Roman Polanski makes a comeback. True, in some ways a throwback to all those private-eye movies, often based on novels by Dashiell Hammett or Raymond Chandler, that supplied the cinema of our formative (or merely impressionable) years with one of its juiciest genres. But *Chinatown* is not just another *Maltese Falcon* or *Big Sleep*, to be dismissed as a contemporary painting that apes, however skillfully, an Old Master. It is, rather, a subtly updated version: an equivalent with significant albeit subcutaneous differences that puts Polanski, after the monstrous fiasco of *What?*, back into the running.

The plot could hardly be more archetypal. The capable private investigator, J. J. Gittes, slightly soiled but basically honorable, is employed by a beautiful woman with a husband problem, a woman who may, in fact, be criminal herself. Gittes has the properly ambivalent relationship with the police lieutenant who is working parallelly, or obliquely, on the same case: once they were partners in uniform, now they nudge each other with a mixture of respect and mistrust. Gittes is sucked into a world of intrigue in which, typically, he gets about as many beatings as he delivers. Finally, though he solves the case, success turns bitter in his mouth. Life is a cracked bowl of mostly rotten cherries.

So what else is new about *Chinatown?* Quite a bit, actually. The hero, even though the time and place is Los Angeles in the thirties (which is to this genre what Paris 1890 was to bedroom farce), is played by Jack Nicholson as an emblematic man of today. Unlike the Bogartian hero, he is not coolly sure of himself all the way down the line. His wisecracks are more brittle, he is occasionally gauche, his aplomb is muted by a sense of moral ambiguity. He can break up at other people's jokes as retold by himself, a childlike trait as remote from Bogey as the somewhat high-pitched voice and thinning hair, both of which render Nicholson's Gittes more fragile, as does his slightly ridiculous name: can you imagine Hammett calling a Spade a Gittes?

The lovely but shopworn heroine, Evelyn Mulwray (Faye Dunaway), is also faintly off-center. Under the beautiful, battered exterior there lurks neither the untouched innocent who can settle down snugly into a happy ending, nor a fascinating wrongdoer for whom the electric chair is the fitting final seat. Even the chief villain is not your typical racketeer, sadist, or madman; his evil has sociopolitical coloration and even a certain pathos; too bad that John Huston, a living *hommage* to *The Maltese Falcon*, gives an essentially lazy, unresonant performance opting for easy charm. The others are mostly genre types, but the police lieutenant (Perry Lopez) is a Chicano, whose position is ipso facto precarious, which brings us back to social implications.

What primarily distinguishes the film from its models is the new sensibility of the director and scenarist, and the new technology, wide-screen and color, which interestingly distort the old simplicities. Thus the "Chinatown" in which the final reckoning unfurls is not so much a place as a concept, a symbol. Gittes, when still on the force, was stationed in Chinatown, where the wary police motto was, "Do as little as possible." In this Chinatown, he loved a woman and tried to keep her from being hurt, but "ended up making sure that she *was* hurt." Throughout the film there are quietly ominous references to this Chinatown where "you can't always tell what's going on," but where your very life is changed even as you endeavor to do as little as possible.

analyzing the title

Gradually, then, we become aware of a Chinatown of the mind, to which, the film says, all roads lead. Unlike Rome, it is not a place to which we want to be led, for in it *we* do not have a Chinaman's chance. Because the film works honestly and contemporaneously with real locations (instead of, say, the fancy opium-den setting, smelling more of studio than of opium, where the Martha Vickers character is shown in *The Big Sleep*), it must use the available China-town of Los Angeles, which is not quite the place of sinister mystery we might demand from an objective correlative. This is somewhat disappointing visually, but has the virtue of forcing us toward the symbolic rather than realistic values of the concept. What is more troubling is that the references to Chinatown seem at times to be dragged arbitrarily into the conversation, and that the var-ious Chinese servants, who also serve as visual reminders, no longer exude the disquieting "Oriental inscrutability" they gave off when private-eyehood was in flower.

Yet it is not just some philosophic overview that differentiates this film from its predecessors. Nor do I mean the greater sexual freedom in language and incident. So, for instance, the film begins with a series of black-and-white stills, mostly of copulation, accompanied by grunting on the sound track. By degrees we realize that we are looking at telephoto snapshots of infidelity being examined by a Gittes client, and that the groans are not the lecher's but the cuckold's. In an old folks' home, we are allowed to glimpse an elderly inmate grabbing a nurse's buttocks. The brief affair between Gittes and Mrs. Mulwray, for all its tactful understatement, is still more suggestive than was once possible: "I didn't see anyone for very long," says Evelyn about her psy-chosexual disarray. "It's difficult for me. . . ."

The main modernity of *Chinatown* is of a different order. Robert Towne's screenplay (so superior to that for *The Last Detail*) is at times much more spec-ulative than the old genre films dared to be: "Politicians, ugly buildings, and whores all get respectable if they last long enough," the aged millionaire-villain will say. Things also get more Rabelaisian: when a policeman taunts J.J. with an unflattering interpretation of how he came by his nose injury, our hero replies, "No. Your wife got excited and crossed her legs a little too quick. . . ." But what really brings the film into the 1970s is the loss of innocence that per-meates its world: the boundaries between right and wrong have become hazy even in the good—or better—people, and the two genuine innocents of the film are both, in one way or another, victimized. The entire world is headed for its Chinatown, and when, in the end, Gittes, faced with a dreadful recurrence of loss, mutters dazedly, "As little as possible," what may have once been shrewd strategy becomes a counsel of universal despair.

Entirely new is the approach to violence. There is less of it than in the Marlovian heyday, and much less than in the Spillanian decadence; what there is of it, however, is more discriminating, disturbing, and real. When Gittes is to be given a warning, an ugly little punk (played by Polanski himself) slices up his nose with a switchblade knife. It happens quickly, too quickly for immediate comprehension, with the full new awareness that speed, brevity, and opacity vastly increase the horror quotient. The sight is grisly, and the aftereffects are precisely observed: J.J.'s nose, for the rest of the film, is bandaged, and though the bandages decrease in size with clinical accuracy, even the big sex scene, with the bandages temporarily removed, has to be played with a nose from which the freshly torn sutures protrude like a carp's whiskers. A lesser villain, whom Gittes roughs up, sports a suitably bandaged head next time round. And the final bullet hole of the film has the true disfiguring ghastliness that could not have been shown formerly. Yet the film is at the other end of the scale from those movies where excess of violence is allowed to immunize the viewer with surfeit.

So, too, the sex is treated with a nice adultness, and the only place where the film becomes childishly preposterous is the very end, when a policeman pulls off the kind of fatal marksmanship that is as improbable as the fatuous nonmarksmanship in certain films by Godard and Truffaut. Otherwise, *Chinatown* is a cogently low-key thriller, in which action and even suspense must take a backseat to atmosphere: a sense of general corruption far more unsettling than the conventionally localized evil of the standard genre film, however explosive it may be.

Historically and visually, the ambience is laudably right. Anthea Sylbert's costumes, and her brother-in-law's, Richard Sylbert's, sets could not look more Los Angeles circa 1935, but without any ostentation. Granted that in few places has time stood so ponderously still as in the capital of film and sunny living unclouded by thought, there are still details here that are wonders of re-creative exactness, whether it is the goose-pimpled brown leatherette covering on binoculars, wooden-slatted Venetian blinds, or stacks of Pears soap in a bathroom cupboard. And never does one of Faye Dunaway's outfits call attention to itself as it would had it been designed, say, by Theodora van Runkle. Jerry Goldsmith's score avoids repetition of an obvious theme (it is, in the ordinary sense, almost tuneless) and can eerily subsume the sound of a leaky faucet in a murdered woman's apartment. Sam O'Steen's editing is happily uncommitted to modish hyperexcitation, and will linger appositely over the desolation of a dry riverbed.

Very fine, too, is the cinematography of John A. Alonzo. It makes use of the wide screen in various cunning ways, managing even to convey strong verticals, as when Gittes is spying on Mulwray from roof- or hilltops; but it can also be cleverly procrustean when it shows just enough of Miss Dunaway's breasts for erotic spice, but not too much to deflect attention from the dialogue. Yet it is not just a matter of framing shots (which, in any case, is more the director's doing), but also of using an ingeniously muted palette, with emphasis on tawny or burnished tones that somehow suggest a bygone era preserved in amber.

The final question is whether a mystery film, however concerned with moral climate and psychological overtones, can transcend its genre. The performances Polanski elicits are certainly unusual. Jack Nicholson has never trod with greater assurance the fine line between professional cynicism verging on sleaziness and a still untarnished self-respect and concern for at least the less demanding decencies of life; he looks wonderfully in period with his hair almost in a center part, and he manages emotional shadings miles above his self-indulgences in *The Last Detail*. Faye Dunaway, too, carries off a neat balancing act as a woman whose sophistication cannot gloss over her woundedness, and whose neuroses and sound instincts are at war beneath a translucent coat of not-quite-chip-proof polish. These people are much more vulnerable than their genre antecedents, which is what ultimately makes for *Chinatown*'s originality and distinction. Still, the hold of the genre is so strong that, even with sensational plot twists kept at a minimum, there simply isn't room enough for full character development—for the richer humanity required by art.

1974

Brendan Gill

Brendan Gill (1914–1997) was the quintessential man-about-town and man of letters. With an insatiable curiosity and appetite for life, he brought a cultivated critical eye to the fields of literature, film, theater, and architecture, and published several novels as well. He was especially passionate about architecture and city planning, wrote a biography of Frank Lloyd Wright, and helped to preserve Grand Central Station and other New York landmarks. For 60 years he wrote criticism and journalism for *The New Yorker*, including a stint as its regular film critic, and was its chronicler, writing a loving book about that institution, *Here at The New Yorker*. A man with a great civic responsibility, Gill also made a point of having fun in life—an attribute that separated him from many of his fellow intellectuals—and this sensual streak was manifested partly in the pleasure he took viewing pornographic movies and collecting erotica, as the essay below suggests.

◆

Blue Notes

For a good many years, I was a movie reviewer for the *New Yorker*, and continue to go to movies with an undiminished and evidently incorrigible zeal, which is to say that I am upset if I fail to see most of the important movies of a given season and that I feel from time to time a nagging desire not merely to have seen certain movies but also to be known to have seen them—to put in my two cents' worth of criticism along with that of my former colleagues. I try to resist this temptation, but there are areas of moviemaking that my old friends curiously neglect, and with pleasure I now volunteer to walk the bounds of one such area, calling attention to a few of the more notable features of a landscape apparently as foreign to most newspaper and magazine reviewers as Cockaigne. What I have in mind are those commercial blue movies that have become a commonplace of our contemporary culture and about which, up to now, there has been an almost total lack of critical discussion. Whenever I raise the question of the radical changes that have taken place in their manufacture and distribution in recent years, it will usually turn out that my friends among the reviewers have no first-hand knowledge of these changes and that what little they possess in the way of opinions is based on hearsay. All this for the reason that they simply do not go to blue movies. Indeed, they are, or affect to be, aggressively indifferent to them. Sometimes they protest that the reason for their indifference is that blue movies are so boring. How can they be sure of this, I ask them, if they refuse to see any? Unhappy at being caught out in a child's dodge, they offer a child's riposte: *everyone* knows that blue movies are boring, and the only mystery is what a person of my supposedly refined perceptions finds of interest in them. With a patience that they no doubt consider irritating, I point out that they have misconstrued the argument, a sure sign of unease: up to that moment, I had not claimed that blue movies were interesting in themselves but only that they could not be ignored as a phenomenon. Lest I be thought to be masking a Puritan prurience behind sociological cant (one thinks of Bishop Potter leapfrogging among the whores in order to improve his education), I then quickly add that a large portion of the blue movies I go to strike me as being at once boring *and* fascinating, and that what proves fascinating in them nearly always encourages me to sit through what proves boring. In that respect, if perhaps in no other, blue movies are not unlike the works of George Eliot.

I go to as many blue movies as I can find time for, and it amounts to a blessing that two of the most important theatres housing hard-core porn in New York City—the Hudson/Avon, for heterosexual blue movies, and the Park/Miller, for homosexual ones—are within a couple of hundred yards of my office. At the moment of writing, another fifteen or twenty porn houses are but five minutes away. How lucky I am that this unexpected period of permissiveness in pornography should have coincided with my life, and how unready I am to have the period brought to a close by some new ruling of the courts! The President's Commission on Obscenity and Pornography, appointed by Johnson, submitted a report to Nixon so little disapproving of pornography and therefore so little to his liking that Nixon immediately rejected it. Open pornography openly arrived at has been in increasing jeopardy during the Nixon administration. A permissive society makes people like Nixon nervous, because they feel sure of themselves only under conditions of repression. These conditions need not be the ones they favor; if they exist, they can be manipulated and made to serve. The threat to freedom of the press and the threat to a continued easy access to pornography are scarcely to be spoken of in the same breath, but they occupy the same ground and will often be found to have the same defenders.

History may see the early nineteen-seventies as the high-water mark of permissiveness in the arts in this country. At present, there is nothing I can think of that a novel or poem is not free to describe, that a play or dance cannot embody, that a movie cannot depict. We are no longer at the mercy of the

Irish Catholic policeman who stops a movie, arrests the projectionist, and testifies in court that the movie must have been obscene because it gave him an erection. (What does that make his wife, who presumably is capable of securing the same response? Or his sacred old mother, who if she had lacked this ability, would have failed to conceive him?) Still, we remain a Jansenist country, in which, as Henry Adams noted long ago, sex remains a species of crime. The police and the courts are eager to resume control over our appetites; prosecutors who should know better continue to equate morality with law. The grating insistence on the part of clergymen and big real-estate operators that the city clean up Times Square may be a hint of hard times to come. The Times Square that these groaners pretend to look back upon with affection never existed; it was a squalid and ramshackle honky-tonk fifty years ago, as it is today, and the groaners were already in full—and, thank goodness, ineffectual—voice. The metaphor for the Square is the statue of Father Duffy there: pigeons shitting on the bronze head of a priest. The question is not "What are they doing there?" but "What is he doing there?" I grant that the Square is more dangerous now than it was in the twenties, but then so is Fifth Avenue, so is Main Street everywhere. The groaners do not really want the Square to be cleaned up; they want it to be wiped out. Their cure for what they consider all the uglier manifestations of the life-force is extermination.

Yeats says that love pitches its mansion in the place of excrement, and this is precisely what all blue movies, even the worst of them, say again and again; ideally, it is all they have to say. And *I* say that we are a timid and fastidious people and are far from having heard the message as often as we need to. But in saying even that much I risk striking the note of the Puritan bully: the mutilating didact, sure that he knows what is good for everyone else, and who, if he likes eating dung, would turn us into a nation of dung-eaters.

Many otherwise sophisticated men are embarrassed to be seen entering or leaving a blue movie house. Hard as it is to believe, this sense of shame is surely one of the reasons that so few of my former colleagues have kept up with the revolution in the genre. By and large, movie reviewers are a bourgeois lot, and while they would not be averse to catching a blue movie or two at the home of that quintessence of bourgeois chic, George Plimpton, they are unwilling to stand at the turnstiles of the not very fashionable little boutique pornie houses—former hardware stores, shoe shops, and delicatessens—that bespeckle the West Forties. They would feel that the eyes of the world were upon them, glittering with disapprobation. ("Nanny spank!") Myself, what I usually feel at the turnstiles is a rueful sense of outrage at the price of admission: three or four dollars at most midtown heterosexual blue movie houses and five dollars at most midtown homosexual houses. In the light of how little the movies have cost to make compared with, say, *Ryan's Daughter*, I cannot fail to feel that I am being flim-flammed. Nevertheless, I pay, for nevertheless it is worth it. On leaving the theatre, many people dart sidelong into the crowd, seeking to efface themselves and their immediate past as quickly as possible. My own tendency is to saunter. Since I have the reputation of being an exceptionally fast walker, my slow pace under the marquee must be a way of affirming that attendance at blue movies is not to my mind a clandestine activity. Grubby, yes, it may be that, but I have long since made my peace with grubbiness. There are a number of things in my life that I cherish and that lack elegance.

Some titles: *The Odd Mother, Little Women, The Coming Thing, Gland Hotel, Cheek to Cheek, All Balled Up.* And in just tribute to that early capital of movie porn, on every blazing marquee: *San Francisco Femmes.*

Nowhere in these notes have I tried to define the word "pornography." And this is wise and not merely craven, for if two people were to discuss the matter face to face it is possible that they could arrive at last at a rough meaning, hedged round with all manner of provisos concerning its applicability to such and such a state of affairs in such and such a time and place. Three people, though they met face to face, would be unlikely to agree on a definition. Pornography is whatever one thinks it is, and what *I* think it is will have to be guessed from the way I write about it. In his biography of Mark Twain, Justin Kaplan speaks of the pornography of the dollar. I think I know what the phrase means, but I doubt if J. Paul Getty would know what it means. Or, rather, to be fair to Mr. Getty (for the evidence is clear that he is far more acute about money than I am), if he were to be right about what the phrase means, then I would be sure to be wrong. In the same fashion, Pope Paul and I do not mean the same thing when we speak of the sacredness of the body. To me that means its continuous, joyous use, in all its passionate carnality; to the Pope it means chastity, the highest expression of which is virginity, both in men and in women. In short, non-use: a gathering of cob-webs, to be broken only by the furtive, unruly finger.

If I am being fair to J. Paul Getty, I may as well try to be fair to the Papacy as well. Paul's predecessor, the jolly and sensual John, would have granted me my definition of the sacredness of the body, only adding that eating and drinking and working and playing and making love must be to the greater glory of God. "No harm in that?" he would have asked me, and "No harm in that," I would have been obliged to reply. John once granted an audience to a large body of journalists meeting in Rome. His message to them: "Now, you gentlemen are journalists, and there is one commandment—'Thou shalt not bear false witness'—that is to be followed with a particular fidelity by you. As for the other nine, pay as little attention as possible to them."

A good deal of nonsense has been written about the audiences at blue movies. As a veteran champion of Women's Lib, I am sorry to say that the most inaccurate articles I have read on the subject have been by women reporters, who in most cases describe what they expected to find and not what, according to my greater experience in this field, actually exists. What Dwight Macdonald has called the parajournalism of Tom Wolfe has infected a younger generation of writers; in Wolfe's terms, serendipity is not the happy faculty of stumbling by chance upon something one wants but the inventing of something one wants that is then stumbled upon by calculation. Writers in the *Village Voice* and elsewhere would have you believe that audiences at blue movies consist largely of lonely, middle-aged men bringing themselves off under rustling raincoats. Let me testify that the pleasure of masturbation appears to be no more commonly indulged in at blue movies than at straight ones. It could be argued, indeed, that the rate of indulgence would be likely to be higher at straight movies, on the grounds that one's fantasy in respect to a desirable but wholly unattainable sex object would be far more intense than one's fantasy in respect to women who combine an appearance of immediate availability with comparatively little allure. (In a similar way, the underwear advertisements in the Sunday *Times* magazine section may be more stimulating to many men and women than the photographs of genitalia in the magazines sold in the shabby storefronts on Forty-second Street.) Nor does the average audience consist of middle-aged men—the range in age will extend from, say, very young, non-English-speaking Argentinian sailors, who are spending a few days in port and can think of nothing better to do at the moment, to very old men, who also have nothing better to do and who tend to fall asleep almost as soon as they sit down, hypnotized not by what they see on the screen but by its harsh light. As for the loneliness of the men in the audience, that is surely in the mind of the beholder; if it is not, then I am at a loss to understand the method by which, in a darkened auditorium, a reporter succeeds in detecting such a characteristic. Loneliness is something I am unable to make out with any degree of confidence in the faces of strangers passing me on a sunlit Madison Avenue, to say nothing of the faces of old friends passing me in the corridor outside my office. My guess is that the audiences at blue movies would be scarcely different in appearance, aptitudes, and appetites from the male portion of any crowd in a subway car or a political rally or a meeting of the P.T.A. I suspect, but cannot be sure, that many of the audience are salesmen idling between appointments; others—those who, glancing at their watches around five in the afternoon, hastily jump to their feet and race up the aisle—may be commuters, on their way home to voluptuous wives in Scarsdale.

What all reporters can agree on is that the great majority of the audiences at blue movies is male. White middle-class women of any age are conspicuously absent. Only one white woman of my acquaintance—a brilliant Englishwoman of twenty-seven—has seen as many as three or four blue movies. "They make me feel sexy," she says. "I was very strictly brought up, so the feeling may come as much from my sense of doing a forbidden thing as from watching sex. I go to skinflicks with a man from the office—married; no big deal—to kill a couple of hours at lunchtime. We bring hot dogs and Cokes and relax. I like everything about skinflicks except the way the man always has to ejaculate outside the woman. I suppose that's to prove he isn't cheating the audience. Naturally, I think of him as cheating the woman."

A good many Puerto Ricans and blacks come in couples to blue movies, nearly always seating themselves at the rear of the theatre and appearing more interested in nuzzling each other than in watching the screen. At homosexual blue movies one sees, understandably, no women at all. As far as I know, there is not a single blue movie theatre in New York that caters to Lesbians; they must make do with the occasional movie of women having intercourse that one encounters in programs combining six or eight so-called "featurettes" or "stagette loops." Even in these movies, the two or more women making love will sooner or later be joined by two or more men, and a heterosexual frolic will then ensue. (In such cases, the men never make love to other men; it is a tradition in blue movies that women are permitted to be indiscriminate in regard to the sex of their partners but that men are not.) Women play no part in homosexual blue movies; one might expect them to be introduced into a plot as possible rivals or as sexual objects to be repudiated, but no—the only authentic feminine note struck is by drag-queens. A large portion of the audience at both heterosexual and homosexual blue movies is Oriental. Unlike white males, Oriental males come into the theatre by two's and three's and talk and laugh freely throughout the course of the program. At heterosexual blue movies, white males ordinarily enter and leave alone, speak to no one, and manifest as little emotion as possible. If some especially gauche sexual gesture is enacted on screen, there may be scattered laughter, almost instantly suppressed; and sometimes, as when an ardent act of fellatio fails to have the desired result and the fellator increases her efforts with evident impatience and a speed of thrusting that seems to threaten actual injury, a universal groan will go up. Otherwise, the conventional posture of the audience is that of the herd:

calculatedly impassive, taking everything in with fixed eyes and giving nothing back.

The behavior of audiences at homosexual blue movies is radically unlike that of audiences at heterosexual ones. Each kind of audience has its favorite rituals and taboos, and although it is a topic risky to speculate on, it would seem to be the case that the homosexual audience, enjoying a much greater freedom of action than the heterosexual audience, is likely to be having a much better time. For the homosexual, it is the accepted thing that the theatre is there to be cruised in; this is one of the advantages he has purchased with his expensive ticket of admission. The atmosphere is perhaps not quite that of a tea-dance on a terrace in the Hamptons, but neither is it that of the Meditation Room at Frank Campbell's. Far from sitting slumped motionless in one's chair, one moves about at will, sizing up possibilities. Often there will be found standing at the back of the theatre two or three young men, any of whom, for a fee, will accompany one to seats well down front and there practice upon one the same arts that are being practiced upon others on screen. One is thus enabled to enjoy two very different sorts of sexual pleasure simultaneously— a boon that Edison, though himself of strongly homosexual tendencies (one remembers those camping trips with Henry Ford), was too inhibited to have made his goal when he set about inventing a practicable motion-picture camera.

It is a sign of the increasing acceptance of blue movies in our culture that *Variety* now lists the most successful of them in its weekly chart of big movie grossers. Throughout the autumn, *Deep Throat* was averaging something like $35,000 a week at the box-office, giving it a place of importance not far below *What's Up Doc* and *Straw Dogs*. Legman's now widely accepted theory that Americans, in their arts as in their lives, prefer violence to sex, is borne out by the fact that there has yet to be a really substantial box-office hit among blue movies. The figures speak for themselves: in the time that it took *Deep Throat* to gross $500,000, *The Godfather* grossed $42,000,000—*Deep Throat* is a silly little fable celebrating life; *The Godfather* is a celebration of blood and death.

Another sign of a general acceptance of blue movies is the number of Upper East Side people who are venturing into Times Square to catch blue movies often at what they believe to be the risk of their lives. A ticket-seller in the box office at the Cameo was quoted recently as saying, "We're getting an altogether different class of people in here these days—the kind of people who call up and ask what time the feature starts."

As blue movies gain in popularity, they become more and more profitable to manufacture and distribute. Already they are claiming attention as a growth industry, like mobile homes and male cosmetics. In a fashion often praised by big business but rarely practiced by it, the money to be made in blue movies has led to increased competition in the marketplace, which has led in turn to a notable improvement in the quality of the product. Of course I do not mean an improvement in its artistic quality. On the contrary, I would be tempted to argue that, following the principle that it is the difficulty of the sonnet that makes for excellence in that form, the present license to depict anything one pleases on the screen has led to a falling off in the ingenuity of the plots of blue movies—never a strong point in the best of circumstances—therefore to a lessening of sympathetic interest on the part of the spectator. In the old Mrs. Grundy days, one had to find some means, however clumsy, to get the performers down to their skins, in order that they could set about making love or at least—and how sad this always seemed!—to simulate making love, with the man's shadowy genitalia, just out of camera range and the girl's tongue licking her lips in transports of passion that she was all too evidently far from feeling. We had time to become familiar with the amateur actors, squeaking away uneasily in their poor little paper-thin roles, and even to identify with their often grotesque problems. We wanted them to be happy, which is to say that we wanted them to score, and we knew that sooner or later they would be able to do so. Nowadays, the protagonists are often to be seen scoring as the movie opens, and scoring in gigantic close-ups of great technical resourcefulness, well-lighted and (to the extent that scoring is subject to instruction) well-directed, and at the same time hard to recognize as human. For the camera-work may well be so superb that at first we will simply not know where we are—can we be approaching the nave of some great Gothic cathedral, hung with pink moss, or is this only a vagina? That immense veined wet redwood, straining to resist the force of some incalculable gale—is it only, at second glance, a penis? A few years ago, we would not have thought "only" a vagina, "only" a penis. The bolder the movie and the better made it is, the more it risks, in 1972, boring us. The threat of anti-climax hovers over the latest and most skilled handiwork of young blue movie makers, prompting us to observe that in the field of pornography, as in so many other fields, prosperity is often the enemy of promise.

Simply as theatre, cunnilingus isn't a patch on fellatio, and it is difficult to see what even the most ardent Women's Lib maker of blue movies can do about it.

People like me who champion pornography on the grounds that it is life-enhancing are constantly being told that it isn't *truly* life-enhancing, because it is only a travesty of the real thing. The difficulty with that argument is knowing what the real thing is. Whenever I ask for a definition, my interlocutor begins to sputter; precisely as "everyone" knows that blue movies are boring, "everyone" knows what the real thing is. But I don't. Or I do and I don't. I live bathed in a continuous erotic glow, and I recognize pornography as among the thousand blessed things that heighten this glow. Like sunlight, like water, like the smell and taste of skin, it helps make me happy. I foresee that with every passing year it will become increasingly precious to me: a vade mecum when the adventure of old age begins.

1976

Richard Corliss

Richard Corliss (b. 1944), who has been *Time* magazine's urbane, trustworthy film critic for many years, began writing about movies for *New Times* and *Film Comment* (where he also served as editor-in-chief). One of his unique contributions was to have highlighted the key role of the screenplay in a movie's artistic success or failure. Having come to critical prominence during a period that deified the director, Corliss provided an indispensable corrective emphasis, first in his anthology *Hollywood Screenwriters*, then in his groundbreaking book *Talking Pictures: Screenwriters in the American Cinema, 1927–1973*, from which the following analysis of *M*A*S*H* is taken. It is both sly and fitting that Corliss would choose a crowd-pleasing film by cult director Robert Altman to dismantle, and in the process scarcely mention Altman, while tracing what he regards as the unconsciously self-satisfied, contradictory attitudes of the movie to the script of Ring Lardner, Jr., a screenwriter whose craft he clearly admires.

◆

*M*A*S*H*

As the vehicle of Ring Lardner, Jr.'s return to the top of his profession—and as a film that received almost unanimous critical praise—*M*A*S*H* deserves two viewings, or none. At first sight, this comedy about a group of medics just behind the lines in Korea may seem cruel but very funny. The second time, *M*A*S*H* seems funny but very cruel. Granted that the surprise of a joke is part of its appeal; but *M*A*S*H* has, in its writing and direction, a style so relaxed and assured that it isn't lost on second viewing. What does become obvious is that this smooth style disguises a bludgeon, which the main characters in the film employ on anyone who disagrees with them.

M*A*S*H follows the surgical and sexual exploits of three lovable medics, known as the Swampmen, and their virtuoso outfit, the 4077th Mobile Army Surgical Hospital. Besides the knitting and purling usual in an operating room, their exploits include saving the life of a Korean baby through an emergency operation, saving the self-respect of a well-equipped dentist through the ministrations of a shapely *dea ex machina*, and winning a football game for the outfit by drugging the opposing team's star player. Grand, fun-loving guys with quick wits and hearts of gold, right?

Not exactly. *M*A*S*H*'s trio of "heroes" (Andrew Sarris's phrase) are also bully boys. Any admiration their coolness may inspire—a coolness that is suggested by having them all act as if perpetually stoned—is tempered by the ruthlessness they show in imposing their style on the recalcitrant uncool. It's true that, like hip vampires, they'll go for the jugular only when they see it exposed (preferably on a red-neck). Thus, their Lieutenant Colonel—a benign, befuddled, absent-minded professional soldier who galumphs rather than glides—is spared the Swampmen's more vicious japes because he takes their hi-jinks and low-blows calmly. But their first tentmate is not so lucky.

Frank Burns is a high-strung surgeon of the Don Knotts variety, who does bad things like pray out loud and bite at the Swampmen when they bait him. When Burns conspires with Margaret Houlihan, the pretty, pompous Chief Nurse, to inform the nearest general of the loose-limbed life style at the 4077th Mobile Army Surgical Hospital, our heroes decide to teach them a lesson in being cool: they bug the tent where Majors Burns and Houlihan are making violent love, and feed their orgasmic groans over the P.A. system! Beautiful? A scream? And then, the next morning, hero Donald Sutherland goads Burns into a rage by asking him if Hot Lips Houlihan is a moaner or a screamer, and if the session was "better than self-abuse"—whereupon Burns lunges at Sutherland and is led off the base in a strait jacket! Fun-ny?

If our laughter at this practical joke sticks in our throat—if we find it impossible to laugh at all—it may not be because we, like Major Burns, can't take a joke. Perhaps we simply don't like to see human beings—even self-righteous or shortsighted ones, even those meant as butts of a general military joke—tortured in such a smug, pesudo-moralistic way. In most comedies, where the dialogue, situations, and characters are stylized to create a critical distance between actor and audience, we don't worry about the pain one character inflicts on another. Charlie Chaplin can fit Eric Campbell's Bluto head into the vise of a Victorian streetlight and turn the gas on; John Wayne can throw a pitcher of scalding water on a stubborn trapper in the burlesque *North to Alaska*; and we accept it without flinching, as a convention of the genre. The broadness of comic style is the film's assurance to its audience that nobody, least of all these fleshed-out cartoon villains, is really being hurt.

But *M*A*S*H* mixes comedy situations with a documentary rigor almost worthy of Fred Wiseman. When a patient in the operating room spurts a vigorous stream of blood, we're meant to gasp, not laugh, and to think it's real. The tendency also applies to the characters: they're not caricatures, they're meant to be real. And, of course, pain and humiliation are two different things. So our reaction to *M*A*S*H*'s first "humiliation" scene is closer to what it would be in a drama or melodrama, as it is in the gas suffocation in *Torn Curtain* or the scalding coffee Lee Marvin throws at Gloria Grahame in *The Big Heat*. Our sympathy inevitably goes to the humiliated majors in *M*A*S*H*, as it does to the victims in films as disparate as *Mr. Smith Goes to Washington* and *The Naked Night*. The heroes of *M*A*S*H* are guilty of a prank that, because of its effect on Major Burns, turns into an atrocity. In what other movie have we been expected to sympathize with the torturers (however likable) and against the victims (however ludicrous)?

This is only Phase One of the neat little trick our boys plan to spring on Hot Lips. As a penance for no particular transgression, the Swampmen rig a falling-screen device to determine Major Houlihan's "natural" color. When the ploy is realized, Hot Lips becomes hysterical and runs to the Colonel's tent to threaten resignation. But the Colonel is in bed with his secretary. "Goddammit, Hot Lips," he shouts, "resign your goddammed commission!" The virulence of this second humiliation—the most horrifying "shower scene" since *Psycho*—and the sense of claustrophobic persecution that Sally Kellerman conveys as Hot Lips, remove it entirely from the relaxed atmosphere of the rest of *M*A*S*H*. Miss Kellerman's (possibly misplaced) conviction as a pent-up, full-bodied woman being pecked at by a kindergarten full of Katzenjammer starlings forces us into the kind of paranoid identification we feel for Stefania Sandrelli, the pregnant girl in *Seduced and Abandoned*. It occurs to us that the MASH surgeons "maintain sanity in the rampant insanity of war" (as Lardner himself put it) simply by driving other people insane. Surely therapy has its limits.

But surely, Lardner would argue, the Swampmen are performing radical therapy on Hot Lips. And, to be sure, Nurse Houlihan is soon liberated—by sleeping with one of the heroes. The effects of this liberation are not entirely positive, however: a woman who, when repressed, displayed a tremulous but real dignity, suddenly becomes an idiot when freed. The movie's idea of redemption is to turn her, and all the other women in the outfit, into affable imbeciles who are only trusted with passing the scalpel, cheerleading at a ballgame, and acting as bedmates. *M*A*S*H* may be the first war film that rejects the back-home female fantasy of What Our Nice Boys Are Doing Over There (a dream necessary for civilian morale during World War II) for the male locker-room and barracks fantasy where all the guys are cool studs, all the chicks are succulent nymphets, all the officers are cheerfully corrupt, and all the trouble-makers are "dealt with." Lardner, and Robert Altman even more so, are guilty of failing to "place" the Swampmen's sexism—a failure that suggests the film-makers simply weren't aware of it.

Pauline Kael, only a shade more enthusiastic than her colleagues, called *M*A*S*H* "the best American war comedy since sound came in"—in other words, since Raoul Walsh's 1926 version of the Anderson-Stallings play, *What Price Glory?* That sounds like a pretty sweeping recommendation, until you stop to examine that genre, "American war comedy." Subtract all the subgenres, those films dealing with noncombat aspects of the military like P.O.W. escapes (*Stalag 17*), civilians in wartime (*Hail the Conquering Hero*), basic training (*No Time for Sergeants*), peacetime "service" missions (*Operation Mad Ball*); throw out the comedy-series fillers (*Buck Privates, Sailor Beware, Francis Joins the WACs, McHale's Navy Joins the Air Force*), and you're left with a handful of combat comedies hardly substantial enough to be considered a genre: Bill Mauldin's *Up Front* movies, the John Ford remake of *What Price Glory?*, *Mr. Roberts*, and a very few others. It's like calling a movie the best horror musical, or the most exciting Negro western.

I think the critics liked *M*A*S*H* for a lot of the same reasons they and the public latched on to *The Graduate* a few years earlier: it's a comedy that looks different. *The Graduate* wasn't the best "generation-gap" comedy of the sixties. It was the first. And *M*A*S*H* is neither a great antiwar comedy nor even an antiwar comedy. Like *The Graduate*, it is a very funny movie—and Lardner deserves credit for the multilayered, mostly humorous dialogue that makes *M*A*S*H* sporadically appealing—whose characterizations lack the depth and consistency we demand when looking for a movie that's more than very funny. As with *The Graduate*, its tone is too distinct and erratic (The Hardy Boys one moment, Satan's Sadists the next) to fit it easily into a genre. And as with *The Graduate*, most critics tended to review a film they wanted to see instead of the film in front of them.

The Mike Nichols movie arrived at a time when opinionmakers like *Time* magazine and the U.S. Census Bureau were beginning to convince us that the half of America under twenty-five was gazing at the half over twenty-five across that infamous chasm, the Generation Gap. It mattered little that *The Graduate*'s Benjamin Braddock was an inert, inarticulate schlemiel right out of the Silent Fifties, or that his girl friend Elaine was a one-cylinder coed with all the smarts of Connie Francis in *Where the Boys Are*. Audiences needed a cuddly, acceptable totem for the rebellious Now Generation, and Benjamin was probably as radical a youth image as Mom and Baby Sis could accept.

M*A*S*H is a hip, unsolemn "antiwar" movie that ends with a crazy football game (a surefire irrelevant climax, as Harold Lloyd and the Marx Brothers could verify) and makes everybody feel good on the way out—just the way Ben's and Elaine's escape from marital catastrophe did at the end of *The Grad-*

uate. But, despite *M*A*S*H*'s clear implication that the war under consideration is not Korea but Vietnam (long hair, "groovy," marijuana), the film is no
more antiwar than *The Graduate* was antibourgeois. Both tell how a cluster of
individuals adapts to an unpleasant environment: the MASH surgeons to the
chaos of army life, Ben and Elaine to middle-class "maturity." Neither group
is even vaguely political; neither film is remotely radical.

Indeed, *M*A*S*H*'s heroes are experts at beating the system, not
Smashing The System. They are saving lives because it's their job, as driving
a tank would be if they'd been teamsters back home. Their civilian counterparts are the publishing, pop-music, and advertising executives who look and
talk weird, but get the job done. Their surgeons' manual is not *The Strawberry
Statement* but *How to Succeed in the Army by Being Really Trying*. And the aura they
exude is less the crackling atmosphere of an SDS meeting than the stale beer
smell of a fifties frat party. All the sideburns, swish gestures, and scatological
jive can't conceal their panty-raid sensibilities. The Swampmen aren't
cleansing Hot Lips of fascist sympathies when they pull aside her shower curtain; they're just initiating her. The 4077th MASH is an overseas Sigma Nu
with unsavory hazing policies. While it's not wrong to find these antics funny—
they often are—it *is* dishonest to justify casual cruelty by associating it with
antiwar activities.

A look at Richard Hooker's novel, *MASH* (no asterisks), suggests how the
brutalizing of the characters took place. In the book, war is just as insane, but
the heroes don't respond to it by torturing the officers they find pompous or
incompetent. The film's two "humiliation" scenes are hardly recognizable, so
subdued are they in the book. (Lardner has said that he wrote in the first
sequence, involving Burns and Hot Lips, while Altman "improvised" the
shower scene.) Hooker also includes a scene in which Hawkeye, the super-cool
hero, blows his cool during difficult surgery—just like the movie's bad old
Major Burns. Hawkeye's fellow surgeons are far more understanding to Major
Burns in the book than they are in the film. Now, there's no reason why the
movie *M*A*S*H* should be faithful to the book. But Hooker's original makes
the same points without any captious brutality. Even assuming the film's
heroes were justified in purging the unit of Major Burns, I can find no reason
for them to humiliate Hot Lips a second time. And isn't it being overly generous to assume that their motives were any more elevated the first time? They
certainly seemed to be enjoying their work.

A case might be made for *M*A*S*H* as a clinically ambiguous study of the
way Joe College and Fred Premed adjust—sell out—to the pervasive and corrupting system called War. But this would certainly not be the cute and cruel

mish-MASH which most critics, anxious for a piece of old-fashioned enter-tainment with the look of "now, baby," prematurely propelled into the vault of great films. Nor would it be the subtly reactionary film that brought Ring Lard-ner, Jr.—the tenacious leftist—back into the limelight toward the end of what may be remembered as the most frustrating career of a major screenwriting talent.

1974

James Baldwin

In his extraordinary essay collections *Notes of a Native Son, Nobody Knows My Name*, and *The Fire Next Time*, James Baldwin (1924–1987) established himself as the most important American essayist of the postwar era. Largely self-taught (he never went to college) he developed an elaborate, piercing prose style that combined Henry James's balanced clauses and the Bible, whose rhythms he had mastered as a boy preacher. Baldwin was also entranced from boyhood with movies. In his book-length meditation on that life-long love affair, *The Devil Finds Work*, he recalled his first movie: "I am fascinated by the movement on, and of, the screen, that movement which is something like the heaving and swelling of the sea (though I have not yet been to the sea): and which is also something like the light which moves on, and especially beneath, the water. I am about seven. I am with my mother, or my aunt. The movie is *Dance, Fools, Dance*." Baldwin's great subject was race, which as an African-American he dissected from every possible angle, including that of film criticism. Witness this assessment of *Lady Sings the Blues* (which James Harvey quotes later in *his* entry).

◆

from
The Devil Finds Work

Lady Sings the Blues* is related to the black American experience in about the same way, and to the same extent that Princess Grace Kelly is related to the Irish potato famine: by courtesy. The film pretends to be based on Billie Holiday's autobiography, and, indeed, Billie's book may make a very fine film one day: a day, however, which I no longer expect to live long enough to see. The film that *has* been made is impeccably put together, with an irreproachable professional polish, and has one or two nice moments. It has absolutely nothing to do with Billie, or with jazz, or any other kind of music, or the risks of an artist, or American life, or black life, or narcotics, or the narcotics laws, or clubs, or managers, or policemen, or despair, or love. The script is as empty as a banana peel, and as treacherous.

It is scarcely possible to think of a black American actor who has not been misused: not one has ever been seriously challenged to deliver the best that is in him. The most powerful examples of this cowardice and waste are the careers of Paul Robeson and Ethel Waters. If they had ever been allowed really to hit their stride, they might immeasurably have raised the level of cinema and theater in this country. Their effect would have been, at least, to challenge the stultifyingly predictable tics of such overrated figures as Miss Helen Hayes, for example, and life, as one performer can sometimes elicit it from another, might more frequently have illuminated our stage and screen. It is pointless, however, to pursue this, and personally painful: Mr. Robeson is declining, in obscurity, and Miss Waters is singing in Billy Graham's choir. They might have been treated with more respect by the country to which they gave so much. But, then, we had to send telegrams to the Mayor of New York City, asking him to call off the cops who surrounded Billie's bedside—looking for heroin in her ice cream—and let the Lady die in peace.

What the black actor has managed to give are moments—indelible moments, created, miraculously, beyond the confines of the script: hints of reality, smuggled like contraband into a maudlin tale, and with enough force, if unleashed, to shatter the tale to fragments. The face of Ginger Rogers, for example, in *Tales of Manhattan*, is something to be placed in a dish, and eaten with a spoon—possibly a long one. If the face of Ethel Waters were placed in the same frame, the face of Little Eva would simply melt: to prevent this, the black performer has been sealed off into a vacuum. Inevitably, therefore, and as a direct result, the white performer is also sealed off and can never deliver the best that is in him, either. His plight is less obvious, but the results can be even more devastating. The black performer knows, at least, what the odds are, and knows that he must endure—even though he has done nothing to deserve—his fate. So does the white performer know this, as concerns himself, *his* possibilities, *his* merit, *his* fate, and he knows this on a somewhat less accessible and more chaotic and intimidating level. James Edwards, dead at the age of fifty-three, in a casting office, was a beautiful actor, and knew, at least, that he was an actor. Veronica Lake was a star, riding very high for a while there: she also died in relative obscurity, but it is doubtful that she knew as much.

The moments given us by black performers exist so far beneath, or beyond, the American apprehensions that it is difficult to describe them. There is the close-up of Sidney Poitier's face, for example, in *The Defiant Ones*, describing how his wife, "she say, be nice. Be nice." Black spectators supply the sub-text—the unspoken—out of their own lives, and the pride and anguish in Sidney's face at that moment strike deep. I do not know what happens in the breasts of the multitudes who think of themselves as white: but, clearly, they hold this anguish far outside themselves. There is the truth to be found in Ethel Waters's face at the end of *Member of the Wedding*, the Juano Hernandez of *Young Man with a Horn* and *Intruder in the Dust*, Canada Lee, in *Body and Soul*, the Rochester of *The Green Pastures* and *Tales of Manhattan*, and Robeson in everything I saw him do. You will note that I am deliberately avoiding the recent spate of so-called black films. I have seen very few of them, and, anyway, it would he virtually impossible to discuss them as films. I suspect their intention to be lethal indeed, and to be the subject of quite another investigation. Their entire purpose (apart from making money; and this money is not for blacks; in spite of the fact that some of these films appear to have been, at least in part, financed by blacks) is to stifle forever any possibility of such moments—or, in other words, to make black experience irrelevant and obsolete. And I may point out that this vogue, had it been remotely serious, had a considerable body of work on which to draw—from *Up From Slavery* to *Let Me Live*, from *The Auto-Biography of an Ex-Colored Man*, and *Cane*, to *Black Boy*, to *Invisible Man* to *Blues Child Baby* to *The Bluest Eye* to *Soledad Brother*. An incomplete list, and difficult: but the difficulty is not in the casting.

My buddy, Ava Gardner, once asked me if I thought she could play Billie Holiday. I had to tell her that, though she was certainly "down" enough for it—courageous and honest and beautiful enough for it—she would almost certainly not be allowed to get away with it, since Billie Holiday had been widely rumored to be black, and she, Ava Gardner, was widely rumored to be white. I was not really making a joke, or, if I was, the joke was bitter: for I certainly know some black girls who are much, much whiter than Ava. Nor do I blame the black girls for this, for this utterly inevitable species of schizophrenia is but one of the many manifestations of the spiritual and historical trap, called racial, in which all Americans find themselves and against which some of us, some of the time, manage to arrive at a viable and honorable identity. I was really thinking of black actors and actresses, who would have been much embittered if the role of Billie Holiday had been played by a white girl: but, then, I had occasion to think of them later, too, when the tidal wave of "black" films arrived, using such a staggering preponderance of football players and models.

I had never been a Diana Ross fan, and received the news that she was to play Billie with a weary shrug of the shoulders. I could not possibly have been more wrong, and I pray the lady to accept from me my humble apologies—for my swift, and, alas, understandably cynical reaction. For, indeed, the most exasperating aspect of *Lady Sings the Blues*, for me, is that the three principals— Miss Ross, Billy Dee Williams, and Richard Pryor—are, clearly, ready, willing, and able to stretch out and go a distance not permitted by the film. And, even within this straitjacket, they manage marvelous moments, and a truth which is not in the script is sometimes glimpsed through them. Diana Ross, clearly, respected Billie too much to try to imitate her. She picks up on Billie's beat, and, for the rest, uses herself, with a moving humility and candor, to create a portrait of a woman overwhelmed by the circumstances of her life. This is not exactly Billie Holiday, but it *is* the role as written, and she does much more with it than the script deserves. So does Billy Dee, in the absolutely impossible role of Louis McKay, and so does Richard Pryor, in a role which appears to have been dreamed up by a nostalgic, aging jazz *aficionado*.

The film begins at the end, more or less: titles over, we watch a series of sepia stills of Billie being fingerprinted, and thrown, alone, into a padded cell. We pick up, then, on a gawky colored girl, alone in the streets of Harlem. She has been sent by her mother to a rooming house, which turns out to be a whorehouse. She does not stay there long—packs her bags, and gets dressed, in fact, as a particularly horny and vocal client is getting undressed. She has seen Louis in this establishment, or elsewhere: in any case, she has seen him. She later meets him again, in a dive where she is one of the singers, and where the singer is expected to pick up money off the tables with her, ah, sexual equipment. Billie cannot do this, which has its effect on the two men in her life, Louis, and Piano Man (Richard Pryor). It is at this point that Piano Man dubs her "Lady," and it is at this point that she has her first date with Louis. A few frames later, she is the black singer with a white band, touring the South. (Billie went on the road with Artie Shaw, but the film version of this adventure is not in Billie's book.) On the road, she encounters the Ku Klux Klan, and sees a lynching. One of the members of the band has been offering her drugs, but she has always refused. After the lynching—an image, and a moment, to which we shall return—she succumbs to the friendly pusher, and returns to New York, hooked. Louis tries to get her off drugs, but does not succeed. Desperate for a fix, she pulls a razor on him, to force him to give her her works; after which he asks her to leave his house. Her mother dies, she gets busted—I think, in that order—Louis returns, and helps bring her back to the living. He also realizes that she needs her career, and helps her to begin again. Since she cannot work in New York, they end up on the Coast, with Piano Man. Eventually, Louis has to leave, on business, and to arrange her date in Carnegie Hall. Left alone with Piano Man, she decides that she wants to "cop," and sends him out to buy the junk. They are broke, and so she gives him a ring, which he is to pawn, to pay for it. Piano Man cops, all right, but doesn't pawn the ring, and doesn't pay for the stuff, and is, therefore, beaten to death before her eyes. The patient and loving Louis comes to the Coast, and brings her back to New York, where she scores a triumph on the Carnegie Hall stage. As Billie is singing, *God Bless the Child*, and as thousands cheer, we learn, from blow-ups of newspaper items behind her, of her subsequent misadventures, and her death at the age of forty-four. And the film fades out, with a triumphant Billie, who is, already, however, unluckily, dead, singing on-stage before a delirious audience—or, rather, two: one in the cinema Carnegie Hall, and one in the cinema where we are seated.

It is not every day that a film crams so much cake down one's throat, and yet leaves one with so much more to swallow.

Now, it is not enough to say that the film has nothing to do with Billie Holiday, since the film's authority—and, therefore, its presumed authenticity— derives from the use of her name. It is not enough to say that the film does not recreate her journey: the question is why the film presents itself as her journey. Most of the people who knew, or saw, or heard Billie Holiday will be dying shortly before, or shortly after, this century dies. (Billie would now be sixty years old.) This film cannot be all that is left of her torment and courage and beauty and grace. And the moments of truth smuggled into the film by the actors form a kind of Rosetta stone which the future will not be able to read, as, indeed, the present cannot.

In the film, we meet Billie on the streets of New York. But we do not know that she was raped at ten, sentenced, as a result, to a "Catholic institution" where she beat her hands to "a bloody damn pulp" when she was locked in with the body of a dead girl. We do not know that she was virtually raped at twelve, and that, at thirteen, she was a "hip kitty." We do not know, from the film, that when she refuses to sleep with the horny and vocal Big Blue, he has her thrown in jail: we know nothing, in fact, of the kind of terror with which this girl lived almost from the time that she was born. The incident with Big Blue is reduced to low comedy, much as is the scene with Billie's mother when she tries on the extravagant hat. Billie's testimony concerning the meaning of this hat is not in the film: "all the big-time whores wore big red velvet hats then—she looked so pretty in it"—nor is the fact that it is the mother who has bought the hat, because "we were going to live like ladies." In the film, Billie auditions as a dancer, and is terrible, and she says so in the book. It is also during this audition that the piano player saves her by snarling, "Girl, can you sing?" and so she sings for the first time in public, and this turns out to be the beginning of her career.

But the scene, as recounted by Billie, and the scene as translated in the film have nothing whatever in common. In the film, for no immediately discernible reason, except, perhaps, ambition, Billie drops into a nearby club, and asks for an audition. She is dressed as Hollywood—though it should certainly know better by now, God knows—persistently imagines cheap whores to dress. She joins the chorus line, disastrously, ending with her black bottom stuck out—after which, etc., she sings, etc.

Billie's testimony is that she and her mother were about to be evicted in the morning and that it was as "cold as all hell that night, and I walked out without any kind of coat." She hits a joint, she is indeed allowed to dance, but solo, "and it was pitiful." Before they throw her out, the piano player does indeed say, "'Girl, can you sing?'—So I asked him to play 'Trav'lin' All Alone'. That came closer than anything to the way I felt." And: "when I left the joint that night, I split with the piano player and still took home fifty-seven dollars—I went out and bought a whole chicken and some baked beans."

The scene, in the film, is far from being an improvement on Billie's testimony, and it has two curious results, neither of which are vouched for anywhere in Billie's book. One is the invention of Piano Man, who, according to the film, remains with Billie until his death. According to the book, she scarcely ever sees him again, nor, according to Billie's evidence, does he ever become one of her intimates. It is conceivable, of course, however preposterous, that this figure is meant to suggest a kind of distillation of Lester Young: but I do not have the heart to pursue that line of country. The other result is that the club-owner, a white man, becomes one of Billie's staunchest supporters, and closest friends. The book offers no corroborating evidence of this, either, though Billie speaks with great affection of such people as Tony Pastor and Artie Shaw. But absolutely none of these people are even suggested in the film—these people who were so important to her, along with Pigmeat Markham, and "Pops" Armstrong, and Charlie Barnet—or the jazz atmosphere of that period of Billie's life, and our lives. The film suggests nothing of the terrifying economics of a singer's life, and you will not learn, from the film, that Billie received no royalties for the records she was making then: you will not learn that the music industry is one of the areas of the national life in which the blacks have been most persistently, successfully, and brutally ripped off. If you have never heard of the Apollo Theatre, you will learn nothing of it from this film, nor what Billie's appearances there meant to her, or what a black audience means to a black performer.

Now, obviously, the only way to translate the written word to the cinema involves doing considerable violence to the written word, to the extent, indeed, of forgetting the written word. A film is meant to be seen, and, ideally, the less a film talks, the better, The cinematic translation, nevertheless, however great and necessary the violence it is compelled to use on the original form, is obliged to remain faithful to the intention, and the vision, of the original form. The necessary violence of the translation involves making very subtle and difficult choices. The root motive of the choices made can be gauged by the effect of these choices: and the effect of these deliberate choices, deliberately made, must be considered as resulting in a willed and deliberate act—that is, the film which we are seeing is the film we are intended to see.

Why? What do the filmmakers wish us to learn?

Billie is very honest in her book, she hides nothing. We know the effect of her father's death on her, for example, and how her father died, and how, ultimately, this connected with her singing of "Strange Fruit." We see her relationship with her mother: "I didn't want to hurt her, and I didn't—until three years before she died, when I went on junk." We know, from her testimony, that she was in love with the husband who turned her into a junkie, and we certainly know, from her testimony, that she loved the Louis who did his best to save her. I repeat: her testimony, for that is what we are compelled to deal with, and respect, and whatever others may imagine themselves to know of these matters cannot compare with the testimony of the person who was there.

She testifies, too: "I had the white gowns, and the white shoes. And every night they'd bring me the white gardenias and the white junk. When I was on, I was on and nobody gave me any trouble. No cops, no treasury agents, nobody."

"I got into trouble," says Billie, "when I tried to get off."

Let us see what the film makes of all this: what we are meant to learn.

Billie's father is not in the film, and is mentioned, I think, only once: near the end of the film, when she and Piano Man are high—just before Piano Man is murdered—and they both crack up when Billie says that her father never beat her because he was never home.

In the book, her father is a jazz musician, mainly on the road, who, eventually, leaves home, divorces, and re-marries. But, when he was in town, Billie was able to blackmail him into giving her the rent money for her mother and herself. And she cared about him: "it wasn't the pneumonia that killed him, it was Dallas, Texas. That's where he was, and where he walked around, going from hospital to hospital, trying to get help. But none of them would even so much as take his temperature, or let him in [but] because he had been in the Army, had ruined his lungs and had records to prove it, they finally let him in the Jim Crow ward. By that time, it was too late." And, later: "a song was born which became my personal protest—'Strange Fruit'—when [Lewis Allen] showed me that poem, I dug it right off. It seemed to spell out all the things that had killed Pop."

This is quite forthright, and even contains, if one dares say so, a certain dramatic force. In the film, on the southern road, Billie leaves the bus to go relieve herself in the bushes. Wandering along the countryside, Billie suddenly sees, on the road just before her, grieving black people, and a black body hanging from a tree. The best that one can say for this moment is that it is mistaken, and the worst that it is callously false and self-serving—which may be a rude way of saying the same thing: luckily, it is brief. The scene operates to resolve, at one stroke, several problems, and without in the least involving or intimidating the spectator. The lynch scene is as remote as an Indian massacre, occurring in the same landscape, and eliciting the same response: a mixture of pious horror, and gratified reassurance. The ubiquitous Ku Klux Klan appears, marching beside the bus in which the band is riding. The band is white, and they attempt to hide Billie, making, meanwhile, friendly gestures to their marching countrymen. But Billie, because of the strange fruit she has just seen hanging, is now beside herself, and deliberately makes herself visible, cursing and weeping against the Klan: she, and the musicians, make a sufficiently narrow, entirely cinematic escape. This scene is pure bullshit Hollywood-American fable, with the bad guys robed and the good guys casual: as a result, anyway, of all this unhealthy excitement, this understandable (and oddly reassuring) bitterness, Billie finally takes her first fix, and is immediately hooked.

This incident is not in the book: for the very good reason, certainly, that black people in this country are schooled in adversity long before white people are. Blacks perceive danger far more swiftly, and, however odd this may sound, then attempt to protect their white comrade from his white brothers: they know their white comrade's brothers far better than the comrade does. One of the necessities of being black, and knowing it, is to accept the hard discipline of learning to avoid useless anger, and needless loss of life: every mother and his mother's mother's mother's brother is needed.

The off-screen Billie faced down white sheriffs, and laughed at them, to their faces, and faced down white managers, cops, and bartenders. She was much stronger than this film can have any interest in indicating, and, as a victim, infinitely more complex.

Otherwise, she would never have been able to tell us, so simply, that she sang "Strange Fruit" for her father, and got hooked because she fell in love.

The film cannot accept—because it cannot use—this simplicity. That victim who is able to articulate the situation of the victim has ceased to be a victim: he, or she, has become a threat.

The victim's testimony must, therefore, be altered. But, since no one outside the victim's situation dares imagine the victim's situation, this testimony can be altered only after it has been delivered; and after it has become the object of some study. The purpose of this scrutiny is to emphasize certain striking details which can then be used to quite another purpose than the victim had in mind. Given the complexity of the human being, and the complexities of society, this is not difficult. (Or, it does not appear to be difficult: the endless revisions made in the victim's testimony suggest that the endeavor may be impossible. Wounded Knee comes to mind, along with "Swing Low, Sweet Chariot," and we have yet to hear from My Lai.) Thus, for example, ghetto citizens have been heard to complain, very loudly, of the damage done to their homes during any ghetto uprising, and a grateful Republic fastens on this as a benevolent way of discouraging future uprisings. But the truth is, and every ghetto citizen knows this, that no one trapped in the ghetto owns anything, since they certainly do not own the land. Anyone who doubts this has only to spend tomorrow walking through the ghetto nearest to his.

Once the victim's testimony is delivered, however, there is, thereafter, forever, a witness somewhere: which is an irreducible inconvenience for the makers and shakers and accomplices of this world. These run together, in packs, and corroborate each other. They cannot bear the judgment in the eyes of the people whom they intend to hold in bondage forever, and who know more about them than their lovers. This remote, public, and, as it were, principled, bondage is the indispensable justification of their own: when the prisoner is free, the jailer faces the void of himself.

If *Lady Sings the Blues* pretended to be concerned with the trials of a white girl, and starred, say, the late Susan Hayward (*I'll Cry Tomorrow*) or Bette Davis (*A Stolen Life*) or Olivia de Havilland (*To Each His Own*) or the late Judy Garland (*A Star Is Born*) or any of the current chicks, Billie's love for her father and for the husband who so fatally turned her on would be the film's entire motivation: *the guy that won you/has run off and undone you/that great beginning/has seen its final inning/*: as desperately falsified, but in quite another way. The situations of Lana Turner (in *The Postman Always Rings Twice*) or Barbara Stanwyck (in *Double Indemnity*) or Joan Crawford (in almost anything, but, especially, *Mildred Pierce*) are dictated, at bottom, by the brutally crass and commercial terms on which the heroine is to survive—are dictated, that is, by society. But, at the same time, the white chick is always, somehow, saved or strengthened or destroyed by love—society is out of it, beneath her: it matters not at all that the man she marries, or deserts, or murders, happens to own Rhodesia, or that *she* does: love is all.

But the private life of a black woman, to say nothing of the private life of a black man, cannot really be considered at all. To consider this forbidden privacy is to violate white privacy—by destroying the white dream of the blacks; to make black privacy a black and private matter makes white privacy real, for the first time: which is, indeed, and with a vengeance, to endanger the stewardship of Rhodesia. The situation of the white heroine must never violate the white self-image. Her situation must always transcend the inexorability of the social setting, so that her innocence may be preserved: Grace Kelly, when she shoots to kill, at the end of *High Noon*, for example, does not become a murderess. But the situation of the black heroine, to say nothing of that of the black hero, must always be left at society's mercy: in order to justify white history and in order to indicate the essential validity of the black condition.

Billie's account of her meeting with Louis McKay is very simple, even childlike, and very moving. Louis is asleep on a bench, a whore is lifting his wallet, and Billie prevents this, pretending that Louis, whom she has never seen in her life before, is her old man. And she gives Louis his wallet. Anyone surviving these mean streets knows something about that moment. It is not a moment which the film can afford, for it conveys, too vividly, how that victim, the black, yet refuses to be a victim, has another source of sustenance: Billie's morality, at that moment, indeed, threatens the very foundations of the Stock Exchange.

The film does not suggest that the obsolete and vindictive narcotics laws had anything to do with her fate: does not pick up the challenge implicit in her statement: *When I was on, I was on, and nobody bothered me. . . . I got into trouble when I tried to get off.* Neither does it suggest that the distinction between Big Business and Organized Crime is like the old ad, which asks, *Which twin has the Toni?* The film leaves us with the impression, and this is a matter of choices coldly and deliberately made, that a gifted, but weak and self-indulgent woman, brought about the murder of her devoted Piano Man because she was not equal, either to her gifts, or to the society which had made her a star, and, as the closing sequence proves, adored her.

1976

Penelope Gilliatt

Penelope Gilliatt (1932–1993) was an English-born writer of novels, stories, and screenplays, as well as a long-time film critic for *The Observer* and *The New Yorker*, a post she shared with Pauline Kael from 1968 to 1979. Her adult, compassionate screenplay for *Sunday, Bloody Sunday* (1971) received an Academy Award nomination. Her film criticism and profiles were collected in *Unholy Fools* (1973) and *Three-Quarter Face* (1980). Gilliatt brought her fiction-writing skills to film criticism, turning descriptions of plot and character into a compact hybrid of review and short story, as may be seen in the following piece from *The New Yorker*.

◆

The Bitter Tears of Petra von Kant

Rainer Werner Fassbinder's *The Bitter Tears of Petra von Kant* (1972) is a film about lesbians which Fassbinder solemnly describes as "strictly autobiographical." It is a lucid, beautiful work of innovation which hides its fondness for its characters under a cloak of august formalism. One remembers at the end that the dedication reads, "A case history of one who here became Marlene." Marlene is an apparently minor character who never speaks—of the six women in the film, she is the mute—but the story, in recall, is about the effect of its events on her sensibility. It is typical of the ricochet movement of Fassbinder's films that at the time we should regard her only as a witness. She is apparently present only as a hand on a glass wall, listening to two women talking about love. Or as an offscreen clattering of a typewriter in her employer's office-bedroom.

Petra von Kant (Margit Carstensen) is a dress designer, twice married. She wakes in her plush double bed looking like a very hung-over ballet dancer: hair pinned back, skeletal body, expressive arms. She complains to Marlene (Irm Hermann), her assistant, that her head aches. Marlene is already fully dressed for work, wearing the Edwardian clothes that one comes to accept as contemporary in this hothouse of ruffles and beads and fur trimmings. Petra demands freshly squeezed orange juice. She has had dreams that seem to weight her like pig iron.

Sit up. Grab the white telephone. Talk to her mother, fibbing about having been up for ages, affecting pleasure at her mother's going to a resort. Marlene obediently brings the orange juice. Petra smokes in bed, in a white nightdress fit for a night club. Then she gets up, starting to get dressed by putting on a curly dark-brown wig. She and Marlene dance together, to a record of "Smoke Gets in Your Eyes." Then she abruptly sends Marlene to the easel, because a costume drawing "has to be finished by noon."

There are fibre-glass figures and costume drawings everywhere in the working part of the room. We are watching a woman who is almost suffocated by stylishness, surrounded by copies of herself. Everything is ersatz. When she is on the telephone about an appointment, she forces a pause so that she can seem to be looking in her diary. When she talks to her mother, she pretends that an order to her assistant was a crackling on the line.

A woman friend arrives from Frankfurt. (The only men in the film are the nudes in the huge Correggio mural beside Petra's brass double bed.) As Petra makes up before a mirror, her reflected face moves about in stylized compositions with her friend's. Their impulsive talk runs against the grain of the deliberated images on the screen. It is a habit of Fassbinder's. They are saying that love is difficult. That expressing love is more difficult. That one would often like to say something affectionate, "but you're afraid of losing a point, of being the weaker one." Petra, completing the change in herself from a childishly fibbing daughter with a hangover to a lonely but beautiful career woman giving advice about marriage, utters thoughts that lie at the heart of Fassbinder's notion of her predicament. If you understand a person, she says, then change that person; only pity what you can't understand. She will never be satisfied by what her friend says about women's trump cards: remembering marriage, she says, "I wasn't interested in conjuring tricks." In her authoritarian solitude, she is looking for equality of company, curiously enough; in her hypocrisies, she is looking for probity. The real thing, that's the answer. Omniscience, that's the answer. Knowing what's going on, not only in yourself but in others.

Yet, all the time, this creation of perfect bones and mascara, seeking to control everything around her, has very little mastery, which is one of the abiding and passionate themes of Fassbinder's apparently unemotional works. The same idea runs through *Fox and His Friends* (1975), a story of male homosexuality. "There are more things in heaven and earth . . ." quote both Petra and Fox. Petra speaks wisely of the uselessness of fidelity under duress, but by the end of the film she is the one applying the duress. Fox—played by Fassbinder himself—shows off about his winnings in a lottery; but a man friend cruelly makes a buffoon of him about his lack of French in a restaurant, then persuades him to buy a place that is a folly of grandness and leads him to ruin. In all the sumptuous sophistication of both Petra's and Fox's experiences, there is much pain, much innocence. Just as Fox is robbed of his fortune by tutelage in good living, so Petra is tormented in her fortunate world of a room, furnished with a copy of a great painting and bald-headed, long-necked mannequins.

Petra falls in love with a working-class girl called Karin (Hanna Schygulla). When she is suddenly abandoned, as she has abandoned others, the nearly intolerable pain perplexes her. She calls Karin a slut. She says that if she'd known things would turn out this way her attitude would have been different. As the friend of much earlier in the film said, "When you foresee the end from the start, is the game worth the candle?" Yes, of course, says the film, because no other route is ever possible: Petra was lonely, and Karin was company to grasp. Fassbinder is defining need without love. "I'm so alone without you," Petra says to Karin. "Alone, without a slut?" says Karin acidly.

With Karin gone, the white pile carpet of the office-bedroom becomes the stage, with Petra crawling over it tippling gin and hysterically clasping the telephone receiver. Clinging to a vestige of power, she refuses to go to Frankfurt when Karin eventually rings. In the meantime, Marlene has been unnoticed, but not unobservant. Much changed, and suffering, she packs her case. Very little. She takes with her a naked mannequin doll that was a knowing birthday present to Petra. Then she leaves, hobble-skirted. Hobble-skirted because of obeisance to femininity? Because she is beguiled by Petra's notion of love, which is a process of demands and reprisals much like the ones played out in *Fox and His Friends*?

Fassbinder's films ache, in spite of their apparent formalism. On the face of it, *Petra* is a theatrical film. Six women, no men; five acts, separated by change of dress; no change of scenery, much change of mood. The set moves from bed to corridor to carpet. In one of the final episodes, when Petra is sprawled on the floor with the telephone, the pile carpet becomes a field of razed earth.

Fassbinder shoots in very long takes. The camera seldom moves. We become obsessed with the contradiction of composed and worldly faces uttering primitive anguish. Heads in close-up will appear to touch and part breathtakingly while intimacy is abstractly spoken of. In pain, there are no mascara smudges. Lovemaking is made emblematic: by the heads of two dressed women briefly bending over one another's shoulder. Everything is terse and minimal. Noun and verb. Fassbinder is concerned here with the sort of love that rests in contest. So his real heroine is not Petra, the victimizer turned victim, but her silent assistant, who has been tortured by the sight of sadistic love's punishments.

This is a political film, as Fassbinder's always are, as well as a sage film about love. Petra believes that what she has earned she can break. In her agony of longing for Karin, the lower-class model who has made a reputation out of working for her and then found it easy to leave her, she stamps on a tray laid with an expensive tea set. All fragments. But she is only breaking a talisman of her elegant ambitions: it is no triumph, because she is not destroying her passion for Karin. The passion is born of capitalism, Fassbinder implies, for Petra still truly believes that she paid for Karin by giving her the benefit of her greater talent and income, constituting a superiority of class in the tournament. The changeover of power is shown by Fassbinder with a curtness veiling sympathy. The dialogue is sharp in a stylized set of scenes. It is often the case that extreme stylization covers extreme pity. This is so of *The Bitter Tears of Petra von Kant*. In a setting deliberately made to seem shallow, his characters deepen: the powerful hypocrite turns into the loser, and the silent employee symbolizing obedience and imitation changes into the rebel and the original. We are watching a more political and more angular *Miss Julie*. Fassbinder makes films with a cutting edge. Henri Langlois, director of the Paris Ciné-mathèque Française, during an *hommage* to him said that he represented "the beginning of German postwar cinema."

1976

IV

◆

Reconsiderations and Renegade Perspectives

The 1980s to the Present

Walter Kerr

Walter Kerr (1913–1996) was one of this country's most revered theater critics, covering plays for over three decades, first for the New York *Herald Tribune* and, when that paper folded, moving over to *The New York Times*. His first reviewing experience, however, happened to be writing a weekly column, "Junior Film Fans," for the *Evanston Review*, which allowed him to see eight movies a week. After retiring from theater criticism he returned to writing on movies in *The Silent Clowns*, a now-classic analysis of the films of Charlie Chaplin, Buster Keaton, Harold Lloyd, and Harry Langdon. Comedy is notoriously a subject that wilts in the presence of analysis; but Kerr, through his richly detailed, felicitously worded descriptions of physical gags, his probing summaries of individual performance style, and his own sense of humor, managed to re-create the spirit of the original works while dissecting their innards.

◆

The Keaton Quiet

Buster Keaton's films were sorely neglected for twenty-five years. In the recent excitement that has come of their rediscovery, there has been a tendency toward overcorrection: he has been hailed, here and there, not only as Chaplin's equal but as Chaplin's superior. This, I think, is waste effort, a misreading of Keaton's very values. Chaplin is likely to retain his preeminence among silent film comedians in part because he is so instantly accessible—no need to introduce or explain him, just run one of his films for a child or a thirty-year-old who has never seen him and response will come like a geyser—and in part because his comedy is contained entirely in his *persona*, a *persona* so multilayered that it cannot be exhausted.

Keaton wants more study because he was himself a student: quizzical, cryptic, dispassionate, a man whose work could never be finished because there was always another corner to be turned. I confess that *I* find his work fascinating above that of all others. But that is a matter of temperament: Keaton was compulsively analytical, a trait that no doubt speaks directly to my own sorry habits of mind. Temperaments can lock in love and stay sane: Let Chaplin be king, and Keaton court jester. The king effectively rules, the jester tells the truth.

Chaplin appropriated film to his own image. Lloyd manipulated it with an architect's knowledgeability. Keaton preferred to function as its conscience. While others were using film to point at themselves or their daredeviltries, Keaton pointed in the opposite direction: at the thing itself. He insisted that film was film. He insisted that silent film was silent. Whatever was idiosyncratic about him—clothes, stance, emotional makeup—would have to find expression in and about these two prime facts.

I have called Keaton the most silent of silent film comedians without quite explaining why. The silence was related to another deeply rooted quality— that immobility, the sense of alert repose, we have so often seen in him. Keaton could run like a jackrabbit, and, in almost every feature film, he did. He could stunt like Lloyd, as honestly and even more dangerously. His pictures are motion pictures. Yet, though there is a hurricane eternally raging about him, and though he is often fully caught up in it, Keaton's constant drift is toward the quiet at the hurricane's eye.

Keaton ran so often during the twelve features he made in the 1920's that the sprint became a trademark: audiences waited for the cue that would, once in every five or seven reels, send him flying. He raced through city streets, outpacing police and traffic; he leapt, at top speed, the hedges that turned into hurdles on a vast college campus; ponds and streams could not break his stride, even though they sometimes left him with a snapping-turtle locked to his tie; mountain gorges were made to be bridged in a single, spread-legged, continuum. The camera makes a tracer bullet of him as he goes; his course leaves an after-image against the sky.

His stunting was so taken for granted and so dangerous that he broke his neck. He broke it during the making of his third feature film, *Sherlock Jr.*, and the shot in which he did it is still in the film. Buster is running pell-mell along the tops of a string of boxcars, thoughtlessly heading for the rear of the train. The last car comes, speeds by beneath him. Lost in midair he dives for the only object available, the spout of a railroad water tower projecting over the tracks. His weight lowers the spout just enough to release its water supply: a cascade hits him with Niagara-like force, hurtling him to the tracks below. In filming, his neck hit one of the tracks and snapped. Because he didn't realize what had happened, the scene plunges on: two men on a handcar whom he has also drenched take after him. Buster hops up and hares off across the fields.

Keaton suffered blinding headaches for a time after the mishap, but because he wasn't otherwise incapacitated he went right on working. It wasn't until several years later, when he was being given a routine insurance examination, that a doctor pointed the break out to him and remarked on how well it had healed.

There are hair-raising moments in *Sherlock Jr.*'s ultimate chase. Buster is on a motorcycle, plunging headlong across a high, narrow aqueduct. In a long-shot we see that ahead of him there is a sizable gap in the structure, perhaps twenty feet wide, one more drop into empty air. A truck on the road beneath is slowly approaching the gap. Just as Buster nears the appalling precipice, a second truck appears from the opposite direction. The two trucks pass each other, inside the gap, exactly in time to provide the winged Buster with a continuing roadway: he whips across their tops to connect directly with the resumed aqueduct. Then, astonishingly, the entire aqueduct begins to fall toward us. Buster rides straight on down with it, meeting the ground with grace and no diminution of speed, tearing off on his thoroughly reckless journey.

A few moments later that journey brings him into obvious collision course with an advancing train. Buster and motorcycle are in the foreground; the camera is close on them, moving at their violent rate. We see plainly enough that it is Buster on the machine. In the background, just as plainly, is the onrushing locomotive, curving inexorably toward the camera. Buster—and camera—whip across the tracks directly in front of the locomotive, clearing it by what seems inches.

It should perhaps be mentioned that Buster is seated on the handlebars of the motorcycle, and that the machine is driverless. Buster supposes that a friend is doing the driving, but a bump in the road has long since dismissed the friend. In fact, during the shooting of the sequence, the actor playing Buster's friend had been unwilling to take the fall from the driver's seat. Keaton promptly placed another actor, dressed as himself, on the handlebars, put on the friend's costume, and took the bump himself. He then resumed his own lone place on the unguided bars.

With one known exception—he could not do the pole-vault into a high second-story window in *College* and hired an Olympic star to do it for him—Keaton used no doubles. The people who worked with him were forever trying to persuade him not to do what he planned to do. He couldn't be talked out of taking an enormous drop, tied to another man, from a cliff into a swirling river for *Our Hospitality*. And when it came time to tumble a massive building façade on him during the hurricane in *Steamboat Bill Jr.*, everyone rebelled. Keaton was using a gag he'd experimented with twice before, though never on this scale: he would stand utterly still beneath the falling structure so that when it landed he would emerge unscathed in the small opening provided by an attic window. "The clearance of that window," Rudi Blesh quotes Keaton as saying, "was exactly three inches over my head and past each shoulder. And the front of the building—I'm not kidding—weighed two tons. It had to be built heavy and rigid in order not to bend or twist in that wind."

Keaton goes on to remember "the whole gang" begging him to forego the stunt. His story editor threatened to quit, his director simply absented himself from the set, and, when Keaton stubbornly persisted in having the collapse photographed, the cameramen operated their cameras while looking the other way. The shot, in the completed film, is stunning.

But it is stunning in a special way, Keaton's way. It is not, for instance, frightening, as a similar shot of Lloyd's might have been frightening. When Lloyd stunted, he meant to terrify; and he increased the audience's agitation by letting us see how agitated *he* was in the situation. When it has fallen, wall and Buster have arrived at an entirely equitable relationship. There is nothing to scream about.

That is, in part, what I mean by Keaton's silence, a stillness of emotion as well as body, a universal stillness that comes of things functioning well, of having achieved occult harmony. But there are more ways of being silent than that.

One can, for instance, keep one's counsel about what is happening outside the frame, intimating that life is still going on out there but making no noise at all in the process. *Our Hospitality* was Keaton's second feature film, and it is filled with reticences. Buster is riding in the last coach of an early nineteenth-century railroad train; a coachman with a horn sits atop it; the roadbed is decidedly bumpy. The rear wheels of the coach come off. The jolt unseats the coachman, toppling him onto the tracks. The carriage drags on a bit till halted. Buster, quite naturally, hops from his seat to help the fallen coachman. He is getting the poor fellow to his feet and dusting him off when something entirely unexpected happens. The rear wheels of the coach roll into the frame to send both men somersaulting into the air.

The wheels, which disappeared from view as the camera followed the train to a stop, have not vanished from the universe. Had we thought that? They have been leading a life of their own all the while out there, remaining in motion because they *were* in motion, following natural law with an unemotional rectitude until they quite properly upend two men who are in their way. But how silent they have been in coming. In Keaton's films we do not hear what we cannot see.

In effect, he could have made us "hear" the onrushing wheels very simply. All he had to do was interpolate a shot of the isolated wheels still rolling along.

We should then have expected them, supplying our own additional dimension, and what we might lose in surprise we would gain in heightened anticipation of the coming tumble. Most other comedians chose to show the looming threat and so gain suspense. Keaton steadfastly does it his way. Keep it a secret till it's happened, let no word of warning be heard.

An identifying close-up in a film always functions as a shout. If a man is reaching for a box of pancake batter on a shelf high above him and, distracted, plucks off a box of popcorn instead—so that the pancakes, when cooked, will flip about like maddened powder puffs—the customary practice of silent film was to intercut a tight view of the wrong box. Every such shot is a weakness, certainly in Keaton's view: an unnecessary headline has been permitted to scream at us, an exclamation point has been inserted directly into the middle of a sentence. Keaton disliked exclamation points: too noisy. If the joke is a reasonable one, there is no need to fire a starting gun. The joke will explain itself, in mute majesty, to those who can see.

Take the Case of the Slithering Rope, also from *Our Hospitality*. Buster is trapped on a ledge halfway up—or halfway down—a precipitous cliff-face. There is a man at the top of the cliff who wishes to shoot Buster, though Buster does not know that. The man throws down a rope, tying it about his own waist, calling to Buster to do the same, which he does. The man is actually hoping to lure Buster into an exposed position, so that he can draw a decent bead on him. Buster tests a few of the projecting rocks about him, finds one firm enough, glances up. The man's pistol is aimed directly at him. Buster grasps the situation instantly and hastily retreats to shelter, inadvertently giving the rope a small tug as he does so. His attention is now called to the rope. It has been taut before. Now it is rapidly slithering downward, dribbling away before his eyes. Buster is much taken with the phenomenon simply because it *is* a phenomenon. As he watches it with such interest, the man's body flashes past him, heading for the river far below. That, it turns out, is quite interesting too. Buster contemplates the matter, attentively alert, until the rope goes taut again, this time from below, and *he* is yanked from his perch to plunge down with the man he is tied to.

Essentially, the comedy is compressed into one sustained frame. There is no cut to the man above to show him being jerked from the clifftop. Buster's face observing a body hurtling by is quite enough. There is a brief cut to the fallen man temporarily caught in a tree and thrashing loose, which means that the rope will go taut again. But the sequence is almost completely silent about critical matters happening off-frame, preferring to focus on Keaton's repose at the dead center of things, a man studying a rope that is behaving oddly.

Keaton's quiet, together with the refusal to *explain* everything, becomes a marvel of implication.

The silences are sometimes quite literal, tongue-tied on the double. Buster, about to leave town in *Steamboat Bill Jr.*, sees the girl with whom he has been tiffing coming toward him on the road. He at once puts his bag down, hangs his head sheepishly, and begins to stammer out some sort of explanation for his recent conduct. Instead of pausing to hear what he might have to say, the girl circles behind him in continuing hauteur and vanishes into a public building. When Buster looks up to face her, there is no one anywhere on the street. After a moment's bafflement, Buster accepts her disappearance forlornly —a mirage, perhaps?—and, picking up his bag, wanders on down the road. The girl, meantime, has had second thoughts, or something like one-and-three-quarter thoughts. She reappears from the building, biting her lip, and begins to follow Buster tentatively, unsure of what she means to do. When he pauses, she pauses. When he moves on again, so does she. She is not getting much closer. Then Buster stops altogether. He has seen his father being thrown into jail: he will have to remain in town and save him. His dead stop has not, this time, stopped the girl; she is within a few feet of him now. Squaring his shoulders with this new task before him, Buster hikes his valise and turns to go home. In the same instant, the girl has turned. There she is, walking away from him. Where in the hell did she come from? There is no answer; she has gone into the building again. Nor has his question been put into words. The whole little dance of indecision, with its exquisite counterpoint, has been made up of visual thrusts and parries alone. The joke is in the rhythm of what we see; our ears, if we had any, would get us nowhere. Keaton's comedies are unheard chords, harmonies struck in space and time and requiring no other form of amplification.

Keaton could chord his cosmos when he was alone on the screen—and he was often alone. In *Seven Chances* he enters a church to be married. There is no one else there. In a shot from the altar-rail toward the arch of the open door, we see his slender, methodical, top-hatted figure rise from the exterior steps, then—without change of pace—march with sure resolution down the center aisle, the glistening curves of the pews seeming to lap gently beside him like sea-spray. At the front of the church he pauses and then, without hesitation, selects a place for himself, very slightly in from the aisle. I do not know why this one place is exactly the right place for Keaton to sit in all of that vacant church. I only know that as he sits the lines and masses of the church go as still as he, grow quiet, freeze. He has placed his weight just where it will counter-

balance the contending tensions about him, seated himself in the one spot that
will halt the earth's busyness.

Keaton would often open up spaces and leave them there until he entered.
Entering, he would change them not at all. He does not disturb their proportions; he fulfills them. In *Battling Butler* there is a very long camera "hold" on
the door of a prize-ring dressing room. We simply stare at the emptiness for a
time. Then, scarcely moving at all, Keaton melts through it. He is no fighter;
he is a fop being forced to fight. He enters in the clothes that belong to him:
top hat, tails, walking stick. A dejected snail, he stops. He carries a horseshoe
in his limp free hand. What had been the emptiness of the room is now the
emptiness of the room plus Keaton. Zero.

Keaton was called Zero—or something like it—when his short films were
first released in France. Outside America, in the early days, comedians were
often given local names, tags that familiarly described them: even now it is possible to buy Laurel and Hardy dolls in Italy that are not called Laurel and
Hardy but Crich e Croch. Keaton's French alias was Malec. Ask a Frenchman
who remembers what the name might have signified, idiomatically and with
affection, and he will grope for a bit with a smile on his face and finally come
up with something like "the hole in the doughnut."

The cipher was not simply a matter of Keaton's composed countenance,
though of course there is an emotional Zero to contend with there. It has also
to do with the cancellation of masses and stresses, horizontals and verticals, by
the equalizing solemnity of his presence: when the façade falls during the hurricane, three inches equal two tons. More than that, Zero works its way into the
stories he tells and the gags he makes use of. In *Sherlock Jr.* he is a small-town
film projectionist who is studying to be a detective. Unfortunately, on his very
first try at detective work he ends up branded the culprit: he is banished from
his girl's house forever. While he is falling asleep in his projection booth and
dreaming of the great sleuth he hopes to become, the girl—in about two minutes of quick thinking—tracks down the real criminal. The film is no more
than a third over, but a simple reversal of role has canceled the film's entire narrative base. All the time he is dreaming of solutions, everything has been
solved.

Our Hospitality is the story of a Southern blood-feud, and Buster finds himself trapped in the home of the family that means to exterminate him. In anybody else's narrative the problem would be to get out of there as quickly as
possible. In Keaton's the problem is to stay *in* the house. He is only safe so long
as he remains under his sworn enemy's roof. Southern gentlemanliness forbids

killing a man while he is your guest. Stalemate—for just as long as Buster does *not* move. At the closest conceivable quarters, bloodlust is at its most quiet.

Individual gags arrive at nothingness again and again and again. He is undersea repairing a leak in a ship's hull, a phantom in a diving-suit performing a slow-motion dance. His hands become dirty. He picks up a pail from the ocean floor, drags it through the encompassing water to fill it, washes his hands in *its* water, then—ever so thoughtfully—empties the pail again. One disposes of what is dirty. And water equals water, with nothing left over.

He is on the run, desperate to reach his girl's house by seven o'clock. Time is of the essence, and what time is it now? At last he passes a clock shop. Salvation. He scans the window eagerly. Dozens and dozens of animated clock faces. Each tells a different time. Universal negation seems to leer at him.

He is waiting on tables at college and has got his thumb in the soup. He is told to bring something he *can't* get his thumb into. He brings coffee. The cup is upside down on the saucer, its rim unavailable. The cup is perfectly centered, the saucer perfectly dry. Deftly, he removes the cup. The saucer at once fills with coffee. Who suspended gravity while Keaton was turning the full cup upside down?

Each of these zeroes breeds its own odd silence, takes on something of the quiet and weightlessness of outer space. Keaton is working *in* space, of course: there are the hulls and clocks and coffee cups to prove it. But he is capable, when he wishes, of turning visible space itself into a momentary void. Faceless, he moves through the nameless. In fact, it wouldn't be stretching things a bit to call Keaton not so much silent comedy's first surrealist as silent comedy's first existentialist. Existentialism posits that existence precedes essence, which means that no man is born into the world with an essential nature already given him, with an identity on tap and an instinctive set of rules to guide him. He is born more nearly a blank—Keaton's face will do as an image—and with no established relationship to any other thing on this planet. But he may be able to make an identity for himself out of those relationships he *does* establish as he puts a first foot down in an unfamiliar universe that is, for him, a void.

The foot goes out and touches something. What is it? It may glide out from under; it may hold. Either way, why? The foot may touch, mysteriously, another foot. Whose? No one else has a sure identity yet, either. Is the spot to be contested or surrendered? Find out. Try the other foot. The whole body may slip dizzily into the abyss, or it may, seraphically, be borne aloft by unexpected headwinds, hidden hands. It is not so much a matter of danger or safety—the void is unpredictably dangerous and unpredictably safe—as it is of gaining necessary knowledge. And see what haunting parabolas the discoveries make!

In *Our Hospitality* Buster is straddling the engine and the coal car of a runaway train. As the train speeds along a river bank, engine and coal car become uncoupled and begin to separate. Buster has one foot on each, and the gap between them is widening. Just before he can be dropped beneath the wheels or perhaps rent in two, the coal car derails and goes tumbling down the bank into the rapids, Buster with it. As the coal car hits the water, it instantly becomes a canoe; without reflection, without transition, Buster calmly paddles it with a coal shovel. He has made his adaptation to the existentially unforeseeable without comment, in perfect silence.

Keaton was not only still when he was doing nothing, he was still *in motion*. Existential man must move in a universe that moves perpetually; unidentified man making his way through the unknowable void is, Jean-Paul Sartre says, condemned to action. Buster, the condemned man, maintains his reserve no matter what is happening. A moment or two later in the same film he has been tumbled out of his improvised canoe and is being carried helplessly along through the rock-strewn rapids to a waterfall. En route, he passes his girl standing on the river bank. With nothing but his head above water and that moving swiftly with the current, he simply looks at her. No cry for help, no struggle to reach her, just mute acceptance of the fact that people in motion tend to pass people standing still. He could be driftwood. Or, perhaps, something a little more knowing than that. I keep forgetting that there is a dog in the picture, and I keep cursing myself for forgetting. The dog, Buster's pet, is firmly established and repeatedly reintroduced. Why does he vanish for me? I think because Keaton effectively usurps his identity: they are too much of a kind to be differentiated. The look in Buster's eyes as he is swept so noncommittally past the girl he dearly loves is the alert yet unprotesting, wounded yet comprehending look of a puzzled spaniel—a spaniel being taken he knows not where, acknowledging necessity without speech. I think there is no more penetrating shot in the film—it goes straight to Keaton's docility—and few funnier.

Keaton's passivity while he was in fact active, his reluctance to insist upon a clamoring identity as he submitted to the rush of the void, his willingness to concede the void an intelligence with which he did not care to quarrel cannot have come from formal philosophizing, certainly not from having read Kierkegaard or solemnly anticipated Sartre. Where, then, did so tight a fit originate, unless we are to say—as we very well may—that Keaton's simple intuitions about the nature of man in the universe were as breathtakingly

516 ♦ WALTER KERR

perceptive as they were, in fate, simple? It is just possible that they came from film itself, from the frame held up to light in the hand.

Film *is* stillness in motion. There is no such thing as a moving picture. All pictures are still pictures. The illusion of movement in film comes from passing a succession of perfectly frozen images before a lens so rapidly, with a convenient eyeblink between them, that we are deceived into thinking that stillness is action. Take the film out of the projector and look at any one frame—as you now must, if you wish to see it at all—and you will see what Keaton may have seen all his life: rigidity at the heart of things, rigidity as the very condition of apparent activity. Keaton may have taken his esthetic—even his attitude toward life—from the knowledge he derived every time he fingered a strip of celluloid. What was printed on the celluloid was immobile, silent as the tomb, an extract and an abstract from the void. It was also, at the same time, part of a continuum, and when the continuum was seen whole— miracle of miracles that this should be possible—what had been indisputably dead leapt to unreal, yet mysteriously persuasive, life. Now Zero moves, has being, joins the tangible—without ceasing to be Zero. Whether he arrived at his identity consciously or not, Keaton became what film is.

1972

J. Hoberman

J. (or Jim) Hoberman has long been senior film critic for *The Village Voice*. As befits his association with an alternative weekly of hip, youth-oriented, anti-Establishment thrust, Hoberman has espoused the experimental, "outlaw," or fringe strains in new cinema, while covering the big studio releases, often with jaundiced eye. Hoberman employs an ironic, theory-aware style that sometimes playfully leaves unclear whether he is praising or condemning a film. Except for Jonathan Rosenbaum (with whom he co-wrote a book on midnight movies), there is no regular film reviewer who has a more knowledgeable overview of film history and its many contemporary tributaries and byways. Hoberman has written book-length studies of Yiddish and Soviet cinema, and, most recently, *The Dream Life: Movies, Media, and the Mythology of the Sixties*. Having begun as something of a visual formalist and auteurist (he was Andrew Sarris's colleague at the *Voice*), he has been shifting of late to a more active preoccupation with political ideology, following the half-buried leads of Rudolf Arnheim and Siegfried Kracauer, in an attempt to uncover links between the fantasies purveyed by the entertainment industry and the policies pursued by America at home and abroad.

◆

Bad Movies

There are a number of reasons to consider bad movies. The most obvious is that tastes change; that many, if not most of the films we admire were once dismissed as inconsequential trash; and that trash itself is not without its socio-aesthetic charms. Then too, bad movies have a pedagogic use value, even though the evolution of film form has largely been based on mistakes. A third reason is that movies, to a certain degree, have a life of their own. They mix the documentary with the fictional, and the worst intentions aspect of one can overwhelm the worst intentions of the other. In other words, it is possible for a movie to succeed *because* it has failed.

With their perverse, pioneering affection for the detritus of industrial civilization, the Surrealists were the first to cultivate an appreciation for bad movies. "The best and most exciting films [are] the films shown in local fleapits, films which seem to have no place in the history of cinema," advises Ado Kyrou in

Le Surréalisme au Cinéma. "Learn to go see the 'worst' films; they are sometimes sublime." This taste for Elixir of Pot-boiler—junky spectacles, cheap horror flicks, anonymous pornography, juvenile swashbucklers, movies "scorned by critics, charged with cretinism or infantilism by the old defenders of rationality"—was based on the innate capacity of such films to produce (if only in random moments) that "crux of Surrealism," *le merveilleux.*

The Surrealists courted disorientation: A film had a dreamlike latent content—and this could be precipitated by deranging or bypassing the manifest content of its storyline. During World War II, the young André Breton used to wander from movie-house to movie-house, entering mid-film, leaving for the next once the plot became apparent. By the time Breton became Surrealism's Black Pope, this practice had been elevated and refined into the principle of synthetic criticism. The ideal Surrealist spectator habitually broke open a film's continuity to liberate individual images from the prison of the narrative. Thus the American para-Surrealist Joseph Cornell created his 1937 masterpiece *Rose Hobart* by distilling a studio adventure film, *East of Borneo* (Columbia, 1931), into twenty-four non-linear minutes and projecting it at silent speed through a piece of blue glass to the accompaniment of the song "Holiday in Brazil."

For all their admiration for the "worst" films, and despite their propensity for deconstructing movies inside their heads, the Surrealists developed no canon of films so incoherent that *they unmade themselves*—films that transcend taste and might be termed *objectively bad.* Surrealist bad movies are lurid, oneiric, delirious. An objectively bad movie is all this and more.

"A bad actor," wrote the underground cineaste Jack Smith, "is rich, unique, idiosyncratic, revealing." The same may be said for the objectively bad film, and for similar reasons. Smith, who began experimenting with bad acting in *Flaming Creatures* (1962), was undoubtedly thinking of his favorite star, the paradigmatic Camp icon Maria Montez. In part, his appreciation for her vehicles is a Surrealist taste. Infantile fantasies like *White Savage, Ali Baba and the Forty Thieves*, and *Sudan* are founts of inane, voluptuously exotic imagery. Smith was moved by their poetry.

But there is another aspect as well. It was precisely because Montez was so unconvincing an actress that Smith valued her performances: "One of her atrocious acting sighs suffused a thousand tons of dead plaster with imaginative life and a truth." The truth is that Montez is always herself. Montez vehicles are unintended documentaries of a romantic, narcissistic young woman dressing up in pasty jewels, striking fantastic poses, queening it over an all-too-obviously make-believe world. For Smith, her inept portrayals of Scheherezade, the Cobra Woman, and the Siren of Atlantis hyperbolized the actual situation of a Hollywood glamour goddess. Montez's transparent role-playing, and her unconcealed delight at being the center of attention, were more authentic to him than the naturalism achieved by *successfully* phony actresses. The often poignant, heightened realism induced by such a failure to convince is the key to the objectively bad film.

The conventional narrative film does not demand anything so gross as a suspension of disbelief; it only asks an indulgent acceptance of its own diegetic, or fictive, space. The badly-made unconvincing film confounds this minimal requirement by ignoring or (more often) bungling the most rudimentary precepts of screen naturalism. I once saw a porn film set in Outer Space that used a suburban kitchen as the set for its rocket control room. The bluntness with which this profilmic reality (i.e., what's in front of the camera) disrupted the diegetic web produced a more vivid sense of science fiction than anything in *2001*.

The theoretician Noel Burch has identified a-conventional narrative films (exceptions to what he calls the "instructional mode of representation") in pre-1905 and non-Western cinema. An early Japanese talkie like *Wife! Be Like a Rose* (1935) may not fully subscribe to the institutionalized codes, but it cannot be considered badly made: the unorthodox eyeline-matches in reverse-angle sequences, odd cutaways and sound bridges, and impossible point-of-view shots are only subtly jarring. An objectively bad film, on the other hand, casually promotes perceptual havoc—as casually as the 3-D cheapster *Robot Monster* (1953) incorporated special effects lifted without modification from the two-dimensional *One Million B.C.*

Objectively bad movies are usually made against all odds in a handful of days on a breathtakingly low budget. Such extreme austerity enforces a delirious pragmatism: homemade sets, no re-takes, tacky special effects, heavy reliance on stock footage. The objectively bad film attempts to reproduce the institutional mode of representation, but its failure to do so deforms the simplest formulae and clichés so absolutely that you barely recognize them. They must be actively decoded. In Edward D. Wood, Jr.'s *Bride of the Monster* (1956), a film that employs so many inappropriate reaction shots that it suggests a combined Kuleshov-Rorschach test, a secretary abruptly picks up a phone and starts talking. Did the director overlook the necessity of dialing? Did he forget to post-dub the sound of the ring? An actress in Oscar Micheaux's *God's Step-*

children (1937) shakes her head and declares "No . . . empathically . . . no." Belatedly, one realizes she has incorporated the script's stage direction into her dialogue.

Poor acting and ludicrous dialogue—though axiomatic to bad film-making—do not in themselves make an objectively bad movie. Neither does an absurd plot; if it did, D. W. Griffith, Josef von Sternberg, and Samuel Fuller would all be bad filmmakers. In fact to be objectively bad, a film must relent-lessly draw one's attention away from its absurd plot. For Walter Benjamin (and even André Bazin), the seamless "equipment-free aspect of reality" that movies presented on screen was actually the "height of artifice." The objec-tively bad film acknowledges this: the lie of "chronology" is confounded by imperfect continuity; "invisible" editing is ruptured by mismatched cuts; *mise en scène* is foregrounded by cloddish bits of business. A good bad movie is a philosophers' stone that converts the incompetent mistakes of naïve dross into modernist gold. Such movies are unstable objects. They ping-pong back and forth from diegetic intent to profilmic event (or to their own jerry-built con-struction) the way a Cézanne oscillates between a representational landscape and a paint-gopped canvas.

Objectively bad films are almost always targeted at the most exploitable or *lumpen* sections of the movie audience (ethnic minorities, teen-agers, sub-literates, 42nd Street derelicts). Like every other sort of movie, however, the best bad films are personal, even obsessive works. Some guy had a story to tell and he was going to punch it across by whatever impoverished means were at hand. "For the budget, and for the time, I felt I had achieved greatness," said Phil Tucker of his $16,000 *Robot Monster*. The best bad movies add nutty ambi-tion and auteurist signatures to their already-heady atmosphere of free-floating mishigas. "There is a very short distance between high art and trash," observed Douglas Sirk. (Who would know better than he?) "And trash that contains the element of craziness is by this very quality nearer to art." A supremely bad movie—an anti-masterpiece—projects a stupidity that's fully as awesome as genius.

These thoughts were prompted in part by the World's Worst Film Festival, held recently at the Beacon Theatre in Manhattan. The series was itself inspired by *The Fifty Worst Films of All Time* and *The Golden Turkey Awards*, a pair of humorous non-books researched by teenaged Harry Medved and written by his older brother Michael. The Medved position—if we discount its patina of *Mad* magazine masochism and resolve to stomach their facetious tone—also suggests that the best bad movies are akin to masterpieces.

"In both cases," according to the Medveds, "the viewer marvels at the range of human imagination and creativity." Another way to put it is that anti-masterpieces break the rules with such exhilaration as to expand our definition of what a movie can be. *They Saved Hitler's Brain* (1958? 1964?), the most structurally inventive film shown at the World's Worst Film Festival, surpasses the temporal complexity of *Muriel* by intercutting two radically different movies. The first is elaborately lighted and was filmed on studio sets by Stanley Cortez; the second, involving a completely distinct set of actors, was shot *vérité*-style in 16mm some six years later. These two strands are densely interwoven, sometimes even within a single scene. Watching it, your head bursts with ideas.

Peter Bogdanovich once produced a similar, if less bewildering exercise in creative geography when Roger Corman commissioned him to add shots of Mamie Van Doren and other Venusian cuties to a womanless Soviet sci-fi film whose rights A.I.P. had acquired. But whereas Bogdanovich's *Voyage to the Planet of the Prehistoric Women* is wittily schematic, *T.S.H.B.* (as its fans in the Beacon lobby were heard to refer to it) is unpredictable and irrational. The logic it entails is so unfathomable, the shifts in its action so abrupt, that you have to pinch yourself to make sure it isn't a hallucination.

The Medveds' most sincere defense of bad movies, slated in the prefaces to both their books, is that "people show greater enthusiasm in laughing together over films they despise than trying to praise films they admire." There's a self-serving aspect to this questionable observation, but its implications are not without interest. By their unintentional "success," bad movies deflate the claims of more serious works—and they are leveling in other ways. It's reassuring, the Medveds suggest, to discover that the "larger-than-life demigods" of Hollywood are also fallible, even clumsy. Beneath the Medveds' glibness is an inchoate protest against the colonization of the imagination by ready-made, seamless dreams.

Obviously the Medveds' appreciation of badness differs from that of the Surrealists, or of Jack Smith. While the former valorized bad movies for their "beauty," and the latter prized bad acting for its "truth," the Medved aesthetic is an affirmation of the American Way: "Absolutely anyone can recognize a lousy film when he sees one."

This democratic assertion raises hopes that the Medved books will be treasures of objectively bad films. But although many of their "Fifty Worst" are bad to the degree that they are laughable, few are bad enough to be pleasurable, let alone radical. The book—from which aspiring screenwriter Michael prudently withheld his name—is mainly a collection of ponderous mediocrities (*Valley of the Dolls, Northwest Mounted Police*), famous flops (Ross Hunter's

Lost Horizon, Myra Breckinridge), and lame performances by well-known stars (John Wayne as The Conqueror, Clark Gable as Parnell).

The Medveds are alive to the qualities of a *Robot Monster*, but they haven't the imagination to distinguish between purely conceptual (hence, unwatchable) absurdities like the all-midget *Terror of Tiny Town* or the Ronald Reagan–Shirley Temple match-up in *That Hagan Girl* and *films maudits* like *Bring Me the Head of Alfredo Garcia* or *Exorcist II: The Heretic*. This is not so much a factor of their petulant philistinism (they include *Last Year at Marienbad* and *Ivan the Terrible* among the Fifty Worst) as it is of the ingrained literary bias which has them habitually judging films by their bad dialogue and humorously negative reviews.

The Golden Turkey Awards, *The Fifty Worst Films*'s more sleekly packaged sequel (it gives prizes in thirty categories from "The Worst Two-Headed Transplant Movie Ever Made" to "The Most Inane and Unwelcome 'Technical Advance' in Hollywood History"), is something of a corrective. Having solicited suggestions from readers of the first book, the Medveds shift the emphasis of their second away from ponderous star vehicles to horror and sci-fi cheapsters—films which labor under the double burden of having to make the supernatural, as well as their own fictive space, appear convincing. Indicative of this reorientation is the canonization of the previously unmentioned *Plan Nine from Outer Space* (1959) and its director Edward D. Wood, Jr. as, respectively, "The Worst Film of All Time" and "The Worst Director of All Time."

Not surprisingly, The Worst Director of All Time was well represented at the World's Worst Film Festival with *Plan Nine*, *Bride of the Monster*, and the 1952 *I Changed My Sex* (also known as *Glen or Glenda?*). Writer-director-editor Wood featured Bela Lugosi in all three; and the presence of this broken-down star (in some respects a tragic male counterpart to Maria Montez) contributes to their atmosphere of rancid glitz. A sense of Hollywood Boulevard Babylon pervades Wood's universe. It's not surprising to learn that he ended up directing hard-core porn, and that his last opus was an 8mm "home study" segment of *The Encyclopedia of Sex*.

Wood evidently played Svengali to an entourage of *Day of the Locust* wierdos. His movies are less the products of Hollywood's Poverty Row than the fantasies of a parallel Skid Row populated by show biz oddities (Criswell, the TV prophet; Tor Johnson, the 400-pound Swedish wrestler; Vampira, the beatnik ghoul-girl), haggard has-beens (Lugosi, Lyle Bettger), and the talentless progeny of the money-men who bankrolled him. The pitifully emaciated Lugosi gives a particularly painful performance in *Bride of the Monster*, playing a mad scientist with a spare lightstand as the centerpiece to his *art povera* laboratory. Against all odds, Lugosi clings to shreds of his professionalism. One watches in horrified admiration as he shifts gears from enraged ranting to bathetic whimpering to insane cackling in a single, brutally endless take, or when he gamely pretends to struggle in the outstretched tentacles of an unmoving rubber octopus.

A casual *mise en scène* of half-dressed sets and visible Klieg lights is Wood's hallmark, and everywhere in his oeuvre one finds a naive faith in the power of montage. Wood was left with only two minutes of Lugosi footage when the star died early in the production of what became *Plan Nine from Outer Space*. His solution was to hire a stand-in, have him wrap his face in a cape, and use the Lugosi material anyway. Wood's action montages are so perfunctory as to be a slap in the face of public taste. *Plan Nine* features a shamelessly lackadaisical battle sequence fashioned out of scratchy World War II newsreels, inserts of wobbly tinfoil space ships, and a uniformed actor peering through fieldglasses, a white backdrop behind him. The "monster" in *Bride of the Monster* is a squid filmed through the glass of an aquarium tank; the bargain basement apocalypse (and utter non-sequitur) that ends the movie is a single shot of an atomic mushroom cloud. With a similar economy of means, every significant moment—and there are many—in *I Changed My Sex* is punctuated with the identical flash of stock-footage lighting. Wood's fondness for dramatic inserts is balanced by a startling refusal to use cross-cutting to create tension. Characters chase each other around the frame instead.

Plan Nine begins with the psychic Criswell shrilly wondering if our nerves can stand the "idea of grave-robbers from outer space," and ends with his declaration that what we have just seen was based on sworn testimony. ("Can you prove it didn't happen?" he asks in a phrase that might have served Wood as his motto.) Sandwiched between Criswell's two appearances are sequences of people knocked out of their lawn chairs by the "death-ray" of an off-screen flashlight; Vampira haunting a cardboard cemetery that, no matter the time of day in contiguous shots, exists as a zone of perpetual night; extras grinning at the camera and pointing overhead to where a flotilla of flying saucers is supposedly strafing their car.

Plan Nine is Wood's most enjoyable movie; but it is the didactic, exploitational *I Changed My Sex* that offers the key to his work. The structure and thesis of this remarkable film are far too convoluted to summarize briefly. Suffice to say that its parallel "case histories" (one a screwball explanation of transvestism; the other a ponderous depiction of a transsexual operation) are set within a thicket of multiple narratives and framed by cutaways to an omniscient Bela Lugosi surrounded by human skeletons and shrieking, "The story must be told!"

The story must be told indeed. *I Changed My Sex* is a possible psychodrama and, at least, a partial autobiography. According to the Medveds, the mustachioed Wood affected women's pantsuits, pantyhose, and angora sweaters, and bragged he had worn a brassiere beneath his World War II combat fatigues. Low budgets and heavy drinking may account for the spectacular lapses of Wood's *mise en scène*, but his artistic personality (a subject surely for further research) was obviously bound up in this most primitive form of make-believe. The unconvincing magic, crackpot logic, and decomposing glamour of Wood's films are in fact a mirror of his own life. Dressed like a tacky transvestite out of *Flaming Creatures*, he played at being a megaphone-brandishing director with the demented conviction of Maria Montez impersonating a movie star. His films, like hers, intimate the full lunacy and pathos of Southern California. He deserves the title of World's Worst Director.

And yet, there is another filmmaker whose anti-masterpieces are so profoundly troubling and whose *weltanschauung* is so devastating that neither the Medveds nor the World's Worst Film Festival are equipped to deal with him. In fact, five decades after their release, his films still have no place in the history of cinema. I refer to the work of Oscar Micheaux.

I think of Micheaux as the Black Pioneer of American film—not just because he was a black man, or because in his youth he pioneered the West, or because he was the greatest figure in "race" movies and an unjustly ignored force in early American cinema. Micheaux is America's Black Pioneer in the way that André Breton was Surrealism's Black Pope. His movies throw our history and movies into an alien and startling disarray.

Micheaux's last film, aptly titled *The Betrayal*, opened in New York in 1948. "There is simply no point in trying to apply normal critical standards . . . or in trying to describe its monumental incompetence as movie-making," wrote *P.M.*, while *The Times* reported that it contained "sequences so gauche as to provoke embarrassed laughter." The *Herald-Tribune* was bluntest: "A preposterous, inept bore . . . Acting that is worse than amateurish but this is not even its worst flaw. Micheaux's dialogue is even worse, with senseless and unmouthable lines; his concept of human beings is absurd and his direction somewhat less artful than one would expect of home-movies. The fact that Micheaux expects one to watch this [trash] for more than three hours is a monstrous piece of miscalculation." Were the above reviews to greet a film opening tomorrow, one might rush to see it on the assumption that only a powerful originality could goad the jaded reviewers of the daily press to such fury. Edward Wood may be the Worst, but Oscar Micheaux (1884–1951) is the Baddest—with all that that implies.

Only the barest facts of Micheaux's life are in the record. He was a native of Illinois who, after several years of work as a Pullman porter, purchased a homestead for himself on the sparsely settled South Dakota plains. Inspired by Booker T. Washington, he began writing a series of thinly novelized autobiographical tracts, which he published and distributed himself. In 1919 his third novel, *The Homesteader*, attracted the attention of one of the several black-owned movie studios that had sprung up in response to the segregated policies of American movie theaters (as well as to counter *The Birth of a Nation*). Micheaux stipulated in the sale of the screen rights that he would direct the film. When the deal fell through, he raised capital among his public and made *The Homesteader* himself.

After this audacious start, Micheaux went on to be one of the most tenacious filmmakers who ever lived. Against all odds, over the next twenty-one years (with *The Betrayal* in 1948), he wrote, directed, and produced some thirty features. His method of distribution was an elaboration of the set-up he'd used to sell his novels: He would drive across the country, stop at each ghetto theater, show the owner his new script, hype his performers ("the Black Valentino," "the Sepia Mae West"), and ask for an advance against the gate. When he had accumulated sufficient capital, he returned to New York and shot the film. Micheaux's silent pictures were more topical, more lurid, and more critical than those of other black filmmakers.

The painful ambivalence of Micheaux's racial attitudes is one reason why his films are rarely screened and less frequently written about. There seems to be a tacit agreement among scholars of black cinema to avoid discussing this aspect of his work—particularly as he is sometimes offered as a role-model for black directors and his name has been appropriated for the award given those artists inducted into the Black Filmmakers Hall of Fame. Donald Bogle, the only black critic to my knowledge who discusses Micheaux's talkies at length, describes them as depicting a "fantasy world where blacks were just as affluent, just as educated, just as 'cultured,' just as well-mannered—in short, just as white—as white America."

But Micheaux's never-never land is underscored with an almost unbearable bitterness. Despite their fantasy overlay, his films are frought with fury and despair. When the madam of a Chicago brothel in *The Exile* (1931) is reproached by her Abyssinian lover for vamping him away from his studies, she contemptuously replies that "there are enough Negro doctors and lawyers already" and

that he'd only end up as a shyster or abortionist. "Colored men will sell out anyone for fifty cents" is a typically blunt comment made in the suggestively titled
Lyin' Lips (1939); and the Harlem chapter of the Communist Party succeeded
in temporarily driving *God's Stepchildren* (1937) off the screen, in part because
of its hero's contention that "only one Negro in a thousand tries to think."

One suspects that Micheaux never reconciled himself to the ugly fact that,
in a segregated white society, his options were severely limited. After all, in his
cultivation of the West and in his success as a self-made entrepreneur, he was
as American as anyone—if not more so. Trapped in a ghetto, but unwilling or
unable to directly confront America's racism, Micheaux displaced his rage on
his own people. In other words, part of the price that he paid for his American-
ness was the internalization of American racial attitudes. Hence his horrified
fascination with miscegenation and "passing," his heedless blaming of the victim, his cruel baiting of fellow blacks. *God's Stepchildren*, the imitation *Imitation of Life* which epitomizes Micheaux's complex, contradictory mixture of
self-hatred and remorse, forms an essential triptych with *The Birth of a Nation*
and *The Searchers*. They are the three richest, most harrowing delineations of
American social psychology to be found on celluloid.

Micheaux's films were willed into existence with such strenuous single-
mindedness, with so massive a determination to make them tell a story no
matter what that, both in form and content, they open up a chasm between
intent and actualization almost unprecedented in the history of film. Intricate
narratives were based around two or three reshuffled sets (usually the homes
of friends), and entire—often violent—scenes were shot in a single take.

Micheaux's films define objective badness. His camera ground relentlessly
on while the key light wandered, traffic noise obliterated the dialogue, or a
soundman's arm intruded upon the frame. Actors blew their cues, recovered,
and continued. Wasting nothing, he re-used footage with impunity, carried the
post-dubbing of his soundtracks to the outer limits of possibility, saved up his
out-takes and fashioned them into second films. Micheaux films seize every
opportunity to announce themselves as constructs. They are embellished with
gratuitous cheesecake, tricked out with "red herring" mystery music, padded
with obscurely dangling parallel action, and rife with lengthy cabaret
sequences which cut his costs by providing the performers he recruited with
"free advertising," in lieu of pay.

As Micheaux's distanciation evokes Brecht, his continuity surpasses
Resnais. Time stops short in an avalanche of unnecessary titles and reaction
shots, accelerates suddenly through the elliptical omission of an expected

action, doubles back on itself in an unannounced flashback prompted by the use of earlier footage in a new context. Scenes climax in a cubist explosion of herky-jerky jump cuts wherein an actor delivering his line appears in a succession of slightly askew angles. Micheaux's sense of timing recalls Thelonious Monk or Earl Monroe, and his narrative strategies beggar one's imagination. Actors play multiple roles, some characters seem blessed with precognitive abilities while others get marooned in alternate universes. The extensively post-dubbed *Ten Minutes to Live* (1932) makes elaborate use of telegrams and deaf-mutes to narrate the two separate stories that intermittently supercede the lava flow of entertainment erupting out of the single set called "Club Libya." *The Notorious Elinor Lee* (1939) reveals a surprise murder in a courtroom denouement that calls a parrot to testify on the witness stand.

"Every picture he made was mortgaged up to the nose," a Micheaux associate remembered. It's as though Micheaux directed his films while looking over his shoulder. His actors, their heads precipitously low in the frame, converge breathlessly at the center of the screen as a shot begins. Lines are delivered in unison, there are awkwardly failed attempts at overlapping dialogue, some actors appear to be reciting their parts by rote or reading cue cards. In *The Girl From Chicago* (1932) an off-camera voice prompts an actor to "give it to her," and his response is to mechanically repeat the phrase.

That Micheaux lacked either the time or the proclivity to invent any but the most obvious bits of business heightens the Kabuki-like quality of the performances. The non-speaking actor in a two-shot is frequently restricted to a single exaggerated tic. Thirty years before Warhol, Micheaux approached *mise en scène* Degree Zero. Left stranded in scenes that are grossly overextended, his performers strike fantastic poses, stare affectingly into space, or gaze casually off-camera.

Edward Wood was a toadstool at the edge of Hollywood, nourished by the movie industry's compost; Micheaux constructed an anti-Hollywood out of rags and bones on some barely-imaginable psychic tundra. The spectacles he fashioned of blacks playing white (which they sometimes did literally, in whiteface) constitute a ruthless burlesque of the dominant culture. The collapse of bourgeois "niceness" that Luis Buñuel's *The Exterminating Angel* or Eugene Ionesco's plays depict, Micheaux's films actually are. Micheaux took the "institutional mode of representation," up-ended it, and turned it inside out. He demystified movies as no one has ever done and performed this negative magic for an audience that, infinitely more than the Medved boys, was victimized by Hollywood's mechanical dreams. The key to Micheaux's originality is that the social criticism that appears with such painful ambivalence in his scripts was triumphantly sublimated onto the level of form. Regardless of his intentions, Micheaux's films are so devastatingly bad that he can only be considered alongside Georges Méliès, D. W. Griffith, Dziga Vertov, Stan Brakhage, and Jean-Luc Godard as one of the medium's major formal innovators.

Three more things: 1) In *The Exile*, Micheaux uses titan of industry Charles Schwab's Riverside Drive mansion to represent the exterior of a Chicago whorehouse; 2) It's been said that Micheaux deliberately left mistakes in his finished films "to give the audience a laugh"; 3) The longer Micheaux made films, the badder they got. I'm haunted by these facts because they suggest that Micheaux knew what he was doing. And if Oscar Micheaux was a fully conscious artist, he was the greatest genius the cinema ever produced.

1980

The Film Critic of Tomorrow, Today

We've been here before. As the aesthetician (and erstwhile movie reviewer) Rudolf Arnheim predicted in 1935,

One of the tasks of the film critic of tomorrow—perhaps he will even be called a "television critic"—will be to rid the world of the comic figure the average film critic and film theorist of today represents: he lives from the glory of his memories like the seventy-year-old ex-court actresses, rummages about as they do in yellowing photographs, speaks of names that are long gone. He discusses films no one has been able to see for ten years or more (and about which they can therefore say everything and nothing) with people of his own ilk; he argues about montage like medieval scholars discussed the existence of God, believing all these things could still exist today. In the evening, he sits with rapt attention in the cinema, a critical art lover, as though we still lived in the days of Griffith, Stroheim, Murnau, and Eisenstein. *He thinks he is seeing bad films instead of understanding that what he sees is no longer film at all.* [emphasis added]

The crisis of film criticism has been variously linked to the consolidation of entertainment conglomerates, the proliferation of home video, the dumbing down of the movie audience, the toxic fumes of film theory, the death of cinephilia, the retirement of Pauline Kael. True enough, but is the crisis not even more fundamentally related to the disappearance of movies?

Not literally, of course. Indeed, the Movies occupy more cultural space than ever before. *Entertainment Tonight* commands as much broadcast time as the evening news. Entire cable stations are devoted to the promotion of new movies and stars—who exert more power and make more money than at any time in human history. Grosses too are generally up and Oscar night, the annual festival of self-congratulation, has become a "feminine" counterweight to the "masculine" Super Bowl in the celebration of national identity. It's almost a patriotic duty to be entertained in America—even a form of unpaid labor. For busy people, there is Time Warner's *Entertainment Weekly* to provide a convenient substitute for actual consumption. Freed from the obligation to see-hear-read all this stuff, you can flip through the magazine, glom the letter grades, and be knowledgeable. You can have opinions.

(And just what is it that you, reader, want to know about a movie that you have never—and may never—see? Is it an account of the narrative action—stopping too short to protect of the various twists and surprises? Is it an amusing description of the physical appearance of the—hot? cold?—stars? A sober evaluation of the competence of the cinematic technique? An assessment of the manifest directorial personality? Is it speculation on the movie's place in—movie?—history, the degree to which it embodies the way we live now? Did you really care if I liked it—and why? Is the question whether to buy a ticket to see the movie now—or wait for video?)

What else is there to say? Familiarity may breed contempt, but commercial cinema trades on prior acquaintance. (In no medium is the stigma of the "difficult"—which ranges from the absence of stars to the presence of subtitles—more damning.) Stars are a form of living trademark, scripts a kind of organized cliche. Genres rule. Movies are made in cycles and recycled as remakes. Anything sold once can be sold again . . . and again. Moreover, the movies are the nexus for an endless series of cross-references and synergistic couplings. Just as movies are now routinely based on old TV series, so plays are adapted from old movies. So-called novelizations used to be written after a movie was released; now they are published before the film is made.

The more old Hollywood movies are sentimentalized as art, the more crass our appreciation of the current crop. A flop is, by definition, an aesthetic failure; quality is synonymous with economic success (or at least notoriety). Although critics continue to grouse over the decline in narrative values, the story-line that everyone in America has learned to follow is the fever chart of box-office grosses. Every major production brings its own ephemeral *Entertainment Tonight* metadrama. Each summer, audiences are invited to be a part of History by queuing up to see *Independence Day* or *The Lost World*—the resonance of these titles!—on their first megamillion-dollar weekends.

A movie is almost by definition a record of that which once was—and how we long for that which no longer exists! Fifty-eight years after *Mr. Smith Goes to Washington*, *Variety* reported that the most trusted man in America was still Jimmy Stewart.

In the moment of national self-analysis that followed Stewart's death most marvelled over his old fashioned virtues, his lack of pretention, the miracle of his actorly "ordinariness," the positive values of his persona. The fact is, however, that stars are our supreme public servants. The mild gossip that doings and vehicles inspire promotes the socially cohesive illusion of an intimate America where everyone knows (and even cares) about each other. The stars—and the entertainment media that showcase them—create what the theorist of nationalism Benedict Anderson has called an Imaginary Community. And not just ours—by 1995, as American movies filled the vacuum left by the declining indigenous film industries of Europe, Latin America, and Asia, foreign rentals had surpassed those of the domestic box office.

In the totalitarian Soviet Union, entertainment was an obvious aspect of the state ideological apparatus—merging politics with show business. Of course, we can't say that of America (at least not on television). Nevertheless, this Imaginary Community—predicated on the existence of shared tastes, feelings, desires—is an economic necessity. For if the prerequisite of mass production is mass consumption, that mass consumption is itself predicated on the production of mass desire—for movies, among other things. And, because virtually all reviewers are compelled (as journalists) to write about films before most people have a chance to see them—thumbs up or down like parody Roman emperors—they are only one more part of a vast machine devoted to inculcating the mass urge-to-see.

Although movie reviews are historically the favor with which newspapers acknowledge the placement of movie advertisements, the ads now in effect commission their own six-word reviews (while serving the secondary function of providing free publicity for the reviewers and, of course, the periodicals or broadcast outlets that employ them). To be a movie reviewer is to strike a Faustian bargain with the industry. You can have your name (and your words) emblazoned on a newspaper ad or poster as large as that of Tom Cruise. Does anyone doubt that many reviewers write to be quoted or paraphrased? Some phantom reviewers exist only as pull quotes. (The industry term for them is "blurb whores.") In 1989, Rex Reed complained to *Variety* that studio publicists had asked him if he would polish a quote; eight years later, *Variety* was reporting that at least one studio had taken to faxing readymade quotes to freelancers, inviting them to attach their name to the one found most agreeable.

United in their need to promote the latest blockbuster, studio press agents and movie journalists enjoy a symbolic relationship. (*Premier*, a periodical at which I worked for a half-dozen years, transformed on-set reportage into a—marginally—more literary form of the studio press book.) Studios typically mark the opening of a major investment by organizing an industry junket, flying reviewers from all over the country to Los Angeles or New York to preview the movie, enjoy a hotel banquet, and then attend a succession of five-minute group interviews with the stars. Categorizing journalists in terms of their use-value, publicists trade early screenings, film clips, and access to the talent for sound-bites and advance superlatives.

The magazine journalist is thus a part of the movie's anticipatory build-up as well the magazine's own competitive struggle to secure the star-image for its covers. Celebrity is the coin of the realm—the ultimate in surplus value which, through the magic of endorsement, transforms, as Marx wrote in *Capital*, "every product of labor into a social hieroglyph." Publicists routinely vet writers, stipulate format and ground rules, and barter for cover placement (and, when they can, other aspects of editorial content). While publicists understand the press as a potential rival in the creation of a star's persona, the underlying assumption is that journalists, like reviewers, are too stupid or star-struck to realize how much more money they could make writing screenplays or even press releases.

Once upon a time, media commentator James Wolcott wrote in the April 1997 *Vanity Fair*, film critics "had the oral swagger of gunslingers. Quick on the draw and easy to rile, they had the power to kill individual films and kneecap entire careers." Then the frontier closed. Faced with the silence of his idol Pauline Kael, Wolcott laments that "movie criticism has become a cultural malady, a group case of chronic depression and low self-esteem." Reinforcing his point is the fact that the vehicle for his screed is a journal devoting an extraordinary amount of space to movies and movie stars without apparently feeling the need for regular film criticism.

In addition to bankrolling remarks, Hollywood studios are primarily interested in recycling movies as theme-park rides, interactive videogames, CD-ROMs, and computer screensavers. This is one meaning of André Bazin's "Myth of Total Cinema." Anticipating by some decades his compatriots Guy Debord and Jean Baudrillard, Bazin foresaw the historical logic by which the movies and their more perfect successors would inexorably seek to supplant the world: Virtual Reality.

The key development, but only thus far, in the Myth of Total Cinema was development of "talking" pictures in late 1927—the magical simultaneity of sound and image is what the Austrian avant-garde filmmaker Peter Kubelka called the Sync Event. It was, in fact, this particular technological advance that prompted Rudolf Arnheim to declare of the film critic that "he thinks he is seeing bad films instead of understanding that what he sees is no longer film at all."

Time Warner and Walt Disney, the world's two largest media conglomerates, were both founded upon the miracle of synchronous sound. Talking pictures brought forth first *The Jazz Singer* and then, the far more durable blackface entertainer, Mickey Mouse. The Mouse is prophetic of Total Cinema's next stage, namely the overthrow of camera authority by computer digitalized imagery: More and more, the future begins to look like Paula Abdul's four-minute "remake" of *Rebel Without a Cause* or the computer-animated Diet Coke ad where her fellow flack Elton John jams with Louis Armstrong for the amusement of Humphrey Bogart. The living party with the dead under the sign of the trademark, the gods dwell among us from here to eternity.

The very name Time Warner suggests the fusion of news and entertainment—indeed Warner's summer 1996 blockbuster *Twister* was featured on *Time*'s cover as the hook for a news report on tornadoes. Rival retail outlet Walt Disney is called the corporate artist supreme—the single most important figure in mass culture, the first to saturate America with cultural trademarks, to use television to create a system of self-perpetuating hype, a creator so universal his quirks must be stamped on our DNA and his Magic Kingdom now incorporates a substantial chunk of midtown Manhattan. (Might we not balance the budget by establishing the American flag as a registered trademark, licensed exclusively to Walt Disney?)

Following Disney, the successful Hollywood movie is an increasingly uninteresting bridge between the multimedia barrage of prerelease promotion and a potential package of spin-offs, career moves, and tie-ins. (Such ancillary income exceeded even the box-office grosses for such megablockbusters as *Batman* and *Jurassic Park*.) As reported in *Time*, Time Warner chairman Gerald Levin heralded the media conglomerate's Christmas 1996 release—an epic synthesis of an animated Looney Tune and a Michael Jordan sneaker commercial —with unusual candor: "*Space Jam* isn't a movie. It's a marketing event." Disney's summer 1997 animated feature, *Hercules*, went even further (while preempting any criticism) by satirizing itself as a marketing event.

Awaiting the fulfillment of Total Cinema, Americans already live in the world of Total Docu-Drama. (Think of it as the live-action and cartoon mix of *Who Shot Roger Rabbit?*) The television induced symbiosis of entertainment, history, and politics is so complete that no one complains when *Star Trek* memorabilia is enshrined, alongside actual moon rocks and Lindbergh's authentic

Spirit of St. Louis, in America's equivalent of the Sistine Chapel—the National Air and Space Museum in Washington, D.C. This technology for manufacturing evidence is what we have to remember us by—shared projections of an imaginary past.

As predicted by George Lucas's *American Graffiti* and demonstrated by his *Star Wars*, as illuminated by the careers of Steven Spielberg and Ronald Reagan, Hollywood is the main repository of cultural memory—and authority. In her introduction to a recent collection of scholarly essays on *Schindler's List*, Israeli professor Yosefa Loshitzky notes that making the film had effectively made Spielberg more than an artist: his "testimony in the summer of 1994 before a congressional committee examining the issue of 'hate crimes' itself testifies to the fact that the most successful commercial filmmaker in Hollywood's history has suddenly achieved 'expert' status on a controversial and complex social phenomenon—purely by virtue of having directed a film whose subject is the rescue of a handful of Jews from the Nazis."

Any news story in the cinema-saturated world can be played like an old-fashioned pinball machine—ricocheted from one mirrored surface to another. Within weeks of the now barely remembered tale of Tonya Harding's alleged assault on her Olympic skating rival Nancy Kerrigan, the *New York Times* reported that no less than ten film production companies "as well as networks and studios" were seeking the rights to the story. Since then magazines have been aggressively shopping the movie rights to material they publish, while the Disney studio has taken the lead in directly commissioning journalists to investigate stories—eliminating the magazine middleman. Similarly, the Heaven's Gate cult (named for a film) is but the bridge from *Star Wars* and *Close Encounters of the Third Kind*, from which it drew its theology, to a made-for-TV movie.

"Fiction seeps quietly and continuously into reality," writes Benedict Anderson, "creating that remarkable confidence of community in anonymity which is the hallmark of modern nations." In the context of a world inexorably transformed into a representation of itself, the big-budget film biography or historical reenactment—once the ultimate middlebrow made-for-TV mode—has come to seem the quintessential Hollywood genre. Self-proclaimed counter-myths like *Patty Hearst, Born on the Fourth of July, The Doors, JFK, Ruby, Malcolm X, Quiz Show, Hoffa, Schindler's List, Panther, Apollo 13, Nixon, The People vs. Larry Flynt*, and *Evita*—as well as their fictional, satirical, or avant-garde counterparts (*Forrest Gump, Ed Wood, I Shot Andy Warhol*) are to the post Cold War Bush-Clinton transition what the Spielberg-Lucas megafantasy had been to the Age of Reagan or what the epic of antiquity to the early fifties—spectacular displays of pure movie might, would-be interventions, contributions to (or, per-haps, substitutions for) a national discourse.

In the absence of what had been considered film, Arnheim reminded the critic of 1935 to recall that "second great task"—often neglected by virtue of the demands required by "aesthetic criticism"—namely, "the consideration of film as an economic product, and as an expression of political and moral view-points." How can we do anything else? As Arnheim's colleague and contem-porary Siegfried Kracauer put it, "the good film critic is only conceivable as a critic of society." (Now, of course, the reverse is also true.)

As explicated by Terence Davies's 1992 masterpiece *The Long Day Closes*, movies are both the most subjective of individual experiences and the most public of public arts. Davies's ten-year-old alter ego is charged by a love for the ineffable—a fascination with that world on the screen we never see.

Is that love gone? It was just past the hundredth anniversary of the Lumière brothers' first public exhibition of their cinematograph when Susan Sontag lamented the death of cinephilia with an article published in the *New York Times Magazine*: "Cinema's one hundred years seem to have the shape of a life cycle: an inevitable birth, the steady accumulation of glories and the onset in the last decade of an ignominious, irreversible decline."

Readers of the *Times* were quick to point out that Sontag's view of cinema was a highly selective one. She maintained, for example, that only France pro-duced "a large number of superb films" for the first twenty-five years of the sound era (and presumably thereafter). She made no mention of current Chi-nese movies or even American independents (or Chantal Akerman or Atom Egoyan or Raul Ruiz or Lars von Trier or Stan Brakhage or Beat Takeshi or Abbas Kiarostami . . .). She capped her career-long disinterest in American movies by mourning the blighted careers of Francis Coppola and Paul Schrader.

As ahistorical as it was, Sontag's piece nevertheless partook of a now-familiar melancholy. The approaching millennium, the AIDS plague, the col-lapse of "existing socialism," and the end of the Cold War have inspired many such obituaries to mark the real or perceived disappearance of many wondrous things—modernism, historical consciousness, oppositional culture, the literary canon, American industry, the Democratic Party, New York City, baseball, the Broadway theater, downtown nightlife, labor unions, print journalism—all to be replaced by the bogus virtual reality of an impoverished cybertopia. In truth, the movies have merged with the spectacle of daily life.

The cinephilia of the sixties is over—it required not only the films of the sixties but also the social moment of the sixties. If the sixties and seventies brought a film culture of unprecedented plurality, the last twenty years have been characterized by increasing self-absorption, a profound ignorance of world cinema, and a corresponding disinterest—among American critics, as much as American audiences—in other people's movies. More disturbing, perhaps, than diminished film enthusiasm is the failure of the sixties film culture, which Sontag herself helped create, to establish itself as a lasting intellectual presence. (After Reagan, one might expect that movieology would be the central pursuit of the age. But there is still something suspect in taking the movies too seriously—except, of course, as a business.)

Sontag's two-page spread included a cover image of *Cahiers du cinéma* but failed to note the French journal's ongoing debate on the nature of movie-love. "Is it necessary to cure cinephilia?" was the question posed by *Cahiers*'s January 1977 issue, which in sampling the writings of Ricciotto Canudo (1879–1923) resurrected a cinephilia no less intense than that of the sixties. "What is striking, characteristic, and significant, even more than the [cinematic] spectacle itself," Canudo wrote in 1911, "is the uniform will of the spectators, who belong to all social classes, from the lowest and least educated to the most intellectual." Canudo saw in movies a "desire for a new *festival*, for a new joyous *unanimity*, realized at a show, in a place where together, all men can forget, in greater or lesser measure, their isolated individuality."

That festival is "Hollywood"—the quaint name for an international mass culture, based in the United States but drawing capital, talent, and audiences from all over the world. A celebration of American military and cultural hegemony, *Independence Day* was the pure cultural expression of the formula PR + F/X = USA #1. As *Independence Day* united America before one movie, so the movie showed America organizing the world to establish July 4th as a global celebration of independence—from what? Surely not Rupert Murdoch, the immigrant lad who bankrolled the flick.

Is movie criticism then inevitably a form of publicity? Or, put another way, is it even possible to position oneself outside the media system? (For most of the nineties, the national film industries that have inspired the greatest degree of cinephilic enthusiasm have been those of the designated outsiders China and Iran.) Who wants to be the festival's spoilsport?

There is a sense in which print criticism is obsolete anyway. After all, that which television ignores can barely be said to exist. While making his bitterly confessional *Ginger and Fred* (1985), Federico Fellini—for decades the popular notion of the individual film artiste—spoke "about the enchanted palace of TV." Taking its title from a pair of star-imitators, *Ginger and Fred* is set in a hermetic, controlled environment—the Cinecittà studio transformed into something like a mall—where entertainment feeds on entertainment. This is Fellini's complaint: In an image-glutted world aspiring to the complete commercial saturation of cable stations like MTV or the E! Channel, the movies have disappeared. Even the great Fellini has been out-Fellinied by TV.

Sneering at the ersatz, *Ginger and Fred* is filled with celebrity imitators—but, as Andy Warhol understood, celebrity is infinitely recuperable. Tim Burton's 1994 *Ed Wood* results from one of the most bankable filmmakers who ever lived expending the credit of his success in sincere, black-and-white tribute to the obscure, tawdry vision of the alcoholic, heterosexual transvestite and sometimes pornographer known affectionately as "the world's worst director." There is no such thing as negative publicity and to be the World's Worst Filmmaker is to personify a particular high concept.

Celebrity is absolute and *Ed Wood*, of course, is absolutely flawless—as fastidiously crafted as any previous Burton production. Burton's painstaking replication of Wood's haphazard compositions suggests a vanished Hollywood landmark, the Buena Park Palace of Living Art where the Mona Lisa or Whistler's Mother are reproduced as garish wax dioramas and the Venus De Milo is improved upon, not only for being colorized, but through the restoration of her lost limbs. *Ed Wood* is the Palace of Living Art in reverse. Art is not reproduced at kitsch; living kitsch is embalmed as art. Deliberately or not, Ed Wood served to deconstruct all manner of Hollywood pretense. *Ed Wood* builds it all back up, better than new—the movie's greatest irony is the liquidation of irony itself.

We know very well that occasionally—and this will also be true in the future—in the hand of an avant-gardist, a narrow-gauge film amateur, or a documentary hunter, a true film is still made, but the work of a critic cannot be concerned with such exceptional cases. It must instead deal with everyday production, which can only be subjected to aesthetic criticism when a production falls into the realm of aesthetics in principle; that is, when it has the possibility of creating works of art. Formerly, good films differed from mediocre ones only insofar as their quality was concerned; today they are the outsiders, remnants, things of a basically different nature from that which normally passes through the cinemas.
—Rudolf Arnheim, "The Film Critic of Tomorrow"

Yes, but . . . how does one resist? Is it by defending underground movies on the internet? Extolling entertainment that refuses to entertain? "*Mars Attacks!* is *meant* to be a kind of anti-entertainment," the critic for the celebrity-driven *New Yorker* wrote incredulously of Burton's megamillion dollar dada jape.

Similarly, the 1996 Jim Carrey vehicle, *The Cable Guy*—a jarringly violent, slapstick meditation on role-playing, performance, and the E! Channel totality —was attacked precisely for its own, unexpected attack on the system that produced it. "The shocking sight of a volatile comic talent in free fall," per the *New York Times* review, explicitly playing a stellar public servant (and architect of the E!-maginary Community), Carrey's $20 million "cable guy" *was* mass culture, precipitating the latent hostility felt even by the festival's most dogged celebrants.

The Mystery Science Theater 3000, for several seasons a regular feature on cable's Comedy Channel, inscribed an animated pair of wise-cracking humanoid spectators over their presentation of the worst, most inept drive-in features of the fifties—including, of course, those by Ed Wood. The aggression that *MST3K* (as its fans abbreviate it) directed at those hapless old movies that fell into its deconstruction machine is the inverse of the idiotic positive "reviews" that blurb whores can be relied upon to lavish on the most disposable current release. *MST3K* is a rearguard action too be sure, but we might learn from it.

Why settle for a mere laudatory blurb when the entire enterprise is available? Total cinema is our second nature and, as Griffith, Eisenstein, and the Surrealists long ago demonstrated, cinematic meaning is a factor of context and juxtaposition—not to mention purposeful derangement. (In a social sense, we might call this reeducation.) Sooner or later—or rather, sooner and sooner—the most elaborate $100 million blockbuster will fall into your hands as a $19.95 video cassette.

Just as the most radical recent examples of film criticism have, by and large, been "found footage" compilations like Craig Baldwin's *Tribulation 99*, Mark Rappaport's *Rock Hudson's Home Movies*, and Chantal Akerman's *Chantal Akerman by Chantal Akerman*, so the most important film critic of the past thirty-five years has, of course, been a filmmaker. "The greatest history is the history of the cinema," Jean-Luc Godard told Serge Daney.

That history will force those critics refusing the role of underpaid cheerleaders to themselves become historians—not to mention archivists, bricoleurs, spoilsports, pundits, entrepreneurs, anticonglomerate guerrilla fighters and, in general, masters of what is known in the Enchanted Palace as "counterprogramming."

1998

Stanley Cavell

In the parade of American film criticism, Stanley Cavell (b. 1926) occupies an anomalous, if significant, position. A Harvard professor of philosophy, he is not, by his own admission, a regular film reviewer or film scholar, yet he has written some of the most brilliant, deeply reflective books in the field. *Pursuits of Happiness*, his best-known work, maps a genre he calls the comedy of remarriage, scrutinizing screwball classics like *The Lady Eve* and *The Awful Truth* with a care for moral choices and character ambiguities usually reserved for texts on the order of Shakespeare's late comedies. Cavell is well aware that many will think him foolish to have taken so seriously what is, after all, "only a movie," but he argues that the movies, being an art form forever fixed, are worthy of being "examined and reexamined . . . read for their possibilities, like a field of battle or a crime scene." Central to Cavell's analysis of these battle-of-the-sexes comedies is his optimistic conviction that good marriages are possible, however long that may take, if they can evolve into a conversation between men and women as friends and equals. Given this emphasis on conversation, it is no wonder that he has focused on movies made in a period that valued well-written, leisurely dialogue.

◆

Cons and Pros: *The Lady Eve*

We can make a start in reading *The Lady Eve* (1941) without considering its generic allegiances and their Shakespearean background. From the name in its title and from the animated title cards we know that Preston Sturges is going to present us with some comic version of the story of the expulsion from the Garden of Eden. And sure enough, the film opens with a young man and his guardian shadow leaving a tropical island on which he has been devoted to what he calls the pursuit of knowledge. That something is mixed up in this knowledge is confirmed at once by the camera's drifting, as if bored, or embarrassed, away from his delivery of his farewell speech declaring the purity of his pursuit, to discover his shadow leading a nubile native down to the shore, the pair sporting chains of flowers. This line of story is picked up as the leading lady attracts the young man's attention by clunking him on the head with an apple, and again by the intimate enmity revealed between the man's snake and the woman's dreams. Their relationship is broken, anyway their plans are, by the man's coming into new knowledge. As if this were not enough, we are shown the fall of the man repeated over and over, and the idea of "falling" is explicitly and differently interpreted by each of two characters (Curly and Eve), as if daring us to interpret it for ourselves. This line of argument has a most satisfactory conclusion in the man's closing declaration that he does not want to know. Had our common ancestor said that in the beginning, there would be no question of endings.

But even if we consider that Shakespearean romance itself tends to invoke the myth of Eden, such considerations merely scratch at the surface iconography of this film. Of course these considerations also merely pick up superficial items in the myth of Eden, or pick them up superficially. The myth is after all about the creation of woman and about the temptability of man. Now *The Lady Eve* is about a con artist (Barbara Stanwyck, introduced as Jean, reintroduced as Eve) who calls herself, because she is a woman, an adventuress; and it is equally about the gullibility of a man (Henry Fonda), forever being called a mug or a sucker. (Jean's name for him is Hopsy; Eve's name for him, and the world's, is Charles). But can the film be seen to be about the creation of a woman?

Jean's central con of this man requires her reappearance as the Lady Eve. Her associate Curly (Eric Blore)—"Sir Alfred McGlennon Keith at the moment"—explains her (re)appearance by telling Hopsy/Charles the story of Cecilia, or The Coachman's Daughter, filling him, as Sir Alfred puts it, with "handsome coachmen, elderly earls, young wives, and two little girls who look exactly alike"—that is, with the very farcing of romance. Jean as Eve continues Sir Alfred's image by asking, "You mean he actually swallowed that?" and is told, "Like a wolf"—as though this story was the biggest of the fruits of the tree of knowledge that he was to be handed. Eve has her own explanation of Charles's readiness to accept her story (that is, to accept her as not Jean), namely, that they really do not look the same to one another as they did on the boat because they no longer feel as they did then about one another. On the boat, she says, "we had this awful yen for one another." Whatever the psychological or philosophical validity and interest of her explanation, it is a fragment of a reasonable view of what romance is. Quoting one editor of *The Tempest*: "For romance deals in marvelous events and solves its problems through metamorphoses and recognition scenes—through, in other words, transformations of perception."* By the time the pair find themselves alone again, riding horses through wooded paths, compelled by the beauty of a sunset to dismount and look, and the man has begun repeating his own self-declared romance to the

*Robert Langbaum, introduction to the Signet edition.

woman (a line of story he had originally feigned to criticize as "dull as a drug-store novel")—a repetition even the horse tries to tell him is inappropriate—by that time it may dawn on us that Preston Sturges is trying to tell us that tales of romance are inherently feats of cony catching, of conning, making gulls or suckers of their audience, and that film, with its typical stories of love set on luxurious ships or in mansions and containing beautiful people and horses and sunsets and miraculously happy endings, is inherently romantic.

Granted, then, that this film does invite us to consider the source of romance, what is the implication? That we, as the audience of film, are fated, or anyway meant, to be gulled by film, including this film? This makes our position seem the same as Hopsy/Charles's. But don't we also feel that our position is equally to be allied with the woman's, at the man's expense? Who are these people and what are their positions?

Let us approach them by getting deeper into this film's identifying of itself with the tradition of romance. Take first the feature of the action's moving from a starting place of impasse to a place Frye calls "the green world," a place in which perspective and renewal are to be achieved. In *A Midsummer Night's Dream* this place is a forest inhabited by fairies, explicitly a place of dreams and magic; in *The Winter's Tale* the place is the rural society of Bohemia; in *The Merchant of Venice* the equivalent of such a place contains oracular caskets; in *The Tempest* it occupies the entire setting of the action, with the framing larger world supplied by narrative speeches; in *Bringing Up Baby*, *The Awful Truth*, and *Adam's Rib*, in addition to *The Lady Eve*—that is, in more than half of the definitive remarriage comedies of Hollywood—this locale is called Connecticut. Strictly speaking, in *The Lady Eve* the place is called "Conneckticut," and it is all but explicitly cited as a mythical location, since nobody is quite sure how you get there, or anyway how a lady gets there. This is Preston Sturges showing off at once his powers of parody and his knowledge of his subject, and giving us fair warning: in his green world the mind or plot will not only not be cleared and restored, it will be darkened and frozen.

Another feature of Shakespeare's late romances is an expansion of the father-daughter relationship. (This goes together with the fact that these late plays emphasize the reconciliation of an older generation at the expense of a central interest in the plight of young lovers. The comedy of remarriage is a natural inheritor of this shift of interest away from the very young.) *The Lady Eve* emphasizes the father-daughter relationship as strongly as *It Happened One Night* and *The Philadelphia Story* do, but it goes quite beyond its companions in the genre by endowing its father—as Shakespeare endows a number of his late fathers—with the power, or to use Shakespeare's word, with the art, of magic.

That Harry's use of cards is meant to stand for a power possessed not merely by a shark but by a magus is declared as he sits on his daughter's bed dressed in a wizard's robe, deals "fifths" for her admiration, describing the trick as "just virtuosity," saying "you don't really need it"; and as she thereupon asks him, in their tenderest moment together, to tell her her fortune, as if for her to ask this man for a professional reading of the cards is to ask him for his blessing. In *All's Well That Ends Well* the heroine has inherited her father's book and knack of magic, which proves to be the key to the happiness she is awarded. The most famous of Shakespeare's father-magicians is the central figure of *The Tempest*, the play in which renewal or reconciliation or restoration is shown to exact the task of the laying aside of magic. I understand an allusion to this task of Prospero's, or a summary of it, when Jean returns to her cabin after a day with Hopsy and announces their love for one another to her father, declaring that she would give anything to be—that she is going, she corrects herself, to be— everything he thinks she is, everything he wants her to be (a declaration coming the day after she had created and destroyed for him the wisdom of having an ideal in an object of love), and then saying to her father, "And you'll go straight too, Harry, won't you?" "Straight to," he asks, "where?" (This mode of allusion or summary might be compared with another allusion from our genre to *The Tempest* that amounts, to my ear, almost to an echo. I am thinking of the late moment of awakening in *The Philadelphia Story*—comparable to the late moment at which Miranda more fully realizes the imminence of her departure into human womanhood and human relationship, exclaiming "How beauteous mankind is!"—at which Katharine Hepburn says, in a sudden access of admiration, "I think men are wonderful.")

I do not require immediate acceptance of Hollywood fast talk as our potential equivalent of Shakespearean thought, and yet I will have at some stage to ask attention for at least one further moment of thematic coincidence between *The Lady Eve* and *The Tempest*, the coincidence of their conclusions in an achievement of forgiveness. Such attention would mean nothing to my purpose apart from a live experience of the film within which it holds its own against the Shakespearean pressure. I mean, at a minimum, that we are to ponder the experience of this man's and this woman's concluding requests to one another to be forgiven; that this bears pondering. Two ways not to bear it are either to conclude that their treatment of one another has been unforgiveable, in which case the ending of the film is either cynical or deluded by the ideology of Hollywood; or to conclude that there is no outstanding problem since human beings are fated so far as they have progressed, politically or privately, to cynicism, insincerity, and delusion in their relations with one another, above all in their dealings with love and marriage, so the film is after all realistic in its assessment both of their needing forgiveness and of their incapacities to grant it.

The unacceptability, or instability, of each of these conclusions (each gnawed at by the other) is a reason, I believe, that a typical reaction to such films is to develop a headache. (Then it may be such a reaction that produces the title "madcap comedies" for such films.) We are not yet ready to try to think our way beyond this reaction, but I mention that Frye calls particular attention to the special nature of the forgiving and forgetting asked for at the conclusion of romantic comedy: "Normally, we can forget in this way only when we wake up from a dream, when we pass from one world into another, and we often have to think of the main action of a comedy as 'the mistakes of a night,' as taking place in a dream or nightmare world that the final scene suddenly removes us from and thereby makes illusory."* *Bringing Up Baby* and *Adam's Rib* also explicitly climax or conclude with a request for forgiveness, and *The Awful Truth* and *The Philadelphia Story* do so implicitly. *His Girl Friday* notably does not, which is a way of understanding the terrible darkness of that comedy.

I should perhaps pause, still barely inside the film, to say that I am not claiming that these films of remarriage are as good as Shakespearean romantic comedies. Not that this is much of a disclaimer: practically nothing else is as good either. But I am claiming a specificness of inheritance which is itself more than enough of a problem to justify. Another two sentences from Frye will locate my claim: "All the important writers of English comedy since Jonson have cultivated the comedy of manners with its realistic illusion and not Shakespeare's romantic and stylized kind . . . The only place where the tradition of Shakespearean romantic comedy has survived with any theatrical success is, as we should expect, in opera."† I am in effect adding that the Shakespearean tradition also survives in film (thus implying that film may provide an access for us to that tradition) and adding as well that such claims are all but completely up in the air, and will pretty much go on being left in the air by what I have been or will be saying here. The claim sits in the quality of one's experience of film, in the nature of film, and I am at best assuming that experience and that nature, and preparing the ground for inviting the experience of others.

I have sometimes found it useful to think of the nature of film by comparing what camera and projection bring to a script with what music brings to

*A *Natural Perspective* (New York: Columbia University Press, 1965), p. 128.
†Ibid., pp. 24, 25.

a libretto. Whatever the strains of the comparison its point here would be to locate what it is, in any medium that can seriously be thought of as maintaining a connection with Shakespeare's plays, that bears the brunt of his poetry. The signal weakness in comparing the poetry of the camera (of, so to speak, the photogenetic poetry of film itself) with the music of opera is that this misses, as the comparison of film with theater generally misses, the mode of uniqueness of the events on the screen. Plays may be variously produced, and productions may or may not change in the course of a run, and may be revived; films can only be rerun or remade. You can think of the events on a screen equally as permanent and as evanescent. The poetry of the final appeals for forgiveness in *The Lady Eve* is accordingly a function of the way just this man and this woman half walk, half run down a path of gangways, catching themselves in an embrace on each landing, and how just this sequence of framings and attractions of the camera follow these bodies as they inflect themselves to a halt before a closed door, and just the way these voices mingle their breaths together. These moments are no more repeatable than a lifetime is. The uniqueness of the events of film is perhaps better thought of in comparison with jazz than with opera. Here the point of contact is that the tune is next to nothing; the performer—with just that temperament, that range, that attack, that line, that relation to the pulse of the rhythm—is next to everything. Of course a session can be recorded; that is the sense in which it can in principle be made permanent. But that session cannot be performed again; that is the sense in which it is evanescent. Succeeding performances of a play arise from the production, not independently from the play; succeeding sessions of a jazz group arise from the state and relations of the players, and if from a preceding performance, then as a comment on it. (Modern performance may negate such distinctions; it does not annihilate them.) I daresay the themes moving from Shakespeare to film are richer than the tunes of jazz. But the matter of life and death, of whether these themes actually survive in film, is a matter of whether they find natural transformations into the new medium, as in moving from life in the water to life in the air. The feature of the medium of film I have just emphasized suggests that acting for film is peculiarly related to the dimension of improvisation, that there is for film a natural dominance of improvisation over prediction, though of course each requires (its own form of) technique and preparation. (This dominance is a specification of a description I have given elsewhere concerning film's upheaval of certain emphases established in theater, namely, that for film there is in acting a natural ascendancy of actor over character. This matter of the film actor's individuality will come back.)

I was talking about the emphasis on the father-daughter relation in these dramas. The classical obligations of the father in romance are to provide his daughter's education and to protect her virginity. These obligations clearly go together; say they add up to suiting her for marriage. Prospero describes or enacts his faithfulness to these obligations toward Miranda with didactic explicitness. In comedies of remarriage the *fact* of virginity is evidently not what is at stake. Yet all the more, it seems to me, is the *concept* of virginity still at stake, or what the fact meant is at stake—something about the possession of chasteness or innocence, whatever one's physically determinable condition, and about whether one's valuable intactness, one's individual exclusiveness, has been well lost, that is, given over for something imaginably better, for the exclusiveness of a union. The overarching question of the comedies of remarriage is precisely the question of what constitutes a union, what makes these two into one, what binds, you may say what sanctifies in marriage. When is marriage an honorable estate? In raising this question these films imply not only that the church has lost its power over this authentication but that society as a whole cannot be granted it. In thus questioning the legitimacy of marriage, the question of the legitimacy of society is simultaneously raised, even allegorized.

The specific form authentication takes varies in the various films. All, however, invoke the continuing question of innocence, sometimes by asserting that innocence is not awarded once for all, but is always to be rewon (I take this to be a way of telling the story of *Adam's Rib*); sometimes by asking what it means to lose innocence, and even to ask how the burden of chastity can be put off, or anyway shared (*The Philadelphia Story* is about the mystery in putting aside what we may call psychological virginity, an issue of Blake's poetry). In "Leopards in Connecticut" (Chapter 3) I argue that *Bringing Up Baby* contains, even consists of, an extended allegory of this question of sharing the loss of chastity; but a fully hilarious consciousness of the problem occurs right in the first of these films, with *It Happened One Night*, where the mutual happiness in the loss of virginity, or the happiness of mutuality, is said to require nothing less than what authorized the tumbling of the walls of Jericho, trumpet and all.

These parodies are themselves further parodied in *The Lady Eve*, as befits its mode, in its use of the "slimy snake" as an object of terror to the woman, conscious and unconscious—an object from which she awakens screaming, saying she dreamed about it all night. We are being clunked on the head with an invitation to read this through Freud. But the very psychological obviousness of it serves the narrative as an equivalent, or avatar, of the issue of innocence. It demonstrates that sexuality is for this sophisticated and forceful woman still a problem. No doubt this pokes fun at the older problem of vir-

ginity; what used to be a matter of cosmic public importance is now a private
matter of what we call emotional difficulty. We live in reduced circumstances.
But the obviousness also, I think, pokes fun at our sophistication, when that
goes with a claim that we have grown up from ancient superstition. If virginity
was a superficial and even idolatrous interpretation of the problem of innocence, with what has our sophistication replaced this idol?

One consequence of our sophistication is that if we are to continue to provide ourselves with the pleasure of romantic comedies, with this imagination
of happiness, we are going to require narratives that do not depend on the
physics of virginity but rather upon the metaphysics of innocence. In practice
this poses two narrative requirements: that we discover, or recover, romance
within the arena of marriage itself; and that a pair be capable of discussing with
interest not merely the promises of love (topics of courtship—described by
Harry in *The Lady Eve* as "whatever it is young people talk about") but the
facts of marriage, which the facts of life they have shared require them to talk
about. Comedies of remarriage typically contain not merely philosophical discussions of marriage and of romance, but metaphysical discussions of the concept that underlines both the classical problem of comedy and that of marriage,
namely, the problem and the concept of identity—either in the form of what
becomes of an individual, or of what has become of two individuals. On film
this metaphysical issue is more explicitly conducted through the concept of
difference—either the difference between men and women, or between innocence and experience, or between one person and another, or between one circumstance and another—all emblematized by the difference, hence the
sameness, between a marriage and a remarriage.

We got into the topics of virginity and chastity or innocence in naming the
father-magician's obligations. The second obligation was that of seeing to his
daughter's education, and really we are already addressing this topic in registering the necessity for philosophical or metaphysical discussion in these film
comedies, because the form the woman's education takes in them is her sub-
jection to fits of lecturing by the men in her life. For some reason Katharine
Hepburn seems to inspire her men with the most ungovernable wishes to lecture her. Four of them take turns at it in *The Philadelphia Story*, and throughout
Adam's Rib Spencer Tracy is intermittently on the verge of haranguing her. His
major speeches take the form of discourses, one of them presenting his theory
of marriage as a legal contract. Rosalind Russell does not escape this fate even
from the Cary Grant of *His Girl Friday*. In *The Lady Eve*, the man's tendency to
lecture nobly is treated to an exposure of pompous self-ignorance so relentless
that we must wonder how either party will ever recover from it. (The woman

describes this exposure as teaching a lesson, the spirit of which is evidently revenge; earlier she had saved him from what he calls "a terrible lesson your father almost taught me," namely, about games of so-called chance. Or was the lesson about disobeying this woman? She expressed particular impatience with him, quite maternal impatience, in saying, "You promised me you would not play cards with Harry again.")

Comic resolutions depend upon an acquisition in time of self-knowledge; say this is a matter of learning who you are. In classical romance this may be accomplished by learning the true story of your birth, where you come from, which amounts to learning the identity of your parents. In comedies of remarriage it requires learning, or accepting, your sexual identity, the acknowledgment of desire. Both forms of discovery are in service of the authorization or authentication of what is called a marriage. The women of our films listen to their lectures because they know they need to learn something further about themselves, or rather to undergo some change, or creation, even if no one knows how the knowledge and change are to arrive. (It turns out not to be clear what the obligations are for suiting oneself for remarriage.) In *It Happened One Night, His Girl Friday, The Awful Truth*, and *The Philadelphia Story* the woman imagines solving the problem of desire, or imagines that the problem will take care of itself, by marrying the opposite of the man she took first—an action variously described as the forgoing of adventure, and choosing on the rebound, and the buying of an annuity. Even if this man is not in fact older than her former husband, he is a father or senex figure, who must be overcome in order for the happiness of a comic resolution to happen. What our films show is that in the world of film if the woman's real father exists, he is never on the side of this father figure but, on the contrary, actively supports the object of her true desire, that is, the man she is trying, and trying not, to leave.

If this acceptance by the father of the daughter's sexuality, which means of her separation or divorce from him, the achieving of her human equality with him, is part of the happiness of these women, of their high capacities for intelligence, wit, and freedom, it also invites a question about the limitations of these comedies, about what it is their laughter is seeking to cover. The question concerns the notable absence of the woman's mother in these comedies. (The apparent exceptions to this rule serve to prove it.) The mothers that do figure in them are, blatantly, the mothers of the senex figures, separation from whom would not be contemplated. No account of these comedies will be satisfactory that does not explain this absence, or avoidance. I offer three guesses about regions from which an explanation will have to be formed. Psychologically, or dramatically, the central relation of a mother and son has been the stuff of tragedy and melodrama rather than of comedy and romance. (Shaw's *Pygmalion*, explicitly about the creation of a woman, is a notable exception to this rule; here the hero and his mother are happy inspirations to one another. But no less notably, if the central man and woman of this play find their way together at the end, it is explicitly to occur without marriage and its special intimacies.) We seem to be telling ourselves that there is a closeness children may bear to the parent of the opposite sex which is enabling for a daughter but crippling for a son. Eve will say to Charles on the train, "I knew you would be both husband and father to me." She says it to deflate him for his insincerity and hypocrisy, but what she says is true, and it is the expression of a workable passion. Whereas no one would be apt to hope for happiness (given the options we still perceive) should a man say to his bride, "I knew you would be both wife and mother to me." Whether you take this as a biological or a historical destiny will depend on where you like your destines from. Mythically, the absence of the mother continues the idea that the creation of the woman is the business of men; even, paradoxically, when the creation is that of the so-called new woman, the woman of equality. Here we seem to be telling ourselves that while there is, and is going to be, a new woman, as in the Renaissance there was a new man, nobody knows where she is to come from. The place she is to arrive is a mythological locale called America. Socially, it seems to me, the absence of the woman's mother in these films of the thirties betokens a guilt, or anyway, puzzlement, toward the generation of women preceding the generation of the central women of our films—the generation that won the right to vote without at the same time winning the issues in terms of which voting mattered enough. They compromised to the verge of forgetting themselves. Their legacy is that their daughters will not have to settle. This legacy may be exhilarating, but it is also threatening.

Complementing the inability to imagine a mother for the woman is the inability to envision children for her, to imagine her as a mother. The absence of children in these films is a universal feature of them. What is its point? One might take its immediate function to be that of purifying the discussion, or the possibility, of divorce, which would be swamped by the presence of children. But what this means, on my view of these comedies, is that the absence of children further purifies the discussion of marriage. The direct implication is that while marriage may remain the authorization for having children, children are not an authentication of marriage. (This is an explicit and fundamental consequence of Milton's great tract on Divorce, a document I take to have intimate implications in the comedy of remarriage, as will emerge. By the way, the only claim among related comedies I know that a child is justified apart from marriage, even apart from any stable relationship with a man, merely on the ground that you bore it and want it and can make it happy, occurs in Bergman's *Smiles of a Summer Night*, I suppose the last comedy to study remarriage.)

But the films of our genre are so emphatic in their avoidance of children for the central marriage that its point must be still more specific. In *His Girl Friday* the woman's choice to remarry is explicitly a decision to forgo children as well as to forgo the gaining of a mother-in-law. In *The Awful Truth*, what room there is for a child is amply occupied by a fox terrier. In *The Philadelphia Story*, Grant's life without Hepburn is said by him to be, or described as, one in which he might as well part with a boat he devoted a significant piece of his life to designing and building—named *True Love*—on the ground that it is only good for two people. He means that to mean that one person is one too few for it, but his words equally mean that three is one too many. In *Adam's Rib*, as the principal pair are preparing some leftovers for supper, having chosen to stay home alone on cook's night off, there is a knock at the door which they know to be their wearisome childlike neighbor from across the hall. Tracy says to Hepburn, "Now remember, there's just enough for two." (I have not included George Stevens's *Woman of the Year* in my central group of comedies of remarriage because I do not find it the equal of the six or seven I take as definitive. But it speaks radically to the present issue. In it Spencer Tracy takes a child back to an orphanage from which Hepburn had adopted it out of concern for her public image as a leading woman. It is equally to the point that the older woman in this film, said by Hepburn always to have been her ideal, is not her mother but marries her father late in life, in the course of this film, in a scene that enables the younger woman to try for a reconciliation of her own.)

I do not think we are being told that marriages as happy as the ones in these films promise to be are necessarily incompatible with children, that the forgoing of children is the necessary price of the romance of marriage. But we are at least being told that children, if they appear, must appear as intruders. Then one's obligation would be to make them welcome, to make room for them, to make them be at home, hence to transform one's idea of home, showing them that they are not responsible for their parents' happiness, nor for their parents' unhappiness. This strikes me as a very reasonable basis on which to work out a future.

(It is perhaps worth making explicit that only when a period of culture is reached in which contraception is sufficiently effective and there is sufficient authorization for employing it conscientiously is it pertinent to speak of marriage quite in this way. There was a time—perhaps lived climactically in the generation of the absent mothers—when for a woman prepared to demand the kind of autonomy demanded by the women in our films, chastity, or anyway the absence of intimacy with men, would have presented itself as autonomy's clearest guarantee. The issue then would have been whether to have a recognized sexual existence at all, and hence, if marriage requires a sexual existence, whether to marry. But then if such a woman as dominates our films does choose to marry, risking children; if, that is, she requires a marriage in which children *can* be made welcome; then she is looking for a household economy which can undergo this transformation without her being *abandoned* to motherhood. This all the more for her puts the issue of marriage before the issue of children. The question of pregnancy is surely one of the reasons that feminism is thought to lack a sense of fun. Yet each of the women of our films is who she is in part because of her sense of fun, a sense apart from which the man in her life does not wish to exist. The question becomes what the conditions are—and first the requirements upon the man—under which that sense of fun can be exercised. So the conditions of the comic become the question of our genre of comedy.)

The insistence of these films on the absence of children seems to me to say something more particular still. Almost without exception these films allow the principal pair to express the wish to be children again, or perhaps to be children together. In part this is a wish to make room for playfulness within the gravity of adulthood, in part it is a wish to be cared for first, and unconditionally (e.g., without sexual demands, though doubtless not without sexual favors). If it could be managed, it would turn the tables on time, making marriage the arena and the discovery of innocence. *Bringing Up Baby*, on my account, is the most elaborate working out of this wish, but the value of it is fully present, for example, in the repeated remark of *The Philadelphia Story* that the divorced pair "grew up together"; and when Spencer Tracy goes into his crying act at the close of *Adam's Rib* (and we already know that their private names for one another are Pinky and Pinkie), he means to be demonstrating a difference or sameness between men and women, but he is simultaneously showing that he feels free to act like a child around this not obviously maternal woman. *The Awful Truth* ends with the pair dressed up in clothes too big for them, then being impersonated by two figurines doing a childish jig and disappearing together into a clock that might as well be a playhouse. This is in turn a further working out of the woman's having in the previous sequence put on a song-and-dance act in which she at once impersonates a low-class nightclub performer and pretends to be the man's sister, thus staking a final claim to have known him intimately forever.

The form taken by the search for childhood and innocence in *The Lady Eve* is given in that fantasy or romance the man tells the woman with its moral that he feels that they have known one another all their lives and hence that he has always loved her, by which he says he means that he has never loved anyone else. His attempt to repeat this story and to draw this moral again in Connecticut with Eve presents the most difficult moment of this comedy, the moment at which, as I put it earlier, their behavior toward one another appears unforgivable, hence the moment at which we may doubt most completely that a happy end for them can be arrived at. Some such moment must be faced in any good comic narrative; Sturges carries the moment to virtuosic heights in this film. And the question we have known awaits us in whether he succeeds in bringing the consequences safely to earth, or in blowing them sky high, in any case whether the film arrives at something we will call happiness for each of this pair and whether we are happy to see them arrive there.

But just what is the difficulty of this most difficult moment? Presumably that in repeating his romantic vision to Eve the man loses all claim to sincerity, which was really all that has recommended him to our attention. His story was hard enough to listen to the first time, when he told it to Jean, but we went with it because the woman's belief ratified it for us. On his repetition of it we do not know whether to be embarrassed more for him or for ourselves in being asked to witness this awful exposure. But how is his insincerity exposed? It is exposed only on the condition that we take him not to know or believe Eve and Jean to be one and the same woman. But must we so take him? I do not, of course, claim that he does know or believe that they are the same, that he is having to do with just one woman. But we have had continued evidence that he is in a trance (his word for this is "cockeyed"); and the fact of the matter is that he *is* saying his words to the same woman. What he says to Jean at the end is hard to deny: "It would never have happened except she looked so exactly like you." Furthermore, the comic falls the man keeps taking are more Freudian clunks on the head to tell us—as in the case of her reaction to his snake—that genuine feeling has been aroused, and moreover the *same* feeling that had been aroused by the woman on the boat whom he encountered by falling and who will once more enter his recognition through that same route of access. So his inner state as well as his external senses tell him that she is the same person. (So maybe the horse stands not merely for a horse laugh but also for the man's own natural instincts, but baffled by his efforts at domestication.) His intellectual denial of sameness accordingly lets him spiritually carve her in half, taking the good without the bad, the lady without the woman, the ideal without the reality, the richer without the poorer. He will be punished for this.

If we understand his perceptions and his feelings to be the same now as then, then we must understand ourselves to be embarrassed not by the openness of his insincerity but by the helplessness of his sincerity. He desperately wishes to say these words of romantic innocence to just this woman, even as she desperately wished to hear them. (This was a piece of her education.) Yet knowing this she feeds him with the fruit of the tree of stupidity. For this she will be punished.

Note the confluence of conventions Sturges activates in making up his story about identical twins. He gets the narrative and psychological complexities of early romantic comedy, with its workings out of misidentifications and climaxes of recognition, together with a succinct declaration of the nature of film by way of showing its distinction from theater. For the stage, a convention allows two people dramatized as identical twins to be treated as though they cannot be told apart. For the screen, where two characters can be played by one person, and even shown side by side (a fact enjoyed in films from *Dr. Jekyll and Mr. Hyde* to *The Prisoner of Zenda*), a comparable convention allows a person to be treated as though he or she *can* be told, so to speak, apart from himself or herself, even where—and here Sturges rubs it in—she looks no different from one role to the other. If we had taken Charles (or to the extent that we take him) simply to believe that Eve was not the same woman as Jean, then (to that extent) we had been gulled as he had been—by the same story of romance; or anyway gulled at one remove from that story—by the film that suggests that he could simply believe such a story. (There are theories that believe so too, that assume that we do not know the difference between projections of things and real things and that therefore projections of reality are "illusions" of it.) How could we have believed this?

You might wish to give some further psychological explanation of the man here, but that would be to compete with him on his own level, for he has what he calls a piece of "psychology" that explains away to himself Eve's strategy. I think the ambiguity about whether he does or does not believe in her difference from herself is as fixed for us as it is for him. What it is fixed by is the photograph Hopsy is shown in order to reveal to him the (criminal) identity of Jean, along with Harry and Gerald. Hopsy learns this identity not from the photograph itself but from reading the caption printed on its back. The information contained in the caption is, of course, not news to us; what is news for us is the photograph itself. As it fills the screen, slightly inflected so as clearly to resist coincidence with the photographic field of the moving film images, what we are shown, and are meant to recognize that we are being shown, is a photograph of Barbara Stanwyck, Charles Coburn, and Melville Cooper. Or at the very least or most we are shown a photograph of Barbara Stanwyck as Jean

Harrington, of Charles Coburn as Harry, and of Melville Cooper as Gerald. (It would be just like Sturges were the object we are shown to be, what it seems to be, a production still from the set of this film.) What this presenting of the photograph means to me is that we have a problem of identification isomorphic with this man's problem, one which lets his deluded or self-manufactured problem get a foothold with us, one which associates us with him in the position of gull. The relation between Eve and Jean is not an issue for us, but the nature of the relation of both Eve and Jean to Barbara Stanwyck, or to some real woman called Barbara Stanwyck, is an issue for us—an issue in viewing films generally, but declared, acknowledged as an issue in this film by the way it situates the issue of identity.

It is a leading thought of mine about the film comedies of remarriage that they each have a way of acknowledging this issue, of harping on the identity of the real women cast in each of these films, and each by way of some doubling or splitting of her projected presence. I have already mentioned Irene Dunne's scene of impersonation in *The Awful Truth*; this bears comparison with Katharine Hepburn's gun moll routine in *Bringing Up Baby*, which refers back to it (by using the name "Jerry the Nipper"). From *It Happened One Night* through *The Philadelphia Story* to *Adam's Rib*, this splitting is investigated as one between the public and the private, where the public is typically symbolized by the presence of newspapers (or a news magazine)—a major iconographical or allegorical item in virtually every one of the films of our genre. It seems that film, in contrast to the publicity of newspapers, symbolizes the realm of privacy. In *Adam's Rib* this symbolism is most explicitly worked out as a split or doubling between what happens during the day and what happens at night, which amounts to a split or doubling between reality and something else, call it dreaming. The idea of the privacy of film is both confirmed and denied in *Adam's Rib*, say it is puzzled, by the showing on the first night of a home movie. (In another of George Stevens's films adjacent to our genre, *Talk of the Town*, the mode in which a copy of a newspaper is presented in order to reveal a hero's identity at the same time reveals newspapers to be things full of borscht. Again, by the way, this moment in which a front-page photo of a wanted man is the object of concern to two men and a woman about to have a meal together must be a reference to a moment in Hitchcock's *39 Steps*. We have here, I believe, one genre claiming its relationship to another.)

From the first of the major films of remarriage, *It Happened One Night*, the genre is in possession of the knowledge that the split or doubling is between civilization and eros. Newspapers are a medium of scandal, but what they mean by erotic scandal consists of triangles, crimes of passion, sensational marriages, and ugly divorces. What our films suggest is that the scandal is love itself, true love; and that while it is the nature of the erotic to form a stumbling block to a reasonable, civilized existence, call it the political, human happiness nevertheless goes on demanding satisfaction in both realms. This is in effect the terrible lesson Jean/Eve teaches Hopsy/Charles. When she vows to her father that she is going to be everything the man wants her to be, she means it as a blessing to them both. When she is treated to his treacherous lack of trust, or his overtrust in the wrong thing, the public thing, she turns the blessing into a curse. As if to say: Even after you know our passion for one another, and our fun together, you are still a sucker for romance and cannot acknowledge that passion may have a past of flesh and blood; very well, I'll show you the reality of your ideal; I'll give you a new perspective in Connecticut; I'll turn the night into an endless day for you. You refused to believe in me earlier, now I'll give you something you will feel compelled to believe; you thought you believed the worst about me before, here is something you will find worse. She is gambling, carrying out her instruction the night of their honeymoon on the train, that he will take the bait that makes the taker mad. Had he found a sense of humor to outlast his credulity and her anger, he would be able to charge her with stalling on her wedding night by putting up a barrier, between her and her husband, of a thousand and one bawdy tales. The possibility that she is stalling further compromises the purity of the lesson she thinks she is teaching, makes it even funnier and, if possible, even uglier.

It is not news for men to try, as Thoreau puts it, to walk in the direction of their dreams, to join the thoughts of day and night, of the public and the private, to pursue happiness. Nor is it news that this will require a revolution, of the social or of the individual constitution, or both. What is news is the acknowledgment that a woman might attempt this direction, even that a man and a woman might try it together and call *that* the conjugal. (It is roughly what Emerson did call that; but then, as you would expect, he did not expect to find it between real men and women.) For this we require a new creation of woman, call it a creation of the new woman; and what the problems of identification broached in these films seem to my mind to suggest is that this creation is a metaphysical enterprise, exacting a reconception of the world. How could it not? It is a new step in the creation of the human. The happiness in these comedies is honorable because they raise the right issues; they end in undermining and in madcap and in headaches because there is, as yet at least, no envisioned settlement for these issues.

How does the film at hand end? How can any happiness at all be found in this revenge comedy?

Before drawing to its, and closer to our, conclusion, I note the most daring declaration in this film's awareness of itself, of its existence as a film. This comes by way of its virtual identification of the images seen on the screen with the images seen in a mirror. One plausible understanding of our view as Jean holds her hand mirror up to nature—or to society—and looks surreptitiously at what is behind her is that we are looking through the viewfinder of a camera. In that case this film is claiming that the objects it presents to us have as much independent physical reality as the objects reflected in the mirror, namely, full independent physical reality. Their psychological independence is a further matter, however, since we are shown Jean creating their inner lives for us, putting words into their mouths ("Haven't we met some place before? Aren't you the Herman Fishman I went to the Louisville Manual Training School with? You aren't?"), and blocking their movements for them ("Look a little to your left, bookworm. A little further. There!"), and evaluating their performances ("Holy smoke, the dropped kerchief!"). We may take the world she has in her hand as images in her crystal ball, but however we take it we are informed that this film knows itself to have been written and directed and photographed and edited. (Each of our films shows its possession of this knowledge of itself. *The Lady Eve* merely insists upon it most persistently.) That the woman is some kind of stand-in for the role of director fits our understanding that the man, the sucker, is a stand-in for the role of audience. As this surrogate she informs us openly that the attitude the film begins with is one of cynicism or skepticism, earned by brilliance, and that she is fully capable of being thus open and yet tripping us up so that we are brought from our privacy onto her ground, where her control of us will be all but complete. Frye notes that the inclusion of some event particularly hard to believe is a common feature of Shakespeare's comedy, as if placed there to exact the greatest effort from his dramatic powers and from his audience's imagination. And it is well recognized that the final two of Shakespeare's romances, *The Winter's Tale* and *The Tempest*, most clearly and repeatedly give consciousness to their own artifice, that they are plays with casts, as if no responsibility of art shall go unacknowledged. Then it may be in their awareness of themselves, their responsibility for themselves, that the films of remarriage most deeply declare, and earn, their allegiance to Shakespearean romance.

Further discussion of the significance of the phenomenon of mirroring in this film would have to take up the passage in which, the morning after Jean's triumph over her father at cards ("Know any more games, Harry?") and her ensuing receipt of Hopsy's proposal on the bow of the ship, she and her father begin an interview (as she is seated before the standing dressing mirrors in her stateroom and her father enters from the far door behind her, reflected in the mirror, and walks toward his reflection across the room to her) looking at one another in the mirror, speaking to each other's reflection first, communicating through the looking glass. What does this mean in the context? The mood is one of sober, even pained, sincerity and tenderness between them, as though the reflection of mirrors is not to be ceded to the realm of appearances but provides an access, or image, of self-reflection and thoughtfulness, of a due awareness of the world's awareness of you, hence of the other side of its reality to you. (The conjunction of mirrors with moments of sincerity, in a world of fashion and gossip, occurs notably in *Rules of the Game*.) In this interview the father warns his daughter that her admirer might not respond well to the truth about her and her father's lives: "You are going to tell him about us, aren't you?" She replies that a man who couldn't accept the truth wouldn't be much of a man. But all the time they and their reflections are visible together to us, showing us that while these two can view the two worlds they move between, the one world from the conning perspective of the other, they may not occupy either wholly, or not at the same time (as with a thing and its filmed projection). Here the camera especially ponders the meaning of a point of view, seeing these people and seeing what these people see at one and the same time, a feat that they have to forgo in order to stand face to face.

One more preliminary to a conclusion, again having to do with fathers and movies and reflections that declare the presence (or distance) of real people. The opening of the shift to Connecticut discovers and follows Eugene Pallette walking down a long flight of period stairs as he sings, thoughtfully, "Come landlord fill the flowing bowl until it doth run over. For tonight we'll merry merry be, tomorrow we'll be sober." Criticism is being challenged to net in mere words the hilarity, the surrealism, the dream perfection of these juxtapositions; of its being just this human being doing just these things in just this setting. Here is Preston Sturges glorying in the modes of conjunction specific to film, and some specific to Hollywood, and indeed to America, making sure that we know that he knows what he is doing. The pivot of these conjunctions is that voice, declared by, of all things, singing, which declares the presence (by absence) of the only man who could possess it, call him Eugene Pallette, who brings with him, on that Tudorish staircase singing that Elizabethanish ditty, the world of Robin Hood in which he was (or perhaps is) Friar Tuck. (Melville Cooper was the Sheriff of Nottingham in the same production.) The existence of this man in that part no more and no less proves the irresponsibility and resourcefulness of Hollywood than the presence of Tudor mansions just north of New York City proves or disproves the irresponsibility and resourcefulness of American captains of business (though in both cases these presences bespeak a particular set of fantasies). By the time this ale merchant finishes his drinking song and his descent into the world, answers a telephone from which he learns that there is to be a party at his house that night, hangs up the receiver and responds by delivering an observation—"Nut house"—to no one in particular, casting a glance at his surroundings offscreen, we can sense that he is speaking for Sturges and that what he is looking at offscreen is a Hollywood sound stage. This memorable establishment of the hero's father as a character in possession of an inner life of independent judgment prepares him for a decisive function in the conclusion to be drawn by this film.

Now, how can this woman accept back her trusting/untrusting man, after what she has done to him? How can she hope for happiness with him, who at the end still does not know what has happened to him, hope that with him all will be well that ends well? She had said early on that he's touched something in her heart, and later on she confesses this awful yen for him. This combination of tenderness and sensuality is just what the doctor ordered for grown-up love in his *Three Essays on the Theory of Sexuality*. This text also contains, near its conclusion, a sentence that may stand as the motto for the entire genre of remarriage: "The finding of an object is in fact the refinding of it." But how does this woman work her way back to it? No doubt the man's very innocence, the completeness with which this mug appreciates her, the fervor as well as the sappy deliberateness with which he twice appeals to her to find an innocent past together, the very fact that he is what her father calls "as fine a specimen of the sucker sapiens as it has been my fortune to see"; no doubt all this, from being an object of her kidding, and of her scorn, finally elicits again her response in kind. And my question is, how?

I take the answer to be given in the man's father's appreciation of her (and the feeling is mutual) as he conveys his son's refusal to meet her sole condition for agreeing to divorce, that he come to her and ask her to be free. Here is a further thematic coincidence with *The Tempest*. (And what does "ask me to be free" mean? Ask me to let him go?; or, Ask me to let myself be free?) The father tells her he thought it was a pretty fair offer and says he thinks she is a sucker to make it. The father's lawyers are aghast at this businessman's sudden artlessness. Harry and Gerald are aghast at this metamorphosis of artist into sucker. She has become what the man is, a member of his species, the sucker sapiens, the wise fool; she has found what Katharine Hepburn at the end of *The Philadelphia Story* calls a human being; she has created herself, turned herself, not without some help, into a woman. She has done it by laying aside her art, call it her artifice; and in her long and passionate declaration to the man as she shuts them behind her cabin door, she virtually repeats his old story back to him, with the ending: "Don't you know I've waited all my life for you, you mug?"—thus confessing herself to be a mug. This concludes her education.

Mug is almost the last word we hear in the film, as it is one of the first, when her father responds to one of her professional questions by saying, with unquestionable wisdom, "A mug is a mug in everything." Her answer at the end of the film is, in effect: If to be at one with humanity is to be a mug, then as E. M. Foster almost put it, better a mug of the confidence game than a mug of the lack of confidence game, a mug of magic, of exemption. I should, of course, like to say that what she gets in return is another magic, not of control, but of reciprocity. But then you would think me a romantic.

But the word *mug* is not quite the last. The last is reserved for the character actually named a mug by the author of the film, anyway named a diminutive or a diminished mug: Mugsy (William Demarest). He has been remorselessly present from the beginning, but at the last possible moment he is expelled (fictionally, not cinematically, not in the same way). His provenance is clear enough. He is the melancholy that comedy is meant to overcome, the mood Frye notes as forming the opening of at least five of Shakespeare's comedies. This film further specifies this mood as the creature of suspicion and literalness. I think of him privately as a certain kind of philosophical critic, almost the thing Iago describes himself to be—"nothing if not critical." And faced with romantic flights of fantasy, with interpretations of feeling and conduct that make up dreamworlds of eternal and innocent love, who is there who will deny the truth of what Mugsy—the spirit of negativity—says?: Positively the same dame.

1981

Richard Schickel

Richard Schickel (b. 1933) has been a film critic for *Time-Life* magazines since 1972 and is the author of 20 books about the movies, including well-received biographies of D. W. Griffith, Walt Disney, Clint Eastwood, and Marlon Brando. He has also written and co-produced television documentaries on Cary Grant, James Cagney, and Charlie Chaplin. A prolific, polished, always happily opinionated writer who wears his knowledge lightly, he remains unduped by the shallow and the shoddy, but realistic in his understanding of movies as the juncture between art and commerce. While Schickel has often invoked his Midwestern background to argue for a respectful, non-snarky representation of American middle-class decency, his approval of *Blue Velvet* and the raucous cinema of Samuel Fuller (whose last movie, *The Big Red One*, Schickel himself lovingly helped restore recently) shows his other side—an earthy appreciation for the visceral, irrational power of movies to work their way into our psyches.

◆

Blue Velvet

I t's a strange world."

That phrase, or some close variant on it, is repeated four times in *Blue Velvet*, either by Jeffrey Beaumont (Kyle Maclachlan) or Sandy William (Laura Dern), the film's adolescent protagonists, through whose ever-widening eyes director David Lynch means us to perceive not merely the strangeness lurking just below the surface of a placid-seeming universe, but to find there as well a profound perversity, an utter rottenness. His business is to radically dislocate their bland assumptions about reality, and through them to radically dislocate the analogously comfortable, conventional expectations—for rational and optimistic narratives, for the lies we insist must be truth—that most of us bring to the movies.

The critics and moviegoers who are outraged by *Blue Velvet*—and they are legion—are those who take it be an act of exploitative social criticism, something like a vilely updated *King's Row*, hypocritically deploring the seamy side of small-town life while actually titillating us with its details. Those of us who think it is possibly a great work—and we are legion, too—regard *Blue Velvet* as (of all things) an act of movie (perhaps even cultural) criticism, a biliously ironic assault on the goopy fantasies with which movies have traditionally solaced those hard-pressed souls enduring either provincialism or adolescence or—worst case scenario—both at the same time.

Not long ago, the director John Boorman unloaded thus on movie reviewers: "I don't think most critics understand the language of film as it's developed. . . . On the whole, they have a very literary approach. They care about the conventional values of narrative and construction and performance, rather than the other virtues that are more important: the rhythm, the flow, the imagery, and the underlying theme. So often they miss it; they miss it altogether."

Boorman is right. And his remarks should be extended to include the people who produce and market movies and the audience as well. We are, most of us, good little citizens, taught from childhood to listen to the rules and obey them. When we go to the movies we instinctively understand that "narrative and construction"—the plot, to use the simplest possible term—is the voice of authority to which we are supposed to respond. In the vast majority of movies it dictates the development of the characters and it is what carries the moral. And it is, of course, the plot that is crucial to the development of the film from first to last; it is the subject of the treatment that is the first cause of the studio's commitment to a project; it then becomes the matter that everyone connected with a movie argues about from first-draft screenplay through final cut; it is what the marketing department adapts as the basis of its ad campaign; it is what viewers tell their friends about; and, yes, it is what reviewers mostly review. For it is the aspect of a movie that is most readily reducible to a few well-chosen judgmental words.

Not so imagery, which arises spontaneously out of the darkness of a director's unconscious and comes at us suddenly, unannounced, in the dreamy dimness of the theater, after which it scuttles away at a speed of twenty-four frames per second—say, who was that masked rider? In other words, imagery is not just—blandly—a carrier of "underlying meaning." It is a sneak and a subversive, capable of undermining everyone's expectations about a movie, including their hopes for a firmly uplifting, morally useful conclusion.

Mostly the American film industry is alert to imagery's potential dangers. Oh, a little hit-and-run attack occasionally occurs, usually in a comedy. But it is only rarely that something like *Blue Velvet* comes a-gnawing at our brains, chomping its way past the high-rent district, where the aesthetic rules and moral imperatives are clearly posted, heading for the slums where the Academy Award nominators fear to tread but where all the really good American movies immortally live, forever feeding our dreams' dislocating visions. Alfred

Hitchcock's thrillers, Preston Sturges's and Howard Hawks's comedies, *films noir*, *The Public Enemy*, *White Heat*, *The Shining*, *Raging Bull*, *The Terminator*—can we accurately plot their plots in a paragraph now? Of course not. But some of their pictures are indelibly burned into memory.

It is that way—but much more self-consciously so—with *Blue Velvet*. Less than six weeks after seeing it I could not recount its story and, frankly my dear, I don't give a damn—something about a psychopathic hood (Dennis Hopper) terrorizing a woman (Isabella Rossellini) who is masochistic putty in his hands, while he and his gang attempt to corrupt a small American city. The logic of the tale, if you analyze it, is full of jump cuts. But its subversive imagery, after the same six weeks in residency, had been granted a lifetime lease inside my skull.

Take the first shot in the picture: It is of a firetruck sliding past the camera, one of the firemen shyly waving at us. The image is silent, off-speed, desaturated. It reads as an artifact, a clip rescued from somebody's thirty-year-old home movie. The same thing is true of Jeffrey and Sandy's attitudes. They are respectively a Hardy boy as Troy Donahue might once have stalwartly played him and Nancy Drew as Sandra Dee might once have perkily interpreted her. Sweetly they stroll shady suburban sidewalks, dreamily they consult in malt shops and convertibles, falling into unacknowledged love while attempting to solve this little mystery they seem to have stumbled across. With this imagery, but without ever overtly announcing his intentions, Lynch pays bleak, vicious homage to the long-lost values of our former popular culture and to the ostensibly good-natured lies it used to tell in order to prop up the idea that adolescence could and should be an age of bland and twerpy innocence, instead of that clueless hell for the hormonally tormented that it actually is.

So *Blue Velvet* is most basically and most obviously a parody of a fifties teen romance—its score and decor, its locutions and locations, all insinuate the point. But in those old genteel fictions the first hint of whatever mischief would soon preoccupy its peppy protagonists was unlikely to be a severed ear, crawling with ants and held up for our edification in a long, barfy close-up. Nor was any young amateur detective likely to become either a voyeur of or a participant in sadomasochistic scenes, as Jeffrey does. Nor was a jay-naked woman likely to turn up on his girl friend's front porch, so traumatizing everyone that they forget to throw a humane blanket over the poor creature, forcing her to stand around nude while the rest of the characters discuss what to do with her.

In *Blue Velvet*, though, Jeffrey and Sandy have their button noses rubbed in all this dirt. And when it's all over, when hero and heroine go into their well-earned concluding clinch, it's not just a hug and a peck. It's a choking soul kiss, endlessly enjoyed. While her father looks on obliviously. While the last of the dead bodies they have helped to create are trundled past them by the cops.

Does anyone doubt that we fifties kids stuck our tongues down each others throats as we grappled breathlessly in cars parked on dark streets late at night? Of course we did. Does anyone doubt that something like the other realities Lynch alludes to also existed somewhere beneath the infamous "normalcy" of the period? Of course they did. But does anyone remember Troy and Sandra being exposed to any of that as they skipped through their technicolor dreams? No way.

It could be argued that Lynch's most basic business is to deny us the falsifying nostalgia that exposure to the cultural artifacts of the past so genially evoke, to deny us the false comforts of falsified history, in the process denying us that "Golden Age" we so often use to measure—and deplore—contemporary reality. In so doing he obliges us to remember that human nature is nearly always pretty awful, that we are nearly always in decline, very often when we most firmly believe we are in the ascendant.

Clearly this is one of the aspects of *Blue Velvet* that disturbs its critics. "Realistic" movies have presented material just as squalid as it does without exciting the kind of hysteria this film generated among its detractors. But realism is in itself an essentially moralistic style, it signals to us that we ought to attend soberly to what's being said, reflect seriously on its implications for our lives. The sheer jauntiness of Lynch's perversity, his jolly deployment of escapist, sentimental, and nostalgic imagery to portray a mad reality does not endear him to people who like their emotions to be cued straight-forwardly and who have a sentimental investment in the styles he's sending up. If these are not a benchmark against which to measure our moral decline over the last three decades, why then one is cast giddily adrift on the great sea of relativism.

Lynch, I am sure, would rather die than break his deadpan expression and admit this, but his work constitutes, finally, a dream—well, minimally, a meditation—about dream factory dreaming. By juxtaposing, interpenetrating, the characteristic reductions of our commercialized 1950s dream work and that strain of our own pop-cultural dream work, which insists on the omnipresence of degraded sexuality and violent aggression down every alley, behind every door, and then by pushing both up to surreal levels of intensity in his presentation, Lynch implicitly asks us to wonder about the lasting validity of all such stylizations. And, perhaps the moral debates they often stir.

There is a suggestion here that every pop-cultural manner is eventually bound to become self-parodying, or at the very least the subject of parody, that we are forever doomed to wake up screaming—with laughter—at what once was so earnestly pressed upon us as some kind of useful truth by our media masters and at the equally earnest efforts of the critics and cultural commentators to explicate its misuses. This is one of the significantly destabilizing elements of *Blue Velvet*.

And it implies another, yet larger, one. We must finally ask ourselves if all these objects we so earnestly weigh and scrutinize for their possible effect on behavior aren't really abstractions, transformations of commonplace reality that, finally, lose touch with that reality and therefore lose their capacity to influence behavior. At some level, humble or grand, depending on the ambition and sophistication of their creators, all movies become not representations of reality, but—like *Blue Velvet*—commentaries on it. If that is so, then shouldn't we see them not as guides to action (which is the simple way that censors are obliged to see them), but as aids to thought (which is, of course, uncensorable)?

Movies are obviously the creations of a mature and calculating capitalism, with all that implies about the crude and exploitative nature of those who guide them through their real-world lives as "product." But in the end—no matter what those guys say and do—the movies willy-nilly constitute themselves as an alternative, or perhaps parallel, universe. It is the peculiar genius of *Blue Velvet*, the work of a shrewd though comparatively primitive postmodernist, who may or may not know exactly what he's doing, that it is the first commercially made American movie to acknowledge this fact, and challenge us to do the same, with all that that implies about the conventions of knowing and judging that we habitually bring into the theater with us.

1995

Sam Fuller: Movie Bozo

White-maned, white-suited, his omnipresent cigar cocked at a jaunty angle, Sam Fuller, encountered in Parisian exile, briefly stilled the stream of consciousness that usually rushed unchecked across his gravelbed larynx. He was searching for something he rarely offered in his movies—a neat summarizing idea. "That's it," he finally offered. "A director takes a song, a lyric, and makes a symphony of it. Does that make sense to you?"

Generally speaking, sure. But not in Sam's case—unless you thought of him as a sort of Charles Ives, drawing on the vernacular only to subvert it with a big, blatting, unforgettable off-key note: the brave soldier who, having fired the last shot of the Civil War, contemptuously spreads his battlefield picnic on a fallen foe's body only to discover it still twitching with life; the beautiful blonde hooker whose wig falls off in a tussle with her John, revealing a perfectly bald pate; the western hero who coolly plugs his lover when the bad guy tries to use her as a shield in a gunfight.

No *High Noon*ish hesitations for him, no code-of-the-West niceties. Or for his creator. Sam didn't strain for (and could never fully explain) these bold, indelibly transgressive images. They just came naturally to an uninhibited spirit shaped by youthful service to tabloids and pulp fiction and hard, decorated soldiering with the First Infantry in World War II.

Haute Hollywood patronized him—low budgets, no Oscars, no life-achievement awards—and the dominant middlebrow critics of his high time, the fifties and early sixties, prissily dismissed him. His career in those days largely depended on Hollywood's old roughneck, lowbrow fringe, with the occasional subvention from someone like Darryl Zanuck, who probably saw in Sam some of the smash-and-grab spirit of his early Warner Bros. days. To them he was simply a guy who could deliver exploitable subject matter and violent (though rarely headlong) action, and didn't care about, or maybe even notice, what else he might be up to.

To everyone else, though, he was a man rummaging the junk heap of American culture, beguiled by the kind of gaudy trash in which they believed the movies should no longer traffic. Or maybe it was worse than that. Maybe it was really a dung heap he was pawing through. In which case, if you were a serious artiste, it was possibly okay to explore it. If eventually you deplored it. Or tacked on a little liberal uplift at the end of the picture. But you weren't ever supposed to be as exuberantly unjudgmental about the vulgarly obsessed creatures scuttling across it as Sam was.

His was, as Manny Farber, just about the only contemporary critic who understood Sam, once put it, "termite art," gnawing away at conventional boundaries, heedless of—likely ignorant of—conventional good taste, which was the province of "white elephant art" (and the Academy Awards). Another way of putting that point is that Sam's people never tried to evade the brutal logic of events—or fate. They accepted whatever cards destiny dealt them in a variety of ways, ranging from the calm to the hysterical, but never, ever with self-pity. Or with anything smacking of piety, liberalish or otherwise.

For me, his key scene is one that stands at the emotional center of *Pickup on South Street*, which is one of the few Fuller films that still gets played occasionally in respectable venues like AMC. That's the one in which Richard Widmark plays a cop-hating pickpocket who dips into a purse on a subway and comes up with a roll of microfilm that Communist spies are passing from hand to hand. This brings the FBI into his life and brings his paranoia to a snarling boil. It also brings the reds to the door of a character played by Thelma Ritter, who is for once not required to play the funny voice of reason commenting on the misbehavior of her social betters. Here she is a profoundly weary woman who sells ties on the street and may or may not have observed something about the missing microfilm. But she's not going to cooperate with the goons threatening her. This is not because she is particularly patriotic. It's because in her exhaustion she just doesn't give a shit about all the things that set other people into passionate motion. She counts the ways she has been worn down by life and then tells her interrogators to go ahead and kill her if that's what they want to do. Eventually—this being a Sam Fuller film—they oblige her.

The scene is wonderfully played by Ritter, who probably never had another passage in which she was for so long the focus of the camera's undivided attention. Certainly she never had one in which her character's history and feelings were so fully exposed. It is also—except for the fact that he didn't usually write monologues—a characteristic Fuller scene. He was good with crane and tracking shots when he had the budget for them, but he was at heart a rather claustrophobic director. He liked dark, tight spaces, like the shabby room Ritter inhabits, liked their oppressiveness, their lack of options. He also liked marginal loners, pushed to the far edge of polite society. And he liked stark, melodramatic choices of the kind Ritter confronts here.

These qualities naturally counted against him when he was at his most fecund in the fifties and sixties. He seemed old-fashioned in his insistence on celebrating the mulishness of the lower orders, in his failure to provide the increasingly middle-class, middlebrow movie audience with bourgeois heroes standing around in their grey flannel suits trying to make fastidious moral choices in a world where the stakes were rarely deadly.

In this connection I think there is an apt comparison to be made between Fuller's *Shock Corridor* and Elia Kazan's *Gentleman's Agreement*. Both are about journalists going underground in order to experience, in the fullest emotional sense, an important story. In the latter film, as everyone knows, Gregory Peck's magazine writer assumes a Jewish identity in order to feel the full impact of anti-Semitism. About the worst thing that happens to him is that he gets turned away from a fancy restricted hotel. In Fuller's movie a reporter gets himself committed to an insane asylum in order to investigate conditions there. Among other things, he witnesses (another of those astonishing Fullerian reversals) a black man driven so nuts by racism that he becomes in his mind a Ku Klux Klansman, spouting the most hatefully racist speeches. Eventually the reporter himself is driven insane by the experience.

Yes, the thing is improbably, crudely melodramatic. But it does follow out the logic of the deception fully and powerfully. To have achieved the same effect, *Gentleman's Agreement*, which brought Kazan an Oscar, but which he has since virtually disowned because of its politeness, would have had to show Peck's character beaten to death (or nearly so) by neo-Nazis.

It's the same way with *Run of the Arrow*, the film that contains that bestartling picnic scene. The would-be diner is Rod Steiger, playing a Confederate soldier so lost to the Lost Cause that he joins the Indians opposing the Yankee army that is trying to pacify them in the postwar West. You could call it "Run of the Logic" I suppose, for nothing occurs in his life to make him change his mind about his old enemies. He remains what he was when we first met him— a violent hater. Sam shows how that emotion twists and stunts him, as single-minded passions tend to do to many of his characters, but he will not grant him, or us bleeding hearts in the audience, a pleasing last-minute redemption. People like this don't reform, can't be talked out of their madness. And what Sam is saying to us is, "Don't go there." Because if you do, you won't come back.

Let me return to some of the other images I mentioned earlier. Take, for instance, that bald hooker (played by Constance Towers). Her condition is the (highly) visible symbol of a profoundly wounded nature, which thwarts her ambition to find respectability. What we learn as *The Naked Kiss* develops is that she was sexually abused as a child, a theme that was (peculiar as it may seem now) utterly untouched in the movies, anywhere in popular culture, at the time the film was released in 1964. Inevitably, this being a Fuller film, she must seek revenge. Inevitably this leads to an end that does not provide her, or us watching, with anything we would recognize as emotional release.

Consider, as well, the woman shot by that implacable gunman at the end of *Forty Guns*. She is played by Barbara Stanwyck, and she is not exactly the local schoolmarm. She is, in fact, a cattle baroness, and she is introduced in the film's brilliantly arresting title sequence riding at the head of the eponymous troop of gunslingers who enforce her will on this range. We soon come to understand that they are also her studs, summoned to sexual service whenever the whim strikes her, which is probably every night. Hey, if you're a baroness, act like a baroness. Home on this range was a lot more interesting than it was in *The Big Valley*.

Be that as it may, it turns out that Barry Sullivan, as an itinerant lawman trying to bring her psychokiller brother to justice, is man enough to replace all of her enforcer-studs. Their relationship is what passes for love in Fuller's world. But he also is what he is—a man with an obsession. So when her vile brother uses Stanwyck as a shield in the climactic confrontation with Sullivan, the latter does not hesitate even for a nanosecond to plug her in order to get a clear shot at him. Sam meant her to die, but that was too much for the studio. They made him shoot a piece in which it was revealed that he only winged her. But, the staging of what preceded it makes the director's bleak intention perfectly clear.

Like a lot of hard guys, Sam was sentimental about kids and animals, and there were vague implications here and there in his work, as more than one critic has observed, that the United States of America might ultimately come out okay. The ideals behind it were sound and maybe capable of eventually straightening out the many kinks its general population suffered. But that was not an idea that became manifest in his films until quite late in Sam's career. For most of it, he was suspect in all the best places as a vulgar sensationalist. Gavin Millar put it this way in the cautious entry he wrote for Richard Roud's *Cinema: A Critical Dictionary*: "There are defenders . . . who believe he deploys these weapons knowingly and with irony. There are others, his equally passionate detractors, who feel that the crudity, illiteracy and melodrama is . . . a true measure of his sensibility." Roud himself could not resist adding that he counted himself among the latter, was indeed "repelled" by Sam's work.

I think this dichotomy is essentially a false one. I don't for a minute think Sam was an ironist. On the other hand, I don't think he was an illiterate. I think he was, in the profoundest sense, a "movie bozo," to borrow Jeanine Basinger's (quite intentionally ironic) phrase. With it she meant, I think, to identify those of us who are committed to film's unique, essentially non- and often anti-literary way of telling stories, telling lives, working on an audience, and are often enough put down by those whose standards are shaped by aesthetics borrowed from the traditional arts. In this us-against-them context, Sam Fuller is one of the great test cases.

By this I mean he was committed, as few were or are, to a full exploration of the medium's inherent melodramatic logic. Almost all movies take us into emotional realms we usually do not explore in life, therefore to confrontations we are usually able to avoid in reality. The idea is always logically to force seemingly normal people, folks with whom we can easily identify, into situations that are illogically deadly—and then see what happens to them. Most movies, having taken them there, let them off the hook, permitting the audience to escape with their heroic-romantic illusions intact. Sam's tendency was to imperil not-so-nice people and then *not* let them off the hook, thereby testing the limits of our commitment to movie logic.

This strikes me as an honorable and courageous thing to do. But also for him the only possible thing to do. For if you are a fatalist about human destiny, how can you do anything but embrace the inherent logic of your medium—no matter how often others evade or elide it? This is something our most interesting filmmakers (Scorsese, Tarentino, the Coen Brothers) have increasingly tried to do in recent years, which is why Sam Fuller's stock has risen among them and among serious cinephiles, too. We have belatedly come to relish the shock of the transgressive, to enjoy seeing the deadly, implicit logic of screen narrative fully manifested before our eyes.

We also like seeing—at this comparatively late date in the history of the medium—someone ignore the conventions—the last-minute rescue or change of heart—by which we are usually released from that logic and sent home happy. It is not important to us that Sam's way of achieving the transgressive effect was usually not subtle. Oh no, one thinks, he's not really going to . . . oh my God, he is. And then we laugh. At the sheer, sometimes childlike bravado of the thing. At the truth that transcends "realism."

In our movie bozo souls we are not "repelled" by Sam's signature sequences but rather revel in their perversity, in the way they liberate us from the sentimental conventions of decades of moviegoing. The question of how "knowing" Sam was when he conceived and realized one of these sequences is rendered irrelevant by the value of the act, the terrible honesty of it.

When I think of his career, another of Sam's great images occurs to me—the soldier's helmet, a bullet hole drilled in its center, that we see under the opening titles of (logically enough) *The Steel Helmet*. We imagine it to be just a piece of battlefield detritus, but then it begins to move and we see that there is a man, Sergeant Zack (played by that Fuller favorite, blunt Gene Evans), underneath—a hard-bitten, hard-used survivor, a crazy glitter in his eyes, who is going to live to fight another day, die another day.

Oh yes, die. No body of American film work is more touched by the certainty of mortality than Sam Fuller's, none is more conscious of the absurdity of goals, ideologies, perhaps even of action itself, given that overwhelming reality. The narrative arcs of his movies so often turn into closed circles, with people ending up pretty much back where they began, and often enough dying somewhere near their starting point. That certainly is true of *The Steel Helmet*, in which a patrol, a veritable UN of racial types, wanders inconclusively through the fog and darkness of the Korean War, as much as anything trying to figure out what—beyond their own survival—their mission might be.

Zack, their leader, was Sam in a sense—scarred but scrambling, tough but gallant, capable of gruff sentiment—and just a little bit mad. For the director, like his protagonist, had no shrewdness, no skill at temporizing talk or pretentious promises—coin of the new, post-sixties Hollywood realm—and he was forced further and further afield to keep working.

But that unquenchable spirit of his kept him going and brought him back from near oblivion in 1980 to make a reasonably big-budget, studio-backed movie about his beloved *Big Red One*. It's a movie that—even in the reedited version the studio released—makes you feel the terror and loneliness of modern warfare—the individual caught in the vast machinery of death, the uncertainty of small-unit camaraderie, ever threatened by the random hits of morality's mortar fire. It is also a movie that ends terribly at a concentration camp, with Lee Marvin's sergeant, a knowing but not cynical veteran of World War I—a guy as hard as any Gene Evans ever played for Sam—rescuing a child, who dies as Marvin gives him a victory ride on his shoulders. Much as Sam believed in the justness of this war and the comradely virtues displayed by ordinary men called upon to fight in it (as he was), he could not end his film on a note of unambiguous triumph, could not avoid this acknowledgment of fate's cruelty.

Typically of this career, his next movie, *White Dog*, was deemed unreleasable, though it is as a powerful a condemnation of racism as anyone ever made. The problem, of course, was its title creature, an animal that had been conditioned to attack black people. The movie is about its successful retraining—one of those uncharacteristically optimistic notes I mentioned earlier—but the idea that basic instincts could be tampered with, made to serve vile ends, was for many unthinkable. We need to believe that the snarling beasts of unreason have long since been put to sleep, that whatever issues still plague us are soluble with a nice little chat—or maybe another law designed to enforce good behavior.

I suppose what I've been saying here is that Sam's glory lay in the fact that he never believed the taint of something like original sin could be erased from human endeavor, that we might occasionally achieve a grace note or two in life but never the amazement of total grace.

How deeply he considered such matters I can't say—nobody, I think, can say. For he reveled in his identity as a man who simply went ahead and made movies in a heedless, hell-for-leather way. Which implies, I think, an instinctive understanding that movies, especially the best American movies, are not about being "true to life," which is the basic bad rap critics have been laying on them for pretty close to a hundred years now. They are most profoundly about being untrue to our publicly expressed ideas about life—and about being true to our secret life, to that pulpy place where our darkest whimsies, our maddest impulses, both deadly and romantic, live. What one finally loved best about Sam was the ease with which he lived and worked in that place, the sense he conveyed through his outrageous imagery that finally there was no other place worth talking about.

He was a paradox—a populist who was never widely popular. And probably never will be. But in his later years European admirers like Godard and Wim Wenders took to casting him in their films, while the Americans who learned from him—the Scorseses and Tarentinos—began to cast him as an artistic hero. Sam, the deadly innocent, the sweet-souled subversive, beamed upon them, for he sensed that in their admiration lay the beginnings of the small corner of immortality that will be always, uniquely his. Some of us will remember him as a filmmaker whose time came too late for his profit, but not too late to honor its prophet—one of the few, true American originals.

1999

Armond White

Armond White (b. 1953), formerly with *The City Sun* and now *New York Press*, has staked out a position as a renegade film critic, the Last Angry Man, unafraid to attack popular favorites or make enemies with colleagues. In his collection *The Resistance: Ten Years of Pop Culture That Shook the World*, White examines hip-hop, music videos, and black independent filmmaking to locate the erratic pulse of political opposition in the culture. Pauline Kael wrote: "Armond White's race-based approach to movies is more than challenging—it can be unnerving. Often when I start one of his pieces I think he's way out of line, but when I go further I see that he's on to something. He's one of the few writers on popular culture who rouse a reader to do some fresh thinking." In his favorable review of Spike Lee's *Do the Right Thing*, White astutely linked the film's effectiveness to its radio-derived rhythms. But lest one mistake him as an all-purpose promoter of African-American directors, he later roasted the very same Lee for *Malcolm X*.

◆

Rebirth of a Nation

Do the Right Thing opens with a funny, erotic sequence in which a woman of color (Rosie Perez) asserts both the integrity of boxing and dancing in time to Public Enemy's rap song "Fight the Power." Pugilistic, political funk sums up the style of Spike Lee's film. His boldest, most accomplished moviemaking yet, it drives home the cultural and political awareness that his first two films (*She's Gotta Have It* and *School Daze*) only suggested. *Do the Right Thing*'s view of a Black New York neighborhood on the hottest day of the year counters most mainstream ideas about America and movies.

Light on its feet, the movie dances among an assortment of characters in a one-block area of Brooklyn's Bedford-Stuyvesant. Young adults, kids, old folks, working people, and idlers all express their dissatisfaction and heat-aggravated temper in a contrapuntal dialogue that makes this movie, like Public Enemy's music, an artful arrangement of cultural fragments. It, too, spars with the complacency of pop tradition in which Black politics or viewpoints never mattered. This charming, dreamlike film means business.

Do the Right Thing is going to trouble people raised on Hollywood's specious idolatry of American democracy. The movie's sentimental style ironically embraces social distress in a more realistic, cautionary way. This is the torpor and tension of 1980s America that *Rain Man, Broadcast News,* and most other Hollywood films that glorify the white middle class avoid showing. Lee himself plays Mookie, who works as a delivery boy for the Italian pizzeria on his block. Sal (Danny Aiello) runs the place as he has for years, along with his two sons, the angry Pino (John Turturro) and cool, timid Vito (Richard Edson). On his rounds, Mookie moves among the block's types: a benign drunk called Da Mayor (Ossie Davis), the nosy-neighbor Mother Sister (Ruby Dee), a quartet of frisky teens, Korean grocers, Latin boys, and a trio of out-of-work men (Paul Benjamin, Robin Harris, and Frankie Faison), whose joshing routines under a sun umbrella in front of a bright red wall work as a soulful Greek chorus.

Lee's own affectionate bemusement weaves these characters together. Even the bickering between Mookie and Tina, his Latin girlfriend (Perez), who berates him for not visiting their baby, seems rapturously intimate. Lee's structure may be schematic, but no filmmaker since Robert Altman has shown such a profound knack for American vernacular. The modulations between harsh, seductive and just plain social talk seem effortless. One sequence shows off this gift in a montage of Black, Italian, Latin, and Jewish epithets. Lee uses language—the sound of urban unease—to intensify his story's social dynamics.

Radio is the key to *Do the Right Thing*'s brilliance. The movie has a high-frequency style jolting with bursts of music, color, humor, and serious ideas. Lee breaks with Hollywood narrative convention and takes his tone from the populist mode of airwave entertainment. That's perfect for a film about urban African-American life. Lee is able to monitor the collective unconscious of Bed-Stuy through Mister Señor Lovedaddy (Sam Jackson), DJ for WELOVE radio station. Spinning r&b platters and broadcasting verbal reports, the DJ comments on twenty-four hours of Black life. More could be made of this device, but it effectively constructs the film in flowing, start-stop rhythms that match the flux of radio—the only mass-communication medium that has been open to Black people. Through this, Lee picks up signals that are remote to established white filmmaking practice. And unlike the casual radio-derived structures of *American Graffiti* and *Radio Days, Do the Right Thing* is tuned in to the ongoing primacy of pop experience. Its person-on-the-street multiplicity suggests the surreal dissonance of dial spinning. The relation to African oral tradition is obvious, but more important is the implication that in post-sixties America, Black people (and Asians and Latinos)—who may be isolated by age, sex, and taste—are still under the sway of a common cultural wave.

The film's emotional undercurrent, represented by persistent pop music motifs, is brand new for American movies. There's more vitality and warmth here than in a typical lament for the downtrodden. Lee brings to cinema the impudent integrity of hiphop. Unlike mainstream (read white) social tracts about America's class system from *Dead End* (1937) to *Saturday Night Fever* (1977), *Do the Right Thing* doesn't condescend to working-class culture. Lee may borrow the unified time frame and basic setting of the tenement plays and folk dramas from earlier eras, but the action he stages and the dialogue he writes are new-jack, thrilling.

"Fight the Power" is heard throughout the film as the theme song of Radio Raheem (Bill Nunn), a towering young Black man who paces Bed-Stuy carrying a formidably huge beat box. "You don't like Public Enemy?" he asks the jivy hothead Buggin' Out (Giancarlo Esposito). Public Enemy's no-half-measures rap screeds define the intensity of young Black male discontent. The group's propulsive, keening sound collages give the taciturn Raheem eloquence. In one of *Do the Right Thing*'s moments of startling wit, Raheem faces the camera and does a *Night of the Hunter*–style recitation on "love" and "hate" and the battle between good and evil. The scene suggests Travis Bickle as a Gentle Giant and would-be poet and fondly evokes the pent-up inarticulateness of underclass youth. As Mookie, Lee himself acts out the charming, hilarious response to Raheem's speech. Mookie, the film's central figure, knows psychic torment when he sees it—even if he doesn't understand it yet—and like Spike Lee, he respects it.

By fetishizing Raheem's beat box, Lee honors the medium that expands the indigenous musical expressions of America's different ethnic groups. This, clearly, is a criticism of the monopoly that other, more socially mobile ethnic groups have made of movies, television, and the print media. It is Buggin' Out's fury over the domineering photographs of Italian movie stars in Sal's Pizzeria ("How come there ain't no Black people on your wall of pride!") that turns the day's events to tragedy. When Sal smashes Raheem's radio—the kid's preeminent means of articulation—all hell breaks loose.

Do the Right Thing is an antiracist taboo buster. Instead of moralizing about races living together in peace—the "official" made-for-TV-movie manner used whenever Hollywood feels like exploiting the problem—it broadcasts the aggrieved exasperations of racism's Black and white victims. Lee doesn't vent gaseous indignation about the confrontation between Radio Raheem and Sal. He makes the ideologies at war frighteningly clear; good and bad intentions fly up and land indistinguishably. In the aftermath, when Mookie speaks up to Sal, the scene's matter-of-fact sorrow is honestly and authentically ambiguous.

It's the true mood of America's disenfranchised and dispossessed. This appalling, funny exchange in front of the burned-down, gutted ruins of Sal's shop may suggest homegrown, political Beckett, but its stylistic peculiarity has a different intent—a thorough rejection of the false optimism in mainstream entertainment.

Like the best rap and punk music of the past decade, *Do the Right Thing* makes personal behavior inseparable from politics. When Mookie notices that his pretty career-girl sister, Jade (Joie Lee), brings out a schoolboy courtliness in Sal, the sexual tension is released in a sibling debate in front of a blaring graffito: "Tawana Told The Truth." New York City's recent racial controversies (such as the Tawana Brawley affair, Howard Beach, and the police killing of Michael Griffiths) are here turned into folklore that's meant to be argued about.

Lee doesn't preach, but he indicates—spectacularly. That flirtation scene between Sal and Jade is watched by a resentful Mookie and Pino in teasing slow motion. Lee uses a Martin Scorsese trope here, as well as in Radio Raheem's showdown with a group of Puerto Ricans and in Buggin' Out's pitched argument with a gentrifying white yuppie (John Savage). His animated camera style builds on the most important things Lee could have learned from his New York colleague: that movies should be culturally specific and that style should serve audience awareness.

Scorsese's Italian-American trilogy—*Who's That Knocking at My Door?*, *Mean Streets*, and *Raging Bull*—brought new elements to American filmmaking: determinedly ethnic, those movies went fearlessly into the hellishness of their characters' particular racial and sexual biases. Until Spike Lee, such raw emotional milieu has been the province of white filmmakers. Even that sequence sampling assorted racial slurs recalls the classroom face-off between Black and white teens in Philip Kaufman's *The Wanderers*.

Lately, white filmmakers like Kaufman have abandoned American subjects for the safe, ersatz sophistication of "European" political movies like *The Unbearable Lightness of Being*. That leaves a Black artist like Lee to fill the gap and correct the balance.

Black America's pluralism is more affectionately and smartly depicted in *Do the Right Thing* than in *School Daze*, and the *Rashomon* structure of *She's Gotta Have It* is replaced by an agitprop fancifulness much like Jean-Luc Godard's eye-popping sixties political comedies (*Made in the U.S.A.*, *A Woman Is a Woman*). All this proves that Lee is on his way to commanding a many-faceted, expressive technique that will answer both the creative and the political imperatives that he refuses to separate. With cinematographer Ernest Dickerson he refashions a ghetto location into a gold-toned, ordered universe of fractious democracy. This small-scale Gotham is actually a greater achievement than Tim Burton and Anton Furst's *Batman* setting; its look emanates from the fundamental modern American experience of territory and dislocation—the personal sense of home that one views with a global awareness of economic and political inequity.

Lee understands this well enough to treat the film's climax as a social uprising, not a riot. Mookie and his community react to police brutality and the general state of frustration by attacking the institution that pathetically symbolizes their deprivation. Sal, the person, is not their target. There's order in Lee's survey of social chaos. Ending with the philosophies of Martin Luther King Jr. and Malcolm X echoing in sweet, bitter counterpoint, *Do the Right Thing* speaks to today's racial crisis as a matter of individual conscience. Daringly, and with lots of wit and style, it uses the aggregate boiling tempers of New York to portray the state of the nation.

1989

Malcolm X'd Again

When *Time* magazine calls a film biography of *Malcolm X* "tepid" and *New York* magazine calls it "solid," only one thing can be said for sure: The figure of the slain Black politician has been thoroughly domesticated. This may be part of a natural cultural process at work despite daily promulgated racism—yesterday's headache becomes today's pillow just as yesterday's tragedy becomes today's big-budget Hollywood extravaganza. The shocking thing is that the agent of this process is Spike Lee, a so-called outspokesperson (Albert Murray's term) who pretends to shake up America's white-dominated culture industry while trying to attain all its benefits, from money to influence.

Sellout is too common a word for an outrage of this shame and magnitude. The full horror of Spike Lee's *Malcolm X* didn't occur to me while watching the film, with its various, silly look-at-me tropes (a wide-screen moonscape; a purely fanciful trip to South Africa to film an endorsement from Nelson Mandela). Since the film has little aesthetic significance, its real meaning and effect can be seen in surrounding media treatments—the numerous talk shows in which Lee and his star, Denzel Washington, reiterate Malcolm X rhetoric while selling their Hollywood product.

This deception happens within the confusion of Black careerism. First, there's the Catch-22 of being important (rich and famous) enough to make people listen to you but saying only marketable things so that you can become rich and famous (important). In the hiphop era, this is most easily accomplished by making art (product) of previously sanctified things—ethics and ethnicity. Genuine artists who have only their lives to trade on constitute a larger part of African-American pop culture than any other ethnic group. The history that bears this out is also a history full of compromises—stemming from both collusion and betrayal. However, the only thing that justifies these desperate acts and these practical facts is the amount of honesty in the art—the raw truth and plain essence that usually get Black artists ghettoized as being difficult, controversial, without crossover appeal.

It's exciting when a Black artist becomes mainstream and can keep up the level of difficulty (like Prince), but unless that happens, there will be trouble. Black artists whose work gets too far away from their personal thoughts and habits risk devaluing the very experience that inspired them. This was probably difficult for Spike Lee to ascertain during his constant battle to affront the white mainstream, but it happened quickly and it was simple. Here's how:

By transforming his impatience with American racism into an easily packaged emblem—the X cap—Lee automatically voided the meaning of the sign. X for exploitation, X marking the spot of buried treasure, X meaning anything but the sorrow of a people without identity. Lee managed to reverse the original intention of the sign by converting it into merchandise. After turning the X into a style that can be effortlessly purchased, and imitated, he shortchanged its value even while it seemed to become profitable.

Acquiring X necessitated no learning, no experience, no private affection or enmity other than recognizing a current fad. In response, a sarcastic white youth was recently seen wearing a cap with the insignia Y.

The culture is filled with so much misrepresentation and dishonesty that, sometimes, it seemed the mere utterance of a fact or a defiant point of view would be sufficient to clear the air and set things right. But now it's plain that no matter how many sound bites broadcast Malcolm X's most challenging thoughts, they unfortunately enter the air as air, not lightning. This doesn't negate the possibility that somebody might hear the words and start to think, yet the context of their new, Time-Warner sponsorship suggests that far more people will hear Malcolm X's words as merely discomforting and will tell themselves, Don't worry: It's just a movie.

Malcolm is killed a second time, in fact, by the misdirected enthusiasm of a Black entrepreneur who thought he could continue Malcolm X's mission by dealing with Hollywood on its own terms. Lee's own ideas are not comprehensive enough to accomplish this assault successfully. The two schisms that defined Malcolm X's career—ignorance/consciousness, religion/worldliness—are not dealt with. Lee, too, wears a cap rather than feeling Malcolm X's spirit.

That explains why, in the film, Washington comes off petty—lukewarm rather than hot, angry, calculating, intimidating, brilliant, ornery, or, in a word, undeniable. Lee has blanded out Malcolm X's character to make him worthy of a big-budget movie that could recoup its cost by attracting (but not offending) millions of viewers. The *Time* magazine critic who called *Malcolm X* "tepid" is the same one who called *Do the Right Thing* "irresponsible"; this demonstrates the no-win conditions of a contest in the mainstream. Lee should have realized that the only thing he had to lose was the deepest, most personal meaning that Malcolm X has for him (if any). Whatever viewers he lost with a too-harsh portrayal would be worth losing (as the *Time* critic proves, Lee never had them on his side anyway).

Malcolm X is compromised by Lee's contradictory hipness. He wants to be accepted by Hollywood while chipping at the ideology for which it stands. It can't be done. Better filmmakers than Spike Lee have failed at it, but unlike such heroic examples as Eric von Stroheim, Orson Welles, and Brian DePalma, Lee has his ego tangled up with Black political imperatives. He's willing to exploit the political ideas that came out of years of suffering and many struggling, hopeful generations for his own aggrandizement.

Despite the political awareness Malcolm X preached, Lee makes no single statement or incident dramatically potent—or personal. This implies that Malcolm X's axioms are mere slogans to Lee. He doesn't proceed by Malcolm X's ideas; he hides behind them using a convenient sense of righteousness to fuel his career assertions and distract from his compromises. The most "imaginative" filmmaking stunts in *Malcolm X* portray, instead, Lee's competition with other filmmakers. Of course, he comes up short, but Lee never looks tinier (or more small-minded) than in the flashback scene of a Klu Klux Klan attack on Malcolm and his family. To seal the moment of racist aggression and Black humiliation, Lee shows the KKK troupe riding off toward a huge illuminated moon dominating the nighttime horizon.

It's an insensible effect, a hollow visual epiphany that coheres with nothing else in the movie. Certainly, to portray the KKK as Halloween goblins goes against the historical facts that *Malcolm X* reinterpreted as examples of real-life, political evil. Instead, this costly visual effect fights one of Lee's own spiteful battles. The moonshot is a perverse quote of Steven Spielberg's *E.T.* that Spike Lee connects to D. W. Griffith and the KKK as a stupid show of his contempt for *The Color Purple*. This kind of iconoclastic gesture requires more than nerve to be successful; it isn't the same throw-down to pop tradition that Public Enemy made, slighting Elvis Presley in "Fight the Power," mainly because Lee doesn't have the artistic ammunition to make Spielberg look trite the way PE made Elvis look pale. In the end, Lee wants to steal the amazement that was central to *E.T.*'s exploration of childhood awe. Does Lee's moonshot mean Malcolm was in awe of the KKK or that Spike is in awe of white filmmakers whose success he envies? The confusion is sheer lunacy.

On this level, *Malcolm X* is a piddling rewrite of movie history. Lee plays a pitiful game of misinterpreting Hollywood's white liberal past as if it were all lies. This narrowness contradicts his stated respect for Malcolm X's evolution from hate to love. In the film's bizarre finale, Nelson Mandela appears speaking to a classroom of Black South African children whom Lee has introduced in a series of close-ups testifying, "I AM MALCOLM X!" This is a rip from the superb 1970 Hal Ashby–Bill Gunn film, *The Landlord*, in which a white liberal visited a proto-Afrocentric academy and, in a series of close-ups, various cherubs stood up to declare, "I AM BLACK AND I AM BEAUTIFUL!"

Spike's version acutely says much less, but it accurately portrays the commercialization of Black consciousness to today's youth. It's an arrested development from self-regard to style (or perhaps from a period of revolutionary awareness to a Halloween-style assumed identity). This is a consequence of Malcolm X's being discovered first by rappers reclaiming Black history in personal disc expressions and their political-artistic renaissance being imitated—co-opted—by Lee, a less serious pop artist.

Lee neglects what rappers have been good at: There's no continuity between Malcolm X and the legacy of Black intellectuals (and no reference to Frederick Douglass or Marcus Garvey). Lee's pop star Malcolm emerges from prison a full-blown thinker-speaker as incapable of personal politics as Lee himself.

This Malcolm X without rough edges is the last thing Amiri Baraka and his group of naysayers expected when they challenged Lee's ability to tell Malcolm X's story, but it's part of the neutralizing they feared. Already those dissenting voices have been lost, crushed beneath the powerful weight of Hollywood hype.

Once again, capitalism is the force that subdues Black individuality. All this current (temporary) interest in Malcolm X rises from Hollywood-generated publicity. Many Black folks are willing to go along with the hype, not for the sake of Malcolm's politics but for the mainstream legitimization. This is the same kind of pride that always trips up Black show business, whether it's

Ice-T siding with corporate interests or Spike Lee deciding he should have the same privilege of spending time and money on a film folly as Oliver Stone and Richard Attenborough.

Lee's essential con job was to refurbish Malcolm X, but Malcolm X was not Martin Luther King Jr. It is misleading—but typically Hollywood—to pretend that Malcolm X matters because of his late ecumenicism. The film would seem to confirm the wide acceptance of Malcolm X and his message, but this acceptance is on a false premise. Spike himself doesn't risk controversy; the proof of his politics-into-safe-entertainment is in his choice of Arrested Development to provide the movie's theme song instead of the more appropriate rapper Sister Souljah. You've got to wonder how many of the stars who turned out for Lee's premiere would be as supportive of a contemporary rebellious Black political pop star like Sister Souljah. Plainly, all this *Malcolm X* hoopla is not a celebration of ideas but of Hollywood commerce.

The only way to redeem this scandalous sellout would be to radicalize moviegoing and movie watching. (Imagine the blistering, charismatic, brilliant Malcolm X that *Chameleon Street* auteur Wendell B. Harris might have created.) With no formal innovations or controversial content, Lee's film has made Malcolm X safe for box offices everywhere. This mediocre film is a setback to all the artistic advances of the hiphop era. Let the mourning begin.

1992

David Denby

David Denby (b. 1943) began, by his own admission, as a follower of Pauline Kael before evolving in a very different direction from his sensation-loving mentor. In his thirty-five-year career as film critic for *The Atlantic*, *Boston Phoenix*, *New York*, and now *The New Yorker*, Denby has elected often to play the role of responsible citizen and family man, brooding about the morality of art, unashamedly outraged at random, excessive violence or the exploitation of women onscreen. With a probity that draws him naturally to the realistic *gravitas* of figures such as documentarian Fred Wiseman, he seems less pleased to be toyed with by post-modernist directorial games.

◆

The Real Thing

In his most recent documentary, *Central Park*, Frederick Wiseman photographs homeless New Yorkers lying on the park's benches and hillsides, covered in blankets, plastic wrappers, and bits of paper—shelter that looks more like a burial mound than protection for the night. It's as if the homeless were carrying the means of their interment around with them, as if their only "home" could be death. This is the kind of harsh insight we have come to expect from Wiseman, who has been chronicling American institutions on film for almost twenty-five years without shrinking from life's grimmer provinces. But apart from such images, the movie is mostly a record of New York exuberance, a celebration of the city's surviving lyrical and idealistic impulses. In his films, Wiseman has often questioned received ideas and images: here he questions the commonplace that American cities are moribund.*

Beginning in 1967 with the notorious *Titicut Follies*, which was shot in the hideous Bridgewater, Massachusetts, facility for the criminally insane, Wiseman has completed twenty-three of these institutional portraits, mostly for public television.† He has made films about hospitals, schools, military installations,

---

*Central Park was shot in the summer of 1988, almost a year before the gang sexual assault on a female jogger in the park.

†All of Wiseman's documentary films, with the exception of *Titicut Follies*, were broadcast on PBS. The films were financed, in varying combinations, by WNET-TV in New York, by the Corporation for Public Broadcasting, the BBC, the National Endowment for the Arts, the National Endowment for the Humanities, and a variety of foundations.

and research institutes; a big-city police force and a juvenile court; a department store, a monastery, a racetrack, a modeling agency. From *Titicut* on, he has proved indifferent both to journalistic convention and audience convenience, working in an austere, provocatively reticent style. There are no titles, narration, music, or explicit commentary of any kind. He never announces his themes; instead, he plunges the unguided and sometimes baffled viewer into the life of an institution, imposing his own dramatic form on the many fragments of behavior he has photographed. In the films, institutional staff and their "clients" are caught in routine moments as well as in situations of extreme stress and even anguish. Through selection and juxtaposition of these little scenes, Wiseman puts together a complex portrait of the institution, a portrait that has the suspense not of narrative but of a sustained, detailed argument about values and experience.

Virtually everything in *High School* (1968), a savagely comic portrait of a "good" public high school in Philadelphia, gathers around a few central ideas: the school's use of banality to control the students, the suppression of the students' sexuality and independence. The movie begins with a teacher starting her class by reading the "thought for the day" ("What I do today is going to change my life tomorrow") and a Spanish class learning the word "existentialism" by rote. The "thought for the day" is banal, but it is also appalling, for we realize that it is the school, not the students themselves, that is trying to change their lives. As Wiseman's joke about existentialism suggests, the students are studying freedom in a way that will discourage them from being free.

These perceptions are repeated and varied throughout the film and reach a climax in the final sequence, in which the principal, a handsome woman with a fine head of white hair, reads to the faculty a letter from a recent graduate, a boy expecting to die in Vietnam. "Don't worry about me," the boy writes. "I'm just a body doing a job." Everywhere in the school, in the classrooms and administrative offices and in the long hallways, we have seen the omnipresent teachers and school officials, frightened and rule-bound, trying to turn out teenagers who will submit to authority. In this case they have apparently succeeded. The boy, in words of self-negation that the principal applauds, has surrendered to the school even the meaning of his own death. *High School* is a sinister and very shrewd portrait of the American pursuit of mediocrity, a film of almost Nabokovian wit.

Over the years, Wiseman and his tiny crews* have spent many months lugging camera and tape recorders through the vast gulag of American ame-

---

*Usually only a cameraman and his assistant; Wiseman takes the sound.

liorative institutions. The blank conference rooms, the barren marching fields, the listless or demoralized or overexcited people waiting on lines or trapped behind desks or ill in bed, become almost a Whitmanesque catalog in reverse, a bleakly witty panoply of American life at low ebb. But Wiseman also finds in these places signs of revolt, and moments of remarkable kindness or competence and even courage.

The cinema, which records the surfaces of things, the actions of the will and the emotions, is a sensuous art form. But Wiseman's work is preoccupied with what one could call spirit. With an intensity usually found only in fiction, Wiseman examines the moral and spiritual life of an institution, revealing the way people are mauled, pounded into shape, ignored, or even ennobled by passing through or working in one of these places; that is, the way people react to authority.

The individuality and eccentricity that appear as a protest in his other films appear as a right in his new film, *Central Park*. Shooting in color, and in natural light softened by summer, Wiseman and his cinematographer, John Davey, photograph fantasists, lunatics, and cranks; birds and fields and nuzzling lovers; politicians and conservationists debating over the fate of the park. The movie is slow, uninsistent, rather pretty, at times wordless, without Wiseman's usually embattled characters and moral sense of urgency. He ignores the history and aesthetics of Olmsted and Vaux's peerless creation, celebrating instead the stubborn flow of life through the park, the open-armed welcome it offers in the midst of the sullen colossus.

Even if this uncharacteristically sensuous film interests us less than many of Wiseman's more relentless portraits, his structural inventiveness is much in evidence. Early in the film, a minister conducting a wedding in the park evokes the opening of Genesis and speaks of "This beautiful garden in the midst of one of the most awesome cities in the world." In the work of another filmmaker, this remark might seem random. But in Wiseman's films, which have many minor characters but no central ones and no narrative, language and imagery are the key structural elements, and the sentence, as the movie proceeds, takes on weight.

Wiseman is one of the remaining practitioners of "direct cinema" or "cinéma vérité"—the documentary method, originating in the early 1960s, of entering a situation or event with lightweight camera and portable tape recorder and shooting whatever is going on, without script or rehearsal or agreed-upon direction. Such surrender to the subject is the pure form of cinéma vérité, more honored in the breach than in the observance. Other famous vérité filmmakers, such as Donn Pennebaker and Richard Leacock, who worked on *Monterey Pop* (1969), or the Maysles brothers in their *Salesman* (1969), *Gimme Shelter* (1970), and *Grey Gardens* (1975), have photographed formal events, such as rock festivals, or have imposed a narrative or other fictional structure on the material in advance (as in *Salesman*). Wiseman, working without a preconceived plan, shoots and takes sound for many weeks, and then spends months editing the raw footage. The finished film typically represents about one twenty-fifth of the footage shot.

The minister's sentence, it turns out, is emblematic. As the film unfolds, Central Park emerges as a specialized Eden—protected and shaped and argued over by city people guarding an illusion of nature in the midst of one of the most violently urbanized environments in the world. Wiseman observes the self-consciousness of city dwellers heavily aware of their distance from nature, anxiously cultivating their patch of ground—the volunteer gardeners tending cautiously to clumps of shrubbery, students of butterfly migration peering intently into the air. People project onto the park their dissatisfaction with city life: the determined women of the Central Park Conservancy, a successful private organization that has raised and spent millions of dollars since 1980 restoring and beautifying the park, are the most fervent of all believers in the idea of the park as a garden—but the garden they have in mind, we begin to see, is that of a country house, or an English park. "It's safe, it's comfortable," says a Conservancy fund raiser, a description half of which is demonstrably false. "You don't see loitering or grafitti," says another.

But what is the park for if it's not for loitering? What we see in the film both is and isn't the Conservancy's vision of the park—clean and handsome now, but also overflowing with disorderly life. By concentrating on the protest groups and religious acolytes, on the ranks of sunning homosexuals and elderly women doing push-ups, Wiseman, who was a law professor and city planner before becoming a filmmaker, appears to be presenting something like Jane Jacobs's vision of the city, in which the polyglot vitality of the park serves as the vessel of our careless democracy.

Many of Wiseman's early films were outraged exposés of humiliation and resistance. The criminally insane locked up in filthy pens and mistreated in *Titicut Follies*; the young draftees in *Basic Training* (1971; a near companion piece to *High School*), inadequately prepared for the war in Southeast Asia that almost no one believed in—these people were plainly victims, trapped or stunned by bureaucratic routine, though their tormentors, bullying or merely dulled and inept, were revealed as hardly less defeated.

Institutions are made up of two classes, the inmates, who usually need or want something, and the staff, who are so habituated to the ways of the institution as to be no longer separable from it. They are a natural place to observe the effects of power in America. The classic *Welfare* (1975), still Wiseman's most powerful film, takes place entirely in a Manhattan welfare office, in which exhausted and dazed petitioners for aid surge forward to make their pleas to be put on the welfare rolls. A few of them are imperious, or enterprising, or shrewdly manipulative, but most of them are just confounded. They want money and shelter, but they also want something that they cannot articulate: dignity or sympathy, perhaps, but also a reasonable explanation of their "case." But this is precisely what the staff at the center—timid, self-obsessed, and obtuse, and themselves victims of the rigid and absurd rules of the welfare system—cannot possibly provide.

Wiseman concentrates on the relations between staff and clients, building up a rhythm of complaint and rebuff that has a ritualistic power. The welfare workers can only woodenly repeat the rules. For the young, educated, mostly female social workers on the staff, as well as for the older, male, supervisors, the desk that separates them from the clients is an essential barrier. It is as if, were they to react at all, to "understand" too much, they could be infected by the dismay and defeat on the other side. What seems like bureaucratic coldness is also a form of guilty panic.

Watching these scenes, one senses that Wiseman has been influenced less by sociology than by literature. In *Welfare*, two bent, quavering old men, having made their way through the city to the center—the wrong center, it turns out—are sent off again, with a curt command, to another office many blocks away. Wiseman holds the camera on their retreating backs as they shuffle to the door. A furious black woman with large eyes and a wall-slamming voice who has been waiting on line for several hours with her confused mother, whom she has been taking care of for many months, launches into an intense and angry aria of frustration and of contempt for the mysteries of bureaucratic regulation that have forced the two women to rush from social security office to court to hospital, and to arrive at last at the head of the line as the welfare office is closing for the night.

The scene is worthy of Dickens. But once we fully register the drawn or puffy faces, the senseless voices that yet make more than sense, the film frees itself of its literary influences. The images of actual people, each observed individually in raw moments of suffering and frustration, create almost overwhelming tension. In some of Wiseman's films, that tension is not quite satisfactorily resolved, but in *Welfare* the language breaks free, defining each character and situation. A few of the petitioners are visibly ashamed, others seem almost exhilarated, defiant of their innumerable disasters, proud of their messy lives their *stories*, and they pour out a flood of imprecation and lamentation. "What do I do *tonight*?" asks a tall man with a long, melancholy jaw who has been turned away, after being promised an appointment for the next morning. He is a therapist or psychic researcher of some sort who has lost his job. "I haven't eaten for three days now—except what I steal. I can't steal a chicken. I can't steal a steak. It doesn't fit in my pocket."

No one could deny Wiseman's extraordinary sympathy for the insulted and the injured of American society. Yet he doesn't romanticize or politicize the oppressed. He shows the tangle and self-destructiveness of lives as they are acted out and on display in the welfare office, and the way these very qualities compound the difficulties in getting on the rolls. But in the face of the staff's contempt and indifference, the clients' rage and assertiveness—their incoherent complaints, their madness even—become a triumph of individuality, a revenge of temperament on power. They refuse to be quiet. They fight or try to beat the system—or at least to leave their fingerprints on it.

Welfare, along with *Titicut Follies*, *High School*, and *Basic Training* are early Wiseman films that are devastating portraits of institutions. For a while, Wiseman seemed a bitter critic of institutional fatuity, destructiveness, and self-perpetuation, and some of his early admirers, like Edgar Z. Friedenberg, saw his work's power as directly proportional to the severity of his attacks. But as Wiseman went on working through the Seventies and Eighties, the early political estimate of his intentions began to seem inadequate—even mistaken.

In a conventional "professional" television documentary, the material is organized in tabular or chronological order; exposition of explicitly defined issues moves clearly from point to point; and the film's attitudes are "balanced" by opinion of a contrary strain. Wiseman ignores that. Selecting and cutting material from his huge quarry of footage, he works with the freedom of a novelist; he "composes" the movie by assembling a complex mosaic whose point of view and theme emerge gradually and by means of the viewer's interpretation.

For example, in *High School*, the Dean of Discipline, a stocky man with a military brush cut, uses his power in all his relations with students, for instance, bullying an unhappy and rebellious teen-ager who has been unjustly accused of stealing into accepting, and even approving of, his punishment. We then see the dean in a classroom teaching history, where he tells the students that collective bargaining began in the United States because of "a lack of communication" between employees and employers. In other words, power has nothing to do with it. Wiseman is not simply exposing the clichés of a stupid or hypocritical teacher. The movie was shot in 1968, and the school was then clearly attempting to hold off what it perceived as cultural anarchy outside its walls. Many of the teachers and administrators are exercising a bland and frightened dictatorship; their speech is deadened as if any sign of life might inspire the students to break out of control.

Meanwhile, dulled and demoralized by the teachers' inability to bring any subject to life, many of the best students are gathered in a class of malcontents where they sit in a resentful torpor—they are also victims of the hypocrisy and authoritarianism promoted in the school.

In such cinéma-vérité films of the Sixties as *Monterey Pop* or *Woodstock*, the camera was jerked this way and that, in pursuit of a spontaneous moment in a sweeping panorama: and often all that one got was isolated moments. Wiseman uses "moments" structurally. The scenes with the Dean of Discipline were shot on several different occasions; they have been pulled out of the flow of events, and they are played one against the other as the film proceeds. In *Welfare*, the scenes in which the clients express their sense of worthlessness are echoed, partly ironically, by later episodes in which the welfare bureaucrats petulantly argue over their status in the system. A passing emotion or idea in a Wiseman film becomes a key element in a form he seems to be devising in front of our eyes. The most tightly organized of the films can be "read" almost as texts, read for their internal life as well as their reflections of the world outside.

In *Law and Order* (1969), a white policeman arrests a black teenager who has been making trouble in his neighborhood; even though the boy threatens to kill him, the cop is having a good time because the neighborhood regards the boy as a menace and jeers at him as he's taken away. In 1969, when the movie was shot, many in the audience may have been ready to see the police-man as a sadistic agent of state power. But this judgment is modified and refined throughout the film, and a far more interesting one replaces it.

As they make their rounds, the police on screen are constantly subjected to abuse (the same officer later admits to a colleague that he's frightened of the boy, who is about to be released from jail). The police are thrown into inco-herent and violent family quarrels for which nothing in their training has pre-pared them and in the wake of which they are invariably found at fault. *Law and Order* is moving, finally, as an expression of a flowing and undoctrinaire sense of life that is almost melancholy in its acceptance of confusion and loss. By the end of the movie, the police appear to be not so much overbearing agents of the state as the inadequate last resort in neighborhoods that are falling apart.

Looking for the secrets of these places, Wiseman discovered not only oppressiveness but also momentary flashes of spirit in the daily life of institutions. *Hospital*, made in 1970, a year after *Law and Order*, turned out to be less the attack on the urban health-care system that might have been expected than a sorrowing introduction to the elemental, intractable moments of life. Many of the urban poor arrive at the hospital wounded or dying, in shock or suffering with multiple problems, or terrified to face a doctor. The big-city hospital (Metropolitan Hospital, near Harlem, in Manhattan), with its patients waiting forlornly in the hallways, is overburdened and almost chaotic. The movie is not reassuring about urban health care, but it shows its staff coping with limited resources rather well. *Hospital* is filled with surprising, simple, and human gestures—a woman doctor, for instance, saying, "There's nothing to be ashamed of" to an old man who has cancer and is too frightened by the physical ugliness of his symptoms to discuss them with anyone. As the hospital workers struggle to cope with the disasters pouring into the emergency room, the viewer begins to realize that he is watching not the dim events of bureaucratic procedure, but large and grave instances of suffering, courage, and endurance.

The material is so strong that it also produces moments of disgust or revulsion, and at times Wiseman's work approaches black comedy. In *Titicut Follies* there is a grim sequence in which a brutal attendant is force-feeding an inmate who has refused to eat. The attendant pours something liquid into a funnel attached to a narrow hose, which is inserted down the throat of a howling and shaking old man. After twenty years I can still see as vividly as I did then that ghastly scene, in which the attendant's cigarette is fixed in his mouth (both his hands were busy), its lengthening ash dangling precipitously over the open funnel. I remember waiting almost without breathing to see if the ash would fall in.

A "sick" joke like that has a mock cinematic suspense—and it is also truly shocking. For a while, Wiseman's work was almost remorselessly black comedy. *Meat* (1976) was an elaborated joke about advanced industrial methods as applied to butchery, a visual essay on the deconstruction of a cow. Slaughtered, sectioned, sliced, chopped, and wrapped, the beasts were transformed into product. *Meat* is a handsome and scornfully witty film—a sly parody of those celebratory industrial documentaries we were all forced to watch at summer camp on rainy days. But the absence of people was limiting.

There are plenty of people in the three-hour *Canal Zone* (1977), an exhaustive study of the American colony living and working at the Panama Canal, but they are seen as examples of humanity as its meanest. Isolated, a long way from home, and threatened by extinction, the American colonials keep up morale with a nonstop diet of drills, award banquets, speeches, and flag-raising. These Americans isolated in Panama have produced a concentrated version of small-city conservatism, Babbittry raised to defensive hysteria. But the pinched faces and pinched attitudes become almost numbing in their sameness. The best case Wiseman can make for them is that they aren't fakes. Even the rebellious gestures central to the earlier films are absent. (In *Meat*, a recalcitrant cow jumps the pen on the way to the slaughterhouse.)

In *Model* (1980), a dead-pan look at the high-fashion racket, Wiseman teases a fetish system that raises artifice above experience; *The Store* (1983) chronicles the snobbish appeals employed by a Dallas department store to sell luxury goods to culturally insecure Texans at ridiculous prices. Wiseman may have enjoyed exposing the very strategies that he disdains for his own work, but the wit here is colder than before, more self-contained—almost prissy. For a while, in the early Eighties, Wiseman seemed to be running out of subjects that could fully engage him.

In his recent movies, Wiseman has returned to the material of his earlier work, but without their bitter irony and the preoccupation with victimization and incompetence. One of his recent projects has been a quartet of documentaries, *Blind, Deaf, Adjustment and Work*, and *Multi-Handicapped* (1986). In *Blind*, which was photographed at the Alabama School for the Blind in Talledega, a pupil, Jason, a little boy of about six, carries a math paper he is proud of out of his regular classroom, down the hall, down a stairway, past many open doors, and into another classroom, where he presents it to a friendly teacher for approval. He then turns around and retraces his steps, receiving from his home-room teacher some free time as a reward. The sequence is accomplished with only a single cut; the camera tails after the boy, noting each encounter and mishap along the way, and long before he reaches his goal one realizes, against all skepticism, that Jason's trip is an epic moment of documentary cinema.

The quartet of films records the heroism both of young children learning to make do without sight or hearing, and, in *Adjustment and Work*, of older people with multiple handicaps, learning to negotiate, say, the corridor of a factory by listening to the sounds coming through closed doors. These are among Wiseman's most moving works. And last year he completed a masterpiece.

The five-hour-fifty-eight-minute *Near Death* (1989) takes place in the intensive care unit of a Boston hospital, where we see the largest gap yet between staff and clients: the doctors possess almost all the power, the patients, attached to some life-sustaining apparatus, have none. One of the patients, Mr. Cabra, a Hispanic with pulmonary fibrosis, is only thirty-two; the others, much older, have suffered either multiple heart attacks or strokes and are struggling for breath. If they are to have any hope of living, not merely staying alive, they must get off the machines. But once they are taken off the machines, they will probably die—if not immediately, then in a few weeks or months. Advanced medical techniques, by extending their lives, have created a remarkable situation in which the only "healthy" thing for them to do is to die. By going off the machines, the patients at least can go home, where surrounded by family and friends, they can face the end of life with some measure of dignity.*

The subject of terminal patients and advanced medical techniques is a commonplace of news reports and soap opera. But Wiseman brings to it an intensity and gravity unknown in television. In this film Wiseman imposes a narrative, placing the stories of four patients end to end instead of intercutting them, thereby removing any suggestion of suspense—this is a film, after all, about the treatment of terminally ill patients.

The nearly dying, breathing through masks or often unconscious, lie silently in an alertly attended limbo. They are far away: visitors and doctors shout down at them as if they were lying at the bottom of a well. In this film, the clients have entirely lost their individuality. Wiseman's attention stays fixed on the doctors. He observes in particular two of them, both young—Dr. Taylor, who is mostly seen quietly trying to explain the patients' situations to their families again and again (the families, unwilling to foreclose on life, cannot take in what is being said), and Dr. Weiss, a lung specialist in his late thirties who, as the movie progresses, is increasingly tormented by his responsibility, and nearly breaks down.

These relatively recent graduates of medical school have been trained to recognize the emotional as well as the medical needs of their patients. Yet it is their courtesy, their sensitivity to the feelings and dignity of the patients—in contrast to an older doctor, who announces a grim diagnosis and disappears—that makes their position the more difficult. The suggestion is, of course, that they, too, will grow hardened if they are to remain sane. But for now these young doctors have to face such dilemmas as: What if the best thing for patients is to accept that any treatment beyond pain-killers and sedatives is useless? The doctors are the victims of an existential paradox: their concern for their patients often obliges them to recommend termination of treatment. But the words for such a recommendation are impossible to say.

Near Death, throughout its immense length, is shot mostly in the intensive care unit. The doctors meet with patients' families; they awkwardly cluster

---

*The situation here should not be confused with the disputed "right to die" that the Supreme Court recently established. As far as we can tell, none of these patients wants to die.

together with nurses for impromptu conferences in the hallways (no room being set aside for this purpose). What is said in these anguished sessions, once, perhaps, the material of their undergraduate bull sessions, is now real and momentous: When can a patient's condition truly be called terminal? Does life have a value in itself—or only life of a certain quality? The movie investigates the morally anomalous condition of being a healer in an age when technology has interfered with the body's natural progress toward death. Arguments in the film are circular, since there are no answers. They are repeated, modified, particularized, extended, throughout *Near Death*'s great length, and the film grows in power as it goes on and on.

And in Wiseman's characteristically bleak way, the movie is funny. As in his other films, language is key. How does a commercial and technological civilization, positive and utilitarian by temperament, speak of death? In America, the dramatic and poetic language of death has gone. The doctors themselves cannot speak of death in part because they are advocating it, the patients and their families cannot, because they deny it. Even more than most of us, all of them are eagerly looking for a euphemism.

In their conversations with one another, the doctors and nurses say, "If we take him off the respirator, and he doesn't fly, I'm loathe to put him back on." A doctor says that treating a patient dying of lung disease with antibiotics is like using "a pea-shooter against an atomic bomb." The sports and military metaphors, morose attempts at cheerfulness as well as denial, suggest how savagely inarticulateness impoverishes us. For though the doctors clearly have considerable delicacy of feeling, they cannot express it.

When the intensive care unit revives a patient whose heart has stopped beating for a few seconds and who was technically "dead," the doctors query him excitedly afterward. "You've already been there. You know death." (We don't hear his answer.) The doctors are curious to know their antagonist, who has become, in this case, also a secret, unmentionable friend. But words elude them.

Other words they use again and again. We hear the word "comfort" with increasing irony. The doctors want to get the patients and their families to accept "comfort measures"—meaning the withdrawal of all treatment, now useless, except for morphine and sedatives. Comfort equals death. A nurse, speaking of the man who "dies" and returns, but who will surely die for good soon enough, says, "Until he comes to terms with the fact that comfort is the way to go, I guess we can get him [back] to where he was." Inevitably, a doctor says, "We're comfortable with that"—i.e., we've done everything we can do. It is, in a way, an apology. Given the squalor and misery in which most people die, the physical ease of mortality in *Near Death*, a high accomplishment of civilization, is, like the doctor's fervor, deeply unsettling: indeed Wiseman's chaste refusal here to heighten our response with music seems almost punitive.

There are moments in every Wiseman film when the great roar of an institution stops, when the director fastens on what might be called its ecology. In *Central Park* the park itself is a living organism that fills and empties, a garden producing great heaps of garbage, collected in shiny black bags under a romantic moon. Wiseman is attentive to the hollows of institutional activity, the quiet hours when the floors are mopped and the walls and lights seem to hum. Do institutions have a soul? Wiseman's camera strains to capture their mystery, much in the way Edward Hopper does in his paintings of lonely places.

His patience pays off in the astonishing things people say in almost all these films. In the wedding in *Central Park*, the groom, a small balding man with a black beard and wire-frame glasses, says to his bride, "I submit myself to you in love, Elaine, and give myself to you, as my wedding gift, my flesh, to exercise your authority over, that I might not deny you pleasure," which is answered by the no less strange, "I shall uphold your honor in the eyes of others, and remember to praise you when I am with them." The ravings of the mad and maddened in *Titicut Follies*, or the violent outbursts in *Law and Order* or *Welfare*, or the surreally banal social gatherings in *Canal Zone*—such moments, as they each become part of the whole expressive, formal work, produce an elation unique to documentary art.

1990

Geoffrey O'Brien

In his books *The Phantom Empire* and *Castaways of the Image Planet*, and in his movie reviews for *The New York Review of Books*, poet and film critic Geoffrey O'Brien (b. 1948) has gone into the attic of the collective subconscious to find bits and pieces of movies, pop songs, and headlines that lodge there. Though he can write film critiques that are impeccably judicious and reasoned, O'Brien has also perfected a wilder post-modernist stew (see "The Italian System" below) comprising lists, surreal connections, darting insights, and social history: film criticism done in the form of open-ended prose poem. In this chapter from *The Phantom Empire*, as in his memoir *Dream Time*, O'Brien seems less concerned to tell his story than his generation's, to capture in alluringly rhythmic prose the detritus of that universal youth-mind—rock 'n roll, horror movies, drugs, sex, sensory overload—all to be retrieved later in the melancholy, Proustian total recall of middle-aged adulthood.

◆

The Italian System

You wandered in memory through a worldwide junk heap of images—like the makeshift souks of *Blade Runner* and *Mad Max Beyond Thunderdome*—trying to recall the big central display window that existed once, in the shiny world before the center failed. There had come an intermediary period full of signs and portents. The display began to wobble, as if there had all that time been only one light source and it was starting to flicker. Or as if a voice were going hoarse, the only voice in the entertainment world with enough authority to recite: "During the reign of Caesar Augustus, Herod the Great was ruler over all Judaea. And there came to him wise men . . ." In the last days of imperial Hollywood, the big show was the spectacle of the show's disappearance.

The Roman Empire photographed its own decay, as Alec Guinness morosely examined the entrails of sacrificed animals, Charlton Heston's corpse was propped up inside his armor to ride into battle against the Moors, and Steve McQueen died trying to hold at bay the inexorable energies of Chinese revolution. So many movies were about the aging and imminent death of their stars. The heroism of cowboys was transmuted into the heroism of the actors still just capable of playing them.

In the same spirit you were meant to admire the self-destructive extravagance with which the remnants of the studios squandered their resources on histories the audience no longer believed in (if indeed it had even heard of them). After another generation, the Roman Empire would exist only as a footnote to movie history: "Ancient political structure on which films such as *Spartacus* and *Ben-Hur* were based, noted for orgies, chariot races, and acid repartee enunciated by British actors."

It was an intolerably protracted farewell to the old money that had commanded legions of extras; that built three-dimensional sets the size of small cities and then burned them down; that when it clapped made all eyes swivel toward the marquees and billboards and magazine covers it monopolized. The pleasure of the late imperial spectacle was steeped in the cruelty of that slow death. You savored the gradual involuntary abdication as you had been taught to savor the death scenes of Garbo in *Camille* or the wounded GIs in *Battle Hymn*.

All signs spoke of the end: the atrophied camera movements, the crowds so huge they became undirectable and milled about listlessly, the lab effects that might once have passed unnoticed but became glaringly evident when blown up to the grandiose proportions of the 70-millimeter frame, the leaden pauses that existed only to emphasize the *duration* of the program, as if in those last desperate days mere length became a survival tactic. "Make it last forever, there may never be another one." *How the West Was Won*, *55 Days at Peking*, *The Fall of the Roman Empire*: the hugeness of history established a scale which could then be applied indiscriminately to elephantine comedies (*It's a Mad, Mad, Mad, Mad World*, *The Great Race*), auto-race movies whose amplitude worked curiously against the grain of their high-speed spins and crack-ups (*Grand Prix*), musicals so disproportionate that they seemed to lose all relation to the human body (*Doctor Dolittle*, *Star!*, *Hello, Dolly!*). Bigness by now was destiny, or malediction. To expand uncontrollably was as malign a fate as to shrink.

The aging studio czars and their accountant successors couldn't control the scale of things anymore. A remorseless stiffening of reflexes had set in. The images were born old. Audiences woke as if from a long slumber to find themselves looking at a state-of-the-art wax museum, the Gimbel's window come to fitful life: a Grace Kelly look-alike with dyed hair lip-synched her dialogue against a slightly grainy rear projection representing New York's fashionable East 78th Street, to which the music of Neal Hefti or Frank de Vol tried desperately to lend animation. The crackle of sexual innuendo slowed to a blind glacial crunch. Where had the other spectators gone, the ones for whom these images had evidently been intended? What plague or systematic program of assassination had kept them from attending?

The latest sophisticated comedy looked like a promotional short for a hotel chain with empty rooms in every major capital. Indeed, Hollywood was going the way of the beloved old New Orleans hotel in *Hotel*, caught between buyout by money men who would trample its soul and the wrecker's ball that would obliterate it. In the last reel Rod Taylor (probably the lone heroic hotel manager in movie history) opted for the wrecker's ball, and then in proper six-ties fashion set about getting stoned down in the bar where the last blast, the party at the end of the world, was just getting into gear. The drinks were on the house.

The trouble in the empire was highlighted by the encounter, in Hollywood's shadow, with another Hollywood, its cheap twin. The Americans now *had* to make movies that were long and ponderous, as if to do anything less would be a surrender as abject as to withdraw from Southeast Asia. The resources had to be wasted to prove that they were still there to waste. But in Europe it was still possible to work with enough speed and violence and crudity to make movies suited to the world they were being shown in. They had sets and music too, and jazzy main title sequences, just like real movies: like a watch sold on the street corner that could almost pass for a Rolex if you didn't examine it too closely.

The European movies playing on Times Square in 1964 formed part of a multi-episode, multinational serial set in The City (a modular megalopolis of which Rome, Frankfurt, Cairo, and New Delhi were interchangeable subdivi-sions) with its computer networks, its hotel chains, its Möbius-strip highway systems, its canned music converting piazzas into wraparound amplifiers, its transnational corporations implementing mind control through synthetic drugs and programmed orgies.

Jets linked its scattered centers. Never had there had been so many shots of jets taking off, always accompanied by electric guitar music. A jet might take off in one movie and land in another. The deplaning passengers might even encounter some of the same actors, or at least actors who resembled them as uncannily as the androids that rogue masterminds were mass-producing in con-cealed laboratories scattered around the globe.

A common vocabulary had been uncovered, a glossary appropriate for any movie made outside the Iron Curtain, a set of cards that could be reshuffled to generate instant screenplay: airport, amnesia, assassination, atom bomb, blackmail, bondage, cavern, criminal gang, desert, drug hallucination, dual personality, explosion, fashion model, fire, impalement, insanity, jewelry, jungle, laboratory, lesbianism, luxury hotel, mutilation, narcotics, nightclub, nightmare, poison, police investigator, prostitute, psychiatrist, rape, religious cult, satanism, secret society, sequestered island, speedboat, strangulation, striptease, telepathy, telephone, tomb, torture.

Within this field of elements things were made to happen by manipulating the rules of fetishism—not changing them, just nudging them into unforeseen corners. It was a live-action encyclopedia, a zoo of captive gestures. Each imprisoned object exerted a familiar but somehow inexhaustible magnetism. This method of filmmaking might be called for the sake of convenience the Italian System.

All the movies ever made constituted a storehouse of images waiting to be appropriated and pasted into place:

Music Box (*The Criminal Life of Archibaldo de la Cruz*, *Two Rode Together*, *The Ghost*, *For a Few Dollars More*). Childhood, the pain of memory. Sets off a magical or hypnotic process; summons the murderer to his task; restores identity to the amnesiac. Must be smashed or drowned. Its violent disappearance is equivalent to a spiritual liberation.

Madhouse (*The Cabinet of Dr. Caligari*, *Spellbound*, *Bedlam*, *Shock Corridor*, *Shock Treatment*, *House of Madness*). The world is a madhouse. The keeper is himself a madman. The inmate's delusion encrypts the solution to an actual crime.

Likewise: the mirror, the dark glasses, the ray that shrinks or makes invisible, the suitcase stuffed with dollars, the tunnel, the harem, the theatrical dressing room, the police station, the scalpel, the snapshot, the painting, the scarf, the glove, the hat, the window, the secluded cabin, the caged animal, the trapdoor (a thick round handle embedded in the floor), the woods (flight), the streetlamp (violence), rain, cyclone . . .

The letter being written, the letter being torn up or burned, the ring, the locket, the blow, the concealed glance of lust or adoration, the look of recognition, the grimace of hidden envy . . .

The skull, the abyss, the barred door. The tattoo. The scar, the mark of the branding iron.

The Italian System, honorifically: because it was at Rome's Cinecittà studio, and subsequently at Rome's outposts in Spain and Yugoslavia (cut-rate outposts of an empire bought out by entrepreneurial barbarians from New Jersey and West Berlin), that the system was brought to its highest level of automatism. All pretense of telling a new story was abandoned in favor of luxuriating in the intimately predictable contours of the old story. It was a sort of unmasking, as if to say: Look how cheap it is, how hasty, how loud, how unoriginal. *È formidabile, no?*

Was it Hollywood's mirror, or had Hollywood itself all along been only a mirror of a lost European splendor that had secretly survived every catastrophe? Which was the authentic fake, the Ur-ersatz? Cinecittà was before Hollywood. It was what Hollywood had fed on. In the beginning—in the bright dawn that was April 1914—were the volcanoes and elephants and Carthaginian battles of Giovanni Pastrone's *Cabiria*, the virgins fed to the flaming maw of Moloch, the erotic soliloquies and operatic slow-motion death of Queen Sophonisba, the energetic exertions of the good-natured, simple-minded giant Maciste.

It was in *Cabiria* that D. W. Griffith found the germ of the idea for *Intolerance*, and if his inspiration hadn't been *Cabiria* it would have been *The Slave of Carthage* or *The Queen of Nineveh* or *The Virgin of Babylon* or *Fabiola* or *Herodias* or *Theodora*. From the beginning the Italians had recognized in film an opportunity to frame mute divas—Lyda Borelli, Pina Menichelli, Italia Manzini— against Mesopotamian wall hangings. They found their paradise early, and embellished it tirelessly with harps, tigers, fans, orchids, baths, patterned carpets, brooches, sandals, slaves, phalanxes, peacocks, gigantic stone idols, poisonous gardens. The images were visual incense: you inhaled them.

Here too was history, but a history that did what it was told, a sensual history freely adapting itself to the silks and fountains in the midst of which it had been resurrected. Beautiful ghosts were brought out to show off their costumes and perform their appointed turn: Nero, Messalina, Saint Sebastian, Faust, Socrates, Julius Caesar, Lucrezia Borgia, Saint Cecilia, and (for a parting burst of carnivalesque color) Ali Baba and Satan. The past was a festival where no desire was denied.

Cinecittà was then concurrent with Hollywood, competing with the relentless American marketing machine, cooperating with it (in a spirit of mutual mistrust) for the location sequences of the silent *Ben-Hur*, with Black Shirt labor stooges stirring up trouble on the set while extras (who, desperate for cash, had lied about being able to swim) drowned to make possible the extraordinary naval battle. Mussolini banned *Ben-Hur* for local consumption anyway, once he found out that the Roman lost the chariot race. In the end it was determined that Italy could do without American movies, and the American market.

But Fascist cultural directives didn't constrict things all that much. In fact, they provided an ideal pretext for continuing to make movies about banquets, vengeance, and slaves, with emphasis added for the moment on the glories rather than the decadence of the Roman Empire. The nostalgia for world domination was transmuted into the creation of miniature worlds: the jungles and deserts of an imaginary Africa, the brocaded bedrooms of Renaissance princesses, and interiors sculpted out of gauze and rock candy to frame the operatic climaxes of *The Crown of Iron* and *Captain Tempest* and *An Adventure of Salvator Rosa*. Here no blow told, death was music, battle was decorative, and all endings were suffused with an exquisitely tearful happiness.

For a time, time froze. Out in the great world great things were done: heroic Phalangists defended Toledo against the Republican onslaught, saintly missionaries planted the seeds of faith in Libyan wastes, nurses tended the wounds of soldiers. As if to demonstrate what gestural code the recruits had been commanded to mime, *Tosca* and *Cavalleria Rusticana* and the life of Verdi came to lend their support. Those in the interior zone—shy, inarticulate young couples, stenographers, defense workers—could still find something to marvel at in the designs and protocols of a modern department store. It would provide the basis of a wistful, ultimately reassuring little comedy: *Their Day in the City*.

Having survived all that, Cinecittà began to look as if it would survive Hollywood as well. It had made itself the surrogate Hollywood, Hollywood's Hollywood, a low-cost recycling plant for every cast-off plot device and visual motif, not to mention every used-up actor and director: drunks, wilted starlets, aging cowboy actors, former colleagues of Griffith and Ince unemployable in the new Hollywood.

It took Italy to reinvent the faces of Rory Calhoun, Guy Madison, Reed Hadley, Brett Halsey, Ray Danton—certifiably American actors designed to impart authenticity to their surroundings—and to juxtapose their faded nobility with the fresher beauty of Genevieve Grad, Helga Line, Wandisa Guida, or Nadir Baltimor, under the imported directorial tutelage (filtered through some unimaginable fracas of multilingual interpretation) of Raoul Walsh, Irving Rapper, Hugo Fregonese, or Jacques Tourneur.

It was as close as movies got to a cultural lineage, this process of spirals within spirals by which you got the myth (the real, original Italian epics, *Cabiria* and *Quo Vadis* and *The Fall of Troy*, that took America by storm in 1914) and the myth of the myth (the improved and homogenized American epics, *Intolerance* and *Ben-Hur* and *The Queen of Sheba*, which in turn found their way back to Italian screens) and then, beyond computing, the myths of the myths of the myths, as each photographed the other's photographs: the Fascist historical epics with their perfect emulation of Hollywood gloss (*Scipio Africanus*, *The Crown of Iron*), the fifties Hollywood spectacles that took advantage of cheap

Italian backdrops and extras (*Helen of Troy*) and the Italian spectacles that took advantage of Hollywood stars (Kirk Douglas in *Ulysses*), the even cheaper Italian imitations of those spectacles (*Hercules, Hercules Unchained, The Loves of Hercules*) that turned unemployed bodybuilders from Muscle Beach into authentic European stars and ultimately—by way of drive-ins and neighborhood chains—back into authentic American anti-stars, the first major figures in the impending anti-aesthetic with its cult of the bad.

The coilings became ever more inextricable: the art movie *La Dolce Vita* mythologized the sleazy underbelly of the Cinecittà world through the emblematic figures of Anita Ekberg and Lex Barker, the Hollywood movie *Two Weeks in Another Town* mythologized *La Dolce Vita* with Kirk Douglas and Edward G. Robinson masquerading as has-beens washed up in Rome, the horror queen Barbara Steele of *Black Sunday* and *Castle of Blood* turned up in Fellini's *8½*, and when Jean-Luc Godard made his solitary concession to narrative filmmaking (entitled, precisely, *Contempt*) it had to revolve around an Italo-American remake of *The Odyssey* produced by Jack Palance and directed by Fritz Lang. (Lang had already made his Italian-style movie, not in Italy but in India, in German: a diptych divided into *The Tiger of Eschnapur* and *The Indian Tomb*, in which the director—scrupulously adhering to the 1921 scenario he was remaking—charted with hieratic precision the process by which a nearly expressionless German architect fell in love with a temple dancer incarnated by Debra Paget and had in consequence to do battle with rajahs and tigers and lepers.)

Two Weeks in Another Town caught the Italian method, in approximately the sense that one contracts a malady. This was entirely appropriate, since the movie's theme was the decline of Hollywood and the spiritual wreckage exposed in the process of that decline. It was as if M-G-M had decided to commit a peculiarly cinematic suicide by filming its own death. Director Vincente Minnelli and producer John Houseman incorporated ghostly references to their earlier collaboration *The Bad and the Beautiful*, just to twist the knife in the wound. They depicted the breakup of their world while remaining faithful until the last gasp to its forms and methods, displaying a loyalty as unwavering as that of disgraced samurai committing *seppuku*.

The bright, easily distinguishable modular units that made up *Two Weeks in Another Town* could serve as an internationally viable glossary of human feeling and knowledge circa 1962. Love: a couple walking at night holding hands against a background of Roman fountains, or lying on a beach sharing a bottle of red wine in a wicker wrapping. Debauchery: Kirk Douglas with his arms around three different women simultaneously, smashing a table, roaring with laughter. The male crisis of middle age: he looks at his hand shaking, or talks to a doctor in a room filled with leather-bound medical books.

George Hamilton means bisexuality, youthful weakness and uncertainty, complicated neuroses. Rome means comical waiters, hustling agents and producers, temperamental starlets, *La Dolce Vita*. Europe, more broadly, means *La Dolce Vita* (noise, orgies, international cast) plus *Bonjour Tristesse* (youthful perversity, jaded middle age) plus *Last Year at Marienbad* (elegant clothes, hieratically slow movements, inexplicable gaps and reversals in narrative continuity). Authenticity: Dahlia Lavi's neighborhood where ragged little boys play soccer in the street, poetic poverty, Neorealist movies from ten years earlier. Anger: Kirk Douglas driving his sports car at high speed toward a (rear-projected) wall. Spiritual rebirth: the car's impact is not fatal and Kirk Douglas is drenched by jets of water from the wreckage of a conveniently located fountain. The sober regrets of maturity—coinciding with the general sense that it is time for the movie to end—are represented by people saying goodbye at an airport in the morning.

They are saying goodbye to the place where they made an imaginary movie somehow more real than the one you just watched. On the edge of self-definition, it's as if a movie were trying to weasel its way out of its own existence—this isn't real, it's the *other* one inside this one that was real, the one you'll never see. The ultimate film festival would then have to consist of ghost movies: the low-budget *risorgimento* period piece that Edward G. Robinson almost finished shooting in *Two Weeks in Another Town*, Fritz Lang's *Odyssey*, the Crucifixion movie that Orson Welles was directing in Pasolini's *La Ricotta*, and the movie that (in Fellini's *Toby Dammit*) the alcoholic actor played by Terence Stamp had flown to Cinecittà to star in: the first Catholic western, "something between Dreyer and Pasolini with a touch of John Ford, of course."

The seductive charm of the Italian fantasy epics, as they infiltrated unsuspecting neighborhoods all over the world, was the experience of watching a movie that was not a "real" movie but rather a movie of a movie, in the same way you might find yourself dreaming that you were dreaming. This was not *Ben-Hur*, it was a curious REM-state deformation of *Ben-Hur*.

For one long interval—the Age of Dress-Up—it was as if a relatively young child with a propensity for storytelling had been cajoled into spinning out a single open-ended tale, an adventure without beginning or end, while a team of screenwriters took notes. To the child's basic outline were added a few adult touches: literary references and a hint of decadent sexuality.

This was how it went. A group of beings who had come from the moon centuries earlier took up residence in a huge grotto. They were ruled by a tyrannical queen who secretly worshipped a fire-breathing mask hidden behind a curtain. She hypnotized everybody in sight, slipped sleeping potion in Hercules' goblet, and cleverly convinced the sacred oracle of the goddess to tell Ursus that Hercules was the one who sold his mother into slavery. A ceremony was to take place at the base of an idol. A pair of Kurdish wrestlers were brought out for entertainment. The queen's personal maid was accused of witchcraft in order that she might be spirited away to the dungeon. She was rescued by a man wearing a helmet in the shape of a wolf's head. Meanwhile the Greek hero was condemned to undergo what was termed "the truth test," which meant that he must engage in mortal combat with a giant gorilla. The conspirators were hiding out in the forest, getting ready to attack the city. Escaped slaves built a stockade. The queen kept going back to the curtain and making smoke come out of it. Maciste confronted the Echo-men, who destroyed people's minds by making loud sounds. It was at this point that the usurpers found themselves surrounded by rebels led by the masked man, who turned out to be the queen's virtuous sister.

The stories, if such they could be called, appeared to have replicated themselves, like androids building androids, as golems finally escaped from human control. It was here—in the midst of this fever dream bearing almost no trace of a controlling intelligence, wedged between the hurling of papier-mâché boulders and bump-and-grind floor shows concocted for the amusement of the queen of Carthage—that the otherness of language made itself nakedly and helplessly apparent. The robot tones of the dubbed voices brought out the alien quality of words. The words were still there—the actors said "sky" and "mercy" and "understand"—but they had been waylaid, ripped brutally from the network of communication in which they had once functioned.

A sitcom lost in space might sound like that, tuned in by an inhabitant of Sirius light-years after the destruction of Earth. The context made almost any statement seem as eerily misdirected as the unanticipated threats and sarcasms blurted out by a mad ventriloquist's dummy. "At times your genius frightens me, Archimedes." "I thought nymphs existed only in mythology!" "Why did I survive my defeat?" "We must be ready to sacrifice all that belongs to us." "I have serious reasons for disturbing your isolation." "Now that Hercules has saved the queen from death, our whole perspective has changed." A speech at the mercy of random lip movements, unable to deviate from an imposed syntax, articulated a free-floating cosmic dread. Significant portions of the landscape lay under a curse. Or as Jayne Mansfield put it in *The Loves of Hercules*, "My people fear the wrath of the gods more than the anger of men."

It was the peculiar way that the West ended. *Seven Against Thebes*, *The Aeneid*, *The Odyssey*, Omphale, the Sabine women, Romulus and Remus, Mutius Scaevola, Coriolanus: it was the last time they would be filmed, not to enlighten an audience presumed to be ignorant and uncaring, but because the cultivated scenarists were running out of stories. As the sword-and-sandal cycle ran its course they grabbed whatever raw material came to hand, Tacitus and Captain Marvel, Sophocles and the Bible and Mandrake the Magician, Tiresias and the Sibyl, vampires and virgins and an endless horde of raucous men-at-arms. The contents of an old cupboard full of irreplaceable artifacts were being briefly held up to the light—for the delectation of uncompre- hending inheritors momentarily amused by gold leaf or a bit of fine carving— before being discarded. All periods of history collapsed into one, enabling Her- cules and Ulysses to wash up on the Gaza coast and encounter Samson. It was the final garage sale of Thrace and Carthage and Byzantium.

The assembly-line workers raked through what survived of the common fund of imagination, the ragged end-pieces of myth and fairy tale, threw in some magic potion, some crucifixion, some winged goddess, some sacrificial maiden, some blind old wise man muttering prophecies to Mr. Universe 1958. There would be no more local languages with their ancient associations and pungent proverbs, there would be only the generic dialect of those indistin- guishable dubbed voices: "Hey, Hercules, throw me a spear!" It was a docu- mentary about the party after the funeral. The spectator inhabited that same Atlantis whose magic decayed upon contact with air, whose systems of secu- rity and ritual foundered while its dark-eyed blighted queen Antinea (Fay Spain in *Hercules and the Captive Women*) murmured in sonorous post- synchronese: "I have never told you the truth, because truth and death have the same meaning for me."

After they had used up everything in the closet of the ancestors, they had to find new stuff to display. The theme of Italian commercial cinema became haste itself, the haste with which they spliced their found materials together. In an explosion of minigenres the industry annulled any possible distinction between the beautiful and the corrupt by perfecting an ultrarefined tawdri- ness, a cinema of poetic cruelty whose practitioners (Mario Bava, Vittorio Cottafavi, Riccardo Freda, Antonio Margheriti, Sergio Corbucci, Dario Argento) would turn out to have been the authentic inventors of the post-postmodern movie: authentic because they invented nothing, because they stole from their own movies, because they were unable to stop obsessively tacking together a recycled dub of a dub of some archaic internalized European narrative.

It happened too fast to track. First there were just Hercules movies. Then there were Maciste movies, Samson movies, Ursus movies, Goliath movies, and, in the wake of *Spartacus*, a steady putter of gladiator movies (*The Gladiator of Rome, The Two Gladiators, The Ultimate Gladiator*) and slave movies (*The Slave, Revolt of the Slaves, Seven Slaves Against Rome*). The wardrobe department wasn't restricted to togas and breastplates; they could also outfit pirates (*Morgan the Pirate, Musketeers of the Sea*), Vikings (*Fury of the Vikings, The Last of the Vikings*), marauders from the Central Asian steppes (*The Mongols, Maciste in the Hell of Genghis Khan, The Mighty Khan*), Arabian Nights characters (*The Thief of Baghdad*), medieval warriors (*The Revenge of Ivanhoe*), Renaissance avengers (*The Seventh Sword*). There were jungle adventures whose casts and crews seemed rapt in a deep trance imparted by the forbidden jewel of the goddess (*The Mountain of Light, Mysteries of the Black Jungle*), and there was even a series of literary adaptations set in the East Indies, based on the adventure novels of Emilio Salgari, a writer whose classic status was apparently unappreciated outside of Italy: *The Pirates of Malaysia, Sandokan Against the Leopard of Sarawak, Sandokan to the Rescue.*

At the opposite extreme from these fantasies were the pioneering gross-out documentaries of which *Mondo Cane* was the most visible: geek shows for global rubberneckers drawn to the scene of any accident, mixing farce, evisceration, and mood music. A variant form of realism offered canned erotica from the striptease parlors of the Western world (*World by Night, Forbidden Venus, Sexy Proibito*): a genre as much about money as sex, promising admission by remote control to otherwise prohibitively expensive clipjoints. ("You'd have to fly to Beirut to see this!") The art of the tease was further perfected in multiepisode sex comedies intended mostly for local consumption: *These Mad, Mad, Mad Women, Let's Talk About Women, Woman Is a Wonderful Thing.*

Foreigners were more likely to see the movies which wanted to pass for foreign, imitations of every variety of American drive-in product featuring genuine imitation American names like Sterling Roland, Fred Wilson, and Tony Bighouse. For a time these were apt to be James Bond imitations, as the primal texts of *Dr. No* and *The Ipcress File* were reworked into *That Man from Istanbul, Our Men in Bagdad, Super Seven Calling Cairo, Requiem for a Secret Agent, Secret Agent Fireball,* and other items evoking the experience of reading an Italian comic book translated into Basic English by a robot with defective wiring.

These merged almost imperceptibly with the intergalactic conspiracy theories propounded by a series of backlot science-fiction thrillers: *Wild, Wild Planet, War of the Planets, Planet of the Vampires.* Swirling poisonous mists achieved with the aid of dry ice and green and purple gelatin filters, androids in Op Art leotards, and the usual banks of beeping and blinking switchboards. The poverty of the devices seemed prophetic of the real future, which would not be a seamless, lovingly crafted Stanley Kubrick production but just such a makeshift knockoff, an international coproduction rigged by a monopoly called United Coproductions, decorating the threadbare interiors of its rocket ships with travel posters of Biarritz and Minorca to remind the hostages of the twenty-first century what Earth had been like.

When there was hardly any money for production design, the cheapest set was the inside of the human mind. That was where the Italians went for location shooting of their horror cycle, into the shadow country of Mario Bava's *Black Sunday* and Riccardo Freda's *The Horrible Dr. Hichcock* and Antonio Margheriti's *Castle of Blood*. In place of plots or sets or special effects, the method had the ingenuity of survival techniques devised by castaways or escaped prisoners of war: to infect everything the camera saw with evenly spread anxiety, sprinkling insomnia and hysteria over perfectly ordinary sofas and windows and staircases. What did they need a script for if they had enough bad mood to poison the atmosphere for a whole planet?

It was enough that the camera slide into the dark, that electronically distorted moans emanate from barely visible attics and cellars, that nameless men in masks and overcoats pull out glistening razors, and that the face of Barbara Steele stare into the lens, looking as if a vampire had nearly finished draining it of blood. (Steele's unmistakable face—with its oversized eyes and its curves curiously askew, moving with extraordinary plasticity through minute variations of gathering terror, mad devotion, seductive coercion, and sadistic glee— was itself a special effect.)

The hero of *Castle of Blood* made a bet that he could spend a night in a haunted mansion without dying. Once he got inside, he became the spectator, watching reenactments of ancient seductions and murders, conversing with beautiful ghostly women who had a disconcerting habit of vanishing without warning. The scenes he witnessed were out of sequence, as incoherent as an unedited movie. To watch *Castle of Blood* was to be inside that hapless protagonist's head and dream with him of being inside a Gothic house that seemed all the more immense for being nothing but a collection of shadows and fragments. No story, just a disconnected anthology of ominous movements: a glide along a banister, a coffin lid opening toward the camera, a zoom into the interior of a closet, a hand stretching slowly forward to unlock a door.

That *Castle of Blood* did not contain a single original visual idea, that it jettisoned coherence and explanation and relied solely upon tone and suggestion, was the secret of its effectiveness. As a member of the audience you had made a bet that you could spend a whole ninety minutes in this movie. The horror lay precisely in these being the same old images, the inescapable companions of terminal claustrophobia.

The airless love talk of Barbara Steele told you that your fate was to be trapped in this very theater, watching *Castle of Blood*—ninety minutes of living death—over and over, as debarred from real experience as the ghosts who inhabited the castle and lured in outsiders so they could feed on them and feel momentarily alive again. As the spectral inhabitants of the castle called out in unison, "We want your blood, Alan, we want your blood," you understand too late that it was indeed *your* blood that had been sought and duly exacted.

No one seemed more aware of this than the director Mario Bava, who became a brand name for a desperate kind of worst-case beauty, a loving attention to the surfaces of *Hercules in the Haunted World, Planet of the Vampires, Black Sabbath, Kill, Baby, Kill!, A Hatchet for the Honeymoon, Black Sunday, Bay of Blood*. Mario Bava (or John Foam, or John Old, as the would-be-American-style credits sometimes called him) made the frame a kind of funerary display, an ornate wreath draped around the death of a loved image. Antique dolls and mechanical toys were arranged with the discreet sensitivity of an experienced funeral home director masquerading as a fashion designer—just as the pointless, compulsively repetitive death rituals of *Blood* and *Black Lace* masqueraded as episodes in a sprightly psychedelic suspense thriller full of bright colors and lovely fashion models.

As for the fashion designer, the impotent aesthete behind it all, he was of course (in *A Hatchet for the Honeymoon*) the strangely calm lunatic whose narration—after a brief and suitably artistic prelude of Muzak and solarized photo effects under the main titles—opened the film: "My name is John Harrington. I am thirty years old. I am a paranoiac." Inadequate, and sublimely aware of its inadequacy, the movie version of life could only cling to the correctness with which it fulfilled the ritual requirements. These included the mindless bantering dialogue through which a victim flirted with her eventual murderer: "I'm just an ordinary girl. I adore luxury. I'm terribly lazy, and I like to amuse myself doing crazy things." "What kind of things?" "I just turned twenty-three and I've had several lovers."

It was in contrast to the empty worldliness of such talk that the murderer's voice-overs attained a certain austere dignity worthy of the director's studious color effects and almost pedantically beautiful displacements of the camera: "Death exists, I can assure you, and that is what makes life a ridiculous and brief dream." As for the audience's role in all this, it was more or less beside the point. The most discreetly mysterious of authors submerged himself in his images as if it were a species of suicide. You could fully enjoy the movie only by imagining that you had become Mario Bava, and that this was your own dream, your own death.

That, finally, was what the Italian marketplace could offer: a cut-rate death more brutal than anyone had yet dared to enact. The three hundred or so spaghetti westerns made between 1963 and 1969 were not there to revitalize Hollywood's tradition but to ornament its tombstone with severed ears and tortured mayors and the wreckage of trains blown up by intellectual revolutionaries. Around here the only savages were white men: cowards, con men, torturers, psychos for hire, railroad men with dead eyes. A dissonant little dance balanced Franco Nero striking a match on the boot heel of a hanged man and a machine gun mowing down a village full of women and children, a blast from a harmonica and a German militarist exported to Mexico intoning with philosophical solemnity: "Look at the sun, it resembles a ball of blood." It might have been an illustrated textbook: *The Joy of Derision*.

But by the time that particular virus ran its course the whole world had caught on. Italy discovered that it was just another Spain, just another Philippines, just another Hong Kong, just another America. A final avatar—Dario Argento, with his further explorations of Bava's science of plotless shock and dismemberment—proved that you could be as ugly as you wanted to be as long as you made it beautiful, that any atrocity was splendid if perpetrated in a Milan art gallery ("Look at this one, it's certainly one of the best examples of cosmic art") or if (like the demonic slashings, hangings, and balewire disfigurations of *Suspiria*) it propounded a satisfyingly decorative color scheme. *Suspiria* held out the hope of an escape from story, a dream or journey that might have been entitled *Art Deco Goes to Hell, Disco Style*, or *Alice in the Wonderland of the Malefic Undead*. Horror was a drug you swallowed in order to participate in an otherwise incomprehensible festival. You felt as if you'd stayed up all night dancing and chanting among maskers and witch doctors.

The drug finally—in *Terror at the Opera* (1990)—induced only a numbing reminder of now unattainable pleasures. Argento's science of the terrible had nowhere to go except as far as the back of the throat, to show the knife coming through from the outside in close-up. By then the decorative element had been reduced to the standard-issue postmodern bank of video monitors, and when the police interrogated a prime suspect—a director of slasher movies—he replied: "I think it's unwise to use movies as a guide for reality, don't you, Inspector?"

Of course it would never end, because it couldn't. Life had to go even if it meant devolution into Mafia revenge pictures, low-cost remakes of World War II, kung fu spinoffs, Terence Hill comedies, exorcism movies, barbarian movies, zombie movies, cannibal movies. In a kind of twilight state—as if in homage to the spirit of minimalism and punk—the artisans of Rome served up elegantly monotonous variations on the themes of mutilation and ingestion: *Slave of the Cannibal God, Cannibal Holocaust, Cannibal Apocalypse, Apocalypse Tomorrow, Anthropophagus, Anthropophagus II, Island of the Living Dead, City of the Walking Dead, City of the Living Dead, Zombie Holocaust, Cut and Run, Trap Them and Kill Them, Make Them Die Slowly.*

But you had already anticipated the inevitable downgrading the night your best friend lost faith in the future after watching *The Last Man on Earth*. He hadn't reckoned on what a soul-killer a quick and cheap dose of despair could be, far more effective than the carefully crafted and artistically serious kind. Somehow you knew that even *that* squalid nightmare would at some future date be regarded as a remnant of a more sensitive, more intellectually expansive age. And it came to pass just as the movies had said.

After Vincent Price dies there will be nobody left on the planet except vampires. The space monsters have figured out how to replicate themselves even after apparent annihilation. The old gods are dead, and after their last pitiful incarnation in the shape of post-synched exiles from Muscle Beach they will never be heard from again. The streets belong to fashion-conscious ax murderers choreographed by Dario Argento against a backdrop of blue-and-pink wallpaper: except that by now even the wallpaper has been obscured by the green foam oozing from the mouths of the demons who just popped out of your television set. It's the end of the world and you're getting off on it.

1993

Paul Rudnick

(aka Libby Gelman-Waxner)

Libby Gelman-Waxner (b. 1957) is the pen name used by Paul Rudnick in his film criticism column for *Premiere* magazine. Rudnick, the comic screenwriter-playwright (*Jeffrey*, *The Addams Family*, *In and Out*), may have created the persona of Libby, the shopaholic, celebrity-obsessed Jewish-American Princess married to a dentist named Josh, as a camp way to poke fun at the vulgarities of suburban consumer lifestyle, but behind this gossipy mask he makes shrewd, pointed criticisms of current movies, puncturing their pretensions and hypocrisies.

◆

A Boy Named Sioux

I have often wondered what would have happened if, instead of having my own room with a canopy bed and a Snoopy phone in Great Neck, I had been kidnapped as a child by Indians and raised as a Sioux. Now, thanks to Kevin Costner's *Dances With Wolves*, I have my answer. In this three-hour cinematic epic, Mary McDonnell plays a white woman who was brought up in a tepee after her pioneer family was slaughtered and scalped. As a squaw, Mary behaves just the way I would: she wears stunning suede outfits trimmed with shells and Ralph Lauren–style Santa Fe fringe; she does her hair in a flattering shag look instead of too-severe tribal braids; and after her first husband dies, she holds out until a white movie star shows up. Mary is called Stands With a Fist because she once hit an Indian girl who gave her a hard time. In my high school yearbook, the Great Neck *Senior Serenade*, I was voted Best Accessories and Most Likely to Marry Within Her Faith, so the comparison is obvious.

In this movie, Kevin plays a Civil War hero and pacifist who moves out to the prairie alone and becomes an honorary Sioux, even without having read any Time-Life books on how the Indians were good guys. Kevin is also the director, and he told *Us* magazine that "this is a bonding film for all. You could put it anywhere in history—the Berlin Wall, Kuwait." At the film's Los Angeles premiere, Melissa Gilbert said that Kevin and his movie "gave me so much inspiration as an actress. We are not just meat puppets! We can do so much." Demi Moore said that she "came out to support Kevin tonight. I just finished producing my husband Bruce's new film. It is all a risk for me, carrying out a vision." Believe me, you don't want to know what Rosanna Arquette had to say. Someday I hope that a Sioux movie director-star will make a film about how he moved to Bel Air and befriended everyone at Kevin's premiere; it could be called *Dances With Low SAT Scores*.

Kevin brings a real Laurel Canyon sensibility to the plains; he directs like a man with a single earring, if you know what I mean. He teaches the Indians to say "Hi," smokes whatever is in their pipes, and lets his hair get long and bleached and blown-dry; when one of the braves gives him a ceremonial necklace, I expected Kevin to say "Cool." He grins and stumbles and faints a lot, so the tribe is bound to find him adorable; he's like Dick Van Dyke in the tall grass. All of the Indians are sweet and gentle and generous, except when they are attacked by a neighboring tribe and are forced to massacre them with hatchets, arrows, and Kevin's rifles. Kevin learns to speak Lakota, a Sioux language, and he sketches and writes in his journal about how the Indians are the only decent people he's ever met. Now, I'm sure that many Indians are just terrific, but Kevin gets a little Shirley MacLaine about everything; this movie is sort of like watching a Ken doll get to know the Care Bears. All of the white men except Kevin are evil soldiers; they shoot Kevin's horse and pet wolf and use the pages of his journal as toilet paper. This makes the audience cheer when Kevin and the Indians strangle the white guys with chains and drown them.

Kevin basically avoids the really tough questions about Sioux life. At one point, the Sioux holy man asks Kevin if he and Stands With a Fist are going to try for a baby right away—did the Sioux make rawhide diaphragms? And while we're at it, what did the Indians use for toilet paper, anyway, not to mention roll-on and cologne? Whenever I see a western, all I really think is, I'm glad it's a movie, because I bet that until the turn of the century, when Johnson & Johnson arrived, the world was pretty gamy.

Sometimes I wonder what my life would be like if I just picked up and moved to the Middle East and became the sex slave of Saddam Hussein; that is just what happens to Debra Winger in *The Sheltering Sky*. This movie is based on a famous novel by Paul Bowles, but the book is one of those flat trade paperbacks instead of the nice, chunky supermarket type, so I don't trust it. Debra and John Malkovich play a bored, rich couple named Kit and Port, which sounds like a rap group; they go to the Sahara looking for an answer to their spiritual ennui. Eventually, they both expose their pubic hair and wear many neatly pressed outfits, even when they're sleeping on dirt floors in foreign-legion outposts. John is a very odd actor; he's like a transvestite who is too lazy to pull on her gown, so he just pouts and slinks around in his underwear. Eventually John dies of typhoid, and Debra behaves like any well-adjusted widow; after a decent interval, she decides to get out of her shell and meet someone new. Of course, in Debra's case, the interval is about fifteen minutes, after which she runs into the desert, hitches a ride with a caravan, and joins the harem of a Tuareg chieftain in a turban. I'm curious about life in a harem, although the movie is not very clear about it—is everything scheduled, like, If it's Tuesday, you must be Fatima? Eventually Debra leaves the harem and wanders around aimlessly, and the movie ends; when the lights went up, everyone in the theater turned to the person next to them and asked, What time is it?

The Sheltering Sky is about existential issues, like Why Are We Here? And What Is the Meaning of Life? and If There's a God, Why Does He Let Movies About Ennui Go On for More Than Two Hours? As my own mother, the beloved Sondra Krell-Gelman would say, You've got ennui? I'll give you ennui—leave me alone, get a job. And yet, once in a while, I too feel a spiritual emptiness, and I too take a journey, usually to the aisle at Gristede's marked COOKIES, CRAX, AND SNAX. Mallomars, I have found, hold most of your larger answers: the plain vanilla wafer part represents arid suffering; on top of that is fluffy white marshmallow, which represents mankind's attempt at creating an artificial happiness to cover pain; it's all sheltered by a coating of pure chocolate, which of course represents love. Some claim that the coating also represents God, but I think of Him as more of a Drake's Yodel, the only perfect food. It's all there, right in the cookie, although despair is never far off because, of course, sometimes Gristede's is closed, and then you have to go into the desert and join a harem, or at least check out whether area rugs are really cheaper in Algeria once you factor in shipping and customs.

Edward Scissorhands is another fable about the human spirit. Edward is a boy who was created by a kindly old man in a castle who gave him shears for hands and died before replacing them with fingers or a less dangerous utensil. An Avon Lady finds Edward and takes him to live in suburbia, where all the housewives are nice to him; Edward falls in love with a blond cheerleader but can't touch her without slicing. Eventually the town turns on Edward and chases him back up to the castle because he's too sweet and innocent to live among creepy human beings who do terrible things like wear stretch pants and want to have sex instead of just hug.

Some people say that this film is an allegory about Jesus or the role of the artist in society. Jesus, if you ask me, actually had something on his mind beside hedge clipping, and I don't remember anyone chasing Picasso, or Warhol, or even Tim Burton, who conceived and directed this movie, back up to his castle. Tim also directed *Beetlejuice* and *Batman*; I've noticed that after a director earns his first $50 million, he usually makes a movie about how tough it is to be a sensitive soul. In real life, people are nasty to black people and gay people and people in wheelchairs, but Tim is only worried about the guys with big eyes and scissors popping out of their elbows. It's really an issue for our times. No one ever suggests that Edward get a pair of really big gloves; no one even X-rays him to see what the kindly old man used as ingredients, aside from Cabbage Patch dolls and videocassettes of *Rain Man*.

All Edward really needs is to meet Kevin Costner, who would befriend him and help him kill all the bad people. Eventually Kevin would glue a manicure kit to his own hands out of empathy and call himself Dances With Band-Aids. And then maybe Edward could date Debra Winger, and she'd ask him for spiritual answers—if she's willing to have sex with John Malkovich on Algerian gravel, then she's up for anything. Let's bring back Pinocchio; at least he sang and danced and didn't represent anything. Life is hard enough without movie directors thinking about life all the time; they could hurt themselves, if you ask me.

1993

David Thomson

David Thomson (b. 1941), the English-born film critic (*Movie Man*, *The Whole Equation*), biographer (David O. Selznick, Warren Beatty), and fiction writer (*Suspects*) who now lives in California, is best known for his irresistible, invaluable *Biographical Dictionary of Film*. First appearing in 1975 and updated many times since, this personally voiced reference work compresses encyclopedic knowledge of actors, directors, and other movie folk into wry, pungent, judgmental thumbnail sketches, some that function as piercingly skeletal short stories about human fate. Indeed, Thomson may be said to have perfected the brief biographical entry as an alternate way of writing film criticism.

◆

Cary Grant

There is a major but very difficult realization that needs to be reached about Grant—difficult, that is, for many people who like to think they take the art of film seriously. As well as being a leading box-office draw for some thirty years, the epitome of the man-about-town, as well as being the ex-husband of Virginia Cherrell, Barbara Hutton, Betsy Drake, and Dyan Cannon, as well as being the retired actor, still handsome executive of a perfume company—as well as all these things, he was the best and most important actor in the history of the cinema.

The essence of his quality can be put quite simply: he can be attractive and unattractive simultaneously; there is a light and dark side to him but, whichever is dominant, the other creeps into view. It may be that this is Grant (or Archie Leach) himself transmitted by camera and screen thanks to a rare willingness to commit himself to the camera without fraud, disguise, or exaggeration, to take part in a fantasy without being deceived by it. But the effect he achieves is one of art; it shows malice, misogyny, selfishness, and solitariness beneath good manners and gaiety; and it reveals a sense of grace-in-humor buoying up a near-sadistic playing upon lesser people's nerves and good nature. For instance, consider the hint of a real madman beneath the playfulness in *Suspicion* (41, Alfred Hitchcock); the masterly portrait of moral fecklessness stopped in its tracks in *North by Northwest* (59, Hitchcock); hurt pride turning into a cold, calculating manipulation of Ingrid Bergman in *Notorious*

(46, Hitchcock), only to relent finally. Consider again the masculine chauvinism that shows through the sombrero-wearing flyer in *Only Angels Have Wings*, (39, Howard Hawks); the merciless delight in teasing in *His Girl Friday* (40, Hawks); the bringing to life of a sheltered, nearsighted bone specialist in *Bringing Up Baby* (38, Hawks); the demented sexual frustration in *I Was a Male War Bride* (49, Hawks); and the hilarious mixture of adult and school-boy in *Monkey Business* (52, Hawks). If this list is confined to Hitchcock and Hawks, that only underlies how no one else has or could have done so well for two directors as radically opposed in attitude. The same disturbing and living ambiguity can be seen in many other films, along with an unrivaled sense of timing, encouragement of fellow actors, and the ability to cram words or expressions in gaps so small that most other actors would rest. Grant could not be the demanding portrait of man that he is but for a technical command that is so complete it is barely noticeable. It is a conclusive failing of the Oscar system that Grant won nothing for a specific performance. Thus, in shame and confusion, in 1969 the Academy gave him a general award "with the respect and affection of his colleagues."

His mother had a mental breakdown when he was twelve, and young Archie found his education at the Bristol Hippodrome with a troupe of acrobats. He went to America as a tumbler in 1920 (his physical aplomb owes much to this training), but returned to the English theatre and only went back to the United States in a musical, *Golden Dawn*. By 1932, he had earned a small contract with Paramount and made his debut in *This Is the Night* (32, Frank Tuttle). After a few more supporting parts, he played opposite Dietrich in *Blonde Venus* (32, Josef von Sternberg) and Sylvia Sidney in *Madame Butterfly* (33, Marion Gering). But it was Mae West who knew him for what he was, choosing Grant to swop taunts with her in *She Done Him Wrong* (33, Lowell Sherman) and *I'm No Angel* (33, Westley Ruggles).

In the second half of the decade, he emerged from support to a fully fledged comedian. He was opposite Loretta Young in *Born to Be Bad* (34, Lowell Sherman). RKO borrowed him to play with Katharine Hepburn in *Sylvia Scarlett* (35, George Cukor), and next year he signed contracts with Columbia and RKO. On this basis, the films flowed: *The Awful Truth* (37, Leo McCarey) with Irene Dunne; *Topper* (37, Norman Z. McLeod) with Constance Bennett; *Bringing Up Baby*, with Hepburn, in a love story as poignant as it is crazy—in this writer's opinion, Grant got better things out of Hepburn than Tracy ever managed; with Hepburn again in *Holiday* (38, Cukor); as a Cockney soldier in *Gunga Din* (39, George Stevens); *Only Angels Have Wings*, making Jean Arthur yelp with anger; with Carole Lombard in *In Name Only* (39, John Cromwell);

My Favorite Wife (40, Garson Kanin) with Irene Dunne; *His Girl Friday*, goading Rosalind Russell into being bearable; *The Philadelphia Story* (40, Cukor), with Hepburn and James Stewart (the wrong man got the Oscar); *Penny Serenade* (41, Stevens), with Dunne again; *Suspicion*, preying on Joan Fontaine; *The Talk of the Town* (42, Stevens), with Jean Arthur and Ronald Colman; *Once Upon a Honeymoon* (42, McCarey) with Ginger Rogers.

None But the Lonely Heart (44, Clifford Odets) was close to Grant's guarded heart: it described a mother-son relationship that reminded him of his own (Ethel Barrymore was very good as the mother); and Odets was a friend. But the film was received as a gloomy failure, something that betrayed or wasted the usual Grant, no matter that the Cockney drifter he played said a lot about Grant's uneasiness. But the failure frightened him away from further interest in production. His Cole Porter in *Night and Day* (46, Michael Curtiz), therefore, was a business-as-usual travesty bio-pic, no matter that Grant knew the real Porter quite well.

Notorious may be the darkest Grant ever offered for popular approval. He was urbanity at the end of its comic tether in *The Bachelor and the Bobby Soxer* (47, Irving Reis) and *Mr. Blandings Builds His Dream House* (48, H. C. Potter), with Myrna Loy as his partner in both. He made *Every Girl Should Be Married* (48, Don Hartman), with Betsy Drake—and soon they were married. In *I Was a Male War Bride*, Ann Sheridan seems sometimes helpless with laughter. On *Crisis* (50), it was Grant's say-so that gave Richard Brooks his directorial debut. *People Will Talk* (51, Joseph L. Mankiewicz) was well suited to his aloof, almost pained intelligence. *Dream Wife* (53, Sidney Sheldon) was a dud. In *To Catch a Thief* (55, Hitchcock), it was just conceivable that he was a cat burglar, yet his fine moral discrimination hesitated when Grace Kelly offered him a leg or a breast. He had such a thing for Sophia Loren that he made two foolish pictures with her—*The Pride and the Passion* (57, Stanley Kramer) and *Houseboat* (58, Melville Shavelson). He was far better with Deborah Kerr in *An Affair to Remember* (57, Leo McCarey) and with Ingrid Berman in *Indiscreet* (57, Stanley Donen).

Apart from *North by Northwest*, the final films were no more than modest exercise for Grant. Retirement recognized the real onset of age, but perhaps he was a little bored by *Kiss Them for Me* (57, Donen); *Operation Petticoat* (59, Blake Edwards); *The Grass Is Greener* (60, Donen); *That Touch of Mink* (62, Delbert Mann); *Charade* (65, Donen); and *Walk, Don't Run* (66, Charles Walters).

Grant made bad or dull films along the way, to be sure—*Born to Be Bad, Big Brown Eyes* (36, Raoul Walsh); *The Toast of New York* (37, Rowland V. Lee); *The Howards of Virginia* (40, Frank Lloyd); *Destination Tokyo* (43, Delmer Daves);

Mr. Lucky (43, Potter); *Arsenic and Old Lace* (44, Frank Capra); *Dream Wife*; and *The Pride and the Passion*. He was rather cheap, and too suspicious—so he missed being in *The Third Man*. He was, very likely, a hopeless fusspot as man, husband, and even father. How could anyone *be* "Cary Grant"? But how can anyone, ever after, not consider the attempt?

1975

Howard Hawks

When critics play children's games—such as selecting the ten best films of all time—the majority behave like dutiful understudies for a Platonic circle, opting for milestone movies, turning points in the art of film. But imagine yourself a Crusoe, as the ship goes down: a ship transporting the movie resources of the world, the S. S. *Langlois*. Put aside thoughts of urgency; there is time in this sort of dream for one Lang, one Ophuls, one Mizoguchi, one Rossellini, one Hitchcock, one Sternberg, one Murnau, one Renoir, one Buñuel, one Ozu, and one Hawks to while away the days on that island.

But a Crusoe needs to be honest with himself, just as Defoe's hero foresaw that money would be out of place on the island but still could not bear to let it go down, knowing that rescue would vindicate his prudence. So, hold the raft while I lay my hands on *Twentieth Century*, *Bringing Up Baby*, *Only Angels Have Wings*, *His Girl Friday*, *To Have and Have Not*, *The Big Sleep*, *Red River*, *I Was a Male War Bride*, *Gentlemen Prefer Blondes*, and *Rio Bravo*.

Too easy, too superficial a response to the total archive, you protest? Quite right. All the way to the island, paddling my raft, I shall be regretting *Man's Favorite Sport* (full of useful aquatic hints) already underwater, quite broken up by the thought of *Monkey Business* left behind, and gnawed at by the loss of *Air Force*, *Ceiling Zero*, and *Scarface*.

Back in the civilized world there will be libraries crowded with works of cinema history that patronize Howard Hawks. The staffs of *Sight and Sound* may still wake in the night shuddering with the memory that they did not bother to review *Rio Bravo*. And those willing to compromise will concede that "Old Hawks certainly does make entertaining films . . ." with the hollow, wide-eyed charity of minds keen to search out the good in every man. But the reservations mount up: Hawks is old-fashioned, subject to the limitations of the entertainment film, prone to a romantic view of men in action; in short, a moviemaker for boys never quite grown up.

The implication is that Hawks was an obedient, placid artisan within a narrow and corrupting framework. Hawks did nothing to deny that interpretation himself. Even the amusing and revealing interview that Peter Bogdanovich did with Hawks did not coax the laconic veteran further than the admission that he always liked to put as much fun and business into his pictures as possible. He disparaged plot and content and barely referred to camera effects. There was no attempt to conceal the stress on masculine values in his films. And no interest in going beyond the understatement shared by most of his characters or in elaborating on the implications and undertones of the recurring, ritualistic situations that obsess him. Like Monet forever painting lilies or Bonnard always re-creating his wife in her bath, Hawks made only one artwork. It is the principle of that movie that men are more expressive rolling a cigarette than saving the world.

The point should be made that Hawks attends to such small things because he is the greatest optimist the cinema has produced. Try to think of the last optimistic film you saw and it may dawn on you that the achievement is not minor. Not that he fails to notice tragedy. The optimism comes out of a knowledge of failure and is based on the virtues and warmth in people that go hand-in-hand with their shortcomings. Death, rupture, and loss abound in Hawks's world, even if they are observed calmly. The unadvertised sense of destruction in *Ceiling Zero* and *The Road to Glory* is the most breathtakingly frank view of depression in the 1930s American film. *Bringing Up Baby*—not for nothing photographed by Russell Metty—is a screwball comedy surrounded by darkness, forever on the brink of madness. *Sergeant York* is a barely admitted story of outraged conscience. *The Big Sleep* contains not only the General, unwarmed in his sweltering hot house, but Elisha Cook swallowing poison. *Red River* is a story of youth usurping age. *I Was a Male War Bride* only comes so close to sexual frustration by making it ridiculous.

The clue to Hawks's greatness is that this somber lining is cut against the cloth of the genre in which he is operating. Far from the meek purveyor of Hollywood forms, he always chose to turn them upside down. *To Have and Have Not* and *The Big Sleep*, ostensibly an adventure and a thriller, are really love stories. *Rio Bravo*, apparently a Western—everyone wears a cowboy hat— is a comedy conversation piece. The ostensible comedies are shot through with exposed emotions, with the subtlest views of the sex war, and with a wry acknowledgment of the incompatibility of men and women. Men and women skirmish in Hawks's films on the understanding that an embrace is only a prelude to withdrawal and disillusion. The dazzling battles of word, innuendo, glance, and gesture—between Grant and Hepburn, Grant and Jean Arthur, Grant and Rosalind Russell, John Barrymore and Carole Lombard, Bogart and Bacall, Wayne and Angie Dickinson, Rock Hudson and Paula Prentiss—are

Utopian procrastinations to avert the paraphernalia of released love that can only expend itself. In other words, Hawks is at his best in moments when nothing happens beyond people arguing about what might happen or has happened. Bogart and Bacall in *The Big Sleep* are not only characters tangled in a tortuous thriller but a constant audience to the film, commenting on its passage. The same is true of all those scenes in *Rio Bravo* when the tenuous basis of the plot is mulled over. That is why, at the end of *Red River*, Joanne Dru interrupts the fight between Wayne and Clift with, "Whoever thought either one of you would kill the other?"

The "style" of Hawks rests in this commenting astuteness; no other director so bridges the contrived plots of genre and the responses of a mature spectator. And because there is such emotional intelligence, such witty feeling, the camera is almost invisible. It is insufficient to say that Hawks put the camera in the most natural and least obtrusive place. The point is that his actors played to and with him, as he sat to one side of the camera that recorded them. His method involved the creation of a performance in rehearsal for which the script was merely an impetus. Whatever the script said, Hawks always twisted it into those abiding tableaux. It was a requirement of the method that he selected actors and actresses who responded to this sort of badgering championship and whom the audience accepted as being grown up. No wonder then that Cary Grant is so central to Hawks's work. But notice how far *Rio Bravo* shows us a Wayne and Dean Martin hardly recognized by other directors. And do not forget the list of people either discovered or brought to new life by Hawks: Louise Brooks (chosen by Pabst for *Pandora's Box* after seeing *A Girl in Every Port*); Boris Karloff; Carole Lombard; Rita Hayworth; Richard Barthelmess; Jane Russell; Lauren Bacall; Dorothy Malone; Montgomery Clift; George Winslow; Angie Dickinson; and James Caan.

The optimism derived from a delight in people expressed in the finding of new faces and the production of new expressions on old faces. In that sense Hawks blended classical narrative cinema and cinema verité. After all *The Big Sleep* was like a home movie, made amid the dark interiors of a Warners studio; that view of intimacy has time and again shattered the supposedly imprisoning circumstances of entertainment movies. Hawks is the supreme figure of classical cinema. Because he is so unassuming an innovator, so natural an entertainer, his work has still not been surpassed.

Which leaves me on my island: with Lombard kicking Barrymore in the stomach in *Twentieth Century*; with Hepburn sinking that long putt in *Bringing Up Baby*; with Grant asking "Who's Joe?" in *Only Angels Have Wings*; with the flower pot coming through the window in *Rio Bravo*; with the slow dawn pan before the cattle drive begins in *Red River*; and with Bacall snapping "help yourself" in *The Big Sleep*.

There's a motto, if you want one: you need only relax old, dull muscles, flex those undiscovered by other movies, and help yourself.

Twenty years after writing the above, I don't want to change a word of it, or do without the Hawks pictures on my island. Nothing I have re-viewed has dated or deteriorated—and I wish I could say as much for most American directors of the golden age. There's only one thing to add: that the mystery of Hawks builds.

The more one learns of his life, the clearer it is that he was a chronic liar and compartmentalizer, a secretive rogue, a stealthy dandy, and a ruinous womanizer. There is still no biography of Hawks, much less a book that sets the mess of his life beside the heroic grace of the films. But such a book might make it easier to appreciate that Hawks was always a maker of comedy and play (even when the tone is tragic). There was an absurdist in Hawks, and a Nabokovian delight in the game for its own sake. Thus, in a very important way, this seeming American may have been against the grain of his time and place. That may help explain why the films grow in wonder.

1975

bell hooks

bell hooks, the pen name for Gloria Watkins (b. 1952), has become one of the most outspoken and resourceful public intellectuals on the American scene today. Distinguished Professor of English at City College in New York, she has dedicated herself to embodying a dynamic synthesis between intellectual discourse and the personal, bringing her perspectives as a feminist, a black woman, a Buddhist, and a political radical to bear on cultural analyses. In this scathing look at the cult movie *Pulp Fiction*, from *Reel to Real: Race, Sex and Class at the Movies*, hooks nails her points about power relations by moving effortlessly between street talk and poststructuralist theory, meanwhile playing with the form and sound of contemporary film criticism.

◆

Cool Cynicism

Pulp Fiction

While all Quentin Tarantino's work so far plays around with the same themes (in regular Hollywood style), his stuff fascinates precisely because of the way each piece distinguishes itself, signifies on previous work—his or that of others. Cinematically, Tarantino is a master deconstructivist. No wonder then that everything he produces has such postmodern flavor and seduces both those who read and those who don't. When it comes to flavor he is definitely an equal opportunity employer. Unlike most contemporary border-crossing, "eat the other" culture bandits, he is not afraid to publicly pimp his wares.

Tarantino has the real nihilism of our times down. He represents the ultimate in "white cool": a hard-core cynical vision that would have everyone see racism, sexism, homophobia but behave as though none of that shit really matters, or if it does it means nothing 'cause none of it's gonna change, 'cause the real deal is that domination is here to stay—going nowhere, and everybody is in on the act. Mind you, domination is always and only patriarchal—a dick thing.

In Tarantino's flicks women's liberation is just another scam, white women wanting to be let in on the deal even as they act just like that Enjoli

617

commercial told us they would: they help "bring home the bacon, fry it up in the pan, and never let you forget" they're a w-o-m-a-n. Check out the white girls in *True Romance* (written by Tarantino) and *Pulp Fiction*. Even when they are absent à la *Reservoir Dogs*, that little opening dialogue about Madonna says it all—a piece of the action, their share of the cut. And black folks, personified simply and solely by black men, are just into a dick thing, wanting to be right there in the mix, doing the right thing in the dance hall of white supremacist capitalist patriarchy. Only the black woman who has no face—Jimmy's wife in *Pulp Fiction*, we see her only from the back—would raise any protest. The fun thing about Tarantino's films is that he makes that shit look so ridiculous you think everybody's gonna get it and see how absurd it all is. Well, that's when we enter the danger zone. Folks be laughing at the absurdity and clinging to it nevertheless. This happens first with *Reservoir Dogs*, which takes the hardcore white patriarchal dick thing and shows it for the vampire culture it really is. And when the white men have eaten each other up ('cause Tarantino would have us all know that when there are no white girls and niggers of all colors around, white boys are busy fucking each other over), it would be hard work for any viewer to see this film as a gleeful celebration of madness. *Reservoir Dogs* has a critical edge that is totally absent from *Pulp Fiction*, where everything is farce. Yeah, like it's really funny when Butch the hypermasculine phallic white boy—who has no name that means anything, who has no culture to be proud of, who comes straight out of childhood clinging to the anal-retentive timepiece of patriarchal imperialism—is exposed. Yet exposure does nothing to intervene on this evil, it merely graphically highlights it. As the work progresses, little Butch is still doing it for daddy—a real American hero.

Tarantino's films are the ultimate in sexy cover-ups of very unsexy mind-fuck. They titillate with subversive possibility (scenes that are so fine you are just blown away—like that wonderful moment when Vincent and Mia do the twist in *Pulp Fiction*), but then everything kinda comes right back to normal. And normal is finally a multicultural world with white supremacy intact. Note that even when the black male arrives at the top, as does Marcellus in *Pulp Fiction*—complete with a lying, cheating lapdog white child-woman wife—he is unmasked as only an imitation cowboy, not the real thing. And in case viewers haven't figured out that Marcellus ain't got what it takes, the film turns him into a welfare case—another needy victim who must ultimately rely on the kindness of strangers (i.e., Butch, the neoprimitive white colonizer, another modern-day Tarzan) to rescue him from the rape-in-progress that is his symbolic castration, his return to the jungle, to a lower rung on the food chain. No doubt had John Singleton, or any homeboy filmmaker, shot a scene as overtly gay-bashing as this one, progressive forces would have rallied en masse to condemn—to protest—to remind moviegoers that homophobia means genocide, that silence equals death. But it's fine to remain silent when the cool straight white boy from the wrong side of the tracks offers a movie that depicts the brutal slaughter and/or bashing of butt-fuckers and their playmates. If this isn't symbolic genocide of gay men, what is? Yet everyone has to pretend there's some hidden subversive message in the scenes. Hello! But that's the Tarantino message: everybody is in the corrupt jungle doing their own sweet version of the domination dance. This is multiculturalism with a chic neofascist twist.

Let's have a new world order in cinema: i.e., flashy flicks like Tarantino's, which kinda seem like the American version of Hanif Kureishi's stylish nihilism, so well done in *Sammy and Rosie Get Laid* and less well done in the rather tedious *London Kills Me*. Here most anybody can get a piece of the action, every ethnicity can be represented, can be fucked and fucked-over, 'cause in the end it's all shit. The real democracy, as *True Romance* tells us loud and clear, consists of a world where everyone has equal access to eating shit. Mind you, some folks come out of the shit smelling like roses, like our death-dealing white gender-equity couple in *True Romance*, who take their nuclear-family values to a warm place in the Third World and relax 'cause that's their way of getting away from it all. But when Jules (Samuel Jackson), our resident black male preacher-philosopher death-dealing mammified intellectual (he does pull out the tit and feed knowledge to everyone in *Pulp Fiction*:— magnificently, I might add—a stunning performance—particularly that closing monologue), decides *he* wants out of the rat race, he doesn't get to leave the plantation with riches in hand. John Travolta's Massa Junior makes it clear he must go his way destitute. 'Cause in the real plantation economy, no matter how many borders are crossed, no matter how many cultures are mixed and how much shit is appropriated (the everybody-is-a-nigger version of "We are the World"), when it comes right down to it Jules as our resident enlightened dharma bum has nowhere to go—no Third World playground he can retire to.

No doubt that retro hairdo he sports throughout the film keeps him from charting a new journey. It's his own signifying monkey. No matter how serious Jules's rap, that hair always intervenes to let the audience know not to take him too seriously. That hair is kinda like another character in the film. Talking back to Jules as he talks to us, it undermines his words every step of the way. 'Cause that hair is like a minstrel thing—telling the world that the black preacher-philosopher is ultimately just an intellectual arty white boy in drag, aping, imitating, and mouthing intellectual rhetoric that he can't quite use to help him make sense of his own life. Well, in steps the interpreter of dreams, Vincent "Lone Ranger" Vega, who has no trouble spelling out in plain speech to his beloved Tonto, alias Jules, that there will be no redemptive future for him—that if he leaves the white-boy setup and abandons his criminal destiny he will just be another homeless black man on the street, a bum. In the new world order Tarantino creates in *Pulp Fiction*, dead white-boy star-culture bandits live again and, like their ethnographic counterparts, know black folks better than we could ever know ourselves.

Well, as Tarantino's work lets us know, it's a sick, motherfucking world and we may as well get used to that fact, laugh at it, and go on our way, 'cause ain't nothing changing—and that's Hollywood, the place where white supremacist capitalist patriarchy can keep reinventing itself, no matter how many times the West is decentered. Hollywood is the new plantation, getting more chic with the times. That Tarantino can call it out, tell it like it is, give the ultimate "read," the on-the-down-low diss, is part of the magic. It's deconstruction at its finest—all dressed up with no place to go. That is, unless you, the viewer, got somewhere you wanna take it, 'cause this is the new crossover model—the new multicultural survival kit. It can be all things to all people. Like you can choose to come away from *Reservoir Dogs* thinking, Later for white supremacy, racism, and fascism, 'cause when that shit is on display anybody can see how funky it is. Or maybe you could even catch that moment in *Pulp Fiction* when Butch and Marcellus are boy-bonding, with the tie that binds being their shared fear of homosexual rape, and think, Doesn't Tarantino just name the homophobia of our times—calling out the way patriarchal homosocial bonding mediates racism? (I mean Butch and Marcellus, they end up like brothers.) But if you choose to look at it all from the right, that's okay too. 'Cause the shit smells the same whether you are liberal or conservative, on the right or the left. There is no way out.

If you don't get the picture, check out the fate of our cross-race boy-bonding team, Vincent and Jules. Throughout the movie we admire their cross-racial, funky solidarity, their shared cool, but this difference don't last: they don't end up as "brothers" 'cause they are both ultimately disloyal to the structure they should uphold (Vincent by taking a break and reading, i.e. sleeping on the job, Jules by wanting to retire into nothingness). The film takes no note of Vincent's death by showing Jules either grieving or seeking revenge. Like all the meaningful emotional ties in the film (Vincent and Mia) this one doesn't count for shit. In the end loyalty sucks. Betrayal delivers the goods.

Well, as the preacher man told us at the end of *Pulp Fiction*, the tyranny of evil does not disappear just because we change the channel. Tarantino shows us in his films that a good cynical read on life can be compelling, entertaining, and downright satisfying—so much so that everyone will come back for more. But as the poet Amiri Baraka reminds us, "Cynicism is not revolutionary."

1996

Kenneth Turan

Kenneth Turan (b. 1946) is senior film critic for the *Los Angeles Times* and for National Public Radio's *Morning Edition*. He is also the author of *Never Coming to a Theater Near You*, a collection of his reviews that specifically celebrates small (for the most part), personal, out-of-the-way films that tend to get overlooked in the age of blockbusters. As a daily reviewer operating in the heart of Hollywood and industry "buzz," Turan is respected for his ability to convey in a few deft sentences the flavor of a movie and for his warm receptivity to the unconventional performance, script, or directing job. But he is also known for giving no quarter when unimpressed, as is evident from this minority review of the massively touted *Titanic*. When it appeared, that film's director, James Cameron, wrote a counter-blast demanding that Turan be fired. Happily, he wasn't.

◆

Titanic Sinks Again (Spectacularly)

To the question of the day—what does $200 million buy?—the 3-hour-and-14-minute *Titanic* unhesitatingly answers: not enough.

Note that despite the hopes of skeptics, aghast at the largest film budget of modern times, money enough to run a full-dress presidential campaign or put a serious dent in illiteracy, the answer is not nothing. When you are willing to build a 775-foot, 90% scale model of the doomed ship and sink it in a 17-million-gallon tank specially constructed for the purpose, you are going to get a heck of a lot of production value for your money. Especially if your name is James Cameron.

More than that, at *Titanic*'s two-hour mark, when most films have sense enough to be winding down, this behemoth does stir to a kind of life. With writer-director Cameron, a virtuoso at large-scale action-adventure extravaganzas serving as ringmaster, the detailing of the ship's agonies (compressed here from a real-life two hours and 40 minutes to a bit more than an hour) compels our interest absolutely.

But Cameron, there can be no doubt, is after more than oohs and aahs. He's already made *The Terminator* and *Terminator 2*; with *Titanic* he has his eye on

Doctor Zhivago/Lawrence of Arabia territory. But while his intentions are clear, Cameron lacks the skills necessary to pull off his coup. Just as the hubris of headstrong shipbuilders who insisted that the Titanic was unsinkable led to an unparalleled maritime disaster, so Cameron's overweening pride has come unnecessarily close to capsizing this project.

For seeing *Titanic* almost makes you weep in frustration. Not because of the excessive budget, not even because it recalls the unnecessary loss of life in the real 1912 catastrophe, which saw more than 1,500 of the 2,200-plus passengers dying when an iceberg sliced the ship open like a can opener. What really brings on the tears is Cameron's insistence that writing this kind of movie is within his abilities. Not only isn't it, it isn't even close.

Cameron has regularly come up with his own scripts in the past, but in a better world someone would have had the nerve to tell him or he would have realized himself that creating a moving and creditable love story is a different order of business from coming up with wisecracks for Arnold Schwarzenegger.

Instead, what audiences end up with word-wise is a hackneyed, completely derivative copy of old Hollywood romances, a movie that reeks of phoniness and lacks even minimal originality. Worse than that, many of the characters, especially the feckless tycoon Cal Hockley (played by Billy Zane) and Kathy Bates' impersonation of the Unsinkable Molly Brown, are cliches of such purity they ought to be exhibited in film schools as examples of how not to write for the screen.

It is easy to forget, as you wait for the iceberg to arrive and shake things up, how excellent an idea it was to revisit for modern audiences the sinking of what was the largest moving object ever built. Numerous films have been made on the subject, with even the Third Reich taking a shot with a version that concluded, not surprisingly, that the sinking was "an eternal accusation against England's greed." As Steven Biel wrote in *Down With the Old Canoe*, a fascinating cultural history of public reaction to the event, "The Titanic disaster begs for resolution—and always resists it."

One reason this version is so long is a modern framing story involving nautical treasure hunter Brock Lovett (Cameron veteran Bill Paxton), who is scouring the *Titanic*'s wreck (it was located in 1985) for a fabulously expensive blue diamond called "The Heart of the Ocean" that was lost on board.

What Lovett turns up instead is a drawing of a nude young woman wearing the jewel. News of that find prompts a phone call from 101-year-old Rose Dawson Calvert (Gloria Stuart), who says it's her in the drawing. Lovett flies Rose (whom Cameron modeled on artist Beatrice Wood) out to join his expedition.

The bulk of *Titanic* is her recollection of what happened before, during and after that great ship went down.

Young Rose (now played by Kate Winslet) boarded the *Titanic* as a 17-year-old wearing a very large hat and metaphorical shackles. "To me it was a slave ship," she recalls, "taking me to America in chains." In plainer English she was being forced by her snooty mother Ruth DeWitt Bukater into a (gasp!) loveless marriage with Cal Hockley, an arrogant and wealthy snob for whom the phrase "perpetual sneer" was probably invented.

Rose may be a 17-year-old, but she knows a thing or two. She makes offhanded references to Freud, a wise gentleman no one else on board has heard of, and during an impromptu shopping spree she managed to buy works by Picasso, Degas and Monet despite Hockley's dismissive belief that they "won't amount to a thing." Clearly, this prodigy of taste and discernment deserves better than Mr. Perpetual Sneer, no matter how rich he is.

Enter Jack Dawson (Leonardo DiCaprio), a madcap artist and cherubic scamp who wins his steerage ticket in a dockside card game. Jack is staggered by a glimpse of Rose, and though a conveniently placed Irish lad advises him "you'd as like have angels flying out of your arse as get next to the likes of her," he's not the kind of young man to give up easily.

Sure enough, despite the presence of 2,200 other passengers and crew, it's only Jack who's around to save the day when a distraught Rose considers suicide in a flattering evening gown. Despite the best efforts of mother Ruth (Frances Fisher) and Hockley's snarling valet Spicer Lovejoy (David Warner), Jack and Rose are irresistibly drawn to each other. She improves his manners (not hard to do), he teachers her how to spit like a man, and they spend quality time in photogenic locations like the ship's towering prow.

Both Winslet and DiCaprio are capable actors (though his brash brat routine is wearing thin) but they are victimized, as is everyone else, by dialogue that has the self-parodying ring of Young Romance comics. "You could just call me a tumbleweed blowing in the wind," Jack says, adding later, "sooner or later the fire I love about you is going to burn out." Most weighted down by this kind of blather are the fatuous Hockley, who has to say things like "you filth" and Bates' Molly Brown, a character so relentlessly folksy she'd be at home on *The Beverly Hillbillies*.

Finally, after so much time has passed you fear the iceberg has slept through its wake-up call, disaster strikes the ship at 11:50 on the night of April 14. Cameron is truly in his element here, and *Titanic*'s closing hour is jammed with the most stirring and impressive sights, from towering walls of water flooding a grand dining room to the enormous ship itself defying belief and going vertical in the water.

These kinds of complex and demanding sequences are handled with so much aplomb it's understandable that the director, who probably considers the script to be the easiest part of his job, not only wants to do it all but also thinks he can. Yet as Cameron sails his lonely craft toward greatness, he should realize he needs to bring a passenger with him. Preferably someone who can write.

1997

Jonathan Rosenbaum

Jonathan Rosenbaum (b. 1943) had what he calls in his affecting memoir *Moving Places* "a movie-drenched childhood and family life, which came from my family running a small chain of theaters in Alabama." Since then he has become one of the most respected and learned, if contentious, film critics on the planet. The author of 14 books on the movies and senior film critic for the *Chicago Reader*, Rosenbaum uses his formidable grasp of international cinema to argue for a more inclusive canon (see his collection *Essential Cinema*). He has long gone to bat for the more unconventional foreign art film that either goes undistributed in the United States or is dumped on the market with a tiny advertising budget and yanked from theaters a week later. As a critic, he has preformed a particularly valuable service in patiently decoding the mysteries of difficult, initially baffling films (such as Kubrick's *Eyes Wide Shut*, Dreyer's *Gertrud*, or Kiarostami's *Taste of Cherry*), partly by going back to their original sources and researching the filmmaking process, partly by sensitive formal analysis and attention to the movie's implicit as well as explicit politics.

◆

In Dreams Begin Responsibilities

Writing about *Eyes Wide Shut* in *Time*, Richard Schickel had this to say about its source, Arthur Schnitzler's 1926 *Traumnovelle*: "Like a lot of the novels on which good movies are based, it is an entertaining, erotically charged fiction of the second rank, in need of the vivifying physicalization of the screen and the kind of narrative focus a good director can bring to imperfect but provocative life—especially when he has been thinking about it as long as Kubrick had"—that is, at least since 1968, when he asked his wife to read it. This more or less matches the opinion of Frederic Raphael, Kubrick's credited cowriter, as expressed in his recent memoir, *Eyes Wide Open*. But I would argue that *Traumnovelle* is a masterpiece worthy of resting alongside Poe's "The Masque of the Red Death," Kafka's *The Trial*, and Sadegh Hedayat's *The Blind Owl*. Like the Poe story, it features a phantasmal masked ball with dark and decadent undercurrents, and like the Kafka and Hedayat novels, it continually and ambiguously crosses back and forth between fantasy

626

and waking reality. But it differs from all three in having a development that might be described as therapeutic—Schnitzler, a doctor, was a contemporary of Freud—making *Eyes Wide Shut* a rare departure for Kubrick and concluding his career with the closest thing in his work to a happy ending. Moreover, the question about the novella isn't whether Kubrick has "brought it to life"—it lives vibrantly without him, even if he has brought it to a lot of people's attention, including mine—but whether he's done it justice, a problem also raised by his films of *Lolita* and *A Clockwork Orange*.

I read *Traumnovelle* before I saw the movie, which hindered as well as helped my first impressions. The last time I tried this with a Kubrick film was when I read Stephen King's *The Shining* before seeing the film and found that King's novel, whatever its literary limitations, was genuinely scary, whereas Kubrick's movie, for all its brilliance, generally wasn't. Yet practically all of Kubrick's films improve with age and repeated viewings, and, scary or not, his version of *The Shining* fascinates me a lot more than King's. I can't say the same about *Lolita*; Vladimir Nabokov's novel improves with rereading a lot more than Kubrick's film improves with reviewing. And *A Clockwork Orange* is a draw: I embrace the moral ambiguity of Anthony Burgess's novel and detest the morality of Kubrick's film, yet I'd rather see the film again than reread the novel. In the case of *Eyes Wide Shut* I'm inclined to think Kubrick has done Schnitzler's masterpiece justice. Allowing for all the differences between Vienna in the 20s and New York in the 90s and between Jews and WASPs, it's a remarkably faithful and ingenious adaptation. Kubrick made this movie convinced that relationships between couples haven't significantly changed over the past seventy-odd years, and whether you find it a success probably depends a lot on whether you agree with him.

I won't attempt a full synopsis, but I have to outline chunks of the first two-thirds of the plot to make certain points. Bill Harford (Tom Cruise), a successful New York doctor, and his wife, Alice (Nicole Kidman), the former manager of a Soho art gallery, attend a fancy Christmas party at the town house of Victor Ziegler (played to perfection by Sydney Pollack), one of Bill's wealthy patients, where each engages in flirtation—Alice with a Hungarian lounge lizard, Bill with a couple of models. Bill recognizes the orchestra's pianist, Nick Nightingale (Todd Field), as a former classmate and chats with him briefly; later he's called upstairs by Ziegler to help revive a naked hooker he's been screwing who's overdosed on drugs. Bill and Alice make love when they get home that night, clearly stimulated by their flirtations, but the following evening, after they smoke pot, Alice begins to challenge Bill's total confidence in her faithfulness by telling him a story that shocks him, about her passionate attraction to a naval officer she glimpsed only briefly when they were at Cape Cod with their little girl the previous summer.

Called away by the death of a patient, Bill is haunted by images of Alice having sex with the officer, and his night and the following day and night turn into a string of adventures consisting of sexual temptations or provocations that come his way with and without his complicity—all of which prove abortive. The dream-line interruptions and certain passing details share some of the same hallucinatory texture—as they do in Schnitzler's story—so that even waitresses glimpsed in a diner and coffeehouse and a gay hotel desk clerk suggest sexual possibilities. The daughter (Marie Richardson) of the man who has just died is engaged to be married soon yet suddenly declares her love for Bill. Wandering the streets afterward, he's harassed by college kids who think he's gay (in *Traumnovelle* the hero is Jewish and the students anti-Semites), then picked up by a prostitute named Domino (Vinessa Shaw). He finally winds up at the Sonata Café, where Nick Nightingale is playing with a jazz quartet. Nick has a gig later that night as a blindfolded pianist at a costumed orgy in a country house on Long Island, and Bill, after discovering the password, persuades Nick to give him the address. He then proceeds to a costume-rental shop to acquire a tux, cloak, and mask, and takes a taxi to the house. Eventually exposed as an intruder, he fears for his life until a masked woman mysteriously offers to sacrifice herself for him.

When he finally arrives home he wakes Alice from a troubled dream involving the naval officer and an orgy in which she participates while laughing scornfully at Bill, which she recounts. It's one of the movie's many indications that the unclear separations of imagination and reality include many rhyme effects between Alice's dreams and fantasies and Bill's reality, as well as rhymes between her fantasies and his (such as her having sex with the naval officer). In fact, though the film initially appears to be mainly about Bill because it follows him around more than Alice, Alice's confession and dream are just as important as anything that happens to him; in some respects, thanks to Kubrick's (and Schnitzler's) careful calibrations in the storytelling, she makes an even stronger impression than he does, especially because she seems more in touch with her fantasy life than he is with his own—and because every other woman in the movie is in one way or another a doppelgänger for her.

Some of the other rhyme effects create disquieting connections—between a sexual invitation at Ziegler's party ("Do you know where the rainbow ends?") and the name of the costume shop (Rainbow) and between the password to the orgy, "fidelio," which suggests the Italian word for "faithful," and Bill's failure to betray her there. (Schnitzler's story is full of comparable echo effects: there the password to the orgy is "Denmark," which happens to be where the hero's wife was tempted to commit adultery.) There's even a subtle, eerie rhyme between a figurine briefly glimpsed on a table in the scene with Marie Richardson and one of the masks at the orgy.

Eyes Wide Shut has a lot to say about the psychological accommodations of marriage—and has a sunnier view of human possibility than any other Kubrick film, in spite of all its dark moments. It depends on a sense of the shared mental reality of a couple that almost supersedes any sense of their shared physical reality, a strange emphasis that's probably the source of most of the confusion felt by everyone in the course of processing the story. (A similar sense of shared mental reality can be found in the title characters of Schnitzler's startling, almost equally masterful 1913 novella *Beatrice and Her Son*.) A list of the things we never learn about the characters is at least as long as the list of things we know with any certainty. We remain in the dark about how the wife happens upon the mask worn by the husband at the orgy, about the accuracy of Ziegler's account of many of those same adventures, and even about whether they happen outside the husband's imagination. Yet there's never any doubt about what transpires emotionally between this husband and wife.

For years, two misleading adjectives have been used to describe Kubrick's work: "cold" and "perfectionist." "Cold" implies unemotional, and it simply isn't true that Kubrick's films lack emotion. They're full of emotions, though most of them are so convoluted and elusive that you have to follow them as if through a maze—perhaps the major reason his films become richer with repeated viewing. He so strongly resists sentimentality that cynicism and derision often seem close at hand, and one difficulty I had with *Eyes Wide Shut* the first time I saw it was accepting the caricatural side of Kubrick—his handling of Cruise's "normality" in the lead role as Dr. William Harford and the mincing mannerisms of the gay desk clerk—as something other than malicious. My memory of Kubrick's mocking inflation of Jack Nicholson's narcissism in the second half of *The Shining* made me think he was being equally diabolical here about Cruise's narcissism, but a second look at the movie has rid me of this impression. Maybe Steve Martin would have made a more interesting Harford; according to Michael Herr in *Vanity Fair*, Martin was Kubrick's first choice for the role twenty years ago. But using a real couple such as Cruise and Kidman had obvious advantages as well.

That Bill Harford lies to his wife about both his lust for the models at Ziegler's party and the reason Ziegler called him upstairs identifies him at the outset as a glib hypocrite who thinks privilege can get him anywhere—which differentiates him somewhat from Schnitzler's hero—but that doesn't mean Kubrick views him with contempt. The remainder of the story may undermine Harford's confidence, but Kubrick doesn't let us know whether his recounting of his nocturnal adventures to Alice near the end of the movie is fully or only partially honest—we don't hear any of it. All we know is that it brings them both to tears.

Ironically, the major difference between Kubrick and Schnitzler may be that Kubrick is more of a moralist, even if he's unusually subtle about it. The only important invented character in *Eyes Wide Shut*, Ziegler, is the only one I regard as unambiguously evil. But Ziegler's evil, unlike mad Jack Torrance's in *The Shining*, is wrapped in impeccable manners, so some viewers may conclude that he's an OK guy. I saw his darker side mainly in glancing hints, such as his momentary reluctance to wait an hour before sending home the hooker after she recovers from her drug-induced coma. He's a charming monster—a statement about class and power and a composite portrait of every Hollywood executive Kubrick ever had to contend with. In this respect, Ziegler is closely allied to the highly cultivated General Broulard (Adolphe Menjou) in *Paths of Glory*—the true villain of that film, in contrast to the more obvious and scapegoated villain, General Mireau (George Macready), who's openly hypocritical and malicious.

The climactic dialogue between Harford and Ziegler in Ziegler's huge town house—a remarkable scene that runs a little over thirteen minutes—has been getting some flack from reviewers who claim it explains too much. But it explains nothing conclusive, apart from Ziegler's Zeus-like access and power—in a billiards room that seems to belong on Mount Olympus, like the château in *Paths of Glory*—and Harford's ultimate remoteness from those reaches; Ziegler holds all the cards, and we and Harford hold none. Critic David Ehrenstein recently told me he thought *Barry Lyndon* was Kubrick's most Jewish movie in its depiction of social exclusion, but that was before he saw *Eyes Wide Shut*.

The second misleading label attached to Kubrick's work, "perfectionist," might be plausible if it were used to describe his choice of lenses, his ideas about décor, or his obsession with prints and projection. But usually it's used to describe his habit of demanding multiple drafts from writers and repeated takes from actors. Everyone seems to agree that such demands stemmed largely from Kubrick's not knowing what he wanted except through negative indirection, but this is a far cry from what's usually meant by perfectionism. His use of improvisation with actors to great effect—most famously Peter Sellers in *Lolita* and *Dr. Strangelove*, but probably also Timothy Carey in *The Killing* and *Paths of Glory*, and Kidman in some stretches of *Eyes Wide Shut*—further complicates this notion of perfectionism, as does his use of handheld cameras for filming violence in movies as diverse as *The Killing* and *Barry Lyndon*, which involves a certain amount of chance and improvisation. Kubrick came of age artistically during the same period as action painting, and in his work classical notions of composing frames and telling stories vie with other aspects of the artistic process that are more random and less controllable. (Paradoxically, Kubrick's perfectionism in some areas prevented him from being a perfectionist in others. He wouldn't allow the Venice Film Festival to show his films subtitled at a retrospective during the shooting of *Eyes Wide Shut* because he didn't have enough time to check the prints, so the festival had to show dubbed versions he'd already approved.)

Convoluted emotions and negative indirection are two ways Kubrick deliberately kept himself innocent of his own intentions, especially in his later movies. Positing himself as the ideal spectator of his own films, he wanted to be surprised by what his writers and actors did, and that entailed refusing to impose interpretations on his stories, striving to keep some particulars of his stories free from his intellect, and ultimately letting his unconscious do part of the work. (Jacques Rivette has used the same modus operandi in some of his own features, especially during the 70s.)

This dialectic between control and lack of control eventually became not only Kubrick's method but part of his subject. As Gilles Deleuze noted in *Cinema 2: The Time-Image*, "In Kubrick, the world itself is a brain, there is an identity of brain and world." Deleuze singles out such central images as the War Room in *Dr. Strangelove*, the computer housing HAL's circuits in *2001: A Space Odyssey*, and the Overlook Hotel in *The Shining* as examples of what he meant, to which I might add the racetrack in *The Killing* and the training camp in *Full Metal Jacket*. Moreover, Deleuze writes, the monolith in *2001* "presides over both cosmic states and cerebral stages: it is the soul of the three bodies, earth, sun, and moon, but also the seed of the three brains, animal, human, machine." And in each film the brain, the world, and the system connecting the two start to break down from internal and external causes, resulting in some form of dissolution (*The Killing*), annihilation (of the world in *Dr. Strangelove* and HAL's brain in *2001*), mutilation (of the brain in *A Clockwork Orange* and the body in *Barry Lyndon*), or madness (*The Shining* and *Full Metal Jacket*, which also chart respectively the dissolution of a family and a fighting unit).

Building on Deleuze's insight, critic Bill Krohn has proposed, in the only plausible account I've read of the structure of *Full Metal Jacket*, that "the little world of the training camp . . . is portrayed as a brain made up of human cells thinking and feeling as one, until its functioning is wrecked first from within, when a single cell, Pyle, begins ruthlessly carrying out the directives of the death instinct that programs the organ as a whole, and then from without by the Tet Offensive, the external representation of the same force." As a result, in the second part of the film "the narrative itself begins to malfunction" along with the group mind, exploding "the conventional notion of character" and drifting off in several different directions.

There's no such narrative breakdown in *Eyes Wide Shut*, which proceeds in conventional linear fashion throughout—though interludes created by a fantasy and a dream Alice recounts are every bit as important as waking events. This time the "brain" belongs to neither a single character (like HAL) nor a group (like the soldiers in *Full Metal Jacket*) but to a happily married couple— to their shared experience and the world created between them—and the threat of a breakdown, which forms the narrative, is eventually overcome. In this case the "identity of brain and world" is more explicit, and negotiating a relationship between the two, between dreaming and waking, is what the movie is all about. Even the title tells you that.

"Among those I would call the 'younger generation,' Kubrick appears to me to be a giant," Orson Welles said in a *Cahiers du cinéma* interview in the mid-60s, after the release of Welles's adaptation of Kafka's *The Trial*. Stressing that *The Killing* was superior to *The Asphalt Jungle* and that Kubrick was a better director than John Huston, Welles added, "What I see in him is a talent not possessed by the great directors of the generation immediately preceding his, I mean [Nicholas] Ray, [Robert] Aldrich, etc. Perhaps this is because his temperament comes closer to mine."

Both Welles and Kubrick started out in their early twenties, both died at the age of seventy, and both completed thirteen released features. Another significant parallel is that both ended up making all the films they completed after the 50s in exile, which surely says something about the creative possibilities of American commercial filmmaking over the past four decades. But in other respects their careers proceeded in opposite directions: Welles entered the profession at the top when it came to studio resources and wound up shooting all his last pictures on a shoestring and without studio backing; Kubrick began with shoestring budgets and wound up with full studio backing and apparently all the resources he needed.

On this basis one could argue that Kubrick succeeded in working within the system while retaining his independence on every picture except *Sparta-*

cus, while Welles retained his independence sporadically, imperfectly, and ultimately at the price of working outside the system. Yet the price paid by Kubrick for his success—a sense of paranoid isolation that often seeped into his work and as few completed features as Welles—can't be discounted. (By isolation I don't mean to endorse the "hermit" myth that the press always attaches to artists who are reluctant to speak to reporters—including Thomas Pynchon and J. D. Salinger as well as Kubrick; I mean his more general habits as a relatively sedentary control freak who spent a lot of time on the phone.)

Inside and outside, interiors and exteriors, form as important a dialect in his work as control and lack of control, which is perhaps one reason the interiors in his films gradually seem to grow larger—from the dingy lairlike apartments of *The Killing* to the château in *Paths of Glory*, from the spaceship in *2001* to the hotel in *The Shining*. This culminates in the palatial interiors of *Eyes Wide Shut*, which contrast with the claustrophobic railroad flat shared by two women and the cluttered costume shop. The throwaway and sometimes artificial quality of the exteriors conforms to the same expressionist system, and if the overall spatial orientation of the interiors at times recalls Welles, it's the Welles who wound up alternating oversize and cramped interiors in *The Trial*. Many reviewers of *Eyes Wide Shut* have been citing Martin Scorsese's *After Hours*—a picture even more indebted to Welles's *The Trial* in its handling of paranoia—but Welles's influence on Scorsese can be taken as a filtered form of Kafka's influence. (Kafka's story, unlike Welles's, is set almost entirely in cramped spaces.) In Schnitzler's novella the two scenes in the costume shop are already pure Kafka, especially in the uncanny way the relationships of the characters shift between the hero's two visits, and Kubrick catches both the queasiness and the unhealthy sexuality of Kafka at least as effectively as Welles did. Perhaps significantly, this is the only scene in which Kubrick allows the story's eastern European origins to come out, most noticeably in the accent and appearance of the shop owner (Rade Sherbedgia).

There are already signs that *Eyes Wide Shut* is dividing critics, sometimes along regional, even tribal lines. Most Chicago critics were enthusiastic—at least until a lack of public support for the film apparently caused a certain backlash—but a good many New York critics weren't, apparently in part because the contemporary New York this movie conjures up—basically shot on sets in England, apart from a few stray second-unit shots of New York streets—isn't their city. It's true that Kubrick—born and raised in the Bronx but for many years an expatriate who refused to fly—didn't go near Manhattan in the 90s, and the movie clearly reflects that. But given the highly stylized and even mannerist nature of his late work, I can't see how this matters much. (There's some disagreement in the press about when he last visited New York. I'm fairly certain I spotted him in Soho in 1980 around the time *The Shining* came out; he was sloppily dressed and was methodically tearing down a poster from a street lamp advertising an interview with him in the *Soho News*.)

The kind of jazz played by Nick Nightingale in the Sonata Café seems a good two or three decades off, and the nightclub itself seems like an improbable throwback to the 50s. It's even more out-of-date than the nightclub jazz in the second feature of Kubrick's former producer James B. Harris, *Some Call It Loving* (1973)—a fascinating cross-reference to *Eyes Wide Shut* in its treatment of erotic dreaming that deserves to be better known. But if we can accept the precise yet highly stylized city of Fritz Lang's *M* as early-30s Berlin—and presumably Berliners of that period did—we shouldn't have any trouble accepting this paraphrase of 90s Manhattan.

Other objections include the film's methodical slowness (especially apparent in the delivery of the dialogue and the dreamlike repetitions of various phrases), its failure to live up to the hype and rumors about its sexual content, and the stupid and tacky digital "enhancements" added to the orgy sequence to fulfill Kubrick's contractual agreement to deliver an R-rated film. The enhancements, by exposing the routine idiocy of the MPAA ratings, may help to foster some overdue reform. At the very least they show how American adult moviegoers are treated like children, unlike their European counterparts who can see *Eyes Wide Shut* without these digital fig leaves, basically for the sake of Warners's money-grubbing, which allows for an eventual "director's cut" on video and DVD, generating more income while avoiding the risk of an NC-17 rating. Apparently corporate indifference to the public's understanding prevented most critics, including me, from seeing this movie until the last possible minute before writing their initial reviews. That Warners has also chosen to conceal the degree to which *Eyes Wide Shut* was unfinished when Kubrick died—he hadn't yet completed the sound-mixing, which, as David Cronenberg pointed out, can't be discounted as a creative part of the filmmaking process—clears the way for critics to complain that the public is being sold a bill of goods.

But Kubrick recut both *2001* and *The Shining* after they opened commercially, and a climactic pie-throwing free-for-all in the War Room in *Dr. Strangelove*, filmed in color, was cut shortly before the film opened. Obviously what constitutes a "finished" Kubrick film has long been somewhat tenuous. Undoubtedly he would have made a few slight adjustments in *Eyes Wide Shut* had he lived longer—he probably would have fixed the bumpy sound-edit at the end of Bill and Alice's lovemaking scene and perhaps shortened the sequence in which Bill is followed by a generic bald man in a trenchcoat—which means that the released version is in some ways a rough cut. But I regard the opportunity to view a Kubrick rough cut as a privilege. What I resent is Warners's refusal to clarify which portions and aspects of the sound-mix were completed by others and how this was carried out—and the only defense I can think of for that is the profit motive.

Most reviews of every Kubrick picture since *2001* have been mired in misapprehensions and underestimations—many of which are corrected years later without apology, one reason he apparently gave up on critics about thirty years ago. This doesn't necessarily mean he was always ahead of his time: one of the best things about *Eyes Wide Shut*—evident in such artisanal qualities as the old-fashioned sound track, the grainy photography, and the exquisite color balances (such as the dark blue lighting of a bathroom behind one of Kidman's monologues)—is that it isn't a film of the 90s in most respects but something closer to what movies at their best used to be. (One might even argue that the film has something substantial to say about virtually every decade of the twentieth century *except for* the 90s.) The Harfords' apartment calls to mind an Otto Preminger noir film of the 40s or 50s, and the costume orgy harks all the way back to silent cinema—not to mention Georges Franju's *Judex*—in its ceremonial intensity.

The film credits a lighting cameraman but no director of photography, which has led critic Kent Jones to surmise correctly that Kubrick shot most of it himself. This is personal filmmaking as well as dream poetry of the kind most movie commerce has ground underfoot, and it's bound to survive a good deal longer than most of its detractors.

2001

Roger Ebert

Roger Ebert (b. 1942) is known to all as television's roly-poly, sweater-wearing movie critic, quick to pan or praise a new release with a quotable sound bite and joust with his review partner (first Gene Siskel, now Richard Roeper). Less appreciated, perhaps, is that he is a highly dedicated cinephile, who can capture in carefully written prose the worldly refinements of an old movie classic such as Lubitsch's *Trouble in Paradise*, as well as unleash free-wheeling blasts of populist spleen in books like *I Hated, Hated, Hated This Movie*. He has been film critic for the *Chicago Sun-Times* since 1967.

◆

Trouble in Paradise

When I was small, I liked to go to the movies because you could find out what adults did when there weren't any children in the room. As I grew up, that pleasure gradually faded; the more I knew, the less the characters seemed like adults. Ernst Lubitsch's *Trouble in Paradise* reawakened my old feeling. It is about people who are almost impossibly adult, in that fanciful movie way—so suave, cynical, sophisticated, smooth, and sure that a lifetime is hardly long enough to achieve such polish. They glide.

It is a comedy for three characters, plus comic relief in supporting roles. Herbert Marshall plays a gentleman jewel thief, Miriam Hopkins plays the con woman who adores him, and Kay Francis is the rich widow who thinks she can buy him but is content to rent him for a while. They live in a movie world of exquisite costumes, flawless grooming, butlers, grand hotels in Venice, penthouses in Paris, cocktails, evening dress, wall safes, sweeping staircases, nightclubs, the opera, and jewelry, a lot of jewelry. What is curious is how real they manage to seem in the midst of the foppery.

The romantic triangle was the favorite plot device of Lubitsch. The critic Greg S. Faller notes that the German-born director liked stories in which "an essentially solid relationship is temporarily threatened by a sexual rival." Here it's clear from the beginning that the gentleman thief Gaston Monescu (Marshall) and the lady pickpocket Lily Vautier (Hopkins) are destined for one another—not only because they like each other but because their professions make it impossible to trust civilians. When Gaston meets Mariette Colet

636

(Francis), it is to return the purse he has stolen from her and claim the reward. She is attracted to him, and he gracefully bows to her lust, but there is an underlying sobriety: He knows it cannot last, and in a way so does she.

The sexual undertones are surprisingly frank in this pre-Code 1932 film, and we understand that none of the three characters is in any danger of mistaking sex for love. Both Lily and Mariette know what they want, and Gaston knows that he has it. His own feelings for them are masked beneath an impenetrable veneer of sophisticated banter.

Herbert Marshall takes ordinary scenes and fills them with tension because of the way he seems to withhold himself from the obvious emotional scripting. He was forty-two when he made the film, handsome in a subdued rather than an absurd way, every dark hair slicked close to his scalp, with a slight stoop to his shoulders that makes him seem to be leaning slightly toward his women, or bowing. His walk is deliberate and noticeably smooth; he lost a leg in World War I, had a wooden one fitted, and practiced so well at concealing his limp that he seems to float through a room.

He gives a droll, mocking richness to the dialogue by Samson Raphaelson, Lubitsch's favorite collaborator. He seems to know he's in a drawing room comedy, and the actresses speak in tune with him. There are exchanges so teasing that they're like verbal foreplay. Consider the early scene where Gaston, having stolen some jewels, returns to his hotel suite to host a private dinner for Lily. He poses as a baron. She poses as a countess.

"You know," says Lily, "when I first saw you, I thought you were an American."

"Thank you," Gaston gravely replies.

"Someone from another world, so entirely different. Oh! One gets so tired of one's own class—princes and counts and dukes and kings! Everybody talking shop. Always trying to sell jewelry. Then I heard your name and found out you were just one of us."

"Disappointed?"

"No, proud. Very proud."

And they kiss. But soon it is revealed that they have both been busily stealing each other's possessions. She has his wallet, he has her pin, and it's like a game of strip poker in which, as each theft is revealed, their excitement grows, until finally Lily realizes she has been unmasked by another criminal and cries out, "Darling! Tell me, tell me all about yourself. Who are you?"

He is one of the boldest thieves in the world. He meets Mariette (Francis) by stealing her diamond-encrusted purse and then returning it. He insinuates himself into her trust, advising her on lipstick and on her choice of lovers (of course he has read the love letter in the handbag). The dialogue is daring in its insinuations:

"If I were your father, which fortunately I am not," he says, "and you made any attempt to handle your own business affairs, I would give you a good spanking—in a business way, of course."

"What would you do if you were my secretary?"

"The same thing."

"You're hired."

Turn up the heat under this dialogue, and you'd have screwball comedy. It's tantalizing the way Lubitsch and his actors keep it down to a sensuous simmer. In the low, caressing tones of Marshall and Francis, they're toying with the words—they're in on the joke, and Mariette is neither a spoiled rich woman nor a naive victim. She is a woman of appetites and the imagination to take advantage of an opportunity. She probably doesn't believe, even then, that this man is who he says. He has a way of smiling while he lies, to let his victims have a peek at the joke. But Mariette is an enormously attractive woman, not least because of her calm self-assurance, and he likes her even as he deceives her.

Their first meeting is a splendid example of "the Lubitsch Touch," a press agent's phrase that stuck, maybe because audiences sensed that the director *did* have a special touch, a way of transforming material through style. What happens, and you are surprised to sense it happening, is that in a drawing room comedy of froth and inconsequence, you find that you believe in the characters and care about them.

Ernst Lubitsch (1892–1947), short, plain, cigar-chewing, beloved, was born in Berlin, was on the stage by the time he was nineteen, worked as a silent film comedian, and in 1915 began to direct. His silent films often starred Pola Negri, who played Madame DuBarry in *Passion* (1919), which made their reputations in America. Mary Pickford brought him to Hollywood in 1923, where he quickly became successful. His best silent films include a version of Oscar Wilde's *Lady Windermere's Fan* (1925) that the critic Andrew Sarris argues actually improves on the original ("it seems incredible") by dropping Wilde's epigrams, "which were largely irrelevant to the plot."

Lubitsch ruled at Paramount in the late 1920s and 1930s (he was head of the studio for a year), embracing the advent of sound with a series of musicals that often starred Jeannette Macdonald. *Trouble in Paradise* is generally considered his best film, but there are advocates for his version of Noel Coward's *Design for Living* (1933), with Gary Cooper, Fredric March, and Miriam Hopkins; *Ninotchka* (1939), with Garbo, a definitive adult; *The Shop Around the*

Corner (1940), with James Stewart and Margaret Sullavan as bickering coworkers who don't realize they're romantic pen pals; and *To Be or Not to Be* (1942), with Jack Benny and Carole Lombard in a comedy aimed squarely at Hitler.

Because "The Lubitsch Touch" was coined by a publicist, no one, least of all Lubitsch, ever really defined it. It is often said to refer to his fluid camera. Watching *Trouble in Paradise*, what I sensed even more was the way the comic material is given dignity by the actors; the characters have a weight of experience behind them that suggests they know life cannot be played indefinitely for laughs. Sarris, trying to define the Touch, said it was "a counterpoint of poignant sadness during a film's gayest moments." Consider the way Gaston and Mariette say good-bye for the last time, after it is clear to both of them that he loved her and stole from her. How gallantly they try to make a joke of it.

Wow. *2002*

Stuart Klawans

Stuart Klawans has been film critic for *The Nation* since 1988. Inheriting a post previously held by such titans in the field as James Agee and Manny Farber, he has honored their examples with his own polished, quirky, erudite, and courtly prose. The tongue-in-cheek mock-pedantry that begins his review of the blockbuster *Gladiator* suggests a characteristic willingness to be bemused rather than outraged by any nonsense the screen has to offer. Klawans' interest in very large movies that go too far manifests itself further in his delightful, well-researched book *Film Follies*, which details the making of many such sacred monsters from *Intolerance* to *Ishtar*.

◆

Gladiator

According to Gibbon, the emperor Commodus spent the early years of his reign "in a seraglio of three hundred beautiful women and as many boys, of every rank and of every province." Later, adding bloodshed to his round of pleasures, he launched a career in murder, beginning with the dispatch of the usual senators, ministers and family members and continuing with the slaughter of beasts. Styling himself the Roman Hercules, he went as a performer into the amphitheater, where he cut down before the public a number of ostriches, a panther, a hundred lions, an elephant, a rhinoceros and a giraffe. He then entered the lists as a gladiator. Commodus fought 735 times and paid himself such a high fee for each appearance that a new tax had to be levied. No harm came to him in the arena, if only because he furnished his opponents with weapons of lead; so it was left to Marcia, his favorite concubine, to rid Rome of Commodus. One night, aided by a chamberlain and the Praetorian prefect, she admitted a professional wrestler to his bedchamber to strangle him as he lay in a drunken stupor.

I say there's a movie here. Unfortunately, Dream Works and Universal disagree with me, and so the public is stuck with *Gladiator*, one of those productions that betray their disarray by crediting three screenwriters, none of whom is Gibbon. *Gladiator* is the tale not of Commodus (Joaquin Phoenix) but of a disagreeably virtuous general, Maximus (Russell Crowe), who from the height of military honor is sold into slavery, made a gladiator and then elevated to the status of demagogue, all without relaxing his expression from a glower.

For its first half hour, *Gladiator* consists of gloomy, sidelit close-ups of Crowe and a handful of other players, who by means of a relentless shot-countershot scheme are prevented from acting with one another. Worse still: While sitting for their portraits, they are made to worry at length about the future of Rome. Will it become a republic again? Will Commodus succeed white-maned Marcus Aurelius to the throne? And who the hell lugged all those statues into "Germania," just to decorate Marcus's field tent? The Germani-ans, if that's what they're called, interrupt the heavy sighs of Roman conver-sation by dying in battle. Orange flames from the imperial lines fly across the gloomy, blue-gray twilight into Germanian territory, giving the signal for slo-mo, strobe-mo and jitter-mo to ensue, until such time as expository dialogue may resume.

"In this hand, Caesar, I hold a shiny new quarter."

"Strength and honor! Will you exchange it for a nickel and two dimes?"

"Where, in all the province of Zucchabar, does a parking meter accept—*dimes*?"

You heard me right: Zucchabar. After valiant, glowering Maximus has been stripped of his command, informed of the sure demise of his family and left for dead, he awakens into the Hollywood version of the Middle East: a place of mud-brick architecture and ululation, where stoop-shouldered, burnoose-clad merchants pass the days in sibilant larceny. Here, as it happens, *Gladiator* tem-porarily springs to life.

Having severed its few feeble ties to reality, the movie is free to become a backstage comedy. What is a gladiatorial contest, if not showbiz? What is the amphitheater in dusty Zucchabar, if not a stop on the bus-and-truck circuit? And who is Maximus's new owner, Proximo (stately, plump Oliver Reed, done up in a turban and several tins' worth of bronzing makeup), if not a two-bit pro-ducer trying to claw his way back to the big time? I do not interpret; I report the surface features of the movie, which include an instructive speech by Prox-imo about getting the audience onto your side.

Meanwhile, back in Rome, Commodus toys with a model of the Colos-seum. Why should an emperor suffer the risks of real warfare, he asks, when he can mount a play war instead? The image shifts from Commodus's toy to a different kind of model: a computer-generated picture of the Colosseum, into which we descend to view the first of the emperor's games. It will be the re-enactment of a battle from the Second Punic War—in other words, a show about history, which stands in relation to the characters in *Gladiator* as *Gladiator* stands to us.

At this point, noting how the movie has collapsed into itself, cinephiles under the influence of too much caffeine might hallucinate a political vision. Doesn't *Gladiator* lay bare the purpose of today's media wars?

Well, no. In the first place, the movie is far too concerned with turning Maximus into a man on a white horse—again, I merely report surface details—who will restore Rome to democracy by becoming a dictator. (Of course, the minute he's seized power, he will abdicate in favor of the Senate and retire to his country home—good little Cincinnatus, covered with blood and scars.) In the second place, the film's satirical impulse twitches fitfully at best. *Gladiator* is no *Wag the Dog*. In lighter moments, it's more like Sternberg's 1928 *The Last Command*, in which an exiled Russian general winds up playing himself on a Hollywood lot.

I wish that Russell Crowe, as the Roman general remade into a showbiz soldier, had been granted the opportunities for sentiment and irony that Sternberg once offered his star, Emil Jannings. Most people assume that films of the silent era were crude and naive compared with today's movies; and yet for all the money and technology that were dumped into *Gladiator*, and for all the logistical skill of its director, Ridley Scott, this picture is a kazoo compared with the symphony orchestra that Sternberg conducted. Crowe is a wonderful actor, as you can see from *The Insider*, or even *L.A. Confidential*. Yet no one in charge of this film thought to allow him an emotion, other than a single-minded desire for revenge and an equally dull rectitude. Crowe gamely wears whatever costume he is given; he tromps around with his arms held out from his sides, like a tough soldier whose muscles ache. And that's about all he can do under the circumstances, other than work his basso into ever more alarming registers. Some might say it's a voice produced midway between diaphragm and testicles; others, that it sounds like a cement mixer that's just stripped its gears. But neither organic nor mechanical similes will do. I must turn to geology: In *Gladiator*, having no other use for his energies, Crowe has made his voice sound like the grinding of tectonic plates.

Or maybe it's just the grinding of teeth. What else could Crowe do, when asked to stand by impassively during "love scenes" with the film's lone female figure, Connie Nielsen? It is the filmmakers' conceit that Nielsen, as the emperor's sister Lucilla, had a premarital fling with old Maximus. Now she is once more tantalizingly close to him and yet out of reach, in a ponderous subplot that turns her into a surrogate for the general's dead wife, with her son completing the imaginary family. It's a role that's as thankless as it is forgettable; and Nielsen fades with it so thoroughly that you'd think she'd been born in a vat, from whatever stem cells they use to grow starlets.

Of course, if you go by Gibbon, members of the imperial household did not let such a small thing as marriage impede their sex lives. Lucilla's mother had inspected most of Rome's manhood for hernias; and who knows what Lucilla herself might have done, in a less duty-bound movie? But just as *Gladiator* denies you the bloodlust it advertises—scenes of carnage, in both field and amphitheater, are programmatically chopped into blurry fragments—so too does it withhold the elements of hotcha that were always a chief pleasure of the sword-and-sandal picture. Like its hero, the film is solemnly pious; and though Christianity this time is noticeably missing from Hollywood's Rome, the sense of morality oppresses as never before.

It needn't have been this way. Even within *Gladiator*, lurid entertainments are present, though concealed. I have it on good authority that the late Oliver Reed bore on the head of his penis a tattoo in the form of a dragon's claw. I mention this adornment only to point out that the tide of life, though doubtless lower now than in the days of Commodus, has not ebbed entirely. Why couldn't Reed have given more of himself to this movie? (He died during the making of *Gladiator*, perhaps from the strain of being changed into a virtuous character.) Why couldn't Russell Crowe have been freed to act? And when will a producer haul a bag of money to Winnipeg, so that Guy Maddin can have his shot at reviving the sword-and-sandal epic? So far as I know, Maddin hasn't brought out a picture since *Twilight of the Ice Nymphs*, whose title alone should tell you how well he could adapt Gibbon.

Let's decline and fall again real soon.

2002

James Harvey

In two books, *Romantic Comedy in Hollywood: From Lubitsch to Sturges* and *Movie Love in the Fifties*, James Harvey (b. 1929) has demonstrated a brilliant knack for bringing alive old movies through sensuous descriptions that allow us to re-view them in our mind's eye and magisterial analyses that dissect the artistry of camera style and performance. This investigation by Harvey of Douglas Sirk's *Imitation of Life* uncovers, layer by layer, the richness of a film that has often been treated as a silly escapist flick about superficial people. By taking Hollywood melodrama seriously, or at least on its own terms, Harvey retrieves the painful ironies of race and class, ambivalent mother-daughter relationships, and other disturbing moral complexities, and the result is film criticism that is anything but escapist.

◆

Imitation of Life

Imitation of Life is the movie that, still today, most evokes the fifties for me. It was a big hit in 1959—the biggest in Universal's history—and it was Sirk's last movie. "I couldn't go on making those Ross Hunter pictures," he said, about his departure from Hollywood that same year. But he made the best one last—the picture where all the discordancies of those earlier ones get triumphantly resolved. In part, it's a movie about its own genre, the tearjerker, about the genteel pop culture that it itself exemplifies—and about the genre as a way of looking at American life, seeing what Sirk saw: the "creative generosity" and optimism, the complacency and willed innocence, the denial of death and the emptying-out of life, the endemic racism. It's above all about different forms of "imitation" ("I would have made it for the title alone," Sirk said), about "phonies" of different sorts, and their opposites, about American blacks and whites and the connections between them. Fassbinder called it "a great crazy movie about life and about death. And about America." Is it ever. And not *only* about the America of forty years ago.

Sarah Jane (Susan Kohner) is white enough to "pass"—that is, if she can get far enough away from her unmistakably black single mother, Annie (Juanita Moore), who thinks "it's a sin to be ashamed of what you are, and it's even worse to pretend." Her mother thinks she's working at the library, but what she's doing instead is singing and dancing under an assumed name at a sleazy joint called Harry's Club, a small underground room, full of smoke and raunchy atmosphere and leering old men—where Sarah Jane, in a black corset, now performs a sexy song, leaning on the tables, posing near a phallic candle, showing lots of leg and cleavage to the appreciative clientele. She's not very good, but she *is* fairly blatant (by the standards of the time) and is having success with her audience.

But for the second time in this movie (which is entering its final half hour), Annie blows her daughter's cover. She's been there, behind a louvered screen, watching the whole spectacle. "Sarah Jane Johnson, get your clothes on and get out of here!" she says—just as Sarah Jane, after her act, is flirting with one of the cute guys at the club. She tries to brazen her way through the embarrassment: the woman's crazy, she says; "make her go away." But Annie's not going anywhere without her daughter. And the men, of course, are amazed—they would never have *guessed* . . . (It's almost kind of titillating.) But anyway she's fired. (This was a time in America when you *could* be fired for not being white.)

And when she packs her suitcases and leaves, guess who's out there waiting for her—in a doorway? "Sarah Jane!" cries Annie, as the girl goes by, furious and silent. "What do you expect me to do when I find you dancing in a low-down dive like that?" What would they say at the teachers' college— "*Think*, honey," she implores. But Sarah Jane retorts that she "wouldn't be found dead in a colored teachers' college." So come home, have coffee, we'll talk, pleads Annie, as they stop and face each other: "Nobody's all right about anything," says Annie urgently, "and nobody's all wrong. Now if you don't want to be a teacher, all right, we'll talk about what you *want* to be." But Sarah Jane isn't having any—she wants to be *white*, and there's no talking about *that*, not with her black mother. She turns away without replying and goes on, leaving Annie behind, calling her and sitting on a nearby stoop. What Sarah Jane doesn't know, as we do, is that Annie is ill—that the movie, in the conventionally tactful and unspecific way of such movies, has already let us know that Annie "doesn't have long."

So Sarah Jane disappears. And as Annie's time dwindles, she determines to see her daughter one final time, and *not* to reproach or dissuade her: "I've settled all that in my mind," she says. I should emphasize that Annie by now— and in spite of what that Harry's Club scene might suggest about her—is almost inarguably the most sympathetic character in the movie. Sarah Jane is her only competition, as the white characters have become less and less so. What starts out, as Fassbinder observed, as a movie about Lana Turner has turned into a movie about Annie, her maid. Who now goes to Hollywood:

private detectives have informed her that her daughter is working (an assumed name again) as a chorus girl at the Moulin Rouge nightclub there. It's a real place, and the next sequence was filmed there on location.

And suddenly there she is: this genteel "colored" matron, in the middle of the crowded glitzy lobby, as jazzy music blares on the soundtrack, and she slips up the staircase past a tuxedoed host greeting people and into a room with a gridded purple ceiling and hot-pink walls and milling couples, all white. She looms above the camera, looking confused, making her uncertain way through the crowd, and looking just like what she is—Somebody's Maid—in her boxy bluish coat and round black hat. The film now cuts between her progress through the lobby and the show inside that we know she is headed toward. It's a confused-looking production number, as we first see it (before she does) in a long shot: a vast multileveled stage where showgirls in massive headdresses move vaguely about to the jittery music amid Dalíesque truncated pillars and stairways, while sprightly chorus girls in feathers dance onto and down a circular runway that takes them out among the audience's tables. Back to Annie in the lobby, looking around. Back to the show: a male dancer in striped coat and straw bowler is leaping and prancing around an insouciant chorus girl who is inciting him with her plume, as the girls on the runway pass by in front. Back to Annie, seeming to find her way now. Then a shot of her from behind, close and low-angled, and we see, as she moves away from the camera and down an aisle through tables, that she is inside the theatre, and then at the edge of the runway. Where she stands, looking up at the chorus girls as they whip by just above her.

Now something else is happening on the runway: in the far background you can see that the chorus girls are being followed by a slowly moving turntable track of showgirls seated in lounge chairs; as they emerge from the wings you can just see Sarah Jane among them. Chugging along, they perch coquettishly on the edges of their chairs, which have high backs—which they rock to the music. They are wearing gold-colored corsets, with long trains that fall between their legs, and they have ice buckets beside them and are pantomiming the pouring of champagne into goblets and drinking. There is some more synchronized-to-the-music business—arch and mischievous and disturbingly pointless. In close-up Sarah Jane shakes her shoulders and winks. On the floor below, a waiter approaches Annie and whispers at her; she follows him back up the aisle, stopping at the end to look back at the stage—where the routine goes on, Sarah Jane looking suddenly distressed. She and the girls rise and go behind their chairs, leaning on them provocatively. Annie goes out. The girls get back into their chairs and stretch out on them, lying prone and rocking as their turntable begins to move them off. The camera moves with it, fixing Sarah Jane in a disturbing overhead view—laid out on her chair, traveling past the politely applauding tables, arching her back, lifting her pelvis toward the camera, raising an arm to hold the goblet aloft, holding the pose until she is shunted into the wings and offstage. As the turntable moves slowly to a stop, she relaxes (also slowly), gets up off the chair, and peels off her long blue gloves—frowning. A carrot-haired friend from the next chair asks her if anything is wrong. No, nothing, she replies—"just a funny feeling." What she doesn't say, of course, is that she thinks she has seen her mother.

The sequence is very short—less than three minutes—but it focuses so much complication of feeling and meaning, in such gathering, stunning, and total control, that it feels a lot longer: the crosscutting between Annie outside and the show inside, both undercutting the glitzy spectacle and at the same time heightening its excitement; then Sarah Jane's performance with its disturbing undertones, and Annie's impassive witness (like some dream reversal of the primal scene: your parents watching *you*); the intersection between public and private meanings, between the show and Sarah Jane's place in it, and the meaning that *both* get from Annie's inapposite, improbable presence. It's not surprising, then, that before the sequence fades out, Annie makes a final apparitionlike reappearance, passing quickly through the backstage wings as Sarah Jane and her showgirl friend exchange reminders about their after-the-show dates ("Don't forget—the guys are picking us up at twelve-thirty").

But at least it's a step up from Harry's Club, isn't it? Classier, "cleaner," bring-the-whole-family as compared to Sarah Jane's brassy self-display at the "low-down dive." So why does it feel so much worse?

For one thing, Sirk shows that champagne routine (the actual show at this place) without any obvious satiric slant but in a way that makes it feel both nasty and dumb. Just as he highlights (through his cutting and angles) the nattering, dithering quality of the big stage show—you feel it's like something gibbering at you. The sleazy life of Harry's Club has emptied out into this chaotic spectacle, the cold mechanistic tease of those relax-a-bed lounge chairs and fake champagne bottles, into the familiar hectic vacancy of popular entertainment.

But that vacancy is finally and importantly what passing for white comes to mean in this movie—and what Sarah Jane is seen to be finally pursuing. And that building revelation is part of what makes the next scene—where Annie visits Sarah Jane in her motel room to say goodbye to her—as harrowing as it is.

It was principally because of the latter scene, and Annie's death and funeral at the end, that the 1959 reviews would say things like "the most shameless tearjerker in memory," *Time* magazine suggesting that theatre owners would "have to install aisle scuppers to drain off the tears." *That* prediction was nearly right: Sirk's film quickly became famous for its uniting effect on big audiences, the way *Psycho* would a year later, though with a very different kind of effect. But *Imitation of Life* made even more money, more than anything out of Universal before it, in fact. "The sobs," as Pauline Kael would later observe, are virtually "torn from your throat."

That's true enough—but on the other hand, as between having such a reaction "torn" from you or "jerked," you could conceivably prefer the former approach—the all-outness of it, the frankness of the aggression. Why not? It would never work that way, of course, if you didn't also believe the pain, didn't feel that the excess embodied a truth of some kind—in the actors, in the scene itself.

Sarah Jane is dressing for that double date when Annie surprises her in her motel room: "It *was* you," the girl says—and then: "Why can't you leave me alone?" "I tried, honey," says Annie. "You'll never know how hard I tried." The look of this scene is almost Dreyeresque: the bare, dimly lit room, with brown wood furnishings, straight right-angled lines, and blue-and-black-inflected colors, a mirror (of course) framed in brown wood, and (at the beginning) the arc of a wooden chair arm in the low-angle foreground, bisecting the frame in an ominous dark curve. Sarah Jane is in a black sheath cocktail dress, Annie in her dowdy coat and hat. Sarah Jane, upset and angry, supposes she might as well pack her bags again, that her mother's already seen the boss about her. No, says Annie, she hasn't, and she means never to interfere with her daughter's life again. But she's expecting someone, says the girl, only partly reassured. "I'll only stay a minute," Annie says. "I just want to look at you. That's why I came." And then: "Are you happy here, honey? Are you findin' what you really want?"

It's said with love, but it's still a terrible question—whether it's yes or no, you feel, the answer has to be unhappy. As it turns out, it's yes. "I'm somebody else!" Sarah Jane answers, distraught—turning around, the camera tilting upward and turning with her until it shows her reflection in the mahogany-framed mirror. "I'm white," she says into the mirror, with her black mother in the bleak gray-wall background of the shot—then repeats the word ("—white, *white!*") with rising hysteria. Then: "Does that answer you?" turning back to her mother—who says that it does.

It's not Sarah Jane's agitation that controls these early moments as much as it is Annie's sorrowful serenity. The scene itself, as you recognize from its beginning, is an almost obligatory, conventional one, with a prescribed shape and development: the renunciation scene, where the heroine (or hero, though rarely) gives up the beloved other—Marguerite sends Armand away, Stella Dallas rejects her daughter, Lorrie, Annie relinquishes Sarah Jane—for what she feels is the other's good. This always involves some painful masquerade— Marguerite doesn't love him, Stella doesn't want her, Annie is just tired, not ill—which amplifies the heartbreak. And the heroine's belief that she is doing the Right Thing is always at least open to question: causing both Armand and Lorrie to suffer cruelly—and relinquishing Sarah Jane to—well, *what*? A life of "imitation" . . .

But someone will come soon: she wants her mother to go now, please—and to promise if they should ever meet again, not to know her. Annie agrees. But Sarah Jane must promise her that if she's ever in trouble or needs help ("—and you shouldn't be able to—get in touch with me"), she will let them know at home. And one more thing . . . Sarah Jane looks frightened: What? she asks. And from this point, as Annie's emotion bears down on her more and more, so does the camera, trapping both of them, as it were, together and separately, almost unbearably it seems at times, in an escalating series of tighter and tighter close shots. Annie says: "I'd like to hold you in my arms once more— like you were still my baby." "All right, Mama—all *right!*" says Sarah Jane, with a kind of irritable distractedness (a response, the way Kohner inflects it, that seems to summon up a whole bygone adolescence), turning to face away and bracing herself against the chair back. And when Annie then hugs her, Sarah Jane—in a close-up—looks half-dazed, almost unhinged, by the impact. "Oh, my baby!" says Annie, sobbing now, "my beautiful, beautiful baby . . . I love you so much. Nothin' you ever do can stop that." And next Sarah Jane is saying "Mama, Mama!" and hugging her still closer. She was right to be frightened . . . Annie's love is a powerful and terrible thing: it can't be a light matter to be its object.

An offscreen knock at the door and Sarah Jane's showgirl friend comes in, dressed up, wearing a fur stole. "Come on, Linda," she says (that's Sarah Jane's current name), "they're waiting." Then, seeing Annie: "Say, listen," she says, in a voice of reasonable grievance, crossing the room to Annie, "if you're the new maid, I want to report that my shower is full of ants." It's perfectly polite, even a little shy, not at all imperious; but the remark lands brutally—for *us*, too—as reminder of one of the larger meanings of what we've just been watching, and it's a surprise. So is Annie's reply: "Oh, I'm sorry, miss," she says, with her lovely smile, "that must be very uncomfortable"—generous, splendid, somehow more noblesse oblige than self-abasing. "But I just happened to be in town, and I dropped in to see Miss Linda. I used to take care of her . . ." And she approaches Sarah Jane, who is standing apart in a half-shadow, facing the camera—Annie beside her now in profile. She'll be running along now, she says, catching her plane, and so forth. "Goodbye, honey," she says to "Miss Linda"—who turns to her, silently saying the word "Mama," as Annie turns away and goes out. The friend, who has been watching all this, is impressed, and comes strolling forward: "Well, get *you*," she says to Sarah Jane. "So, honey child, you had a mammy . . ." "Yes," says Sarah Jane, crying quite openly now, leaning with her back against the door that has just closed behind Annie. "All my life." Fade-out.

This coda with the showgirl friend is also conventional: multiplying the painful masquerades (Annie must pretend again, and Sarah Jane too this time) ups the emotional ante, giving you an extra pang or two. And you're aware of the manipulation—and, in this case at least, the cleverness (e.g., the several meanings of "mammy," and of "All my life," and the adroit use of them; the instinctive snobbery of the showgirl's reaction). But you're equally aware of how the truth of the performances and the scene itself (the wasting-and-destroying aspect, the final hopeless impasse, of parent-child love) trumps the self-declaring artifice, even redeems it—and that's part of what makes the scene moving altogether: the refraction through a conventional form.

Oddly enough, Sirk himself claimed, when I asked him, to have been surprised when he heard how emotionally audiences were reacting to his film. That was the American audience, he pointed out (the Germans, apparently, remained dry-eyed—the movie failed there). He was still puzzled, he said. "It may be. It may be—I have no talent for sentimentality. So perhaps I simply don't recognize it." I thought then that he was being disingenuous—how could he *not* know? (Later he wanted to omit this exchange from the published interview.) But today I'm not so sure. These scenes with Annie and Sarah Jane have the same formal absorption and intense artifice, the peculiar mixture of coldness and passion, both fracturing our attention and concentrating it powerfully, that mark his best work—in *Written on the Wind*, for example, as different as that movie otherwise is from this one.

And it was those two extraordinary performances from Kohner and Moore. Kohner's dark, vulpine prettiness and angry, intelligent eyes make a remarkable contrast to Moore's air of acquiescence. Sarah Jane is the severe one, with a nice-girl-going-on-tough-cookie quality that's both upsetting and moving—and that gives an entertaining ironic edge to those public performances of yielding sexuality she gives. Moore, with her broad brow, deep-set, large eyes, and high, wide cheekbones, has the kind of face that looks both beautiful and bountiful at once—with such a force of genuine good nature that the Lana Turner heroine's early capitulation to it seems foregone. But you notice, as the movie goes on, that Annie never, even at her most radiant, looks unwatchful. Nor, even at her most nurturing and "mammylike" does she ever seem less than the smart and authoritative woman she is—almost certainly the smartest person in the film. And to the degree that the character assumes a kind of monumentality—the film's representative of historical suffering and injustice ("How do you explain to your child, she was born to be hurt?")—Moore makes it seem (as it should) the opposite, as if the monumentality were assuming *her*. Both actors in their different ways have this kind of sincere, unfaked power. And the rapport between them makes their scenes together one of the wonders of the movie era.

They were both Sirk's casting choices: the studio wanted Pearl Bailey for Annie, and for Sarah Jane, Ross (it's true) wanted Margaret O'Brien (a *young* old star for a change). By comparison to those, Sirk's candidates were both unknown and untried. Moore (then thirty-six—two years younger than Turner, the star) was a former singer and chorus girl who'd been doing small roles (mostly maids, of course) in minor movies, occasionally in a major one like Raoul Walsh's *Band of Angels* in 1957, appearing briefly as a sexy wanton slave who taunts Yvonne De Carlo, the virginal heroine. "Sirk really stuck his neck out for me," she said in 1998. And his patience, she said, was inexhaustible: she recalled being so nervous at the start of shooting that he had to do twenty-two takes of an insignificant early scene with Lana Turner (who was also patient). "He'd say to me, 'You know, if you're no good, Juanita, the movie's no good.'" He was simply the kindest man she had *ever* worked for, she said, before or since. But that's not the way Susan Kohner remembers her experience with him: he was very tough on her (Moore and Heymann both corroborated this)— stern and remote and demanding and, to the twenty-two-year-old she was then, sort of frightening, certainly intimidating. But whatever he was up to in all this, she admits, he seems to have gotten what he wanted from her on the screen. The movie was the peak of both actresses' careers—unhappily, there were never such roles again for either of them (they were *both* nominated for the supporting-actress Academy Award that year; Shelley Winters won).

It was—once again—a remake of an earlier Universal movie by John Stahl. The original, starring Claudette Colbert, was released in 1934 and was a great success—though nothing to touch the remake's. Both movies, based on the Fannie Hurst novel, follow the fortunes of two mothers and their two daughters. Both of them begin when the white heroine, a struggling widow, takes in a homeless black woman to be her housekeeper, along with her light-skinned little girl. The two girls grow up together, and in each version meet the same sort of problem: resolving to "pass," in the one case, and in the white daughter's case, falling in love with her mother's boyfriend. In both pictures the white mother rises to riches and the black mother dies, with a spectacular funeral near the movie's end, and her repentant daughter sobbing over her coffin.

In the Stahl original—which closely follows the Fannie Hurst novel—Bea (Colbert) opens a pancake house on the Coney Island boardwalk, using the secret recipe that her new housemate and cook, Delilah (Louise Beavers), has shared with her. Soon they are selling it in boxes, with Delilah's grinning face on the outside ("Aunt Delilah's Pancake Flour"), and Bea is running a company. But when she offers Delilah her rightful share in the business, the woman refuses, preferring her station as Bea's housekeeper and live-in friend.

Annie, on the other hand, gets no such offer. Sirk's version makes essential changes in this material: instead of a businesswoman who becomes a magnate, the Lana Turner heroine is an actress who becomes a star. But in spite of this fundamental revision, the remake reproduces all the dramatic highlights of the Stahl film, and even many of their details (Sirk never watched the original, he claimed, but the many writers assigned to his film did), but always in an inflated, hyperbolized way. The climactic funeral, for example, is much longer and more operatically rendered in the Sirk version. As is the black mother's death scene: in the Stahl film, she goes rather quietly, slipping discreetly away to the accompaniment of distant "darkie" singing, while Colbert stifles her sobs in a trailing chiffon handkerchief at some nearby windows; whereas Annie has quite a lot to say before *she* goes, and when she finally does, the heroine collapses at her bedside, screaming her name.

In both movies the black mother catches her little girl "passing" at school by turning up unexpectedly at her classroom. The humiliated child in the first version then walks slowly, agonizingly, up the schoolroom aisle, past the whispers and stares of her classmates, to where her mother waits for her at the door; in the next scene, they are back home again. But in Sirk's film, the girl dashes past her mother, grabbing her coat in the cloakroom and rushing out into the falling snow, her mother following, while an offscreen choir shrills and ululates in alarm—in a deep-focus long shot that foregrounds a bright red fireplug. And the effect—like a visualized howl—is stark, beautiful, appalling.

And the original of the Harry's Club scene—the one where you first see the grown-up daughter "passing"—could hardly be more opposite. In the Stahl film, Delilah finds Peola—as the Sarah Jane figure is called in both the novel and the 1934 movie, where she is played by a "real" (i.e., technically) black woman, Fredi Washington—working as the cashier in a tearoom. When Stahl's camera first picks her up there, she is sitting at her register by the door, facing the customers in the dining room, leaning forward on her elbows, looking heartbreakingly happy, and smiling into space—in a private rapture of achieved gentility. That is, until her mother comes in, and asks her what she's doing there—with the predictable results.

The fact is, as this tearoom epiphany suggests, that Peola's situation registers as almost unrelievedly dreary. Where Sarah Jane—angry, rebellious, sexually provocative—is movie-size "tragic," Peola seems mostly depressed (an *angry* black woman would have been too disturbing a figure in 1934 to be offered as sympathetic). When *she* faces a mirror in order to deny her own blackness (another moment echoed in the later film)—"Am I not white!" she says in her velvety alto voice and painfully "correct" English—she sounds plaintive and heartsore, more defeated than defiant.

And Stahl evokes the trap of her life with marvelous economy again and again. The first time we see her as a grown-up, it's the occasion of one of Bea's lavish house parties, with Peola and Delilah in their quarters below-stairs—listening to the party music as it drifts down to them from above. Delilah is dressed up, wearing a corsage—still, there seems to be no question of her or her daughter actually *going* to the party upstairs (they're still ahead of Annie—who cooks and serves for the parties at her place). Peola is stretched out on the couch reading. But her mother, sensing her moroseness, says with blundering benignity: "Come on, honey—*I'll* dance with you." I'm reading, retorts Peola—can't you leave me alone? But the moment evokes at one touch all the pitiableness of the daughter's life and prospects.

The Delilah, Louise Beavers, is certainly the "mammy" type, as it was conceived in those days (Delilah calls her mistress "honey chile," for example, and even offers to share her rabbit's foot with her)—like her contemporary and colleague Hattie McDaniel, she was relegated through her long career mostly to carrying trays and playing comic maids. But where McDaniel could be acerbic and formidable, and even tantalizing (as with Paul Robeson in *Show Boat*), Beavers is wistful and childlike and lost-looking—Mammy without sting or threat, a loveable primitive. Her Delilah is lumbering and overweight and slow-witted ("Just two hundred pounds of mother, fighting to keep her baby," as the Colbert heroine embarrassingly describes her; Delilah corrects her: "Two hundred and forty, ma'am"), as good-hearted as she is long-suffering: just the kind of mother who would have been an embarrassment to a daughter like

Peola even if she'd been white. It's just that sort of mundane, shaming point—not an outrage but a nasty little truth—that Stahl's quiet realism excels at making.

"Realism" is always relative, of course. And while it's true that Stahl's heroine, in the course of her rags-to-riches-to-heartache story, eventually becomes quite movie-star-glamorous (wearing swank soigné gowns and striking languid poses), she at least doesn't become the toast of Broadway, as Lana Turner does. It's the restraint and comparative true-to-lifeness of the Stahl version that make many people (Pauline Kael among them) at least prefer it to Sirk's and Ross Hunter's—with its unrelenting flamboyance and obvious falsities and Hollywood gloss. The tearoom turns into a low-down dive. Delilah turns into Juanita Moore's Annie, a figure of unshakable dignity (and thin, too). Peola has become "white"—that is, played by an actress the audience knew to be white. And the heroine has the kind of romantic and professional career that's closer to Danielle Steel than to Fannie Hurst.

But there is an irony directed at this heroine that has no counterpart in either the book or the earlier film. You've seen it before, of course, in Sirk's earlier Ross Hunter movies, directed at the Jane Wyman heroine, but less controlled, less focused and coherent than it is here. Lora's rise to stardom, for instance, is almost offhandedly preposterous, treated in a way that highlights its daydream unreality. She is a struggling, unemployed actress when she first meets Annie and brings her and Sarah Jane to live with her and Susie, then only eight, in their coldwater flat. When she finally lands a part in a play, she almost loses it at rehearsal. The playwright, David Edwards (Dan O'Herlihy), objects to the way she's acting her scene; she tells him that the scene is unactable: "You're far too good a writer to have such a scene in your play." He is, of course, impressed by this ("You've got spunk," Lou Grant once said to Mary Richards. "I *hate* spunk!"). "Tell me—what would you do with that scene?" he asks her. "I'd cut it," she replies briskly, "drop it entirely."

> EDWARDS: That's not a bad idea. Let me think. Yes—but the scene has a couple of lines that are important . . .
> LORA: Give them to Amy.
> EDWARDS: Yes—it *would* work! Huh! Think *you* could play Amy?
> LORA [*thrilled*]: Amy?
> EDWARDS: Of course we'll have to work very hard together, Miss Meredith . . .

It's the role that makes her a star. And the movie charts her rise to even greater heights in a montage: showing her taking successive curtain calls, against improbable backgrounds in equally improbable costumes (in a bonnet and hoop skirt, in an apache dancer's tight black skirt and blouse, in a leopard-skin coat against painted palm trees, and so on), her name and face appearing above show titles like *Summer Madness* and *Sweet Surrender* and (nicest of all) *Born to Laugh*. "A sophisticated actress in this part would not have been any good," Sirk told Michael Stern, about the casting of Lana Turner. "This character is supposed to be a lousy actress. She got to where she is by luck, or bullshit, or, what-do-I-know, by dumb audiences."

On her way up, Lora has a brief, sophisticated affair with Edwards, the playwright. The other men in her life are Allen Loomis (Robert Alda), her cynical, lecherous agent, whose advances she spurns ("You're trying to cheapen me—but you won't!"), and photographer Steve Archer (John Gavin), her true love (or at least the one in the genre position to be), the one who wants to marry her and whom she rejects to pursue her career. In any case, she is seen to be neglecting her daughter, Susie (Sandra Dee)—prompting the girl to fall back on her mom's friend Steve, and then to fall in love with him: a potentially disruptive development once Lora decides at last to marry him, but one that only Annie seems to know about at first.

A typical Lora-and-Annie scene: It's after one of Lora's big parties, when she is rich and famous and reclining on a sofa in her boudoir, wearing a rose-colored, fur-trimmed lounging robe, her feet up and resting in Annie's lap, at the other end of the sofa. Lora reminisces: "You and I have been through a lot together, haven't we?"—as Annie massages her feet for her. Both daughters are growing up, and the years, as Annie says, are flying by. But Annie herself looks unwell—there are dark circles under her eyes, and Lora asks if she needs any money. Annie says no; thanks to Lora she is "well fixed," she says, with enough money for both Sarah Jane's college education and her own funeral. "Oh, Annie, that *funeral* again!" says Lora. "It's the one thing I've always wanted to splurge on," says Annie—and she's made a list of all the friends who will come to it. Lora takes notice of this: "It never occurred to me that you had many friends—you never have any visit you." But Annie says she knows all kinds, hundreds even, through her church and all the lodges she belongs to. They are both standing now, in a medium two-shot, with Lora reflected in a mirrored door behind them. "I didn't know," she says quietly. "Miss Lora" (as she always calls her, even on her own deathbed), Annie replies gently, "you never asked."

That's a recurring theme about Lora. "What do *you* know about controversy?" Edwards challenges her, apropos of a script with a "colored angle." "Nothing!" she replies. "And I don't *want* to know. I only know that it's a good script and they're not easy to find." Lora is as much characterized by general unawareness, by blindness to matters both near and far from herself, as Colbert's heroine was by her clearsightedness, by her unsleeping perceptiveness and good sense. Where it's the black woman who is childish in the Stahl film, here it's the white one.

Lora is unaware not only of Annie's rich life outside their home, but of the one she leads inside it as well. Beginning with their coldwater flat, where Annie not only sustains the "family" morally and emotionally but even materially. When Lora is out of work and making rounds, not only does the unsalaried Annie take care of the two little girls and generally be the "housewife," cleaning and cooking and taking phone calls ("Miss Meredith's residence"), she also earns money for them as well—addressing envelopes, taking in washing, schmoozing the tradesmen they owe money to, and so on—enabling Lora to pursue her "dream," without noticing.

Nor does Lora ever notice—though *we* are certainly invited to—how much, however discreetly, Annie runs *her*. But constant visitor Steve is aware of it— as we see early on. He and Annie are sitting together one night at the kitchen table in the coldwater flat (he's watching her address envelopes), waiting for Lora to get home from one of her discouraging work-hunting days. It didn't go well today, either, and Lora breaks down, going directly to Annie, to be soothed and comforted in her arms, while Steve looks on. But then Annie rises, returning to the kitchen—the camera following her as she passes Steve, to show her signaling him with a movement of her head and eyes to go to Lora. Which he promptly does. And in a few minutes, she also lets him know— through the open kitchen door, and with the same eye movement—when it's time for him to go home. Which he promptly does. She doesn't have to tell *him* twice . . .

Annie, for Lora, will always remain partly invisible—will always be much like the legion of unseen but indispensable menials who underpin *any* comfortable life. *Except* that the two women are friends—that part of Annie is not invisible to Lora (as it was to Lucia Harper about Sybil in *The Reckless Moment*). But friend or not, Annie is still Lora's cook and maid. And later on, when Lora is a big star, she becomes her dresser too. Around their splendid new suburban house, she wears a uniform. Neither woman, of course, would be likely to question such arrangements (Annie even refuses Lora's offer of another servant to help her). Annie, unlike her daughter an implacable conservative, "knows her place"—more honestly, at least, than Lora is willing to know it. They may indeed have been, as Lora says, "through a lot together." But it's not (nor could you even imagine it) Annie who is getting the foot massage.

What Lora brings to her perception of the outside world is not insight or even a desire for it ("And I don't *want* to know") but a rather indomitable will. "Maybe I should see things as they really are, and not as I want them to be," she says, in a rare early moment of faltering. But faithful Steve comes to her rescue again: "If I know *you*," he says, grinning and leaning over her, "they'll have to be the way you want them." "Thanks, Steve," she replies—the danger past—"you're so good for what ails me."

One night during the Christmas season, just before the little girls' bedtime, in the tiny living room of their flat, Annie is holding Susie and Sarah Jane on her lap and telling them the story of Christ's birth. Lora is occupied learning lines, walking back and forth with a script in her hand. Sarah Jane interrupts her mother's narrative with a question: Was Jesus white or black? *This* gets Lora's attention—something to be corrected, and quickly. "Well, it doesn't matter," she says, gently but firmly, addressing both children. "He's the way you imagine him." Of course. But the little girl's disturbing specificity persists: it seems that Annie has told them that Jesus was a real person, not a "pretend" one, as Susie puts it. And now Susie too wants to know what color Jesus was. An impasse—which even Annie seems unwilling to break. Until the camera moves in on Sarah Jane's face, looking spookily rapt (low, ominous music). "He was like me," she says softly, with centerless absorption, "—*white* . . ."

Little Sarah Jane (Karen Dicker, the child who plays her, is remarkable) is clearly a "troubled" child: self-willed, obsessional, even verging on delusional. But as this scene invites you to notice, her He's-white-like-me obsession is not far from Lora's whatever-you-want-Him-to-be complacency—different ways of bending reality to your will. Sarah Jane—and as she grows up and becomes Susan Kohner, it becomes even clearer—is Lora's true counterpart, her real "imitator." And she even goes into showbiz.

But the movie sometimes shows a kind of animus toward Lora that it never shows toward Sarah Jane—and shows it even crudely at times. In the scene above, for example, when Annie, telling the Christmas story, gets to the birth itself and says (offscreen), "'Heavenly hosts sing Hallelujah!,'" Sirk shows Lora coming upon herself in a nearby mirror—and regarding the image with satisfaction. Later on, when Sarah Jane, after that motel-room scene with Annie, leans back crying on the door that has just closed behind her mother, an image (in a simple black dress) of tragic devastation, the scene fades in and out on Lora, coming through a door in her home, wearing Day-Glo orange, a sleeveless blouse and toreador pants and girlish headband (one of the most outlandish of the star's advertised thirty-four costumes), her hand held to her ever-more-plasticene-looking hair.

This last juxtaposition might even seem like a meanspirited joke, even if an unintended one (a reflex of a general aversion), if it weren't that just such ironic juxtapositions—mostly much subtler ones—are at the heart of the way the whole movie works, from early on. As when Annie and Sarah Jane the child come home from the grammar school, after the girl's imposture has been humiliatingly exposed. Lora is already home with Susie, who is out of school too, and in bed. The situation is just as it all was in the Stahl version—with a crucial difference: in the Sirk movie it is clear, in the midst of Annie's and Sarah Jane's upset, that the white mother and daughter are merely playing at calamity, both of them knowing that Susie's sickness is a sort of game. "Why, you're *practically* normal!" says Lora, looking at the thermometer, and the two of them falling into collusive giggles as a result—while the distraught Sarah Jane and Annie go by in the background.

And this is an early foreshadowing (one of many) of a notion that becomes more insistent in the film as the characters age: the idea that Annie and Sarah Jane have what even Lora herself will later call some "very real problems"—in contrast to Lora and Susie, who have the problems of narcissism, of the spoiled and self-absorbed, of Lora's vanity and ambition, of Susie's sentimentalism. In contrast, in Stahl's film that whole mother-and-daughter-in-love-with-the-same-man is taken straight and treated very seriously, as in soap-opera tradition. And the Colbert heroine, in the movie's final sequence, resolves to give the guy up (at least temporarily), reconciling with the daughter and reaffirming her first commitment, to being a mother. (In the novel, the mother gives him up to the daughter.) The parallel moment in Sirk's movie is *very* different. "I'll give him up!" says Lora, dramatically. "Oh, Mother, stop acting!" says Susie (Sandra Dee's one moment of triumph in the movie). And that, it seems, takes care of *that*—we never hear about it again anyway. Susie goes away to school to recover (and out of the movie), only returning for Annie's funeral at the end.

No black movie actors have been *more* misused than Paul Robeson and Ethel Waters were, James Baldwin wrote in 1975 (in *The Devil Finds Work*). And partly, he argues, that was *because* of their talent and power on the screen—they brought too much "reality" with them, posed too much of a threat to the prevailing Hollywood falsity, having "enough force, if unleashed, to shatter the tale to fragments." Major black artists were segregated in their movies as they were in society, put in "special" sequences apart, in their own musical numbers (the Nicholas Brothers, Lena Horne, et al.), for example, or, as in a multistory film like Julien Duvivier's *Tales of Manhattan* (1942), in their separate episode, as Waters and Robeson were in that film, in a story about a Negro shantytown, at the end of the movie (where they could be more easily excised by southern exhibitors)—and kept at some distance from the white stars in the same film, like Edward G. Robinson and Henry Fonda and Ginger Rogers.

It's Rogers that Baldwin zeroes in on, comparing her face on the screen to an ice-cream confection: "something to be placed in a dish, and eaten with a spoon—possibly a long one. If the face of Ethel Waters were placed in the same frame, the face of Little Eva would simply melt." The important thing becomes, then, to keep "the black performer" away from her, "sealed off into a vacuum."

Well, that seal is certainly broken in Sirk's film—as it was and had been in many other movies of the fifties, but hardly in any of them to quite such effect as here. For one thing, Turner's face at times seems vacuous enough to make Rogers look like Falconetti. And Moore, though younger than Waters was in 1942, less roguish and more conventionally beautiful than her predecessor, is every bit as authoritative and resonant, it seems to me. Turner's face, of course, never "melts"—even metaphorically: it looks too impermeable for that. It's Moore's face that succumbs to age and dying, while Lora's only looks younger. But the contrast, of course, is not to the white woman's advantage (as it is, as much as it exists there, in the Stahl movie). It enacts for us a familiar and central experience: the sense some people give you—whether they are good or bad—of a certain moral and personal authority and size. There are, after all, superficial "characters" in life as well as in fiction. And Juanita Moore on screen has that sort of authority, of course. So in her tortured adolescent way does Susan Kohner. Lana Turner and Sandra Dee, in different ways, lack it. It's the discrimination between shallowness and depth, between what we can take seriously and what we can't, in ourselves and others. And it's often the difference between the movie stars we like or are interested by and those we can't or aren't. And it's that sort of discrimination—the continuing contrast, for example, between Lora's fussy, driven emptiness and Annie's unfailing dignity and inwardness—that Sirk's movie is finally organized around: the juxtaposition of Lora and Annie and of (though to a lesser extent) Susie and Sarah Jane.

Because it is, as Sirk said it was, a movie *about* imitation, about living superficially. And Lora has gained the kind of life that our American plenitude often seems to promise us, to hold out as an ideal: an achieved shallowness. It's not that Lora, like everyone, doesn't have serious crises in her life—it's more that she doesn't believe in them, tending to act rather than live them, what a feminist critic approvingly calls "her refusal to suffer." It's a negative condition that the black characters in the movie implicitly criticize—both by being in a world quite apart from it, as Annie is, and by "imitating" it disastrously, as Sarah Jane does. And Annie especially, for all her considerable misguidedness, embodies the kind of tragic recognition that almost everyone else in the movie resists and opposes: the sort of meaning, according to Baldwin again—in *The Fire Next Time*—that the Negro in America carries with his skin and history, and suffers for, because he reminds "the white American" of precisely what the latter does not *want* to be reminded of at all. Namely, "reality—the fact that life is tragic . . .": ". . . simply because the earth turns and the sun rises and sets, and one day, for each of us, the sun will go down for the last, last time . . . It seems to me that one ought to rejoice in the *fact* of death—ought to decide, indeed, to *earn* one's death by confronting with passion the conundrum of life . . . But white Americans do not believe in death . . ." ("Oh, Annie, that *funeral* again!")

But to respond only to the irony about Lora—as audiences now tend to do, almost exactly reversing the way the audience in 1959 took her—is really to misunderstand the movie, I think. She's a phony, perhaps—and she may be ineducable in certain areas. But who isn't? Still, Lora is no monster (as, in a way, Annie *is*). On the contrary, she's a genuinely nice person, open and generous, a warm and unfailing friend to both Annie and Sarah Jane, and by her lights, dim as they may be, a good and loving mother. And she cares about Sarah Jane, it's clear, almost as much as she does about Susie. And Turner makes all this very believable.

So that when Sarah Jane tells Lora—on the night that Lora is having some important people over—that she's sorry but she can't help her mother serve because she has a date tonight, Lora seems more pleased than not: "A *date*?" she repeats, brightening instantly (she and Annie have been concerned about the apparent absence of boyfriends). She is standing below the white-railinged stairway of her spacious new house, looking up at Sarah Jane, who is standing on the level above, looking down. (Turner looks terrific here—and regal, in a shoulderless white gown with a wide blue strap across the chest.) "Is it the Hawkins boy?" she asks the girl eagerly. It's the wrong question: Sarah Jane frowns in response—what Hawkins boy? The son of the chauffeur down the road, says Lora—he's been asking her about Sarah Jane. "No," says Sarah Jane, rather sullenly, "it's with someone else." (It turns out to be with the very white Troy Donahue, who doesn't know she is "colored," and beats her up when he finds out.) "Oh," says Lora, turning away, a little disappointed her guess wasn't right, reflecting now on the inconvenience: "Well, all right . . . you run along. I'll try to manage here." As the doorbell rings.

Sarah Jane goes back to the kitchen, where Annie, in her uniform, is busy preparing the food, laying out plates—and looking exhausted. And the girl gets the same sort of line from her mother: "Look, honey, why don't you go over to the party at the church? . . . You're young, you shouldn't be sittin' around. Miss Lora feels the same way—she'll lend you her car." "Oh, she will? How nice of her!" Annie persists: "I'd be happy knowin' you're meetin' nice young folks." But Sarah Jane knows about those nice young folks at the church: "Busboys, cooks, chauffeurs!" she retorts angrily. "Like Hawkins!" "I don't want to fight with you, honey," says Annie. "Not tonight—I don't feel too good." And she asks her to take a tray of hors d'oeuvres in to "Miss Lora and her friends." "Why, certainly," says Sarah Jane, very sarcastic, "anything at all for Miss Lora and her friends." And by the time she gets to the living room, where the small group is gathered, she is balancing the tray on her head and doing a darkie imitation—to the dismay and embarrassment of Lora and her guests. She's just showing them something she learned from her "mammy," Sarah Jane says—"who l'arned it from Old Massa, befo' she belonged to *you*!" And she goes out again.

But Lora is furious. She follows Sarah Jane back to the kitchen, where Annie says wearily that she heard the whole thing. So what was that all about? Lora asks the girl. "You and my mother," says Sarah Jane, "are so anxious for me to be colored, I was going to show you I could be." What she was *being* was "childish," Lora says—and she doesn't understand how she could want to hurt her mother so, "or me." "I told her she has to be patient," Annie says, "—things'll work out." "*How?*" says Sarah Jane—who is by this time more ashamed than defiant. She turns and appeals to Lora: "Miss Lora, you don't know what it means to be—different." Lora's reply to this is quick and indignant: "Have *I* ever treated you as if you were different?" she demands. "Has Susie? Has anyone here?" This question—addressed as it is to someone who has just called her "*Miss* Lora" (as Annie and Sarah Jane always do)—seems just another example, though flagrant, of Lora's habit of incomprehension. It's Sarah Jane's reply that is startling. "No," she says, slowly and uncomfortably, "you've been wonderful . . . but . . ." But *what?* But Sarah Jane doesn't finish the sentence—she doesn't know *what*. Some ideologically minded critics have found this moment wanting: Sarah Jane, writes one, "should attack Lora for treating Annie as her servant." Sure she should—except for the fact that Annie *is* her servant. And for the same reasons, known to us all, that Hawkins is inevitably a chauffeur, and that the party at the Negro church will inevitably be attended by busboys and cooks (and that Juanita Moore's career will go downhill after this role, in spite of her Academy Award nomination). To be sure, Lora's kind of unconsciousness helps to sustain these arrangements— but within their constraints, and on the "personal" level, Lora has been unimpeachable, and more, in her relations with Annie and Sarah Jane—even "wonderful," as Sarah Jane has just put it. What *else* could Sarah Jane say or think? It satisfies Lora. "Then don't *ever* do this to us again," she says, "—or to yourself." Then adds, tearfully, tenderly: "It won't *solve* anything, Sarah Jane . . ." And she goes out again, back to her guests.

This is a bigger Lora moment than it sounds like—implying more imagination than we've come to expect from her. And Turner is surprisingly touching here: the sudden inflection of pained tenderness toward Sarah Jane is powerful. It's Lora's most sympathetic and appealing moment so far—the first time we've been invited to see Lora too as someone trapped in a racist mythology and culture. Not as fatally as Sarah Jane and Annie, but just as surely.

Annie sits down wearily—at left-screen foreground—saying nothing. Sarah Jane approaches, bends down to her, crouching and looking up into her face, which now looks collapsed, impassive, drained. "Mama?" says Sarah Jane. Annie's eyes are cast down, her mouth slightly moving. "Try to understand," the girl pleads. Annie turns her head and looks at her. "I didn't mean to hurt you," says Sarah Jane, and throws her arms around her neck: "I love you!"— burying her face on her shoulder, Annie still in the foreground, hugging her back. "Oh, I know, baby," she says, patting the girl's shoulder, looking more wastedly beautiful than ever. And then she offers Sarah Jane her typically shattering sort of comfort, with its mixture of love and total insufficiency: "Oh, I know baby. You're just like a puppy that's been cooped up too much. That's why I wanted you to go to the party . . ." And it's a terrible moment—we register that right along with Sarah Jane. "Oh, Mama," she says, drawing back and looking at her hopelessly, ". . . don't you *see* that won't help?"

Of course, Annie doesn't *see*. Not-seeing, in one form or another—from Lora's "Is it the Hawkins boy?" to Sarah Jane's "You've been wonderful . . . but . . ."—has been the connecting thread through this whole sequence. And this is where you get your strongest sense yet that the incomprehension doesn't belong only to Lora: they are *all* trapped in it. And with that perception, the movie's tone has shifted from a detached, ironic sort of observing to something more involved, more like sympathy. And now, you can no longer depend on Lora being excluded from it.

But that doesn't prevent Annie—as the movie goes on—from beginning to look at her (Lora, when she speaks, is usually looking off) with a certain (and growing) subtle, final lack of interest. Not that she flags in her concern or ministrations for both Lora and Susie, or defaults on her role of nurturer, advisor, supporter, listening to their problems and offering her judgments (she approves of Steve, and disapproves of Edwards, the playwright). But you can see that she's wearing out, and that they are wearing her down more or less. Even when she's in her sickbed confined to her room, Susie is there too, nattering away about her crush on Steve, sitting in the foreground of the shot, and (like her mother) looking off as she talks and eats dinner from a tray—while Annie, in the background, is propped up against the headboard of her bed, looking ravaged and ill and even a little irritable for a change. It's not that she isn't listening to Susie; it's that she'd rather go to sleep, and soon does. Soon Lora is visiting her too, to talk about Susie (you begin to feel they're chatting her to death!).

But at her last moments, it's Annie (at last) who commands the room and the audience (which includes doctor and minister, Steve and Lora)—even the camera (the shots of the others are from her point of view). And she does it with an almost frightening power. With Lora crouching and sobbing at her bedside, Annie has a kind of dry-eyed fierceness that makes you think of a prophetess at a shrine ("You're dying, not crying," Sirk had told Moore, when she played the scene too moistly at first) as she gives them all her last instructions. Steve must find Sarah Jane again (he will, he assures her); Lora must tell her that Annie knows now that she was selfish, and that "if I loved her too much, I'm sorry." She leaves her fur stole to the preacher's wife, and her pearl necklace to Susie, for her wedding: "Our weddin' day, and the day we die, are the great events of our life." And fifty dollars for Mr. McKinney. Who?—Lora is baffled. It's the milkman who gave them a break on their bills when they lived in their coldwater flat. "You've been so good!" Lora says on a sob. Annie hopes so: she wants to "be standin' with the lambs and not with the goats on Judgment Day." And finally, she's left detailed written instructions about that big funeral she wants, and tells Steve to get the envelope from her drawer.

> STEVE: . . . I've got it, Annie.
> ANNIE: I wanta go—the way I planned—especially the four white horses, and a band playin'—no mourning—but proud and high-steppin'—like I was goin' to glory!
> LORA [*sobbing*]: *No!* I won't listen! There isn't going to be any funeral! Not for a long, long time! You can't leave! I won't *let* you!
> ANNIE: . . . I'm just tired, Miss Lora. Awfully tired . . .

And that's all. She seems to drift off. But the passing is an event we see only as it registers on Lora's face, in close-up, as she watches—and then screams, calling Annie's name, her face turning into a kind of rictus mask of horror and grief, sobbing and burying her head in the bed next to Annie—as the camera pans from her face in death to Sarah Jane's framed photograph on the table next to her. Dissolve to a church interior and the funeral in progress—on the unmistakable (as it was in 1959) and thrilling sound of Mahalia Jackson's singing voice.

So it was finally Lora's turn to be a little frightening. That scream at Annie's bedside is startling—and yet in a way feels overdue. The face is not, after all, so impermeable. And you're brought to the recognition that Lora's friendship with Annie was probably the deepest thing in her life, beyond even Susie's place there—at least from what we've seen. (And forget Steve.)

And yet—also from what we've seen—it's in some ways even less than a friendship. Annie's place (however Lora may have denied it) was so fixed that her relation to her "Miss Lora," even at their fondest and closest, had something quite impersonal about it. As the movie makes clear: at best Lora only half-apprehends Annie, showing neither curiosity about nor interest in her other life—the black one. And that indifference hardly seems to change even after it's been pointed out to her ("Miss Lora, you never asked"). But then it hasn't been as necessary for Lora to *know* about that life as much as to have it in the background of her own quite different one. Like a beloved pet, Annie is both remote and intimate to her at once: a ground of Lora's reality, as it were. So that her death is a loss of *meaning* as well as of a friend—just the sort of meaning that gets defined by the funeral that follows.

It's the most famous set piece in the movie (it's what people always remembered from the earlier one, too)—extending the heart-wringing effect even above and beyond Annie's death scene. Not only into the funeral service —with Jackson in a pulpit singing against stained-glass windows, the coffin amid banks of flowers below, the familiar faces (even the milkman's) in the crowded pews—but past that into the funeral cortege itself, and the dramatic and unexpected return of Sarah Jane, throwing herself on her mother's coffin in an agony of regret and remorse, declaring "I killed my mother!," until Lora gathers her into the funeral car, with herself and Steve and Susie. Then the funeral parade, spectacular by any standard—even Annie's, you would suppose —with the majestic and ornate glass-windowed hearse, the marching band from the colored lodge, and, best of all, those four high-stepping black-plumed white horses. No mourning—going to glory. And the streets along the way crowded with mourners, almost all of them black, many shown in close-up, weeping and doffing their hats, paying tribute to Annie.

It's another example, an extended one, of pulling out all the stops (the Stahl movie confined itself to the church facade and a glimpse of the horses). But Sirk denied to me that that was anything like the intention. "The funeral itself is an irony," he said. "All that pomp." It's certainly true that it comes as slightly jarring when the otherwise levelheaded, no-nonsense Annie first tells us and Lora that her funeral is "the one thing I want to splurge on. I really want it elegant." It's too close to one of those Negro clichés—like Delilah's rabbit's foot or Rochester's dice—that now makes us squirm, that even did in 1959: a white person's patronizing idea of black culture and folklore, and sort of cute as well, good for a condescending chuckle at least. But in this film any whiff of condescension, any suggestion of a picturesque ignorance in action, is disposed of at the first notes of Mahalia Jackson's surging and billowing voice lifted into the words of the spiritual—

> *Soon I will be done—*
> *Trouble of the world, Lord,*
> *Trouble of the world . . .*
> *I'm going home to live with God.*
> *No more weepin' and wailin' . . .*
> *No more weepin' and wailin' . . .*
> *I'm going home to live with my Lord . . .*

In the end, it seems, Annie is as unknown to us as she was to Lora—and that feels right too. Annie, you realize, stands for something you don't quite understand or apprehend—for something dimly perceived perhaps, but clearly opposite to the emptiness and sterility of the white characters' lives. Even *they* know that—and Lora in particular, whether she remembers it or not (probably not). In any case, Annie's funeral has become so resplendent, visually and aurally, that it comes to seem almost the equivalent of Dietrich's "What does it matter what you say about people?"—seeming in the end to have as little to do with the character of Annie as with that of Mahalia Jackson. But of course quite unthinkable *without* either of them . . .

There is at least one extraordinary, half-hidden (of course) and very Sirkian touch during the funeral procession—which is shown in a montage of different points of view, one of them (very brief) through the display window of a store from the inside. Just visible are the outlines of some mannequins arrayed in things like knights' and ladies' outfits, and on the window itself the store's logo reads COSTUME RENTALS—only for us, printed in reverse—and beyond that the uniformed band, the plumed horses, the hearse and coffin. "All that pomp" is right. Annie has become in the end not only that generic hope of hers, a Judgment Day "lamb," but an impresario, even an artist ("I really want it elegant"), giving us, and orchestrating to its details, this final but strange and beautiful show.

Apparently, there was to be one more and final sequence after this one. Susan Kohner showed it to me in the final shooting script she used in the original production and has saved. It's a scene between Lora and Steve (and parallels a similarly placed and concluding scene in the Stahl film between Colbert and Warren William). Lora announces her intention to adopt Sarah Jane and her wish now to postpone their wedding, so that she can take both Susie and Sarah Jane "away from here . . . This place, the people, New York—the memories are still too strong for the way we all feel now. I don't have the answers yet—I only know they both need love and understanding—and a mother. That's what I intend to be, Steve." Maybe she'll go back to her hometown in Iowa. She'll go in for country living again—cooking and washing and ironing. And Steve laughs—calling her "ham clear through to the bone." At first affronted by this, she laughs too. They both laugh, then kiss, and then kiss again—for the final fade-out.

No one to my knowledge has ever seen this scene, and Kohner is pretty sure that they never even filmed it. How could they—even at Universal—after Mahalia Jackson?

2001

Kent Jones

Kent Jones (b. 1960), a film critic, programmer, and screenwriter, writes regularly for *Film Comment, Cahiers du Cinéma, Traffic,* and the Canadian-based *CinemaScope* and has acted as a cosmopolitan, one-man bridge between the American and the international film press. A graduate of the NYU film studies program, Jones programs movies for Lincoln Center's Walter Reade Theater, serves on the New York Film Festival selection committee, and has also co-written and co-produced several documentaries for director Martin Scorsese. His passionate criticism is marked by a partisan commitment to the cutting edge of global cinema and an informed historical respect for the past glories of film. In the example below, he circles around Wong Kar-Wai's *In the Mood for Love,* replicating its tango-like structure of theme and variation with particular sensitivity to the film's establishment of mood and its intrinsically musical nature.

◆

Of Love and the City

The word is that *In the Mood for Love,* Wong Kar-wai's latest urban fantasia about two neighbors whose spouses are having an affair, is a departure for the director. For aficionados, it's a welcome return to the contemplative tone of his earlier mood-drenched period piece, *Days of Being Wild.* True enough. *In the Mood for Love* is composed with a more sedate camera than the tactile handheld pov of the previous movies, and it shares with *Days of Being Wild* a Viscontian immersion in the ambience and mores of Hong Kong in the early Sixties. But in all other ways, the new movie is entirely consistent with the director's development since *Chungking Express.*

The last few films in particular feel like reconnaissance flights over dangerous interpersonal territory, getting off vivid snapshots of emotional stalemates in play. wkw has perfected a giddy technique, which appears simultaneously to delve into and flit past the repetitive avoidance strategies and game playing of lonely individuals or couples (at times, he seems like a healthier, more sensual Egoyan). Not uncommonly for a modern filmmaker, he has less of an aptitude for emotional gradation and development than for rough and ready, lunging portraits of emotion-as-action. His films are made up of moments that seem to have been grabbed out of time, as though he's almost always just missed it.

What makes the movies feel like special events, and what makes Wong Kar-wai feel like the Jimi Hendrix of cinema, is the way every emotional tone is blended into the swirling color and motion of city life. As a city filmmaker, he's without peer. He understands the city as more than just evidence of Western infiltration (Edward Yang), as a physical entity that exerts its influence over human affairs (Tsai Ming-liang), or as a romantic repository of dreams (Woody Allen). He sees it—guiltlessly—as the natural state of contemporary men and women, operating at the correct speed, the sedate rhythms of rural life being a thing of the past. And just like Hendrix with his endless bag of tricks, effects segue into one another with matchless fluidity, and the viewer/ listener gets a quick trip to heaven. During moments like Tony Leung's fast-motion elevated train ride through the glittering Taipei night at the end of *Happy Together*, questions of representation drop away and film viewing gives way to pure ecstasy. Like Tarantino and Wenders, those other art hero epiphany-builders, wkw is continually going skyward, exploding his exclusive, up-to-date form of cinematic beauty over the narrative like a fireworks display. What makes him a genuinely great director is the fact that his fusion of speed, color, and vision, always linked to desire, dictates both the form and the subject matter of his work.

The fluidity is still there in the supposedly "classical" *In the Mood for Love*, as is the merging of emotional and physical (meaning urban) space. This time, the director's eye gets quick fixes on states of decorum, good manners, polite-ness, swallowed feelings, which register fleetingly but vividly. There's a piercing moment early on (one among many) where Maggie Cheung's Mrs. Su is sitting in her neighbors' crowded room, a beehive of activity, nonchalantly reading the paper. There's a faint smile on her face to signal the appearance of calm. Her carriage is erect, her back arched and barely touching the back of the chair. Meanwhile, she's wearing a dress in which it's virtually impossible to be comfortable.

In the world of 1962 Hong Kong, which is so overcrowded that people rent out rooms in their apartments to middle-class couples, where the old folks watch the younger ones like hawks with culturally ordained authority, appear-ances are all-important. The film gets directly at the feeling of always putting up a good front, of being on guard against disappointing people, by isolating small physical events in corridors, tiny rooms, restaurants, offices, street corners. This time, the viewer isn't carried along by the gorgeous restlessness of the camera (best exemplified by 1996's *Fallen Angels*) or the Polaroid-ish visual scheme that reached its peak with *Happy Together*.

In that film, Chris Doyle's cinematography suggested a happier, more modishly color-saturated Robert Frank job (Doyle is one of two cinematographers listed on the credits of *In the Mood for Love*, and it's debatable how much of his work survived the final cut). But wkw's visual music hasn't disappeared—it's just spikier this time, more rhythmic than melodic. *In the Mood for Love* moves with elliptical stealth. Very often, the only indication that time has passed is the color of Maggie Cheung's outfit: she wears the same style of Mandarin, or cheong sam, dress throughout the movie, and unless you're paying very close attention, you may not notice that a change from blue to red or green has signaled the passage of days, weeks, sometimes months.

The strategy gives every moment real emotional urgency. In the matter of Cheung's Mrs. Su and Tony Leung's Mr. Chow, you start to ask: How much has changed with the passing of time and how much has stayed the same? How many times will these kind, proper, self-deprecating people displace their longing—for their spouses, for each other, for emotional freedom—with another ritualized walk to the local noodle-shop followed by another night alone? Every wkw movie has its own brand of sumptuousness. This one is more restricted than ever before in its locations (it's almost all interiors) and visual focus. In the previous films, part of the thrill was wondering where the camera was going to alight next, and the knowledge that a scene was more likely than not to end up in a spatial configuration radically different from the one in which it began. A good portion of *Happy Together* takes place indoors, too, but Doyle's camera finds so many small wonders that it feels as vast as a rain forest. In *In the Mood for Love*, the camera is pinned down, obliged to repeat the same povs again and again on repeated activities and behaviors, like musical refrains—Leung and Cheung knocking on each other's doors and talking to each other's offscreen spouses, Leung's wife barely glimpsed behind the partition at the hotel where she works, Cheung walking down the steps of the noodle-shop and wiping the sweat from her brow with the back of her hand.

But even within the film's locked-down symmetries (which replace wkw's usual lachrymose voiceover as a structuring device), every shot remains a quietly ravishing event. Cheung passing her hand over her husband's back as he plays mahjong, then sitting on the edge of his chair, in slow motion: a sad, graceful moment, where the line of her body conveys the sense of a woman playing the dutiful, admiring wife. The palette may be more restrained than in the previous movies (heavy on grays, whites and beiges, with great swathes of red), but every object glows as ecstatically as ever. Dramatically, *In the Mood for Love* isn't terribly different from *Happy Together*, which had a similarly fraught, episodic, improvisational shoot. Once again, the structure is theme and variations; once again, the focus is the predicament of a couple.

The earlier film was about two wayward souls wedged between staying together and parting. The new film is about two people who've built their identities on foundations of niceness, who suddenly find themselves stranded and clinging to each other, but who are finally too self-censoring to give in to romance. Whereas most of *Happy Together* consists of Liu-fai and Ho-ping's dance of devotion and rejection, most of *In the Mood for Love* is given over to Mr. Chow and Mrs. Su's dance of longing and fear, interestingly refracted through an odd dramatic device: each one playacts the role of the other's spouse, in order to understand the affair, or possibly (intentionally? un-wittingly?) re-creates its dynamics. Every other character—Li-zhen's philan-dering boss, Chow's happy-go-lucky friend, the nosy landlady ("Young wives shouldn't stay out so late—people will start to wonder")—is a satellite, and the husband and wife go almost unseen, their offscreen voices used as rhythmic punctuations in a movie that feels less like a narrative than a beautifully drawn-out musical improvisation—Wong Kar-wai's "Blue in Green."

Both films lean more heavily on one character than the other. *Happy Together* was Leung's picture, but *In the Mood for Love* belongs to Cheung, whose beauty lights up the movie like the polar star lights up a winter sky. Cheung is one of the few modern actresses who understands her own physical beauty as an expressive instrument, and who also has the smarts and intuition to take it somewhere substantial. There have been plenty of portraits of repres-sion in the movies, but they've rarely been as filled-out or as radiant as this one.

Acting for Wong Kar-wai is a totalizing experience—since there's no script, the actors and the director are creating characters, a dramatic arc, and a new expressive vocabulary all at the same time. Cheung and wkw have found as graceful and supple a throughline for her Su Li-zhen as it's possible to imag-ine. Even more than for Leung's Chow, with his gelled hair and immaculate bourgeois wardrobe, the clothes make Li-zhen: they dictate the way she moves, and the rigid tension with which she displaces her anger and her desire. Cheung understands that the machinery of repression can't reveal itself too readily, but can only be divined through her character's strenuous efforts to keep it up and running (in comparison, Leung plays the Mr. Nice Guy act a little too broadly at times). She understands the inherent sadness of being a "good person." There's a moment late in the film where she's framed in a win-dow, as carefully as Dietrich was framed in the shadows for her final *Shanghai Express* prayer. It's a portrait of beauty at the service of a thankless goal: to draw a veil over a heart that's sacrificed itself to the happiness of others. Cheung's is a genuinely heroic piece of acting, and it puts the vaunted best actress award at Cannes to shame.

Where *In the Mood for Love* differs from *Happy Together* is in its decenteredness and lack of resolution. The further the new film moves from the core dilemma in the cramped apartment, the more diffuse it gets. Chow's move to Singapore feels vague, as does Li-zhen's phantom visit to his apartment while he's away at work. This is the film's ultimate almost, the capper to a series of near-intimate moments where inner propriety dampens passion. Which would be perfect were this just another movie about two people who don't sleep together. But there are quite a few layers of complexity generated between these characters. Are they actually in love with one another? Or are they in love with the idealized images of their spouses they project onto one another? Or are they just friends who share a need for love and companionship in the abstract? The film touches on all these possibilities, and when it's at its most powerful it suggests that they all exist side by side. This delicate, not-so-brief encounter, probably long forgotten by both Chow and Li-zhen (there's a strong sense that all the action is being remembered—it has something to do with the film's breathless movement forward), deserves to be sifted from the ashes of time, in the same way that the story itself was sifted from the myriad possibilities wkw threw down during the epic shoot. It's all there, but a little fancy intellectual footwork is required to tie everything together. Near the end, when we've skipped ahead to the troubled, destabilizing year of 1967, Li-zhen goes back to her old apartment house with a child in tow.

A few months later, Chow comes to visit their former landlady, who's left for America. He's told that her old apartment is now occupied by a woman and her son. He thinks nothing of it and leaves. The near-miss is a timeworn, instant heartbreaker, but it feels odd here—if they were to meet again, what would they say to each other? Would they sleep together? Or would they just keep on being polite? As for the coda, where Chow whispers his secrets into the wall of an abandoned temple at Angkor Wat, it doesn't really carry much weight (hilariously, there's a "Tell your secret!" section on the official *In the Mood for Love* website).

For some people, the spatial, geographical, and rhythmic change-up is perfect. To these eyes, it feels like a failed version of *Happy Together*'s final side trip through Taipei, as off the mark as its model was on the money. In a sense, *In the Mood for Love* tries to duplicate *Happy Together*'s similarly improvised final form: one couple's dynamics are replaced with another's; Hong Kong on the eve of June 1997 becomes Hong Kong on the eve of the Cultural Revolution and the escalation in Vietnam; the Taipei subway becomes a Cambodian temple; and the falls at Iguazu find their equivalent in the secret desires locked in Li-zhen's heart, betrayed by her too-eloquent body language and mournful

gaze. But where the geographical displacement of *Happy Together* gave resonance to the whole idea of going home, the idea of leaving doesn't do much
for *In the Mood for Love*, which probably would have found a more fitting resolution with a staccato move, a sudden rupture. On the other hand, why complain? This is as intoxicating, as exquisitely nuanced, and as luxuriously sad as
movies get.

It's been a while now since Wong Kar-wai first cast his spell of melancholy
urban enchantment over America's more adventurous moviegoers. When he
first broke with *Chungking Express* in the mid-Nineties, it was like tuning into
a fresh signal on a new frequency: his filmmaking felt as though it was driven
by a seductive urge to dissolve the viewpoints of director, camera, lonely-
hearted hero, audience, and screen into one throbbing, super-sensitive entity.
wkw made quite a team with his dp Chris Doyle (actually, there's a third, less
flamboyant silent partner: production designer/editor William Chang). Young
directors from all over the world wanted to work with Doyle—plenty of older
ones, too. His cinematography had a personality, even a mind of its own. The
more love-struck neophytes wanted to be Wong Kar-wai, the handsome guy in
the colorful sports shirts, forever smiling from behind his dark glasses, who
made movies on the fly starting with nothing more than an inspiration, like a
painter or a sculptor or a choreographer.

Now, in the year 2000, his newness is a thing of the past, the imitators who
tried to perfect the slurred-motion effect of *Chungking Express* have come
and gone, and he hasn't made the kind of impact we all hoped he would in the
American market: this was one secret cinephiles never wanted to keep to
themselves. For those who love his films, it's hard to separate them from the
legends behind them: the insane financing schemes, the endless shoots, the
patient, devoted casts and crews, the hours and hours of material shot and discarded, the marathon editing sessions in an effort to beat the Cannes deadline.
It's difficult not to see each movie as the final result of a long, heroic
undertaking. And the stories and myths endow them with a certain interactive
splendor. Somewhere, there's an alternate universe where the character played
by Stanley Kwan in *Happy Together* is alive and well, and Maggie Cheung and
Tony Leung make love with abandon. I'm sure these moments and characters
are just as fully achieved as their corollaries in the finished films. This is an
artist who's generous to a fault, compiling a stock of grace notes and delivering
the finished films, and the sagas of their creation, like gifts to his audience.

2001

John Ashbery

John Ashbery (b. 1927) has written some 20 volumes of poetry that constitute one of the most sublime and original bodies of work in contemporary American verse. His poems have a teasing, opaque surface, an experimental openness to language's seemingly self-generative capacities, a mastery of high-low tonal variation, and a melancholy wonderment at the uncanny fact of existence, even (or especially) at its most banal. Ashbery has also been an art critic for *Art News*, *New York*, and *Newsweek*, honing a transparent, modest, user-friendly voice of commentary that surfaces as well in his occasional film criticism. This appreciation of *The Seventh Victim* shows, among other things, how a major writer such as Ashbery may seek out movies that echo his own literary aesthetic: the surrealism of everyday urban life, the "muddled yet marvelous" collision of tenderness and menace, the uncovering of a conspiratorial plot which purports to explain the randomness of life, but never does, and the artifice that offers a deeper authenticity. He could be describing his own poetic method when he writes about this movie: "We gradually get the feeling that the ground under our feet is unstable."

◆

On Val Lewton's *The Seventh Victim*

Like Paris, New York is always ready for its close-up. Somehow the city never fails to look good on the screen, where it quickens excitement the way the place itself does. This is sometimes true even when the film is obviously shot in a studio. The "Riverside Drive" backdrop in an early scene of everybody's favorite cheapo film noir, *Detour*, adds a note of romance, though it is obviously a photograph and a crude one at that. And at least two of Val Lewton's low-budget programmers for RKO, *Cat People* and *The Seventh Victim*, convey a haunting New York ambience, though they were shot thousands of miles away.

Lewton's films, in a genre awkwardly labeled "psychological horror," are cult favorites today, but in their time (the early 1940s) they were considered B-movies. Though Lewton was billed as a producer, it was he who imposed a distinctive style on his films. Besides the two mentioned above, *I Walked with a Zombie* and *The Body Snatcher* have become classics of the genre. My favorite, however, is *The Seventh Victim*.

I first heard of it when a fellow Harvard student, Edward Gorey, recounted its plot in his unforgettable delivery, constantly interrupted by strangulated giggles and gasps, a few years after its 1943 release. In those pre-TV and -VCR days, if you missed seeing a B-movie when it first came out, you had pretty much lost your chance of ever seeing it. Television, of course, would soon arrive and begin recycling Hollywood's archives, so that children born after the forties grew up with a cinema literacy that those born in the twenties like me missed out on. It wasn't till the mid-eighties and my first VCR that I was able to buy a commercial VHS cassette of *The Seventh Victim* and find out what Ted Gorey had been gasping about all those years before.

Directed by neophyte Mark Robson (who would go on to commercial fame with the likes of *Peyton Place*, *Valley of the Dolls* and *Von Ryan's Express*), it tells the eerie saga of young Mary Gibson (the late Kim Hunter in her first role) as she leaves her boarding school to go to New York in search of her older sister, Jacqueline (the obscure Jean Brooks, sporting a dazed expression and Morticia Addams hairdo). After the obligatory, always electrifying logo of the RKO radio tower (accompanied by the opening notes of Beethoven's Fifth Symphony), Roy Webb's angst-laden score (recently released on a CD) surges forth to accompany a quotation from John Donne: "I runne to Death and Death greets me as fast / And all my pleasures are like yesterday." The opening shot is of a staircase (borrowed from the set of *The Magnificent Ambersons*) at Highcliffe, a boarding school. Mary is confronted by a tide of prattling schoolgirls as she makes her way up to the headmistress's office. The latter explains that Jacqueline is behind with Mary's tuition; Mary says she has been without news of Jacqueline and wants to go to New York to question her associate, Mrs. Redi. The headmistress doubts that she'll learn anything from "that woman," but gives Mary permission to go, offers to help with her expenses and says she can always return to school as a teacher. After Mary leaves the office, the headmistress's assistant, Gilchrist, follows her to the staircase and warns her not to come back, saying that she had once been in a similar situation and rued having returned to Highcliffe; she is cut short by the headmistress's angry call of "Gilchrist!" Mary goes down the staircase and out the door, pausing to bestow an affectionate smile on the big grandfather clock in the hall.

This short scene contains a number of the small anomalies that finally make the film such a disorienting experience and contribute to the fascination it has held for its fans (including Carol Reed and Jacques Rivette, who reportedly screened it for the cast of his movie *Duelle*). The headmistress is actually being kind. But her appearance and tone are sinister. We wonder in passing what she knows about "that woman," Mrs. Redi, and how she knows it, though we soon forget this detail as the story unwinds. Nor do we learn why Gilchrist urges Mary to leave, nor why the headmistress summons Gilchrist back with such urgency. (Neither actress appears in the film again.) Mary's affection for the grandfather clock is also unexplained.

We soon learn more about Jacqueline's disappearance and the satanic cult she has become involved with in Greenwich Village, but these mysteries tend to get sidetracked by small discrepancies of plot and motivation, and by erratic strands of dialogue. Tom Conway, the real-life alcoholic (and brother of George Sanders) who plays Dr. Judd, at one point irrelevantly remarks to a receptionist that he doesn't treat alcoholics: "Dipsomania can be rather sordid." We hear nothing further of dipsomania or the receptionist's problem (her father drinks), but this odd exchange contributes to our sense throughout the film that people are saying anything that comes into their heads, and that the apparent mysteries of the plot are perhaps only a smokescreen for other, ill-defined ones. We gradually get the feeling that the ground under our feet is unstable.

To make matters worse, the original film was cut clumsily to fit into its second-feature slot, adding to the narrative chaos. Some of these cuts are evident; others are not. Natalie (Evelyn Brent), leader and hostess of the sedate devil-worshipping cult that meets in her Greenwich Village duplex for tea and classical music (shades of *Rosemary's Baby*), has only one arm. It has been suggested that missing footage would reveal that she was once a dancer who lost the arm in an accident, which drove her to satanism, but the story seems more engrossing when you don't know this detail.

After arriving in New York, Mary calls on Mrs. Redi, a proper-seeming matron who has taken over Jacqueline's cosmetics factory, La Sagesse ("Wisdom"; its trademark is a satanic emblem). Redi claims not to know Jacqueline's whereabouts, though the latter is in fact being kept prisoner in the factory for having revealed occult secrets to her psychiatrist Dr. Judd and, it turns out, is facing execution: six other cult members have been similarly condemned and Jacqueline may well become the "seventh victim."

The spiraling complications of the plot take Mary on a scary trip through a studio-bound Manhattan which, as so often, seems more realistic than location filming would have produced. Particularly memorable is the Fourteenth Street station of the IRT subway, where Mary boards a train at night and is soon fleeing from two formally dressed revelers who are supporting the corpse of a murdered man. She dines with a poet, Jason, and a lawyer, Gregory Ward (who turns out to be Jacqueline's husband; he is played by Hugh Beaumont, the future Ward Cleaver of the sixties sitcom *Leave It to Beaver*), in a Perry Street Italian restaurant called the Dante, which features a mural copied from Henry Holiday's famous painting of Dante's first encounter with Beatrice along the

Arno. Beatrice in the mural is a dead-ringer for Mary, but, as usual, this coincidence is left unexplored, while red herrings continue to pile up. (A curious one is a scene outside the "Ivy Lane" theater, obviously an allusion to the Village's still-extant Cherry Lane Theater, above which Kim Hunter lived in later life!)

In the film's most famous scene, Mary is confronted in her bathroom shower by Mrs. Redi (brilliantly played by an actress named Mary Newton), who has come to tell her to stop looking for her sister and return to school. While Mary listens naked under the dripping nozzle, Mrs. Redi, wearing a hat and coat, looms as a menacing shadow against the shower curtain, her voice cold and ominous. (It has been said that Hitchcock, who knew Lewton, got the idea for the shower scene in *Psycho* from this episode.) Eventually Jacqueline is summoned before the assembled Palladists and told she must drink poison from a wineglass. Just as she is about to do so, young Frances, who is loyal to Jacqueline, smashes the glass and bursts into tears. (This cameo is magnificently acted by Isabel Jewell, the hard-boiled blonde in a hundred forgotten and otherwise forgettable B-movies.)

Jacqueline is allowed to leave, but told she will soon have to pay the price for her betrayal. A member of the group follows her through the oddly empty streets, at one point seizing her wrist and brandishing a knife. Jacqueline breaks free and makes it back to her room above the Dante. In the final moments of the film, Mary and Ward declare their love for each other, Mary insisting that it can never be consummated on account of Jacqueline. Jacqueline's neighbor Mimi (Elizabeth Russell, who produced a memorable frisson as Simone Simon's nemesis in Lewton's *Cat People*) emerges coughing from her room in evening dress, determined to go out for a last desperate night on the town, just as a thud from Jacqueline's room tells us that she has finally committed suicide with the noose she kept suspended for that eventuality. We hear a woman's voice intoning the Donne couplet that prefaced the film.

Muddled yet marvelous, *The Seventh Victim* is one of the great New York noir movies. (Though it is classified a horror film, the horror is kept under wraps; as in all the Lewton films, there is barely a splash of gore.) Even though the backgrounds are artificial they have a compelling authenticity. In his 1929 Surrealist novel *Hebdomeros*, de Chirico wrote: "A false beard is always more real on the screen than a real beard, just as a wooden and cardboard set is always more real than a natural setting. But try telling that to your film directors, avid for beautiful locations and picturesque views; they won't know what you are talking about, alas!" Despite its second-tier cast and modest production values, *The Seventh Victim* captures the weird poetry of New York in a way that few films have ever done.

2004

Carrie Rickey

Just as the 1980s saw a generation of independent filmmakers who had started out in art school (David Lynch, Gus Van Sant, Jane Campion), so too there were film critics such as Carrie Rickey (b. 1952) who had gravitated into the field from art history. Rickey alternately covered movies and the gallery scene for *The Village Voice* before becoming senior film critic at *The Philadelphia Inquirer*, a post she has held for over 15 years. Intrigued by the effects of gender on style, she is presently working on a study about the differences between male and female filmmakers, which grew out of the essay below. In it, placing herself mischievously in the role of Darla, the girl who invades the boy's clubhouse, she analyzes a crop of macho buddy movies as both an evolving genre and one that is as old as the hills.

◆

Ratpacks and Pack Males

Mexican soldier of fortune, shocked that his American *jefe* would run guns to counterrevolutionaries:

"Would you give someone a gun to kill your father?"

"$10,000 cuts a lot of family ties."

—Pike (William Holden) in *The Wild Bunch* (1969, screenplay by Walon Green and Sam Peckinpah)

Anybody who says money is the root of all evil doesn't have it! Money can't buy happiness? Look at the fucking smile on my face. Ear to ear, baby. You wanna hear details? I drive a Ferrari 355 cabriolet. I have a ridiculous house on the South Fork. I've got every toy you can imagine. And best of all, kids, I am liquid.

—Jim Young (Ben Affleck) in *Boiler Room* (2000, screenplay by Ben Younger)

You're in a privileged position to learn a thing or two if you can keep your mouth shut and your eyes open . . . If this shit shakes you up, I'll drop you at Rampart so you can pitch a bitch to the Captain and get a nice job lighting flares and measuring wrecks. Decide now if you want to be a wolf or a sheep.

—Alonzo (Denzel Washington) in *Training Day* (2001, screenplay by David Ayer)

The history of American movies is in part the history of guys running in gangs, in wolfpacks and in posses searching for . . . just what, exactly? Tony Montana (Al Pacino) in *Scarface* defined American manhood thus: "First you get the money, then you get the power and then you get the women." But if it were merely about the pesos, the prowess and the pussy a man wouldn't need the company of men. He travels fastest who travels alone—or so they say. Yet in the way a tree falling in the forest needs a witness to hear it, so, too, a man in the wilderness needs another man or men to witness his fall or rise. Or so the movies say.

Whether you call them buddy pictures or action flicks, the testosterone testaments of men performing manly deeds outdoors are a bracing contrast to those so-called chick flicks, the estrogen flashes in which women talk about their inner lives in interior spaces. In the syntax of classical Hollywood cinema, men embody action and women interrupt it. Which may be why it's easier to cite male "feelings" movies—i.e., *Bang the Drum Slowly* and *Stand by Me* (both of which, of course, take place on the road)—than it is female "action" pictures (after *Aliens*, then?). Typically, buddy films exclude or marginalize women while chick flicks include and are preoccupied with men. As an exercise in gender-trending, try imagining the scenarios in this issue—*Boiler Room*, *Training Day* and *The Wild Bunch*—with all-female protagonists. Can't? Neither can I. But I do believe that understanding masculinism is a feminist act. It's instructive to be a gal in no-woman's-land.

Almost inevitably, American movies about men in packs have frontier settings. Often it's the West, as in *The Wild Bunch*, where Pike (William Holden) and his posse elude the authorities at a succession of campsites and villages just across the Rio Grande in Mexico. But just as often the frontier is virtual, as in the cinderblock strip mall in *Boiler Room*. There the boys, nomads in suits on speakerphones hustling worthless stock to suckers, pitch their telecommunications tent in a Long Island industrial park in the ethical frontier fifteen miles and a million light years from Wall Street legitimacy. Similarly in *Training Day*, the turf patrolled by LAPD detective Alonzo Harris (Denzel Washington) and his young recruit, Jake Hoyt (Ethan Hawke) is an unpoliced state where lawmen and lawless make their own rules. That borderland so aptly described as "the meeting point between savagery and civilization," by Frederick Jackson Turner in his 1893 thesis, "The Significance of the Frontier," is the *sine qua non* of the American male-action flick. Only in the frontier can a man experience that twin rush of the adrenal and hormonal. Only in the frontier can a man choose what kind of man he is, whether the wilderness will master him or whether he will master it. Only in the frontier can a man experience the challenge of maintaining a moral code in an immoral world.

Even *Ocean's Eleven*, both versions, features its respective ratpack burrowing through that ultimate frontier town of Las Vegas. By contrast, non-American movies about men in pairs or packs (*Going Places* and *Y Tu Mamá También* come to mind) do not use the landscape as a correlative for character, they do the reverse by using the setting to show the protagonists' alienation from their contexts. In American male-action flicks, landscape is character. Think of the men on horseback stumbling across the sands and arid arroyos in *The Wild Bunch*, unchanged men in changing times, the very ground they travel upon shifting under them. Think of the cops who fail to stay within the lines—and the lanes—of the streets they cruise in *Training Day*. Or of the Wall Street watering holes where Seth (Giovanni Ribisi) of *Boiler Room* waves wads of cash, grunts tribal grunts and feels out of place, a bridge-and-tunnel barbarian at the gates rather than the Manhattan citizen he aspires to be.

The casual iconographer of men-in-packs films cannot fail to note that on the visual level it's largely about the wilderness, the weapons and the wheels. (Or hooves. Yet whether steed or car, horsepower revs up these films.) Men size up the tools packed by other men much as they size up their vehicles. Men in these movies are always watching other men, whether it's Deke (Robert Ryan) spying on Pike via binoculars, or Jake keeping his eyes open and mouth shut as Alonzo plays cock of the walk, ditto Seth, saucer-eyed, at the cocky charisma of Jim (Ben Affleck). The implicit question is, do his tools and transport better equip him for the frontier than mine prepare me? Pike packs a Winchester and rides tall astride a chestnut stallion. In *Training Day*, Alonzo wears twin Glocks, symbolic biceps that he flexes to impress and intimidate Jake; Alonzo's "office" is a 1977 lacquer-black Monte Carlo, Darth Vader on wheels. (Jake's rusted blue junker lacks the protective skin of Alonzo's chrome-plated tank, but it is Jake's car that survives.) In *Boiler Room*, Seth is dazzled by the Ferraris flaunted by the brokers at J. T. Marlin, and also by the way they play their phone handsets, power tools of the trade, instruments used to seduce and to bilk.

One might well ask about these movies where the men are men, the women are whores and the money is stolen, do females factor in the calculus? Not much, with the exception of Debbie (Nia Long), the secretary in *Boiler Room* who serves as a confidante and moral compass. They're either biddies (the temperance workers in *The Wild Bunch*) or babymakers (Jake Hoyt's wife in *Training Day*) or bitches in heat who attach like iron filings to the magnet of corrupt male power. (In defense of the B-word: Both *Boiler Room* and *Training*

Day use the expression "pitch the bitch." In *Boiler Room*, it's used as a warning—"don't pitch the bitch," as in don't sell to women because they're too high-maintenance. In *Training Day*, "pitch a bitch" means to complain. Bitch, bitch, bitch: Noun, verb, sex object.)

To a female, the maleness of these films is transgressive and thrilling. Watching them I feel like Darla of *The Little Rascals* allowed to crash the He-Man Womun-Hater's Club. One hears the maleness in the phallic language—"you two-bit rednecked peckerwood" is a put-down in *The Wild Bunch* while the *Boiler Room* barbarians pump themselves up by calling each other "big, swinging dicks." One sees masculinity's lethal charisma in the preening-rooster performances of antagonists Pike, Alonzo and Jim, surrogate Bad Dads for young heroes (Angel, Jake and Seth) hunting for authority figures. One intuits that the secret password of the fraternity is explosive laughter—especially that of Pike and Alonzo—that tears through flesh like a fusillade of 9mm bullets. (Note to aspiring screenwriters: These are films in which one brutal laugh is worth a thousand words.)

But most of all one experiences the maleness in story structure and editing rhythm. I'm not the first and I won't be the last to note that the structure of the men-in-packs film might be compared to sex. It's about building tension through dialectical editing, escalating to an orgasmic finale. But as significant as the build-up is the letdown: All three of the films end with a reflective coda that feels positively post-coital, elegiac. (Perhaps here is the place to note that David Ayer's first draft for *Training Day*, much more pensive than the final film, might have been the exception, but the studio demanded a conventional shoot-'em-up denouement, which for this viewer is not as dramatically satisfying as Ayer's original in which the showdown between Alonzo and Jake is psychological, not physical. And in which Jake begins and ends his longest day by seeing himself reflected in the eyes of his wife.)

Historically, in movies directed by women as far-flung as Dorothy Arzner, Penny Marshall and Gina Prince-Bythewood, the Big Dramatic Moment takes place in what seems like real time, typically in a continuous take where tension between characters builds inside the frame. In the men-in-packs movies (which, with the exception of Kathryn Bigelow's *Point Break*, typically are man-made), the dramatic tension is ratcheted up through lightning editing. The Big Dramatic Moment occurs in transfigured time. Transfiguring the tempo suggests that these characters exist outside the time/space continuum; it exalts them into myth. *The Wild Bunch* was influential in this regard. In the late '60s, the average American movie had 600 cuts. *The Wild Bunch* has 3,600. Peckinpah shot his showdowns from six different angles and as many film speeds, giving him the ability to compress and elongate the same sequence by taking a slo-mo shot and accelerating it with blitzkrieg cuts. The editing simulates the spurt of ejaculation, the spray of gunfire, the splatter of blood. It's about discharge—in every meaning of the word. While director Antoine Fuqua films the assassination of Alonzo in *Training Day* in a bullet-riddled tribute to Peckinpah, for *Boiler Room*, writer/director Ben Younger uses a hip-hop soundtrack and shock cuts to convey the jumpy rhythms—and jangled central nervous systems—of its men.

Before, I mentioned the elegiac codas. From *The Wild Bunch* to *Road Trip*, men-in-packs sagas are almost inevitably about the death of a masculine ethos. Pike, Alonzo and Jim are pitching lifestyles that no longer are viable, they are father figures literally or symbolically killed off in these riffs on *Oedipus*. (In *Boiler Room*, Seth needs to follow the example of Jim, the mentor, in order to re-connect with his real father, a judge who sits in judgment of him.) Each of the men who once were eager initiates of these fraternities sees that his invincible mentor is all too vincible, sees that the pack no longer has power. Each must, in the way of all myth, blaze his own path.

Significantly, in these films He who is watched dies and He who watches lives. This is the way Hollywood constructs the male double-bind: At least since *OK Corral*, He who is the spectator feels impotent but lives; He who is the spectacle feels potent but dies. (Contrast with the female double-bind—circa Salem—She who is not a witch, drowns; She who is, floats and gets hung.) Men travel in packs not because misery loves company or because there is safety in numbers. Men travel in packs in order to watch the spectacle—and *schadenfreude*—of the Alpha Male go South.

2003

Gilberto Perez

In his essays and reviews for such scholarly periodicals as *The Yale Review*, *Raritan*, and *London Review of Books*, as well as in his densely suggestive book *The Material Ghost: Films and Their Medium*, Gilberto Perez (b. 1943) has narrowed the gap between movie love and academia, criticism and theory, and in the process has established himself as one of the most reliable, intelligent observers of film culture today. He grew up in Havana, Cuba, a city passionate about the art of film, before moving to the United States where he has lived and taught for many years. Here, he takes a characteristically methodical approach to a lesser-known John Ford movie, describing its complexities and the subtle pleasures they give in language that is both lucid and learned.

◆

Saying "Ain't" and Playing "Dixie": Rhetoric and Comedy in *Judge Priest*

In *Judge Priest* (1934), the second of three movies he made with John Ford, Will Rogers is the title character, William Priest, a judge in a small Kentucky town some years after the Civil War. At one point in the movie he is discussing with a friend the challenge he faces in the upcoming election. "He's a spellbinder and a silver tongue from way back," says the judge about his opponent. "I'm just a, well, an old country jake who's kind of a baby kisser. [They laugh.] I ain't got much to offer the boys in the . . . in the way of rhetoric." "I understand he doesn't approve of your grammar," says the friend. "My grammar?" replies the judge. "First thing I learned in politics was when to say 'ain't.'"

Knowing when to say "ain't," the judge says he "ain't got much to offer . . . in the way of rhetoric." His opponent, the spellbinder with the silver tongue, is of the florid, orotund school, and of that kind of rhetoric, it is true, the judge hasn't much to offer. But he is master of another rhetoric, and knowing when to say "ain't" is part of that mastery. It's clear the judge will beat his opponent in the election, as he beats him in the courtroom in the central action of the movie, because he's the better rhetorician. His is the kind of rhetoric that pretends not to be rhetoric, the kind that is all the more persuasive for seeming not to be trying to persuade. When he tells his friend that saying "ain't" is not a matter of grammar but of political savvy, the judge is in effect admitting to that other kind of rhetoric, acknowledging that his plainness of speech and colloquial manner are something calculated to have an effect. And Ford's movie lets us know all along that this rhetoric that seems not to be trying is indeed a very effective form of persuasion, that it's not innocent but calculated, that in pretending not to be rhetoric it's being cunningly rhetorical.

The judge's political opponent is the prosecutor of a case in which he alleges the judge is biased: "I call upon you, Judge Priest, to vacate the bench during this trial and yield your place to a qualified judge." Judge Priest is visibly shaken. After all these years, he's being deemed unqualified to sit on the bench. He takes out his handkerchief, fumbles with his pipe, wipes the sweat off his face. He is at a loss for words. At length he rises, walks toward a portrait of Robert E. Lee up on the wall, and haltingly recalls how, after fighting in the Civil War "for what we thought was right," he returned to his home town, put up his shingle, and before long was sitting on that bench. "Maybe I did have a hankering for the spirit of the law . . . not the letter . . . but as far as I know nobody ever found cause to complain . . . till now." Gradually we come to recognize that this man whose feelings have been hurt is turning those hurt feelings into rhetoric. He's giving a performance. He instructs the jury to "forget everything that I've said . . . my feelings have no place in the . . . in the records of . . . of this trial"—which of course only serves to impress those feelings more firmly in the minds of the jury. Those hurt feelings are by no means false. Judge Priest is being quite sincere. But at the same time he's being quite rhetorical. He's all choked up with emotions when he asks another judge to "come up here . . . and take . . . take my p . . . my place on . . . on the bench." We scarcely know whether to cry or cheer, cry over the genuine emotion or cheer the consummate performance. Ford is asking us to admire the judge as a man of feeling, and to admire him all the more because he knows how to make those feelings effective in a public situation.

In *Judge Priest* two kinds of rhetoric, the judge's and his opponent's, are set in contrast. The contrast is not merely between plainness and verbosity, or between colloquial and high-flown language. Rhetoric, the film makes clear, is not merely a matter of language. The judge's pauses, his hesitations and repetitions, are as eloquent as his words. Rhetoric is not only language but also gesture, movement, action. Rhetoric is performance. And like all performance, it's addressed to an audience. Judge Priest is a great rhetorician because he knows his audience and knows how to play to that audience.

The judge is made to step down from the bench during the trial of Bob

Gillis, a man we know is innocent. But the testimony of three—three who ganged up on him and are now accusing him of assault—goes against him, as does the fact that Gillis keeps to himself and has few friends in the town. Moreover, he doesn't say much at the trial in his own defense; he refuses to give testimony that would be likely to exculpate him because he doesn't want to involve a nice young woman named Ellie May. The judge is fond of Ellie May and has been encouraging her romance with his nephew, Rome—short for Jerome—against the objections of Rome's mother, who disapproves of a young woman whose father is unknown. Rome, fresh out of law school, is Gillis's defender at the trial. This is a small town—neither the number of lawyers nor the circle of relationships is large. And, as much as a story about justice, this is a story about family, about a community not very much larger than a family, and about the ties of blood that bind such a community.

Things are looking bad for Gillis at the trial—only the summations remain—when Judge Priest receives a visit at home from Reverend Ashby Brand (Henry B. Walthall, who played beside Lillian Gish in *The Birth of a Nation*). The reverend has something to tell him about Gillis that leads the judge to intervene in the case. He writes an anonymous letter to the prosecutor and entrusts Jeff Poindexter, a black man he has brought into his service (Stepin Fetchit), to deliver it without revealing its provenance. The letter discloses that Gillis was once convicted of murder and sentenced to life imprisonment, a fact that the prosecutor naturally wants to bring to the attention of the jury, and so the next day he reopens the case and calls Gillis back to the witness stand. This gives Judge Priest his chance. He comes forward and announces himself to the sitting judge as associate counsel for the defense. He has no questions to ask Gillis, but he has tricked the prosecutor into allowing him to call Reverend Brand as a witness. The reverend now tells the story of Gillis's release from a chain gang to join the depleted Confederate army, and of his fighting with truly exceptional courage in the last days of the Civil War. Meanwhile Judge Priest has arranged for Jeff Poindexter to play "Dixie" right outside the courtroom, so that everyone can hear it as a rousing background to the story of Gillis's bravery. The reverend also makes known that Gillis is Ellie May's father and has been secretly providing for her. Of course Gillis is acquitted—and not only acquitted, but welcomed into the community as a hero of the lost Southern cause.

To be sure, what Gillis did in the war has nothing to do with the case being tried. The judge wins the case not by evidence or by argument but by staging a performance. This time as director more than as actor, he puts on a show, complete with stirring musical accompaniment, a shameless manipulation of the allegiances and emotions of his audience. When I recently showed *Judge Priest* to a class, the students liked the movie but objected to this rhetorical manipulation. They had expected the judge would unearth some decisive piece of evidence or significant judicial precedent, or maybe bring forward an expert or a key eyewitness whose testimony clears up the facts, which is what lawyer heroes usually do in courtroom dramas. The students expected the judge's rhetoric to address the facts of the case, but instead it engages the feelings of the audience. It would have been easy enough for Ford and his scriptwriters to contrive the finding of evidence or the enlisting of factual testimony that would have made the judge a more conventional lawyer hero. But they chose not to do that. They chose not to make the judge into a detective, which is what the lawyer hero is most of the time, a digger into evidence, a detector of facts, the hero of a positivist ideology. Nor did they make him into a philosopher, an upholder of abstract principles, a manager of reason aimed at a universal humanity, the hero of an idealist ideology. Rather they made Judge Priest into a hero of rhetoric. Rhetoric is mostly effective—which is to say, most rhetorical—neither when it merely adduces facts that presumably speak for themselves, nor when it merely invokes principles that presumably speak in the same way to everyone everywhere, but rather when it speaks in the terms of a concrete social situation to the particular human beings who are in that situation and are part of that society.

Plato condemned rhetoric as deception. He similarly condemned poetry and painting, but many who balk at that nonetheless go along with his condemnation of rhetoric. In the *Poetics* and the *Rhetoric*, Aristotle came to the defense of those arts, but primarily defended them as arts of language—tragedy as the art of the poet, not the actor, rhetoric as a matter of discourse, of the content and form of words, and only secondarily of their delivery before an audience. Aristotle would not have thought so well of Judge Priest's rhetoric because it depends too much on performance. But, as the proof of the pudding is in the eating, the test of rhetoric is in the audience. Rhetoric as such is not to be judged by principles but only by effects.

In *The Eloquence of Color*, her brilliant book on rhetoric and painting in the French seventeenth century, Jacqueline Lichtenstein puts forward Cicero, the great orator of republican Rome, as the classical defender, not only against Plato's condemnation but against Aristotle's condescension, of rhetoric as an art of performance. Delivery (*actio*) was for Cicero the most important thing in oratory; he liked to cite another famous orator, Demosthenes, who, when asked about the parts of oratory, is said to have answered that delivery comes first, second, and third. "Delivery, or action, which includes an audible and a visible aspect, since it consists of voice and gesture, derives not from a rhetoric of discourse," Lichtenstein comments, "but from an eloquence of speech in which the body participates with all its expressive forms." She contrasts Cicero's bodily rhetoric with Plato's disembodied philosophy:

Plato tried to rid philosophy of the risk from the body and from images, from all the effective and affective forces set off by speech. . . . The emotive body reduced to silence by philosophy, the direct and physical relation to the other ruled out by the mediations of writing, and the theatrical expressivity annihilated by the abstractions of a disincarnated theory—these are elements that Ciceronian rhetoric tries to bring back into speech. In the Ciceronian oratorical art the various modalities of physical expression like bodily gesture and tone of voice can finally regain their claims to wisdom and dignity.

Plato divided truth from eloquence, but Cicero stressed the truth of eloquence:

Because it passes beyond traditional distinctions of nature and artifice, of reality and illusion, of being and appearing, Ciceronian eloquence brings us to a universe of tangible representation in which the staging of the body and of discourse has sincerity as its condition and real emotion for effect. No one can make another believe a cause to be just without sharing the belief, at least during the speech. Through many examples and varied formulations, Cicero never ceases to repeat it: the orator must not only be *actor* but also *auctor*; he must himself feel the effects of the passion whose gestures he imitates in order to make its effects felt by his audience.

Cicero had a point when he argued that, by valuing only principles and discounting effects, philosophy becomes ineffectual, that it renders itself impotent by renouncing the power of eloquence. Even if eloquence requires sincerity, however, even if one grants Cicero's contention that the effective orator must feel what he would have his audience feel and believe what he would have his audience believe, this may yield real emotion but not necessarily justice or truth. Plato had a point, too.

The term *Ciceronian* customarily refers to a style that is profuse, flowing, Latinate, ornamental. A tourist guide is called a *cicerone*, my dictionary tells me, "from the usual loquacity of guides." *Ciceronian* would not seem to be the term for Judge Priest—it's much more like his verbose opponent. And yet the judge's rhetoric is no less ornamental than his opponent's, and if it seems otherwise it's only because the judge makes a more effective use of ornament. Although his language may be plain and colloquial, not what we would call Ciceronian, it comes with all the ornament of his pauses, his gestures, his inflections of voice, all the embellishment of delivery he's master of. The judge is Ciceronian in his rhetoric of performance. I may not be doing him a favor by calling him that. *Ciceronian* isn't exactly a term of praise—but then neither is *rhetorical* usually a term of praise. If *Ciceronian* means ornamental, so does *rhetorical* mean ornamental. Plato likened rhetoric to cosmetics. Rhetorically he was disparaging rhetoric. The comparison had behind it the breach he posited between appearance and reality. Cicero called that breach into question, but by and large the philosopher has prevailed. To this day rhetoric is suspect as ornament is suspect. One may dispute Plato's metaphysics and one may dispute his disparagement, but he was not wrong to make the comparison. The fates of rhetoric and ornament are fittingly bound up together. A defense of rhetoric must also be a defense of ornament.

When the judge turns into rhetoric his hurt feelings over vacating the bench, it's real emotion he communicates to his audience, bearing out Cicero's claims for the truth of eloquence. We sympathize with the judge and feel that his opponent is treating him badly. But his opponent is right to maintain that the judge has a bias in the case. This doesn't mean that the judge wouldn't have been able to rise above that bias and conduct the trial fairly, but his opponent has reason to ask him to step down. The judge's hurt feelings do not speak to the issue of his vacating the bench. They are real emotion but they are not the truth of the matter. The feelings of a corrupt judge might have been just as hurt. The real emotion is an embellishment.

It's the same with the reverend's testimony. The reverend speaks with sincerity, with real emotion, and he arouses real emotion in the audience. He's speaking the truth, the truth about Gillis's bravery in the war, but that truth does not speak to the issue of Gillis's innocence or guilt in the charge of assault. It's not the truth of the matter but an embellishment. And the musical accompaniment of "Dixie" is flagrantly an embellishment. We know that Gillis is innocent and that all this embellishment is in the service of a just cause. We know the judge is a good man. But what if Gillis were not innocent? What if the judge were not a good man? Couldn't the same embellishment, the same manipulation of the audience, be put in the service of injustice? If Judge Priest is a hero of rhetoric, what kind of hero is this, winning not by principles but by effects, not by truth but by ornament?

Judge Priest is a hero of comedy. Rome and Ellie May, young lovers meeting with opposition from the older generation, are the stuff of New Comedy. New Comedy is very old—it was new in ancient Greece—but has endured through the centuries, from Plautus and Terence to Shakespeare and Molière to the romantic comedies of the screen. As Northrop Frye has written, "New Comedy normally presents an erotic intrigue between a young man and a young woman which is blocked by some kind of opposition, usually paternal, and resolved by a twist in the plot . . . a discovery in which the hero becomes wealthy or the heroine respectable." In *Judge Priest* we have the young lovers, we have the blocking parental figures—not only Rome's mother but also, more indirectly, the judge's opponent, who is prosecuting Ellie May's father and whose daughter is the woman Rome's mother would like her son to marry— and we have the twist in the plot, the discovery that makes the young woman respectable and happily resolves the situation. That the hero is the judge, the older man rather than the young lover, isn't much of a departure from a genre whose young lovers, as Frye remarks, are often not very interesting, paling beside other, more vivid characters. *Judge Priest* is of course a courtroom drama as well as a comedy, but the action of comedy, as Frye notes, is a social contest

not unlike the action of a lawsuit, in which plaintiff and defendant construct different versions of the same situation, one finally being judged as real and the other as illusory. This resemblance of the rhetoric of comedy to the rhetoric of jurisprudence has been recognized from earliest times.

The trial of Gillis fits nicely into the plot of the comedy. It leads to his acquittal and social vindication and at the same time to the revelation that he is Ellie May's father, which enables the young lovers to come together with the blessing of the community.

What may be more of a departure from the configuration of New Comedy is the governing role the judge plays in his society. The chief representative of the older generation, not only is he not a blocking figure, he sides with the young lovers not from the sidelines but from the center, from a position of power in the society they are up against. At the end of *Tartuffe* the king intervenes to set things right, but the judge is setting things right in *Judge Priest* from the very beginning. Not that he assumes the position of a king or lord: his authority has the democratic cast of a man of the people. As outlined by Frye, the plot of New Comedy begins with blocking figures in control of society, figures of undesirable authority such as the *senex iratus* or heavy father and the *miles gloriosus* or braggart warrior (a type found in *Judge Priest* among the Confederate veterans telling war stories); and it ends with the formation of a new society around the triumphant young lovers. Judge Priest, however, is in control at the end as he was at the beginning, a benevolent authority presiding over the world of the movie. He may be seen as a figure out of romance, a wise old man like Prospero in *The Tempest*. But the old Kentucky town depicted in *Judge Priest*, though invested with a bygone sweetness, is a human society with its share of imperfections and limitations, prejudices and problems —not the idyllic and enchanted land of romance. And the judge, unlike Prospero, has nothing arcane or occult about him, nothing of the magician: his skills and power are worldly, not otherworldly. His only magic wand is the one most thoroughly implicated in actual human society—his rhetoric. Will Rogers comes up in Frye as a type of satirist, the rustic who exposes the pretensions of society; the society in *Judge Priest* is rural rather than urban, and the judge is a leader rather than an outsider, but he still subjects its way to comic puncturing. If Judge Priest is a Prospero, the wise old man of romance, he is a Prospero brought down to the domain of comedy.

According to Frye, "the movement of comedy is usually a movement from one kind of society to another." That doesn't happen in *Judge Priest*. But comedy, I would argue, is more accepting and less subversive than it sounds in Frye's account; it may often be irreverent or unruly, but it is seldom revolutionary. In my view, what happens in *Judge Priest* is what more often happens in comedy: not the formation of a new society but merely a renewal of the existing one. Take a classic boy-meets-girl comedy, *It Happened One Night*, made the same year as *Judge Priest*. It begins with the heroine's overbearing rich father as a *senex iratus*, but as the plot develops the old man is shown to have been right about the phony his daughter wanted for a husband, and in the end he's the one who sets things right between her and the hero; rather than the old man's antagonist, the hero is his chosen successor, a young version of himself who will perpetuate his lineage. *It Happened One Night* seems to me typical of New Comedy in the way it leads not to the overthrowing of a social order but to its rejuvenation. New Comedy pits a young couple against the dictates of convention, but the conflict is conventionally resolved. The community is disturbed but not disrupted, and its values are revitalized by the disturbance and reaffirmed at the happy ending. Youth wins but its victory only strengthens the social fabric and ensures its continuation. That's what happens in *Judge Priest* under the judge's benevolent manipulation. And the very instrument serving him to bring about a renewal of his society is bound up with it and becomes part of the comedy: *Judge Priest* is a comedy of rhetoric.

This comedy of rhetoric may be most evident in the exaggerated verbosity of the judge's opponent (played by Berton Churchill, who a few years later was the banker in *Stagecoach*, another pompous representative of the establishment coming in for Ford's lampooning), whose rhetoric during the trial is repeatedly punctured by the spitting of a drunken juror (Francis Ford) into a spittoon that keeps being moved out of his reach and that he keeps managing to hit with a resounding noise. But the humor isn't just at the opponent's expense: it extends to the judge's own rhetoric as well. I have called the judge Ciceronian in his rhetoric of performance, but the way we are made aware—and aware that he's aware—of his rhetoric as a performance, involving not just a flowing sincerity but a certain feigning, a matter not merely of real emotions but of calculated effects, undercuts the Ciceronian truth of eloquence. The reverend's testimony is Ciceronian in its earnestness, but the judge's use of the reverend's testimony is a knowing manipulation of an audience, not outright deception but surely a bit of a cheat. The comedy of the judge's rhetoric comes from our amused awareness that it's a bit of a cheat. It was for cheating that Plato earnestly condemned rhetoric, and it was in terms no less earnest that Cicero defended it. In the terms of comedy, Ford acknowledges that rhetoric cheats and asks us to recognize the need for that cheating in society. Gillis went to trial with the community prejudiced against him. It's very hard to argue a community out of a prejudice. Had he attempted that, the judge would have been right, but he would have lost the case. Instead he played to another prejudice of the community and won the case. We approve of his ends and smile at his means.

Both the rhetoric and the comedy reach a high point with the playing of "Dixie." Wearing an elegant raccoon coat and a vest given to him by the judge in compensation for his musical services, Jeff Poindexter steals a bass drum from the Confederate band getting ready to play on Memorial Day—which happens to be the last day of Gillis's trial—and sets himself up outside the courthouse with the drum and a tambourine, by a large window so that his playing carries inside and can be heard loud and clear. At the right moment in the reverend's testimony the judge signals to Jeff that the music is to start. Jeff is joined by other black musicians, one playing a banjo, another a fiddle, as the sound of "Dixie" rises into the courtroom. The joke here is not on the blacks playing the music of the Southern Confederacy. The joke is on the white Southerners whose sentiments are being swayed by this music, by this performance the judge has arranged and Jeff has orchestrated on behalf of Gillis. Twenty years later, in *The Sun Shines Bright* (1954), Ford returned to the character of Judge Priest. Will Rogers was long since dead, and Charles Winninger played the part. Next to this different judge—"little Billy Priest," one character calls him, which no one would call Will Rogers—Stepin Fetchit is again Jeff Poindexter. When a young black man fond of playing the banjo is brought before the judge on charges of vagrancy, Jeff gets him to play "Dixie" on his banjo to sway the judge in his favor, the same rhetorical ploy used by Judge Priest in the earlier movie. This time the joke is on the judge.

Stepin Fetchit is an actor who has been maligned for his portrayal of a type that some find demeaning to his race. Some find all types demeaning and think that people should be portrayed as individuals. But types are a representation of people in society, of individuals as part of a group. Comedy especially calls for types in its rendering of the human accommodation to society, an accommodation not without its troubles, but the troubles allow for laughter when seen as something shared. To be against types is to be against comedy. Still, it cannot be denied that some types are objectionable. What about Stepin Fetchit? He is alleged to portray black people as dumb and lazy. But his character is neither dumb nor exactly lazy. In the white supremacist society in which he lives, he must play dumb—or else he would be seen as surly or insolent—in order to get away as much as he does with doing what he wants. His dumbness is a mask that Fetchit subtly lets us see through so we can glimpse the intelligence beneath. And as for his being lazy, in that regard Jeff Poindexter is at one with Judge Priest. They're both easygoing Southern types. Their relaxed quality, which matches Ford's own directorial style, is construed positively. Neither Jeff nor the judge subscribes to the work ethic, which doesn't mean they don't work, only that they're not hard driving and ambitious like the judge's opponent. At the beginning of *Judge Priest*, Jeff is brought before the judge and falls asleep in the courtroom as the prosecutor carries on. "Sheriff, wake him up there," says the judge, who has been reading the comic pages of a newspaper. "If anybody's going to sleep in this court it'll be me." Jeff's appearance in court leads to no conviction but to his going fishing with the judge.

Across the differences that divide them, Jeff and the judge are akin. One black and the other white, one low and the other high in the hierarchy of their society, the two are counterparts, doubles of each other. When a suitor comes to visit Ellie May, the judge, who lives next door and is hidden behind some bushes, stages a dialogue between Jeff and himself designed to scare the suitor, trick him into running away so that Rome can take his place by Ellie May's side. In a gesture of complicity, Ford's camera moves to reveal that we have been hearing the judge alone playing both parts in this dialogue, taking turns as himself and as Jeff—which conveys a sense of his identification with Jeff. Far from being dumb, Jeff is a variant of that traditional figure of comedy, the clever servant, the *dolosus servus* or tricky slave of Roman comedy, Harlequin in the *commedia dell'arte* or Figaro in *The Barber of Seville*—except that Jeff is paired with his master the judge, who is himself something of a Harlequin or Figaro scheming on behalf of the young couple, something of a trickster giving the affairs of society a turn for the better. At the same time that he represents the law, the judge partakes of the resistance to the law, the incipient anarchy, represented by Jeff. It's that dash of anarchy that makes the judge's rhetoric successful. His opponent's is a rhetoric shackled by decorum and convention. The judge's is a rhetoric that takes liberties, that doesn't break the law but doesn't play strictly by the rules. It's the rhetoric of a trickster.

Will Rogers and Stepin Fetchit are very good together, both in *Judge Priest* and in their next film with Ford, *Steamboat Round the Bend* (1935), which was made just before Rogers's death in a plane crash. With the room to improvise they enjoyed under Ford's direction, the two actors palpably had a good time playing off each other—surprising each other, as Fetchit put it in a newspaper interview at the time. And more than "a remarkable harmony of acting styles," as Joseph McBride has described it, the rapport between Fetchit and Rogers— who was himself part Cherokee and quite proud of it—represents a rapport between the races, a harmony bringing black and white together, albeit within a hierarchy that places white above black.

The harmony may be all very well, but the hierarchy is not, and the harmony may be taken as a justification of the hierarchy. *Judge Priest* may plausibly be looked upon as an apology for a society that, while relegating blacks to an inferior position, allows individuals of different races to get along together and even to develop a warm rapport with one another. Stanley Kramer's liberal drama of the civil-rights era, *The Defiant Ones* (1958), is about two escaped convicts chained together, one white (Tony Curtis) and the other black (Sidney Poitier), who start out hating each other but in the end come to form a bond of human fellowship. *Judge Priest* starts where *The Defiant Ones* ends: the judge and Jeff form a bond of human fellowship when they go fishing together. And Ford shows happening naturally within society what Kramer can only imagine happening in extreme circumstances outside society. Kramer removes his characters from society so that the racial problem can be solved by their coming to terms with each other as individuals. Like other liberals, he assumes that racism is nothing but the belief that persons of another race are humanly inferior, so that the recognition of a common humanity will serve to dispel it. Tony Curtis's racist in *The Defiant Ones* is Southern white trash. Judge Priest is a better type of Southerner yet he's not exempt from the racism of his milieu. Admirable though he is personally, his unquestioned privilege as a white man can only be called racist (I don't use the term as an insult, merely as a description). He's a more interesting portrait of a racist precisely because he's a sympathetic figure: racism is not confined to the obviously reprehensible. (Nor, of course, is it confined to the South: none of us is exempt from the racism of our milieu.) Judge Priest is no bigot—he doesn't believe that blacks are humanly inferior. He has an easy human affinity with them. As individuals he and Jeff have no problem, and they cannot solve the racial problem as individuals. The problem is plain to see—on account of their race blacks are socially inferior.

The judge relates to them as a good master relates to his servants. The problem is social, and removing the characters from society is not a way of solving it but of avoiding it. If *Judge Priest* is an apology for a racist society, it's an apology that doesn't dissemble the racism of the society. It puts its finger on the problem even though it leaves it unsolved.

Judge Priest contained a scene in which the judge saves Jeff from a lynching —a triumph of rhetoric against force, bearing out Cicero's claims for the civilizing power of eloquence—but the studio (Fox) cut out the scene for fear of displeasing audiences in the South. All that remains is a mention of it the judge makes in an exchange with Jeff. Planning his strategy for the last day of Gillis's trial, the judge asks Jeff if he can play "Dixie" on his harmonica. Jeff says yes and adds he can also play "Marching through Georgia." He's taunting the judge with "Marching through Georgia," which, as Jeff well knows, is a tune of liberation for blacks but also a reminder for Southern whites of defeat and devastation by Sherman's invading army. "I got you out of one lynching," says the judge as the scene fades out. "Catch you playing 'Marching through Georgia,' I'll join the lynching." This exchange makes clear that Jeff is no fool. From the moment the judge asks him, he's quite aware that his playing "Dixie" is an accommodation to the racism of the society in which he lives. "Dixie" is the tune of the milieu in which he was nearly lynched, and he brings up "Marching through Georgia" as a counter tune. Both Jeff and the judge know, and know the other knows, that something very serious is being alluded to. Yet their exchange is humorous. If it were not, Jeff might indeed have been lynched to the tune of "Dixie" for playing "Marching through Georgia." Comedy helps. Treating the world humorously doesn't do away with its wrongs, but it serves to ameliorate and conciliate. It doesn't erase the difference between Jeff and the judge, but it allows for a certain equality between them. It's the wisdom of comedy that the two of them share that enables the harmony they enjoy together.

Will Rogers was one of the most popular Americans of his time. More than an actor, a top box-office attraction in the movies, he was a figure on the national scene, heard on radio and read in daily newspapers, even talked about as a presidential candidate. Many people identified themselves with him. Or he identified himself with them: he was popular as a populist, homespun and down-to-earth, a figure of the common man speaking common sense. Identification, as Kenneth Burke has argued, is central to the workings of rhetoric. Persuasion by a speaker, a picture, a work of fiction, comes about largely through identification. And identification with a speaker or a depicted character, an emotion or a perspective on things, is elicited in the audience largely through prior identifications made by the speaker—as when, in Burke's example, a politician says to an audience of farmers, "I was a farm boy myself"—or by the picture or work of fiction. Like the politician speaking to the farmers, Will Rogers identified with his audience before his audience identified with him. And *Judge Priest*, beginning with its title—and with a shot preceding the titles, a head-on view of the judge addressing us and calling the court to order—identifies itself in various ways with its protagonist judge before we come to identify ourselves with him.

It may be said that every work makes an identification with its protagonist simply by making him or her the protagonist. But there are different degrees and different kinds of identification. Of course we identify with the hero, but if we didn't in some way identify with the villain, too, the conflict between them wouldn't have much dramatic force. It may also be said that every movie star calls forth the audience's identification, but surely people don't identify themselves with Greta Garbo or Cary Grant in the same way they identify with Will Rogers. The identification Ford makes with Rogers's Judge Priest—I don't mean Ford the actual person but Ford the implied author of the movie, the governing intelligence we sense behind the camera—is especially strong and of a special kind. A governing intelligence dramatized in front of the camera, Judge Priest is not only the protagonist: the way he presides over the movie identifies him with the author or director.

To the rhetoric of a film or play, the means by which drama sways its audience, the actors are usually central. In this film Will Rogers is unusually so. When the judge vacates the bench under pressure from the prosecutor, the rhetoric of hurt feelings he addresses to his audience in the courtroom is the film's rhetoric as well, addressed to us through the actor commanding our attention. After asking another judge to take his place, our protagonist leaves the courtroom, and we see him in long shot from behind, darkly framed by the door as he puts on his hat and goes down the steps toward the sunlit town square in the background. It's a lovely shot that Ford holds on the screen in a felt gesture of sympathy for the judge. With as much sincerity as the judge exhibited in the courtroom performance that this shot brings to a conclusion, the film's visual rhetoric is here identified with the judge's rhetoric. This identification with Judge Priest isn't subjective. It's not an identification with his individual point of view: rather we see him from the collective point of view of his audience in the courtroom turning to look at him as he departs. We are identified with that audience, are as moved by his performance as they are, and share their lingering last look at the judge we and they feel shouldn't be departing. The emphasis isn't so much on how the judge himself feels as on how he's made his audience feel. It's an identification with the judge's rhetoric fittingly assuming the perspective of those he has affected.

In another scene the film makes a more subjective identification with its presiding figure. After the feigned dialogue with Jeff succeeds in scaring away Ellie May's suitor, the judge goes up alone to his darkened bedroom and looks out the window, and, in a point-of-view shot through his eyes, we see Rome and Ellie May down in the garden. The sight of the young couple he has contrived to bring together reminds the judge of his own youth, and when again he looks out the window and again we see through his eyes, a ghostly image from the past takes over the present, and in Rome and Ellie May's place we see an apparition of the judge as a young man beside the young woman he married. The judge lights a candle that illuminates the portrait of his dead wife and children on his bedroom wall, and his reflection appears on the glass over the portrait, like a ghost from the present over the imprinted image of the past, as he starts talking to his wife: "It's been a long time, honey, since . . . you and the . . . babies . . . went away." This may be the most moving of the several scenes in Ford's films enacting a conversation with the dead. Will Rogers is wonderful. With barely contained emotion—emotion made more affecting by the attempt to contain it—the judge tells his dead wife about his nephew's return and points out that Rome is just the same age their son would have been: "I guess it's . . . Rome coming home . . . what makes it seem more lonesome than . . . ever around here." Not wanting to show himself in this mood in front of his wife, he changes the subject. Gazing with a smile at the portrait on the wall, he tells her that the fellow who "enlarged that tintype . . . sure did a pretty job . . . I wish you could see it, honey." Noticing a blemish in the oval frame, however, he disparages the fellow who "put that gilt on there" and promises to "get that fixed" as he blows out the candle and leaves the room to continue the conversation in the cemetery.

In a move of identification with the character, sentiment in this scene is allowed to take over from comedy, the judge's personal, private sentiment, which the film enters into and shares with us. When his feelings are getting too personal, too painful for him in the privacy of his bedroom, the judge moves to the more public space of the cemetery. There, sitting by her grave, he still has a private conversation with his wife, but about more public matters: "People are funny, honey . . . always got their eyes set on something"—Rome on Ellie May, Rome's mother on the prosecutor's daughter she wants for her son, the prosecutor on the judge's job—"some of them are going to be disappointed." The judge puffs on his pipe and talks about the honeysuckle he smells. Then the film cuts to a more distant view, and from behind a tree at

screen center near the judge's wife's grave, Bob Gillis appears carrying a bou-
quet of flowers, the camera panning with him as he walks toward another
grave. Cut to a frontal view of Gillis as he reaches the grave he came to visit
and stands over it; cut to an analogous frontal view of the judge watching and
reporting to his wife, whose grave from this angle seems to blend with the tree
rising beside it, now at the edge of the screen framing the view like an outgrowth of her spirit. Cut back to Gillis, who bends down with his offering of
flowers; cut back to the judge, who informs his wife as the scene fades out—
and informs us, like a narrator entrusted by the film to fill us in—that the grave
Gillis came to visit is Ellie May's mother's. An identification is made here
between the judge and Gillis. The men each visiting a woman's grave, the
loner Gillis and the lonesome judge are joined together in the community of
their privacy. In the bedroom the film's identification with the judge brought
us into community with his privacy. In the more public space of the cemetery
the judge's privacy connects with another's, the identification with the judge
opens out into an identification between him and Gillis, and the community
of privacy links up with the life of the community.

The judge's personal story harbors sadness, yet out in the community he's
a hero of comedy. The comedy is shaded by the sadness, by the recognition
that all's not quite well even though it ends well enough. Nowhere is the film's
identification with its protagonist more evident than in the way the judge
arranges the happy ending. The reverend's testimony to the accompaniment
of "Dixie" that wins the day in court and wraps up the plot is a "spectacle," as
McBride writes, "stage-managed by Judge Priest, serving as the director's onscreen surrogate." Here as previously in the film, Judge Priest concurs with
Demosthenes and Cicero that in rhetoric what counts the most is delivery, the
speaker's performance before an audience—except that previously the judge
was the speaker, the performer of his rhetoric, and here he's the director of
the performance. Allowed by the sitting judge to talk without interruption, the
reverend becomes the narrator of a flashback illustrating in images the story
he tells, with his face superimposed as a vignette, an unusual device that
enhances our identification with the audience in the courtroom: we see the
face before them and at the same time see the images he evokes in their
minds. More than they, however, we're aware that behind the reverend as narrator stands the judge as director, whose arranging hand in these proceedings
we're better placed to recognize. We may be swayed as they are by the judge's
rhetoric, but our response is qualified by the irony that comes from seeing it
as rhetoric—seeing the judge giving Jeff the cue to start the music, seeing the
black ensemble playing "Dixie" out in the street—the amused irony of unde-

ceived comedy. Crowning touch of the judge's rhetoric, "Dixie" accompanies not only the reverend's words in the courtroom but also the images rendering his narrative on the screen: it becomes part of the film's own rhetoric, identified with the judge's and acknowledged like the judge's to be a manipulation. The film's close identification with the judge and what he represents—the good and the not so good, the humaneness of his character and the racism of his milieu—is combined with the distance of comedy.

Every society has its hierarchy. A society pledged to equality—such as the United States or the old Soviet Union—may want to deny or dissemble this, but a hierarchy is nonetheless in place. Comedy disturbs hierarchy. It brings down the high and gives play to the low. It recognizes the injustices of hierarchy and holds them up to laughter. Jeff and his fellow blacks playing "Dixie" at the climax of *Judge Priest* humorously declare the injustice of their situation, the fact that the Confederate glory whose tune they sing for their supper rests on the backs of their race. But the laughter of comedy carries another recognition—the recognition of limits. Comedy knows that society harbors wrongs, but it knows, too, that there are limits to their righting, and its laughter is both a mockery and an acceptance. Comedy says that society admits improvement only up to a point, and that beyond that its wrongs are to be lived with. The endings of comedy may be happy, but part of the reconciliation they bring about is a reconciliation to injustice.

Judge Priest is a figure of tolerance. We're able to appreciate this despite being unable to see what must have been his finest moment, the rescue of a black man from a lynch mob, omitted by a studio as timorous as the judge is courageous. He succeeds in overcoming the social prejudice against Ellie May and against the loner Gillis, who turns out to be her father. He has a kinship with Jeff and a genuine sense of fellowship with the blacks in the community. But he does not attempt—there is nothing he could do, within the terms of his society—to change the racial hierarchy that keeps blacks in an inferior position. He is reconciled to that injustice. We of course are not, and we may object to a comedy proposing such a reconciliation. But let's not indulge in that easiest of self-congratulations, a feeling of superiority toward the past. How many films can we put beside *Judge Priest* that have given us such a vivid portrayal of an interracial community and of blacks as integral to that community? *Do the Right Thing* (1989) comes to mind as one, but I can't think of many others. The blacks in *Judge Priest* are inferior socially but not humanly, and they're not token individuals but part of a living texture of social interrelationships. They are at the bottom of a racist hierarchy, it is true—the film knows that as well as we do, even though, like its judge protagonist, it takes no stand against it. *Judge*

Priest sees the flaws of the society it depicts, and if it asks us to accept them, it's not because it approves but because it also sees that, under the circumstances, there is nothing else to be done. Such is the spirit of comedy. This is the way things are, not the way they should be. Under changed circumstances, it may be a different story. The happy endings of comedy promise a better society, and the change for the better that concludes *Judge Priest* leaves open the possibility that further changes for the better may come about in the future.

Plato condemned rhetoric in terms of an ideal society where truth and reason would prevail and embellishment could only get in the way. In such a society—which few of us would want to live in—there would be no politics. Cicero defended rhetoric in terms of practical politics, but he still idealized the truth of eloquence. Ford shares neither idealism. His comedy of rhetoric takes place in the realm of the imperfect. It recognizes that society has flaws and that rhetoric must work with the flaws of society. Its laughter both exposes and accepts those flaws. We laugh at the discrepancy between rhetoric and truth at the same time we cheer rhetoric's ability to help the cause of truth. Things are not perfect, but within the limits of the possible they turn out well. Like politics, rhetoric is the art of the possible. It must build its persuasions on the beliefs of society, which it may bend to its purposes but cannot afford to break, or else it may succeed as reason but will fail as rhetoric. It's the wisdom of comedy to celebrate the possible without making it into something grander. Cynicism about politics—and about rhetoric—is widespread in our society. Ford's comedy of rhetoric—and of politics—is not cynical. Its undeceived celebration of the possible, the change for the better that negotiates an imperfect situation for the best, counters a cynicism that by disdaining politics lets things remain unchanged.

2004

A. O. Scott

A. O. Scott (b. 1966), *The New York Times'* senior film critic, received that post largely on the basis of his uniformly intelligent and balanced book reviews, and since then he has demonstrated a knack for writing equally well about movies on a daily deadline schedule. As a film critic, Scott keeps his bookish cultivation in the background, preferring, if anything, to make whimsical references to popular culture, especially the animated cartoon shows he watches as a parent at home. With a rare (for a critic) good nature that wears well over time, he generously conveys his enthusiasm for pictures that have at least some good things in them rather than trolling sourly for their flaws. Here, in Scott's deft handling of the controversies surrounding Mel Gibson's *The Passion of the Christ*, we see him confronting, defusing, and refusing to indulge in the hot rhetorical froth engendered on both sides by the movie, while taking its artistic measure. In his analysis of *Sideways'* popularity, he turns a knowing searchlight on the sometimes-narcissistic practice of film criticism.

◆

Good and Evil Locked in Violent Showdown

There is a prophetic episode of *The Simpsons* in which the celebrity guest star Mel Gibson, directing and starring in a remake of *Mr. Smith Goes to Washington*, enlists the help of Homer Simpson, who represents the public taste (or lack of it). Homer persuades Mr. Gibson to change the picture's ending, replacing James Stewart's populist tirade with an action sequence, a barrage of righteous gunfire that leaves the halls of Congress strewn with corpses. The audience flees the theater in disgust. I thought of Homer more than once, with an involuntary irreverence conditioned by many years of devotion to *The Simpsons*, as Mr. Gibson presented his new movie, *The Passion of the Christ*, to carefully selected preview audiences across the land, making a few last-minute cuts, and then taking to the airwaves to promote and defend the film. It opens today nationwide.

Given the Crucifixion story, Mr. Gibson did not need to change the ending.

The Passion of the Christ is so relentlessly focused on the savagery of Jesus' final hours that this film seems to arise less from love than from wrath, and to succeed more in assaulting the spirit than in uplifting it. Mr. Gibson has constructed an unnerving and painful spectacle that is also, in the end, a depressing one. It is disheartening to see a film made with evident and abundant religious conviction that is at the same time so utterly lacking in grace.

Mr. Gibson has departed radically from the tone and spirit of earlier American movies about Jesus, which have tended to be palatable (if often extremely long) Sunday school homilies designed to soothe the audience rather than to terrify or inflame it.

His version of the Gospels is harrowingly violent; the final hour of *The Passion of the Christ* essentially consists of a man being beaten, tortured and killed in graphic and lingering detail. Once he is taken into custody, Jesus (Jim Caviezel) is cuffed and kicked and then, much more systematically, flogged, first with stiff canes and then with leather whips tipped with sharp stones and glass shards. By the time the crown of thorns is pounded onto his head and the cross loaded onto his shoulders, he is all but unrecognizable, a mass of flayed and bloody flesh, barely able to stand, moaning and howling in pain.

The audience's desired response to this spectacle is not revulsion, but something like the cowering, quivering awe manifested by Mary (Maia Morgenstern), Mary Magdalen (Monica Bellucci) and a few sensitive Romans and Jerusalemites as they force themselves to watch. Disgust and awe are not, when you think about it, so far apart, and in Mr. Gibson's vision one is a route to the other.

By rubbing our faces in the grisly reality of Jesus' death and fixing our eyes on every welt and gash on his body, this film means to make literal an event that the Gospels often treat with circumspection and that tends to be thought about somewhat abstractly. Look, the movie seems to insist, when we say he died for our sins, *this* is what we mean.

A viewer, particularly one who accepts the theological import of the story, is thus caught in a sadomasochistic paradox, as are the disciples for whom Jesus, in a flashback that occurs toward the end, promises to lay down his life. The ordinary human response is to wish for the carnage to stop, an impulse that seems lacking in the dissolute Roman soldiers and the self-righteous Pharisees. (More about them shortly.) But without their fathomless cruelty, the story would not reach its necessary end. To halt the execution would thwart divine providence and refuse the gift of redemption.

Anyway, this is a film review, not Sunday school. The paradox of wishing something horrible to stop even as you want it to continue has as much to do with moviegoing as with theology. And Mr. Gibson, either guilelessly or ingeniously, has exploited the popular appetite for terror and gore for what he and his allies see as a higher end. The means, however, are no different from those used by virtuosos of shock cinema like Quentin Tarantino and Gasper Noé, who subjected Ms. Bellucci to such grievous indignity in *Irréversible*. Mr. Gibson is temperamentally a more stolid, less formally adventurous filmmaker, but he is no less a connoisseur of violence, and it will be amusing to see some of the same scolds who condemned Mr. Tarantino's *Kill Bill: Vol. 1* sing the praises of *The Passion of the Christ*.

Mr. Gibson, from the moment he began speaking publicly about this project, emphasized his desire to make his *Passion* as realistic as possible. To that end the dialogue is in Aramaic and a dialect of Latin, which takes some getting used to but which dispenses with the stilted, awkward diction that afflicts so many biblical epics. The absence of identifiable movie stars (with the exception of Ms. Bellucci, who comports herself with fitting modesty) also adds an element of verisimilitude. But the style and tone of *The Passion* are far from what is ordinarily meant by realism.

The first part, which takes place in the murk and gloom of night (shot by the superb cinematographer Caleb Deschanel), has the feel of a horror movie. As Jesus prays in the garden of Gethsemane, the camera tiptoes around him like a stalker, and John Debney's score is a high-toned creep show of menacing orchestral undertones and spine-jabbing choral effects. A slithery, effeminate Satan (played, the end credits reveal, by a woman named Rosalinda Celentano) slinks around like something in a Wes Craven nightmare, and Judas, reeling from his betrayal, is menaced by demon children with pointy teeth and milky eyes.

When daylight dawns, the mood shifts from horror-movie suspense to slasher-film dread. Throughout, Mr. Gibson lays on Mr. Debney's canned sublimity with the heaviest possible hand, and he indulges in equally unsubtle visual and aural effects. Judas's 30 pieces of silver fly through the air in slow motion, and the first nail enters Jesus' palm with a thwack that must have taken hours of digital tweaking to articulate. The thuddingly emphatic storytelling (along with the ancient languages) makes the acting almost beside the point, though it is hard not to be impressed by Mr. Caviezel's endurance.

The only psychological complexity in this tableau of goodness and villainy belongs to Pontius Pilate and his wife, Claudia, played by two very capable actors, Hristo Naumov Shopov and Claudia Gerini, who I hope will become more familiar to American audiences.

Is *The Passion of the Christ* anti-Semitic? I thought you'd never ask. To my eyes it did not seem to traffic explicitly or egregiously in the toxic iconography of historical Jew hatred, but more sensitive viewers may disagree. The Pharisees, in their tallit and beards, are certainly shown as a sinister and inhumane group, and the mob they command is full of howling, ugly rage. But this on-screen villainy does not seem to exceed what can be found in the source material.

Mr. Gibson a few weeks ago reportedly expunged an especially provocative line of dialogue that referred to the Jews: "His blood be on us, and on our children." That line comes from the Book of Matthew, and it would take a revisionist to remove every trace of controversy and intolerance from a story that rests squarely on the theological boundary separating Christianity from Judaism.

That Mr. Gibson did not attempt to transcend these divisions may be regrettable, but to condemn *The Passion of the Christ* for its supposed bigotry is to miss its point and to misstate its problems. The troubling implications of the film do not arise primarily from its religious agenda: an extreme, traditionalist Roman Catholicism that has not prevented *The Passion* from resonating, oddly enough, with many evangelical Protestants.

What makes the movie so grim and ugly is Mr. Gibson's inability to think beyond the conventional logic of movie narrative. In most movies—certainly in most movies directed by or starring Mr. Gibson—violence against the innocent demands righteous vengeance in the third act, an expectation that Mr. Gibson in this case whips up and leaves unsatisfied.

On its own, apart from whatever beliefs a viewer might bring to it, *The Passion of the Christ* never provides a clear sense of what all of this bloodshed was for, an inconclusiveness that is Mr. Gibson's most serious artistic failure. The Gospels, at least in some interpretations, suggest that the story ends in forgiveness. But such an ending seems beyond Mr. Gibson's imaginative capacities. Perhaps he suspects that his public prefers terror, fury and gore. Maybe Homer Simpson was right after all.

2004

The Most Overrated Film of the Year

In the next few weeks you will surely read—perhaps even in the pages of this newspaper—a great many articles about the Oscar race, and about how this year, for various esoteric reasons, no clear front-runner has emerged in the major award categories. (As the archive of earlier, similar articles suggests, this often appears to be the case, but for all I know, this year it may actually be true.) In the meantime, though, the movie critics of America, a collection of cussed individualists and ornery contrarians (some of them my best friends) have expressed themselves with unusual unanimity. At least as far as most critics are concerned, whether making their own personal 10-best lists or voting in their regional awards-giving groups, the movie of the year is *Sideways*.

As of this writing, *Sideways*, Alexander Payne's funny-sad story of two buddies on a ragged wine-tasting tour in central California, has been named best picture by critics' groups in New York (both print and online), Toronto, Los Angeles, Boston, San Francisco, Chicago and Florida. If you take into account the acting, writing and directing prizes the critics' groups confer, Mr. Payne's film has won more than 40 awards, four times as many as any other contender. It is perched atop the annual Film Comment survey of 80 prominent English-language critics. According to a frequently updated chart at moviecitynews.com, it has also appeared on more year-end top 10 lists than any other picture.

Now this is very good news for Mr. Payne, a smart and adventurous filmmaker (his other movies are *Citizen Ruth*, *Election* and *About Schmidt*), for his longtime writing partner, Jim Taylor, and for the cast of *Sideways*: Thomas Haden Church, Sandra Oh, Virginia Madsen and especially, Paul Giamatti, who plays Miles, a failed novelist treading the narrow boundary between wine connoisseurship and alcoholism. The movie is well written and flawlessly acted, funny and observant (if also, at two hours and three minutes, a bit long for a four-person comedy). It also seems to me, through no fault of its own—indeed, through its real and modest virtues—to have become the most drastically overrated movie of 2004.

I don't just mean that the critical praise is out of proportion to the quality of the film. While that seems to me to be true—beyond the movie's occasionally slack pacing, I would cite a coy ambivalence about its main characters as its principal flaw—it would most likely be true in any case. The accumulated passions of people who are paid to have opinions about movies can sometimes place an undue burden of expectation on both the objects of those passions and the readers to whom they are communicated. Each of us, in proclaiming something or another the best movie of the year, is giving voice to a personal enthusiasm, and also tugging at your sleeve, as if to say, "Hey, be sure to check this one out." If 10 or 40 of us—in packs and phalanxes and carefully polled battalions—are saying the same thing, you may start to feel badgered and beleaguered, and by the time you get around to seeing the movie in question —whatever its merits—you may be more inclined to shrug than to swoon. But the risk of inflated expectations is one critics should always be willing to take, since if we hedged or soft-pedaled our opinions, we would hardly be doing our jobs. Overpraising good work is surely a more forgivable sin than underpraising it.

Still, the reaction to *Sideways* is worth noting, less because it isn't quite as good as everyone seems to be saying it is than because the near-unanimous praise of it reveals something about the psychology of critics, as distinct from our taste. Miles, the movie's hero, has been variously described as a drunk, a wine snob, a sad sack and a loser, but it has seldom been mentioned that he is also, by temperament if not by profession, a critic.

The contrast between him and his friend Jack is partly the difference between an uptight, insecure epicurean and a swinging, self-deluding hedonist, but it is more crucially the difference between a sensibility that subjects every experience to judgment and analysis and a personality happy to accept whatever the moment offers. When they taste wine, Jack is apt to say "tastes good to me," and leave it at that, whereas Miles tends not only to be more exacting in his judgment ("quaffable but not transcendent," which is about how I feel about *Sideways*), but also more prone to narrate, to interpret—to find a language for the most subtle and ephemeral sensations of his palate.

This makes him, among other things, an embodiment of the critical disposition, and one of the unusual things about *Sideways* is that, in the end, it defends this attitude rather than dismissing it. Yes, the film pokes fun at Miles's flights of oenophile rhetoric—all that business about asparagus and "nutty Edam cheese"—but it defies the usual Hollywood anti-intellectualism in acknowledging that, rather than diminishing the fun of drinking, approaching wine with a measure of knowledge and sophistication can enhance its pleasures. There is more to true appreciation than just knowing what you like.

In one of the film's best-written and most beautifully played scenes, Miles launches into a paean to the pinot noir grape that is also, evidently, an account of himself. Criticism always contains an element of autobiography, and it is not much of a leap to suggest that more than a few critics have seen themselves in *Sideways*. (Several have admitted as much.) This is not to suggest that white, middle-aged men with a taste for alcohol are disproportionately represented in the ranks of working movie reviewers; plausible as such a notion may be, I don't have the sociological data to support it just yet. But the self-pity and solipsism that are Miles's less attractive (and frequently most prominent) traits represent the underside of the critical temperament; his morbid sensitivity may be an occupational hazard we all face.

In *Sideways*, a good many critics see themselves, and it is only natural that we should love what we see. Not that critics are the only ones, by any means, but the affection that we have lavished on this film has the effect of emphasizing the narrowness of its vision, and perhaps our own. It both satirizes and affirms a cherished male fantasy: that however antisocial, self-absorbed and downright unattractive a man may be, he can always be rescued by the love of a good woman. (What's in it for her is less clear.)

There is nothing wrong with entertaining this conceit, and *Sideways* does it artfully enough. And of course, the critics respond to other stories as well. Or do we? For the most part, the groups that did not choose *Sideways*—the Village Voice Poll, for example, and the Washington film critics—selected *Before Sunset* and *Eternal Sunshine of the Spotless Mind*, both variations on the theme of a moody, cerebral fellow graced by the kind of romantic love he probably doesn't believe in and can hardly be said to deserve. Film critics, for our part, clearly have plenty of self-love to go around.

2005

Manohla Dargis

In successive stints as film critic for *The Village Voice*, *LA Weekly*, *Los Angeles Times*, and now *The New York Times*, Manohla Dargis has risen to the top of the movie reviewing Establishment in fairly short order, without compromising her youthfully savvy print persona and her informed appreciation of the avant-garde. Using a vibrant prose style that sends off verbal sparks, she dives into her insightful critiques, exposing treacle, and demolishing stereotypes with a quick, slashing wit. She is especially sensitive to backlash treatments of women. At the same time, she is fascinated with the primal pleasures of cinema: glamour, visual panache, and kinetic movement. Here she presents the best possible case, sympathetic and forcefully articulate, for Wes Anderson's cultish *The Royal Tenenbaums*, offers a funny critique in verse of a Dr. Seuss film, and pinpoints the complex meta-genre allure of David Cronenberg's *A History of Violence*.

◆

High Hopes

Wes Anderson is an authentic original—an eccentric and heretical talent. Now 31, he has directed only a handful of films, including an extended version of a short called *Bottle Rocket* and two other features, the oddball romance *Rushmore* and now, *The Royal Tenenbaums*, about a family of former prodigies. As with the earlier films, the new one is funny enough to be taken for a comedy, but there's a deep vein of melancholia to its drollery, an ineluctable air of sadness. Written, as all Anderson's films are, with his close friend, the actor Owen Wilson, the film revisits the same passions that animate the earlier work—friendship, innocence, love, ennui—this time through adult children who, having never got over growing up, live in a haze of disappointment. Their pathos is that while their genius has faded, they can never succumb to ordinariness—the grind from 9 to 5, the right girl or boy to love—which is also their glory. Erstwhile genius has turned them into tragedians of their own existence, however farcical or quotidian, yet that early promise has been its own sort of benediction. Even at their most woebegone, the Tenenbaums live in radiant hope that their lives can again be something other, something different, something better.

This is no easy thing, either for an individual to live or for an artist to convey, particularly without pity or condescension. It's impossible if you don't love your characters as Anderson does—generously, and with aching tenderness. For all their mistakes, missteps and spasms of outrageous narcissism, his gentle misfits remain human, never more than when at their worst: *The Royal Tenenbaums* begins with Etheline Tenenbaum (Anjelica Huston) asking her husband, Royal (Gene Hackman), to move out of the house. Royal breaks the bad news to the couple's three young children—two boys, Chas and Richie, and a girl named Margot—while seated at the head of the family's vast dining table. Framed against a swirl of red velvet wallpaper, his ubiquitous cigarette clamped in its holder, Royal comes across less like a grieving husband and father than like a chief operating officer who's not only accepted the truth of a losing proposition, but moved on already. "It doesn't," he admits with a shrug, "look good." "Was it our fault?" asks one of the kids. "No," Royal answers, before dispensing a nonchalant twist of the knife: "Obviously we made certain sacrifices as a result of having children."

Wearing a toupee that curls around the top of his head like a sleeping wombat, Hackman makes a peculiar father, though he's realer than most movie dads—meaner, too. The actor tends to play men who run cold or blistering hot, and who often embrace both extremes at once, which helps to explain why so many of them shiver with menace no matter what temperature they're running. Hackman's Royal may not be a monster, at least by the child-rearing standards of the late-1970s backdrop against which the story is launched, but he's oblivious, careless on the edge of cruelty. That Royal doesn't sentimentalize his three children, and wouldn't begin to know how, means that he also doesn't condescend to them. For better and, often, for worse, he treats them like little adults, as equals—and sometimes, calamitously, as rivals. But all this fair play doesn't leave much room for kindness. Royal dismisses one of Margot's fledging theatrical efforts, then tries to bandage the wound with a lie that neither of them believes: "That's just one man's opinion." It's Margot's 11th birthday, and she's just received the gift of her own imperfection; it's a gift that will keep on giving.

In Anderson's first feature, also titled *Bottle Rocket* (1996), there's a scene in which the character played by Owen Wilson, Dignan, decides to risk imprisonment in order to save a downed colleague. Dignan and his friends have just failed, sensationally, to rob a cold-storage company. They didn't need the money, but they did need a reason to get up in the morning, a reason to feel special. Mostly, though, they needed one another. Dignan's friend (played by Owen's brother, Luke Wilson) tries to stop him from going back in the building, but he refuses: "They'll never catch me, man, 'cause I'm fuckin' innocent." He's caught, of course, but in doing so Dignan confirms his own freakish innocence, as well as his poignancy. In that instant he finds a reason for being, an escape hatch to a more perfect world, maybe even transcendence; he becomes, in other words, yet another American hopeful buoyed by the specter of his own promise. The moment may be fantasy, a reverie, but as with the Tenenbaum childhood, it glitters with possibility. In the new film, Owen Wilson returns, this time as Eli Cash, a friend of the Tenenbaum children who's spent his entire life wanting to be one of them. Now a famous writer of anguished Cormac McCarthy–style prose, Eli still yearns to be a Tenenbaum, to find a place where he can safely hide from the outside world. Like Dignan, he longs for a way out of the here and now.

Set in a gently fictionalized New York (the taxis are all heaps from the Gypsy Cab Co.), *The Royal Tenenbaums* unfolds primarily inside the family's sprawling brownstone, a warren of startling color, fanciful bibelots and objets trouvés. As in *The Magnificent Ambersons*, one of the story's touchstones (Salinger's Glass family is another), the house tells a crucial part of the story, first through the grandeur of its turrets (there's even a family flag), then 22 years later, after the children have grown, through its genteel dilapidation. By then, Royal is long gone and the children have scattered. Chas (Ben Stiller) is lost in his work; Richie (Luke Wilson) is literally adrift, a passenger on a transoceanic ship; back in the city, Margot (Gwyneth Paltrow) spends hours in a tub as her husband, Raleigh (Bill Murray), taps on the locked bathroom door. Each of the children has spectacularly failed, and failure has sealed them in solipsism: Margot enjoyed early success as a playwright but soon fizzled, while Richie went from tennis champion to burnout during one calamitous match. Entrepreneur Chas has endured a more brutal comeuppance: He lost his wife in a plane crash. Always the straightest Tenenbaum, he has become a neurotic protector of his sons, to the point where he can no longer distinguish between genuine peril and the bumps of everyday life.

Chas eventually figures out the difference, but only after he returns to the Tenenbaum home and surrenders to adulthood. In *Rushmore*, there's another prodigy who earns his comeuppance, losing a woman he loves to his surrogate father (Murray again); but in losing, he becomes the very child he'd desperately tried to outgrow. In Anderson's films, adults and children rarely figure out how to play the roles that age has assigned them, and who can blame them? In *The Royal Tenenbaums* the prodigies have become disappointed adults because they're stuck in the dreams of childhood—stuck there precisely because the dreams were so seductive. We first meet the kids through a series of fast, funny montage sequences: There's Margot in fur and kohl eyeliner reading Chekhov and writing, Chas wheeling and dealing in Brooks Brothers, Richie racking up trophies. The sense of detail in these sequences is beautiful and fastidious, recalling the obsessiveness you sometimes see in children's play, in the fantastic worlds they create from glass animals and figurines. But as the silky-voiced narrator (Alec Baldwin) guides us through these dioramas of precocious talent, it becomes increasingly evident that the museum is also something of a mausoleum.

It happens to all of us, the fall from grace. Much depends on what happens next, naturally, but much depends on how you remember it—as comedy, tragedy or, as Anderson has, both. The world of *The Royal Tenenbaums* initially seems as unreal and at times almost as precious as that inside a glass paperweight. And it's clear from the sheer verve—the giddiness, even—with which he films the children's early years that Anderson is as comfortable tucked inside his meticulousness as the Tenenbaums are tucked inside the family home—he's more comfortable in a world of his own making than with the world beyond. But, like Chas, Richie and Margot, he's starting to shake things up. By the time the children are grown, Anderson has loosened his style, almost as if he, too, were finally free of the constraints of so much early perfection. The framing seems less fastidious, the camera movements more gestural, while the vapor of self-congratulation that perfumed the Tenenbaums' childhood has been blown away by the truth of adult lives in all their pain and new-found grace. In a film that verges on greatness, it is a sign of terrific faith, as well as of Anderson's promise as a director, that when one of the characters in *The Royal Tenenbaums* wears hospital pajamas after a detour into grief, the words over his heart read "recovery area."

2001

Not-So-Nice Kitty

Why oh why did they make it like that,
oh why did they ruin *The Cat in the Hat*?

A sweet silly story with a girl and a boy,
the book was created for wordplay and joy.
The artist behind it was a Geisel called Seuss,
a genius cartoonist and baby-boom Mother Goose.
The movie takes place in a bright-colored town,
a twee little burg unblighted by frowns.
The girl and the boy are quiet as slugs,
when along comes a Cat dressed up in a rug.

The Cat is played by the comic Mike Myers,
a zany Canuck whom I tend to admire.
Myers shambles in like the Cowardly Lion,
but Bert Lahr never stooped to a studio tie-in.
Soon a tale of daydreaming tots,
becomes a fiasco riddled with rot.
No one in Hollywood likes humor that's clean,
so the jokes in this film are lowdown and mean.
When the Cat sees a mom who's hotter than Hades,
his hat swells up to the size of a Mercedes.
A joke about poop is ever so limp,
and the gag with the hoe is fit for a pimp.
It is fun to have fun with the MPAA,
but dirty is dirty and that's all that I'll say.
Thing One and Thing Two are creepy and crude,
they look like the critters from Cronenberg's brood.
When these Things run amok like a couple of ids,
there's simply no saving these home-alone kids.
As their bodacious mom who's too hot for the room,
Kelly Preston radiates va-va-va-voom.
Unlucky for her there's a guy named Quinn,
a bachelor type who really wants in.
Quinn is played by the Baldwin called Alec,
an actor whose presence is decidedly phallic.
Quinn eyeballs the mom with a notion to bed,
without him onboard the film would be dead.
If directing bad movies were a sin to confess,
Bo Welch would say oops for making this mess.
Critics are paid to suffer bad art,
no matter how icky it is from the start.
"So all we could do was to
Sit!
Sit!
Sit!
Sit!
And we did not like it.
Not one little bit."

(*With apologies to Theodor Geisel.*)

2003

Once Disaster Hits, It Seems Never to End

A masterpiece of indirection and pure visceral thrills, David Cronenberg's latest mindblower, *A History of Violence*, is the feel-good, feel-bad movie of the year. The story of a seemingly average American family almost undone by cataclysmic violence, the film takes place in a surreal and mercilessly brutal land, Anytown, U.S.A., that has been repeatedly soaked in blood only to be repeatedly washed clean. The great kick of the movie—or rather, its great kick in the gut—comes from Mr. Cronenberg's refusal to let us indulge in movie violence without paying a price. The man wants to make us suffer, exquisitely.

Mr. Cronenberg also wants us to have a good time, and it's this tension between cinematic pain and pleasure that helps make *A History of Violence* such a sensational moviegoing experience. The film, which hinges on an upstanding citizen and reluctant mystery man, Tom Stall (brilliantly played by Viggo Mortensen), takes it as an article of faith that we, the multiplex allegiant, have been long-reared on the ways and means, giddyups and brutalizing downs of the action movie. Decades of mainlining blockbusters have, for better or perhaps for worse, inured us to the image of bullet-chewed bodies and the pop-pop-pop of phony weapon fire. For the contemporary movie connoisseur, film death is now as cheap as it is familiar. To which Mr. Cronenberg quietly says, "Oh, yeah?"

Loosely adapted by Josh Olson from the 1997 graphic novel by John Wagner and Vince Locke, the film opens with two men exiting a motel room. The younger man (Greg Bryk) is dressed in a T-shirt and jeans; the older (Stephen McHattie) wears the black suit of a funeral director and a Beelzebub Vandyke. Although it's day, probably morning, each also wears the scowls and sagging expressions of men who have long been hard at work. And back to work they go: the older man heads to the motel office to check out while the younger drives their late-model convertible a few dusty yards. When the older man returns, he sends the younger one to fetch water. They're almost ready to hit the road, but, first, there is killing to do.

There is a lot of killing in *A History of Violence*, none more troubling than the first murder, which takes place inside that motel office turned charnel house. In its outrageous brutality, this inauguration into the spectacle—and entertainment—of death signals that Mr. Cronenberg's film isn't the usual bloody cinematic joy ride. There is, it soon emerges, nothing usual or routine about *A History of Violence*, which at first plays like a stock genre picture (or an outtake from *Pulp Fiction*), only to grow progressively freakier and hair-raisingly nasty. A master of conflicting, contradictory moods, Mr. Cronenberg has a history of turning genre, particularly horror, inside out and upside down, and he applies his cool intelligence and prodigious craft to the action movie like a French deconstructionist moonlighting as John Woo.

The killers ultimately get theirs, as monsters almost always do in Hollywood movies, receiving their villainous comeuppance from a figure of outwardly impeccable rectitude and gentleness: Tom Stall. Happily married with a sexy, adoring wife, Edie (Maria Bello), and two charming children, the teenage Jack (Ashton Holmes) and a towheaded pipsqueak named Sarah (Heidi Hayes), Tom runs a diner straight off the yellowing cover of a *Saturday Evening Post* in a town as cozy and sleepy as one perched on an old studio back lot. Here, the townsfolk greet one another with a smile and a wave, and youngsters share ice cream sodas like Mickey and Judy. There isn't a Wal-Mart or McDonald's in sight—no boarded-up storefronts, no toxic waste dumps, no despair, no bums, no bad men.

Although the sign above the front door of Stall's promises "friendly service," these villains receive something altogether different when they enter the diner early one evening. In a furiously paced scene that tears a hole in both the character and the town's pacific façades, Mr. Cronenberg establishes that he can outgun Mr. Woo and then some with a sensationally choreographed shootout. The encounter leaves both desperados dead—Mr. Cronenberg lingers on one man's ripped away face for a few squirmingly uncomfortable seconds—and Tom is declared an "American hero." The media descends in short order as do three men (including Ed Harris) whose sunglasses, black town car and tough-guy accents suggest we're not in Kansas (or Hollywood) anymore, but somewhere north of David Lynch's *Mulholland Drive* and far west of Lars von Trier's *Dogville*.

Like both those films, *A History of Violence* explores the myth and meaning of America (or at least a representative facsimile) through its dreams, nightmares and compulsive frenzies. But where Mr. Lynch invariably imbues the violence in his films with eroticism, mixing in lipstick with the blood, and Mr. von Trier has recently let didacticism get the better of his ideas, Mr. Cronenberg plays it cool. He knows that movie violence turns us on: we kiss to the bang-bang. There's something undeniably exciting about Tom's heroic actions, so much so that they effectively produce a veritable contact high, first spurring his son to stand up to a bully and, a while later, inspiring some intensely rough sex that will leave his wife covered in abrasions. But there is something irredeemable and soul-killing here, too.

A History of Violence might have easily been called *A History of America*, but it would sell both Mr. Cronenberg's art and his purpose short to reduce this film to an ideology. While transparently set in small-town America (Ontario passing for Indiana), the sheer unreality of the hamlet initially makes it clear that this story is not taking place in the here and the now, but in a copy of the world that looks—wouldn't you know it—a lot like a movie. Mr. Cronenberg, a Canadian, is taking aim at this country, to be sure. But he is also taking aim at our violence-addicted cinema, those seductive, self-heroicizing self-justifications we sell to the world. Perversely, though, the more violent this film becomes—in time, the blood flows all the way to Philadelphia—the more real Tom and his family seem. He kills, therefore they are.

That sounds far grimmer or at least more relentlessly grim than this shrewd, agile, often bitingly funny film plays. Ornamented with ghoulish comedy (a "live bait" sign posted at a murder site) and superbly acted by all the principals, including, in a nice surprise, William Hurt, who delivers a beautiful showboat of a performance late in the film. *A History of Violence* finds Mr. Cronenberg at the top of his form. Few directors working today know more about the erotics of screen violence than this filmmaker, who can make your head spin and your pulse quicken with a single edit. Fewer directors still bother to acknowledge that the canard "it's only a movie" is not only an article of bad faith, but also a deceptively comforting one. Movies, Mr. Cronenberg understands, make meaning: they entertain, therefore we are.

2005

Stephanie Zacharek

Stephanie Zacharek is a senior writer on film for the web magazine *Salon* and one of the most respected and quoted web film critics. Earlier, she had written on film and music for *The Phoenix*. As the review below demonstrates, she is keenly alert to the way movies operate (sometimes discordantly) on our nervous systems and intellects, and she is willing to bring her own very personal, visceral responses to her analysis of watching a film. Like Pauline Kael, Zacharek uses as a starting-point the seductions of certain screen actors or directors—the elements that "grab" audiences and give movies their appeal—while exploring candidly the nagging doubts that may linger in the back of a veteran critic's mind.

◆

United 93

Paul Greengrass' *United 93* is a movie made with tremendous care, and with almost boundless sensitivity to persons living and dead. But just hours after seeing the picture, I'm finding it hard to care about Greengrass' integrity: I've never had a more excruciating moviegoing experience in my life, and as brilliantly crafted—and as adamantly unexploitive—as the picture is, it still leaves you wondering why it was made in the first place.

The movie's press notes suggest a number of explanations: In telling the story of the fourth plane to be hijacked on Sept. 11, 2001—en route from Newark, N.J., to San Francisco, it crashed in a field in Shanksville, Pa.— Greengrass wanted to commemorate the lives lost at the hands of Islamic terrorists on that day. He also wanted to map, in a very personal way, the emotional contours of a less-than-two-hour span in which the world changed drastically. But I went into *United 93* with a feeling of dread, and ultimately, I'm not sure Greengrass did much more than pluck at that dread with dogged, if scrupulous, persistence. I walked out of *United 93* feeling bereft and despondent; my stomach muscles had tensed into a seemingly immovable knot. But the picture didn't make me feel anything I hadn't fully expected to feel. Greengrass, a director I deeply respect, hadn't made a great movie (as he did in his portrayal of another real-life event, the superb 2002 film *Bloody Sunday*); he had simply fulfilled a prediction, and that isn't nearly enough.

Greengrass is an extraordinarily gifted filmmaker, and there are moments

in *United 93*, particularly at the beginning, where his craftsmanship is both subtle and admirable. As much as I wish I hadn't had to see *United 93*, I'd rather
see this material in Greengrass' hands than in those of almost any other filmmaker. For obvious reasons, the story of United Flight 93 demands a certain
amount of conjecture. Greengrass (who wrote the script as well as directed)
went about his research fastidiously and honorably, using information gleaned
from the 9/11 Commission Report but also relying heavily on interviews with
civilian and military personnel involved in the day's events. Greengrass also
spent a great deal of time interviewing the victims' families, learning what he
could from them about the hostages' last moments: Much of that information
came from the calls made by the victims, from cellphones and plane phones,
in the midst of the hijacking. Greengrass took great pains to reassure the victims' families that he'd get the story right—he has said that his goal was to
reach "a believable truth"—and for all my misgivings about *United 93*, his
respect for both the survivors and the victims is evident.

Greengrass cast mostly unknown actors in *United 93*. One exception is
Christian Clemenson as passenger Thomas E. Burnett Jr., who has appeared
on *Veronica Mars* as Abel Koontz. And some real-life figures, among them air-
traffic controllers and military personnel, appear as themselves. Perhaps most
notable is Ben Sliney, the manager of the Federal Aviation Administration's
operations command center in Herndon, Va. On Sept. 11, 2001, Sliney had just
been appointed to that position; it was his first day on the job, and his performance here suggests a masterly and controlled channeling of the feelings he
must have had as he faced this daylight-nightmare challenge: What must it be
like when your job is to respond, calmly and efficiently, to the unspeakable?

Greengrass has a feel for the way the mundane so readily gives way to the
tragic. We see the passengers and crew getting ready to board the doomed
flight, doing all the things most of us do as we hang around in airports: Some
slouch in their chairs, reading books or newspapers or fiddling with their bags;
others make last-minute work or personal phone calls, possibly more out of
boredom than out of necessity. The pilots (played by J. J. Johnson and Gary
Commock, pilots in real life) chat idly about the recent ups and downs of the
weather as they make their way toward the plane. Onboard, the attendants call
to one another from across the cabin ("Do you have sugars up there?") or wish
out loud that they could be at home with their babies instead of working.

These early moments give the movie a portentously chilling shape and
texture: Sometimes it seems as if 99 percent of our conversation is just boring
work talk, and yet even our boring work talk is a way of defining our lives.
Later, when the passengers and attendants realize what's happening and begin

to make anxious calls to their loved ones, the movie veers into a sharper dramatic pitch—and yet I'm not sure those final phone calls are necessarily more moving than the unassuming casualness of those earlier conversations. (Greengrass needs to dramatize those fervent phone calls, and yet he does dance a bit too closely to milking them for dramatic value—it's an insoluble problem for any filmmaker.)

The action in *United 93* cuts between the plane cabin, a thin shell of isolation and vulnerability, and various sites on the ground: Those include the FAA's Herndon command center and a military command center in upstate New York, as well as air-traffic-control centers in Boston and New York and the control tower at Newark International Airport. (In one moment that's startling even though we're set up for it, the Newark controllers glance across the river and see fat plumes of smoke billowing from the World Trade Center. We see it from the same distance they do, an emblem of both Greengrass' fidelity to the characters' point of view and his tact.) The sequences set in the cabin—even before the hijackers spring into action—are so tense they're nearly unbearable to watch. Whenever Greengrass cuts back to the safety of the ground—even as the air-traffic controllers and military personnel slowly come to realize that two earlier flights have been hijacked—the movie relaxes slightly, and we do too. We know the worst is yet to come, and we know exactly what the worst consists of. So we grasp at every reprieve from it.

Greengrass doesn't portray the four hijackers (they're played by Khalid Abdalla, Lewis Alsamari, Omar Berdouni and Jamie Harding) as monsters, but as human beings who have chosen to act like monsters. The picture opens with two of them praying in their hotel room, a faceless, neutral space whose very beigeness seems unwelcoming to anyone's God; still, their prayers have the rhythm of habit and conviction—although that comforting rhythm may also suggest the utter absence of thought.

But the hijackers—even the tall, handsome one, who betrays a flicker of recognizably human apprehension in the early moments of the flight—are very much "the other" in *United 93*. None of the other passengers pay these men a bit of attention, but we're hyper-aware of their presence, simply because we know what's coming. Greengrass, to his credit, doesn't do any fancy two-step around the fact that these men committed murder in the name of Islam. He's unafraid to make the link between the terrorists' religion and the barbarism they carried out for its sake. "In the name of God," one of the hijackers says flatly as he slits the throat of a flight attendant.

Although the violence in *United 93* is affecting, Greengrass keeps stern control over it, showing only as much as we need to see. (The murder of that attendant is shown from the back.) And Greengrass addresses the notion of heroism only glancingly: The passengers' bravery is presented as more personal than patriotic, the desire to save their own lives and the lives of their fellow passengers. And the movie's climactic sequence, in which several of the bigger, stronger passengers attack two of the terrorists, jolts us with a terrifying charge. We need the catharsis the scene offers, but Greengrass never allows us to lapse into moral superiority. Greengrass doesn't allow a comfortable distance between ourselves and these desperate passengers. When they lunged for one of the terrorists, I found I'd curled my own hands into fists, as if expressing some atavistic desire to choke the life out of him myself.

United 93 is not an apolitical movie: Greengrass, who's English, takes care to point out that both the FAA and the military—fumbling to do their jobs to the best of their ability in a time of crisis—were stymied by government incompetence and lack of communication. And while Greengrass must have his own strong personal feelings about how the U.S. government has co-opted the events of 9/11 for its own purposes (he's too politically astute a filmmaker *not* to have such feelings), *United 93* isn't intended to make a statement on the war on terrorism. And yet Greengrass refuses to be an apologist for terrorism. He isn't interested in retrofitting explanations for the events of 9/11: He accepts these murders as a deplorably inhuman act perpetrated by religious fanatics, never shying away from how much pain they caused, particularly to the families directly involved.

All of Greengrass' artfulness and conscientiousness should add up to an astonishing movie. But as I watched *United 93*, ticking off the things I was grateful Greengrass *hadn't* done, as well as toting up the things I could see he did well, I realized that even though Greengrass seems to be tackling a larger, more globally significant subject here, this movie doesn't feel nearly as expansive in scope as his remarkable, and deeply unsettling, 2002 *Bloody Sunday*. *Bloody Sunday* is an account of the Jan. 30, 1972, massacre on the streets of Derry, in which 13 unarmed civil rights protesters were killed by British paratroopers. Greengrass has a gift for capturing the essence of true chaos—he doesn't try to tease sense out of it, which would only deny the awfulness of that chaos and play into the comforting fallacy that a belief in goodness, human or otherwise, can explain away horrific events. And so, in *Bloody Sunday*, when we see British soldiers firing live rounds at terrified civilians, suddenly and without provocation, we can hardly believe what we're seeing—in the context of the basic moral templates we try to live by, it makes no sense whatsoever, and yet the reality of it is undeniable.

Bloody Sunday has a you-are-there immediacy that dissolves the decades between then and now: When Greengrass shows us a teenage boy dying in the backseat of a car that's been stopped at a roadblock, it's a tragic vision that provokes outrage, but it also draws sorrow from the deepest part of us. In comparison *United 93*, an evocation of a far more recent piece of history, feels weirdly constrained. The picture is "about" a single momentous, horrific event, and its intensity is undeniable. But while *United 93* offers a horrifyingly realistic evocation of pain and fear, it doesn't open itself out to any greater, more expansive truth. And it offers us no hope of transcendence. *United 93* spells out for us horrors that previously we could only have imagined, as if imagining them could never be enough. It's an expertly made picture that I wish I could stamp out of my mind. What's the value of artistry that sucks the life out of you? YES.

2006

Nathan Lee

Nathan Lee is perhaps the most exciting and representative spokesman for the younger generation of film critics. Initially he held the film desk at *The New York Sun*, an alternative newspaper, then worked as a second-string reviewer for *The New York Times*, and is now (with J. Hoberman) senior film critic for *The Village Voice*. Lee writes with colloquial verve, passion, and energy about all movies, but especially the most cutting-edge independent and international cinema. He is ever on the lookout for films that will break the conventional mold aesthetically and have a liberating political or sexual dimension. In the example below, he champions a picture that was more popular with critics than the public, arguing than it is less about serial killings than about data processing and the ways that media impinge on and construct our contemporary world—including, in a self-reflexive manner, the movies themselves.

◆

To Catch a Predator

In the unforgettable *Zodiac*, three shots stand out. The first comes early, climaxing a brisk introduction to one of the film's primary settings, the offices of the *San Francisco Chronicle*. Gliding through hallways with the suavity you'd expect from the director, David Fincher, and the cinematographer, Harris Savides, the camera assumes the point of view of an object inside an overflowing mail cart. It is August 1, 1969. The first of many letters and cryptograms by a serial killer calling himself the Zodiac has been delivered to the newspaper.

The second shot, captured by helicopter or perhaps digitally composited, is an aerial view of a taxi motoring through San Francisco. Starting at the intersection of Mason and Geary, the God's-eye-view follows the vehicle to the corner of Washington and Cherry, at which point the passenger, the Zodiac, shoots the driver, Paul Stein. Patterned with a series of space-collapsing dissolves, the sequence is scored to disembodied voices on a talk radio program discussing the man—the media phenomenon—that has gripped the city in fear and fascination.

The third, arriving about halfway through the film, literalizes the theme of the first two, and indeed of *Zodiac* itself: the relationship of man to media.

Several years have passed; the body count has mounted; the letters have piled up. The efforts of Homicide Inspector Dave Toschi (Mark Ruffalo) and his partner William Armstrong (Anthony Edwards) have failed to turn up a suspect. A tracking shot follows them through the offices of the San Francisco Police Department, the other nexus of the film. The image is layered with a digital scrawl of letters, phrases, and symbols from the Zodiac missives, literally engulfing the heroes in a text that has thus far led nowhere.

Thus far: There is much more to come. With a runtime of over two and a half hours, this relentlessly swift film super-charges every minute with a maximum of minutiae. Dizzyingly dense, intricate in the extreme, *Zodiac* is the most information-packed procedural since *JFK*, though far more restrained when it comes to theorizing. The screenplay, meticulously engineered by James Vanderbilt, has been adapted from a pair of books by Robert Graysmith (played here by Jake Gyllenhaal), a cartoonist at the *Chronicle* who glommed on to the Zodiac case and eventually took it on as his life's work. Everything has been checked against verifiable sources, then staged with the utmost fidelity and precision; note how Fincher resists dramatizing the events in Paul Stein's cab, sticking to a representation of his known route. The result is an orgy of empiricism, a monumental geek fest of fact-checking, speculation, deduction, code breaking, note taking, forensics, graphology, fingerprint analysis, warrant wrangling, witness testimony, phone calls, news reports. "I felt like I was stuck in a filing cabinet for three hours," complained one viewer. Exactly!

A remarkable feat of concentration, *Zodiac* is a fully mature triumph for reasons that bring us back to that trio of signature shots. Their explicit virtuosity stands out in a surface that forgoes the visual sweep of *Seven*, *Fight Club*, or *Panic Room*. Mechanical as he can be, Fincher tends to the operatic: big emotions, massive denouements, portentousness, flamboyance. *Zodiac*, by contrast, plays out with the cool calibrations of a 12-tone piano suite, advancing with a detached, mathematical precision capable of great variety and nuance, yet controlled by a strict discipline. It's a film that never raises its voice because it needs to speak clearly and carefully. It's got a hell of a lot to say.

Talk to Fincher and he'll tell you he just wanted to tell a damn good story. Mission accomplished. Yet it's his very lack of pretense, coupled with a determination to get the facts down with maximum economy and objectivity, that gives *Zodiac* its hard, bright integrity. As a crime saga, newspaper drama, and period piece, it works just fine. As an allegory of life in the information age, it blew my mind.

The medium is the message in *Zodiac*. That's what those three shots mean, and why they're delivered with extra rhetorical emphasis; the Zodiac is never given an attention-grabbing p.o.v. shot, but his communiqué is. A serial-killer flick that isn't really about a serial killer, a procedural keyed to the psychology of *procedure* more than the men engaged in it. *Zodiac* is an information system of bewildering complexity laid out for our contemplation. It's an epic, reflective analysis of how one canny lunatic triggered an all-consuming flood of data that swept up, and drowned, three different entities: the media, the police, and one man's life. *Zodiac* returns the serial-killer flick to its roots in Fritz Lang's *M*, a movie likewise preoccupied with technology, symbols, spatial patterns, communication systems.

Anyone expecting a reprise of *Seven*-style shivers and Grand Guignol psychodrama will be gravely disappointed. Yet common to both films is the notion of their villains as the inevitable manifestation of a troubled zeitgeist. *Seven*'s John Doe seeks to chastise the debased, apathetic modern world through a kind of radical installation/performance art; an appreciative audience, shocked at his subversive daring, is an essential component of his project. His provocation is basically an extremely twisted publicity stunt. "We are talking about people who are mentally ill," protests Brad Pitt's wrathful hothead. "We are talking about people who are fucking crazy." "No, no we are not," replies Morgan Freeman's world-weary detective. "We're talking about everyday life here."

Compared with his colleagues in the serial killer pantheon, the Zodiac was something of an underachiever. His true forte was marketing, complete with a spiffy logo. "The thing that was so stunning about the Zodiac was not what he did but how he hyped it," says Fincher, reached by telephone on the set of his new movie in New Orleans. "The letters themselves are amazing graphic examples of that. They're riveting. They're the reason we're still talking about this guy, not the body count." Like *Seven*'s John Doe, the Zodiac is in it for the publicity; the most intriguing detail of his story isn't what he did to his relatively few verifiable victims, but rather the likelihood that he claimed responsibility for murders he read about in the news. "What's the one thing we know about the Zodiac for sure?" asks a character at the end of the film. "That he reads the *Chronicle*."

This helps explain why *Zodiac* is less concerned with delving into the inner lives of its characters than observing their operative role in larger phenomena. Fincher denies the audience a strong, sympathetic hero. He's at least as interested in the yellow-on-gray color scheme of the *Chronicle* office as he is with the psychological shadings of his protagonists. "Fincher paints with people,"

Gyllenhaal recently griped to *The New York Times*. "It's tough to be a color." That doesn't mean that *Zodiac* is inhuman, only that it applies attention evenly across the whole canvas, the big picture; it's a panorama, not a portrait.

The most ingeniously designed narrative in many moons, *Zodiac* is structured in three parts without conforming to the conventional trajectory of a three-act narrative. The first section details the effect of the Zodiac on the media, filtered through the experience of Graysmith and Paul Avery (Robert Downey Jr.), a jaded reporter assigned to the story. Part one climaxes with the rupturing of the media's sense of its own inviolability: The Zodiac sends a letter, and a swatch of blood-soaked fabric, directly to Avery.

The middle part focuses on the police investigation, with a wealth of circumstantial evidence pointing to Arthur Leigh Allen (John Carroll Lynch), a convicted child molester now employed at an oil refinery. *Zodiac* makes a convincing case for his guilt, though the mechanics of a whodunit are more important here than who, definitively, done it. If part one scrutinized media manipulation, part two delineates the limits of law enforcement, the lunge and parry of a police procedural destined to go unresolved. The section fades out at the 1971 premiere of *Dirty Harry*, a film incorporating the Zodiac mythos. "You're going to catch him," Graysmith says to Toschi in the lobby. "No," he replies in resignation. "They're already making movies about it."

By the time we get to section three, the sheer volume of information has grown exhausting—which is very much the point. *Zodiac* ends with the story of Graysmith's continuing mania for the truth. It is only here, nearly two hours into the tale, that a recognizable human story enters the picture. Delaying that contact is one of *Zodiac*'s shrewdest maneuvers; by the time we're dropped into Graysmith's drama, we're almost as overloaded with information as he is.

Toschi remains only nominally involved in the case. Avery has retired to a houseboat and the bottle. Graysmith's persistence is pitched somewhere between the admirable and the unhinged. As ever, the Zodiac takes his toll. Mrs. Graysmith (Chloë Sevigny) leaves Robert to stew in an apartment heaped with "Zodiac crap"; from first date to breakup, the way she's sidelined from the story may seem a cliché of the genre, but it makes perfect, poignant sense in a movie with a deft sense of elision.

In its final stretch, as it zeroes in on the processes of a single consciousness, *Zodiac*, that endlessly resonant glyph, functions as a movie about its own process. Graysmith's obsession is mirrored in Fincher's; the movie soldiers on, accumulating still more facts, unearthing new connections, pushing deeper into the labyrinth, chasing the ghost. The director's cut is going to be amazing —and intolerable.

Zodiac exhausts more than one genre. Termite art par excellence, it burrows for the sake of burrowing, as fascinated by its own nooks and crannies as *Inland Empire*. While it mimics the look of 35mm film, it is appropriately, perhaps inevitably, a product of the high-def-video imagination. The movie operates with the back-and-forth insistence of a scanner arm, gathering, filtering, digitizing, and storing an immense catalog of analog enigmas. It might have been titled *A Scanner Darkly*.

"The ending for me," says Fincher, "was always, At what point can you, personally, call it a day, Robert?" The film ends with the publication of Graysmith's book on the Zodiac, a final twist in the Arthur Leigh Allen theory, and a set of on-screen title cards that twist the theory yet again. As for Graysmith, the Zodiac lives on. Reached by phone from his home in San Francisco, the author mentions *Shooting Zodiac*, a book he's finishing about the production of Fincher's film.

2007

David Bordwell

David Bordwell is the Jacques Ledoux Professor of Film Studies, University of Wisconsin-Madison, and has long been one of our country's most eminent film scholars. He has written or co-written (with his longtime partner Kristin Thompson) over 15 books, including in-depth studies of Dreyer, Ozu, and Eisenstein, investigations of the poetics of cinema, such as *Figures Traced in Light* (2005) and *On the History of Film Style* (1997), and textbooks, such as *Film Art: An Introduction* (2006). Preoccupied by formal and stylistic issues rather than thematic ones, Bordwell has managed to bridge the gap between academic scholarship and general readership, partly by his accessible writing style and partly by his enthusiasm for unstuffy subjects such as Hong Kong cinema. His openness to new technologies may be evidenced by the fact that he keeps a website or blog, davidbordwell.net, from which the following posting on DVDs is taken.

◆

New Media and Old Storytelling

To what extent has the DVD changed viewing habits and movie storytelling?

As everybody knows, a DVD offers more interactivity than a movie you watch in a multiplex. In a theatre, the movie rolls on, unaffected by anything you may do. But with a DVD you can pause the film, run fast forward, skip to a particular second, shuffle chapters, even play the thing in reverse.

Most minimally, the DVD offers greater convenience. You can zip back to replay a bit you might have missed or halt the film so you can answer a phone call. But some of us wonder if this new interactivity harbors more radical implications. Does the new flexibility of use allow us to experience the film in new ways?

In a mystery film, say there's a clue at the half-hour mark. During a theatrical screening, we're moved forward with no time to ponder it. Watching the film on DVD lets us pause the film, ponder the clue as long as we like, and maybe track patiently back to earlier scenes to test our suspicions about what that clue means. Or suppose you decide to sample the film, browsing through the opening bits of several chapters? More radically, suppose we decide to watch the DVD in reverse? Nothing stops us, and we'd have an experience of the story very different from that of someone who watched the film in the normal order. Doesn't this all suggest that it's hard to generalize about what the "ordinary" viewer's experience of a movie might be nowadays?

Now consider the craft of fictional filmmaking. The movie's creators make choices about what story information to impart, when to impart it, and how to impart it. They assume that the viewer follows the story in the order mandated by theatrical projection, scene 1, then 2, 3 and onward. Likewise, the pace of uptake is set by the film—no slowing down or speeding up at the viewer's will. But given the new conditions of digital consumption, these assumptions may be wrong. So shouldn't the filmmakers take those conditions into account? And more specifically, haven't some filmmakers already taken them into account? In other words, hasn't the DVD transformed cinematic storytelling?

Questions like these matter to me. I've long argued, along with Kristin, that mainstream US filmmaking, dubbed "classical Hollywood cinema," has cultivated a sturdy and pervasive narrative tradition. That tradition depends on sharply delineated characters pursuing well-defined goals. This commitment in turn creates a plot that displays linear cause and effect: In pursuing goals, the protagonist makes one thing happen, and that makes another thing happen, which in turn triggers something else. The mainstream tradition lays these actions and reactions along a fairly rigid structural layout, and the film's narration constantly reiterates the characters' traits, their goals, important motifs, and the overall circumstances of the action.

But now home video allows our consumption to be highly nonlinear. By skipping or skimming DVD chapters, we may not register the plot or narration as the makers intended. Doesn't this make hash of goal-directed action, character arcs, and all the other features of classical storytelling? Might we not be moving toward a "post-classical" cinema?

Let's tackle the question first from the standpoint of the viewer. I think we can get help by recognizing this basic point: The DVD made a movie more like a book.

It sounds odd to say this, because we think of digital media as replacing print. Yet consider the similarities. You can read a book any way you please, skimming or skipping, forward or backward. You can read the chapters, or even the sentences, in any order you choose. You can dwell on a particular page, paragraph, or phrase for as long as you like. You can go back and reread passages, and you can jump ahead to the ending. You can put the book down at a particular point and return to it an hour or a year later; the bookmark is the ultimate pause command. We tacitly acknowledge the resemblance between the DVD and the book when we call the segments on a DVD its chapters, the list of chapters an index, and the process of composing the DVD its authoring.

With these similarities in mind, we can ask: How many people, on first contact, would sit down to watch a film in a nonlinear way?

My hunch: Just about as many people who would buy or borrow a book and then proceed to read it in a nonlinear way. True, if you have a nonfiction book in hand, you might find certain chapters to be more intriguing than others and move straight to those. Similarly, confronted with the menu of a DVD documentary on penguins, some viewers might want to start with the chapter labeled Mating Habits.

But with a fictional film, as with a novel, we're much less inclined to graze and browse. We might sample the novel before buying or borrowing it, but I'd bet the portion we're most likely to sample is the opening chapter. With a fiction film on DVD, some viewers might sample a distant chapter opening, but I expect that soon they'd settle down to watching from start to finish. This is more or less what happens with literary fiction. I don't mean to say that all consumers of fiction move at the same pace or read the same way. I'm just indicating that following the mandated order, page by page or shot by shot, is the default in nearly all cases.

This suggests that pausing is the most common way we play an interactive role. When reading a book you might call out to your friend and reread a particularly striking description or funny dialogue exchange. When watching a film, you might stop and replay some images to enjoy them again. Another common act is probably quickly "paging back"—rereading or re-viewing a bit that just preceded the pause to remind ourselves of what's going on at the moment.

Our purpose in starting a book or film at the beginning is to get into the story world and start to think and feel in relation to the information we get about it. But we don't have to take that as our primary purpose. More extreme acts of "creative" spectatorship are tied to different purposes than learning about the story world. I suppose that teenage boys might well rent *300* when it comes out on DVD and fast-forward looking only for the scenes showing carnage or naked ladies, the same way that my high-school contemporaries rummaged through Terry Southern's *Candy* digging out the good parts. But this doesn't seem to be a radically new way of using any medium. Scanning a text for immediate gratification rather than narrative involvement was common well before DVD.

Of course we students of cinema use the DVD commands in order to study a film, spooling back and forth to analyze it. But that usage isn't a radical reworking of consumption either. Typically before we start to analyze a movie, we've already experienced it in the ordinary linear way. Students of literature read a text straight through before they analyze it in a back-and-forth way.

Finally, I'd suggest that a highly unorthodox mode of consumption, like setting out to watch a film in reverse at 8x speed, would become boring fast. As with so many things in life, just because you can do something doesn't mean you'd enjoy it.

Speculation 1: The actual uses that people make of DVD interactivity are limited; traditional beginning-to-end consumption is the default.

Speculation 2: Pausing, paging back, and scanning for the good bits suggest that the most frequent DVD interactivity is familiar from other media, particularly books.

Let's now consider things from the side of the creators. Knowing that films are seen on DVD, don't filmmakers adjust their art and craft to this new medium? Of course they can provide revised versions, or directors' cuts, along with alternative endings, deleted scenes, and other material that shed light on the film and the production process. But does the DVD format change the very act of conceiving and executing the story presented by the film?

Yes, in certain respects. In *The Way Hollywood Tells It*, I argue that the viewer's possibility of rewatching a film with little fuss encourages ambitious filmmakers to "load every rift with ore," to pack in details that might not be noticed on a single viewing. One of my examples is the 8:2 motif in *Magnolia*. Likewise, the looping time schemes of *Donnie Darko* and the reverse-order plotline of *Memento* are amenable to being picked apart after several viewings. But before home video, you as a viewer could scrutinize such movies by just going back to the theatre and watching the film over and over, very attentively.

Clumsy as it seems, film nerds of my generation did this. When we were lucky, we might get a film in our hands and go through it reel by reel. I remember my thrill as a junior in college when I discovered, after rerunning a 16mm print of *Citizen Kane* on my apartment wall, that the snowstorm paperweight that Kane clutches on his deathbed is sitting on Susan's vanity table the night he first meets her. Welles had, as it were, planted this clue for attentive viewers to spot. Granted, the random-access aspect of DVD allows this sort of fine-grain scanning to be done more easily, but it's not different in kind from threading up a Films Incorporated print one more time.

This sort of scrutiny enriches the film in a very traditional way. Films that sustain this sort of attention, from Buster Keaton movies to *Hiroshima mon amour* and *The Silence of the Lambs*, long predate the arrival of DVD. Throughout *Play Time* Tati sprinkled details and gags that reward many viewings. When Paul Thomas Anderson and Christopher Nolan bury details in their films, or when *The Simpsons* flashes a jokey sign past us, they're practicing a time-honored strategy of teasing the viewer to return to the work to get something more out of it.

There are, though, more radical cases. In an essay, "The Book as Object," the experimental novelist Michel Butor pointed out that the fact that the book is an object to be manipulated at will allows stories to be dense and difficult. Why not write novels that demand that the reader search backward to identify characters or find details? Along the same lines, once a film becomes a book-like object, it can be composed to encourage multiple replays not merely to appreciate little touches but just to make bare sense of what's going on in it. *Memento* and *Primer* would seem to be instances—films designed to encourage extensive, not to say obsessive, re-viewings simply in order to build up a full understanding of the story. Again, however, the DVD serves not as a unique format for such a film but as a tool that makes replaying a lot easier than would several visits to the theatre.

There are other possibilities tied to the format itself. The DVD of Max Allan Collins' *Real Time: Siege at Lucas Street Market* was designed to permit the viewer some choice of camera angle in certain scenes. At a few points we're permitted to enlarge the monitors of different surveillance cameras in order to follow one or another strand of action. Still, in *Real Time*, the plot action is clear and redundant in the classical manner, so even if you don't enlarge the screens, I suspect that you won't miss much.

Butor suggested that since a book is an object, all in hand at once, a plot could be composed to permit many, equally valid points of entry and exit, on different pages. Such seems to have been achieved by the DVD version of Greg Marcks' *11:14*. The film follows five characters in a small town as their lives intertwine. The plot is broken into five segments, each one following a character up to the critical moment given in the title. In carrying it to DVD, Marcks chaptered it so that you could skip among storylines at will. He explains in an email to me:

> It's a feature on the DVD that I called "character jump," which allows you to jump to what another character is doing at that same moment in time. Theoretically you could watch the film in an endless circuitous loop because the end is simultaneous with the beginning.

During some scenes of *11:14*, a JUMP icon appears. If you press Enter, the scene switches to another character's storyline—either earlier or later in the theatrical version's running time. Once in that story, the icon stays on for a bit so that you can return to your point of departure if you want. Presumably for reasons of engineering and disc space, the number of JUMP options remains fairly small. Still, it's a fascinating effort, and it does seem to offer the possibility of your restructuring the plot in fresh ways.

Even in *11:14*, however, the story possibilities are closed. As in a *Choose Your Own Adventure* book, you're hopping among trajectories that are already designed. The opening sequence remains the opening for every option; no Butor-style starting in the middle. Furthermore, the trajectories themselves are linear, running along a cause-effect pattern very familiar to us from classically constructed stories. We find such stable patterns in branching or multiple-draft narratives like *Run Lola Run* and *Sliding Doors*. I argue in *The Way* that even the reverse-order disjunctions of *Memento* sort out along lines to be found in film noir. It's very hard to abandon principles of classical narrative entirely.

Let's also recall a simple point. Even though the book format offers the sort of mind-bending manipulations Butor celebrates, most literary fiction remains traditionally plotted and narrated. Likewise, we should expect that the arrival of the DVD permits filmmakers who want to tell orthodox stories in orthodox ways keep on doing so. The line of least resistance is straightforward linear presentation.

Speculation 3: The ease of DVD replay can encourage filmmakers to pack their films with more details that repay rewatching. The result might be films that are "hyperclassical"—still more tightly woven than we tend to find in the studio years.

Speculation 4: Some filmmakers have made their storylines hard to follow on a single viewing, encouraging DVD replays so we can figure out what's going on. This strategy makes the films less classical in construction, to a greater or lesser extent.

Speculation 5: A few filmmakers have utilized DVD features to allow greater interactivity than a theatrical screening would grant. In most cases, however, this interactivity proceeds along classical lines. We follow, however nonlinearly, protagonists with goals, confronting obstacles, conflicting with others, and arriving at a definite conclusion along a definite path.

Despite all the options provided by DVD, I'd argue that even in the age of digital media, spectators enjoy their greatest freedom not in the way that they manipulate films but in the ways they can interpret them. But even an epic blog has to stop somewhere, so I'll leave that matter for another time.

2007

SOURCES AND ACKNOWLEDGMENTS

Great care has been taken to locate and acknowledge all owners of copyrighted material included in this book. If any owner has inadvertently been omitted, acknowledgment will gladly be made in future printings.

Renata Adler. Cold Blood: Cheap Fiction: *New York Times*, January 28, 1968. Copyright © 1968. Reprinted by permission of the author.

James Agee. The Song of Bernadette; Annual Wrap-Up of 1944; A Great Film; The Lost Weekend; Shoeshine; Day of Wrath: *Agee on Film: Reviews and Comments* (New York: McDowell, Obolensky, 1958). Copyright © 1941, 1942, 1943, 1944, 1945, 1946, 1947, 1948, 1949, 1950, by The James Agee Trust. Copyright © 1958 by The James Agee Trust. Copyright renewed by Teresa Agee, Andrea Agee & John Agee, 1986. Reprinted by permission of The James Agee Trust.

Cecilia Ager. Parachute Jumper; Hallelujah I'm a Bum; Ladies They Talk About; Our Betters; King Kong; Night Flight; Camille; The Last of Mrs. Cheyney; Personal Property; Another Dawn; A Day at the Races: *Garbo and the Night Watchman*, Alistair Cooke, ed. (New York: McGraw-Hill, 1937). Copyright © 1937. Reprinted by permission of Laurel Ager Bentley.

Eugene Archer. A King in New York: *Film Culture* #16 (January 1958). Reprinted with permission of Anthology Film Archives, New York.

Rudolf Arnheim. The Film Critic of Tomorrow: *Film Essays and Criticism* (Madison, Wisconsin: University of Wisconsin Press, 1997). Copyright © 1997. Reprinted by permission of University of Wisconsin Press.

John Ashbery. On Val Lewton's The Seventh Victim: *John Ashbery: Selected Prose* (Ann Arbor: University of Michigan Press, 2004). Copyright © 2004 by John Ashbery. Originally appeared in *Modern Painters* (Autumn 2003). Reprinted by permission of Georges Borchardt, Inc., on behalf of the author.

Alexander Bakshy. The "Talkies": *The Nation*, February 20, 1929. Reprinted with permission from *The Nation*. For subscription information, call 1-800-333-8536. Portions of each week's *Nation* magazine can be accessed at *www.thenation.com*.

James Baldwin. *from* The Devil Finds Work: *The Devil Finds Work* (New York: Dial Press, 1976). Copyright © 1976 by James Baldwin. Copyright renewed. Used by arrangement with the James Baldwin Estate.

David Bordwell. New Media and Old Storytelling: Copyright © 2007 by David Bordwell. Reprinted by permission of the author.

Vincent Canby. Midnight Cowboy: *New York Times*, May 26, 1969; The Wild Bunch: *New York Times*, June 26, 1969; Easy Rider: *New York Times*, July 15, 1969; Z: *New York Times*, December 9, 1969; They Shoot Horses, Don't They?: *New York Times*, December 11, 1969; Patton: *New York Times*, February 8, 1970; Zabriskie Point: *New York Times*, February 10, 1970; Is *Fiddler* More De Mille Than Sholem Aleichem?: *New York Times*, November 28, 1971. Copyright © 1969, 1970, 1971 by The New York Times Co. Reprinted with permission.

Stanley Cavell. Cons and Pros: The Lady Eve: *Pursuits of Happiness* (Cambridge: Harvard University Press, 1981). First published in *New Literary History*, summer 1979. Reprinted with permission of the author. Stanley Cavell is Professor of Philosophy, Emeritus, Harvard University.

Richard Corliss. M*A*S*H: *Talking Pictures* (New York: Overlook Press, 1974). Copyright © 1974 by Richard Corliss. Reprinted by permission of The Overlook Press.

Arlene Croce. Pather Panchali and Aparajito: *Film Culture* #19 (1959); A Note on La Belle, La Perfectly Swell, Romance: *The Fred Astaire & Ginger Rogers Book* (New York: Galahad Books, 1972). Copyright © Arlene Croce. Reprinted by permission of Arlene Croce.

Manohla Dargis. High Hopes: *LA Weekly*, December 14–20, 2001. Copyright © 2001. Reprinted with permission of the author; Not-So-Nice Kitty: *Los Angeles Times*, December 19, 2003. Copyright © 2003 Los Angeles Times Syndicate International. Reprinted by permission; Once Disaster Hits, It Seems Never To End: *The New York Times*, September 23, 2005. Copyright © 2005 by The New York Times Co. Reprinted with permission.

Barbara Deming. The Reluctant War Hero: *Running Away from Myself: A Dream Portrait of America Drawn from the Films of the 1940s* (New York: Grossman Publishers, 1969). Reprinted by permission of the Barbara Deming Literary Estate, c/o Judith McDaniel.

David Denby. The Real Thing: *New York Review of Books*, Vol. 37, No. 17, November 8, 1990. Copyright © David Denby. Reprinted by permission of the author.

Hilda Doolittle. The Passion of Joan of Arc: *Close Up*, 3.1 (July 1928). Copyright © 1928, copyright © 2005 by The Schaffner Family Foundation; used by permission of New Directions Publishing Corporation, agents. Reprinted by permission of New Directions Publishing Corp.

Roger Ebert. Trouble in Paradise: *The Great Movies* (New York: Broadway Books, 2002). Copyright © 2002 by Roger Ebert. Used by permission of Broadway Books, a division of Random House, Inc.

Ralph Ellison. The Shadow and the Act: *The Collected Essays of Ralph Ellison* (New York: Modern Library, 1995). Copyright © 1953, 1964, renewed 1981, 1992 by Ralph Ellison. Used by permission of Random House, Inc. Originally published in *The Reporter* (December 6, 1949).

Manny Farber. Underground Films: *Commentary* 24 (November 1957); White Elephant Art vs. Termite Art: *Film Culture*, 1962; Kitchen Without Kitsch (with Patricia Patterson): *Film Comment* 16.6 (November–December 1977). Reprinted by permission of the author(s).

Otis Ferguson. It's Up to the Kiddies: *The New Republic*, May 16, 1934; Stars and Garters: *The New Republic*, October 24, 1934; Artists Among the Flickers: *The New Republic*, December 5, 1934; Arms and Men: *The New Republic*, January 25, 1935; Words and Music: *The New Republic*, October 2, 1935; In a Dry Month: *The New Republic*, November 13, 1935; Cagney: Great Guy: *The New Republic*, October 13, 1937; Through the Looking Glass: *The New Republic*, October 27, 1937; Walt Disney's Grimm Reality: *The New Republic*, January 26, 1938; Hitchcock in Hollywood: *The New Republic*, September 16, 1940; For Better, for Worse: *The New Republic*, September 30, 1940; Handsome Is . . . :*The New Republic*, February 10. 1941; Citizen Welles: *The New Republic*, June 2, 1941; Welles and His Wonders: II: *The New Republic*, June 16, 1941.

Brendan Gill. Blue Notes: *Film Comment*, January 1973. Copyright © 1973 by FILM COMMENT Publishing Corporation. Reprinted by permission of the Film Society of Lincoln Center.

Penelope Gilliatt. The Bitter Tears of Petra von Kant: from "Fassbinder," *The New Yorker*, June 14, 1976. Copyright © 1976. Reprinted by permission of the Gilliatt Estate.

Paul Goodman. Griffith and the Technical Innovations: *Partisan Review*, May–June 1941. Reprinted by permission of the Howard Gotlieb Archival Research Center, Boston University.

James Harvey. Imitation of Life: *Movie Love in the Fifties* (New York: Alfred A. Knopf, 2001). Copyright © 2001 by James Harvey. Used by permission of Alfred A. Knopf, a division of Random House, Inc.

Molly Haskell. The Woman's Film: *From Reverence to Rape: The Treatment of Women in the Movies* (New York: Holt, Rinehart and Winston, 1974). Sophisticated Interiors: *Film 71/72: An Anthology by the National Society of Film Critics*, David Denby, ed. (New York: Simon and Schuster, 1972); Melancholy Males or Movies About Men Turning 50: *The Guardian*, October 10, 2003. Copyright © 1972, 1973, 1974, 1987, 2003, by Molly Haskell. Reprinted by permission of Georges Borchardt, Inc., for the author.

J. Hoberman. Bad Movies: *Film Comment*, July 1980. Copyright © 1980 by J. Hoberman. Reprinted with permission of the author; The Film Critic of Tomorrow, Today: *The Crisis of Criticism*, Maurice Berger, ed. (New York: New Press, 1998). Reprinted by permission of the New Press.

bell hooks. Cool Cynicism: Pulp Fiction: *Reel to Real: Race, Sex, and Class at the Movies* (New York: Routledge, 1996). Copyright © 1996. Reproduced by permission of Routledge / Taylor & Francis Group, LLC.

Kent Jones. Of Love and the City: *Film Comment*, 37.1 (January–February 2001). Copyright © 2001 by FILM COMMENT Publishing Corporation. Reprinted by permission of the Film Society of Lincoln Center.

Pauline Kael. Band of Outsiders: *The New Republic*, September 10, 1966; Funny Girl (Bravo!): *The New Yorker*, September 28, 1969; Trash, Art, and the Movies: *Harper's*, February 1969; McCabe & Mrs. Miller (Pipe Dream): *The New Yorker*, July 3, 1971. Copyright © 1966, 1969, 1971 by Pauline Kael, renewed 1996, 1999. Reprinted by permission of Gina James.

Stanley Kauffmann. The Misfits: *The New Republic*, February 20, 1961; L'Avventura: *The New Republic*, February 20, 1961; Lola Montes: *The New Republic*, May 3, 1969. Reprinted by permission of *The New Republic*, © 1961, 1969.

Walter Kerr. The Keaton Quiet: *The Silent Clowns* (New York: Alfred A. Knopf, 1972). Copyright © 1975 by Anntess Enterprises Ltd. Used by permission of Alfred A. Knopf, a division of Random House, Inc.

Lincoln Kirstein. Dancing in Films: *New Theatre*, September 1936. Copyright © 2006 by the New York Public Library (Astor, Lenox and Tilden Foundations). Reprinted with permission.

Stuart Klawans. Gladiator: *The Nation*, May 22, 2002. Reprinted with permission from *The Nation*. For subscription information, call 1-800-333-8536. Portions of each week's *Nation* magazine can be accessed at *www.thenation.com*.

Siegfried Kracauer. Introduction: *From Caligari to Hitler* (Princeton: Princeton University Press, 1947). Copyright © 1947 by Princeton University Press, 1975 renewed PUP, 2004 rev. & exp. ed. Reprinted by permission of Princeton University Press.

Nathan Lee. To Catch a Predator: Copyright © 2007 Village Voice Media. Reprinted with permission of the Village Voice.

Meyer Levin. The Charge of the Light Brigade: *Garbo and the Night Watchman*, ed. Alistair Cooke (New York: McGraw-Hill, 1937). Copyright © 1937. Reprinted with kind permission of Tereska Torres Levin and JABberwocky Literary Agency, PO Box 4558, Sunnyside, New York, 11104–0558.

Vachel Lindsay. The Photoplay of Action: *The Art of the Moving Picture* (New York: Macmillan, 1915); The Artistic Position of Douglas Fairbanks and *The Thief of Bagdad* Production: *The Progress and Poetry of the Movies* (Lanham, Maryland: Scarecrow Press, 1975). Copyright © 1975 by Scarecrow Press. Used by permission.

Pare Lorentz. Anna Christie: *Judge*, April 5, 1930; Good Art, Good Propaganda: *McCall's*, July 1940. Reprinted by permission of Pare Lorentz, Jr.

Dwight Macdonald. 8½: *The Two Hundred Days of 8½* (New York: Macmillan, 1964). Copyright © 1964 by Dwight Macdonald, renewed 1993 by Michael Macdonald and Nicholas Macdonald. Reprinted by permission of Michael and Nicholas Macdonald.

Jonas Mekas. The Creative Joy of the Independent Film-Maker; Renoir and Plotless Cinema; Marilyn Monroe and the Loveless World; On Andy Warhol's Sleep; Not Everything That Is Fun Is Cinema; On Bresson and Une Femme Douce: *Movie Journal* (New York: Macmillan, 1972). Copyright © 1972. Reprinted with permission of the author. Originally published in *The Village Voice*.

H. L. Mencken. *from* Appendix from Moronia: *Prejudices: Sixth Series* (New York: Alfred A. Knopf, 1927). Copyright © 1927 by Alfred A. Knopf, a division of Random House Inc. Used by permission of Alfred A. Knopf, a division of Random House, Inc.

Hugo Münsterberg. The Function of the Photoplay. *The Photoplay: A Psychological Study* (New York: D. Appleton, 1916).

Geoffrey O'Brien. The Italian System: *The Phantom Empire* (New York: W.W. Norton & Company, 1993). Copyright © 1993 by Geoffrey O'Brien. Used by permission of W. W. Norton & Company, Inc.

William S. Pechter. These Are a Few of My Favorite Things: *Movies Plus One* (New York: Horizon Press, 1982). Copyright © 1982 by William S. Pechter. Reprinted by permission of the author; Buñuel: *Twenty-Four Times a Second* (New York: Harper & Row, 1971). Copyright © 1971 by William S. Pechter. Reprinted by permission of the author.

Gilberto Perez. Saying "Ain't" and Playing "Dixie": Rhetoric and Comedy in Judge Priest: *Raritan*, Spring 2004 (Vol. 23, No. 4). Copyright © 2004. Reprinted with permission.

Donald Phelps. The Runners: *Covering Ground: Essays for Now* (New York: Croton Press, 1969). Copyright © 1969 by Donald Phelps. Reprinted by permission of the author.

Harry Alan Potamkin. "A" in the Art of the Movie and Kino: *New Masses*, December 1929; Remarks on D. W. Griffith: *Révue Du Cinéma*, February 1931. Reprinted by permission of the publisher from *The Compound Cinema: The Film Writings of Harry Alan Potamkin*, ed. Lewis Jacobs (New York: Teachers College Press, 1977), pp. 120–124, 454–457. Copyright © 1977 by Teachers College, Columbia University. All rights reserved.).

Carrie Rickey. Ratpacks and Pack Males: *Scenario*, January 2003. Copyright © 2003 Carrie Rickey. Reprinted with permission of the author. Carrie Rickey is a film critic for *The Philadelphia Inquirer*.

Jonathan Rosenbaum. In Dreams Begin Responsibilities: *Chicago Reader*, July 3, 2001. Copyright © 2001 Chicago Reader, Inc. Reprinted with permission. All rights reserved.

Paul Rudnick (aka Libby Gelman-Waxner). A Boy Named Sioux: *If You Ask Me* (New York: St. Martin's Press, 1993). Copyright © 1994 by the author. Reprinted by permission of St. Martin's Press, LLC.

Carl Sandburg. The Cabinet of Dr. Caligari: *Chicago Sun-Times*, May 12, 1921; Nanook of the North: *Chicago Sun-Times*, October 21, 1922; A Woman of Paris: *Chicago Sun-Times*, January 12, 1924; Manhandled: *Chicago Sun-Times*, July 18, 1924; The Temptress: *Chicago Sun-Times*, November 24, 1926; What Price Glory?: *Chicago Sun-Times*, December 27, 1926 and January 15, 1927. Reprinted in *The Movies Are: Carl Sandburg's Film Reviews and Essays*, 1920–1928 (Chicago: Lake Claremont Press, 2000).

Andrew Sarris. The Birds: *The Village Voice*, April 4, 1963; La Guerre Est Finie: *The Village Voice*, February 2, 1967; Falstaff and Countess from Hong Kong: *The Village Voice*, March 30, 1967. Reprinted in *Confessions of a Cultist: On The Cinema*, 1955–1959 (New York: Simon & Schuster, 1970). Copyright © 1970 by Andrew Sarris. All rights reserved. Reprinted

call 1-800-333-8536. Portions of each week's *Nation* magazine can be accessed at *www.thenation.com*.

Kenneth Turan. Titanic Sinks Again (Spectacularly): *Los Angeles Times*, December 19, 1997. Copyright © 1997 Los Angeles Times Syndicate International. Reprinted by permission.

Parker Tyler. Double into Quadruple Indemnity: *Magic and Myth of the Movies* (New York: Henry Holt and Company, 1947); Warhol's New Sex Film: *Sex, Psyche, Etcetera, in the Film* (New York: Horizon Press, 1969). Copyright © 1947, 1969. Reprinted by permission of the Estate, c/o Collier Associates, P.O. Box 20149, West Palm Beach, Florida, 33416.

Robert Warshow. The Gangster as Tragic Hero: *Partisan Review*, February 1948; A Feeling of Sad Dignity: *Partisan Review*, November–December 1954. Reprinted by permission of Paul Warshow.

Armond White. Rebirth of a Nation: *LA Weekly*, July 7, 1989; Malcom X'd Again: *The City Sun*, December 2, 1992. Reprinted in *The Resistance* (Woodstock, NY: The Overlook Press, 1995). Copyright © by Armond White. Reprinted by permission of The Overlook Press.

Edmund Wilson. The New Chaplin Comedy: *The American Earthquake: A Documentary of the Twenties and Thirties* (Garden City, New York: Doubleday, 1958). Copyright © 1958. Copyright renewed 1986 by Helen Miranda Wilson. Reprinted by permission of Farrar, Straus and Giroux, LLC.

Martha Wolfenstein and Nathan Leites. Got a Match?: *Movies: A Psychological Study* (Glencoe, IL: Free Press, 1950). Copyright © 1950 by the Gale Group. Reprinted by permission of The Gale Group.

Stephanie Zacharek. *United 93*: This article first appeared in Salon.com, at *http://www .Salon.com*. An online version remains in the Salon archives. Reprinted with permission.

INDEX